434-435- book's lifetime potential

Book Marketing Handbook   VOLUME TWO

Dedicated to Ruth, Les, Mark, and Debbie

Book Marketing Handbook

VOLUME TWO

Over 1,000 More Tips and Techniques
for the Sale and Promotion of
Scientific, Technical, Professional,
and Scholarly Books and Journals

Nat G. Bodian

R. R. BOWKER COMPANY
New York & London, 1983

Published by R. R. Bowker Company
1180 Avenue of the Americas, New York, N.Y. 10036
Copyright © 1983 by Xerox Corporation
All rights reserved
Printed and bound in the United States of America

Library of Congress Cataloging in Publication Data
(Revised for volume 2)

Bodian, Nat G., 1921–
  Book marketing handbook.

  Includes indexes.
  1. Book industries and trade—Handbooks, manuals, etc.
2. Advertising—Books—Handbooks, manuals, etc.
I. Title.
Z283.B58   070.5'2   80-17504
ISBN 0-8352-1286-6 (v. 1)
ISBN 0-8352-1685-3 (v. 2)

Short Contents

Contents

3. TESTING: GUIDELINES, OPTIONS, TECHNIQUES, CASE HISTORIES

4. MAILING LIST DETERIORATION AND GROUP MOBILITY: CASE STUDIES

5.   FORMATS FOR PROMOTION

6.   INVENTORY REDUCTION SALES AND PRACTICES

14. HEADLINE WRITING: GUIDELINES AND IDEAS FOR SCI-TECH, PROFESSIONAL,
AND BUSINESS BOOKS

15. COPY FITTING: GUIDELINES AND TABLES

Part III Marketing and Promoting Professional and Reference Books

16. MARKETING STRATEGIES

Part V   Outlets for Professional and Scholarly Books

Part X   Marketer-Author Relations

37. WORKING WITH YOUR AUTHOR

Part XI   Book Marketing and Promotion Cogitation

38. MORE SHOPTALK: A POTPOURRI

Appendixes

Preface

Why an entirely new second volume of *Book Marketing Handbook*? What does this new volume cover that the first volume did not? The answer lies in the aims of the first volume, how well they were met, and reactions to *Volume One* within the publishing industry.

The primary aim of *Volume One* of this handbook was to fill an industry need for a practical reference guide for the marketing and promotion of professional and scholarly books and journals. Another objective was to define the parameters of book and journal marketing, an imprecise grey area varying in scope from one publishing establishment to another.

With the publication of *Volume One*, the professional and scholarly publishing community finally had a book it could call its own. *Book Marketing Handbook, Volume One* not only addressed itself to the special needs of professional and scholarly book publishers, but it also targeted one of their most pressing concerns, *marketing*. *Volume One* enjoys wide use as a reference tool not only by book and journal marketers, but also by an extensive cross-section of publishing staffs at many levels, from copywriters, publicists, and exhibits managers to editors, publishers, and managing directors. It may be found on the business reference shelf in hundreds of libraries and has also been adopted as a textbook in publishing education courses and used as a reference source in seminars for publishing mangement.

The appearance of *Volume One* in the fall of 1980 also marked another phenomenon. Its publication helped destroy the myth that professional and scholarly book marketing know-how, acquired only by on-the-job experience, was a collection of secrets one kept to oneself and carried from one job to another. In *Volume One*, those so-called secrets were called by their true name, techniques, and were brought out into the open to be understood, shared, and utilized by all.

Another beneficial outgrowth coinciding with the death of the "secrets" myth has been that, in the less than three years since the appearance of *Volume One* of *Book Marketing Handbook*, the professional, sci-tech, and scholarly publishing community has experienced more meetings, seminars, workshops, luncheon sessions, and information exchanges directly related to book and journal marketing technique than most longtime publishing professionals could recall in the preceding twenty years.

Visible proof of this phenomenon was the creation, in the year following the publication of *Volume One*, of the Professional Publishers Marketing Group (PPMG), an organization of marketers from over fifty publishing establishments nationwide who meet regularly to discuss and exchange ideas on marketing technique. PPMG founder Peter Hodges directly attributes the inspiration for the organization to *Book Marketing Handbook*.

Throughout the preparation of both volumes of this handbook, Dr. Irving Louis Horowitz, author, educator, and publisher, has been a loyal and staunch supporter of its objectives. Writing about *Volume Two*, Dr. Horowitz said, "I have always taken the position that (one's) first work . . . is intensely personal . . . but the second work represents a serious commitment." His words ring true. Much of the content of *Volume One* is based on personal experience gained during twenty years of book and journal marketing. By comparison *Volume Two* represents a serious commitment to expanded coverage of book and journal marketing technique for the industry as a whole. Every segment of professional and scholarly publishing has been included in this volume: commercial, university press, and learned society. Within each of these classifications, the reader is provided with a wealth of studies and case histories from large and small publishing operations alike.

Many chapters in *Volume Two* carry the same headings as those in *Volume One*. Lest the reader be deceived, however, it should be stressed that all of the content under these headings represents entirely new material, case studies, and practical approaches to techniques outlined briefly in *Volume One*. Thus, the ideas and information contained in *Volume Two* not only stand apart from those presented in *Volume One*, but they expand on and demonstrate practical applications for the rules and guidelines defined in the earlier work. New chapters in this volume discuss formats for promotion; cooperative mailings; package inserts, book inserts, and envelope stuffers; headline writing; copy fitting; the school market; journal subscription studies; how to estimate a book's lifetime sales potential; and guidelines for reaching international markets.

This new volume also sheds light on the distinctions within the various markets served by professional and scholarly publishers. For example, while *Volume One* gave general coverage to libraries, *Volume Two* examines the different marketing techniques for college, public, special, and school libraries. Additionally, this new volume addresses many aspects of book and journal marketing that were touched on only briefly in the first volume, in response to feedback from readers and reviewers—all industry professionals—of *Volume One*.

Another valuable feature of *Volume Two* is the presentation of the findings of numerous tests, market surveys, and readership studies that will be immediately applicable to effective marketing procedures for professional and scholarly books and journals. In many instances, information is presented that previously appeared in publications or reports that were directed to very small or specialized audiences, or were only available to a limited audience and, therefore, unknown to the larger body of book and journal marketers. The first "public" appearance of this information provides book and journal marketers with an array of practical working tools that will enhance their professionalism. The listing of sources also gives the marketer ample opportunity for further investigations.

This work could not have been accomplished without a great amount of help, encouragement, and support from many, both within the publishing industry and in various other areas. I take this opportunity to express my gratitude to all of them, and, most importantly, to my wife, Ruth Bodian, who patiently read, advised, and provided invaluable help during the two and one-half years this volume was researched, assembled, and written.

Among the many others, I wish to extend special thanks to: Peter Hodges, Warren, Gorham & Lamont; Allan Wittman, Macmillan Publishing Company; Bill Begell, Hemisphere Publishing Company and chairman of the Professional and Scholarly Publishing Division of the Association of American Publishers; Paul Nijhoff Asser, the STM Secretariat, Amsterdam; Mary Curtis, Wiley Journals Division; Irving Louis Horowitz, Transaction Books; Glenn Matthews, College Marketing Group; Steven Lustig, IBIS Information Services; Ray Lewis, *ZIP Magazine*; Chandler Grannis, contributing editor, *Publishers Weekly*; and Carole Cushmore and Betty Sun of the R. R. Bowker Book Division.

I am no less indebted to my many colleagues at John Wiley & Sons in New York, Toronto, Chichester, Brisbane, and Tokyo for encouragement, suggestions, and criticisms.

Also to Dimity Berkner, UNIPUB; Irv Berkowitz, Co-op Mailings, Inc; Peter Black, Business Publications Audit of Circulation, Inc.; Les Bodian, Department of Psychology, University of Maryland; Patricia Broida, Columbia Books Inc.; Charles Bussman, Compass Publications; Terry Coen, Market Data Retrieval; Robert A. Day, ISI Press; Charles Dall'Acqua, National WATS Services; Jenifer Deroche, Special Libraries Association; Donald Farnsworth, McGraw-Hill Book Company; Dan Fischel, Gordon & Breach Science Publishers; Lynn Frankel, Prentice-Hall; Abbot M. Friedland, Princeton University Press; Elaine Fulton, National Association of Parliamentarians; Neal Gray, Medical Economics Books; C. Rose Harper, The Kleid Company; Dee Hjermstad, DeRoe Associates; Kenneth Hurst, Prentice-Hall International; Susan Hunter, W. B. Saunders Co.; Debra Kaufman, American Can Co. Corporate Library; Milton Kaufman, Internal Revenue Service; Edward Keller, Sherago Associates; Edward Langer, American Society for Metals; Jim Langford, University of Notre Dame Press; Ed Langlois, Camera-Ready Composition Co.; Nancy Laribee, Matthew Bender & Co.; David Lavender, Industrial Hygiene News; Leonard Maleck, Times Mirror Book Clubs; Bruce Marcus, Marketing Consultant; Barbara Meyers, American Chemical Society; Randal K. Miller, Institute for Scientific Information; Marc Paszament, Clark Boardman Company Ltd.; Angelo Rollo, Specialty Printers of America; (the late) Harold Roth, library consultant; Moshe Y. Sachs, Worldmark Press; John Stockwell, McGraw-Hill Book Company; Brook Stevens, MIT Press, Leigh Stoeker, Little, Brown & Co.; Vivian Sudhalter, McGraw-Hill Book Company; Beverly Todd, University of Oklahoma Press; Hank Troemel, McGraw-Hill Book Co. Ltd., Hamburg; Tim Vode, publicist; Bill Walker, Metropolitan Museum of Art library; Willis Walker, Van Nostrand Reinhold Co.; and Julie Zuckman, Journal Division, MIT Press.

Introduction

Getting a good book into the places where it is wanted and needed is no simple task. Rather it is one that is challenging, often exciting, and always eminently worth doing. How to do it well is the subject of both volumes of *Book Marketing Handbook*, which should be used together, since the second expands importantly upon the first in every aspect of the multi-faceted marketing process.

The book marketer, of course, operates within the context of the book publishing house, and plays a major part in defining that context. Marketing properly begins before there is a finished book. The decision to go ahead with an idea and to publish hinges in part on market research. As the book develops, so do marketing plans and budgets, and thus the company's operating plan, for a season or for much longer, deeply involves the marketers. Both volumes of the handbook provide extensive information about the process of anticipating markets and testing channels of sale and methods of selling through which marketers help create and then execute their company's plan.

The book publishing house (and its marketing and other departments) exists in several larger contexts: those of the book industry as a whole, the publisher's own segment within that industry, and the various markets the publisher seeks. A knowledge of facts and figures about all of these matters serves not only to help publishers maintain a sense of proportion, but also to make necessary calculations about marketing and some of the editorial, design and manufacturing considerations.

It is because publishers have demanded such information over the years that data have been collected and analyzed by industry and government sources, especially by the Association of American Publishers (AAP), Book Industry Study Group (BISG), R. R. Bowker Company, and the U.S. Department of Commerce. For example, the AAP's annual industry-wide statistical report indicates that book publishers' total receipts for 1981 were over $7.7 billion. Of this total, those divisions of the industry that this handbook addresses in particular accounted for approximately 30 percent, computed here on the basis of divisional figures in the same report: professional books as a group, about 14.8%, including technical/scientific books (5.1%), medical books (3.3%), and business and other professional books (6.4%); university press books, 1.1%; and college texts and materials, 14%. (Techniques described in this handbook apply in varying degrees to other divisions of publishing, notably mail-order publications and book clubs, which accounted for about 8.5% and 7.4% of 1981 industry sales, respectively.)

BISG estimates suggest that, at the same time, 1.6 billion books were purchased in the United States (unit sales). Here the percentage of unit sales represented by the same kinds of publishers is very different: professional (all types), 3.1%; university press, 0.5%; college, 5.6%; mail order, 3.4%; and book clubs, 12.2%.

Most marketers need as much demographic information as they can get. Government sources provide much of it, as can be seen in the annual *Statistical Abstract of the United States* of the Department of Commerce. But the book market researcher usually needs still more specialized information. Accordingly, this volume of *Book Marketing Handbook* suggests many channels to be explored and names agencies, commercial and other, that give access to them.

At this point the marketer is working not only in the context of publishing but also in that of marketing as a profession, applying that profession's skills and techniques to books. It is upon these more detailed areas that Nat Bodian concentrates. Both volumes cover all the major areas with nuts-and-bolts examples. Major areas of coverage are: direct-mail promotion and use of mailing lists, direct response techniques, book advertising, types of outlets, exhibits at professional meetings, journals, and international sales. In *Volume Two*, all these areas are discussed in the context of more extensive, more up-to-date, and often more sophisticated examples than were used in the first volume, thereby helping the marketer to make distinctions among different methods or variations thereof, under variable circumstances.

Certain areas are greatly expanded: for example, marketing strategy, promotional copywriting (along with long lists of effective phrases and headlines), design, use of catalogs; and formats for promotional material—to name a few. Changes in the economy and technology make it appropriate to give more information about certain contemporary tools of marketing: credit cards, still proliferating, yet fraught with new problems; handling sales to meet the need for inventory reduction; solicitation by telephone; the swiftly widening use of "800" numbers for obtaining telephone responses to promotion; and other techniques. All of this underlines one of the most important points about book marketing that is made in this handbook: that while successful marketers by no means underplay the tried and true methods, they also have to apply enough imagination, flexibility, and sheer zest to act upon changing situations and new opportunities.

In such an effort, individual marketers are not alone; they are part of a professional community of many marketers who, as the author points out, are aware that they have more to gain from sharing experiences than from trying to keep secrets. The spirit of cooperation was eloquently demonstrated to Nat

Bodian as he prepared *Volume Two* of this handbook, for which scores of willing colleagues supplied information.

Books, whether or not they are in competition with each other, stimulate interest in still other books; thus does the world of book markets change and grow, to the common benefit of author, publisher, and reader.

CHANDLER B. GRANNIS
Former Editor-in-Chief
Publishers Weekly

Part **I**

Professional and Scholarly Book Promotion by Direct Mail

1

Overview and Techniques

The retail exposure of specialized books is so limited that direct marketing by the publisher becomes almost a necessity.

John P. Dessauer, *Book Publishing, What It Is, What It Does,* 2nd Ed., R. R. Bowker, 1981.

1:01   Direct Mail: Techniques that Produce Better Results

In the first volume of *Book Marketing Handbook,* the opening section identified *direct mail* as the most powerful marketing tool available to the publisher of technical, scientific, professional, scholarly, and reference books. In it, we explained the preference for direct mail as the opening section of the book because, while there are more than 19,000 book outlets in the United States, a scarcity of good technical bookstores existed. As this volume was written, the number of bookstores stocking the "short-discount" professional or reference book has increased somewhat, thanks to their "discovery" (see 22:02) by the major chains. However, experienced book professionals will still take bets that you can't find 100 good technical bookstores in the United States, or some insist, not even 50.

In *Volume One,* the emphasis in the direct-mail chapter was on definitions, rules, formulas, and guidelines—in other words, the reasons for using direct mail, the "laws" for successful direct marketing, incentives to help direct mail produce better results, mailing strategies, direct-mail components and formats, and the like.

In *Volume Two,* the emphasis in this opening chapter is on *technique,* tried and proven ways you can utilize to produce better results. Its aims are to show you how to do better what you are presently doing. If you are a novice, it will show you how to get started in direct-mail book promotion with the same advantages that seasoned professionals have—the advantages of knowledge and experience.

Much of this chapter is derived from on-the-job working experiences of the author and various other book marketing professionals in publishing establishments throughout the United States who are willing to share their experience and the lessons they have learned.

A number of valuable entries are the result of questions posed by readers of *Volume One* who encountered problems in direct marketing to which no answers could be found in the earlier work—and who took the time and trouble to let us know. To those who asked the questions, "Thank you! The answers are included in this and succeeding chapters, and you have made it possible for your colleagues to benefit also from this added information."

In the entries that follow in this chapter, you will find many valuable gems. One of the more valuable, we think, is one that confuses so many in the publishing community: the difference between *direct mail* and *direct response*. Other entries in this chapter of special interest include how and when to choose between package and self-mailer . . . evaluating the effectiveness of direct-mail campaigns . . . how and when to use different classes of postage . . . checklists for various aspects of direct-mail promotion . . . a variety of case histories . . . white mail and the echo effect . . . tips on credit-card usage and telephone numbers in promotions . . . and much more.

Essentially, this first chapter on direct-mail technique picks up where *Volume One* leaves off. It is designed to answer in brief, easy-to-absorb entries the myriad nagging questions that come up on the job every day, to provide you with enough guidelines to use the direct marketing tool with confidence and a minimum of risk, and to benefit by the lessons of scores of others who have learned easier, more effective, and less costly ways to achieve good results with direct-mail book promotions.

1:02   **Ending the Confusion Between Direct Mail and Direct Response: A Clarification**

There appears to be confusion among many in the publishing community concerning the difference between publisher *direct mail*, on the one hand, and *direct response*, on the other. It is surprising how many mix the two terms and use them interchangeably. Actually they are very different and serve entirely different purposes.

Direct-response mailings have a single purpose—to generate direct responses from those to whom they are mailed. Many types of professional and reference books lend themselves to direct response (also referred to as direct orders or mail orders) and produce profitable returns when such offerings are properly targeted. Some of the more successful mailers among the large publishing houses claim a cost to net sales ratio of as much as one-third, or $3 in sales for every dollar spent.

Direct mail, on the other hand, is really a shortened form of the term *direct-mail advertising*. Its function to the publisher is essentially the same as publisher space advertising: to place advertising about the publisher's offerings in the hands of a targeted audience, with response a secondary consideration.

- Mailings to libraries fall in the realm of direct-mail advertising, as most libraries order through wholesalers or jobbers.
- Mailings to many groups of individuals produce sales in indirect ways, through the "echo effect": A mailing to college professors will influence sales, but ultimately bookstores will stock and sell the books to students.
- Mailings to individuals in academic and other institutions often result in recommendations for acquisition by their institutional library.
- Mailings of professional and business books to individuals in business and industry may produce little direct response, but ultimately the response may reach the publisher through company purchase orders bearing only the purchasing agent's signature.
- Mailings to all types of individuals who influence purchases by others rarely produce a strong traceable response. As a study among scientist/readers of *Current Contents* (19:16) indicates, for every direct book order placed through the order coupon by a reader of *Current Contents*, six other orders are placed by other means.

Marketers in a number of publishing establishments consider that obligations to authors have been met when one or more direct-response mailings have included the author's book, and that when such promotions fail to produce a good response the book lacks sales potential. The reality may be that the book has excellent sales potential, but it just is not a direct-response or *mail-order* product. It may well be that its natural audience(s) does not as a general practice buy and pay for books for which they receive mail announcements.

It is generally assumed that when a publisher agrees to publish an author's book, the publisher will meet the definition of "publish," which is *to make public*. This definition carries with it the implied understanding—although this may not always be possible or feasible—that the book will be made public to its true or intended audience or readership.

Once and for all, it should be made clear to all in publishing who interchangeably use the terms direct response and direct mail in the belief that the first also covers the second—it does not. Direct response can be an important aspect of book marketing and of direct-mail advertising, and for many publishers it can be extremely profitable when the right books are effectively promoted to the right audiences. But direct response is only one of many ways that direct-mail advertising can be used to good effect by book marketers, and it should always be viewed as a means—never as an end.

**1:03   Direct-Mail Advertising and the Echo Effect:
Planning Guidelines**

A well-known commercial house ventured into a previously untried advertising medium, and its initial efforts produced a high rate of response. However, when overhead was assigned under the company's accounting policies, the effort was considered ineffective. It is hazardous for any professional and scholarly publisher to evaluate advertising in any medium solely on direct reponse. The marketing of professional and scholarly books occurs largely in a selling environment that manifests itself through the echo effect.

This means that, whatever the promotional medium, generally its effect is reflected in orders received by the publisher through various routes such as bookstores, wholesalers/jobbers, industrial purchase orders, library direct orders, telephone orders, over-the-transom orders from individuals, college adoptions, and the like. Thus, in publishing establishments where each direct-mail campaign must meet predefined criteria to be considered successful, thinking must be changed to consider the echo effect.

Many types of books sell well through the mails—self-improvement books, state-of-the-art professional books, books aimed at personal interests or that upgrade professional skills, to name a few. These invariably do well when matched with the right lists. However, there are also many categories of professional and scholarly books that do not lend themselves to mail order. Such books generate most of their response through the echo effect. Such titles must still be budgeted for mail advertising but with less emphasis placed on traceable response. These include books in the earth sciences, theoretical books, and books purchased by businesses, institutions, laboratories, government agencies, and libraries.

In effect, the professional and scholarly publisher should view a direct-mail advertising program on two different levels. One level of the direct-mail program can and should be linked to direct response and should be directed to potential mail-order buyers. The other level of the program should be considered announcement advertising and should not necessarily aim at producing a high level of measurable response to be considered successful. Response to this second level of mailings will manifest itself in different ways, and its effect can only be measured, if at all, through inventory shrinkage of the promoted titles.

Publishers and book marketers must stop thinking about direct response as the only game in town and start thinking about direct-mail promotion as a two-level effort designed to achieve different ends. Unless they do, books that lend themselves to mail order will continue to be heavily promoted, while other, equally deserving titles that do not lend themselves to mail order will either be neglected or underpromoted and, ultimately, become outdated and die after achieving only a small fraction of their true sales potential.

1:04 **Hodgson's Advice:**
Study Techniques that Have Proved Successful to Others

If you are just entering or are new to the medium to mail as a tool of book promotion, you will profit from the sage advice of one of the long-time authorities in the field, Dick Hodgson. In his introduction to the booklet *202 Tips for Direct Mail Advertising** (Advertising Publications, Inc., 1955), Hodgson wrote:

There are few set rules for getting assured results from the direct mail medium. What works for one [mailing] may lay a big fat egg for the next one ... tips serve only as an opportunity to analyze your own direct mail methods to see if there aren't some changes which may bring better results ... don't be misled by a single change which seems to bring immediate results—there are too many factors involved to *prove* that the change was the only reason for the success.

In 1980, Hodgson, writing in the introduction to his classic *Direct Mail and Mail Order Handbook*, 3rd Ed. (Dartnell), restated the premise thusly:

There are no real RULES for success. ... In direct mail there are few limitations ... the advertiser is the "publisher" and can pretty much establish his own boundaries ... beware of any who would preach hard-and-fast rules. ... But, on the other hand, study the techniques which have proved successful for others ... to provide direction in the wide-open spaces of direct mail creativity.

1:05 **More "Laws" for Successful Direct-Mail Book Offers**

The following "laws" for succesful direct-mail book offers supplement the ten presented in *Volume One*. The word law, wherever used, implies general principles based on experience, as no rule or law in direct-mail promotion has universal application.

1. An offer with a free trial examination will produce a higher rate of response than one that requires payment.
2. Response to any promotional offering of professional or scholarly books is closely tied to the perceived immediate usefulness or value of the titles to the recipients.
3. Response improves when postage is affixed by meter imprint as opposed to printed indicia.
4. Multititle mailings of scientific books to individuals with research grants generate more multiple-copy orders than similar mailings to individuals within the same institutions or to nonresearch individuals in the same field.

---

*Tips were by Franklin C. Wertheim and many others, including this author.

5. Response to direct-mail promotions will always be better when mailed to known buyers within a given field or interest group than when mailed to any other list of names in the same field or interest area.

6. Response will be substantially higher and much faster on catalog mailings to libraries containing a special offer, deal, or discount, when the offer is mentioned on the outside envelope, wrapper, or mailing cover.

7. A first volume in a series with flat sales can be reactivated when included in a joint mail offering with a new second volume at a discounted "set" price.

1:06   The Echo Effect

Any marketing director or sales manager or promotion manager or copywriter working in an academic or professional publishing house who does not know what 'the echo effect' is has not read Nat G. Bodian's Book Marketing Handbook *and should buy a copy.*

Gordon Graham, Chairman, Butterworth & Co.,
in *The Bookseller*, March 13, 1982.

Our detailed explanation and coverage of the echo effect in *Volume One* prompted a lengthy review entitled "The Echo Effect" in the British weekly book trade journal *The Bookseller*, by Gordon Graham, an internationally respected authority on the marketing of scientific, technical, and medical books and chairman and chief executive of Butterworth & Co. (Publishers), Ltd., in Kent, England. (For readers unfamiliar with the echo effect, the term refers to the secondary sales effect that targeted publisher mailings have by reverberating through all of the other outlets where books are normally sold. One of the visible ways in which orders generated by the echo effect of publisher promotions are received is explained in the next entry on "white mail.")

Case histories of publishers' studies of the echo effect are presented in *Volume One*. In a Wiley study, older sci-tech titles with declining sales patterns showed sharp sales gains in bookstores for the entire year following their inclusion in Wiley direct-mail promotions. In an MIT Press study of the echo effect, half of the press's current list was included in a series of mailings to scientific and technical lists. Following the mailings, increased echo-effect sales were recorded in virtually all sales outlets. The study showed these increased sales to have been the direct result of inclusion in the mailings. In a more recent study of echo effects (reported in 12:18) six of seven survey respondents reported buying books offered in *Current Contents* from other sources.

1:07   White Mail: One Visible Form of the Echo Effect

"White mail" is one of the visible ways by which orders generated by the echo effect of advertising and promotion reach the publisher. The term white mail, used frequently in publishing-marketing discussions, represents incoming orders received "over the transom"—that is, orders that have no identifiable source.

White mail derives its name from the fact that many such orders are received in publishing establishments on plain white sheets of paper, either handwritten or typed. The term is also applied to untraceable orders received on postcards and company or institutional purchase orders.

In some houses that rely heavily on direct mail to market books and loose-leaf materials to business professionals, projected response from direct-mail promotions may also include an add-on allowance for anticipated white mail.

White mail orders may also result from sources other than space advertising or mail promotion—for example, publicity, book reviews, word-of-mouth, convention exhibits, listings in abstracting and indexing services, even a literature reference in a published scientific paper. One publisher of advanced scientific books conducted a buyer survey and discovered a measurable percentage of white-mail orders had resulted from the buyers' having seen the book in a library.

1:08   Evaluating Cost-Effectiveness of Direct-Response Mailings

What constitutes a successful return from a direct-response mailing? While many book marketers aim for a percentage based on the total number of pieces mailed, the more experienced sellers of books by mail consider successful any mailing that brings in a dollar in net sales for a cost of 40¢ to 43¢. A few marketers are able to show better ratios, such as $3 for every dollar. These results are sometimes achieved by using different formats, such as card decks (see also 8:03 and 8:04) or order stamps (gum-backed, postage-like stamps that are affixed to order cards), but when the extra effort is figured in, the averages are often about the same. Some others have attained this average (on paper) by burying some of the preparation costs under overhead.

It is readily apparent that percentages become meaningless when you offer high-priced works as opposed to lower-priced ones. You need far fewer orders when your book prices average $25 to $35 than you do when they average $7.50 to $12.50. You also need far fewer orders when you are selling a journal subscription that has an 80% renewal average.

Response percentage may be even lower when a mailing includes a high percentage of academics. Results from this group are often better reflected by echo effect than by direct response. Academics routinely suggest acquisition of mail offerings to their institutional libraries, or they place special orders through the school bookstore. A high percentage of academics, especially in the sciences, also do outside consulting and often recommend books for reference or training programs to the organizations they serve.

*See also 8:03 and 8:04.

1:09   Risks in Free Examination Offers: A Rule of Thumb

The element of risk exists with all free examination offers. When you offer books for a free examination period, be prepared to write off a certain amount of your response for nonpayers. One rule of thumb: The more specialized the mailing, the lower the risk. Other factors determining risk include the quality of the lists of specialized prospects, price of product, and whether or not the list contains known mail-responsive buyers.

A mailing to many categories of scientists or engineers, for example, will generate a negligible loss factor. One expects that the reason is that the professional is not willing to jeopardize personal credit status, especially in an area such as books, which they depend upon to keep up-to-date and avoid professional obsolescence. There are exceptions, however: This writer has had a bad experience with design engineers, and another book marketer experienced a high degree of bad debt in psychology mailings. Experience is a good teacher, but current book-buyer lists tend to be fairly good.

1:10   Essential Ingredient of Every Free Examination Offer

When you offer books for free examination in your mail promotions, include a space for the signature of the person sending in the examination request. Here's why: Should the recipient of the book later deny ever ordering the book(s) and refuse to return or to pay, you have the signature as proof of the order. Save the signed examination order requests until payment is received or the return credited.

1:11   Key to Content of Mailings: Special Interests of Recipients

Some publishing establishments show poor judgment in selecting the content of mailings targeted to scientific and technical specialists by including promotional matter in unrelated areas that are not likely to have any interest to the recipient. In *Volume One*, we cited an 18-enclosure mailing to chemists in which virtually none of the specialized book offerings was related to chemistry. As *Volume Two* was being written, a readers service inquiry placed in response to a book advertisement in a scientific journal brought a five-enclosure reply in which only one of the five pieces was in any way remotely related to the subject of the books in the advertisement.

It can be both profitable and productive to include in your targeted mailings to lists of scientific and technical individuals self-help books and books that offer career guidance or improvement of personal skills (see entry following for a detailed discussion). However, books in unrelated scientific and technical fields may not only be unproductive but may also harm the publisher's image.

1:12   Tap Personal Interests for Extra Sales in Sci-Tech Mailings

Do not restrict your sci-tech mailings to books specifically within the subject area or discipline of the mailing. Where space permits, be sure to include selected business books, particularly in mailings directed to scientists, engineers, and researchers in rapidly changing areas of science or engineering. Recipients of your mailings, particularly those in the rapidly changing high-technology areas, counsels one mailing list specialist, "are hungry for information and they are anxious to keep up with every type of management technique they can get their hands on."

Scientists and engineers are also interested in self-help books that offer career guidance or improvement of personal skills. The author's own experience in many mailings to this audience reinforces this theory. In many a sci-tech mailing, business and self-improvement books have matched and sometimes even bettered the response to titles specifically in the subject area of the mailing. When you have a number of business or self-improvement books for inclusion in a sci-tech mailing, group them under a common heading, such as "References for Your Professional Library," or "Useful Professional References," or "Professional References, Handbooks, Manuals."

1:13   More Ways to Help Increase Response from Book Mail Offerings

1. Include an expiration date in each mail offering. State on your offer that all prices are guaranteed until the expiration date shown.
2. If the book is an annual or serial, include on the order vehicle an option of placing a standing order, or an order for the next volume, or for the previous volumes, or for future supplements as issued.
3. If the book is part of a set, or can be grouped with related titles, offer the group as a set at a special discounted "set" price.
4. If the order form enumerates each item in the offering, include an additional ordering line or two for a related title or titles.
5. Include a sweepstakes offering.
6. Include postage stamps as ordering vehicles. To order, the recipient will paste the stamp bearing an illustration of the desired book on the order card.

**1:14   Simple Device for Making a Mailing
Piece Do the Work of Two or Three**

The simple addition of routing instructions or a routing card can make a single mailing piece do the work of two or possibly three. Following are some routing devices that have been used successfully to enable a single mailing piece to reach two, three, or even more prospects.

1. Affix routing instructions to the mailing face or envelope. For example:

   Please forward to:

   ( ) Marketing Manager
   ( ) Advertising Manager
   ( ) Publicity Director

2. Affix routing instructions to the face of each enclosure within the same mailing package:

   Please route to:

   _____

   _____

   _____

3. Create a mailer with a double business reply card affixed. Instruct the recipient to use one card for response and to forward the same mailing piece and the second card to a friend or colleague.

4. Enclose a separate routing card with specific instructions for forwarding. Example:

   TO THE LIBRARIAN:

   I recommend that the following books be ordered for the library:

   Author _____   Title _____
   Author _____   Title _____
   Author _____   Title _____

   From _____ Dept. _____

1:15   When to Consider Using First-Class Postage Instead of Third-Class Bulk Mail

1. When the book is an annual and will date quickly.

2. When the mailing includes a prepub offer and requires a more predictable delivery.

3. When a high-ticket item is offered and the added postage is warranted.

4. When you want to convey the "importance" of first-class mail either through first-class postage or first-class postage combined with a "first-class mail" overprint on the envelope.

5. When a mailing will require prepayment, and the earlier cash flow justifies the added postage expense for early orders.

6. When a book has competition from a similar or related title being offered at or about the same time by another publisher.

7. When the books in a multiple-title mailing have text adoption potential and must reach book selectors during a decision-making season.

8. When a mailing is done late in the year and you want to avoid Christmas-season mail delays.

9. When the book promoted in a mailing is designed to tie in with a newsmaking event or date, and thus the delivery date is vital to its success.

10. When the mailing is designed to coincide with an activity involving the author, such as receipt of the Nobel Prize or an appearance on a nationwide TV show in which the book will be discussed or mentioned.

11. When an author of a book, for business or personal reasons, offers to subsidize the difference in cost between first- and third-class mailings.

12. When the mailing is used to test the responsiveness of a number of mailing lists and a fast follow-up is planned.

13. When a new edition is planned and the mailing is being done to reduce inventory of the earlier edition.

14. When the information in the book being promoted focuses on government data that may drastically change with an upcoming election or a change in government administration.

15. When the lists being used include addresses lacking ZIP codes.

16. When you want to test the reliability of several new lists. "Nixies" come back free on first-class mail.

17. When you want your mail to be forwarded to a recent new address.

18. When your personalized letter contains a date.

19. When a high percentage of deliverability is a critical factor in a mailing.

1:16   Should You Ask for Telephone Number on Order Form?

Should you ask for a telephone number on an order form? "Never," says one marketer of high-priced loose-leaf services. "We ask for as little information as possible on the order forms. We don't want to scare them off." Another marketer of publications directed primarily to the legal profession takes a different viewpoint: "We always ask for the phone number on the order form, and 80% of the time we get it."

Both marketers said they also include a credit-card payment option on all order forms (VISA and MasterCard).

1:17   Changes in Publisher Use of the Credit-Card Option

When we took up the subject of credit cards as an ordering option in *Volume One*, use by publishers in direct-mail promotions was relatively small. Reactions over their value were mixed among the marketers polled. Since the credit-card entry for *Volume One* was written, increasingly book marketers have taken to using the credit-card option in their direct-mail promotions and in promotions that do not have an exposed order card.*

As the earlier entry in *Volume One* indicated, the value of the credit-

---

*American Express charges are not permitted on an open-faced card; a sealed envelope is required.

card option increases as the price of the promoted product rises. With inflation and increasingly higher book prices, so many professional and reference books are offered at prices well beyond $25 that credit-card use has taken a strong hold. One example of a journal subscription offer featuring the credit-card option is shown in Figure 1. This has become increasingly evident in book displays at meetings and conventions, where the use of charge orders has been rising steadily. To match this increase in credit-card use, more and more publishers have available at meetings credit-card forms that fit the standard imprinter machines provided to exhibitors.

One scientific publisher, in a mail survey to its periodical subscriber audience, asked whether they would like to order books by credit card. Thirty-nine percent of the respondents said they would.*

Credit-card use is obviously here to stay. A few marketers include notations in their printed promotions to encourage credit-card purchases by stating that such purchases are considered prepaid orders on which the publisher pays shipping charges.

1:18   **25 Action Headings that Will Draw Attention to Your Order Forms**

Your reply or order form has a better chance of being used if you include a heading that urges some kind of action. Following are 25 suggested headings for your reply/order forms for professional and scholarly book offerings.

1. Check and Return This Form Promptly
2. Clip Coupon. Mail Today
3. Don't Delay! Mail This Card Today
4. 15-Day Free Examination Offer
5. Fill in and Mail Today
6. Fill Out Now. Mail Coupon Today
7. Free 15-Day Trial Examination
8. Handy Mail-Order Coupon
9. Just Mail the Card Today
10. Mail Card at No Risk—Send No Money
11. Mail Coupon for "On Approval" Examination
12. Mail Coupon for 15-Day Free Trial
13. Mail Your Order Today
14. Order Now for Immediate Shipment
15. Order Today! Money Back if Not Fully Satisfied

---

*In the same survey, readers were asked about ordering books using the publisher-supplied book order form in each periodical. Only one in seven respondents said they ordered books direct; six in seven indicated they ordered listed books through other channels.

FIGURE 1. Increased use of the credit-card option and the toll-free 800 number in periodical subscription promotions to individuals is epitomized in this full-page advertisement in the September 13, 1982 issue of *Current Contents* (*CC*), devoted entirely to these two convenient subscription options. A *CC* subscriber survey two years earlier had shown that 39% of the survey respondents said they would like to be able to order books listed in *CC* by credit card.

16. Satisfaction Guaranteed or Your Money Back
17. Send No Money—Mail Coupon Now
18. Send Now for Free Examination
19. Special No-Risk Offer
20. Tear Off and Mail This Card—NOW!
21. Examine 15 Days at Our Risk—Rush Coupon
22. Mail No-Risk Coupon Today
23. Mail This Card for 15-Day Free Trial
24. Send No Money—Just This Card
25. Mail Free Trial Coupon Today

1:19   **Coupon/Order Form Elements for Direct-Response Book Promotions: Checklist**

1. Company name and address on all order forms/coupons. If the form is a business reply envelope (BRE), it is sufficient to have name and address on the mailing face. For wallet-flap BRE, see 1:24.
2. International Standard Book Number (ISBN) for each title on order form as identification check. If no ISBN is used as identification, use catalog number or order number.
3. Author/title/volume number/edition/series name (where space permits). If space is very limited, supply at least ISBN/order number or key/author name.
4. Book price, consistent with price shown for same book elsewhere in ad or promotion piece. If no firm price is available, show a tentative price and indicate that it is tentative.
5. Sales tax requirement as applicable.
6. Terms of payment available:
    (a) Prepayment required or credit-card option
    (b) Open credit: invoice sent with book(s)
    (c) Optional cash prepayment
7. Statement of postage and handling charge as applicable.
8. Statement of free examination period.
9. Statement of returns policy on prepaid orders.
10. Future availability dates on not yet published titles.
11. Expiration date of offer.
12. Disclaimers as applicable (see entry following):
    (a) Price subject to change without notice
    (b) Territorial restrictions, if any
    (c) Requirements for international orders
13. Appropriate campaign/mailing list/media keys for tracking.

1:20   **Disclaimers, Restrictions, and Conditions**
       for Book Order Forms: Checklist

PAYMENT:

( ) Examination copies not sent to post office box addresses without prepayment.

( ) Payment must accompany orders with post office box addresses.

( ) If order totals $ _____ or more, enclose _____% partial payment, or attach company/institutional purchase order.

( ) Prepayment required. Price includes shipping.

( ) Orders from individuals must be accompanied by payment.

( ) Foreign payment must be in U.S. currency, by U.S. bank draft, international money order, or UNESCO coupons.

( ) Prices are payable in U.S. currency or its equivalent.

( ) Add $ _____ handling charge for books.

( ) Bill us plus postage, or Check enclosed, less 5%, postage prepaid.

( ) Charge orders are not considered prepayment.

( ) MasterCard/VISA orders are considered prepayment.

( ) All major credit cards are accepted.

PRICE:

( ) Price subject to change without notice.

( ) Minimum charge order: $ _____ .

( ) Price guaranteed until (date).

( ) U.S. prices are subject to exchange rate fluctuations.

OFFER:

( ) Offer valid in United States only, or Offer good only in United States and Canada.

( ) Order cannot be processed without your signature.

( ) Order subject to acceptance by (publisher).

( ) Offer expires (date), or Prices good until (date).

( ) Order subject to credit department approval.

( ) Order includes both basic and additional upkeep service such as new editions or additional companion volumes, or I do not want upkeep service.

( ) Premium offer extended for cash-with-orders only.

( ) Continuation order may be cancelled at any time without penalty or obligation.

DELIVERY:

( ) Please allow _____ to _____ weeks for delivery.

( ) If order cannot be filled within _____ days, payment will be refunded.

( ) If address is a post office box number, give street address; we ship by UPS.

SPECIAL REQUIREMENT:

( ) When ordering by letter or purchase order, please attach this form completed.

1:21 Value of Publisher Imprint in Direct-Mail Promotion: Case History*

In the early 1970s, a newly established subsidiary of a prestigious publishing establishment planned a large mailing utilizing a package containing a letter printed on its new stationery. The name of the parent organization was mentioned on the letterhead, but in a barely noticeable typesize.

During the course of mailing plans, it was discovered there was insufficient stationery bearing the new imprint. To make up for the shortfall, a portion of the mailing was done on stationery borrowed from the parent organization.

When the campaign results were evaluated, it was found that the response from that portion of the mailing on the parent company's letterhead was nearly twice that of the response from the mailing sent on the stationery of the newly established, unknown subsidiary.

1:22 "Plastic" Idea for Generating Book Orders

Create a plastic card resembling a credit card and mail it to previous book buyers, to selected lists of prospective book buyers, or to members of a specialized group or society within your field. On the face of the "Discount Card," include the name, affiliation, and address of the individual to whom the plastic card is mailed. Also include on the face of the card the name and address of the publishing establishment and an expiration date. On back of card, use some form of this copy:

This card, when returned with your order for (quantity) or more (publisher's name) books, entitles you to a ___% discount. This card is for the exclusive use of the individual named on the card and may not be transferred or assigned.

*See also 12:21.

1:23   Catalog Order Form that Touches All Bases

One catalog order form that touches all bases is issued by MIT Press. The form:

- States that orders from individuals must be accompanied by check, money order, or credit-card number.
- Offers refund in full if the customer is not satisfied and returns the book within ten days.
- Requires that libraries and institutions attach a signed purchase order.
- Specifies that textbook examination requests must be on departmental stationery and sent to a special department at the press.

1:24   Pitfall of Wallet-Flap BRE that Can Impede Response: Two Case Studies

If you plan a mailing using a wallet-flap reply envelope and put ordering information on the back under the flap, make certain that the gummed portion of the flap does not cover any of the printed area.

We recall a multibook promotion we tried some years ago, and the gummed flap adhered to the envelope exactly where the two lines bearing the customer's name and address were given. Fortunately, the problem was discovered when the initial order was received (and the customer's name and address destroyed). Careful opening or steaming of the remaining orders prevented further losses.

In another instance, a New York City–based publisher of professional and reference books used a wallet-flap BRE inviting credit-card orders that required the buyer's signature. In this instance, the gummed flap directly over the line where the customer's signature appeared.

The lesson learned is that to prevent mishaps, you should allow at least half an inch between live or fill-in area on the back of a wallet-flap envelope and the space where the gum adheres to the envelope.

1:25   How to Summarize and Evaluate Your Direct-Mail Campaigns

Book marketers employ various systems for summarizing direct-mail campaigns. Whatever system is chosen, it is useful to have a summary of your mail campaigns, not only for budgeting purposes and as a record of results achieved but also as a guide for planning subsequent mailings in the same subject area or discipline or to the same mailing list.

In searching out titles to include in upcoming mail campaigns, you may want to review best-sellers of past campaigns for once popular titles that may merit a fresh effort, or the once successfully tested list that might again be used because related titles have subsequently been published that parallel the appeal of the best-sellers when the list was used earlier.

On the next page is a suggested direct-mail campaign summary form that touches most bases of a professional and/or scholarly mail campaign. It can be modified or revised to suit your particular requirements.

1:26   Guidelines from USPS that Get Your Mailings Delivered Faster*

1. Capitalize everything in the address, eliminate all punctuation, and use the common address and state abbreviation.
2. Single-space address block. Put one or two spaces between the character groups and at least two (but not more than five) spaces between the state abbreviation and the ZIP Code.
3. If address includes a data line unrelated to the address, place it *above* the address.
4. If address is to a foreign country, place the name of country on the *last line* of the address block.
5. If address includes both a post office box number and a street address, the mail will be delivered to the address, be it the box or the street number, that appears immediately above the bottom line.
6. ZIP Code must be correct for the address given.
7. When window envelope is used, only the address should be visible through the window. Make sure the addressed insert fits the envelope to prevent shifting. Try to keep a one-quarter-inch clearance between address and window edges.
8. Avoid italic or script types in printed addresses.
9. Include return address with ZIP Code.

1:27   How to Convert Price-Increase Announcement into a Selling Tool

When a general price increase announcement is planned, consider using the price increase as a selling tool to generate orders *prior* to the effective date of the increase. Mail to known book buyers and other prime prospects in the areas affected by the increase and announce "before" and "after" prices, giving the recipient at least 60 days to order before the increases go into effect.

1:28   Response-Boosting Devices Gaining Use in Professional Book Marketing

Two widely used consumer response-boosting devices have been gaining increased attention in the direct-response marketing of profes-

Memo to Mailers, January 1981.

DIRECT-MAIL CAMPAIGN SUMMARY

Mailing Title _____   Job Number _____

Mailing Date _____   Campaign Evaluation Date* _____   Print Quantity _____

Mailing Lists Used†

Name of List	Size of List	% of Return
1.		
2.		
3.		
4.		
5.		
Total	Quantity _____	Return _____ %

Summary of Sales Results (best-sellers by dollar volume)‡

Author/Title	Dollar Volume	@/Unit Price	Total Units Sold
1.			
2.			
3.			
4.			
5.			
6.			
7.			
8.			
9.			
10.			

Gross (Dollar) Sales for Campaign: $_____   Total Units Sold _____
(If books sold on free examination basis, allow for returns and show gross and net figures)

Mailing Description/Format:

Total Number of Titles in Mailing: _____
Overall Cost of Mailing: _____
Cost per Title   _____
Average Book Price per Order   _____
Average Dollar Volume per Order   _____
Average Number of Units Sold per Order _____

Comments:§

---

*Allow at least 12 weeks from mailing date.

†On rental lists, optional entry might state list source, rental cost, and the like.

‡Some prefer two summaries, one by dollar volume and one by units sold.

§Separate space should be provided for comments and to show titles with zero sales because they were not yet published or out of stock during campaign period.

sional and reference books: stamps and sweepstakes. Both require added time, effort, and expense not incurred in conventional book marketing practices. However, as marketers test and find that these devices can increase response by as much as 20% or more, their desirability as marketing tools becomes increasingly attractive.

Use of *sweepstakes* in the promotion of professional and reference books was initiated by John Stockwell at McGraw-Hill in 1982; it involved a mailing that offered responders a choice of prizes, led off by a personal computer (donated by a computer manufacturer for the publicity benefits involved). Word of its success spread quickly, and other sweepstakes promotions were launched by Wiley in New York and by Warren Gorham and Lamont in Boston in the same year.

Such promotions were heralded by mailing envelopes bearing such identifications as "WG&L Sweepstakes" and "Here is your chance to win! . . . a complete Apple II Computer System or any one of over 100 other valuable prizes."

Stamps, long used by medical publishers in various ways, spilled over into nonmedical professional and reference book promotions by other publishers. One establishment bound a sheet of stamps into the centerfold of a 40-book catalog mailing and found in a split test that it did 20% better than the portion of the mailing with no stamps. This highly versatile method of book promotion, largely untried by publishers outside the medical field, is explained in greater detail in other parts of this handbook (see index entry for stamps).

1:29   Sweepstakes Response and Contest Management: Advice from Nash

"Sweepstakes," says Ed Nash in his book *Direct Marketing* (McGraw-Hill, New York, 1982) is "one sure booster to the number of responses." He indicates that a prize of as little as $10,000 has boosted response rates by 30 to 50%, and that larger prizes, selected creatively, have done even better.

"If you use a contest," Nash cautions, "consult a contest management company like Ventura Associates or D. L. Blair to help you select prizes, set up rules, and administer the contest.* The legal restrictions are very exacting, and an independent management and judging organization will be well worth the small cost."

A separate entry on a card-deck sweepstakes promotion appears in 5:18.

1:30   Guidelines to Use of Stamps in Promotion

Because of the increased interest in the use of stamps for book and journal promotion, we met with and posed a number of questions that

---

*Ventura Associates, Inc., was the judging organization for all three 1982 professional reference book sweepstakes conducted by various publishers.

book or journal marketers might ask to the New York representative of *Specialty Printers of America*, the primary supplier of stamps to the publishing industry. Questions and answers follow:

Q. Who can use stamps as a promotional vehicle?

A. Any multititle book publisher or any journal publisher.

Q. What is considered a minimum number for a stamp promotion?

A. For any stamp promotion, we wouldn't advise any quantity under 10,000.

Q. What determines the number of stamps on a sheet?

A. There is no minimum quantity; you can have anywhere from 1 to 120 stamps. You can have as few as one book on a sheet—a "tip-on" stamp that is designed to encourage a "Yes" or "No" response and forces the recipient of your promotion to make a decision right away.

Q. If I decided to try a one-stamp promotion with a letter, how would my lettershop be able to use it?

A. It's tipped on to a letter by any lettershop that has a Cheshire labeling machine.

Q. Can you use stamps in a low-budget promotion?

A. You can use a stamp in a promotion that will have a manufacturing cost of as little as $600.

Q. If there any optimum number of stamps to use on a sheet?

A. No. Some book publishers have used 18, others 20, some 30. Doubleday has used 120 stamps on a sheet; Book of the Month Club has used 60 on a sheet.

Q. How about color? Do you have to use full color in stamp promotions?

A. No. One medical book publisher has been using one color ink (black) on colored stock. Most other book publishers use two colors, but a publisher that had been using two colors has now gone to four colors.

Q. When people ask for rule-of-thumb estimates, what do you base them on?

A. I usually figure on a sheet of 50 stamps, as many publishers seem to favor this amount.

Q. If I were to consider a 50-stamp book promotion, two ink colors, based on 1982 prices, what would they cost approximately?

A. Of course, prices are subject to change. But at 1982 prices, a sheet of 50 would cost $1,500 for 10,000. It would go up to $2,000 for 50,000, and only up to $3,000 for 100,000. There are many variables in determining price, but these should give a good idea.

Q. Who are some of the publishers who have been using your stamps?

A. Saunders, F. A. Davis, Mosby, Wiley, Christian Herald Association, Rodale Press, History Book Club, and Times Mirror Book Clubs.

Q. If I use stamps, but have only a few books, do I have to use a full sheet?

A. No, you don't need stamps on the entire sheet. It can be part stamps, part heading, signature, or advertising copy, or any promotion of your organization. One publisher uses part of the sheet for a return mailing label, and another as a tear-out request form for a publishers' catalog.

Q. What are some of the key factors that determine cost in a stamp promotion?

A. Every job is quoted individually based on such factors as size, number of ink colors, color of stock, perforation patterns desired, and folding requirements.

Q. Is there any charge for an estimate on a job?

A. No, we will be glad to discuss with you any promotion you are planning that involves the use of stamps, to make suggestions, and to show you how you can integrate the stamps into the promotion in the most cost-effective manner possible, based on our experience with houses in the publishing industry.

Q. How do I go about getting an estimate?

A. Call Specialty Printers of America at 212-697-0820, or write to us at 201 East 42nd St., New York, NY 10017.

1:31   What You Need for a Promotion Involving Stamps

1. A mechanical or image for each stamp on one board.

2. An assembly of all of the images on a single board would be ideal and save you money. If you supply, for example, 30 different photographs for 30 different books to appear on a single stamp sheet, you must pay much more than if you were to supply the single board with everything on it.

3. If you plan to have your stamps printed in four-color process, it is best to supply 35mm slides or reflective art, if not finished film.

4. Also supply a folded sample (just a piece of paper mocked up in pencil), with instructions to the stamp printer on how you want stamp sheet folded.

1:32   Some Stamp Formats Used in Book and Journal Promotions

1. Folded sheet of stamps shrink-wrapped on top of book.
2. Folded sheet bound into catalog.
3. Stamps tipped on to cover letter, to be affixed to reply card.
4. Folded sheet, inserted loose in envelope, with reply order card.
5. Souvenir sheet of illustrations (on stamps) picked up from book.
6. Folded sheet with standard letter package.
7. Premium device: "Yes" or "No" stamp with or without other stamps having other uses.

**1:33   Legitimacy Rate of BRCs
in Professional/Reference Book Promotions**

Nearly 95% of all business reply card (BRC) orders received from professional and scholarly audiences are legitimate. This was the finding of a multiyear study based on over a quarter of a million such cards received by one eastern commercial publishing establishment.

During the period of the study, approximately 88.5% of all orders were properly completed and bore the signature of the respondent. All those BRC orders lacking a signature were returned with a postpaid envelope and the signature was requested on the order. Another 6.5% responded, bringing the overall total to just shy of 95%. The percentages shown for the study did not take into account a minute percentage of BRCs returned blank by pranksters.

The study suggests that mail marketers should allow for a 5% factor for false orders in mail-order book offerings involving BRC response vehicles.

**1:34   Addressing Techniques to Ensure Mailing Reaches
Correct Individual in Company or Institution**

Many mailing lists provide just an organizational name. The addition of an "Att:" line indicating a job function or title becomes essential if the promotion piece is to reach its intended recipient.

In some promotions, the intended recipient can be any one of several people. How do you handle this? The answer is to add routing instructions, which frequently are followed. How the routing instructions on your promotional piece should be worded depends on whom you want your mailing to reach. In a medical promotion, for example, it could be three individuals on three different levels of authority.

A wide range of routing instructions is possible. To get some good ideas, watch the mailings sent by people who sponsor seminars. They have refined the technique of routing instructions, so that their announcements have a good chance of reaching at least one likely prospect in the organization to which they mail.

Here are some examples of routing instructions used in recent mail promotions. They may provide some guidance:

Handbook
   A brochure bearing Library of Congress Cataloging in Publication data also had this routing line added: *Pass this card to your librarian to request acquisition.*

Science publisher announcement
   If you have received a duplicate, please route this to a colleague who you feel may be interested in our publications.
      TO: _____
      FROM: _____

Sponsor of Career Development Seminar
Attention Mailroom Personnel:
Please reroute if necessary. If undeliverable to addressee, this announcement should go to Vice President, Administration, or Director of Human Resources.

Publisher of Teacher Periodicals
Route to:
( ) Teachers' Lounge   ( ) Teacher (Grade _____)
( ) PTA   ( ) Librarian   ( ) Purchasing Agent

Loose-Leaf Publisher
Mailroom: If the person on the label is no longer employed at your organization, please route this informative brochure to his or her replacement or department supervisor.

Publisher of Manual on Documentation Methodology
Self-mailer addressed to Marketing Manager had this routing instruction in lower lefthand corner of mailing face:
Attention Mailroom. If undeliverable as addressed, please route to DP Manager, DP Marketing Director, DP Education Manager, or Documentation Department. Thank You.

List Compiler:
Your new mailing list catalog
Please route to:
( ) Mailing List Buyer
( ) Advertising Manager
( ) Sales Manager

2

Mailing List Science
for Book Promotion

Mail order [is] one of the most skillful, interesting methods of marketing or selling that exists, because it is a science. . . . I don't know why I shied away from it all these years. What I should have done was to proceed with developing a mailing list and mail order business, because ultimately, that is what is going to save the small independent publisher . . . unless we develop our own means of marketing, small publishers . . . will not survive. First and foremost, that means mail order.

George Braziller, Founder and President,
George Braziller, Inc., in "Publishing
Voices," *Publishers Weekly*, January 15, 1982.

The single most important element in any direct mail campaign is the list selection system. Improving art and copy can increase response up to 50%; format up to 150%; but the list can increase your response 1000%!

Adapted from Clark-O'Neill *Indicia*

2:01   Mailing List Science: Its Role in Success
of Publisher Mailing Efforts

Attendance at one of the summer publishing workshops included a number of promotion people. One participant reported she was surprised at the high degree of ignorance shown by those present when she spoke briefly on the subject of direct mail and the use of mailing lists. The questions raised were so elementary, she said, that she couldn't believe these same people were involved with the expenditure of budgeted promotion moneys.

It is becoming increasingly apparent to those in book marketing and promotion, particularly in the professional and scholarly areas of publishing, that direct mail is the most effective tool. It is also clear that the body of knowledge and experience accumulated by those laboring in these areas of the book distribution system should in some way be set down, defined, and explained for those just entering the field and those to follow.

We created the term mailing list science in *Book Marketing Handbook*, 1st Ed. (*Volume One*) and defined it as:

An understanding of the general body of knowledge covering practices and procedures involving mailing lists—acquisition, testing, use, maintenance, and evaluation—in conjunction with the marketing and promotion of [professional and scholarly] books.

This chapter is aimed at disseminating that understanding of the practices and procedures involved in the use of mailing lists for professional and scholarly book promotion. It has no level; its appeal is to beginner and professional. Both aspire to the highest degree of response in a mailing effort; both deserve to attain it. Knowledge, experience, and correct practice can help make it possible.

2:02   List-Rental Practices and User Obligations

Mailing list rentals, unless otherwise specified, are for one-time use only. Virtually all list-rental agreements specify that a list is not to be reused for any purpose other than the specific mailing for which it was rented. In most cases, release of the rental list is subject to the approval of a sample mailing piece. Some list compilers/owners will, for a small additional fee, rent a list in duplicate. A limited few will, *with prior agreement*, rent a list for multiple usage or for unlimited use during a one-year period.

It is standard practice for list owners/compilers to seed their lists with decoy names. This ensures they will have knowledge of any unauthorized usage of a rented list.

Mailing list houses or suppliers invariably include a statement in their offerings that your rental of their list constitutes an agreement that you will not reuse the list or any portion of it without consent and payment for each additional use.

Some list owners, such as Technical Publishing Co., require in advance of a list rental that renters submit a letter on business letterhead stationery agreeing to their list rental conditions.

If your rental order specifies that the list be forwarded to a lettershop for mailing, the list owner may require, in addition to or in place of your written agreement, a letter from the lettershop on its stationery stating the list will not be copied, reused, sold, or used by anyone other than the original renter.

2:03   **The Importance of List Guarantees:**
What You Should Know about Compilers

In Chapter 2 of *Volume One*, we cautioned that a list "guarantee" is
not a guarantee of delivery by the list compiler; rather, it usually
means that you will receive a refund of postage or a certain amount for
each undelivered piece returned to the compiler that exceeds the
percentage guarantee. For example, a 90% guarantee means the refund will be made on returned pieces in excess of 10% of the list.

Rather than rely on guarantees, it is advisable to depend on the
reputation and integrity of the compiler. Compilers may view a mailing list in either of these ways:

1. For the list compiler who is conscientious about offering clean, cur-
    rent lists, the list guarantee represents a timely opportunity to
    make corrections promptly and to ensure that the list is a little
    cleaner for the next user.
2. For another class of list compilers who recompile from a new direc-
    tory as issued each year, the "guarantee" merely represents an
    added cost of doing business with a partly out-of-date list.

Make every effort to deal only with compilers who are conscientious
about list cleaning and maintenance. Avoid the others.

2:04   **A Convenient Single Reference Source for**
Virtually Any Type of List

If you mail with any frequency and want a convenient single source for
virtually any type of mailing list, you should consider a yearly subscription to Standard Rate and Data Service's *SRDS Direct Mail List
Rates and Data*. With your annual subscription you receive every
other month, on odd-numbered months, the combined* volume containing over 40,000 business lists and over 10,000 consumer lists. You
also receive 24 of the semimonthly *Update Bulletins* with new data not
previously reported and information on new lists that have just
become available.

Entries in the *Subject/Market Classification Index* are arranged
alphabetically, from "accountants" to "zoologists," for quick retrieval. They are also in a title/list owner index, in alphabetical sequence. The list title is the title supplied by the list owner. There are
also separate sections on co-op mailings, package insert availabilities,
and private delivery systems.

*The one-volume format combining *Business Lists* and *Consumer Lists* in a single bimonthly volume became effective May 1983. Previously, these were published as
separate volumes and at different times of the year, since the start of *SRDS Direct Mail
List Rates & Data* in July 1967.

The SRDS mailing list "catalog" was born at the urging, and with the cooperation of, the Direct Mail/Marketing Association and the American Association of Advertising Agencies (AAAA) Direct Mail Committee. Both organizations provided experience, advice, and counsel in helping to create the present highly workable format.

If you offer or wish to offer your own lists for rent, you can get free listings in *SRDS Direct Mail List Rates and Data* by completing an SRDS listing questionnaire for each list. Your list will not be included if you do not supply list counts and rental prices, if your lists do not supply ZIP Codes, or if you only wish to make your list available on an exchange basis or to selected applicants only.

DATA AVAILABLE ON EACH LIST

1. Personnel—Names of individuals to contact, as well as authorized agents or list managers.
2. Description—Characteristics of list, special features, list arrangement, ZIP Coding sequence, and identification if list is computerized.
3. List source—When, where, and how developed or derived.
4. Quantity and rental rates—Total names, price per 1,000, combination rates, special selection rates, and minimum order requirement.
5. Commission, credit policy—Agency commission, broker's commission, cash discount policy, deposits (if any) with amounts and conditions, credit conditions.
6. Method of addressing—Detailed information on addressing methods, impression selections, and rate differential, if any.
7. Delivery schedule—Availability, time lag or delivery, guarantees, and/or special considerations.
8. Restrictions—Conditions of availability and conditions regarding reuse or security.
9. Test arrangement—Rates, premiums, minimum number required, returned material.
10. Lettershop services—Services performed, mailing instructions, returned material.
11. Maintenance—Updating procedures, guarantee (if any) on delivery, refund conditions, duplication conditions.

**2:05   International Thomson Data Bank:
Additional Source for Direct-Mail Book-Buyer Lists**

Another noteworthy source of direct-mail book-buyer names is the International Thomson Data Bank (ITDB), available from Mailing List Marketing, Oradell, NJ, beginning in 1983. The ITDB names represent the combined lists of buyers of professional books by mail from the various publishing organizations that belong to International Thomson Organisation, Ltd. (ITO), companies in the United States.

A major segment of this data bank of book buyers is the approximately 150,000 book-buyer names, organized by subject areas of books bought in the last two years, from Van Nostrand Reinhold (VNR).

VNR book-buyer names are classified according to such subject selections as art instruction, woodworking, chemical engineering, civil engineering, electrical/electronics, construction management, mechanical engineering, energy conservation, plastics and polymers, business and management, DP software, architecture, and psychology.

Some other data bank book-buyer classifications that are not part of the VNR lists include biochemistry, chemistry, geology, energy, environment, metalworking, materials handling, textiles and clothing, home economics, vocational education, construction professional (by interest category, such as carpentry, plumbing, and the like), and architecture.

Business-related categories include accounting, investments, taxation, finance (general), and legal. The "legal" list, numbering more than 190,000 names, includes buyers of books in banking law, real estate law, and tax and patent law, as well as subscribers to newsletters on banking law, tax law, legal current events, and legal practice. Virtually all names are of attorneys and legal libraries.

As an added service of ITDB, Mailing List Marketing offers a free international list referral service. If you need a list in Great Britain, Canada, Australia, South Africa, France, West Germany, or Denmark, Mailing List Marketing will research the resources of International Thomson Organisation, Ltd., worldwide. If ITO has the list, it will let you know whom you are to contact and how many names are available.

For details and further information, contact: Manager, Mailing List Marketing, Medical Economics Co., Inc., 680 Kinderkamack Road, Oradell, NJ 07649; 201-262-3030.

**2:06   Tool for Checking Mailings and List Rentals:
The Mail Monitoring Service**

If you wish a positive check on your mailings and list rentals, you can obtain such service at a fairly reasonable charge through a mail monitoring service. A subscription to such a service provides you with an individual identifiable decoy name and address in one or more cities. When one of your mailing pieces is received by the service's agent in the city or cities specified, the date is noted on the envelope and the piece is returned unopened to you by first-class mail. Receipt of such a return enables you to ascertain:

- If your mailing was delivered.
- How long it took to be delivered.
- If the components of the mailing were properly included.
- If there was an unauthorized use of your list.

One such monitoring service is U.S. Monitor Service, 43 Maple Avenue, New City, NY 10956; 914-634-1331. It offers monitoring service in 27 cities from Albany, Atlanta, and Baltimore in the East to San Francisco and Seattle in the West and in the Toronto, Canada, area.

2:07   Seeding or Salting:
Protection Devices for Improper List Usage

When you rent your mailing lists to others, it is important to monitor each rental for improper use. This is done by inserting decoy or dummy names in each of your lists. The practice of inserting these names is called list *seeding* or list *salting*. Decoy names may be real or fictitious.

The larger the list, the greater the need for additional names to be scattered throughout the list. Here's why: If only one or several decoy names are inserted and they are all in one city or geographic region, often in a single state, you will not be able to detect improper use of the list in areas outside the areas in which the decoy or dummy names have been inserted.

In *Volume One* of *Book Marketing Handbook*, we cited two ways of monitoring list rentals: by inserting names in the list that would bring samples of each mailing to a cooperating friend, relative, or employee and by enrolling the cooperation of an actual customer, but using a fictitious middle initial so that mailings with that initial would be reported back to you.

Here are additional ways to monitor or otherwise protect your mailing lists against improper usage:

1. Use names furnished by a mail monitoring service in selected, scattered cities in different parts of the country.
2. Include a unique decoy in specific rentals for added protection against list-rental misuse.
3. Periodically change decoy names on your lists as an aid in identifying cases of list misuse.

2:08   List Misapplications You Can Detect with Decoy Names

1. Whether list was used one time only.
2. Whether list was used within authorized time period.
3. Whether list was used by unauthorized third parties.
4. Whether list was used for mailing of the sample submitted.
5. Whether list was not used, and possibly diverted to other purposes.
6. Whether list was misused for any purpose whatsoever.
7. Approximate duration of misuse of list.

2:09   Telltale Signals That Offer Advance Warning of List Pitfalls

Book-buyer lists compatible with your own publishing program will usually generate more response to any book offering by mail. But a claim that a list is actually of book buyers should never be taken on faith alone. Other factors must be considered. One recalls an instance of a "book company" that promoted its rental list of "buyers and inquirers," with the statement in its offering that the buyers portion of the list could be obtained separately at a somewhat higher price. The implication in the offering was that the buyers were book buyers. However, in the description of the combined list, the text read "buyers and inquirers for books and related materials." Use of "and related materials" was a signal that the buyers being offered were not necessarily book buyers, regardless of the fact that the words "book company" were part of the list owner's name.

Two other statements in the advertised list offering provided clues as to the type of buyers the list offered. One was a statement of an "average unit sale of $10" and the other was the maintenance claim that the list was "cleaned every 6 months."

If your publishing program stresses mainly high-priced texts or professional references, a $10 unit sale may not necessarily be the right audience for higher priced books. The list-cleaning claim offered a second signal. In the field of engineering, which this list covered and in which the annual rate of mailing list deterioration is around 50%, a six-month cleaning is advance warning that the list could be as much as 25% undeliverable, depending on how long ago it was last cleaned.

When inquiring about or examining an offering of specialized mailing lists, especially of book buyers, be alert for telltale signals that offer advance warning of possible pitfalls in the list under consideration.

2:10   How to Detect and Prevent Costly List-Count Errors

When you plan a mailing utilizing lists with varying requirements and from different sources, have the lists sent directly to you, rather than to your mailing house. This will enable you to have each list checked to establish that it is in compliance with the specifications on your order, that no wrong lists have been substituted, that no foreign names are included if the order specified U.S. names only, that no libraries are included if you asked for names of individuals only, and the like.

It will also enable you to ensure that the list counts delivered are reasonably close to the amounts ordered and on which your print run was based. It is possible, especially with some association and society lists or when only certain segments of a larger list are ordered, that the counts may vary considerably from your original estimates. When such checking reveals wide discrepancies, errors can be corrected and often there is ample time to change the print order to coincide with actual counts.

2:11   **When a Professional or Scholarly Group
Won't Rent Its List: Alternatives**

1. Advertise in its publications, if it accepts advertising.
2. Ask if the group will accept an insert with its next mailing.
3. Set up a co-op sales arrangement and let the group offer the book itself.
4. A subscription to the organization's periodical may include an annual membership directory issue.
5. Exhibit at its annual meeting. A free drawing at the booth could produce a large number of names.
6. Ascertain if your author has access to a membership list through membership or other contacts.
7. Offer a one-time exchange of one of your own lists in a compatible market. The organization may be interested for possible membership recruitment.
8. If the group's membership is mainly academic, rent lists of academic instructors in all areas related to the subject or discipline.
9. If the group won't release the list, ask if it will do the actual mailing for you at an agreed-upon price.

2:12   **When to Extract a Premium for a List Exchange: Criteria**

If you specialize in a field, subject, or discipline, your book-buyer lists will have greater potential than those of a publisher with a widely diversified list that is not known for specialization in any single discipline or subject area. Should you consider an exchange with such a publisher, you may exact a premium for the added value of your buyer lists over those of the nonspecialist publisher. Also, if you maintain a list of multiple-book buyers, this will have an added value over the names of one-time book buyers.

2:13   **How to Get the Most Out of Lists Used
for Professional and Scholarly Book Promotion**

"A buyer is a buyer is a buyer." What he or she has already bought tells us more about what he or she is likely to buy than all the demographic statistics available.

Ed Burnett, in *The Handbook of
Circulation Management*, ed. Barbara Love,
Folio Magazine Corp., 1980.

In numerous tests, book-buyer lists outpulled other lists in the same subject area or discipline. It is therefore to your advantage to favor book-buyer lists whenever possible for your book promotions. However, a word of caution is in order: If the book-buyer lists you rent are maintained by year of purchase, your biggest pull will always be from book buyers of the previous year. In a subject or discipline where there is a high list deterioration factor (deterioration index), a buyers' list two years old will pull considerably less than a one-year old list of names, and a list that is three years old will pull even more poorly.

Where you have the advantage of ordering lists by year, order names one year old or less, or, for larger coverage, two years old or less. Certainly it is inadvisable to order any list that contains names more than three years old, even where it is claimed the list has been cleaned and updated.

Another good reason to limit book-buyer list rentals to recent years is buyer needs. Book buyers who had great book needs as students or as professionals just starting out may be less inclined to purchase books after several years in professional practice, or their book-buying patterns may have changed vastly after three years.

It is also advantageous to seek out lists from publishers whose buyer lists are for books in areas that closely parallel your own publishing program. Obviously, if you publish primarily for engineers, the buyer list of a primarily textbook publisher will not serve as well as the list of a publisher of professional references and handbooks.

In my own comparisons of two buyer lists from competing publishers, the university press with a publishing program compatible with that of my own company consistently outpulled the buyer lists of a commercial publisher, whose books in the same subject areas were in part at a somewhat lower level.

2:14   Is Merge/Purge Right for Your Mailings?

Is merge/purge a vehicle for improving the quality of your mailings? Perhaps. This process, which combines two or more lists into one composite to eliminate duplications, is not for everyone. It becomes viable for lists from different sources only when list counts are substantial and the elimination of duplicate names provides a good saving over the cost of the merge/purge run.

Most lists used by professional and scholarly publishers are too small to consider a merge/purge run, unless one is merging lists from the same supplier, and this can be done at little or no cost.

Both of the major college faculty list suppliers, College Marketing Group (CMG) and The Educational Directory, have a merge/purge capability for all list orders from their data base. This is true also of Bowker Mailing Lists and of other list suppliers who offer a wide variety of options from a single data base, as do the various licensees of the American Medical Association lists.

So, to answer the question for professional and scholarly book and journal promotions, "yes" to merge/purge if you are ordering various lists from the same data base and if you want to give up the capability of tracking the various segments of the list separately; probably "no" to merging outside lists. If you are using outside lists and you suspect there may be a fairly large overlap, stagger the mailings of the two lists by perhaps a week or ten days so that even with duplications you get a double impact for your mailing and retain the capability of tracking each list separately.

2:15   Another Money-Saving Factor to Consider with Merge/Purge

If you are planning mailings involving large lists and are going to utilize the services of an outside computer service bureau for merge/purge to clean the list and eliminate duplicates, inquire about the availability of a further screening to detect inaccurate ZIP Codes. According to Ray Lewis of *ZIP* magazine, this may affect 2 to 5% of a typical list (depending on how the original data were entered). He advises also that a similar percentage of "bad addresses" can often be eliminated by carrier-route coding lists.

2:16   Lists from Paid or Controlled Circulation Publications: Which Are Better?

Given your choice of a mailing list from a controlled or from a paid circulation publication within the same field, which offers the best names for your direct-mail promotion?

The latter list owner may argue that he offers the better prospect as each name represents an individual who wants the publication enough to pay for it. The former list owner claims his list is better because, in order to obtain a free subscription, the subscriber must complete a detailed questionnaire that provides more information about his work profile than could either a paid circulation or a compiled list.

The controlled circulation list, the owner maintains, also can pinpoint exactly what the subscriber does, his title, the products or instruments he works with, specifies, or purchases, and their value, plus essential information about the company or institution he works for.

2:17   Why Response Pattern Will Fluctuate from a Known Responsive List

Even when you mail repeatedly to the same list with scientific or professional book offerings, the response can vary widely among mailings. The reason is that the response is dependent mainly on the perceived usefulness of the various titles within your offering to the recipients.

A study of responses from repeated mailings to the same list of scientific book buyers over five years showed an average response of from 1.1 to 1.5% generally. However, the response has been as low as 0.8% and as high as 4.3% for selected individual mailings. In the case of the 0.8% response, the mailing had little new to offer over a similar mailing made some months earlier. In the case of the 4.3% response, a number of major new reference works in the field were announced.

Lesson: Your multititle scientific and professional mail offerings must include works that are perceived to be of immediate value or benefit to the recipients if you want them to respond in substantial numbers. Benefit-oriented headlines help.

2:18   Regression Analysis: Use with Mailing Lists*

Regression analysis is a methodology enjoying increasing use in mailing list selection by those who undertake large mailings to improve bottom-line efficiency and profitability. It is based on Pareto's law, which states that, in any given activity, 70 to 80% of the activity is usually produced by 20 to 30% of the participants.

By employing this mathematical concept to large mailing lists, some mailers are able to reduce a large list by two-thirds, while giving up only a very small percentage of the gross sales that a mailing to the larger list would have yielded.

The elements used for regression analysis in direct mail are ZIP Codes and sales related to the purchases within ZIP Codes, such as regency, frequency, and monetary value of the average purchase. These three elements are aggregated by ZIP Code. Then, with the aid of a computer, all ZIP Codes are compared for relative productivity.

The mailer then sorts all ZIP Codes in descending sequence, with the most profitable or responsive ZIP Codes appearing first, and then decides at which point to limit the size of the mailing.

2:19   How to Target Address to Book's Prime Prospect

When promoting a highly specialized professional book, you can best reach your prime target by mailing to a job function. The more specifically the job function can be tied to the theme of your book, the greater your chances will be for reaching the prime prospect within the organization addressed.

Occupational titles within a single engineering discipline cover a wide range of responsibilities. For a book in the field of civil engineering, for example, you would do better to avoid "civil engineer" as a job function and, instead, directly address such specific functions as construction engineer, drainage engineer, environmental engineer, soil mechanics engineer, site development engineer, structural engineer, surveys engineer, utilities engineer, water supply engineer, and the like.

Promotional mailings directed to libraries are most frequently addressed to the attention of the acquisitions librarian. Although this may hold true for most small libraries, in the large ones, the acquisitions librarian may be concerned only with the mechanics of acquisition and not at all involved in title selection. In such instances, your

---

*Based on article, *VECTOR®* in the Clark O'Neill Indicia, August 1981.

best bet is to tag your mailing for a specialized book to the "head of collection development" for the book's subject or discipline.

OCCUPATIONAL TITLES IN MANUFACTURING

Titles tend to vary according to the number of employees. The accompanying table indicates titles that seem most appropriate for mailings where the number of employees is known or specified when renting the list.

Number of Employees

1–49	50–99	100–499	500–999	1,000 and Over
Production Manager	Plant Manager	Vice President, Operations	Vice President, Operations	Vice President, Operations
Sales Manager	Marketing Manager	Vice President, Marketing	Vice President, Marketing	Vice President, Marketing
	Industrial Engineering Manager	Vice President, Research & Development	Vice President, Research & Development	Vice President, Research & Development
Comptroller	Comptroller	Vice President, Finance	Vice President, Finance	Vice President, Finance
Owner/ President	Owner/ President	President/ Owner	Vice President, Corporate Relations	Vice President, Corporate Relations
	Personnel Manager	Director, Industrial Relations	Vice President, Industrial Relations	Vice President, Industrial Relations
			President	Chairman

OCCUPATIONAL TITLES, BY INDUSTRY, FOR LARGE AND SMALL COMPANIES

Transportation, Communication, Utilities

Large Companies	Small Companies
Chairman and Chief Executive Officer	President
President and Chief Operating Officer	Vice President
Executive Vice President	Vice Presidents, Equipment, Labor Relations & Personnel, Transportation, Legal, Sales & Marketing, Comptroller
Senior Vice Presidents, e.g., Operations	
Vice Presidents, Human Resources, Law, Marketing, Transportation, Sales, Public Relations	Executive Secretary
	Treasurer
Vice President, Treasurer, Comptroller, Purchasing	Purchasing Director

Finance, Insurance, Real Estate

Large Companies (Insurance)	Small Companies (Banks)	Small Companies (Insurance)
Chairman of the Board, Chief Executive Officer	Chairman of the Board President and Chief Executive Officer	President
President		
Executive Vice President	Executive Vice President	Executive Vice President
Senior Vice Presidents (for specific activities: Corporate Services, Computer Systems, etc.)	Senior Vice Presidents	Vice President, Secretary
	Vice President	Vice President, Treasurer
Vice President, Secretary	Vice President, Correspondence	
Vice President, Treasurer		
Purchasing		

Data Processing Companies

Large Companies	Small Companies
Chairman of the Board and Chief Executive Officer	Chairman of the Board, Vice President
President and Chief Operating Officer	President
Vice Presidents	Senior Vice President
Secretary	Vice President, Treasurer
General Counsel	Vice Presidents
Vice President, Finance	Vice President, International
	Secretary
	Controller

Construction Industry

Large Companies	Small Companies
President	Chairman of the Board
Senior Vice Presidents, e.g., Sales	Treasurer
Vice Presidents	President
Vice President, Project Management	Vice President
Vice President, Project Operations	Secretary
Vice President, Process Engineering	
Vice President, Engineering	
Vice President, Procurement	
Vice President, Sales	
Vice President, Secretary	
Vice President, Finance	
Group Vice Presidents	
Treasurer	

2:20   Simple Way to Clean House Lists

On all mailings using house lists, always include somewhere on the response vehicle a line "Please remove my name from your mailing list," or words to that effect. This will enable prompt elimination of people who for various reasons—retirement, lack of interest, wrongly included, etc.—are no longer prospects and diminish the effectiveness of your promotional efforts.

2:21   First-Class Mailing Ensures Highest Percentage of Delivery: Case Study

When a list has been acquired with great difficulty or at great expense or when a high degree of deliverability is a critical factor in the mailing, use first-class mail. It has been found that first-class mail will be delivered or forwarded, whereas third-class mail to the same address, no matter how identified, may not.

In a study by the Doubleday Book Division in 1980, 80% of 1,948 pieces of mail sent by first-class mail were either delivered, forwarded to a new address, or not returned by the customer or postal service. Each of the 1,948 pieces in the mailing had been sent to identical addresses in a third-class bulk mailing two weeks earlier and were returned as "undeliverable." Each of the pieces in the earlier third-class bulk mailing had the envelope endorsement "Forwarding and return postage guaranteed." The reasons stated for the returned mail varied considerably, including "not at this address," "no such number," and the like.

2:22   Medical List Selection Options Advancing List Science

In the broad spectrum of professional and reference book promotion, no business, profession, or field offers a wider range of list selectivity options than the American medical profession.

Book marketers dealing with medical professionals can assemble almost any profile imaginable and obtain a list that meets the profile requirements with precision.

Clark-O'Neill, Inc., in its computerized selection options for American Medical Association (AMA) doctors, offers nearly two score options to cover variables ranging from age, sex, race, and marital status, to geographic location by city, state, county, ZIP Code segmentation, to age ranges of doctor's children and median home value.*

The writer recalls a successful test campaign in a medical field in which the selection included only primary practitioners of that subject (lists were also available in which the same subject was a secondary and tertiary specialty). At the same time, the mailing went only to

*In *SRDS Direct Mail List Rates and Data*, Business Lists section, Standard Rate & Data Service, Inc., 5201 Old Orchard Road, Skokie, IL 60077; 312-470-3100.

those in a certain age bracket and in selected cities by population size. Responses were then measured by the size of the city as well as other factors.

One marketing director of a large medical publishing establishment has a direct-response program geared primarily to doctors within five years of graduation from medical school. Most of the numerous medical promotions go to physicians under 25 years of age or to residents. Virtually no mailings from this house are ever sent to physicians over 55 years of age. The company is eminently successful in its efforts.

Mailing list usage, a fly-by-the-seat-of-the-pants business not too many years ago, is emerging as a true science. Those book marketers who make an effort to understand it and to use it effectively can reap immense rewards.

2:23   College Faculty as Market for Professional and Reference Books: Study Result

Marketers of professional and reference books that are not textbooks tend to overlook college faculty as a prime market. Often their reasoning is that because mailings targeted to college faculty often produce poor traceable responses, college faculty lists are not as good as lists of book buyers or membership/subscription lists rented from professional societies or business publications.

It is a fact that mailings targeted to college faculty do generate substantial sales, but it is often difficult to tie them directly to the mailings that triggered them.

One year-long study by a publisher of professional and reference books produced an interesting result. During the course of the year, all mailings in the various scientific and engineering disciplines included approximately 15% college faculty names. While response from the college faculty lists frequently did poorly when compared with the response from other lists in the same mailing, it was found at year's end that nearly 30% of the U.S. sales of that publisher came through college stores.

2:24   Ordering Guidelines for College Faculty Lists

- List counts change constantly; phone first and verify approximate count before issuing order.
- Include with your order relevant job number(s) and the address of the lettershop if lists are to be delivered there. Specify on the mailing label the name of your key contact at the lettershop and include the line "For (your company) Job No. _____."
- If more than one list is being ordered, indicate whether the lists are to be delivered separately or merged into one composite.
- Indicate the type of labels on which lists are to be supplied.

- If key coding is desired on labels, supply key code for each list.
- If the list supplier offers options for two- and/or four-year college names, specify which grouping is desired. Specify "all" if you want both.
- If the list supplier offers the option to choose between faculty in teaching and/or in research, specify the list segment desired. If you want both, indicate "all."
- If the list supplier offers both U.S. and Canadian names, specify on your order "U.S. names only" or "U.S. and Canada."
- If the list supplier offers lists by size of school enrollment as an order option, specify which selection, if any, is desired.

2:25   **The Educational Directory Lists of**
University Press Book Buyers

The Educational Directory (ED) now offers a greatly expanded range of book-buyer lists culled from its 35 member university presses. The book-buyer lists in more than 150 subject categories include more than 140,000 individuals who have bought scholarly, technical, professional, and academic books within the two most recent years. At least 75% of the names are buyers within the current year.

The broad range of subjects cover topics from African studies, agricultural economics, and the American Indian to veterinary science, women's studies, and zoology. There are separate categories for various subjects in history, in literature, and in regional studies.

In addition, there are four special categories of particular appeal to book marketers:

- High schools that buy university press books (2,756)*
- Bookstores that buy university press books (2,644)*
- University press "sale" book buyers (16,073)*
- Multiple book buyers (2,022)*

All book-buyer lists of ED are guaranteed 100% deliverable and may be integrated with other lists on the ED data base, which include college and university faculty, libraries (college, public, and special), and administrators (presidents, deans, and department heads).

For information on the Educational Directory's book-buyer lists, contact the Educational Directory, One Park Avenue, New York, NY 10016; 212-889-8455.

2:26   **New List Selection Options Available for College Mailings**

Because the Educational Directory (ED) list catalog is in loose-leaf form to accommodate periodical updated supplements, list users are inclined to overlook new list selection options periodically added to the ED data base. Larry Fees, director of Educational Directory, cites

*List counts as of late 1982 may be different at the time you need them. Call ED and verify count at time of use.

these unique new selectivity options, now available with ED college faculty lists, at no extra charge:

- Institutional affiliation or control: Federal; State; Local; State/local; State-related; Independent, nonprofit (private); For-profit (private); Religious (by affiliation: Roman Catholic, Jewish, Friends, Episcopal, Baptist, Lutheran, Presbyterian, Southern Baptist)
- Institution's highest level of degree offering: Four- or five-year baccalaureate degree program; First professional degree; Master's degree; Beyond master's but less than doctorate; Doctorate; Undergraduate, non-degree-granting institution; Graduate, non-degree-granting institution; Postdoctoral, research only; Two-year, but less than four-year, degree program
- Predominant sex of institution's student body: Male; Female; Coed; Coordinate (separate colleges for men and women)
- Institution program: Complex program, doctoral emphasis; Complex program, with emphasis in a range of postbaccalaureate programs; Complex program, professional emphasis; Chiefly postbaccalaureate program; Varied, some postbaccalaureate programs; Undergraduate, baccalaureate program; Two-year program, academic emphasis; Two-year program, vocational emphasis; Two-year program, mixed academic/vocational emphasis

2:27 Prime Source for Targeted Lists of Mathematicians

If there is an audience for one or more of your books in one of the specialized branches of mathematics, you will want to know about the lists of mathematical specialists available from the American Mathematical Society (AMS). These lists, in more than 60 branches of mathematics, include names of subscribers to AMS publications, seminar participants, reviewers, math department heads, and buyers of AMS books. Each time an AMS book is purchased, that subject classification of the book is added to the name on the list. Each name may contain up to five subject classifications. If a non-AMS member book buyer does not make another purchase within two years, the name is dropped from the list.

Lists can be supplied for any geographic area. Location should be borne in mind when you order, as about 40% of AMS names are from outside the United States (5% Canada, 35% foreign). AMS lists carry a 99% guarantee. Write for AMS list brochure to Sales Department, American Mathematical Society, Box 6248, Providence, RI 02940; 401-272-9500, ext. 221.

2:28 New CMG Data Base: Major Development in Professional and Scholarly Book Marketing

A major development in the field of professional and scholarly book marketing in the latter part of 1982 and in early 1983 was the emergence of College Marketing Group (CMG) of Winchester, Massachusetts, as a data base of book-buyer names culled from leading publishers throughout the industry and offered in previously unheard-of segmentation options.

These book-buyer names, of which there were more than 1.5 million by the end of 1982, had been virtually impossible to obtain a few years earlier from most of the participating publishers. Yet, now, with nearly 40 publishers participating, the names are offered in many hundreds of selection options and from a single source.

College Marketing Group, prior to the establishment of its new CMG Data Base Division, had enjoyed a reputation since 1968 as a reliable supplier of college and university faculty lists to the U.S. publishing community. All of the book-buyer names in the new CMG data base may be integrated with the CMG's college professor, librarian, continuing education, college administrator, and medical laboratory lists.

Book-buyer list selections in virtually any subject area in which professional and scholarly books are published may be integrated with any college faculty or other lists in the CMG data base to avoid duplication and to ensure pinpoint accuracy in targeted promotional mailings.

Additional details on the CMG data base lists are included in 28:11, 28:12, 28:14, 28:15, 28:17, and 29:05. For detailed information on CMG data base offerings, see 42:03.

2:29   **Most Mailings to Ad Agencies
Are a Waste: Study Result**

Many publishers consider advertising agencies prime prospects for all types of business books, newsletters, references, and similar material. Yet most of this mail is discarded unopened, if the findings of the following study are to be considered.

During a one-year period, approximately 1,800 pieces of bulk third-class promotional mail was received by a small retail advertising agency in northern New Jersey. It was handled in the following manner:

• Approximately 80% was discarded unopened.

• Approximately 20% was opened and noted.

• Of the 20% opened and noted, about half was addressed to an individual by name currently employed at the agency; the other half was addressed by job function or job title.

• Of the 80% discarded unopened, about half was addressed to individuals no longer employed at the agency (some had been gone for as long as five and six years); about half was addressed to the agency by name only with no individual's name or job function specified and no routing instructions.

- In those instances where an individual's name was used (whether correctly or incorrectly), there were often duplicate copies of the same mailing piece.

Study Indications: In a high-turnover business such as an advertising agency, your mailing has a better chance of being opened and noted if it is directed to a job title or job function.

3

Testing: Guidelines, Options, Techniques, Case Histories

Marketing people can make or break a book. They can become so absorbed in the habitual that they forget to be daring, to take chances, to try the unusual. Where, they must constantly ask, is the hidden—not obvious audience? Where are the unexplored markets?

> R. Miriam Brokaw, Princeton University Press,
> in "Letters," *Scholarly Publishing*, October 1981.

3:01   Testing: Tool for More Effective Book Marketing

Testing has been used as a marketing tool by the advertising industry for more than 40 years. Yet, as a tool in book marketing, it has been greatly underutilized. This chapter is intended to make the book marketer aware of testing as a tool of effective book marketing and of its many facets.

For large-scale users of direct mail, testing of mailing lists is a way of life. Today, however, the combination of rising costs and greater specialization in professional and scholarly book publishing makes it more essential than ever for book marketers to refine their practices so that every dollar expended achieves its highest potential in terms of sales. Testing is one way to make this possible.

If you are considering testing, these basics should provide guidance for whatever tests you undertake: Your tests should:

• Provide measurements relevant to your promotion objectives.

• Consider in the evaluation of results the nature of the target audience tested and their normal response mechanisms.

• Cover an adequately large sample size.

Consider relevant measurements. Don't undertake a test of anything that, when results are evaluated, will not contribute to more efficient future efforts in the same area. Arthur Rosenfeld, president of Warren, Gorham and Lamont (WGL),* put it aptly when, speaking to an audience at AAP's Midwinter Meeting in February 1982, in Washington, D.C., he said, "Learn from your failures."

Second, you should consider the test evaluation in the light of the target audience and the usual response mechanisms for such an audience. Consider a test of two lists, one to a professional group and one to a group of librarians. Professionals frequently respond well to publisher promotional literature. However, librarians more often choose to order from a wholesaler or library jobber. Or consider a test of response vehicles, such as postpaid business reply envelopes (BREs) as opposed to reply envelopes, where the customer must supply postage. You may test several audiences, among which are attorneys. Tests have shown that most audiences respond more readily to a postpaid BRE, whereas testing by several legal publishers have shown that mailings got better response from attorneys when no postpaid BRE was provided.

Third, consider size of sample for the test. The sample tested should be representative of the entire group, both geographically and demographically. A geographic test of a group largely based in one part of the country will not reflect accurate results if an area is tested where the group has small representation. Or consider this: Older engineers long established in their profession may be less responsive to a book offering a "refresher course" than a group of young engineers only a few years out of college, especially if the field is a rapidly changing one.

So test, but test with a purpose. Don't restrict your testing only to lists. Test other areas where you feel testing can improve the efficiency of your efforts and stretch your budget dollars. The entries in this chapter will help you to be more aware of the possibilities.

Peter Hodges, marketing director at WGL and one of the industry's leading authorities on testing in conjunction with professional book marketing, offers this gem for readers of this volume: "Everything I tell you [about professional book direct mail promotion] may be right for me, but for you it may be wrong. Take nothing on faith. Test to be sure."

3:02   More List-Testing Guidelines

- When testing a single state, group of states, or geographic region, the test may not be valid unless the nature of the group is considered in the area selection. Certain groups or industries tend to be clustered in specific geographic area, such as those in mining, agriculture, or communication services. Others may be clustered within a single city, such as federal government offices, headquarters of national associations, or book publishers.

*Rosenfeld left WGL November 1, 1982 to become president and editorial director of International Thompson Professional Publishing in New York City.

- When you are testing a small list and want to speed up response, use first-class mail. To obtain results even more quickly, perhaps by another day or two, include a toll-free 800 number and display it prominently in your offering. Impulse buyers often react to a mailing offer as soon as it is received, and the more prominently the 800 number is displayed, the more likely a recipient will utilize it.

3:03   Market Testing: How to Search Out Untapped Markets for Specialized Books

Most marketers of specialized books think in terms of lists and mailings for market testing. There is another route to testing for secondary or untapped markets for that specialized book. It lies in the careful monitoring of responses from promotions and other ordering for that book and implementation of a follow-up procedure in untapped areas that suggest possible market potential.

If you have a book on energy management, your known markets, according to the author's questionnaire, are among builders, architects, and engineers. But you notice that among the orders and inquiries for this book are a number from managers or operators of residential properties and from real estate firms.

You look into Standard Rate & Data Service's *Business Publication Rates and Data* (monthly) and you see that Category 19A is "Building Management and Real Estate." You see, too, that it contains over a score of publications and that, in the "Direct Response Section" of that same directory there are also several co-op card decks under 19A. You decide to test this market.

HIGH ROAD TO A MARKET TEST

If your budget permits, buy a one-card participation in one of the co-op card decks. If you can't afford that, buy a fractional page and insert a pubset quarter-page ad in one of the smaller publications for about $180.

LOW ROAD TO A MARKET TEST

You can't afford to take much out of a tight budget, so you should find out which of the various periodicals in the 19A classification takes classified advertising and will carry your advertisement under a special heading, such as "Product Offerings," "Professional Services," or just "Books." You prepare a tight, benefit-packed mail-order ad of eight or nine lines. You are merely testing the market, so don't offer the book for sale, just offer literature. When you get responses from the ad, send a news release with a coupon on the bottom, if you don't have a special piece of literature on the book. This will cost you as little as $40 to $50, sometimes even less. One publisher promoted a highly specialized book costing $50 for an entire year using this method and attributed most of the 1,500 unit sales of the book to this one source. A toll-free number in the classified ad will help, but you should add a department or key so you can track the responses from the test ad.

3:04   Various Types of Letter Tests: Examples

- Personal vs. personalized
- Personalized vs. mass-produced
- Long letter vs. short letter
- Signed letter vs. unsigned letter
- Letter with postscript vs. letter without postscript
- Traditional letter saluation vs. letter with headline
- Standard letter vs. Reply-O-Letter
- Two-color letter vs. one-color letter
- Ink-color test for second color on letter
- Letter with or without response vehicle
- Letter set flush left and right vs. letter set flush left, ragged right
- Letter printed on two sides of one page vs. two-page letter printed on one side only on two sheets
- Freestanding letter vs. letter printed on cover or panel of larger mailing piece

3:05   Envelope Tests Used in Book Promotions

- Conventional business corner card vs. blank (no corner card)
- Envelope with teaser copy vs. envelope with no teaser copy
- Envelope with typed address vs. printed mailing label
- Envelope with handwritten address vs. printed mailing label
- Envelope on white wove stock vs. envelope on colored stock
- Window envelope vs. regular full-faced envelope
- Envelope with name of individual on corner card vs. envelope with company name on corner card
- Conventional envelope package vs. package in which envelope is affixed to flier printed on card stock and mailed flat

3:06   Envelope Teaser Copy: Test Results in Occupational Education Mailings

A number of book marketers in the professional and educational fields place little value on the use of teaser copy on mailing envelopes. Some use none. A limited number even omit a printed corner card, presumably with the view that a blank envelope will look more like a personal communication.

However, a marketer in the field of occupational education discovered through testing that teaser copy on envelopes containing his new book announcements increased response from course instructors or curriculum coordinators by 15 to 18%. The envelope teaser copy usually highlighted a key feature of the book.

3:07   No-Risk Way to Test Effectiveness of Co-op Mailing

When you are invited to participate in a cooperative mailing, it is sometimes possible to set up a test arrangement on a per-inquiry basis. Under such an arrangement, replies to the mailing go back to the sponsor, to whom you pay an agreed-upon amount for each inquiry received. Responses to book offers usually take the form of orders. High-ticket or multivolume works may offer detailed information in the form of a flier or prospectus. Journal or periodical offers may work best with an offer of a sample issue.

3:08   Business Reply Card Test: Premium vs. Pass-Along

A promotion for business books included two attached tear-off business reply cards (BRCs). The first was for ship-and-bill orders; the second offered a premium for prepayment. In a follow-up mailing of the same promotion, the two reply cards were changed. One card was a standard order form with no premium for prepayment. The second card was essentially the same, except that it also carried the suggestion that the mailing piece with this card be passed along to a friend or colleague. The second mailing with the changed reply cards brought a considerably higher response.

Lesson: If you want the recipient of your book or journal promotion to take some action, suggest it in the copy.

3:09   Format Tests for Law Book Promotions:
Two Case Histories with Same Results

Attorneys, probably because they have ready access to secretarial help, prefer to use their own postage and envelopes when responding to law book promotions and react more readily to a coupon than to a business reply card. Here are two case histories that bear this out.

PARKER & SON

Parker & Son, a California law book publisher, had been using card stock for its mail promotions so that the removable order form was a business reply card. In 1977, it tested two mailing formats. One used the standard format—a piece printed on 8 pt. coated cover stock with a tear-off reply card. The other format used 70 lb. offset stock with a perforated order coupon instead of a reply card. Both formats used the same offer and copy.

1977 Test Result   828 orders, 44% with payment, were generated by the business reply card format, while the perforated order coupon format produced 880 orders, 66% with payment.

Parker repeated the test in 1979 with a slight variation. Instead of testing percentage of prepaid orders, total sales and cost per thousand were tallied in the 1979 test.

1979 Test Result   The business reply card format generated total sales of $11,723 at a cost of $260 per 1,000, for a cost ratio of 1.5:1. The perforated order coupon format generated total sales of $9,685 at a cost of $180 per 1,000, for a cost ratio of 1.8:1.

NEW YORK LAW JOURNAL SEMINARS-PRESS

Paul Siman, of New York Law Journal Seminars-Press, reported in 1981 (in *PPMG News*) that he had made the same format change after testing—replacing reply cards with coupons requiring postage and mailing envelope—and found that prepaid orders were up an average of 30%.

Furthermore, Siman said, he substituted 60 lb. white offset stock for the 7 pt. bulk stock previously used in order to reduce production costs. He reported three additional benefits from the change:

• The increase in prepaid orders cut his billing expense.

• The return/cancellation rate was reduced.

• Collection and bad debt expense was reduced.

3:10   Postage Test: Split Between First Class and Third Class

A marketer of professional books and publications in the field of taxation embarked on a postage test to ascertain whether the added cost of first-class postage could improve response of his numerous promotional mailings to this market. A substantial chunk of his annual budget was involved. His promotional vehicle for the test used a Reply-O-Letter* format in a split run, with half the mailing on each list going by metered bulk third-class mail and the other half going by first-class mail with postage stamp affixed. The test consisted of 70,000 pieces and involved a 20,000-name customer list and 50,000 names from six rented lists.

RESULTS

In the mailing to the 50,000 names on the six rented lists, the half of the mailing sent by metered bulk third-class mail outpulled the half with first-class postage. In the mailing to the 20,000 customers, the

---

*A "Reply-O-Letter" is a patented mailing format that is designed to facilitate replies and is available from the Reply-O-Letter Co., Inc., 1860 Broadway, New York, NY 10023. It features a die-cut opening on the face of the letter and a pocket on the reverse. An addressed reply card is inserted in the pocket so that the name and address thereon show through the die-cut opening.

half sent by first-class mail heavily outpulled the half of the mailing using bulk third-class postage.

EVALUATION

The marketer making the test theorized the difference in results this way: "In the case of our customers, they get 'tons' of our third-class mail, but when it's first class, they probably thought it was an invoice or renewal notice and, therefore, it merited special attention."

CONCLUSION

Mail first class when it serves a useful purpose; otherwise metered third-class bulk mail will usually do as well or, as in this test, better.

3:11   List Tests: With and Without Stamp Sheet Enclosures: Case Study

Early in 1982, a New England medical publisher did a split test mailing to approximately 15% of a large list in a medical specialty that comprised approximately 10,000 names.

Five thousand names were randomly selected and sent a book flier that contained six 8½" × 11" panels and folded down to 8½" × 11", printed in two ink colors. The cover panel contained a letter, and the remaining panels contained copy describing 32 different medical books, each with a cover illustration.

Another 5,000 names were randomly selected from the same list and sent the same flier, to which was added a sheet of stamps, each illustrating in four colors the cover of one of the books in the flier. The fliers with stamps outpulled the fliers without stamps by 2.8%.

3:12   Some Other Stamp Tests Used in Book Promotions

- A medical book publisher enclosed a sheet of stamps, on which each stamp contained ordering information for a different book, with outgoing book shipments. The simple one-color nonillustrated sheet of stamps paid for itself many times over and is still widely used after two years. (For a more detailed entry, see 9:08.)
- A professional and reference book publisher mailed half of 100,000 catalog mailings with a conventional postpaid order form; the other half contained a sheet of book stamps bound into the catalog centerfold. The test half with the stamps required that the stamp bearing the two-color cover illustration of the desired book be removed and pasted on a blank space on the order card. The half of the test using stamps outpulled the other half by 20%.
- A book club tested two packages—one with and one without stamps—for an introductory club offer. The package with stamps outpulled the other by 50%.

3:13 Offer Tests: Book Mailings with and without Free Examination Option

In two loose-deck postcard mailings by the College Marketing Group (CMG) in 1980, a postpaid business reply envelope returnable to CMG made possible a comparison of responses to books with and without a free examination offer. These were the results, based on offerings by many participating publishers:

- In a mailing to 50,000 special education book buyers, the 10% of the deck offering books on a free trial basis (15- or 30-day free examination) produced over two and one-half times more orders per card than those cards in the same deck that did not offer free examination.
- In a deck mailing to 50,000 medical book buyers only 2 of 43 books in the deck were offered for free examination. These two cards outpulled the other cards in the same deck by a margin of 20 to 1!

3:14 List Testing by Telephone

If a list would normally give a 1% return, a telephone test of that list will not show any measurable improvement and would be largely a wasted effort. However, if a list is known to yield a 5% return, a telephone test of that same list could increase the yield to as much as 20 to 25%. Such is the advice of a telephone marketing expert who heads his own phone marketing organization.

3:15 Protective Technique for Shoddy List Rental Practice

In *Volume One* of *Book Marketing Handbook*, we issued a warning against a relatively rare type of list renter who may supply dynamite names for a test and give you garbage when you go back for the rest of the list.

One protective mechanism suggested was to order a certain segment of the list by ZIP sequence. By request, here is an enlargement and clarification of how you can effectively use this method: You order a certain segment of a larger list by ZIP sequence, say from 00000 to wherever your test quantity, be it 2,000 or 3,000, ends. Then make a photocopy of the last page of names on the test list.

When you order the balance of the list, start with the lowest ZIP number on the photocopy sheet, and compare those names with the names on the first sheet of the reordered list. If the names and addresses are essentially the same as on the test portion, you have the same list.

4

Mailing List Deterioration and Group Mobility: Case Studies

4:01   Mailing List Deterioration:
        Key Factor in Direct-Mail Success

In *Book Marketing Handbook, Volume One*, we posed a simple success formula for selling books by mail: the offer (the right book); the message (factual, convincing copy); and the list (the right audience). We contended that whatever the mailing format, the ultimate success or failure of any mailing is tied to these three basic factors.

This chapter focuses on the third part of the three: the list. We want to drive home the lesson that even with a terrific offer and a convincing and well-prepared message, unless your list delivers its message to the right audience, no mailing can succeed.

The lesson seems obvious. But it isn't.

Suppose you have a terrific, high-priced book and a beautiful mailing piece describing it. You mail to a list of 10,000 names. You would be very happy with a 2% response, or 200 orders. But you use a list compiled from an old directory in a rapidly changing field, and only one of four pieces in your mailing actually reaches its intended recipient.

Not only is your response cut by three-fourths to 0.5%, or 50 orders, but the cost of three-fourths of the mailing, including postage, that was wasted will most likely exceed the value of the resulting orders. The mailing is a total loss.

The example demonstrates the importance of mailing list deterioration. Think "deterioration" when you think lists. How old is the list you are using? What is the age of the directory from which it was compiled? How frequently, if at all, has the list been cleaned? And, most important, how reliable is the list source from which the list is being rented?

Give credence to the reliability of the list compiler. How long has it been in business? Which of your competitors have been using its lists? Check with other publishers who have used the lists to see whether there were any problems.

And, above all, avoid being your own list maven. Don't think that, because an author has given you a three-, four-, or five-year-old directory from a professional organization in which he holds membership, you have stumbled upon a gold mine. These old lists can sow the seeds of failure for a mailing effort.

So how do you avoid high-deterioration lists?
- Use lists that are used frequently and regularly cleaned and maintained. As some of the later comments in this chapter indicate, some lists are recompiled as each new edition of a directory is issued with no effort to clean between editions.
- Use lists from professional societies.
- Use lists from large, reliable, and established compilers and directory publishers.
- Use lists from book publishing competitors in your own area who will rent them to you.
- Use the book-buyer list data base of College Marketing Group, which combines the book buyer lists of many established commercial publishers.
- Use the book-buyer lists of the Educational Directory, which offers the combined book-buyer lists of the university presses.

4:02   Mailing List Degeneration: A Commentary by Ray Lewis*

Volume One of this handbook cited the generally accepted practices for evaluating the accuracy of mailing lists. This factor, called "list degeneration," will vary greatly according to the list used and to general economic conditions.

Until the 1982 economic downturn, people were physically moving at the rate of about 10% a year. Professional and technical people were moving even faster, and the rates of change within companies often were very high, as job responsibilities shifted, new plants and offices were opened, and people were promoted.

This has now slowed down a bit. But if you consider that many of the so-called compiled lists are from directories that may be out-of-date when issued and may not be changed for a year or more from that date, you can see how 20% or more of these lists can be inaccurate. This means 20% of the pieces you mail may end up in the mailroom wastebasket, or may be thrown away if undeliverable (third-class mail).

*Ray Lewis is editorial director of *ZIP, The Magazine of Effective Direct Marketing*. His publication is the most widely circulated of the three major publications in its field, reaching nearly 40,000 subscribers monthly.

The older the information on a list, the more likely it is to be obsolete. If we posit a general rate of change, our "deterioration index" is then 10% times the age of the list (in years).

For engineers, nurses, scientists, college professors, and other highly mobile professional groups, you should double this rule-of-thumb index. Therefore, allow 20% times the age of the list.

Quite a bit of money is wasted, not only for list rental but also in costs for postage, printing, envelopes, inserting, and the like—costs that amount to about 25¢ to 30¢ per piece.

If you subtract the date of the source input for the list you plan to use from the date you expect the piece to arrive in the hands of the prospective buyer, you get a fairly accurate picture of the percentage of undelivered pieces you can expect.

For a mailing to a list 12 months old, with an estimated deterioration index of 20%, only 80% of this list would be deliverable. You therefore need to figure on a higher rate of response in order for your mailing to be cost-effective.

Professional list managers and brokers will often be able to tell you the rate at which a given list changes. When dealing with compilers, ask specifically about the date of the original compilation of a list or list segment that you are considering.

4:03   List Offering Poses Risk from High Annual Deterioration: Case Study

In the mid-1960s we ceased using a multidisciplinary list of scientists when we learned through inquiry that the list was cleaned only when a new edition of the directory from which it was compiled was issued. The list had been maintained on plates used in the compilation of the new edition.

Fifteen years later, the directory names were still being offered, now online. When we learned of the online offering, we again inquired about the frequency of list cleaning. We were assured that the list was clean because it was compiled from a recently published, new edition of the directory.

We recalled that we had calculated the deterioration rate of the prior edition of that same directory, issued several years ago. It was then over 40%, and we wondered how clean such a list would be in the years between editions.

The lesson of this entry is that when you plan to use any list, especially on a large scale, as we had when over 50% of our catalog mailings went in this direction, ask first: When was the list last cleaned? It is a small investment in your time that can pay big dividends.

4:04   Mobility among Scientists in Leadership Roles: Survey Result

In 1978, 93 scientists who had contributed to a major reference work in their field were contacted by mail. Four years later, a mailing to this same list disclosed the following changes: 15 (16.1%) were at a different address; 7 (7.5%) were retired and no longer active; and 2 (2.2%) were deceased. The four-year list deterioration rate was 25.8%, or approximately 6.5% per year. The discipline as a whole has an annual mobility rate of 15%. The indication is that a list of scientists in leadership roles is less likely to change over a number of years than an across-the-board list that includes more highly mobile, younger professionals.

**4:05   List Deterioration in the Arts and Humanities:
Case History**

A publisher in the arts and humanities was considering a mailing list merger with another establishment that had a much smaller list. He felt he had much to offer—a list containing more than 100,000 names. When the intended partner in the merger requested a breakdown of the list by year, he thought he could not deliver, and that his list had been maintained as a single composite grouping.

He consulted the list service bureau he had engaged two years earlier. Luck was with him, for the service bureau's computer had entry dates for all names added during the preceding two years. When this segment was extracted from the larger list, approximately 22% of the total remained.

Then the intended list partner asked how often the list had been cleaned. The list owner made another discovery: nixies that had accumulated over a two-year period had not been sent to the list service bureau for purging. When this was done, the list became even smaller. The merger of lists did not take place.

The lesson here is that if you maintain mailing lists of buyers and prospects, be sure to include the date each name is entered into the system. Furthermore, if you use your list often, purge the nixies from your list as quickly as they are received, or at least before each new use of the list.

4:06   Annual Mobility Rate of Landscape Architects

Landscape architects are a very mobile group, says Linda Robertson, membership director for the American Society of Landscape Architects. Address changes for the society average about 100 per month, which gives the 5,000-member society an annual mobility rate of 24%.

4:07   Annual Mobility Rate of Special Librarians

The membership of the Special Libraries Association (SLA) is 11,500. In a recent year, according to Jennifer Deroche of the SLA Membership Department, there were about 4,000 address changes, for an annual list deterioration rate of about 35%.

4:08   Annual Mobility Rate of Attorneys

The annual change rate for the 162,000-member mailing list of the Chicago-based American Bar Association (ABA) has varied in recent years between 15 and 19% for an average of 17%, according to Robert Taylor, ABA director of direct response marketing.

4:09   Annual Rates of List Obsolescence in Business and Industry: Two Indicators

"The real world of U.S. business is changing at the rate of one percent every three weeks. That rate of change," says a market data retrieval publication issued in 1980, "comes close to 20 percent a year. To put it another way, any list of companies verified by telephone data checks today will be 10 percent out of date six months from now."

Dick Hodgson, reporting on list obsolescence in industry in the 3rd edition of his classic *Direct Mail and Mail Order Handbook*, points to McGraw-Hill circulation records, which show that, for every 1,000 key persons in industry, each year "only 435 stay put in the same job, same company, same location."

4:10   The High Mobility Rate in Book Publishing

The annual rate of job change among titled book publishing personnel is about 25%.* This is due largely to the fact that a change of jobs usually brings with it a salary increase of 20% or more, whereas annual increases within the same company may amount to an average of 7 to 10%.

And this situation has not changed over the years. In the mid-1960s, the promotion manager of the U.S. branch of an international scientific publishing house was "rewarded" for outstanding accomplishment by the board of the international group: They voted him an annual salary increase of $1,000 per year for five years. The annualized rate for the period was less than 8%—and this for outstanding accomplishment!

A clear example of the high mobility rate in publishing is the following: When a 1966 group photo of the McGraw-Hill College Division, including both management and field staff, was examined 15 years later, only 18 of the 111 individuals in the photo, or 16%, were still employed by McGraw-Hill.

4:11   Alternative to Direct Mail when List Mobility Is High

With a book or periodical of sufficient price and a targeted audience with a high rate of mobility, you may find telephone marketing a

---

*See also 40:02 in this volume and 4:19 in *Volume One*. Also refer to the *PW* Special Survey, "Publishing's Revolving Door," by Stella Dong (*Publishers Weekly*, December 19, 1980).

viable alternative to direct mail. Through this medium you can achieve instant results from among those prospective buyers you are able to reach. *Army Times* faced this problem in marketing the circulation for its publications aimed at career military personnel, as these individuals are usually transferred every three years. *Army Times* relies almost entirely on the telephone for its subscription marketing as well as renewals.

4:12   **Some Occupational Areas Where Compiled Lists
Must Be Viewed with Caution**

Because of the high rate of mobility in some occupational areas, any lists compiled from directories embracing these fields should be used with caution. They may have a high rate of obsolescence even before the directory has come off press.* Personnel turnover in advertising agencies is reportedly very high. In placing list orders or undertaking list compilation from directories in fields subject to high mobility, you stand a much better chance of having your mailing delivered if it is addressed to a job title or job function, rather than to an actual name.

Lists of names containing writers, commercial photographers, or artists that are compiled from directories older than the current year entail a high degree of risk. Some directories in these three areas were reported to have changes affecting more than 70% of the list between annual editions, and the fact that a new directory will be issued within a year makes it unlikely that the compiler will clean the list repeatedly in the short time span between editions.

4:13   **Lists Compiled from Directories:
Pitfalls, with Selected Examples**

As discussed earlier, directories have a high annual rate of deterioration and become obsolete even as the compilation process is being completed. As Dick Hodgson says in his *Direct Mail and Mail Order Handbook,* "In using directories for list compilation it is important to remember that . . . it takes a long time to edit and publish any major directory, and during this time span many names and addresses change . . . then, the majority of directories are not revised for another year and sometimes not more often than every five years."

We do not question the validity and importance of the directory as the starting point for list compilation. But we also feel that an understanding of the list-compilation process and of the ways in which directories become outdated can be helpful to the list user in considering any directory for list compilation or in renting a list compiled from any directory.

The examples in the following entries provide insights into how some compilers and data-base managers view use of directories for list compilation, and are designed to contribute to that understanding.

*For additional information on high-mobility professions, refer to the table in 4:27 in *Volume One, Book Marketing Handbook.*

4:14   **List Compilation from College Catalogs**

A number of publishing establishments use as their primary source of
college faculty names the directories issued by the colleges. This is
both a wasteful and an impractical source for building mailing lists.
The primary reason is that somewhere between a third and a half of all
colleges issue their catalogs every other year.

When one considers that the annual turnover rate of college faculty
is more than 21%* and that most college catalogs are prepared and
issued before the start of the academic year for which they are issued,
it becomes apparent that the college catalog is a poor source for
faculty list compilations.

If you already maintain lists of college faculty and have no effective
vehicle for updating changes, it is now possible, through College
Marketing Group, to order any segment of the college faculty market
and to obtain just the names of faculty members added as of any date
you specify. Write to College Marketing Group, 50 Cross Street, Winchester, MA 01890.

4:15   **Lists Compiled from School Directories**

Because of diminishing school enrollments and subsequent school closings, at least 5 percent or more of the entries on lists compiled from
school directories are out-of-date. As a result, says Terry Coen of
Market Data Retrieval, a school list compiler, at least 5% of any mailing to school lists compiled from a directory is undeliverable.

4:16   **Annual Change Rate in Association Directory**

Columbia Books, Inc., when queried for this volume on the annual rate
of change in its annual directory, *The National Professional and Trade
Associaton (NPTA) Directory*, replied: "We do not keep exact statistics about the percentage of change in our entries each year.
However, at least 50% of the associations we list in our directory
undergo some kind of change during the course of a year. They may
move, have a new phone number, a new executive director, put out a
new publication, or disband, merge with another organization, or split
and form two separate organizations."

4:17   **Annual Proliferation and Cessation of Journals and Serials**

Ulrich's International Periodicals Directory data base contained
109,622 entries, for both periodicals and serials, at the end of 1982. Ac-

*The annual rate of address change for 523,777 U.S. college professors in the College
Marketing Group data base, according to a 1979 study, was 21.35%. This study was
prepared for 4:11 in *Volume One*. That same entry showed a 19.3% annual mobility rate
for the 1964–1965 academic year, based on an independent study.

cording to Iris Rugoff, manager of Bowker Online Services, 5,000 new entries are added each year, whereas 12,000 titles ceased publication between 1974 and 1982, an annual rate of 1,500 per year.

4:18   **Phone Directory List Compilation: A Pitfall**

To be deliverable, a mailing address must carry the name of an official post office or named branch or station. Many communities in the United States, possibly as many as 100,000, do not receive mail in their own names. Yet community names are used in many phone directories. Consider this pitfall when using a phone directory as a list source.

4:19   **Use, But Don't Rely On, Directories—Robert Howells**

Robert Howells of IBIS (International Book Information Service), who contributed the article "Building and Using Mailing Lists" to *Scholarly Publishing* (July 1980), contends that directories should be used for list building, but should not be relied upon. A directory published in January 1980, he says, might have a 1980–1981 date, leading those using it in December 1981 to think of it as being up-to-date, when, in fact, the research may have been done during 1978–1979. Thus, it may be up to three years out of date and 60% inaccurate.

4:20   **Compilers Don't Use Nixies to Update Lists—Angelo Venezian**

Marketers who rely heavily on directory list compilers should heed this comment from Angelo R. Venezian, president of the list brokerage firm bearing his name, whose article "The List Business" (*DM News*, June 15, 1981) contained this statement: "List compilers do not use nixies to update lists. Lists deteriorate monthly. List compilers put up a new list each year rather than update them."

4:21   **We Don't Treat Nixies. We Recompile Each Year**

National Business Lists (NBL), one of the largest compilers of lists from directories, reported in its *NBL Marketing Guide* that 72.8% of the more than 10 millon entries in its data base remain unchanged each year, and that even within this group, nearly 20% undergo status changes, such as change in SIC (Standard Industrial Classification) number, financial strength code, or corporate branch status. How does NBL keep up with these changes? We questioned an NBL official, E. William (Bill) Carney, and got this response, "Except in certain pockets of our list, we don't treat nixies. We recompile each year."

4:22   **U.S. Mailing-Address Deterioration Rate**
         Nationally and by Region

Volume One of *Book Marketing Handbook* (entry 4:25) reported that
American households change their addresses at the rate of 18.6% a
year, based on a 1976 study by Census Bureau demographers. It con-
trasted the high U.S. rate with that of Australia (15%), Japan (12%),
Great Britain (11.1%), and Taiwan (9.1%). It also indicated that
Ireland had the lowest mobility rate (3.1%).

More recent studies, released by the Census Bureau at the end of
1982, indicated that the U.S. rate of address change is holding, but at a
declining rate. In the year ending October 1980, the annual rate of address change for U.S. households was 18%. In the year ending October
1979, the rate was 19%. In the year ending October 1978, the rate was
20%.

Americans in different parts of the country change their addresses
at greatly varying rates. According to the same late 1982 Census
Bureau report, the "recent mover" rate for households in the West was
23%. The most stable U.S. geographic region was the Northeast, with
a mobility rate of only 13%. For the North Central states, the annual
rate was 16%. In the South, 19% of households changed their address.

5

Formats for Promotion

5:01   **Type of Mailing Format Determines Speed of Response: Options**

The format you select for your professional and reference book promotions has an important effect on the length of the mail response curve.

- If you're looking for a sudden response to wrap up a campaign quickly, do an individual promotion piece for one book.
- If you have a number of books to offer and can't afford to promote each individually, try a card deck. The loose-deck format will give you very fast response—about half the total response will come within four to five weeks after mailing date.
- If time is not important, try a catalog format. This format will pull much longer, has a "pass-along" readership you won't get with a deck mailing, and often provides a higher quality response probably because the catalog permits more space for descriptive copy than a postcard.
- If you're looking for a format that will force the recipient to make a "yes" or "no" decision on a special offer, include a tipped-on double stamp with your mail offering and invite the recipient to remove and mail back the return card with either the "yes" or the "no" stamp pasted on it.

For other entries in this volume related to promotion formats, see 1:32, 23:10, 23:12, 23:14, 28:16, 30:15, 34:01, 34:05, and 34:06.

5:02   **Popular Formats for Professional and
Scholarly Book Promotion: Checklist**

( ) Direct-mail package (traditional).

( ) Personalized letter.

( ) Self-mailer: series of 8½″ × 11″ panels, folded down to 8½″ × 11″ mailing size. Usually two, three, or four panels, sometimes with separate tear-off order form.

( ) Self-mailer: series of 8½″ × 11″ panels, as above, but folded once more to reach a 5½″ × 8 ½″ mailing size.

( ) Single self-mailer cards, from standard postcard to oversized card.

( ) Broadside folded down to self-mailer size.

( ) Card deck: pack of loose postcards in paper or polyvinyl envelope (loose format).

( ) Card deck: bound-deck format. Usually two or three cards on a page, perforated and bound into booklet.

( ) Mail-order catalog, self-cover, at least 0.007 inch thick stock.

( ) Mail-order catalog, paper stock with bound-in order card or envelope.

( ) Subject catalog or seasonal catalog, self-cover.

( ) Catalog or offering booklet, hard cover.

( ) Dover format (series of 11″ × 17″ fliers, folded down to fit into #10 envelope).

( ) Flier printed on back of book jacket.

( ) Reply-O-Letter format (reply card in pocket of die-cut letter).

( ) Syndicated stock formats available from various printers or envelope manufacturers.

( ) Letter-Gram or News-Gram format.

( ) News release format.

( ) Newsletter.

( ) Newspaper.

( ) Wrap-around: promotional four-page cover over regular catalog cover, designed to draw attention to special project.

5:03   **Unconventional Formats that Worked in
Professional Book Promotions**

POP-UP SELF-MAILER

Used by Matthew Bender & Co., Inc., for its book *Courtroom Toxicology*. When the self-mailer was opened, the headline, book title, and accompanying illustration popped up as the top panel unfolded.

SWEEPSTAKES (LETTER ENCLOSURE WITH CARD DECK)

Used by McGraw-Hill Professional and Reference Division. Persons who placed orders for books also had chance at winning an Apple computer (donated by Apple for the advertising value from promotion).

STAMPS

Little, Brown & Co. uses one of the simplest direct-response formats, a sheet of stamps bearing cover illustrations of 30 to 35 medical books, along with a postpaid reply card. To order any book, the recipient pastes any stamp on the order card and drops it in the mailbox. The stamp sheet is folded twice and mailed in a #10 envelope. Stamps are printed in four colors of ink.

HYBRID CATALOG/BOUND DECK

The Bureau of National Affairs uses a hybrid format that is both catalog and bound-card deck. Each catalog page, which is the size of two postcards, features a single book. Sandwiched between each two book pages are two removable perforated order cards, one atop the other. The top reply card is for the book featured at left, the bottom reply card for the book featured at right. A catalog of 14 book offerings has 14 matching cards. The self-covered catalog includes an 800 (toll-free) number on each card and offers each book on 45-day approval.

UNUSUAL RESPONSE FORMAT

Used by W. H. Freeman and Co. in an annual mathematics catalog, this format featured a centerfold consisting of a two-page bind-in on postcard stock. Each $8\frac{1}{2}'' \times 11''$ page contained three removable perforated reply cards:

- The first (postpaid) card addressed itself to the instructor with the heading "For Possible Class Adoption." It contained this copy: "I am teaching the course described below, for which this text may be adopted. Please send me a complimentary copy."
- The second (postpaid) card offered "for examination and possible class adoption, complimentary copies of (low-priced) Scientific American Offprints."
- The third (not addressed or postpaid on reverse side) was headed "For My Personal Use" and indicated that if the books purchased were adopted for classroom use, the publisher would cancel or refund the charge. It offered a 15% discount and required payment with the order. The reverse side of the card was blank, except for the statement, "For Your Personal Library."

POSTCARD-SIZED SELF-MAILER

A small publisher of nursing texts issues modest postcard-size self-mailers, printed black on card stock. The folded mailer, measuring 4″

× 6″ opens flat to 6″ × 12″. Each of three inside panels features a different title, as does the concealed panel on the inside flap. The exposed back panel has illustrations of the covers of titles featured inside under an appropriate headline.

5:04   Alternatives to Classic Letter Mailing Package Format

You need not feel you are "married" to the classic mailing/package format. Any number of variations are available to you that are more economical and may be more effective. Here are a few possibilities that worked in book and journal promotions:

- Letter with BRC or BRE only; flier omitted.
- Letter only, with BRC (or BRE) and flier omitted.
- Letter only, with order form as bottom part of letter (no BRE).
- Letter with order form as bottom part of letter and BRE enclosed.
- Letter on four-page 11″ × 17″ sheet, with letter on page 1 and continued on page 4. Flier printed on two inside pages.
- Letter on four-page 11″ × 17″ sheet, with letter on first three pages, flier on fourth page.
- Letter of any length, with typewritten copy running around book illustrations, either to the right or left. Keep illustrations small so they do not interfere with the copy. Include BRC or BRE.
- Letter, four-page miniature version, folded into quarters and inserted with card-deck mailing. Folded size should be equal to card size.
- Letter package, with 8½″ × 11″ flier rigid, flat, and mailed outside package. Envelope-package affixed to lower third of flier.

5:05   Nonletter Mailing Formats: Examples

1. Self-mailer
2. Self-mailer hybrid (perforated removable reply envelope)
3. Catalog: subject/seasonal/annual
4. Card deck: loose deck/bound booket
5. Postcard: conventional/oversized/picture/announcement
6. Broadside
7. Simulated newspaper
8. Simulated periodical
9. Booklet
10. Book jacket overprint
11. Poster in mailing tube

12. Statement stuffer

13. Package insert

14. Sheet of stamps, each an order coupon for one book

5:06   Which Is Better: Package or Self-Mailer?

The design options available to you for your mail promotions may not always be a matter of personal preference. The best format may be dictated by the terms of sale of the book(s) being offered. If you require payment with order, or a formal purchase order on company stationery, or written request on institutional stationery, your mailing format will have to be one that permits enclosure of a business reply envelope (BRE). If, on the other hand, you extend credit, or ship books for free examination, or accept a written-in purchase order number or credit card number, a self-mailer with detachable business reply card (BRC) will usually be the less expensive format.

The booklet or catalog, used as a self-mailer, permits both types of response devices. The reply card can be part of the catalog or booklet cover. Or if high-bulk paper is used that will meet postal requirements for postcard thickness, the reply card can be incorporated into one or more pages. The reply envelope can also be a bind-in item. If the catalog or booklet has a self-cover, the BRC or BRE will usually be bound into the centerfold.

**5:07   Most Responsive Positioning of Titles in
             Multititle Self-Mailer Format**

A sci-tech publisher, who has relied on a self-mailer format for single-subject mailings that include 30 to 60 titles per mailing, recommends this positioning of titles within the mailing for optimal response:

- New or forthcoming books with substantial sales potential should be displayed on front or feature panel.
- The most active (in sales) related titles published in the last season prior to the mailing should follow immediately thereafter.
- Best-selling titles from the backlist in the same subject area should fall in the next order of presentation. These backlist titles should be integrated with new or forthcoming titles of limited potential, such as a limited-appeal conference proceeding or an upcoming title from an ongoing series with a fairly even sales pattern.
- Next, popular titles of general appeal that are not necessarily directly related to the subject of the mailing theme, such as self-improvement books.
- Journals related to the subject of the mailing (if you publish same).

An alternative format is to have the main panel featuring new titles be followed by compartmentalized groupings of titles according to their subject headings within the mailings. For example, individualized headings within a physics mailing, such as general physics, solid state physics, optics, acoustics, and electricity and magnetism. Compartmentalizing enables the specialist to go directly to those titles of special interest first.

**5:08   Self-Mailer Format for Direct-Response Book Campaigns:
Some Pros and Cons**

"We favor using a self-mailer when we have something to say of immediate news value. This format says, 'Hey!—Look at me!' " This approach is favored by the marketing head of a leading publisher of books and subscription services in business, finance, and taxation.

A direct-response book marketer who mails to a wide range of scientific and technical audiences as well as to general consumers has developed a different philosophy regarding use of the self-mailer format. Here the self-mailer has been found most cost-effective when used for professional audiences. Where mailings involve general consumer audiences, the marketer says, "They require a harder sell than a self-mailer can offer," and the traditional letter package format is favored.

**5:09   Pitfall to Avoid When Order Card Is
Part of Self-Mailer Cover**

With escalating postage costs, more and more catalogs are going out as self-mailers, with the back cover serving as mailing face and a return order card as part of the cover.

If you are mailing this way or planning to use a catalog in this format, with postal indicia and mailing label affixed so that the removable order card comes back to you with the mailing label portion, be sure that the return address and postage portion does not fall inside the reply card area, but rather outside the lines of the perforation.

The reason for this is that when the customer completes, removes, and mails the order card, and it still contains the return address and indicia portion of the original mailing, the customer may well receive his or her own order card a second time. This has happened.

5:10   Failings of an Overdesigned Self-Mailer: A Critique

The 5½″ × 8½″ self-mailer was issued late in 1982 by a scientific professional society. A slick-looking two-color job printed on 70 lb. white offset stock, the mailing opened to 8½″ × 11″ on the first unfolding, with the mailing face and order form sharing one 8½″ × 11″ panel.

The other five panels of the six-panel mailing contained a total of fourteen book offerings, ten of which were symposium proceedings and the other four multi-author "advances" volumes in the same series. What came through more strongly than the copy was the heavy black and red background patterns—either red panels crisscrossed with white lines or black panels crisscrossed with red lines.

In each panel, two or three titles were listed, either in 8 or 9 pt. type. In every instance the contents were also listed in either 5, 6, or 7 pt. type. In no instance did the typeface for the contents match the type size used for the descriptive matter, and the typefaces for adjacent titles in each panel did not match. In each panel the composition was set solid, occupying in one panel only about 15% of the available space. Most of the emphasis was placed on the background color designs; the 5, 6, and 7 pt. typefaces made the contents difficult to read.

The feature panel carried two titles under a one-word headline: "NEW!" The second, third, and fourth panels (the open spread) had the headline "NO-RISK 15-Day Money-Back Guarantee" over the first, a toll-free 800 number over the second, and "ORDER these books today!" over the third. A typical headline word, "New!" might have looked good atop one of the panels, but instead it was placed at the very bottom of the third panel in red ink on black background.

The order card, returnable to a "Distribution Office," requested that orders be prepaid and listed the 14 titles in 6 pt. type. It also required mailing in a customer-supplied envelope.

This elaborate and costly mailing is a clear example of a job in which the designer prevailed. He (or she) had created an elaborate artistic concept and "shoehorned" the book offering into it. This type of effort should be avoided. Typically, it produces very few orders, but looks great in a scrapbook or portfolio. A much simpler effort would have done as well—or perhaps even better.

Lesson: Design your mailings to inform the reader and to sell, *not* to satisfy artistic whims. Another lesson: The idea of asking for an order, presenting copy, and then stating that the book is new is backwards. In selling, first you state that it is new, then you describe what is new, and then you ask for the order, in *that* order.

5:11   Catalogs: How and When to Use Them for Greatest Benefit

The catalog is offered by publishers in a variety of formats and seasonal presentations. The general or comprehensive catalog is offered by most publishers on an annual or sometimes semiannual basis. It is an essential reference tool for bookstores and libraries, but it is not an effective selling tool.

The *subject catalog* is a useful reference for publishers of professional and scholarly works, as it enables the scholar, instructor, or professional to find available titles under subject headings that cater to his or her special interests.

Mail-order catalogs are offered by many publishers and are mailed periodically. They deal with forthcoming titles and best-selling books from the backlist in special areas. Most mail-order catalogs have self-covers and can be mailed without envelopes. Frequently, the back cover serves as the removable order form. Mail-order catalogs work best when they include effective headlines and excerpts from reviews from well-known publications within the field.

Catalogs need not be elaborate. One or two ink colors usually will suffice. Illustrations of book jackets help. Always include order forms and repeat ordering information in more than one place in the catalog in the event the catalog is passed along to someone after the order form has been removed. An 800 toll-free order number will enhance the sales appeal of any catalog. Credit-card options will increase the amount of prepaid orders.

Seasonal catalogs usually provide detailed listings of titles for the forthcoming season (usually a six-month period), and more often than not they coincide with a spring or fall list. Seasonal catalogs often also include listings from the preceding season. One scholarly publisher included a subject listing of all books published in the previous year in his spring catalog and a subject listing of spring titles in the fall catalog. Thus, recipients were informed of books of both the upcoming six-month period and the preceding six- or twelve-month period. Such catalogs were produced in a single edition for all outlets, including libraries, bookstores, and individuals. The catalog had a 5½" × 8½" format with a self-cover.

In some of the major houses, *specialized catalogs* are issued for different outlets. A trade catalog, for example, is issued in the spring and fall expressly for bookstores. Some publishers issue library catalogs, whereas others produce catalogs for accounts in nontraditional outlets, for industrial training programs, or for educational purposes.

If yours is a small house and you cannot afford to issue a comprehensive catalog, rely on an *annual price list* for your entire list and simple, one-color seasonal announcements for your forthcoming titles. Some printers have standardized catalog formats and will print 5,000 copies of an eight-page 8½" × 11" catalog for under $500, or 16 pages for about $850, on 50 lb. white offset paper. One such house is Vividize, Inc., 23 Campbell Drive, Dix Hills, NY 11746. Vividize and other such houses will customize the catalog to any number of pages in multiples of four and will supply the copies in lots of 5,000 to keep your catalog costs extremely low. Call Vividize at 212–895–5122; outside New York State, call toll-free 800-645-5522.

5:12   **Catalog Format Change Causes Problems: Case History**

The publisher of a successful and rapidly growing list of scientific, technical, and professional reference books had been issuing his seasonal catalogs in the same established format for many years. The spring catalog announced forthcoming titles for a six-month period under appropriate subject headings. Each page carried a running headline of the book's subject. The catalog also carried by subject a listing of titles published in the previous calendar year. The fall catalog also carried a six-month listing by subject and a subject listing of publications from the previous six months.

The format worked well and each 80,000-copy edition was widely used by librarians, booksellers, and the scientific and technical community to whom it was mailed. However, the publisher felt the seasonal catalogs had a drabness and engaged a well-known designer (of books) to redesign the seasonal catalog.

When issued, the new format was visually attractive but extremely difficult to comprehend. The running headlines, usually atop each page, ran instead down the outer edges of the pages in reverse type. There were also variations in the way the information on each book was presented.

The redesigned catalog resulted immediately in a number of complaints that it was difficult to find information in it. Not only did booksellers and librarians complain, but so did the commission reps. They said the material was too hard to locate for the catalog to be of much use as a sales tool.

The previous format was restored with the next seasonal catalog, and no further complaints were received.

Lesson: When you have a promotional vehicle with an established format that is working well, don't change it without a compelling reason.

5:13   Are Catalogs Necessary? Some Thoughts on Usage and Value

Reliance on catalogs by publishers of professional and scholarly books varies from house to house. There is no uniform rule or set of guidelines that may be deemed to be generally applicable.

Many university presses rely heavily on catalogs. For some it is their sole mail promotion vehicle. The mailing program of one university press consists of monthly catalog mailings, updated to reflect new titles. Another relies heavily on a yearly sale catalog that runs from Christmas to August. Many houses issue separate catalogs announcing forthcoming spring and fall lists.

The general practice is to issue a general annual catalog, arranged by subject. A popular by-product is separate, smaller subject catalogs which are used to answer mail inquiries and as convention handouts. Some houses with substantial lists have in past years issued general catalogs in alternate years.

Full-list catalogs can be a major expense, often difficult to justify, and troublesome when budgets are tight. Marketers sometimes see the catalog as a necessary evil, knowing they can't be without one and still can't afford it. How does one prove that the catalog, which costs many thousands of dollars to produce, generates even a single sale?

With a large and rapidly changing list covering many subject categories, the annual catalog is a must. In houses where the list is small and the annual changes modest, a general catalog might be done in alternate years if the years skipped can be covered by a catalog-updating supplement.

Where does one send the big, costly general catalog? In one house the annual general catalog goes automatically to bookstores the first week in January.* It is also sent to library accounts, but other libraries must request a copy. (For information on catalog use by public libraries, see 23:09.) A few are sent to conventions, both for reference and on request.

When this writer was associated with a small, new house with fewer than 400 titles, it managed successfully for a number of years to issue only spring and fall announcement catalogs and no general catalog. Each spring catalog contained an annotated subject listing of the previous year's publications. Each fall catalog contained selections from the first half of the year only in a separate reference index. Requests for a general catalog were usually satisfied by spring catalogs, which had full listings for the preceding years. The seasonal catalogs, produced in quantities of 80,000, cost pennies to produce, and no general catalog was issued in the first five years after the company was started.

5:14   **Journal Catalog Format Serves United States and United Kingdom**

An international publishing establishment with journals programs in both the United States and Europe has come up with an interesting journals catalog format that serves a multitude of purposes. Because of the company's broad scope, journals originate from five different sources in the publishing operation.

The journals catalog is 16 pages, measuring $3\frac{1}{2}'' \times 8\frac{1}{2}''$ in booklet form with a hard cover. More than 75 journals are listed alphabetically by title after a double contents page, which alphabetically lists the journals by outlet origin. As each journal appears in the regular catalog, a large letter, in a reverse type box, identifies the division or branch of the company from which the journal originates. Medical division journals, for example, are identified by the letter "M."

The back cover has two perforated order cards that may be removed and used for submitting subscriptions. The cards are folded in and tucked under the back cover. One card, for U.S. subscriptions, is an addressed postpaid BRC. The other card, "Outside the U.S.," bears the address of the U.K. branch of the publisher and requires postage.

The catalog is mailed in a standard #10 envelope. It is also used as a handout at exhibits and conventions. Addresses of the publisher's branches and an 800 toll-free telephone number appear in the inside covers of the journals catalog.

5:15   **Quick, Inexpensive Way to Produce Book Fliers**

A device popular at a number of publishing establishments is the "quickie flier," which can be produced quickly and inexpensively, usually on one side of an $8\frac{1}{2}'' \times 11''$ sheet of paper. It consists of a repro-

---

*When general price changes take place during the year, it is best to coordinate catalog issuance date to coincide with price change date.

duction of the book jacket, alongside of which is the front-flap copy (to which has been added page count, ISBN, pub date, and price). The bottom of the sheet usually contains an order blank.

In at least one house, the mechanical is made up in this format by the artist at the same time that the jacket art is produced. A mechanical for each flier is forwarded to the marketing department, where multiple copies are made on white or colored paper as desired. Some publishers using this practice have found that, by routinely sending 100 or 200 such fliers to the author, they receive numerous extra orders for the book, as the author is usually the best salesperson for his or her own book.

5:16   **New Directory Announcement:**
Checklist of Essential Ingredients

( ) Features
( ) Important new information not previously included
( ) Change in size from previous edition
( ) Expanded fields of coverage, if any, in new edition
( ) Number of new entries
( ) Number of changes in preexisting entries
( ) New chapters/sections added, if any
( ) Changes in format or organization, if any
( ) Contents current as of (give most recent date)
( ) Excerpts from reviews of previous edition(s)
( ) Awards or special honors won by prior editions
( ) Advantages over competitive works
( ) Compelling benefit-oriented headline
( ) Order form
( ) Sharp illustration of directory
( ) One or more sample pages or spread

5:17   **Inside-Out Package Designed to**
Ensure 100% Readership: Case Study

We reported in *Volume One* on studies indicating that doctors personally handled most of their mail, discarding about 40% without examining it. It is likely that accountants and tax and other business professionals probably discard just as high a percentage of their "uninteresting" mail.

Knowing this, how does one get professionals to examine 100% of a book promotion mailing package before discarding it? It seems impossible, but one loose-leaf publisher in the tax accounting field has found a way to do it.

Here's how: The classic package consists, as we know, of an envelope containing a letter, folder, and a response device (BRC or BRE). If the envelope package is discarded before opening, obviously the folder will never be seen.

But what if, instead of the folder being *inside* the package, it is printed on rigid card stock and mailed flat *outside* the package? And suppose that the envelope that normally contains the folder is instead tipped onto the outside of the flat self-mailer, covering only the lower third of one side of the mailer?

That's what the Research Institute of America did in the fall of 1982 (see Figure 2). The folder was mailed flat, as an 8½" × 11" self-mailer, printed in black and red ink on card stock. The envelope, a #7¾" monarch (3⅞ × 7½") with die-cut window opening on 24 white wove stock, was tipped onto the lower third of one side of the card. Above the envelope, a strong benefit-oriented headline in 36 pt. bold type, printed black over red, preceded the name of the offering, "Tax Guide," which was printed in 216 pt. type, dropped out white on a red background. The back of the 8½" × 11" exposed flier was devoted entirely to benefits from the subscription guide.

Inside the envelope, in addition to a four-page letter with a postscript premium offering in one color ink, there is also a 7" × 10" sheet on 50 lb. white offset stock listing the contents of the guide and the premium offered in the postscript. It invites a subscription on an enclosed postage-paid certificate.

The "certificate" in this instance is a postpaid reply card, to which the recipient's mailing label has been affixed and positioned to show through the die-cut window envelope. The offer is a subscription deal calling for eight quarterly billings of $49.50 each, over a two-year period, for the tax guide and updating services.

5:18   **Format/Approach for Sweepstakes Offering in Card Deck**

In the fall of 1982, Warren, Gorham & Lamont, Inc. (WG&L), in Boston, launched a card-deck sweepstakes offering in a white booklet/envelope in a 4¾" × 7" format (see Figure 3). The corner card bore the imprint "WG&L Sweepstakes" over the return address and the teaser copy. The left half of the face stated in four colors, "Here is your chance to WIN! . . . a complete APPLE II COMPUTER SYSTEM or any one of over 100 other valuable prizes."

The 58 card-deck enclosures* included 57 offerings for WG&L publications on returnable postpaid cards. The fifty-eighth card, not postpaid, was headed "Official Entry Card" and included sweepstakes instructions and two separate check-off boxes above respondent's name and address:

---

*The 57 publication-offering cards were returnable to WG&L. The fifty-eighth, the "Official Entry Card," was returnable to an address furnished by the contest management company.

( ) Yes, I'm ordering from the enclosed card(s). Please enter me in the Sweepstakes.

( ) No, I'm not ordering now but enter me in the Sweepstakes anyway.

A separate, enclosed mini-letter of four 5½" × 7" pages (11" × 7" flat) folded down to 3½" × 5", the same size as the cards in the deck. It carried color illustrations of the three different types of prizes and a "Dear Professional" letter in black ink with the blue-ink signature of an individual with no title. The letter postscript reminded readers to send for any free offering in the deck "on a FREE trial examination."

The WG&L loose-deck offering devoted entirely to business books duplicated the format of two earlier sweepstakes offerings (for architecture and construction books) issued by the McGraw-Hill Professional and Reference Book Division in November 1981 and in June 14, 1982.

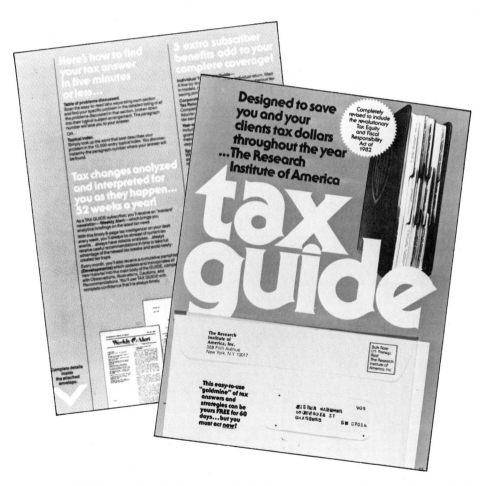

FIGURE 2   Folder in the form of a rigid 8½" × 11" card is mailed "outside" the package, and the envelope is affixed to the flier in a mailing by the Research Institute of America. The "inside-out" package virtually ensures notice of the flier, even by those who discard the mailing without opening it.

FIGURE 3 Paper mailing envelope, first page of a "Dear Professional" letter, and sweepstakes entry card used in sweepstakes card-deck promotion of Warren, Gorham and Lamont. Aside from the entry card, the deck contained 57 separate card offerings of WG&L loose-leaf products in the areas of business, taxation, and finance.

5:19   Format/Approach for Sweepstakes Offering in Book Catalog

In September 1982, Wiley launched a catalog sweepstakes offering. A 16-page self-cover, self-mailer booklet was prepared for five different subject areas. Each offered approximately 40 to 50 books and was printed in black ink, except for the sweepstakes offering, which was highlighted by a second ink color.

The 7″ × 10¼″ booklet bore the conventional catalog cover copy, but had overprinted in a second color: "Win: Help Us Celebrate! Enter the John Wiley & Sons 175th Anniversary Sweepstakes. See page 2 for details."

The inside front cover (page 2), printed in one color of ink as was the rest of the catalog, carried the listing of prizes: an IBM personal computer (first prize), a GE 10-inch television set (second prize, 5 winners), a Samsonite luggage ensemble (third prize, 10 winners), a pen (fourth prize, 50 winners), and a tote bag (fifth prize, 1,000 winners). Rules were listed.

On the back cover (see Figure 4), which constituted the removable order form for the catalog, a second-color rectangular panel stated: "Win: No purchase required." It then included two check-off boxes: "( ) YES. I've indicated which books I want and please enter me in the sweepstakes" and "( ) NO. I don't wish to order now but enter me in the sweepstakes." As a legal requirement, all cards—whether book orders or sweepstakes entries only—required postage be affixed for mailing.

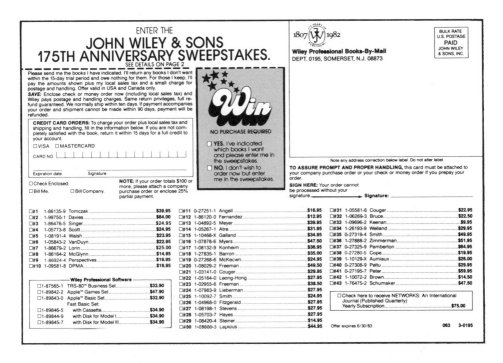

FIGURE 4 Catalog sweepstakes offering has an entry blank and book order form on the same card. Mailed at about same time as the WG&L sweepstakes (5:18), this offering was tied to the publisher's 175th anniversary celebration. The catalog had 50 offerings in contrast to the 57 in the card deck.

6

Inventory Reduction Sales and Practices

6:01   **Importance of Inventory-Reduction Sales in
        Professional and Scholarly Book Publishing**

Inventory-reduction sales, mentioned in a single entry in *Book
Marketing Handbook, Volume One*, are given a full chapter in this
volume. One reason is their increasing importance to publishers of professional and scholarly works as a means of reducing surplus inventory. Another reason is that for one category of publishers, the university press, the special-offer sale may often be a means of survival.

All classes of professional and scholarly publishers and—yes, even
the loose-leaf publishers in the business fields—conduct different
types of sales to reduce inventory.

Various case studies of different types of sales, offerings, and formats are presented in this chapter. They represent the works of commercial houses, professional societies, and university presses. They
offer a wide range of sale concepts that are readily adaptable to your
own surplus inventory problems and the prospect that, by combining
features from several, you can come up with your own "original" version that will top all of them.

Most special-offer sales are produced in catalog format, i.e., in a
bound booklet. Most are designed to stimulate movement of slower
backlist titles. Many of these fail because the outer wrapper fails to
identify the offering as a "sale" offering.

Academic libraries receive a steady volume of sale catalogs and are
likely to give them high priority over seasonal or general catalog mailings. The likely reason is that most sales offer overly generous dis-

counts that enable the library to fill out its collection at bargain-basement prices, and most offers expire reasonably quickly.

Harlan Kessel, marketing manager at the University of California Press, says that special offers are essential if you want to sell scholars books for their professional use. Adds Kessel, "Today's buyer of scholarly books is a bargain hunter. We have found that mailing pieces without a special offer produces little response."*

6:02   **Ways of Reducing Surplus Inventories of**
        Professional and Scholarly Books

1. Discount sales

2. Sell-offs to reprinter

3. Scholar's Bookshelf participation (see 6:03)

4. Remainder sales

5. Charitable contributions (see 6:04)

6. Sell to author at special price

7. Use as premiums

8. Coupon programs (inclusion of "special offer" as discount-coupon bind-in or freestanding insert with other mailed offerings)

6:03   **Mail-Order Outlet for Surplus Inventory**
        of Scholarly Imprints

A convenient source to which you can sell your surplus inventory of slow-moving titles is The Scholar's Bookshelf in Princeton, N.J. This mail-order operation issues catalogs of deeply discounted scholarly works in two categories: the humanities and fine arts and science and technology. Each catalog includes more than 1,000 offerings. If your books are included, orders per title will usually reach quantities of 100 to 250 copies. Send information about your excess stock titles to: Abbot M. Friedland, The Scholar's Bookshelf, 195 Nassau Street, Princeton, NJ 08540; 609-921-1631.

6:04   **Contributions of Books to Recognized Charities:**
        Practices and Procedures

In recent years, publishers have witnessed the emergence of the "independent consultant," one who specializes in structuring programs for contributions of books to qualified charities in conformity with the special Internal Revenue Service rules applicable to inventory contributions. The consultant is paid by the publisher for these services.

The program includes a monitoring process to ensure that the re-

*Speaking at the annual meeting of the Society for Scholarly Publishing, San Francisco, June 1981.

cipient uses the contributed books appropriately, that the books are contributed at a time when their value can be supported under IRS examination, and that they are not used in a manner inconsistent with required business practices of the publisher.

Here is how the independent consultant works: He or she submits to a publisher a list of recognized charities that will accept book contributions. The consultant then suggests which charities are appropriate for which of the publisher's titles, and suggests also the quantity of each title to be contributed. Titles so contributed must be on the publisher's active list and must be a relatively small fraction of the lifetime sales of the title.

The publisher ultimately receives a letter from the charity regarding the disposition of the contributed books. This letter serves as a substantiation for the IRS of the deduction, which may not exceed twice the unit cost.

6:05   Use of Sales in Loose-Leaf Publishing

One area of publishing where sales are rarely, if ever, held is in the loose-leaf field. The reason, of course, is that loose-leaf publishing is a subscription service. The goal is not so much to sell the basic book or books as it is to sell the updating services that follow.

However, one loose-leaf publisher has conducted experiments with a special type of sale. Subscribers to the loose-leaf service, after a period of four or five years, received a new, three-volume edition of the complete, updated book, priced at $145. The new edition was issued when the supplements became unwieldy in relation to the size of the original book.

To attract new subscribers, special mailings were made in a split test "To New Subscribers Only" offering the three-volume work with a discount coupon. Half the mailing had a coupon offering $25 off; in the other half the coupon offering was $50 off. Test results were not available.

6:06   Criteria for Successful Sale Offerings to Libraries

1. Allow ample time for response: at least 90 days from date of mailing.
2. Offer discounts larger than those normally given by library suppliers.
3. Do not insist on prepayment.
4. If sales are final, indicate conditions under which returns will be permitted.
5. If quantities are limited and may not be sufficient for all, indicate available quantities to avoid disappointment.
6. If incentives are offered for special types or combinations of purchases, keep these within reason.

7. Utilize catalog format.

8. Clearly identify the sale offering on the face of the mailing envelope or catalog cover.

9. State the conditions of sale clearly in an easy-to-find location.

10. Use a special order form or reply envelope to identify readily orders from the sale offering.

11. Avoid mixing sale and nonsale offerings in the same mailing piece.

12. If older titles are offered, indicate whether these are superseded by new editions.

13. Avoid complicated layouts or type arrangements.

14. Keep the type area on the page to a modest width to allow for marginal notations.

15. Keep to alphabetical arrangement by author or editor under subject headings.

16. Always include the year of publication for each title.

17. Always include ISBN number for each title.

18. If the descriptive copy is short, include favorable review excerpts in addition to or in place of copy.

19. Have each entry clearly indicate the saving by showing both the regular price and the sale price.

20. Prominently state the range of savings on the sales announcement in terms of percentages, such as "50% to 80%."

21. Give a believable reason for the sale; avoid such frivolous titles as "Whale of a Sale!"

22. A check-off order form requiring only an "x" simplifies the ordering process and can increase sales.

23. If prepayment is required, state that library or institutional orders will be acceptable without payment or if accompanied by a purchase order.

24. Provide an incentive on shipping charges for orders over a certain size.

25. Offer an additional discount if orders reach a certain amount, or offer different added discounts if orders reach certain dollar levels.

26. If a bind-in order envelope is used, repeat the mailing address several places throughout sale offering, especially if the sale address is different from your usual address. This can encourage subsequent orders, that could be tied to the sales offering, after the order envelope has been removed.

6:07   **How a University Library Responded to 51 Publishers' Sale Offerings: Case Study**

In the late 1970s, the library at the University of Massachusetts in Amherst received and reviewed 51 different publishers' "special sale" offerings within a six-month period. Sigfried Fuller, associate director of the library, analyzed the various offerings and reported these findings:*

1. Twenty-two of the 51 offerings were from the university presses.

2. Eleven catalogs produced substantially higher percentages of orders for the titles listed.

3. Ten catalogs were moderately successful. Fuller states that these ten could have done two to four times better if the titles presented were closer to the library's basic requirements.

4. Twelve catalogs yielded few orders because of the mix with seasonal announcements of new publications and other problems that posed ordering difficulties.

5. Eighteen catalogs were rejected out-of-hand as having too many deficiencies to waste time inspecting them.

The important lesson from Fuller's study and report is that two out of five publishers' sale offerings were moderately successful or very successful. Three out of five offerings were largely wasted. The tragedy of this lesson is that the catalog mailing efforts wasted on the three-in-five probably cost as much or more to produce than the two that were moderately or very successful.

This lesson points up the need for this chapter and, more importantly, for this book on techniques. Book marketers who are willing to devote time and attention to technique and to the needs and interests of the people to whom they send their promotions can be successful. Those who do not heed technique or customer needs are bound to fail. In either case, whether the end result is success or failure, the cost in dollars is about the same. But what makes the difference either way is knowledge.

6:08   **How Engineering Book Buyers Respond to Sale with Incentives: Case History**

A "clearance sale" was conducted of 100 once popular but now slow-selling backlist engineering books via a sales catalog. In addition to the moderate to substantial discount offers on each book in the sale catalog, a number of incentives were included for orders above certain dollar amounts. In addition, buyers were offered free shipping in any order over a certain dollar minimum.

The mailing went to four lists comprising approximately 150,000 names. Three of the lists contained names of previous buyers of engineering books. The fourth list was subscribers to an engineering periodical in the same field as the books offered on sale.

*Sigfried Fuller, "Special Sale Catalogues and Library Customers," *Scholarly Publishing* 8, no. 2, January 1977.

SALE RESULTS

- Orders received totaled approximately 2% of the mailing.
- Average number of books per order: Two (in contrast to an average of one book per order for nonsale mailings to the same lists).

CONCLUSIONS

- Incentives and bargain prices help sell slow-moving backlist books to engineers.
- Lists of book buyers responded better, at an average of two books per order.
- The list utilizing the periodical subscriber names yielded about 15% fewer books per order.

Case Studies of Inventory Reduction Sales:
Techniques, Formats, Offers

6:09   **A Unique, Innovative Special Sale Program**
        that Works: Case Study

The unique and most innovative special sale program we have encountered is that conducted annually by MIT Press. It begins with a hefty sale catalog that is mailed each year right after Christmas.

The sale lasts from January 1 through June 30, a sale period that is about four months longer than those of most other publishers (Figure 5A). The 300-book sale catalog carries a June 30 expiration date. However, orders are honored through the end of July.

The reasoning for the extension beyond the posted expiration date is that most libraries' fiscal year budgets run from July 1 to June 30 (see 10:06). Those libraries that can't afford to buy during the first six-month term of the sale are able to do so in July, the first month of the new fiscal year budget.

According to Brook Stevens, book promotion manager at MIT Press, "the sale works fantastically well." The sale catalog is mailed to in-house lists, lists of known book buyers, members of professional and scholarly organizations, libraries, and periodical subscription lists.

In addition, an experiment tested successfully in 1978 has provided tremendous additional impetus to the sale. In that year, MIT Press placed a one-sixth-page advertisement in *Scientific American* announcing an "MIT Annual Book Clearing" and offering the sale catalog to all who complete and return the coupon at the bottom of the advertise-

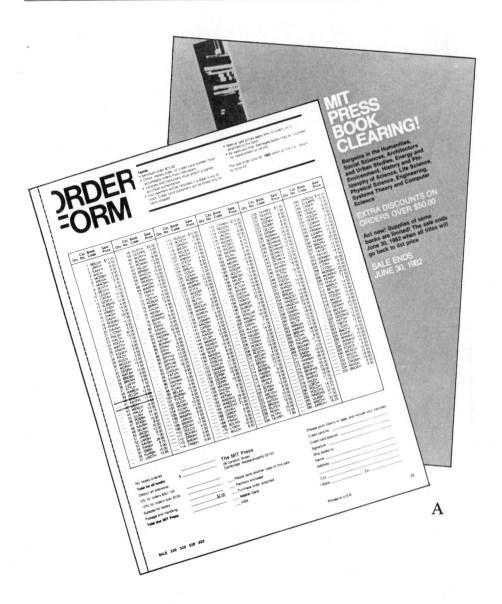

FIGURE 5(A) Cover and order form of annual MIT Press sale catalog. The sale has a six-month duration, but orders are accepted through the seventh month. The sale catalog is mailed to lists and also offered in advertising placed in scientific publications.

MIT's Annual Bookclearing!

Great bargains on fine University Press books in the Humanities, Social Sciences, Architecture and Urban Studies, Energy and Environment, History and Philosophy of Science, Life Science, Physical Science, Engineering, Systems Theory and Computer Science.

Don't miss this unique opportunity to acquire books for general reading as well as hard-to-find technical and professional books at substantial reductions.

Note: This offer is good only in the United States and Canada.

The MIT Press
28 Carleton Street
Cambridge, MA 02142
(Tel. 617-253-2884)

Please send me your sale catalog:

Name _____
Address _____
City _____
State _____ Zip _____
(Please type or print)

B

Hacker Art Books

announces

OUR FAMOUS ART BOOK SALE

Our 32-page illustrated catalogue is filled with over 700 beautiful and important art books in all fields—out of print and rare books, antiques, painting, sculpture, ceramics, jewelry, limited editions, architecture. African art—many of the rare collectors' items available only from us at prices reduced as much as 70%. A unique opportunity to acquire these superb volumes, lavishly illustrated with color plates, gathered from the world over, at these incredible prices.

Hacker Art Books, Inc.   5
54 West 57 Street, N.Y. 10019 • 212-PL 7-1450

Please send me the catalogue at no charge.

Name_____

Address_____

City/State/Zip_____

C

FIGURE 5(B) Advertisement in *Science News* offers MIT's sale catalog to all who request it. Such advertising produces numerous inquiries and good sales results.

FIGURE 5(C) MIT Press advertisement offering its sale catalog is based on sale catalog offerings used for more than 30 years by Hacker Art Books. The Hacker advertisement offering the sale catalog appeared in October 26, 1982, in the *Wall Street Journal*. The format is unchanged from the first such advertisement, which ran in the *New York Times* in 1952.

ment.* The response from that first advertisement produced catalog inquiries that resulted in $20,000 worth of book orders.

The initial success of the advertisement in *Scientific American* offering the sale catalog led to expansion of the sale catalog advertising program. The catalog is now also offered in *Science News*, which reaches more than 170,000 scientists and science-oriented individuals (Figure 5B). The resulting catalog requests and orders are reported to constantly do "extremely well." One effort was made to offer the MIT sale catalog to a non-science-oriented book audience,† but the offer did not do well and was discontinued.

As only a few new titles are added to the sale list each year, older books are repeated year after year. Sales on some of the older ones are beginning to taper off. However, buyers of sale books are an enthusiastic book-loving lot. In past offerings, they have bought old textbooks, old engineering tomes, and superseded editions of current titles that were selling well. Superseded editions reportedly sell very well.

Here is a sale catalog program that has dared to be different, to offer more books than most others, to run for a longer period than most others, and to innovate in distribution technique. All of these new techniques have worked for this prestigious university press. There is little question that the reputation of MIT Press contributed materially to the success of this innovative, long-running sale program. But the example is clear. Experiment, innovate, dare to be different—and you can be successful.

6:10   **Bender Anniversary Used as Theme for Inventory-Reduction Sale: Case Study**

An appealing and successful inventory-reduction technique was that used by Matthew Bender in 1982. It cleverly used the occasion of its ninety-fifth anniversary as the theme for an inventory-reduction sale. A wide range of its high-priced loose-leaf works was offered, for a limited time, for $95 each.

Figure 6 shows the various elements included in this anniversary offer mailing. The usual corner-card area of the mailing envelope bore an imprint that invited the recipient of the #10 envelope to "Help Us Celebrate Our Anniversary: Matthew Bender 95th." There were two different envelopes—one for previous buyers and one for prospects. The customer envelopes bore this added imprint over the address label area: "Thanks for being our customer!—Look inside for a special money-saving offer." Mailings to prospects had this envelope imprint

---

*The idea of advertising a sale catalog originated with Hacker Art Books, Inc., a New York City–based publisher of books in art history. Hacker ran the first ad offering its sale catalog in the *New York Times* in 1952 (Figure 5C) and has been repeating these offerings in various media, including the *Times, Wall Street Journal*, the *New Yorker, Art and Antiques*, and other publications, for more than 30 years. Seymour Hacker of Hacker Art Books says the advertisements account for approximately 5% of the total distribution of his sales catalogs.

†MIT Press advertised, but later discontinued, its sale catalog offer in the *New York Review of Books*.

FIGURE 6 Matthew Bender's ninety-fifth anniversary package offer uses separate envelopes for customers and prospects, using the same letter inside for both. The offer, mailed early in 1982, had a May 15 expiration date. An accompanying 11″ × 17″, four-page listing contained 52 numbered offerings. Twenty-seven offerings were for books priced from $50 to $75 and offered any two for $95, in keeping with the anniversary theme. Twenty-five offerings made two-volume works priced normally at $120 to $170 available for $95 per set, again in keeping with the anniversary theme.

angle-printed across the first third of the envelope: "What does $95 buy?—Plenty, if you act now. Look inside for details." Return address was printed on the back flap of the envelope.

The inside package contained a four-page letter explaining the reason for the sale: "We're celebrating our 95th anniversary with a special offer for you!" An accompanying four-page enclosure, of the same size and stock as the letter, listed 52 one- or two-volume titles. Where a single volume had a list price of between $60 and $75, the $95 sale price bought any two. Where double-volume works were priced at $120 to $170, the regular price was crossed out by simulated handwriting in red-ink overprint on black that stated "now $95."

A postpaid business reply card bore this heading in bold reverse type: "95th Anniversary Special Offer Order Card." To order, the respondent was asked to circle the numbers (1 to 52) desired: 1 through 27 for two single volumes, and 28 through 52 for each two-volume title. A separate box asked the respondent to check off: "( ) I do not want Additional Upkeep Service." Another check box bore this message: "( ) Save 10%. Full payment (plus applicable sales tax) is enclosed. Amount enclosed $____." The order card bore an expiration date for the offer and a 30-day return privilege.

6:11   Missing Ingredient in University Press "Special Offer": Case Study

A "special offer" mailing by a prestigious eastern university press featured five different books in the same field. It offered a 20% discount on prepaid orders received within a five-month period. A credit-card option was offered, and a flat charge of $1.50 for postage and handling was added per order. The offering was attractively prepared on $8\frac{3}{8}'' \times 15\frac{1}{2}''$ two-color coated stock. However, there were two shortcomings. First, the cover copy on the folded piece read "VITAL BOOKS FROM," with emphasis on the word "VITAL." Given the prestige of the imprint, had emphasis been placed on the university press name, the piece would have been considerably more effective. The other missing ingredient was the lack of publication dates for any of the books offered. When the press was queried about this omission, a member of its direct-mail department responded, "As a rule publication dates are not listed in our brochures, especially when our books are recent publications." In the offering in question, only two of the titles were from the current year. The others were one to six years old. Although a full refund was offered "after a 10-day examination period," it is likely that the omission of publication dates had a negative effect on response.

6:12   American Affiliate of German Publisher

The American affiliate of a 140-year-old German scientific publishing establishment conducted a "Spring Mathematics Yellow Sale," with a July 30 expiration date, of specially selected mathematics books.

It included a choice of one or more bonus books for various dollar amount purchases. Discounts on selected mathematics books ranged from 20 to 50%. Additionally, a mathematics or statistics calendar was offered free with any order over $60, a free bonus book or calendar with any order for $75, two free bonus books for $125 orders, and up to eight bonus books and both calendars for an order of $550 or more.

An 8½″ × 11″ self-mailer booklet format, printed one-color (black) on newsprint, was used. The copy advertising the "Yellow Sale" on the front cover carried this subtitle: "A golden selection of our famous yellow books at savings up to 50% off list price plus free books of your choice."

6:13   West Coast Commercial Publisher

A West Coast commercial publisher conducted an "End-of-November Sale" mailing that offered 30 discounted mathematics titles. Teaser copy on the cover of the self-mailer read, "Save!—25 to 30% on selected high quality professional reference books." The inside head-line read, "From now until January 31, you can build your professional library at a special savings of 25 to 30% off the regular list price of selected timely works. It's our way of saying 'Thanks for helping us grow.' " The mailing was made in mid-November with a January 31 expiration date.

The self-mailer was printed in two colors on 80 lb. colored offset stock. It measured 11″ × 17″ flat and was folded twice to make the 5½″ × 8½″ format with self-cover.

Only one of the 30 offerings, a symposium proceeding, was from the current year. All the others were two to six years old. All 30 titles in the sale offering were priced at 25% below list price. A provision on the removable postpaid order card offered an added 5% discount for orders over $50. Books were offered for 30 days' free examination with a credit-card option.

6:14   Multiline Commercial House

A multiline commercial publisher issues a monthly new book announcement, in wire-stitched booklet format, to a wide range of libraries. From time to time, one of the monthly announcements will include a bound-in sheet of coupons offering selected titles at approximately 60% discount off the list price. The discounted titles are considered to have excessive inventory and were published in prior years. Libraries are instructed to order directly from publisher and that offerings are not subject to further discount. The coupon copy states that the offer is good for 60 days. The expiration date shown is approximately three months from the mailing date.

6:15   Professional Society Publishing Division

The book publishing division of a professional society in the natural sciences conducted an "Inflation-Fighting Book Sale." The promotional format differed from the usual sale catalog in that this one was printed in two colors on individual 8½″ × 16½″ 50 lb. white offset sheets.

The sheet folded down to form a 5½″ wide × 8½″ high self-mailer, forming a six-panel piece with self-cover. Each of the three panels had a separate list of offerings with a different discount. There was a 25% discount panel, a 30% discount panel, and a 50% discount panel. One of the panels contained a return order form that required an envelope for mailing. It invited credit-card charges (VISA and MasterCard).

6:16   Advanced Research Scientific Publisher

A New York affiliate of a Netherlands-based scientific publishing firm conducted an annual "June Library Sale" for overstocked backlist titles from its parent company and various copublished, imported British works.

The sale offered a wide range of titles in various scientific disciplines and in advanced mathematics. Books were generally high-priced. Discounts ranged from 25 to 75% off list prices. Each entry was extremely brief, giving only title, author, pubdate, list price, sale price, and a terse one-sentence description.

Mailings were targeted to college, large public, and special libraries and included a postpaid BRE identified with the sale offering. Mailings for the June Library Sale were made annually in May, with a July 31 expiration date. Orders received by August 15 were honored. Sales generated by each of the annual mailings were approximately three to four times the cost of the mailing.

A format consisting of four 8½″ × 11″ pages (11″ × 17″ flat) that folded down for mailing in a #10 envelope was used. The imprint on the outer envelope usually carried variations of the theme "June Library Sale: Save up to 75%!"

6:17   Professional and Reference Book Publisher

An eastern professional and reference book publisher mails several sale catalogs each year. Each sale catalog is in a particular subject area and is mailed to lists of book buyers within that area. Catalogs contain 35 to 50 titles that are more than one year old and considered to be in surplus inventory. The sale expiration date is approximately 90 days from the mailing date.

The sale catalog takes a 7″ × 10¼″ booklet format and is printed one-color on sufficiently heavy white offset stock so that back cover/perforated postpaid order card meets USPS requirements for postcard thickness.

6:18   Case Study and Evaluation of a Sale Campaign
that Failed: Lessons Learned

An eastern publisher includes in its list a large number of symposium proceedings of an international society. In late 1981, a "Special Offer" space advertising and direct-mail campaign was launched to reduce inventory overstock on 14 proceedings volumes. These books, ranging in age from the current year to more than four years old, were offered at discounts over 70%.

The full-page advertisement containing the special offer was run in the November 1, 1981, issue of *Library Journal* (*LJ*) and repeated in the publisher's Winter Bulletin, mailed December 8, 1981, to more than 18,000 libraries, bookstores, and individuals. The special offer also occupied a two-color two-page spread in a subject-related catalog mailed to four different lists of nearly 15,000 prospective (individual) buyers on October 28, 1981. All promotions showed a January 31, 1982, expiration date.

The special offer campaign produced a total of 21 book orders that carried the special offer discount. Of the 21 book orders, 15 of them (71%) were received in the two months following the January 31 expiration date.

What were the factors that made this special offer a failure? We see at least three.

One factor was the very short time between offering dates and termination date. The earliest offer allowed only two months. The first advertisement in *LJ* allowed only two months. The Winter Bulletin, dropped in the mail on December 8, probably wasn't delivered until January, which left little or no time for response.

A second factor was the bad timing of the Winter Bulletin. Mailing at the height of the Christmas mail crush meant, at best, postponement of delivery. Very little third-class bulk mail gets through in December.

A third factor was that symposium proceedings are poor sellers in any sale offering. Our own experience has proven this time and again. Here was a mailing with 14 proceedings volumes. Had the special offering been "sweetened" with some other more salable books, the symposium volumes might have ridden on the coattails of library orders for some of the other books being offered.

Lessons: When you do a sale offering to libraries, allow a minimum of three months, possibly longer, to give librarians a chance to let the offering go through the machinery necessary to get approvals and place orders prior to cut-off date. Avoid mailing at the height of the Christmas mail rush or, if you must, spend the extra money and mail first class. "Sweeten" every sale offering with some desirable volumes that will find quick appeal with your audience. Books of lesser appeal that would not normally be ordered by themselves may well ride on the coattails of orders for the more desirable books.

7

Cooperative Mailings

7:01   What Is a Co-op Mailing?

A cooperative, or co-op, mailing is a mailing to a specialized list or market in which the mailing vehicle, an envelope or some other carrier,* contains the offerings of more than one advertiser. The co-op sponsor may charge a fixed amount per insert for participation, and must be given a supply of inserts from the advertisers sufficient to cover the number of units to be mailed. A size and/or weight requirement is usually involved—i.e., the insert must be of a specific size so that all components of the carrier will be uniform and under a certain weight, such as up to half an ounce.

One co-op sponsor (see 7:02), who specializes in promoting book publishers' offerings to bookstores, schools, and libraries, will also provide the insert, and the participant may purchase advertising space on it.

In some other types of cooperative mailings, the participants may share the cost of the mailing based on degree of participation or some other agreed-upon formula.

IBIS Information Services (see 7:03) does international mailings to libraries with publisher-supplied literature or on standard 3″ × 5″ cards that IBIS provides and prints using data supplied by the publisher.

Standard Rate and Data Service (SRDS) views sponsored card decks as co-op mailings and includes them in both its monthly *Business Publication Rates and Data* (under the heading, "Direct Response Advertising Media") and in its *Direct Mail List Rates and Data*, published bi-monthly in odd-numbered months, under the heading "Co-op Mailings and Package Insert Programs." The package-insert programs contained in that same SRDS section may be useful for

---

*Most card-deck sponsors favor polybags rather than envelopes as carriers for their co-op deck offerings.

general-interest books, but do not seem to offer much potential for professional or technical works directed toward their specialized audiences. Avoid the SRDS "Co-op Mailings and Package Insert Programs" section if you are looking for co-op card-deck availabilities. This section contains about 15% of the card-deck listings that appear monthly in the *SRDS Business Publication Directory.*

7:02   Inexpensive Way to Mail to Libraries and Bookstores

If you have a modest budget, are just starting out, or have only one or a few titles for the particular market covered, there's an inexpensive, convenient way to mail to a variety of lists, ranging from those for college, public, and school libraries and bookstores to retail music stores, at a fraction of what the postage would cost if you did the mailing yourself.

You can participate in the monthly or periodic cooperative mailings of Direct Mail Promotions, Inc., 342 Madison Avenue, New York, NY 10017. These cooperative mailings have been going out regularly since 1966, and they have been used repeatedly by scores of publishers, both large and small, year after year. Figure 7 shows Direct Mail Promotion's invitation to participate in its mailings.

Here's how they work. You supply a printed insert on an 8½" × 11" sheet in sufficient quantity to cover the list being used. Your insert, along with a maximum of nine others, is enclosed and mailed flat in a 9" × 12" envelope. The oversized envelope saves you the folding cost. A printed sheet that can be folded in half to 8½" × 11" is also accepted.

If you have something other than the specified sizes, call Joe Morton at Direct Mail Promotions (212-687-1910), and he will try to work it out with you. Morton tries to give complete satisfaction. He supplies postal receipts and invites new customers to check him out with the Better Business Bureau, of which he is a member.

Typical mailing costs, at the start of 1983, were $550 for a mailing to either 5,000 large public libraries or to 5,000 libraries of public school systems or $450 to 4,000 bookstores.

If you wish to participate in a mailing and have no insert to provide, or do not wish to provide one, there is an alternative way to mail that is a true bargain. In most mailings, Morton includes one or more sheets with a printed heading "4-Star Value Bulletin." Under the heading are four quarter-page (4" × 5") areas in which you can advertise. A quarter-page insert, if you provide camera-ready copy costs $300 and gets mailed to 5,000 public libraries and 2,500 college and university libraries—7,500 libraries in all.

**7:03   Foreign Co-op Mailings to Libraries
in English-Speaking Countries**

IBIS Information Services, New York, offers a wide range of cooperative mailings to special libraries in foreign countries on an alternate-

MEMBER: DIRECT MAIL MARKETING ASSOCIATION   Phone: (212) 687-1910

DIRECT MAIL PROMOTIONS Inc.

342 MADISON AVENUE • NEW YORK, N.Y. 10017

DIRECT
MAIL

THE PERSONAL MEDIUM

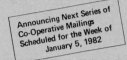

Announcing Next Series of Co-Operative Mailings Scheduled for the Week of January 5, 1982

This letter is being sent in reply to your recent
inquiry regarding our Co-operative mailings to Schools,
Colleges and Libraries.

As requested, we are enclosing information plus a
Reservation Form.

We are now working on our current series of mailings.

Since we limit each mailing to ten (10) Participants,
we will appreciate receiving from you an expression of
your wishes using the enclosed Reservation Form.

Because of our limit of 10 participants in each mailing,
we suggest your entering your reservation as soon as
possible so that you will not be disappointed by our
closed reservations.

Should you require any additional information, please
contact the writer.

Looking forward to hearing from you, I remain,

                                   Cordially yours,

                                   L. J. MORTON

P. S.   Small publishers find our FOUR-STAR BULLETIN
         very effective. For $300.00 we will send your
         4X5 advertisement from your camera ready copy to
         5000 Public Libraries plus 2500 College and
         University Libraries. We also do the printing.
         Early reservations suggested.

Our 15th Year

CONSULTANTS AND CREATORS OF DIRECT MAIL AND MAIL ORDER ADVERTISING

FIGURE 7   Letter from Direct Mail Promotions, Inc., which conducts cooperative mailings to bookstores and college, school, and public libraries at extremely modest prices. When the publisher does not wish to supply its own insert, Direct Mail Promotions will print an announcement on its own insert from publisher-supplied copy.

month basis. Mailings are available in 22 subject categories, for which lists of special libraries in colleges and universities, research centers, and government and company libraries with special interests in that subject are used. You can participate in any mailing by subject to libraries within two geographic areas: (1) the United Kingdom, Western Europe, and Israel and (2) other English-speaking areas.

MAILING OPTIONS

- You can mail your own promotional material by supplying printed mailing inserts in bulk to IBIS's U.K. mailing house. Your insert is then mailed with the promotional material of other publishers in one of 22 special library cooperative mailings by subject area.
- You can mail Publishers Information Cards (PICs), printed by IBIS. You promote a single title or series on a standard 3″ × 5″ card, blank on one side (Figure 8). Each card gives information on one title or series, including a brief description of the scope, contents, readership, and author, as well as ISBN/ISSN, price, and name and address of publisher. The typesetting and printing are done by IBIS from information you supply. You card is mailed with those of other publishers in the special library cooperative mailing according to your choice of 22 available subject areas. The accompanying table itemizes the 22 subject categories and lists the number of special libraries* by subject in each of two regions:

Subject Selections	UK, W. Europe, and Israel	Other English-Speaking Areas
Art and architecture	2,800	1,300
History	3,000	1,300
Philosophy	1,500	800
Law	2,600	1,100
English language and literature	1,500	1,200
Religion	1,600	800
Geography	2,000	1,100
Sociology and anthropology	2,400	1,100
Psychology and psychiatry	2,700	1,200
Education	2,400	1,600
Politics	1,700	900
Economics	2,800	1,300
Management and business	2,700	1,400
Medicine	5,800	1,500
Biological sciences	2,900	1,400
Mathematics	2,700	1,400
Physics	2,800	1,200
Chemistry	2,900	1,300
Electrical engineering	2,700	1,300
Mechanical engineering	2,100	1,300
Civil engineering	2,600	1,300
Chemical engineering and industrial chemistry	2,900	1,200

*University central and public libraries in the same regions can be added to your special library cooperative mailing.

KUCK, J.A. ed.
The Determination of sulfur in the presence of other elements or simultaneously with them. Microchemical research papers of contemporary microanalysts in Bulgaria, Czechoslovakia, Hungary, Poland, Roumania & the Soviet Union/edited by J.A. Kuck; trs. fr. Bulgarian, Czechoslovakian, Hungarian, Polish, Roumanian & Russian by Kurt Gingold. — Gordon & Breach, 7.78. — 466p.: figs., tabs.; 23 cm. — Methods in microanalysis ser. Vol. 6. — ISBN 0-677-20770-0 Cloth: $64.00 USA/Canada, £35.60 elsewhere, non-net.

SCOPE: This volume is devoted exclusively to the analysis for sulfur in organic substances. It contains methods which apply not only when sulfur is the sole hetero element present, but also when it is combined with one or more other hetero elements.

CONTENTS: (include) The determination of sulfur by oxidative methods; The determination of sulfur by reductive methods; The determination of sulfur by catalytic desulfurization; The determination of sulfur in the presence of other elements; Titration for sulfur by means of new indicators; The simultaneous determination of sulfur with other elements; Colorimetric methods for sulfur; Instrumental methods for sulfur.

READERSHIP: Analytical chemists & other scientists who need to use analytical techniques.

EDITOR: Fairfield University, Connecticut.

© P I C S Ltd 1978   2372/040978   Prices net unless otherwise stated.

G|B

Gordon and Breach

SCIENCE PUBLISHERS LTD.

41/42 William IV Street, London WC2

FIGURE 8   IBIS Information Services' Publisher-Information Card mailed in alternate months to special libraries in English-speaking countries. The publisher supplies advertising copy to fit the 3″ × 5″ card. IBIS provides typesetting and printing and mails, along with similar cards of other publishers in any one of 22 subject categories to your choice of two geographic regions: (1) the United Kingdom, Western Europe, and Israel or (2) other English-speaking countries worldwide.

COSTS

Costs in 1981 were 25¢ per address for an insert weighing half an ounce or less and 34¢ for an insert weighing up to 2 oz. Postcards, depending upon the number of cards mailed, were about 23¢ per address in 1981.

For complete information contact IBIS Information Services, Inc., 215 Park Ave. S., New York, NY 10003; 212-505-7620.

7:04   Co-op Mailings to Scientific Researchers

Co-op Mailings, Inc., will bring your message to 19,000 scientific researchers in colleges and universities and industrial, government, and nonprofit laboratories for $695 (price subject to change). For an added $45, it will handle all production details and supply proofs. You supply up to 125 words, a glossy photograph, and first-class business reply card permit number. The loose postcards are mailed in card-deck format.

You can reach virtually the entire scientific research audience through the more comprehensive ACS Lab Universe Sales Cards. These quarterly card-deck mailings reach 75,000 laboratories at a cost of approximately $1,200 (price subject to change).

For information on Co-op Mailings, Inc., call Irv Berkowitz at 201-666-3111, or write to Co-op Mailings, Inc., P.O. Box 248, Hillsdale, NJ 07642. For details on the ACS Lab Universe Sales Cards, call Clay Holden at 213-325-1903, or write to Centcom, Ltd., GSB Building, One Belmont Ave., Bala Cynwyd, PA 19004, to the attention of Jim Byrne.

The Co-op Mailing, Inc., card-deck reaches researchers in physics, chemistry, biology, and the earth sciences. The ACS Lab Universe deck mailing reaches more than 40,000 industrial labs, and approximately 15,000 university and clinical/medical labs each, as well as more than 3,000 government labs.

7:05   **Co-op Card-Deck Mailing to Public Libraries**

The only co-op card deck now being mailed to public libraries is the bimonthly mailing from Rickmar Publishing Co., P.O. Box 187, Mount Prospect, IL 60056. (Mailing subject to cancellation when there is insufficient participation. Call first and confirm before scheduling.) For just $375, at the time of this writing, Rickmar will include your card offering in a mailing to 15,000 libraries. This includes all public libraries and about 500 army/navy service libraries.

Mailings are scheduled every other month, in September, November, January, March, May, and July. When there are insufficient participants, Rickmar may double up and do only four mailings, so the mailing dates cited may be imprecise.

Ed Vogeney produces these deck mailings in conjunction with a business that sells tape decks to the library market. The mailings have been issued since May 1980. He says the publishing community has largely overlooked his deck mailings, but that among those few who did participate were Dartnell and McGraw-Hill.

If you are interested in the library card-deck mailing, call Vogeney at 312-577-3653. For the mailing, publisher-supplied negative (right reading) is preferred; if illustration is included, it should not require more than a 110-line screen for reproduction.

8

The Card Deck as a Tool
of Book Promotion

8:01   The Card Deck:
Unique Book-Selling Vehicle for the 1980s

The card deck—a collection of loose postcards measuring $3\frac{1}{2}'' \times 5\frac{1}{2}''$ and usually numbering 30 to 80, is seen most frequently in a polybag. Most of the 300 to 400 commercially sponsored decks are issued by publishers of specialized business publications and mailed to their circulation. Individual cards are sold to advertisers and, usually, the participation cost per card is 10 to 20% less than the cost for advertisement in the sponsoring periodical.

Virtually all of the commercially sponsored decks are listed in monthly issues of *SRDS Business Publication Rates and Data*, grouped by subject, together with circulation and pertinent insertion data.

The original intent of the card deck, when introduced by McGraw-Hill in conjunction with several of its publications in 1959, was to generate sales leads for advertisers through literature offers. As recently as 1982, one of the larger commercial sponsors of decks, making mailings of close to 200,000, still cautioned potential advertisers in its prospectus that deck offerings were *not* designed to sell.

However, a number of professional and scholarly book publishers have found that the card deck is a sales tool—and a powerful one at that. The popular use of card decks by book publishers as a selling vehicle did not begin until the mid-1970s. Today, it is rare to receive any commercially sponsored deck in which there are not at least several book offerings. A commercially sponsored deck in the business field in 1982 contained 80 cards, of which over one-third were book offerings of various publishers.

McGraw-Hill Book Co. is credited with being the first book publisher to issue an all-book deck offering. This effort started modestly in the early 1970s. The idea was later adapted by Wiley-Interscience and then spread to other professional and scholarly book establishments. Today, at least a score of book publishers have issued their own decks.

Recently, book publishers producing their own decks have started to branch out and become syndicators, by "sweetening" their own deck with the offerings of other advertisers.* One book publisher/syndicator limits outside participation to no more than 20% of a deck offering. It has claimed that the 20% outside participation produced enough income to pay the entire cost of the deck. Another excludes participation by other book publishers.

Originally, all loose-deck mailings were encased in paper envelopes. In the early 1980s, the polybag emerged as the most popular vehicle for loose-deck mailings, although a few publishers still favor the slightly more expensive paper envelopes.

The first card decks in bound-booklet format were introduced by Cahners Publishing Co. shortly after McGraw-Hill had introduced the loose deck. The booklet consisted of postcard pages (three cards per page) and was mailed to 31,000 subscribers of *Metalworking* magazine.

Book publishers tried and then quickly moved away from bound-deck mailings, when, in testing, they found that loose-deck mailings were more than twice as effective.

The first syndicator of exclusively loose decks not tied to a magazine's circulation was Co-Op Mailings of Hillsdale, N.J., in 1965. This syndicator is still active in educational mailings (see 25:06).

The entries following in this chapter continue the pattern established in *Volume One* of *Book Marketing Handbook*. The comprehensive presentation in that volume introduced the card-deck concept to hundreds of publishers, provided guidelines for using decks and estimating response, and gave results of early format tests showing the clear edge that loose decks have over bound decks.

This second volume vastly expands that body of knowledge on card-deck usage for professional and scholarly book promotion. The information in this chapter describes the latest thinking of publishers who are successful card-deck users and provides detailed responses to questions on card-deck promotion posed by book marketers to the author since publication of *Volume One*.

Topics covered in this new presentation on card decks include new approaches to evaluating card-deck participation costs; guidelines for figuring card-deck response rate; test results of the echo effect of a publisher's card-deck promotion; the value and importance of headlines and illustrations in deck offerings; advantages of single vs. multiple-book listings on a single card; best timing for deck mailings promoting books; the first "position" studies ever undertaken to show the relationship of response to a card's position in a deck; and pointers on how to create and syndicate your deck.

---

*In February 1983, Virginia Pepis of the Wiley Direct Response Marketing Department conducted a publisher deck mailing to Wiley engineering bookbuyer lists in which *all* participants were competitors and non-publisher advertisers.

For other entries in this volume relating to card decks, see 5:18, 7:05, 9:09, and 24:15. For a test of response to a medical card-deck mailing with and without a free examination offer, see 3:13.

8:02   **New Approaches to Evaluating Card-Deck Participation Costs**

In *Volume One* of *Book Marketing Handbook* we mentioned that some marketers were evaluating card-deck costs by using a factor of 1.5¢ per name as an average. Costs per name over that price were considered in the high range; those under that average were deemed in the low range. However, as publishers' use of decks has increased, the 1.5¢-per-card rule of thumb has given way to a different view of card costs. As the size of the mailing increases and the list becomes less specialized, the cost per card tends to go down. When the list size is much smaller and the target audience more specialized, the cost tends to go up.

Thus, when you use an *IEN* (*Industrial Equipment News*) card, you reach nearly 200,000 individuals who are spread over 22 different SIC business and industrial classifications and hold various levels of responsibility in areas ranging from administration to production and purchasing. The average cost per name at the time of writing for this group was 1.1¢.

The average cost per name reached for five different, widely scattered deck mailings, each of which reaches audiences ranging from 125,000 to 290,000, was 1.2¢. However, when you averaged five somewhat more specialized deck mailings with circulations ranging from 35,000 to 50,000, the cost per name was 2.6¢. A third group of five smaller and more selective mailings reached more specialized audiences with circulations ranging from 17,000 to 25,000 and showed a cost per name of 3.3¢.

So, when considering a card-deck participation, avoid a single standard for all your participations. The more specialized and selective the audience, the more you can expect to pay per card. But, often, the higher priced card may be a bargain, whereas the lower cost per name may not be.

8:03   **Figuring Response Rate for Card-Deck Promotions: Guidelines**

How do you figure the response rate from a card deck? Whether you sponsor your own deck or buy a participation in someone else's, it is best to forget percentages and, instead, to think of response in terms of cost-to-net-sales ratio.

Let's assume you need a maximum cost of 40% for a promotion to be considered profitable. You'll then need $2.50 in net sales for each dollar spent on the promotion. If it costs $400 to produce and mail 1,000 card decks, you'll need a net response of $1,000 in sales to achieve your profit objective.

If the average book offering in the deck is priced at $25, you will need 40 orders per 1,000 decks. If your mailing produces more than 40 orders per 1,000 decks and you are not reaching the desired $1,000 in net income, the majority of the ordering may be for the lower priced books in the deck. The solution here is to substitute higher priced books for those in the lower price range.

Use this formula as well when you buy a participation in a syndicated desk. You can use this formula, too, for your promotions of loose-leaf publications or periodical subscriptions. You multiply the order value (potential income), taking into account returns and non-payments, by units sold. This total is then matched against the cost of the promotion.

8:04   **Cost-to-Net-Sales Ratio on 100 Participations**
        in Co-op Deck Mailings: A Study

A study of 100 publisher participations in cooperative card-deck mailings in a recent year indicated an overall cost-to-net-sales figure of 43.8%. Ninety percent of the offerings were for scientific and technical books, and 10 percent were for business books. Of the 100 offerings, 68 were new titles and 32 were best-selling or very active backlist titles.

8:05   **Techniques for Cutting Cost of Booklet Deck**
        Participation by 75% or More

Card-deck promotion is great, you say, but who can afford it—especially for some of your titles with limited potential. For example, you have your eye on one marketplace-type booklet deck that is issued as a stitched booklet with three cards on a page and that is mailed to a prime audience for perhaps a dozen or more of your titles. But at $1,300 per card, the cost is out of reach.

Here's a way you can get around the high cost, reach your audience, and make the impossible possible. Accumulate enough of your budget to be able to buy a triple card, which frequently will cost about two and one-half times the cost of a single card. This gives you a full page in the booklet, for which you utilize only the lower one-third as the business reply card. In the upper two-thirds of the page, run descriptions of your various titles, perhaps six on each side, with corresponding order numbers that you repeat on the card. The card at the bottom, then, becomes an ordering vehicle for 10 or even 12 different titles. Even if you only come up with ten titles and the triple-card page costs $3,000, your pro-rated cost per title is only $300 instead of $1,300. With a dozen book offerings, your cost is down to only $250 per book, and that's a lot cheaper than $1,300. Who says you can't afford card-deck promotion!

8:06   **When Limited Budget Prohibits Use of Co-op Deck: An Alternative**

Although cooperative card-deck promotions can be highly effective for certain appropriate books, this form of promotion is often beyond the reach of many small publishers with limited budgets.

If you are confident that you have a title that is highly suited for a particular co-op deck promotion but the cost per card is beyond your reach, try contacting the sponsor to arrange a participation on a per-order basis. Tell the sponsor you are willing to arrange for the response to be returned to him and that you are willing to pay a certain amount for each order received. Sometimes it may be possible to set up such an arrangement on a test basis, i.e., with the promise of regular participation in a future co-op deck if the test proves satisfactory.

8:07   **Sponsoring Your Own Card Deck:**
Keeping Costs under Control When You Lack Sufficient Product

If you would like to produce and mail your own card deck, as opposed to buying an occasional card or two in deck mailings sponsored by others, here are some ways to keep costs under control when you feel you lack sufficient product:

1. Mix new and recent titles with formerly successful backlist titles.
2. Promote your pertinent journals.
3. Offer cards to other publishers in exchange for cards in their future deck mailings, for space in their mailing promotions, or for advertising space in their publications.
4. Syndicate, i.e., sell individual cards to other publishers or advertisers. Aside from helping to cover printing and mailing costs, you can "freshen up" your offering, especially where your list does not change materially from one deck mailing to another.

8:08   **Cost to Sponsor Your Own Deck:**
What It May Take to Break Even

If you plan to sponsor your own deck and offer individual cards for sale to others, how much should such a promotion cost? Solar Press, Inc., a Naperville, Ill., card-deck printer, provides this estimate.

Let's say you are planning a deck with 40 loose cards, to be mailed to 50,000. Cards will be printed one-color on two sides and mailed in a clear polybag with a two-color front and a one-color back and with an address card on the face.

The total production and mailing cost, which includes postage, will be approximately $12,000 (based on mid-1981 paper and postal costs). Add to these costs promotional sales aids, marketing and sales expense, list preparation, billing and collection, and overall coordination costs. These additional costs, says Solar Press, will run around $10,000, based on the assumption that the card-deck coordinator is someone who takes on the project in addition to other activities.

We think such a card-deck promotion can be done for reasonably close to $12,000 without all those extra costs. This means that if you can sell 15 of the cards in your deck at $800 each, your cost is basically covered on the remaining 25 cards. Even with some of those added costs that contribute to the $10,000, you can keep your own expenses relatively small.

8:09   How Publisher Solved Problem of Low-Priced Books in Deck: Case History

If you use or are considering the use of co-op card decks for your book promotions, sooner or later you will find you have certain low-priced books on your list that may have great sales potential in the market to which the deck is being mailed but that simply cannot pay their way, no matter the response.

Here is how one publisher has been solving that problem. He takes two books, both squarely in the market of the co-op card deck, but both too low-priced to carry their weight in a normal deck offering with free examination privilege. Each book is then made into an offering on one side of a single card that includes descriptive copy, illustration, and ordering information. Each side also includes three more ingredients:

1. The instruction "SEND TO," with complete publisher name and address.
2. A prepayment requirement: I enclose $____.
3. An additional postage and handling charge.

Reporting on one such mailing, the publisher, who also issues a monthly periodical in the same subject area, said,

We have discovered no appreciable difference in the rate of sales using this approach versus a standard card with business reply address. Any slight less return on any mailing is more than compensated for by the cost savings. In our most recent mailing [after 10 weeks] our income thus far is exceeding our costs by 48%.

He added further,

We have found our method of advertising on both sides of a card particularly advantageous when selling low-priced books. With a tighter promotion budget for such books, we can stretch our dollars, getting in effect two messages delivered for the price of one. By eliminating the business reply mail feature we receive only paid orders, thereby avoiding return postage costs, follow-up invoicing costs, and in the case with low-priced books, occasional collection costs or losses. Audience and subject matter have much to do with the matter. In our case we have a highly selective audience and the right subject matter. The reader is interested and is willing to pay the postage and send a check. The postcard serves as an effective means to earn his attention.

8:10   **Best Mailing Months for Publisher-Sponsored Card-Deck Mailings**

If you are planning to sponsor your own card-deck mailings, more than likely you will find that these four months—January, February, March, and September—are the most cost-effective. This judgment is based on a year-long study of close to 20 publisher-sponsored card-deck mailings in ten different subject areas involving business, architecture and engineering, and the social sciences. More than two million units were mailed in all. The judgments of response in these mailings was based on the cost-to-net-sales ratios, which were about equal for all four of the most cost-effective months.

8:11   **The Echo Effect of Publishers' Card-Deck Promotion:**
College Marketing Group Test

Do card-deck mailings devoted exclusively to professional and scholarly books generate indirect or echo sales, and, if so, how much? In 1980, Glenn Matthews of College Marketing Group (CMG) found his answer to this question in a test made in one of three deck mailings of books, each to 50,000 names culled from publishers' book-buyer lists.

All three decks had been targeted to professionals in such fields as special education, business, and medicine, who were in a position to purchase books with money other than their own, or who were able to mark book selections for a secretary, purchasing agent, or library with a recommendation to order. All deck mailings included, in addition to the individual cards, a postpaid business reply envelope returnable to CMG.

For the echo test, two of the book offerings in the special education deck omitted the publisher's name and address, so that orders could only be received by CMG. Ultimate sales of the two books, based on orders received by CMG, were $3,665.40. A little more than $700 was the postcard response. More than $2,900 came through purchase orders from various sources. The ratio of indirect sales to direct orders was a little better than 4–1, for an echo effect of over 400%!

8:12   **Pitfalls of Book Promotions on Postcards**

High-priced reference works that require a lot of explanation and loose-leaf publications with various types of ordering options do not lend themselves easily to the very restricted space of a postcard. Some co-op deck sponsors have tried to overcome this by offering a double card with a fold or a triple card with two folds, which eliminates the problem but doubles or triples the cost of the card.

Another pitfall, say marketers who have used both decks and catalogs to promote books with free examination offers, is that book returns and bad debt are more prevalent from deck than from catalog offerings.

8:13   **Relationship of Position of Card in Deck to Response:**
         Study Results

Is the position of a card in a deck of any special benefit in a book promotion mailing? When the question was posed by a book marketing
professional, the author of this handbook undertook a study of responses from more than one million decks representing nearly 500
card-deck book offerings and covering a broad range of scientific and
professional subjects.

The study was based on ten different card-deck mailings that were
devoted exclusively to books and mailed to from 100,000 to 120,000
names each on more than a dozen different lists. Book prices in the ten
mailings ranged from $9.95 to $79.95, with 40 to 50 books offered in
each deck. All areas of the physical sciences, engineering, business,
data processing, and nursing and health care were covered in the mailings. Each of the mailings was devoted to a different theme.

Answers were sought to these questions: Is the last-card position in
a deck, like the fourth or back outside cover in a periodical, a preferred
position? And does the position of a particular card in a deck have any
bearing on the response?

FINDINGS

Last Card in Deck Position   In not one of the ten mailings did the last
card in the deck equal the highest scoring, both in terms of unit
response and dollar volume.

Response vis-à-vis Position in Deck   A remarkably even pattern of
response emerged for cards positioned in the first half of the deck as
opposed to those in the back half of the deck. In every one of the ten
mailings studied, the unit response of the ten highest response cards
was twice as good in the front half of the deck as in the back half.

On a weighted response from all ten mailings, which represented a
combined mailing of 1,250,000 decks, 67% of the highest response
cards were positioned in the front half of the deck and 33% were in the
second half. Taking the position results mailing-by-mailing, one deck
had eight of the top ten high-response cards in the first half, five of the
mailings had seven of the top ten high-response cards in the first half,
and four deck mailings had six of the top ten cards in the first half.

8:14   **Pricing and List Response Patterns**
         from Card-Deck Promotions: A Study

Three business and professional book card-deck mailings were made at
approximately the same time in 1980. Each mailing consisted of more
than 100,000 units, with each containing approximately 50 book titles.
Each was mailed to approximately ten lists, some of which consisted
of book buyers and others of subscribers to professional publications
in the field. Analysis of the results of the three deck mailings disclosed
the following for the 150 book offerings:

1. In all three mailings multiple-copy orders boosted the average number of books per order received to 1.1, although the lists and audiences were different.

2. The average gross sale in each of the three mailings was approximately $25. (Prices ranged from $15 to $60 in the first mailing; from $10 to $50 in the second; and from $13 to $39 in the third.)

3. Price did not seem to be a factor in the ten top-selling titles. Best sellers were priced in this order: (first mailing) $27.95, $24.95, $65.00, $21.95, $57.95, $16.95, $25.95, $21.50, $15.95, $20.95; (second mailing) $27.95, $24.95, $65.00, $21.95, $57.95, $16.95, $25.95, $21.50, $15.95, $20.95; and (third mailing) $34.95, $12.95, $24.95, $37.50, $31.95, $32.50, $29.95, $30.50, $22.95, $12.95.

4. In all three mailings the book-buyer lists outpulled business periodical subscriber lists by a combined average of 22% (38% in the first deck mailing, 11% in the second deck mailing, and 17% in the third deck mailing).*

8:15 Should Illustration Be Included in Deck Mailing? Three Viewpoints

Two marketers were questioned on the value of a book illustration in card-deck promotions. Said the head of direct marketing for one leading professional and reference publishing house, "Use a photograph if the jacket looks interesting or it is fairly attractive; otherwise no." Another point of view was expressed by the direct-response manager of another major professional and reference publisher, who is also a major user of card decks: "I won't promote a book without showing it. People want to know they're buying a 'thing'; I want them to know what they're geting. It's a focal point on a card; it exists."

Doug Wilhide addressed the question of illustrations in his article "Direct Response Cards Come of Age" in the August 1981, issue of *Industrial Marketing*. Said Wilhide, "You may have to choose between a product picture and a long headline. If the product . . . *can* be shown in the space, show it. Otherwise make the headline work as the visual element." (Wilhide was writing in his capacity as copywriter for Colle & McVoy Advertising, Minneapolis.)

Examination of professional and reference book promotions in various card decks over a one-year period indicated that more than 90% of the book offerings on cards did include an illustration.

8:16 Do Multiple-Book Listings on a Single Card Pay Off?

Do multiple-book listings on the same card in a deck pay off? The answer is both "yes" and "no," depending on the circumstances, as we will show.

---

*The third deck mailing also included a list of executive seminar attendees. In that particular mailing, the book-buyer lists outpulled the list of executive seminar attendees by more than 80%.

One direct-response marketer tested multiple offerings for scientific and technical books that were ganged on a card and got poor results. Her conclusions: "Good results on a book in a card deck generally require a minimum of several sentences of descriptive copy. When such an offering does not include sufficient information, the response suffers."

Another leading publisher of professional and reference books found that ganging a number of books on a single card in a deck did pay off, although the circumstances were special: (1) All of the books were handbooks with highly descriptive titles; (2) the offer came from the leading publisher of handbooks, and (3) all of the handbooks listed had previously been promoted individually in both space and direct-mail promotion.

The multiple-book listing format on one card is a favorite of some book clubs. The McGraw-Hill Book Clubs, in participations in co-op deck offerings, have been listing as many as nine books on a single card (stating title, author, and club price) under such headings as "Buy one great book—GET ONE FREE."

An outstanding case study of the use of multiple titles on a single card in a deck appears in 8:26. As this study shows, the multiple listings were tied to in-depth descriptions of each of the titles listed on the card in a publication advertisement mailed almost simultaneously to the same audience.

CONCLUSIONS

A book in a deck offering, with no supporting circumstances, needs a minimum amount of descriptive copy (at least 100 to 150 words) for the offering to be comprehended and effective. A strong headline greatly enhances that effectiveness, and a clear, recognizable illustration often can help.

EXCEPTIONS

- When the book's title is a form of advertisement that by itself fully explains the content of the book (such as a handbook).
- When the book is a new edition of a well-known standard reference work and a simple listing may be sufficient to prompt a previous buyer to reorder.
- When a book is part of a free or special offer (such as for book clubs) and requires no descriptive or "selling" copy.
- When the offer is tied to another promotion, for example, a mailing that occurs simultaneously with a space advertising campaign for the book(s) listed.
- When the offer is tied to an offering advertised elsewhere (see 8:26).

8:17   **Pitfall of Multibook Offerings on Card in Deck: Problem/Solution**

If you plan to place more than one book on a single card in a deck offering, be alert to a serious pitfall of such practice and a way to overcome it. One publisher who offered two companion volumes on a single card with separate check-off boxes reported that a large number of the responses were returned fully completed with all of the ordering information, but without either of the two preference boxes checked. A way to avoid this problem when you make more than one offering on a card is to add a line directly over the "Name" line stating something to this effect: "Check title(s) of your choice before completing."

8:18   Importance of the Headline in a Card-Deck Offering

As vital as the headline is for routine promotions of professional and business books, it becomes even more important in a card-deck offering. The reason: Severe copy limitations imposed by the small area available for descriptive copy tend to place the major emphasis on the headline, which must work in concert with the book's title. When a book illustration is included on the card as well, as is frequently the case, the entire selling message may be limited to perhaps five to ten lines of 6 or 7 pt. type.

Any extra time spent on developing a compelling headline for a card-deck offering is well invested. The headline should focus on the prime benefit of the book and have enough strength to trigger an interest in the book even before the copy is read. Tests have shown that the most effective card offering combines a compelling benefit-oriented headline with a free trial examination offer. If faced with the choice of either illustration or headline, opt for the headline.

8:19   Technique for Getting 30% More Advertising
Area on Card in Deck

There may be occasions when a publisher wishes to qualify response from a card-deck offering, such as when a complimentary examination copy of a book is offered, or when publisher wishes to encourage the recipient to order from a library jobber or visit a bookstore. This "braking" action is accomplished by requiring that the respondent affix his or her own postage to the reply card. Under such circumstances, the reward to the publisher is bonus of 30% additional copy area on the card. This "bonus" is the first 1¾ inches on the left of the address side of the card, which may be used for the respondent's name and address and qualifying information, or for any other advertising matter. The post office only requires 3½ inches on the right-hand side of the address area on a card when postage is affixed by the respondent.

8:20   New Technique for Order Form in
Business Card-Deck Offerings

A new technique for the order-form portion of business card-deck offerings made its appearance late in 1982. This was the phenomenon of overprinting, in a light benday of the ink color, on the order area of the postcard an instruction to "tape business card here." In a deck mailing by *Marketing Bulletin Board*, over one-third of the offerings in the 106-card deck bore some variation of this instruction, although most stated "tape business card here." One deck participant covered the entire print area (3½" × 5") with "selling" copy, thereby omitting the ordering portion of the card completely, which was replaced with the single one-line instruction: "For your free catalog, please tape your business card to this side and mail today."

**8:21   Production Pointers and Pitfalls
for Syndicated Loose-Card Deck***

If you are launching a card-deck promotion and plan to syndicate, or to offer to advertisers through one of your journals, here are some production pointers and pitfalls to consider.

1. You can avoid many production problems by having all participants supply film negatives geared to your printer's requirements.

2. Avoid offering proofs. Failure of an advertiser to approve proofs can hold up the entire mailing. And with material supplied on film, there should be no need for proofs.

3. If you do not offer proofs, arrange for one responsible individual to check each card to see that each front and back are properly matched and that correct key numbers and artwork are properly inserted.

4. If any lists in your mailing program require a change in the print run, or if you have any advertising cancellations, inform the printer immediately. Printers run on tight schedules, and last-minute changes can delay the entire project.

5. Get the mailing labels into the hands of your printer early enough for him to meet his printing/mailing schedule without delays.

6. If a card buyer insists on supplying his own preprinted cards, be sure they are to your printer's specifications, and that he will accept preprinted cards for the mailing. It is preferable to show your printer a sample in advance so he can examine it for suitability.

7. Your choice of either of the two basic encasements for a loose-deck mailing will have little or no effect on return. Whether you use paper envelopes or polybags is largely a matter of preference or cost (see 8:24).

8. If a second color is desired in your deck mailing, use a printer who can deal with a second color at little extra cost. Some cannot print a second color without affecting considerably the overall printing cost of the mailing.

---

*Material for the ten pointers is based on an article in the October 31, 1978, issue of *Print Buyer & Production Manager's Newsletter* (3255 South U.S. 1, Ft. Pierce, FL 33450). The article was based on information supplied by the Solar Press, Naperville, IL 60540.

9. You can lower some of the costs of a deck mailing by getting estimates for printing with and without paper stock supplied. Then
check with a paper mill or merchant to find out paper cost. It may
be more economical to order the paper separately and supply it to
the printer yourself.

10. Your deck mailing will require a number of working days. Find out
from your printer how many working days will be needed from
final proof to actual mailing and set your mailing schedule accordingly.

**8:22   Production Tips: When You Buy a Card
in Someone Else's Card Deck**

Virtually all publishers of card decks request that material be submitted in the form of negatives. The most frequently specified format
is for right-reading negatives with the emulsion side down. Other acceptable formats are camera-ready art, Scotchprints, repro proofs, and
repro stats.

Screens For halftone illustrations, most publishers specify 110-line
screens as desirable or as the maximum. Others request 100-line screens
and state a maximum of 110-line. A few specify 110-line screens as
desirable and 133-line as the maximum. If no screen is specified, use the
110-line screen.

Illustrations Most prefer a velox in position. For specific requirements, contact the individual publisher, or refer to *SRDS Print Media
Production Data* or to *SRDS Business Publication Rates and Data.*

8:23   Card-Deck Mechanicals: Sizes Most Frequently Used

We examined the size of the copy area on more than 100 commercially
sponsored decks and the size requirements indicated by the deck spon-
sors. More than 25% use a standard $3\frac{1}{2}$" $\times$ $5\frac{1}{2}$" postcard but gave no
requirements for the copy area. Among those who specify a maximum
copy area in their requirements, nearly 25% indicated 3" $\times$ 5". The
next three sizes specified were in this order: $3\frac{1}{8}$" $\times$ $5\frac{1}{2}$", $3\frac{1}{4}$" $\times$
$4\frac{3}{4}$", and $3\frac{1}{4}$" $\times$ $5\frac{1}{4}$".

**8:24   Planning Your Own Loose Deck?
Which Type of Wrapping Is Best?**

The vast majority of loose card-deck sponsors favor polybag mailers
over paper envelopes. Polybags are more economical and the decks can
be inserted by machine. But there are other reasons: Polybags tend to
be more colorful and to generate more excitement. A book publisher's
test of polybags vs. paper indicated a better response to the polybags.
Still, there are those who favor the paper envelope, which, they feel,

more closely conveys the idea of a letter and is less likely to be discarded before examination. One deck printer serving more than 40 clients reports that more than 70% specify polybags. Evidently the polybag is here to stay. Some recent innovations include perforated seals that permit ease of opening and bags that can be resealed. One pitfall of polybags was discovered by a sponsor who reported that during a siege of below-zero temperatures some of the bags broke open.

8:25   First Use of Card Deck Exclusively for Books

The first user of a card deck exclusively for book promotion was John Stockwell of McGraw-Hill's Professional and Reference Book Division. His first all-book deck mailing was made in the early 1970s. He recalls testing a 19-card deck against a 19-book promotional mailing. Although the deck cost twice as much, it produced twice as many orders. Stockwell subsequently doubled the size of his deck to 38 cards, and discovered a linear increase in business but at a smaller incremental cost. Subsequently, he increased the size of his all-book decks to as many as 60 cards. In 1981, he achieved another first in card-deck promotion of professional and reference books by using a sweepstakes to increase response.

For the "First All-Book Card-Deck to Offer Everything Gratis," see 24:15.

8:26   Most Books Ever Offered on Single Card in Card Deck

The record for the most books ever offered on a standard-size card in a card deck is held by Wiley-Interscience with its listing of 28 books and multivolume sets (see Figure 9). The record was set* in the fall 1982 card-deck mailing of the *Journal of Chemical Education*. The standard 3½" × 5½" card listed the 28 single titles and multivolume sets under the heading "Free 15-Day Examination of these Wiley-Interscience Books Advertised in Sept. Issue of *Journal of Chemical Education.*" The deck mailing was made shortly after the mailing of the September issue of the *Journal of Chemical Education*, in which the books on the card were advertised in a two-page spread. On the postcard, each single title or multivolume set had a check-off box, full or abbreviated title, ISBN number, and price. It was highly cost-effective.

In the late 1970s, the McGraw-Hill Professional and Reference Book Division had listed 28 handbooks on an oversized (3½" × 7½") card. That card listed only the title with a corresponding check-off box and the price under the headline "Handbooks You Can Stake Your Reputation On—From McGraw-Hill."

*That record was set by this author.

FREE 15-DAY EXAMINATION of these Wiley-Interscience books advertised in Sept. issue of *Journal of Chemical Education*

Wiley-Interscience, Dept. 092
605 Third Ave., N.Y., N.Y. 10158

Please send book(s) I have checked to use FREE for 15 days. I'll either keep and send payment indicated, plus my local sales tax and a charge for postage/handling. Otherwise, I'll return it within the trial period and owe nothing. (Offer valid in U.S. only).

Sign: _____
         (Order invalid unless signed.)

Name _____

Company _____

Address _____

City _____

State _____ Zip _____

Prices subject to change without notice. 3-2173

- ☐ Txt *Pharmaceutical* Anal *3Ed* (1-09034-4).....$55.00
- ☐ Aquatic *Pollution:* Intro Text (1-05797-5)......$38.95
- ☐ Princip *Color* Technology *2Ed* (1-03052-X) ...$33.95
- ☐ *Aquatic* Chem *2Ed:* paper (1-09173-1) $27.50
- ☐ *Carbon 13* NMR Spectro *2Ed* (1-53157-X)....$29.50
- ☐ Pattys *Hygiene 3Ed 5Pt 3V Set* (1-87350-0) ...428.95
- ☐ Fund Princ *Polymeric* Materials (1-08704-1) ..$32.50
- ☐ Dicty *Chromatography 2Ed* (1-87477-9) $39.95
- ☐ *Electrons* in Chem Reactions (1-08474-3).....$35.00
- ☐ Intro Mod *Liquid* Chrom *2Ed* (1-03822-9) $43.95
- ☐ *Inorganic* Chem: A Modrn Intro (1-61230-8)...$34.95
- ☐ Literatur Matrix of *Chemistry* (1-79545-3).....$30.00
- ☐ Health *Hazards* in Industry (1-06339-8) $30.95
- ☐ *Reagents* for Org Synthesis V10 (1-86636-9) $39.50
- ☐ Physical Chem of *Surfaces 4Ed* (1-07877-8) ..$39.95
- ☐ Princip ot *Polymerization 2Ed* (1-05146-2) ...$39.95
- ☐ *Kinetics* and Mechanism *3Ed* (1-03558-0).....$32.00
- ☐ *Pharmaceutical* Cal *2Ed* paper (1-07757-7) ...$17.50
- ☐ *Statistics* for Experimenters (1-09315-7) $35.95
- ☐ Minicomputr in *Laboratory 2Ed* (1-09012-3) ..$29.00
- ☐ *Statistics* for Research (1-08602-9)............$31.95
- ☐ Advncd Inorg *Chemistry 4Ed* (1-02775-8).....$34.95
- ☐ *Medical* Botany (paper ed) (1-86134-0) $14.95
- ☐ *Protective Groups* in Org Synth (1-05764-9) ...$37.50
- ☐ *Antibiotics,* Chemoth, Antibactl (1-87359-4) ..$49.50
- ☐ *Directory* of Publishg Sources (1-09200-2) ...$27.50
- ☐ *Nuclear* & Radiochem 3Ed ppr (1-86255-X) ...$29.50
- ☐ Dicty *Spectroscopy 2Ed* (1-87478-7)..........$39.95

FIGURE 9   Card from "Chemical Education Cards" deck mailing in September 1982 to the circulation of *Journal of Chemical Education*. The card was placed by Wiley-Interscience and offered 28 individual volumes or sets. All had been advertised in a two-page spread in the September 1982 issue of *Journal of Chemical Education*, which had been mailed earlier.

8:27   First Users of Sweepstakes in Conjunction with Loose-Deck Professional Book Mailings

Sweepstakes, although in wide use for various contest promotions to consumers, were not used for professional and reference books until November 1981. John Stockwell of the Professional and Reference Book Division of McGraw-Hill, originator of the book promotion card deck, incorporated a sweepstakes offering into a card-deck mailing of books on architecture and construction.

That first sweepstakes offering contained 59 book cards, plus an order entry card, and a folded-down four-page letter illustrating and describing the prizes. The cards printed in one-color ink on white stock. The letter was printed in four colors of ink to highlight the prizes, which were headed by an Apple computer. The success of that first card-deck sweepstakes offering prompted a second, similar mailing in April 1982 that contained 71 cards plus entry form.

By September 1982, the Boston-based business book publisher Warren, Gorham & Lamont, Inc., duplicated the successful McGraw-Hill offering by issuing a card-deck mailing for business books. It consisted of 57 book offerings plus an entry form card and letter (see 5:18).

8:28   **Evolution of Card Deck as a Book-Selling Tool: Highlights/Dates**

- First use of card decks as a promotional vehicle: McGraw-Hill Publishing Co., in 1959, in conjunction with several of its periodicals.
- First use of card deck in bound-booklet format: Cahners Publishing Co., in 1960, a booklet of postcard pages (three cards to a page) to 31,000 circulation of *Metalworking* magazine.
- First use of card deck for book promotion: McGraw-Hill's Professional and Reference Book Division, in the early 1970s, by John Stockwell.
- First use of all-book card deck offering everything gratis: Wiley Technical and Occupational Publishing Group, in December 1980, by James Gaughan.
- First syndicator to loose decks exclusively (not tied to periodical subscriber circulation): Co-Op Mailings of Hillsdale, N.J., in 1965.
- First Study of bookselling echo effect using card deck as test vehicle: College Marketing Group in 1980, by Glenn Matthews.
- First studies of relationship of position of card in deck to response: Nat Bodian of Wiley-Interscience for *Book Marketing Handbook, Volume Two*.
- Most cards ever mailed in single deck: 140 in deck produced by Solar Printing Co., for technical publication.
- Most books ever offered on single standard-size card in card deck: 28 by Wiley-Interscience, in October 1982, deck issued by *Journal of Chemical Education*.
- First detailed annotation of card-deck availabilities, by subject, issued on periodic basis: Standard Rate & Data Service's *Business Publication Rates and Data*, in its monthly issues, beginning in November 1971.*
- First all-book card deck incorporating a sweepstakes offering: McGraw-Hill's Professional and Reference Book Division, in November 1981, by John Stockwell.
- First all-business book card deck incorporating a sweepstakes: Warren, Gorham & Lamont, Inc., in September 1982.

---

*The November 1971 issue carried 113 card-deck listings. By early 1983, the number of listings had increased to 426.

9

Package Inserts, Book Inserts, Envelope Stuffers

9:01   Package Inserts, Book Inserts, and Envelope Stuffers:
        How and When to Use Each to Best Advantage

PACKAGE INSERTS

Package inserts may be included with mail-order shipments of either your own or someone else's merchandise. When your package inserts are shipped with someone else's merchandise, you have these advantages:

- You reach an active mail-order buyer.
- Your insert in someone else's package has the implied endorsement of the shipper of that package.
- You reach a market with identifiable characteristics at a very reasonable cost.

When you insert in packages with your own outgoing mail-order shipments, your cost is practically nil, except for the cost of the insert. Your package insert will do much better if a postpaid order form is included. Include a selection of your best-selling titles across your entire list, and your insert will be appropriate for any retail shipment. If a sufficiently large assortment of books is included in the insert, a return of $4 to $5 in orders is not unusual for every dollar spent on inserts.

If you plan an insert or package-stuffer program along product lines, and your books are shipped from a source other than your main premises, you might want to indicate the subject area of that product on the invoice so that the packer can include subject-related stuffers in the shipment.

BOOK INSERTS

If your planned insert features a book or books directed to a specific audience, it is best to place the insert directly in a book in the same broad subject area. Other book-insert possibilities include a continuation order for subsequent volumes in a multivolume work or series and a journal announcement/subscription offer. Book inserts are less costly if machine-inserted during the binding process or if book is shrink-wrapped, atop the book, under the film wrapping. If done at shipping center, hand insertion will cost considerably more.

ENVELOPE STUFFERS

An added low-cost source of revenue is the promotional enclosure in the same envelope with a letter, statement, or invoice. Stuffers can be used effectively to promote books of broad general interest, to announce related books or series with journal invoices, or to promote a journal in outgoing mail to customers in a related business or discipline. A statement or invoice stuffer generally has the advantage of going out by first-class mail. Other types of envelope stuffers generally accompany one or more primary pieces from a single mailer.

9:02   One Form of Envelope Stuffer: The Co-op Mailing

A cooperative mailing is one form of envelope stuffer. The envelope stuffer usually consists of a group of offerings united by the common desire of each participant to reach the audience to which the mailing is directed. Cooperative mailings are sometimes sponsored by a single mailer (see Chapter 7 for detailed information on co-op mailings) who, for a fee, may include perhaps ten or more inserts in the same package.

A number of companies will, for a fee, include the advertising literature of others. These may be found under the listing "Co-op Mailings and Package Insert Programs" in the SRDS *Direct Mail List Rates & Data Directory.*

Two companies that specialize in mailing the printed literature of book publishers in grouped envelope mailings are Direct Mail Promotions, Inc., 342 Madison Avenue, New York, NY 10017 (see 7:02); and IBIS Information Services, Inc., 51 East 42nd Street, New York, NY 10017, which conducts co-op mailings to international markets.

9:03   How to Use Catalog as Package Insert

If your establishment has prompt order fulfillment, consider producing subject catalogs on lightweight paper and including a subject-related catalog with each book shipment. The customer who is pleased with the book and speed of order fulfillment is likely to buy your other books in the same subject area.

9:04   **Successful Package-Stuffer Format for Professional and Reference Books**

A publisher who has a substantial volume of mail-order sales has had considerable success with a package stuffer that is randomly inserted with outgoing shipments to individual book buyers. The insert is a 16-page saddle-wire stitched booklet with self-cover in a 5″ × 6¼″ trim size, printed on 75 lb. high-bulk white offset stock. A message in letter format with a "Dear Customer" salutation always appears on the inside front cover and highlights the content of the booklet. The back cover is a perforated tear-off postpaid business reply card with check boxes listing each title by entry number, ISBN, and price. Each version of the stuffer contains 36 numbered book offerings, three of a subject on each page. The stuffer is always printed in black and one other color of ink. The subject matter for each page is given in the second color atop each page, centered and separated from the book descriptions by a 2 pt. horizontal rule. All other text is printed in black ink.

9:05   **Handbook Insert that Generates Orders for Related Titles**

A publisher of handbooks uses a unique book insert in a format that is easily adaptable to related books in a single subject area or field. The format consists of eight continuous postpaid postcard order forms that are accordion-folded and perforated for easy separation (Figure 10). The accordion-folded deck has a nonmailable cover card that features a brief copy block under the headline "7 Success-Proven Ideas to Help You. . . ." Attached to the cover card are seven separate order cards, one for each of seven handbooks. All are offered for 15-day free examination.

9:06   **Publisher's Package-Insert Program: Study Results**

In the early 1980s a publisher of professional books in business, architecture, the natural sciences, and engineering started a package insert program. A booklet-type insert was included with all outgoing retail orders. Over a three-year period, four separate package-insert campaigns were launched. Each booklet-insert contained approximately 40 titles. Each title in the insert was an acknowledged best-seller within its subject area or discipline. To allow for a comparison of the various campaign results, the same number of pieces were used in each campaign. Book prices in the campaigns ranged from a little more than $5 to nearly $100. Each of the campaigns tracked for the study followed the preceding one by several months so that the four campaigns in the package-insert program covered all seasons of the year.

FIGURE 10 Handbook insert used by Dartnell consists of eight postcards accordion-folded to a single 3½″ × 5½″ postcard size. Seven of the eight cards feature individual manuals with postpaid address copy on the reverse side. The eighth card is a cover with the heading "7 Success-Proven Ideas. . . ." The reverse side of the cover card invites the recipient to "try these time-saving programs to growth FREE for 30 days." Most of the handbooks were priced at $69.50, one at $59.50.

STUDY RESULTS

- Overall percentage of response for all four campaigns: 2.6%
- Average number of books per order for all four campaigns: 1.5
- Average price of each sale per order, all four campaigns: $29.

THE INDIVIDUAL CAMPAIGNS

	Percentage of Return	No. of Books per Order	Average Gross Sale per Order
1st Campaign	2.8	1.8	$22
2nd Campaign	1.4	1.4	$17
3rd Campaign	3.0	1.4	$37
4th Campaign	1.9	1.4	$40

- In the first two campaigns, a number of books in the $6 to $7 range were included, which kept the average gross sale per order much smaller than in subsequent insert campaigns.
- In the third campaign, the lower priced books were eliminated and the much higher priced books included. The two top revenue producers in this campaign were priced in the $75 to $100 range.
- In the fourth campaign, while the number of books per order remained constant, the percentage of response dropped by nearly one-

third. This was attributed to the fact that the fourth campaign was a duplication of the third and may have reached many of the same buyers a second time.

HOW CAMPAIGNS WERE TRACKED

Tracking for each campaign began simultaneously with the start of each insert campaign and continued for approximately eight weeks after the last insert in each of the four campaigns had been mailed (about 20 weeks in all, per campaign). Response generally ceased about four weeks after the last insert had been mailed.

LESSONS LEARNED FROM PACKAGE-INSERT
PROGRAM TO RETAIL BOOK BUYERS

- A package insert should include acknowledged best-selling titles.
- Subject matter should cover a wide spectrum of topics to appeal to as wide a range of interests as possible.
- Costs of an insert program are less than those of a catalog-mailing program, as the former involves no list rentals, no postage, and either very nominal or no mailing costs. (The return from a package-insert program is somewhat better than the return from a catalog mailing.)
- Response will continue four weeks after the last insert has been mailed.
- Higher priced books in an insert program will produce a higher average gross sale per order at little or no risk to the percentage of return.
- Time of year has no effect on the rate of return from a package-insert program.

9:07   **Book Insert/Postcard Produces More Than $30,000 in Prepublication Orders: Case Study**

When a new edition of a classic scientific reference book was planned after a lapse of 15 years, it was discovered that due to the information explosion in the field the work could not be reissued in one volume. The manuscript would require well over 3,000 pages, and the decision was made to issue the updated edition in three separate parts over a two-year period.

To help capture sales from the buyers of the first part of the new edition for the second part to follow over six months later and the third a year after that, a book insert was used in the first part. The insert, a postpaid order card, invited the buyer to place an order for the subsequent parts. The card was inserted at the bindery. When the second part was printed, a similar order card was inserted to invite orders for the third and remaining part, which would follow a year later.

Use of the inexpensive postcard insert in the first and second parts

Stick with Little, Brown
for the best in medical literature

You know how useful our books are . . . so make a wise investment and stock up on some more. Are you looking for a comprehensive reference that covers all aspects of your specialty? A handy spiralbound manual that concentrates on clinical essentials? A textbook that prepares a solid foundation for future professional growth? We have all three and more—written by the most distinguished authors in medicine. Choose from the popular titles listed below.

To order . . .
1. Detach the appropriate stamps.
2. Moisten and affix to any Little, Brown order card or correspondence with us. We'll ship your order and bill you later. Or save—by enclosing a check—and we'll pay postage and handling. Either way, our 30-day approval policy guarantees complete satisfaction or a full refund.
Prices are subject to change.

Samter **Immunological Diseases,** 3rd Edition #769843/ 51-93M1, $70.00	Earley & Gottschalk **Strauss and Welt's Diseases of the Kidney,** 3rd Edition #203149/ 57-91AB1, $85.00	Masters & Johnson **Human Sexual Response** #549878-89AD1, $17.50	Masters & Johnson **Human Sexual Inadequacy** #549851-89AC1, $17.50	Snell **Atlas of Clinical Anatomy** #802093-94AC1, $27.95	Cone **History of American Pediatrics** #152897, IN PRESS—due Spring 1980	Washington University **Manual of Medical Therapeutics,**2nd Edition #923966-88AD1, $11.95
King **Why Not Say It Clearly: A Guide to Scientific Writing** #493465-93R2, $5.95	Reller, Sahn, & Schrier **Clinical Internal Medicine** #739707-89A1, $15.00	Leaverton **A Review of Biostatistics: A Program for Self-Instruction,** 2nd Edition #518522-87X1, $6.50	Alton **Malpractice: A Trial Lawyer's Advice for Physicians (How to Avoid, How to Win)** #035009-88D1, $12.50	Wallach **Interpretation of Diagnostic Tests: A Handbook Synopsis of Laboratory Medicine,** 3rd Edition #920444-88Z1, $10.95	Bochner, Carruthers, Kampmann, & Steiner **Handbook of Clinical Pharmacology** #100633-94V2, $10.95	Samuels **Manual of Neurologic Therapeutics** #769908-92W1, $12.95
Gantz & Gleckman **Manual of Clinical Problems in Infectious Disease: With Annotated Key References** #303518-89K1, $12.95	Gardner & Provine **Manual of Acute Bacterial Infections: Early Diagnosis and Treatment** #303275-88V1, $12.95	Hoenig & Payne **How to Build and Use Electronic Devices without Frustration, Panic, Mountains of Money, or an Engineering Degree** #368075-92X1, $11.50	Friedman **Problem-Oriented Medical Diagnosis,** 2nd Edition #293563-90U1, $12.95	Spivak & Barnes **Manual of Clinical Problems in Internal Medicine: Annotated With Key References,** 2nd Edition #807141-88Y1, $12.95	Schrier **Renal and Electrolyte Disorders** #774758-90X1, $18.50	Doyle & Dennis **The Complete Handbook for Medical Secretaries and Assistants,** 2nd Edition #180823-91D1, $15.00
Jacox **Pain: A Sourcebook for Nurses and Other Professionals** #455903-87C1, $17.50	Bandman & Bandman **Bioethics and Human Rights: A Reader for Health Professionals** #079987-94G1, $10.95	Masters & Johnson **Homosexuality in Perspective** #549843-89Z1, $17.50	Strauss **Familiar Medical Quotations** #819158-92J1, $19.95	Wilkins & Levinsky **Medicine: Essentials of Clinical Practice,** 2nd Edition #940917-89Q1, $25.00 Cloth / Wilkins & Levinsky **Medicine: Essentials of Clinical Practice,** 2nd Edition #940909-99F1, $15.00 Paper	Colton **Statistics in Medicine** #152498-94F1, $19.95 Cloth / Colton **Statistics in Medicine** #152501-88S1, $14.50 Paper	Brooks, Manseau, & Principe **Nurses' Drug Reference** #109738-87Z1, $22.50 Cloth / Brooks, Manseau, & Principe **Nurses' Drug Reference** #109754-91A1, $11.95 Paper
free catalog! Get the entire list of all Little, Brown's Medical, Nursing, and Allied Health books when you return this stamp.		Kolodny, Masters & Johnson **Textbook of Sexual Medicine** #501549, $18.95 (T)	American Psychiatric Association **A Psychiatric Glossary,** 5th Edition IN PRESS—due Spring 1980	**Little, Brown and Company** Medical Division 200 West Street Waltham, Massachusetts 02154 Attention: Rita Connolly		

FIGURE 11 Stamp sheet used by the Medical Division of Little, Brown & Co. as book enclosure with medical book shipments. The sheet was folded in half, placed atop the front cover of outgoing book, and shrink-wrapped with the book. The original stamp sheet enclosure had 20 stamps. The sheet illustrated here was used in 1982 and contains 33 stamps.

of the three-part work resulted in several hundred prepublication orders for the subsequent parts of the multivolume work and produced traceable sales in excess of $30,000. This sum represented only a small portion of the total sales generated, as the overall price of the three-part work was well over $200 and this type of sale is usually placed with a company or institutional purchase order, which is difficult to track.

9:08   Sheet of Stamps as Book Enclosure: Case Study

The use of stamp enclosures for a scientific book promotion was initiated in 1980 by the Medical Division of Little, Brown & Co., Boston. A sheet of 20 stamps promoted general-interest medical books. Each stamp specified author, title, order number, and price. The stamp sheet was placed atop the front cover of each outgoing medical book shipment and shrink-wrapped with the book, so that the stamps would be visible as soon as the book was taken out of its wrapper.

At the top of the sheet ordering instructions asked that the recipient tear out the stamp and paste it on any order card, letterhead, or correspondence sent to the publisher. Many stamps came back affixed to invoices that also accompanied the book shipments.

The stamps as book enclosures did remarkably well, according to the publisher, and the program has been enlarged and refined and continues to be used.

A sheet used in late 1982 (Figure 11) was printed on goldenrod stock and contained 33 book offerings on individual stamps, as well as a return label stamp addressed to the publisher and another stamp for requesting a free catalog. The sheet carries the headline "Stick with Little, Brown for the best in medical literature," and gives ordering instructions atop the one-color (black) all-type sheet.

9:09   Sweepstakes Insert with Card Deck

In late 1982, Warren Gorham and Lamont, Inc., included in its regular card-deck mailing, which contained 57 cards offering its publications, a fifty-eighth card that served as an "official entry card" for its sweepstakes. In the same card-deck, which was wrapped in a white (paper) mailing envelope, a mini-letter insert illustrated the sweepstakes prizes and invited participation. For details, see 5:18.

10

Timing and Seasonality
of Book Promotion Mailings

10:01   Timing: A Common Problem in Book Promotion Planning

A common problem of novice and professional alike in promotion planning is timing. A promotion that is properly timed to reach its intended audience can be highly effective, whereas the same promotion at another time may have a disappointing response. An apt example comes to mind immediately of a sale offered by a small publishing house that was beautifully promoted in two colors, but that set an expiration date two days after the receipt of the mailing.

A good offer to the right audience will always produce results. The rules and guidelines that follow in this chapter represent experience, testing, and the results of efforts that have worked. But, like our explanation for the word "law" when used in conjunction with book promotion, there are no hard-and-fast laws on timing—only guidelines to what has worked well in the past.

This was a lesson we learned while writing *Volume One*. Discussing timing with a veteran book marketing professional, we told him we avoided mailings during the latter part of November because we feared they would be caught up in the Christmas mail rush. He responded that he liked to mail between November 20 and December 5 because so few other (competitive) promotions were received in the mail at that time, and that his mail responses were better than usual.

10:02   Timing of Promotion for Books in Production

You lose much of the momentum from your mailing if the new books announced in your promotion are not available for shipment during the promotion-response period. When announcing forthcoming books in a direct-response mailing, you should include only those titles likely to be available within 90 days of the mailing date. If you ask for payment with orders from individuals, mention on the order form or response device that payment will be refunded if the book cannot be shipped within 30 days (variable, according to your policy) of receipt of order.

The 90-day period is not applicable to orders from libraries and institutions, which usually will accept shipment of previously ordered book long after it has been announced. The author recalls one instance in which an announcement of a new edition of a handbook generated many library orders and was delayed nearly two years, during which time the price nearly doubled. Yet, when librarians were queried just prior to the new publication date, most still wanted their original order filled.

If your mailing includes an academic audience, bear in mind that the instructor is likely to be angry if a book has been announced as available prior to the starting date of a course and the ordered copy fails to arrive by the time the course has started. Academics consider textbooks and related materials crucial to the success of their educational endeavors.*

10:03   Timing for Mailings to College Stores: Tips from a Store Manager

"The big problem," reflected the manager of a major university bookstore, "is that publishers send us a lot of material—catalogs, brochures, and the like—in September. By that time, we have our book requirements for the fall semester and they're already on the shelf. In September, I'm busy on the floor handling the flood of customers. I have no time to look at publisher literature, whatever its merit.

"If the publishers had sent me that same material in June or July, I would have given it more serious attention. I have all my fall book orders in to the publishers by mid-July. Then I take a couple of weeks holiday to the end of July. By August the books start coming in and we're busy getting them shelved. If there's any spare time, I use it for ordering odds and ends in August and September so we can be all set for the rush of students at the start of the fall semester.

"Yes, September is a bad time for the publisher to mail literature to the bookstore. Another bad time for publisher literature is in January, at the beginning of the second term. By then it's already too late to do anything for the spring term, and a lot of mailings the publishers send to me in January I don't get a chance to look at until March or April.

"Now, for those publishers who mail in late November or even early December, the timing is good, because this is a quiet period in terms of the number of customers coming into the bookstore, and I have more time to make book selections for stock for the upcoming semester.

*According to the 1980 College Textbook Survey prepared by Crossley Surveys, Inc., for the Association of American Publishers, the Book Industry Study Group, and the National Association of College Stores.

"Once the book rush starts in September or January, the bookstore is flooded with special orders and special requests, and so much time is spent with customers, I have no time to look at publisher announcements of new books.

"A lot of publishing people think the summer's too quiet for mailing to the college bookstore, so they mail when they think things pick up. But if they mail when things pick up, it's too late for us in the bookstore to have any time to look at it."

10:04   Timing of Textbook Promotions to Academics: General Guidelines

Planned textbook promotions should reach academic instructors early enough to allow them sufficient time to examine books of interest in February and March for fall semester adoptions and in October, November, and December for spring semester adoptions. Do not hesitate to mail at any time during the academic year if you have an offering that is timely, important, or presents new, helpful information.

10:05   Timing Promotions for Fall College Text Adoptions: Survey Results

If your books have textbook potential and you are seeking adoption for the fall semester, you've probably missed the boat if you publish in the spring. The reason is that most fall textbook adoption decisions (77%)* must be submitted to the college store by April or May, and faculty members usually will not make an adoption decision without actually examining the book. Your best bet is to announce forthcoming textbooks in promotions from November through January and have books available for sampling from February through April for fall adoption.

Exception to above In schools where text adoptions are made by committee, such committees generally meet annually (65%). Some meet every two years (20%), and a smaller percentage (15%) meet every three years. Adoption decisions usually take effect one year after committee selection.

10:06   Timing and Seasonality of Library Book Ordering: CBE Survey Result

According to a survey conducted by the Combined Book Exhibit (CBE), the biggest month for library ordering is July, followed by September and January, in that order.

---

*All statistical data presented here are based on the 1980 College Textbook Survey prepared by Crossley Surveys, Inc., for the Association of American Publishers, Book Industry Study Group, and the National Association of College Stores.

"July ranks first," says Edward Malinowski, president of CBE, "because that is the beginning month of the fiscal year budget for most libraries. July is when all the action starts."

Library buying patterns were determined from responses to a questionnaire distributed to librarians in the Combined Book Exhibit display at the American Library Association's Midwinter Meeting in Denver in 1981. Of the approximately 200 survey respondents, 46% were from public libraries, 45% from academic libraries, and 9% from special libraries.

10:07   High School Library Ordering Cycle: Timing Book Promotions to Fit

Mailings to high school librarians are most effective when mailed from January through March, with delivery timed for no later than April. Here's why: Many school librarians start working on their fall book orders in April or May. They usually make up one consolidated order, which they place with their jobber (usually a single contractor). As the order must be processed through the board of education, it does not reach the jobber until summer and is thus reflected in publishers' summer sales to jobbers, who order for delivery to the schools before the start of the school term in September.

10:08   Timing for Mailing to High Schools: Tips from a Long-Time Mailer

"In over 17 years of mailing to high schools," says Irv Berkowitz of Co-op Mailings, Inc., of Hillsdale, N.J., "I have found there are three optimum times to mail to high schools.* The prime time is the September period. The second-best time is the January period. The third-best time is around late February/early March. I base this on the theory that budgets are made and submitted in December, but bounce back for modification in March and are locked in in June. In high school promotion, it is generally agreed that the major publishers make their big push in September and, if you want to be in the running, then you mail in September."

10:09   Timing Promotion of Conference Proceedings

Because conference and symposium proceedings usually have a short sales life (and modest sales potential), promotion should be timed for the months immediately prior to and after publication. The active sales life of published conference proceedings is about two and one half years. However, most of the sales occur during the first 12 months after publication. After early promotion, additional efforts will generate virtually no response. It is better to wait out the trickle of library

---

*Postcard-deck mailings to high schools by Co-op Mailings, Inc., are made in September and January. See 25:06.

orders resulting from "books received" listings and reviews and to save your promotion money. Listings of proceedings publications in other related promotions on a space-available basis may help, but only in a limited way.

10:10   Timing of Special-Interest Book Club Mailings: Two Views

A long-time director of a special-interest book club that caters to hobbyists favors January and February as the best months for mailing. His second choice is the period starting in late August and stretching to early October. He also favors April and July as good mailing months. A university press director (see 27:07) offering books dealing with history, literature, business, and contemporary topics mails in January and July to club members and in October and May to a vastly larger alumni list.

10:11   Two Publishers' Reference Works Reveal Similar Seasonal Sales Patterns: Case Study

A year-long study was made in 1981–1982 of library buying patterns for two compatible reference works, offered by two different publishers. Both sold primarily to school and public libraries.

Reference work "A" was in its launch cycle during the 12-month study. The first three months of the study were still part of the prepublication offer period. The year-long study represented the third through the fourteenth months of a projected 60-month active life cycle for the newly published work.

A four-year-old reference work, "B," during this study was in its declining cycle. The first seven months of the study represented the last seven months of the projected 60-month life cycle. The last five months of the study were "carry-over" months beyond the projected life cycle of "B" and prior to the issuance of a new edition.

As Figure 12 shows, the first three months for work "A" were peak, or "up," months that represent the closing of a six-month prepublication offer. The extremity of the decline in sales in the fourth month resulted in part from termination of the prepublication offer. August was the best month of the year for work "A." August was also the "high" month of the year for work "B," which had no sales incentives then in effect.

September was second lowest month of the year after May for work "A." September and May were tied for the lowest month of the year for work "B." October, February, and March all were "up" sales months for both works. November, April, and May were all "down" months for both works.

STUDY CONCLUSIONS

1. August is a peak buying month for a basic reference work aimed at school and public libraries.

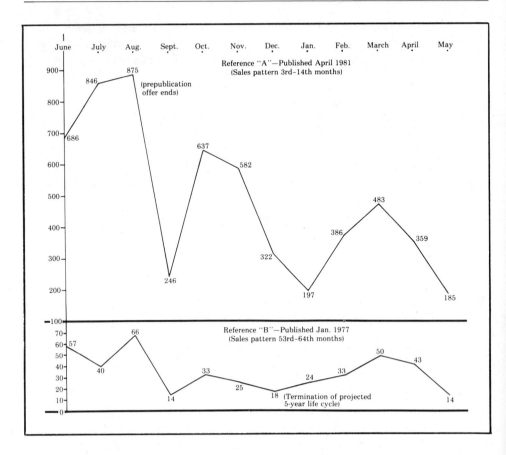

FIGURE 12 Seasonal sales patterns of two publishers' reference works show remarkable similarities.

2. Seasonal buying patterns for two different library reference works at opposite ends of their life cycles bore remarkable similarities.

3. The seasonal similarities suggest that promotion for similar library reference works would do best if timed for these three mailing periods: May through June (two months preceding peak sales period) is the best time, followed by August and September (two months preceding fall sales peak) and the third best period, January and February (two months preceding spring sales peak).

10:12 Best Months for Selling By Mail: Seasonality Studies by Subject

In recent years, Americans have turned to the mails for buying a wide variety of products. Seasonality studies for products sold through the mail are conducted annually by the Kleid Co., New York–based list brokers. Following is a summary of the heaviest mailing months based on the most recent annual study. Information was provided by C. Rose Harper, president of Kleid. It should be noted that December mailings are made usually in late December.

Mailing Category	Four Best Months 1981–1982				Four Best Months 1980–1981			
	1	2	3	4	1	2	3	4
Business/Finance	Dec.	Jan.	July	Apr.	Jan.	Dec.	Feb.	Sept.
Cultural Reading	Dec.	June	Sept.	Feb.	Dec.	July	June	Aug.
General Reading	July	Dec.	Jan.	Sept.	July	Dec.	Jan.	June
Self Improvement	Dec.	Sept.	Jan.	Feb.	Jan.	Dec.	July	Feb.
Home Interest	Feb.	Jan.	July	Sept.	Jan.	Feb.	Sept.	Oct.
Parents and children	July	Jan.	Dec.	Aug.	Dec.	July	Jan.	Aug.
Hobbies/related subjects	July	Dec.	Jan.	Feb.	July	Jan.	Dec.	Aug.
Entertainment	July	Aug.	Sept.	Dec.	Jan.	Sept.	July	Dec.
Educational/technical/ professional	June	Dec.	July	Oct.	Dec.	July	Aug.	Jan.
Fund-raising	Nov.	Oct.	Aug.	Sept.	Jan.	Sept.	Oct.	Nov.

MONTHLY PERCENTAGE OF TOTAL MAILINGS

Mailings Month of	Business/ Finance	Cultural Reading	General Reading	Self-Improvement	Home Interest	Parents and Children	Hobbies/ Related Subjects	Enter-tainment	Educational/ Technical/ Professional	Fund-Raising
Jan.	11.0	9.4	18.8	13.1	14.8	18.9	15.5	7.4	5.3	6.4
Feb.	7.0	9.5	4.7	9.3	18.2	11.4	7.4	8.2	5.2	12.9
Mar.	6.3	4.0	3.5	2.2	2.6	2.5	3.8	7.1	4.4	6.3
Apr.	8.7	2.1	1.5	2.4	5.3	1.4	3.2	5.1	8.4	6.6
May	8.4	1.6	3.5	1.5	2.4	8.4	3.8	2.3	1.1	5.4
June	5.9	14.5	3.1	5.6	8.9	3.3	6.5	4.5	33.2	1.7
July	9.4	8.6	26.0	7.3	12.4	23.2	22.9	17.5	9.9	7.1
Aug.	6.9	3.4	2.4	9.0	8.9	12.3	7.2	13.8	3.6	11.3
Sept.	8.5	13.4	11.9	15.9	9.7	1.7	9.0	12.0	4.5	10.6
Oct.	8.0	7.8	0.1	1.3	8.9	2.9	2.5	8.4	9.0	11.5
Nov.	5.8	4.6	1.9	1.6	.9	0.4	0.8	5.0	4.9	13.6
Dec.	14.2	21.1	22.6	30.8	7.0	13.6	17.4	8.7	10.5	6.6

11

Tips on Lettershops,
Typography, Production

11:01   **More Ways to Expand Your Know-How**

Reader response to the chapter "Tips on Lettershops, Production, and Paper" in *Volume One* indicated a strong interest in and need for more understanding of the mechanics—the "nuts and bolts"—of organizing a printed promotion and dealing effectively with suppliers. The entries following are presented to help fill that need.

The following entry will tell you what you need to know in dealing with printers and discusses basic, clearly defined terms and printing trade customs associated with the terms. Other entries include more tips on getting the most out of your lettershop and, to round out your knowledge of the production process, tips on ink color selections and ink-related terms encountered in preparing printed promotions. These are followed by entries designed to familiarize the beginner with the production process and to provide professionals with convenient checklists for everyday activities, including tips on readability of type, on better typographic design, and the ranking of popular typefaces used in headlines and/or body copy.

11:02   **What You Need to Know in Dealing with Printers:**
Terms/Definitions/Trade Customs

QUOTATION

An estimate given by a printer on a job under consideration, a quotation is usually valid for 30 days before being subject to review.

PREPARATORY WORK

Discussions between you and the printer regarding any pending job and involving layouts, dummies, copy, and the like. Such work remains the property of the printer, including any ideas indirectly derived from them. They may be used only with payment of an agreed-upon amount to the printer.

ORDER/ORDER CANCELLATION

Request to a printer to do a job. Once you have placed a verbal or written order with a printer, you cannot cancel the order except on terms that compensate the printer for any expenses incurred up to the time of cancellation.

COMPOSITION

The setting of type in a form suitable for printing. Estimates are given for composition based on original, clean copy or manuscript that has been typed double-spaced on one side of 8½ " × 11 " uncoated paper. Any work involving copy that deviates from this standard, such as mathematical equations or scientific formulas, graphs, tables, and the like, must be reestimated unless the printer/compositor knows that special elements are required at the time the estimate is prepared and has covered these in writing in the estimate.

ALTERATIONS

Changes in text matter already set, or any other modification of the original specifications for a job in progress. Such alterations require additional payment.

PROOFS

Proofs are sample impressions of a composition job that are supplied by the compositor/printer for checking and correction. The number of sets of proofs to be supplied is usually prearranged. One set of proofs, marked "master set," is intended for corrections and must be returned to the compositor with your approval or "approval with corrections," and must bear your signature. Once you return an approved set of proofs with your signature, the compositor cannot be held responsible for errors. You should know also that the supplier cannot be held responsible for errors in any job you order if you fail to return proofs with corrections, or if you instruct your compositor to proceed with a job without submitting proofs.

PRESS PROOFS

This is an actual press sheet drawn from the press just before the start of the pressrun. If you want press proofs, be sure to request them in the printer's original quotation; otherwise you should expect to be charged for them. If you are willing to be available at the press at the time of makeready, you can examine a sheet for any form at no charge.

If you do so and you make any changes or corrections or cause any time to be lost, you should expect to be charged for it.

DELIVERY TOLERANCES

No printer prints the exact number of pieces you order. Every job is either overrun or underrun, and there are trade practices governing these. On print quantities up to 10,000, a printer may be up to 10% over or under, and any quantity that does not exceed that percentage is considered acceptable. You are usually billed for the exact quantity shipped, whether it is over or under the run requested, and are expected to pay for that amount. If you are printing to match a specific number of names in a mailing and your order specifies "not less than" the number you will require for the mailing, the printer's percentage for overrun should be doubled. On quantities over 10,000, the tolerance percentage should be agreed upon in advance.

MATERIALS FURNISHED BY CUSTOMER

Many jobs are quoted on the basis of customer-supplied paper, camera-ready copy, film, or other materials pertinent to the job. Such materials must be manufactured, packed, and delivered according to specifications provided by the printer in the quotation and as required for satisfactory completion of the job. If this is not done and causes delays, you are expected to reimburse the printer for any additional cost caused by delays, impaired production, or specification deficiencies.

TERMS

Payment (net cash) is due to a printer for a completed job 30 days from the invoice date, unless other terms have been agreed upon and specified in writing. If you have claims against the printer due to defects in a job, damages, or shortages, you should make these in writing within 30 days of delivery. Your failure to make such claims within this period is considered by the trade to be full acceptance and admission that the job was satisfactory and fully complied with all terms, conditions, and specifications.

11:03   More Tips on How to Get the Most Out of Your Lettershop

1. Never place an order asking for completion (either for mailing or delivery) "as soon as possible." This term can mean a day, a week, or a month and is too vague. Always give a specific date.

2. The mailing date you specify usually will be observed if all the materials for the mailing are delivered to the lettershop on time (preferably five days before the scheduled mailing date) and if postage for the mailing has been provided.

3. When issuing an order for a mailing package, be sure it includes clear instructions for insertions that describe the sequence, facing, and the nesting of the various parts of the package.

4. As soon as printed samples become available, be sure you supply a sample package that is stapled or taped together in proper sequence.

5. If your lettershop is also your printer, know the press capabilities of the shop and plan each promotion to utilize fully the most suitable press for the job.

6. When planning a mailing utilizing selected, low-bid suppliers (for envelopes, printing, computer letters, and other elements) in different geographic locations, be sure to allow sufficient time for all the components to reach the lettershop in advance of the planned mailing date.

7. If your shop is doing a self-mailer that includes either Canadian or Mexican addresses, be sure you have provided the shop with the right-size mailing envelopes in which to enclose this portion of the mailing (mailings to Canada and Mexico must be in sealed envelopes).

11:04   Tips on Ink and Color Selections

When you are planning printed promotions, it is helpful to keep the age and nature of the recipient in mind. One publisher received a notice from an older engineer who complained he had difficulty reading a flier printed in orange-colored ink on white paper. Although a steady customer of the publisher, he said he would ignore any notices that were difficult to read. Doctors, who are inundated with mail and who must read on the run, appreciate larger type and well-leaded lines that permit information to be grasped easily.

What colors offer the best and worst contrast? Following is a list of color combinations in diminishing order of legibility. It should be noted that within each color there are many shades and the contrast will vary if a lighter shade is used. It is best to match the color you plan to use against the paper stock before you have the job printed; even better, supply a PMS number or actual color sample.

1. Black letters on yellow
2. Green letters on white
3. Blue letters on white
4. White letters on blue
5. Black letters on white
6. Yellow letters on black
7. White letters on red
8. White letters on green
9. White letters on black
10. Red letters on yellow
11. Green letters on red
12. Red letters on green

**11:05   Ink-Related Terms Encountered in Working
with Printers and Printed Matter**

body   Viscosity of ink.

chalking   When the pigment on a printed piece dusts off because of overly rapid vehicle absorption into the paper.

drier   A substance added to the ink to speed the drying process.

fountain solution   Solution used in the offset press fountain to dampen the offset plate and keep nonprinting areas from accepting ink.

hickeys   Spots or imperfections in offset printing caused by dirt on the press, dried ink skin, paper particles, etc.

ink fountain   The device on a printing press that stores and supplies ink to the printing rollers.

length   Ability of ink to flow.

opaque ink   An ink that conceals all color beneath it.

PMS colors   A selection of more than 500 standard ink colors that can be accurately mixed from ten basic inks in varying combinations. PMS (Pantone Mixing System) colors are specified by number.

pigment   Color particles in powder form.

tack   Transfer of ink from rollers to blanket to plate to paper.

tints   Various even-tone areas of a solid color. The strength of the tint is usually expressed as a percentage of the color.

varnish   Protective coating applied to a printed sheet for protection or appearance.

vehicle   The fluid component in a printing ink that acts as a carrier for the pigment.

**11:06   Popular Typefaces Used in Advertising Headlines:
Reader/Professional Preferences**

Among the more popular typefaces used for advertising headlines in specialized business publications, which is preferred by readers? Which by the people who specify the faces? To find out, a survey was conducted for Cahners Publishing Co., Boston, using ten typefaces selected by a panel of graphic production professionals. Two separate audiences were surveyed: one comprised 3,000 readers of specialized business publications, and the other consisted of 300 agency art directors. The ranking based on responses from 306 readers and from 87 art directors is shown on the next page.

CONCLUSION

Readers of advertising in engineering, technical, and business periodicals prefer Caslon Bold over other typefaces for headlines, whereas art directors prefer Helvetica.

Headline Typefaces	Ranking by Readers	Ranking by Art Directors
Caslon Bold	1	2
Helvetica Medium	2	1
Franklin Gothic	3	6
Optima Semi	4	3
Souvenir Demi	5	4
Avant Garde Demi	6	5
Century Bold	7	9
Egyptian Bold	8	7
Clarendon Bold	9	8
Kabel Black	10	10

11:07   Popular Typefaces Used for Advertising Body Copy: Reader/Professional Preferences

Among the more popular typefaces used for body copy in specialized business publications, which is most preferred by readers? Which by the art directors who select the typefaces? As a companion study to the survey of headline typeface preferences, a separate study* was made of preferences for body copy typefaces among the ten most popular selected by a panel of graphic arts professionals. Those surveyed included 3,000 readers of specialized business publications and 300 agency art directors. Following is the ranking of preferences for body copy typefaces, based on responses from 306 readers and 81 agency art directors:

Body Copy Typeface	Ranking by Readers	Ranking by Art Directors
Helvetica	1	2
Garamond	2	3
Melior	3	4
Century	4	1
Times Roman	5	6
Universe	6	5
Optima	7	7
Avant Garde	8	8
Caledonia	9	9
Bodoni	10	10

CONCLUSION

Readers of advertising in engineering, technical, and business periodicals prefer Helvetica over other typefaces for body copy, whereas art directors prefer Century.

*The survey was done for Cahners Publishing Co., Boston.

11:08   Tips on Readability of Type: Research Results*

- Reverse type (white printing on black background) reduces readability by 10.5% compared with black printing on a white background.
- Type that is set in lowercase letters is read 13.4% faster than type set in all caps. (The difference is due partially to the fact that much reading is done by word recognition, and words set in lowercase type are more easily recognized.)
- There is no difference in reading comprehension between copy that is set flush left or right and copy that is set flush left and ragged right. The studies that led to this finding included tests with ragged right copy with divided words and ragged right copy with no divided words.

11:09   Tips for Better Typographic Design

- Long lines need more leading than short lines.
- Long lines require larger type than short lines to be read easily.
- Type is more readable when the line length is somewhere between 1.5 and 2.5 times the number of letters in the alphabet. The optimal number of characters is close to 39,† and some favor no more than 60 characters per line.
- Lowercase or small letters are easier to read than capital letters.
- There are few significant differences in readability if the printing is high in contrast to its background.
- Serif typefaces are easier to read than sans-serif faces.
- The maximum leading between lines of type should not exceed the spacing between words on a line.
- An alphabet set in capital letters will run approximately 50% longer than one set in small letters.
- A line set in all caps will accommodate one-third fewer letters than a line set in lowercase type.
- Black print on a white background is more legible than white print on a black background.

11:10   Type Bibliography

Cahners Advertising Research Reports. Boston: Cahners Publishing Co., 1981.

The Chicago Manual of Style, 13th ed. Chicago: The University of Chicago Press, 1982.

---

*Studies were conducted on behalf of *Cahners Advertising Research Reports* (Boston: Cahners Publishing Co., 1981).

†For any suitable type size the average eye span—the line width perceivable with one fixation of the eye muscles—is about 1.5 alphabets of normal width, lowercase characters. Lines much longer than two alphabets require extra physical effort to read.

Graham, Irvin. *Encyclopedia of Advertising.* New York: Fairchild Publications, 1952.

Lem, Dean Phillip. *Graphics Master*, 2nd ed. Los Angeles: Dean Lem Associates, 1977.

Melcher, Daniel, and Nancy Larrick. *Printing and Promotion Handbook*, 2nd ed. New York: McGraw-Hill, 1956.

Pocket Pal, 13th ed. New York: International Paper Co., 1983.

Printing Elements and Methods. Boston: S. D. Warren Co.

Schlemmer, Richard M. *Handbook of Advertising Art Production*, 2nd ed. Englewood Cliffs, N.J.: Prentice-Hall, 1976.

Skillin, Marjorie E., and Gay, Robert M. *Words into Type*, 3rd ed. Englewood Cliffs, N.J.: Prentice-Hall, 1974.

Stanley, Thomas Blaine. *The Technique of Advertising Production.* New York: Prentice-Hall, 1940.

Stevenson, George A. *Graphic Arts Encyclopedia*, 2nd ed. New York: McGraw-Hill, 1979.

Typography and Design. Washington, D.C.: U.S. Government Printing Office, 1951, revised 1963.

Wijnekus, F. J. M. *Elsevier's Dictionary of the Printing and Allied Industries.* Amsterdam, 1967.

11:11   Production Tip for Cost-Effective Sale Catalog

If you are planning a sale catalog mailing, your greatest economy will come from planning a catalog with a self-cover in a paper stock that will mail at the current third-class bulk rate of 10.9¢ per piece for up to 2 oz.

You can keep your sale catalog under 2 oz. by using a 50-lb. offset stock or, at slightly extra cost, a 60-lb. offset stock. If you want a bind-in order envelope, consider a cost-cut or a cut-out order-form page, which the recipient must then mail in his or her own envelope. The following list gives the number of pages you can have in a self-covered catalog to have it weigh in at less than 2 oz. Bear in mind that if you include a bind-in reply envelope, a weight allowance must be made. Have your printer make up a bound dummy in advance to ensure the weight does not exceed the 2-oz. limit.

Paper Stock	Trim Size	Number of Pages
50 lb. offset	8½ × 11″	24 pages
50 lb. offset	5½ × 8½″	48 pages
60 lb. offset	8½ × 11″	16 pages
60 lb. offset	5½ × 8½″	32 pages

11:12   How to Understand and Specify Perforations in Your Printed Promotions

Perforations are used in printed promotions to facilitate quick and easy removal of a card or order form by tearing or cutting. The perforation is done by a separate operation on machines that punch rows of tiny holes. The perforated line is usually printed in ink as well. Be sure it appears on the mechanical. The perforations are specified in number of teeth per inch. Most removable reply cards utilize a 10- or 12-tooth perforation, or an 8-tooth large-gap perforation. Some other sizes include 16-tooth and 18-tooth perforations.

11:13   More Ideas on the Use of Color in Promotions

- Response will increase when you add a second color to a letter mailing or promotion for a major work.
- Consider changing ink color, paper stock, paper color, or all three when you repeat a promotion that may reach the same audience.
- When repeating a card-deck mailing that is virtually unchanged from an earlier one, change the colors on the mailing envelope.
- Use a different color for the paper and ink used for the reply device in a package mailing.
- If you want your promotion to attract a lot of attention, red is considered the most attention-getting color, followed by green.
- Avoid use of light-colored inks on dark stock.
- Blue ink is a favorite of male audiences; blues and violets appeal to older audiences.
- Red ink is a favorite of female audiences; reds and orange are suitable for younger audiences.

11:14   Way to Mail in Half the Time at No Added Cost

When you mail frequently or in large quantities with tight mailing deadlines, or if you have to tie your mailings to seasonal or fiscal schedules, the key to successful planning is often how well your letter-shop meets your mailing-deadline requirements.

If your shop renders generally satisfactory service but has problems meeting short deadlines, consider dealing with two lettershops, using one as your primary mailing source and the other as a backup. If shop A cannot meet your deadline because of other commitments, often shop B can. Furthermore, when you have simultaneous deadlines for different mailings, utilize both lettershop staffs by giving one mailing to each. This can also work for very large mailings, of which each shop handles half. As lettershop rates tend to be competitive in most areas, the two-shop system is often one way to cut in half the number of working days required for your mailing without increasing your cost.

A word of caution: The two-shop system requires that you consistently give work to both shops. The quality of service the shop provides is often related to the volume of work the shop is getting from you: Shops tend to give preferential treatment to good clients.

11:15   **Time-Savers that Can Help Speed a Mailing**

1. Order mailing lists promptly as soon as the mailing date is set.
2. Verify that the desired paper is in stock or, if special order is required, can be received in time to be available for the scheduled printing date.
3. Supply folding dummies to support written folding instructions.
4. Approve press proofs at the printshop, where minor corrections can be made on the spot, and save time that would be spent on pickup and delivery of proofs.
5. Specify precise delivery dates and obtain assurances that these will coincide with your scheduled mailing date, particularly when various ingredients of a mailing are coming from more than one supplier.

Part II
Book Advertising Techniques

12

Advertising Techniques, Studies, and Case Histories for Business and Scholarly Publications

---

Advertising is a key tool of publishers who resort to direct selling.... Such advertising can benefit even retailers ... by sending them customers who prefer to obtain the book locally.

John P. Dessauer, *Book Publishing:*
What It Is, What It Does, 2nd ed., R. R. Bowker, 1981.

Reviews are not a substitute for advertising. Whereas the regular reader is inclined to look for and read book reviews, accompanying advertisements are needed to promote books to the occasional reader.

Peter J. Curwen, *The UK Publishing Industry,*
Pergamon, 1981.

12:01 20 Questions to Ask Yourself before You Place a Book Advertisement*

1. Is the publication targeted to reach the book's primary or secondary audience?

2. Does the book have a timely appeal or offer benefits of value to the audience it will reach?

3. If the aim of the advertisement is to obtain orders, is adequate information included on terms for ordering?

---

*If the answer is "no" to any of the 20 questions in this entry, think twice before releasing the advertisement.

4. Does the descriptive copy for the book include pertinent bibliographic data, including price, page count, and publication date/year?

5. Is there something in the copy at the end of the advertisement that invites orders or gives ordering information?

6. Does the advertisement contain a key that will permit tracking of response?

7. If the ad includes a special or prepublication offer, does it specify an expiration date for the offer?

8. Does the advertising include the signature of a key individual within your organization to whom mail or telephone inquiries can be addressed?

9. Does the advertisement have a compelling headline that is not too long, too "cute," or a bragging claim?

10. Is the advertisement timed to run at an appropriate time of year or season?

11. Has a position been specified on the insertion order to prevent the ad from being "buried" in the publication and tc ensure its exposure to a high degree of readership?

12. Is the advertisement set in a clean, readable typeface?

13. If the book contains information of a highly specialized nature, is the author's business or professional affiliation, or credentials, given?

14. Is the advertisement being sent to the publication far enough in advance of publication deadline or, if late, has an extension been obtained?

15. Does the advertisement meet the publication's specifications?

16. Is the advertisement correctly addressed to the individual and address designated by the publication for submission of advertising?

17. Is the advertising copy tailored to the special interests of the publication's readership, whether it be user, adopter, or library?

18. Is the copy set in a clear, readable typeface in line widths not more than one and a half to two alphabets?

19. Is your press clearly identified as the sponsor of the advertisement?

20. Is the advertisement cost within the budget allocation for the book(s) advertised and, if not, can the expenditure be justified without causing problems?

12:02   Guidelines for an Effective Textbook Advertisement: Checklist

( ) Is it going to a publication that will reach the book's target audience?

( ) Does the timing of the insertion allow an adequate period for examination before the book is needed?

( ) Does the advertisement copy address itself to the individual who can influence the adoption?

( ) Is the headline one that does not insult the intelligence of the reader?

( ) Does the copy adequately describe the book's form, content, and level?

( ) Are your book's benefits and advantages over competing works incorporated into the copy?

( ) Does the advertisement reflect the time of year in relation to typical decision-making dates?

( ) Does the ad include clear instructions for response?

( ) Does the ad include a name or department for tracing the response?

( ) Has the ad copy incorporated comments, if available, from an individual well known in the field, from a major university, or from a school known to excel in the subject?

12:03   A Device that Can Help Your Ads Sell More Books

The inclusion of a person's signature on your ad coupon gives a print-media book advertisement the "person-to-person" contact that works so well for direct-mail letter offerings. A specific name enables the reader of an advertisement to feel that he or she will be dealing with a person, rather than a company, when placing an order. Some publishers' advertisements use fictitious, rather than actual, names. These have been used to identify a department, copywriter, or even a specific advertisement.

The use of a person's name in a book advertisement can aid the selling process, especially if the ad's intent is to produce direct orders. A name lends credibility—it implies that the customer has someone to turn to if a question or problem arises. This useful bookselling device should not be overlooked.

12:04   Innovative, Cost-Effective Ad Format Sells
Professional Books: Case History

Top honors for the most innovative and cost-effective space advertising format for the mail-order sale of professional books in the past decade goes to McGraw-Hill. Its unique ad format held up through repeated use over several years and has attracted a host of imitators.

The format consisted of a full-page advertisement for assorted professional books—as many as 27 within a single insertion—that was framed entirely within a heavy broken-line border as a coupon (Figure 13). Each insertion carried a commanding one- or two-word headline running into the border on the top and bottom. In effect, the entire ad was a coupon.

The idea originated with Paul Burns at McGraw-Hill. During a planning session with Vivian Sudhalter, head of McGraw-Hill's creative

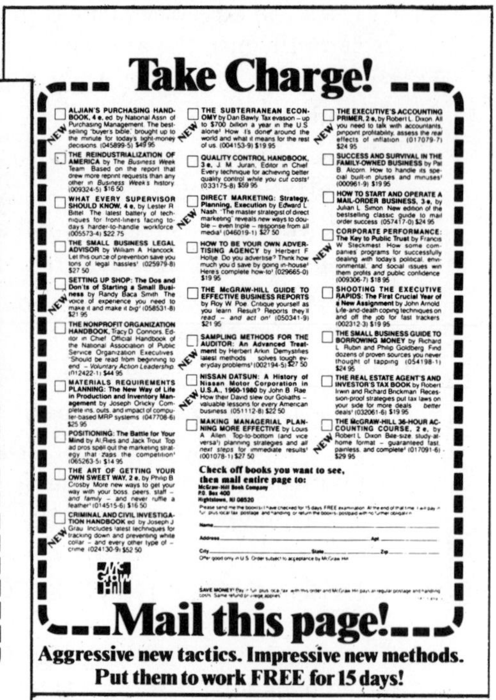

FIGURE 13 Award-winning advertising format used by McGraw-Hill in 1981 and 1982 for professional and reference books. Numerous top and bottom headline changes were used for different offerings in various publications, but the "ad-within-a-coupon" format, which proved very effective, remained unchanged.

services, Burns proposed, "Let's make the whole ad a coupon."
Sudhalter executed the idea with the aid of Chris O'Malley, and the
first insertion appeared early 1981. From the very first insertion, the
advertisement proved more cost-effective than anything they had
tried in memory, and they knew they had a winner. Advertising insertions in this format continued through 1982.

In succeeding insertions, not only did the content of the ads change
but also the top and bottom headlines, so that, in effect, each ad was
totally different from the others. Yet the format was identical. Some of
the winning headline combinations included "Clip" (at top) and "Zip"
(at bottom), "Tear Out!" (at top) and "Mail!" (at bottom), or "Step
Up" (at top) and "To Success!" (at bottom). With the last version, this
copy was added in 30 pt. boldface type under the coupon: "Mail this
page today for a FREE 15-DAY LOOK at business tools that cut you
an edge!"

A problem in the later ads, according to Sudhalter, was having to
come up with a set of concise, attention-grabbing top and bottom
headlines that would jump off the page and catch the eye of the casual
reader. But the challenge was met, and the ad format was repeated successfully and cost-effectively, and was widely imitated. In one 1982
publication, the McGraw-Hill advertisement ran in the same issue
with three imitations of the format by other advertisers.

The initial version of the advertisement was a two-time award winner in McGraw-Hill's internal "Professional Recognition Awards"
competition for 1981. An outside panel of mail-order and book marketing professionals (including this author) awarded the advertisement
first prize in two different categories: general layout and general effectiveness.

12:05   **Another Important Way to Get Preferred Treatment
for Your Space Advertising**

In *Volume One* of *Book Marketing Handbook*, we listed ten ways you
can get preferred treatment for your space advertising, based on con-
versations with various business media production managers. Burton
Cohen, former production manager at Marcel Dekker, Inc., after
reviewing the ten tips in *Volume One*, offers yet another that he says
will serve the advertiser even better than all the others:

Get the name of a contact person at the publication with the best clout to get
your ad set up right. Don't just send your ad to: Advertising Department;
send it to a contact person at the publication who is responsive and will give
you results.

12:06   **The Reader's Service Card as a Selling Tool
for Professional Books**

A bookselling technique that has established itself among the tools
available to marketers of sci-tech and professional books is the use of

the reader's service card in some business, trade, and special-interest publications.

The reader's service card is a bound-in reply card on which many numbers are shown, and is returnable (usually postpaid) to the publication in which it appears. Periodical publishers refer to this card as a "reader's service card," but to the trade and to most advertisers, it is a "bingo card." This name was coined because the arrangement of numbers on the card suggests the arrangement of numbers on a bingo card.* Each number on the reader's service, or bingo card duplicates a number used in the same periodical. The number is usually used with an advertisement, but it may also be used with an editorial note offering literature, information, or a service.

The reader circles on the card the numbers signifying offers of interest and mails the card to the periodical for forwarding to the advertiser (or organization mentioned) for appropriate action.† Bingo-card responses not only produce inquiries for the advertiser but also give the periodical a vehicle for measuring its value to the particular advertiser as a medium for its product or service.

Some book publishers, through special arrangement with a periodical that carries reader's service cards, have been asking readers to circle a reader's service number under a particular book within an advertisement to order that particular book for a free trial examination.

The technique was first used in the late 1960s, at the suggestion of this writer, in conjunction with the book section of the annual *ACS Lab Guide*. It was dropped after one issue. This writer then reintroduced the practice in the late 1970s in advertisements for a multipart high-priced reference book in *Industrial Hygiene News*. The ads for each part in the multivolume reference work included the line "Circle No. XX to Order for 15-Day Trial Examination." The advertisement was repeated over a number of years in the same publication and enabled the publisher to achieve a remarkably high degree of market penetration with the advertised work.

As virtually all of the readers of the publication were qualified professionals within the field of the reference work, the volumes sent on-approval had an acceptance factor of more than 90%. Surprisingly few of those who habitually circle bingo-card numbers complained of receiving "unordered merchandise," and the relatively few who did quickly withdrew their complaint when sent a copy of the advertisement bearing the line "Circle No. XX to Order," as well as a copy of their bingo card showing the circled number with their signature.

In the spring of 1982, *Industrial Hygiene News* assistant publisher David Lavender, at the request of this writer, isolated reader's service numbers offering books for free examination on the bingo card from other numbers on the card by printing them in a separate box on the card under the heading "By circling the numbers below, you are ordering the products for trial examination" (see Figure 14). This eliminated

*One publication used "Bingo-Gram" as the name for its reader's service card.
†Advertisers are not charged for this service.

Circle Numbers Of Items On Which You Wish To Receive Additional Information

DO NOT USE THIS CARD AFTER SEPTEMBER 20, 1982

1	26	51	76	101	126	151	176	201	226	251	276	301	326	351	376	401	416	431	446	461	476
2	27	52	77	102	127	152	177	202	227	252	277	302	327	352	377	402	417	432	447	462	477
3	28	53	78	103	128	153	178	203	228	253	278	303	328	353	378	403	418	433	448	463	478
4	29	54	79	104	129	154	179	204	229	254	279	304	329	354	379	404	419	434	449	464	479
5	30	55	80	105	130	155	180	205	230	255	280	305	330	355	380	405	420	435	450	465	480
6	31	56	81	106	131	156	181	206	231	256	281	306	331	356	381	406	421	436	451	466	481
7	32	57	82	107	132	157	182	207	232	257	282	307	332	357	382	407	422	437	452	467	482
8	33	58	83	108	133	158	183	208	233	258	283	308	333	358	383	408	423	438	453	468	483
9	34	59	84	109	134	159	184	209	234	259	284	309	334	359	384	409	424	439	454	469	484
10	35	60	85	110	135	160	185	210	235	260	285	310	335	360	385	410	425	440	455	470	485
11	36	61	86	111	136	161	186	211	236	261	286	311	336	361	386	411	426	441	456	471	486
12	37	62	87	112	137	162	187	212	237	262	287	312	337	362	387	412	427	442	457	472	487
13	38	63	88	113	138	163	188	213	238	263	288	313	338	363	388	413	428	443	458	473	488
14	39	64	89	114	139	164	189	214	239	264	289	314	339	364	389	414	429	444	459	474	489
15	40	65	90	115	140	165	190	215	240	265	290	315	340	365	390	415	430	445	460	475	490
16	41	66	91	116	141	166	191	216	241	266	291	316	341	366	391						
17	42	67	92	117	142	167	192	217	242	267	292	317	342	367	392						
18	43	68	93	118	143	168	193	218	243	268	293	318	343	368	393						
19	44	69	94	119	144	169	194	219	244	269	294	319	344	369	394						
20	45	70	95	120	145	170	195	220	245	270	295	320	345	370	395						
21	46	71	96	121	146	171	196	221	246	271	296	321	346	371	396						
22	47	72	97	122	147	172	197	222	247	272	297	322	347	372	397						
23	48	73	98	123	148	173	198	223	248	273	298	323	348	373	398						
24	49	74	99	124	149	174	199	224	249	274	299	324	349	374	399						
25	50	75	100	125	150	175	200	225	250	275	300	325	350	375	400						

By circling the numbers below, you are ordering the products for trial examination.

700	704	708	712	716
701	705	709	713	717
702	706	710	714	718
703	707	711	715	719

FIGURE 14 The reader's service card of *Industrial Hygiene News* has specially assigned numbers for free examination book offers in a separate box in the lower right-hand corner to ensure that readers do not receive unordered books.

any confusion as to what the reader meant by circling numbers.

A variation of this technique has been used for a number of years by *Science News* in conjunction with its two-page centerfold advertisements of science-related books. Under each book in the advertisement is the line "To order, circle (alphabet letter) on Reader Service Card." The letter of the alphabet under each book in the advertisement matches the same letter on the bound-in facing postpaid order card, returnable to *Science News* or to the publisher if a paid ad.

12:07 When You Offer Books through Reader's Service Card: Guidelines

If you decide to use a reader's service card as a bookselling vehicle, be sure to follow these time-tested problem-solving guidelines:

1. Discuss what you plan to do with the publication that sponsors the reader's service card so there will be no misunderstandings later should anyone complain about receiving unordered merchandise.
2. Make certain that the publication's reader's service card calls for a signature. This may be your only proof that a reader has ordered the book(s).

3. Be sure that the instruction to circle the book offer in your advertisement includes the words "To order."

4. If there are any conditions for orders, state them in the advertisement. For example, if the number of books ordered cost more than $50, and you require a 25% deposit for all orders over $50, state this clearly in your advertisement. Otherwise your shipping center may request a deposit that could conflict with the free trial examination terms of your advertisement.

5. Although "false shipment" complaints are rare from this type of offer, one does occasionally come up after repeated use of this technique. In such an instance, it is best to resolve the complaint with a phone call. Invariably one call will do it, and this may save needless correspondence over a protracted period of time that sometimes involves the U.S. postal service, the periodical, the Better Business Bureau, or others.

6. As proof of the customer's order, usually a copy of the advertisement plus a copy of the reader's service card showing the signature are sufficient.

7. All bingo-card book offers should have a stated free trial examination period that is reasonable, usually 15 or 30 days.

8. In a "worst-case" situation, offer to refund the return shipping costs if the book is an expensive one; otherwise, just cancel the charge—it may be the odd exception to an otherwise successful offering.

9. If bingo-card book offers pose unusual problems, request that the sponsoring publication add a footnote to the bingo card to this effect: "Please note: Certain numbers on this card are for trial examination of books or other products."

12:08   Placement Techniques that Ensure High Readership for Your Advertisements

The best position for your book advertising will vary from publication to publication. A good position is one that will attract the highest number of the publication's readers. A bad position is one that is likely to be seen by only a small segment of the readership or to be overlooked entirely because it has been sandwiched between other attention-commanding entries, be they advertisements or features.

Often you can ascertain which sections of a particular periodical have a large readership by examining available readership surveys. Many society and professional publications conduct such surveys periodically and make them available to potential advertisers without charge.

Check the sections of the publication with the most readership according to the survey. In one survey of an engineering society publication checked by this author, readership of the book review section was 17%. The section containing news about the society had a readership of 96%. When the author advertised in one issue on the page facing the society news page, readership for the ad was 16%, compared to a readership of all advertising in that issue of 10.9%. Readership of the issue's lead book review was about the same as that for the author's book advertisement.

Most periodical readers are likely to turn first to the page listing its contents. If you are able to get the page facing the contents, you are likely to attract perhaps the highest number of readers attainable. Such a position may not always be available or it may require a space reservation far in advance, but is worth the effort. Entry 12:09 lists this author's determination of best and worst advertising positions.

12:09 Positioning Guidelines for Book Advertising in Periodicals

What are the best positions for your book advertising in professional and scholarly periodicals? No two marketers will agree. However, these are this author's preferences, based on more than 20 years' experience placing thousands of advertising insertions:

BEST POSITIONS

- Fourth cover
- Left-hand page facing the table of contents
- First right-hand page facing the table of contents
- Left-hand page facing the start of the book review section
- Left-hand page facing association news in any professional association publication
- Right-hand page facing editorial page or column, preferably as far forward as possible in the journal

LEAST-FAVORED POSITIONS

- Left-hand page facing another advertisement in color
- Left-hand page following a two-color ad
- Any page, left or right, facing another full-page advertisement
- Any section of a periodical that caters to only a small segment of the publication's circulation

12:10 Readership of Book Advertising in Scientific and Engineering Periodicals: A Comparison

The chances that a book advertisement will be read are considerably higher for a scientific research journal than for an engineering periodical. This has been indicated by a number of readership studies.

One study conducted by *Civil Engineering*, a monthly publication of the American Institute of Civil Engineers, indicated a 12.2% advertising readership in studies conducted annually over a ten-year period. During this same period the average readership for book advertising was double the 12.2% figure.

A study by Health Industries Research, in Stamford, Conn., examined 15 scientific research journals in the life sciences and showed the "exposure potential" (the chance that an average reader of a journal would see an advertisement) ranged from 29% (for *Federation Proceedings*) to 63% (for *ASM News*). The average advertising exposure potential for all 15 journals was 46.4%, nearly four times that of *Civil Engineering*.

In four readership studies of *Science* that were conducted over four years from 1978 through 1981 by Ballot Research Co., Mamaroneck, N.Y., the average "advertising recognition score" for the four issues studied was 42.9%.

It becomes apparent from these studies that book advertising in general has a higher readership than nonbook advertising and that advertising exposure potential is higher for a scientific research journal than for engineering publications. This is true probably because much if not most of the advertising is about books and publications directly related to the field, discipline, or special interests of the readers of the journal, whereas advertising in engineering publications tends to deal with engineering products or services.

The studies conducted by *Civil Engineering* did show that the readership for book advertising was double the overall average readership for all advertising. It is likely that that same ratio would hold in other engineering disciplines if the publications in those branches of engineering contained more professional book advertising. This conclusion is borne out by the September 1980, survey done for *Engineering Times* by McGraw-Hill Research in New York, in which a cross section of that publication's 80,000 professional engineers/subscribers were polled on their readership of technical, engineering, or professional books: 94.5%* said they relied on books, and only 3.5% indicated that they did not. Respondents to the survey indicated regular readership in one or more of 50 different engineering publications.

12:11 Readership of Multiple-Page Ads Compared with Single-Page Ads Run Separately: Study Result

Which attracts a higher readership—a multiple-page advertisement in a single issue of a publication or the same number of single-page ads in successive issues of the same publication? Dr. D. Morgan Neu addressed the question in his report "Readership of Multi-Page Ads," which appeared in the May 1982, issue of *Art Direction.*

Based on a study of readership of multipage advertisements, Neu reported that three-page advertisements (right-hand page followed by

*The actual percentages by discipline were 96.4% for civil engineers, 95.8% for mechanical engineers, and 94.9% for electrical engineers.

a spread) "had a total projected score of 72 per 100 issue readers, whereas three one-page advertisements in three different issues would have a total of 90 accumulated ad-notings per 100 issue readers." "Four-page advertisements" (two successive two-page spreads), he added, "had a total projected score of 81 whereas four one-page advertisements in four different issues would have a total of 120 accumulated ad readings per 100 issue readers."

Neu concluded: "Unless there is an overriding reason for a multipage advertisement, [you get] a substantially [larger] . . . audience by using the same amount of space in one-page units in separate issues than by using the total space in one issue." Neu is a vice president of Starch, INRA Hooper, Inc., an advertising research organization based in Mamaroneck, N.Y.

12:12 How to Convert the Coupon or Order Form into a Selling Tool

With a little imagination, the coupon in your space ad or the response vehicle in your mail promotions can be transformed from an ordering tool into a selling tool. Here are some tested ways. You are limited only by your imagination in the ways you can expand this list and increase your sales.

1. If the book is a serial, include options for placing a standing order, an order for the next or previous volume(s), or an order for future supplements as issued.
2. If the book is part of a set or can be grouped with related titles, offer a small saving on a "set" price for the group.
3. Add a separate order line for a related title or titles.
4. Include an incentive to order at a preferred price for any order placed before a specified date.
5. Include a cash discount, free standard shipping, or other inducement for cash with order.
6. Include a discount for multiple-copy orders, or special prices for orders for specific quantities or orders over a certain dollar amount.

12:13 Occasions When a Coupon Should Not Be Used in Advertising

1. When you advertise to libraries, which usually order through wholesalers or as part of a specialized ordering system.
2. When you advertise in a scientific journal. Most are library or archive copies whose readers are either forbidden or reluctant to deface them.
3. When an advertisement appears on a periodical cover. Most recipients will not cut the cover of a periodical.
4. When it is likely that the coupon may appear back-to-back with important editorial matter and therefore can or will not be removed.

5. When the coupon offers an expensive reference work and a formal purchase order is desired.

6. When a bind-in order card appears adjacent to the advertisement.

7. When the readers of the advertisement are not the ultimate users of the book(s).

8. When the audience is so diverse (consumer, wholesaler, bookseller, librarian, educator) that a "universal" coupon might not be appropriate.

9. When you advertise in the publication of a dealer or distributor (unless orders are directed back to the publication's sponsor).

10. When your advertising is directed to a specialized audience only, and response on an identifiable letterhead is essential to qualify the order or inquiry.

12:14   Advertising Bearing Coupons in Scientific and Scholarly Journals: A Word of Caution

A word of caution is in order regarding the placement of coupon-bearing advertisements in scientific and scholarly journals. In the earlier volume of *Book Marketing Handbook*, we warned against the use of coupons for advertising on journal covers because of the reluctance of librarians, scholars, and scientists to deface a cover by removing a coupon.

We repeat this advice for advertising inside many types of scientific and scholarly journals. In publications such as the many American Chemical Society research journals, advertising is ganged with other editorial matter (contents, editorials, letters) at the front of the journal. In such journals, there is always a high degree of likelihood that your advertising coupon will appear back-to-back with important editorial matter, and such positioning would partially negate the usefulness of the advertising coupon.

There are three things you can do: (1) Arrange with the periodical in advance to have your advertisement-with-coupon be printed back-to-back with another advertisement; (2) omit the coupon altogether; or (3) in place of a coupon, include a toll-free 800 number. Scientists and scholars who want the advertised materials will not hesitate to use the telephone to order books and materials of professional interest.

12:15   Book Advertising in Tabloids vs. Magazines: Is One Format Better?

In many fields in which publishers of business and professional books advertise, there are publications available in both standard magazine and newspaper tabloid sizes. Does either format have any advantage over the other?

Although it is difficult to relate response from advertising to the format of the publication in which the advertisement appears, it has been the experience of this author over many years that in fields where both formats existed and were competitive, the tabloid format produced a better response—for certain subject areas, namely, engineering, the natural sciences, and data processing.

The question was raised with another marketer who promoted and sold business books and who recalled many successful experiences with several tabloid-size publications printed on newsprint. He theorized that tabloid formats provided a stronger pull for book advertising "because people want to get rid of it," and therefore read the advertising sooner. He added, "They tend to throw out publications that look like newspapers or are printed on newsprint, but save magazines printed on coated papers."

One class of business periodicals that relies on the tabloid format is the product-oriented tabloid. Most present product information with reader's service numbers tied to a "bingo," a reader's service card, through which the reader may order the product information offered. Most have little or no editorial matter and, when they do, it is often relegated to the back of the publication.

A conversation with the editor of a leading product-oriented tabloid expressed this reaction to the high and rapid rate of response from such publications:

The product-oriented tabloid is a necessary-evil type of publication that you go through and discard. People who receive them are looking for information on a specific product, usually. They see the tabloid primarily as a buyer's guide whereas the magazine is seen as a thing you have to take your time to read, so you set it aside to read later—sometimes immediately—sometimes after reading one article.

Readers of product-oriented tabloids are not interested in editorial matter, so we place editorial matter at the end of our publication so as not to hamper readership.

The editor recalled one advertisement complete with reader's service number that had been producing a high rate of response and that was placed among pages containing other advertising. When the advertisement was placed adjacent to editorial matter, the response fell off materially.

12:16   How to Authenticate a Business Publication's Circulation

How can one be certain that circulation figures given by a publication are accurate? Two guarantors of accuracy regarding circulation figures are the Audit Bureau of Circulations (ABC) and Business Publications Audit of Circulation, Inc. (BPA).

A publication's affiliation with ABC indicates that the circulation figures have been audited by the ABC and that circulation records are maintained under the uniform standards, rules, and procedures required by ABC. An ABC audit is generally used for paid-circulation publications and for those not requiring breakdowns of the circulation.

Affiliation with BPA means the publication submits to an annual circulation audit by BPA, during which the name, company, industry, and job title of every reader of the publication are verified. The orientation of BPA is to industrial and trade magazines, because it provides more detailed classifications of the readers. More than 750 publications belong to BPA.

12:17   Pass-Along Audits:
New Phenomenon in Measuring Advertising Readership

Increasingly in the 1980s and beyond, a new phenomenon will become a factor in measuring advertising readership for business and professional publications. It is the pass-along audit, offered by Business Publications Audit of Circulation, Inc. (BPA).

The pass-along audit identifies and characterizes the people who see a single copy of a publication after the primary subscriber. Through such an audit, a publication can identify a heretofore unknown segment of its circulation and offer a potential advertiser an audited readership figure that may be well in excess of its paid or controlled circulation.

The first pass-along audit was done in May 1982 for that month's issue of *Architectural Record*, which has a circulation of 74,332. This inaugural audit involved only the 3,982 copies that were addressed to businesses or companies. The audit produced 2,661 qualified responses. The total pass-along rate for the 2,661 copies to other individuals was 4,668, or 2.8 individuals per copy. Interestingly, 211 of the primary recipients reported their copies served 844 individuals (4 each), 185 reported their copies served a total of 925 individuals (5 each), and 200 reported their copies served a total of 1,200 individuals (6 each).

As more publications of quality begin using the BPA pass-along audit (for which the publication pays), the term pass-along will take on more meaning for marketers of books and periodicals who are seeking the most coverage for their advertising dollars.

12:18   Ratio of Echo Effect to Direct Orders in
Scientific Book Ordering: Survey Results

In 1980, the Institute for Scientific Information (ISI) probed the book-buying patterns of subscribers to its *Current Contents*, most of whom are in various research and development branches of science and engineering.

Current Contents (*CC*) is published in seven editions by discipline. The study surveyed a statistical cross section of the 35,000-subscriber base. Each *CC* issue carries the contents of recent issues of scientific and engineering periodicals relating to each of the disciplines (life sciences, clinical practice, and others).

Along with the contents of the periodical, each *CC* also carries the contents of selected new (mainly multiauthor), pertinent scientific books. The book section, "Current Book Contents" (CBC), includes an ordering coupon and invites subscribers to order the books listed directly from the ISI office in Philadelphia. Orders thus received are forwarded to the books' publishers for shipping and invoicing.

Three-fourths of those responding to the survey reported they bought books listed in CBC. The ordering patterns of book-buying respondents follow:

- One in seven said they ordered books through ISI.
- Two in seven said they ordered books directly from the publisher.
- Nearly four in seven said they ordered books through their organization's purchasing channels.

The ISI survey findings suggest to advertisers of scientific and engineering books that for each direct book order resulting from a listing in a publication that asks for direct orders, the number of indirect orders through the echo effect can be many times as great. More important, the survey indicated that half or more of the indirect orders may reach the book's publisher through untraceable institutional purchasing.

This ISI survey also contains a message for advertising copywriters of scientific and engineering books aimed at the research/development market: This audience will readily buy a book from a listing of contents only without descriptive copy.

12:19   Technical Book-Buying Patterns of Professional Engineers: Survey Result

If your list includes books in civil, mechanical, and/or electrical engineering, professional engineers as a group constitute a prime market. A survey conducted by McGraw-Hill Research in September 1980 sampled 80,000 registered professional engineers (see also 12:10). The results showed that 95% of the respondents indicated they read or use technical, engineering, or professional books in their area of expertise. Furthermore, 55% indicated they read or use books outside their area of expertise. A single publication that covers the total professional engineer market is *Engineering Times*, a publication of the National Society of Professional Engineers. Advertising rates and information are available from Sherago Associates, 1515 Broadway, New York, NY 10036; 212-730-1050.

12:20   Quality of Advertisement May Be Key to Readership: Case Study

In 1979, a subscriber survey was conducted by *The Physics Teacher* to measure the readership and degree of interest in both editorial features and advertising. More than 65% of those surveyed responded.

Among ten editorial features, the three highest scoring were read thoroughly by 70%, 50%, and 40% of the respondents, respectively. The highest scoring feature was the editorial.

Among the advertisers were six publishers. We extracted from the survey scores for each of the six to determine which of the ads were read thoroughly (to allow for comparison with the editorial features). We also evaluated the ads in terms of the percentage of respondents with a current interest in the publisher's advertised products. We surmised that those with the highest current interest would be readers of the advertisements. But were they? The accompanying table gives the scores.

Advertisement	Read Thoroughly (%)	Current Interest (%)
A	23	12
B	13	26
C	13	20
D	12	33
E	8	17
F	6	23

In ad A, why did 23% read the ad thoroughly when only 12% had current interest? In ad F, why did 6% read the ad thoroughly when 23% had current interest? Our guess is that the answer is in the headline and quality of presentation of the advertisement. The leading advertisement was thoroughly read by nearly twice as many people as had current interest in the publisher's advertised products. The poorest advertisement was thoroughly read by about one-fourth of the 23% of those with current interest.

Lesson: Take extra care with the preparation of the advertising you place. An advertisement (advertisement A), if properly presented, can attract twice its potential current-interest audience. A similar advertisement (advertisement F) with less appeal could attract only one-fourth of its potential audience. The way you present your advertisement can make the difference.

12:21   **When to Emphasize Publisher Imprint in Scholarly Book Advertising**

When you advertise a book in a scholarly journal, which merits the most emphasis, title and author or the publisher's imprint? If you take the view of Abbott M. Friedland, marketing director of Princeton University Press, the main emphasis should be placed on the publisher's imprint. "Specialists," says Friedland, "are very aware of the publishers in their field, in contrast with general readers who are not. For this reason," Friedland commented in *Scholarly Publishing* (vol. 12, no. 3, April 1981), "a publisher's advertising in a scholarly journal should emphasize his name, for a specialist reading the journal is as likely to be stopped by a familiar imprint in an ad as by a particular title or author."

Friedland's long career as a marketer of scholarly books lends much authority to his comment, but he speaks with the authority of a world-class scholarly publisher. Obviously, the prestigious press with a strong position in a particular field, or in scholarly publishing in general, may well wish to capitalize on the imprint name to lend an aura of importance to books advertised in a scholarly journal.

On the other hand, in fields where the publisher is little known or is known to have weak coverage of a particular field, emphasis of publisher imprint will add little to a book by an author well known in the field, or to one that is important, new, innovative, or beneficial to the audience reading the journal.

12:22   Marketer's Low-Cost Solution Helps Sell Out Problem Book: Case History

The 1980 book in question was about a specialized area of maritime shipping and was due off press at close to $40. It didn't fit the rest of the marketer's list, and its limited potential did not seem to warrant a separate promotion campaign. What could be done about this problem book without taking too big a bite out of the budget?

The marketer located a shipping magazine in Standard Rate & Data Service's *Business Publication Rates and Data* and spoke to its advertising representative. When she mentioned to the advertising rep that the book was by several people prominent in shipping circles, the rep suggested a mini display ad in the "People" section of the publication. There was not much one could say in such a small space, which cost less than $100, but in went the ad—a listing and an offer for a free flier with the publisher's name and address. Inquirers received a multipage news release with an order coupon attached.

The offer pulled, and the ad was repeated in the "People" section for a year, and then for most of another year in the classified section. At the end of two years, all 2,200 copies of the print run had been sold.

12:23   Two-Inch Display Ad Turns Losing Project into Cash: Case History

In the mid-1960s a U.S. publisher purchased from a Dutch publisher a share of the editions of two rare old atlases, authentically reproduced in facsimile editions and priced at $135 each. The atlases received highly favorable reviews in various media, but virtually no sales materialized. After a period of inactivity, a number of mail offerings were made, mainly to the library market and at increasingly larger special sale discounts. Each produced a small flurry of sales, again followed by complete inactivity. Finally, when the marketing manager was instructed to dispose of the atlases in any way possible, he tried a 2-inch display advertisement in the *Wall Street Journal* (see Figure 15). The headline said, "Save $195 on rare facsimile atlases." Cash was requested with the order for postpaid shipment. The 2-inch advertise-

SAVE $195 ON RARE FACSIMILE ATLASES

. . . a unique gift, collector's item or conversation piece—below cost

World's two most historic atlases. Each a true facsimile of the rare first edition. Six-color reproductions in oversized format (11½x16½), opulently bound in Scotch-grain leather and buckram, gold embossed. . . . World's first land atlas produced by Ortelius in 1570 ("will become a collector's item"—Saturday Review Syndicate), and world's first sea atlas produced by Waghenaer in 1584-1585 ("every one a masterpiece"—Yachting) . . . Limited edition sold at $270 per set. Publisher sacrificing last 100 sets at $75.00/set, postpaid and insured. American Elsevier, Dept. J, 52 Vanderbilt Ave., New York, N.Y. 10017. MU 6-5277. Payment must accompany order. N.Y. add tax. Money back if not satisfied.

FIGURE 15 *Wall Street Journal* advertisement that was placed repeatedly and effectively to deplete inventory of high-priced facsimile atlases.

ment produced orders well in excess of its cost, and it was repeated until the entire inventory was sold. Although the project was a losing proposition, a valuable lesson was learned: Books of quality, at the right price, will find a market.

12:24   Advertising and the Unsellable Book: Case Study

No amount of advertising will move an unsalable book.

> John P. Dessauer, in
> *Publishers Weekly*, January 29, 1982.

Time and time again, the validity of John Dessauer's sage advice has been learned the hard way by hopeful marketers and, even more often, by publishers who maintain that, given enough advertising, any book can be sold.

In 1982, a publisher of a relatively high-priced business directory was dismayed to learn that after nearly a year since publication less than 15% of the edition had been sold. Even worse, sales in the preceding quarter were only 36 copies, of which 19 were traceable to a single 50,000-piece promotion effort.

In the twelfth month after publication an all-out effort went into reviving the sagging sale of the book. A solo coupon advertisement with a strong benefit-oriented headline and an 800 toll-free number for free examination orders were inserted in half a dozen publications simultaneously. These included the business sections of the *New York Times* and the *Washington Post*, as well as the east and west coast editions of the *Wall Street Journal*.

Net sales in the three months following the advertising blitz were 88 copies. The effort proved that advertising can be made to work—but at a price. More than $2 was spent in this instance for each dollar of net sales produced. The lesson learned here is that, contrary to Dessauer, "Advertising can be made to move an unsalable book—if you're willing to forget about profit."

12:25   Who Says Space Ads Can't Sell Books?
Case History of Record-Breaking Ad Proves the Opposite

Many marketers are convinced that advertising of scientific and technical books has two main purposes: to make the book known to its intended audience and to appease the author. They view it more as a necessary evil than as a selling vehicle that can compete on an equal basis with direct mail.

This is a case study of an ad that defied the rules and broke the records. A recounting of its history provides some valuable lessons on the advertising of scientific and technical books, and, at the same time, offers proof that advertising, under the right conditions, can effectively compete with direct mail.

The advertiser: Wiley-Interscience
The book: *Patty's Industrial Hygiene and Toxicology*, 3rd ed.
The advertising vehicle: *Industrial Hygiene News*
Size of advertisement: Full (tabloid) page
Number of insertions: 22, in consecutive issues from March 1978 to
July 1982
Average traceable dollar return for all insertions: Over 3 times cost.

DETAILS OF THE AD CAMPAIGN

The headline, "The One Essential Reference for Every Industrial Hygienist!" never changed during the entire run (22 insertions), nor did the three-column format (Figure 16). As the ad started with the first of what was to be three volumes, the first column carried descriptive matter, and the second and third columns carried the contents. Subsequently, as the additional volumes were published, a column was devoted to each of the three volumes. The first volume was published in April 1978; the final part of Volume 2 was published in March 1982.

Ordering exceeded $15,000 in response to the first ad insertion and remained high through all subsequent insertions. Sales did not drop below $5,000 until after the nineteenth insertion.

Most of the ordering resulted from the circling of bingo, or reader's service, card numbers that appeared under each volume offered in the insertions. The line for each volume read "To order for free examination circle No. 000." A different number was assigned to each volume.

Late in the advertising run, arrangements were made with the publication to isolate the numbers used for book ordering from other numbers on the publication's reader's service card, which then bore this special headline "By circling the numbers below, you are ordering the products for free trial examination."

Surprisingly, over the three and one-half years that the advertisement ran without separate book-ordering numbers on the bingo card, the number of "accidents" reported by readers who complained they had not ordered any books was less than half a dozen. And even then, in one instance, the reader who claimed not to have ordered the book he received eventually paid for it (and the other parts of the set).

March, 1978 Page 21

Coming in April...from Wiley

The One Essential Reference for every Industrial Hygienist!

THIRD REVISED EDITION

PATTY'S INDUSTRIAL HYGIENE AND TOXICOLOGY

Volume 1: General Principles

George D. Clayton and Florence E. Clayton, Editors

An authoritative handbook and reference designed to provide the industrial hygienist with a complete guide to methods of evaluation, record keeping and control, as well as historical background.

This new Third Edition updates the second edition published 20 years ago. Coverage has been vastly broadened to include new topics, developments, and legislation.

Each of the 27 contributors to this new Third Edition is a recognized authority in his respective field, and each has contributed his expertise to this all-inclusive volume.

The wide array of subjects covered reflect every aspect of industrial hygiene, including: • air pollution • agricultural hazards • atmospheric contaminants • pulmonary effects of inhaled dusts • occupational dermatoses • legislative trends • reports and record keeping • epidemiology • abnormal atmospheric pressure • noise and conservation of hearing • lighting • radiation • also . . . chapters on: • controls • ergonomics • calibration of instruments • quality control.

Volume 1: General Principles
1504 pp., approx. 400 figures
April 21, 1978 (1-16046-6) $75.00

In preparation:
Volume 2: Toxicology (Jan. 1980)
Volume 3: Industrial Environmental Analysis (April 1979)

WILEY-INTERSCIENCE
a division of John Wiley & Sons, Inc.
Att: Nat Bodian, Dept. 092
605 Third Ave., New York, N.Y. 10016
In Canada: 22 Worcestor Road
Rexdale, Ontario

VOLUME ONE—CONTENTS

1. *Industrial Hygiene: Retrospect and Prospect* (Frank A. Patty). 2. *Legislation and Legislative Trends* (William E. McCormick, American Industrial Hygiene Association). 3. *Industrial Hygiene Records and Reports* (Paul D. Halley and Peter Wolkonsky, Standard Oil Company, Indiana). 4. *The Industrial Hygiene Survey and Personnel* (Lucian E. Renes, former Dir., Industrial Hygiene Services, Phillips Petroleum Corp., Oklahoma). 5. *Epidemiology* (Mario C. Battigelli, School of Medicine, University of North Carolina & John F. Gamble, AL-FORD, West Virginia). 6. *The Mode of Entry and Action of Toxic Materials* (Bertram D. Dinman, Dir., Aluminum Co. of America, Pennsylvania). 7. *The Pulmonary Effects of Inhaled Inorganic Dust* (George W. Wright, M.D., Consultant, Colorado). 8. *Occupational Dermatoses* (Donald J. Birmingham, Wayne State University, Michigan). 9. *Physiological Effects of Abnormal Atmospheric Pressures* (Albert R. Behnke, Jr., San Francisco Medical Center, California). 10. *Industrial Noise and Conservation of Hearing* (Paul L. Michael, Pennsylvania State University). 11. *Nonionizing Radiation* (George M. Wilkening, Bell Laboratories, New Jersey). 12. *Ionizing Radiation* (George M. Wilkening). 13. *Lighting for Seeing* (C.L. Crouch, Illuminating Engineering Research Institute, New York). 14. *Air Pollution* (George D. Clayton, Clayton Environmental Consultants, Inc., Michigan). 15. *Agricultural Hazards* (Clyde M. Berry, College of Medicine, University of Iowa). 16. *Odor Measurement and Control* (Amos Turk, Consulting Chemist, Connecticut & Angela M. Hyman, Rockefeller University, New York). 17. *Industrial Hygiene Sampling and Analysis* (Robert D. Soule, Clayton Environmental Consultants, Michigan). 18. *Industrial Hygiene Engineering Controls* (Robert D. Soule). 19. *Air Pollution Controls* (John E. Mutchler, Clayton Environmental Consultants, Michigan). 20. *Heat Stress-Its Effects, Measurement, and Control* (John E. Mutchler). 21. *Respiratory Protective Devices* (Darrel D. Douglas, Los Alamos Scientific Laboratory, New Mexico). 22. *Ergonimics* (Erwin R. Tichauer, New York University Medical Center, New York). 23. *Potential Exposures in Industry—Their Recognition and Control* (William A. Burgess, School of Public Health, Harvard University). 24. *Quality Control* (William D. Kelley, National Institute for Occupational Safety and Health, Ohio). 25. *Calibration* (Morton Lippmann, Institute of Environmental Medicine, New York University Medical Center. 26. *Industrial Sanitation* (Maurice A. Shapiro, University of Pittsburgh, Pennsylvania). 27. *Fire and Explosion Hazards of Combustible Gases, Vapors, and Dusts* (Joseph Grumer, Pittsburgh Mining and Research Center, Pennsylvania). *Useful Equivalents and Conversion Factors. Conversion Table for Gases and Vapors. Index.*

Mail Coupon for 15-Day Free Trial Examination!
Circle **114** For Trial Examination

Please send PATTY'S INDUSTRIAL HYGIENE AND TOXICOLOGY: Vol. 1: General Principles for 15-DAY FREE EXAMINATION

(Restricted to the continental U.S. and Canada.)
☐ Clayton/HYGIENE, 3RD. ED., Vol. 1 (1-16046-6)

☐ Payment enclosed, plus sales tax. Wiley pays postage/handling. We normally ship within 10 days (after publication). If shipment cannot be made within 90 days, payment will be refunded.
☐ Bill me ☐ Bill firm or institution

Mail to: **WILEY-INTERSCIENCE**, Dept. 092, 605 Third Ave., New York, N.Y. 10016

NAME ____
AFFILIATION ____
ADDRESS ____
CITY ____ STATE ____ ZIP ____

Price subject to change without notice. 092-A8557-51

Circle **114** For Trial Examination

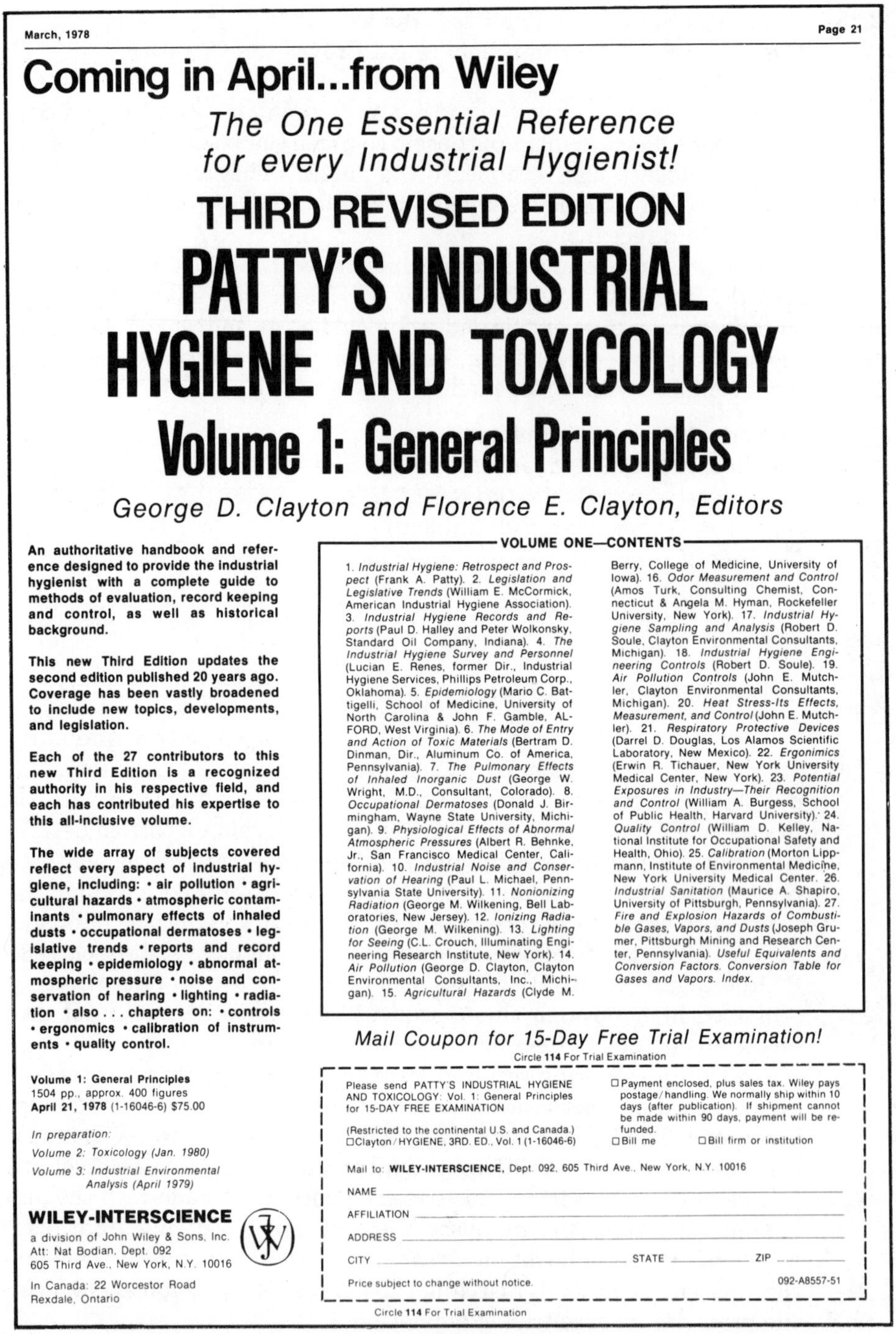

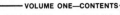

FIGURE 16 Illustration of successful advertisements for *Patty's Industrial Hygiene and Toxicology*, 3rd ed., that ran virtually unchanged in every issue of *Industrial Hygiene News* from its premier issue in March 1978 through July 1982. The first advertisement (A) shows the original 1978 insertion when only the first volume of what eventually became a three-volume, five-part

work was about to be published. The second illustration (B) shows a final insertion just after the fifth and final part of the five-part work was published, in July 1982. Copy and layout by Nat Bodian; pubset arrangements at *Industrial Hygiene News* handled by David Lavender.

SUMMARY OF ACCOMPLISHMENTS

- Longest running and most successful ad format for a published scientific reference work.
- Average traceable dollar return over the 52-month life of the advertisement was over three times the advertising cost—better than most direct-response mail efforts for similar works.
- Introduction and extended use of bingo (reader's service) card numbers as a book-ordering vehicle in a business publication.

WHY THE ADVERTISEMENT WORKED—AN EVALUATION

- The book, a work on industrial hygiene, was perfectly matched to the audience of 65,000 qualified industrial hygienists.
- It was a new edition of a work that had been in existence for 30 years and was widely known among readers of the advertising.
- The name of the author of the earlier two editions, Frank A. Patty, who has been acclaimed as the father of modern industrial hygiene, had been worked into the title of the new edition, *Patty's Industrial Hygiene and Toxicology*, for instant recognition.
- Extensive, up-to-date information was being offered in an expanding field. The advertising medium worked closely with the advertiser and responded affirmatively to suggestions for ad improvement, such as separate numbers on the bingo card for book orders.
- The advertiser was willing to continue the advertising without a break and without diluting a winning format by inserting other related titles in the same field over a more than four-year period.

13

Copywriting: Ideas, Guidelines, Alternatives for Professional and Scholarly Book Promotion

---

13:01   New Ideas in Advertising and Promotion: How to Find Them and Make Them Work for You

Marketing success requires momentum. But for acceleration, your efforts must be fueled with new ideas. New does not necessarily mean original. It means, rather, that you should be ready and able to take established concepts and to realign them in new relationships.

Where do you turn for new ideas? Everywhere! To be a producer of new ideas, you must develop an insatiable curiosity. If your responsibility involves advertising, be interested in what everyone else is advertising. Watch for ads that strike you as having good headlines, layouts, or formats. Watch for different ways in which ad elements are assembled. Collect samples of advertising you consider to be new, unusual, innovative, or whose repeated use implies effectiveness.

If you are involved in direct-mail promotion, be aware of what your competition is doing. Make an effort to obtain and study mailings done in branches of publishing other than your own. Watch what other mailers are trying. Perhaps there is an idea you can use for your next promotion in the way a reply envelope is bound into a mail-order catalog, in the way a science magazine is making a subscription offer, in the way a book club is offering you a membership, or in the sweepstakes mailing by a company selling magazine subscriptions.

The newspapers and periodicals you read, as well as your everyday mail, provide constant exposure to a wealth of ideas, concepts, and proven approaches. With imagination, many can be adapted to your own efforts.

Cultivate an awareness for promotion ideas. Learn to recognize and appreciate ideas that are different. Maintain your own idea file. And start to think in terms of ideas. Remember—there is no such thing as a new idea; there are only old ideas realigned in new relationships. Think of ideas as new tools you have available to work with, and you will find your horizons constantly expanding, your work environment more enjoyable, and your efforts more productive.

For other entries in this volume, relating to copywriting, see 14:01, 14:06, 14:07, 23:14, 29:04, and 30:12.

13:02   **How to Write Good Ad Copy for Professional
          and Scholarly Books**

The ability to write advertising copy for professional and scholarly books is not a gift. It is an acquired skill. The only prerequisites are a reasonable command of English grammar and language, some degree of imagination, and a desire to learn.

The best way to acquire the skill is by study and practice. We use the term study not in the usual sense of learning in school or from a text, but rather study of commodities readily available free of charge—the periodicals and direct-mail pieces in which other professional and scholarly advertising appears.

Study what other publishers in your field are already using. Study headlines for clues on how to start the opening sentence of your own copy. Study sentence structure, wording arrangements, and length of copy. The copy approaches used by other publishers in your own field generally reflect tried and proven approaches that are being used because they have been found effective. They reflect the experience not only of the copywriters but also of their supervisors, who are often seasoned copy pros.

Start a collection of various copy approaches for various types of books. Look for differences in copy concepts and approaches between, for example, engineering handbooks, on the one hand, and theoretical books in the social sciences, on the other. Note that all professional and scholarly book copy does not fit a pat formula, but many books within a given subject or discipline may more or less follow the same form of advertising presentation.

Once the form of presentation becomes recognizable to you, it is only a matter of time and practice before you have mastered it and can apply it to virtually any other book within the same subject area or discipline.

There is much good copy being written—and much bad copy as well. You need not be an expert to recognize copy that is good. Good ad copy will catch and hold the reader's attention and interest. Appealing to the reader's interests gets a message across that is sufficiently compelling to make the reader want to order or at least take a look at the book.

Good copy informs, describes, provides the facts, outlines benefits to the reader, and possibly gives other reasons why the book advertised should be given consideration. When you recogni.. copy that has these attributes and it looks good to you, clip and save it or make a copy of what you like.

Refer to your good examples for ideas, inspiration, and stimulation when you have a writing assignment in the same subject area. When this procedure has been repeated often enough, eventually your feeling of what is good copy will call up images or ideas from your mental inventory of ideas. As you continue to sharpen your copywriting skills by repeated practice, eventually your copywriting style will become instinctive.

13:03 Copy Strengths that Help Sell Professional and Reference Books to Libraries

You can strengthen the effectiveness of your copy if it defines clearly or emphasizes the following:

- Purpose, scope, and audience of book.
- Timeliness of subject matter.
- Advantages over other works in same field. Stress the newness of the contents, especially in rapidly changing fields or subject areas.
- Credentials of author, especially if he or she is an authority in the field.
- Format of your book(s), if material is presented in a different, more convenient format than that of competing works.
- Value of your book in strengthening a specific reference collection.

13:04 Copy Essentials for Announcement of New Edition of Encyclopedic Reference Work

1. Does the announcement's cover or enclosure feature the major benefit of the new work?
2. Are excerpts from good reviews of previous editions included?
3. Is the work an updated version of previous edition, or is it entirely rewritten. Is this made clear?
4. If revised from a previous edition, what percentage of the contents is new?
5. Does the copy mention how many years have elapsed since the previous edition?
6. If it is the first edition in many years, does the copy stress or draw attention to changes in the field since the last edition?
7. Are the editors/authors of the new edition the same as for the previous edition? If so, is this mentioned? If not, are the credentials of the new editors/authors given?
8. Is the new edition in the same style/format as previous editions, and is this mentioned?

9. If the bibliography has been updated, does the copy mention what percentage of it is taken up by new entries?

10. Has any of the previous editions won awards or been approved or recommended by any library or professional group in its field? If so, is this mentioned?

11. What new features have been added to this edition?

12. What exclusive features does this edition contain?

13. Is the new edition larger than the previous edition and, if so, is this mentioned?

14. Will the new edition make the previous edition obsolete?

15. If the new edition complements a prior edition, will the earlier edition continue to be available after publication of the new edition?

13:05   Copy Strategies for Special-Interest or Hobby-Oriented Book Clubs

If you find yourself with an assignment to write copy for a special-interest or hobby-oriented book, it will pay you to consider the strategy used by Times Mirror Book Clubs. Leonard Malleck, director of the clubs, spells it out.* If you think of your selling copy as love letters, then:

• Longer copy is better than shorter.

• You are writing about activities your readers love; provide a wealth of detail.

• Promise more of the "real thing" when your readers get the book.

• Include lots of pictures.

On the philosophy behind this successful copy strategy, Malleck says it is not necessary to sell the activity. Instead, you reinforce the satisfaction the reader will derive from that activity. What your copy should be selling is the means to achieve that satisfaction.

Referring to Elmer Wheeler's classic sizzle/steak theory, Malleck admonishes that his clubs' customers are "already sold on the sizzle: we sell them the steak."

Malleck's advice on a special-interest book club mailing piece is to make it a valuable and useful document. Make it something that will contribute to the readers' special interest even if they don't buy the book, and, above all, make it interesting. The cumulative effect of this copy approach is that you establish a rapport with your book club customers that ultimately pays off in sales.

*These statements were made by Malleck in a talk given before a New York University course (1978) on direct marketing; they were also reported in "Everything You Always Wanted to Know about Book Clubs," *Direct Marketing*, March 1979, pp. 98–114.

13:06 **Copy that Works for One Market
May Be Inappropriate for Another**

You prepare and send a mailing to a book's primary market and it works. You try the same mailing to a secondary market and it doesn't. Why?

The answer, according to Ed Nash,* is that you have to consider the book as more than one book. Speaking before the Professional Publishers Marketing Group in New York on May 18, 1982, Nash explained that a mailing to a book's primary market may require a totally different copy approach than when the mailing is offered to a different market. He added that a technical book deals not only with a rational need but also with a psychological need—namely, self-image—for the security of knowing the book is there should the need for it ever arise.

13:07 **Copywriting for an Engineering Audience:
Why They Buy Professional Books**

There are three important reasons why a practicing engineer will buy a book from personal or from an employer's funds:

1. The book will help solve an immediate engineering problem.
2. The book will help the engineer to update professional skills or knowledge.
3. The engineer feels threatened in his or her job by lack of knowledge and feels the book will help.

These findings emerged when marketers in the Professional and Reference Book Division of McGraw-Hill called in a group of six practicing engineers in April 1981 for an informal discussion of the factors that prompted them to buy books on engineering subjects. From this session at McGraw-Hill came the suggestion that engineering texts aimed at the professional market include such features as more "real-life" or practical examples, less theory, and a minimum of mathematical development from basic principles.

In most instances, the decision to buy an engineering book is based on several critical chapters in it. Often a technical book at the forefront of a field contains as little as one or two chapters that are truly important to a prospective buyer. The promotion for the book should focus on these critical chapters and not on those that build up to or elaborate the important contents.

How do engineers feel about book jackets? If the book is written by an author with prestigious affiliations, the jacket is valuable if it tells

---

*Nash is author of the highly acclaimed *Direct Marketing* (New York: McGraw-Hill, 1982). He is also head of direct marketing at BBDO (Batten, Barton, Durstine & Osborn).

the prospective buyer something about the author—professional affiliations, specialized experience, and writings—that indicates to the buyer that the author was competent to write the book.

13:08   Copy Tips for Direct-Mail Promotions to Overseas Markets

1. Copy should be simple, clear, and concise.
2. Copy should be in the language of the book. Avoid using a foreign language to promote books written in English, as recipients of that promotion piece may think the book is written in their own language.
3. Use American English, not British English.
4. Avoid using the specialized jargon of any field or business; it may not be applicable in other countries.
5. Try to get someone other than an American to preview your copy who would recognize language that will not be understood overseas.
6. If you intend to use testimonials or excerpts from reviews, they should be by internationally respected individuals, internationally prestigious institutions, or internationally recognized journals.

13:09   Improving Readability of Your Mail Promotions: Guidelines

1. Keep lines short. Because most people read words in clusters, a short line is easier for the eye to pick up than a long one. Eye-camera studies have shown that text is more readable if the columns are the width of 40 characters or less. (see 11:09).
2. Keep margins ragged right. Text looks less formal and more inviting when set ragged right rather than flush right, although studies indicate no difference in readability (see 11:08).
3. Use a typeface with serifs. Sans-serif typefaces are more difficult to read and make it easier for the eye to skip lines in text. (For headlines, however, a sans-serif face can be used, as there is little likelihood that the eye will jump to another line.)
4. Use lowercase type for headlines. Headlines set in lowercase can be read faster than headlines set in all capitals or initial capital letters.
5. Leave widows in. "Widows open up copy, let in a little more space," says one expert. "The opinion that you must avoid widows is an old wives' tale."
6. Conserve on color. Sometimes a touch of color, perhaps just in a headline, or an occasional spot here and there is more effective than a heavy mix of colors.
7. Favor darker color ink for text. Where different colors of ink are used, use the darkest color for text and other reading matter, such as the contents.

8. Avoid reverse type. Reverse type is much more difficult to read than black on white (see 11:08) for text matter, but can be used for a short blurb, feature, or headline.

13:10 Why It Doesn't Pay to Knock the Competition in Your Ad Copy

Many writers of advertising copy hold that it is legitimate to knock the competition if it helps to boost your product. It has long been this writer's conviction that knocking the competition not only is unethical and inappropriate, but also utilizes the advertiser's budget money to draw attention to a competitor, when, in fact, the reader of the advertising may not even be aware of the competitor. In other words, giving exposure to your competition in your advertising can be counterproductive.

It has been the practice of this author in his advertising to apply the psychology of advantage by identifying the strengths of a book compared to the competition and by incorporating these into the advertising copy (see Figure 17). Readers familiar with the competition will recognize the advantages of your book over what they already may know about the competition. Readers who are unfamiliar with the competition will see these strengths as features of your book without having been informed about competitive works. By making reference to the competition, which may lack some of the features of your book but may offer other benefits to the reader, you could be drawing the reader's attention to what you are knocking rather than selling.

If the reader is already sold on the competition, your criticism may be viewed with skepticism anyway, as many readers almost instinctively doubt claims of superiority in product advertising paid for by the owner of that product.

13:11 How to Avoid Duplication of Copywriting Effort

In some publishing houses, a central promotion department may service various departments or divisions of the company. As such, the department may have a number of copywriters, and it is possible for more than one copywriter to be working simultaneously on projects involving the same book. Overlapping or duplication of effort can be avoided in these instances if the writers are referred to a central file or "copy bank" where all copy, once written and approved for all titles, is kept on file. This central file should be readily accessible to all copywriters. Files should be identified as "approved copy," "approved space ad copy," or "approved direct-mail copy." It may also be desirable to further identify copy written for professional or scholarly books according to its intended audience, such as "for library media," or "for business publications/professionals." Before a new copywriting job is undertaken, each copywriter should check the copy bank for available approved copy.

FIGURE 17 When the serial publication of a competing work was postponed, Wiley's advertising for the *Kirk-Othmer Encyclopedia* (also a serial publication) concentrated on the theme of continuity by featuring prominently the publication dates of all the remaining volumes in its series. No reference was made to any competing work, but to those active in the subject area of the two works, the message was clear.

**13:12 Potent Adjectives that Enrich Professional
and Scholarly Book Promotion Copy**

accurate	fully documented	remarkable
authoritative	fundamental	revised
balanced	hands-on	self-contained
basic	helpful	self-help
best-selling	highly successful	self-study
breakthrough	how-to-do-it	self-teaching
classic	important	simple to use
clear	in-depth	single source
compact	indispensable	solid
complete	informal	standard
comprehensive	informative	state-of-the-art
concise	informed	successful
convenient	introductory	systematic
copiously illustrated	invaluable	thorough
daily (reference)	jargon-free	time-saving
definitive	lively	timely
detailed	lucid	unified
down-to-earth	meticulous	unique
dynamic	monumental	updated
easy to follow	much-needed	up-to-date
easy to understand	multifaceted	useful
easy to use	new	valuable
effective	nontechnical	well documented
encyclopedic	objective	well illustrated
essential	outstanding	well referenced
exhaustive	perceptive	well researched
expanded	popular	working
extensively rewritten	practical	workable
first	problem solving	work-saving
first of its kind	profusely illustrated	

13:13 Action-Verb Sentence Starters to Help Keep Copy Tight

Cites	Elaborates	Reflects
Collates	Evaluates	Reports
Communicates	Examines	Reveals
Compares	Explains	Reviews
Compiles	Explores	Shows
Considers	Focuses	Spotlights
Covers	Furnishes	Stresses
Demonstrates	Gives	Suggests
Describes	Highlights	Surveys
Details	Illustrates	Summarizes
Discloses	Offers	Synopsizes
Discusses	Outlines	Teaches
Displays	Presents	Treats
Documents	Provides	

13:14   Alternative Words for "Book"—Prescription for "This-Book-Itis"

Most copywriters suffer from "this-book-itis." Especially where the copy involves scientific, technical, or scholarly works, the rule seems to be to start every sentence with "This book." Here are more than 40 alternatives for the word "book" you can use in promotion copy. Using these examples as a starting point, turn your own imagination loose and see how far you can stretch this list.

account	manual	study
aid, learning aid	monograph	summary
analysis	new version	survey
anthology	one-volume library	synthesis
best-seller	overview	text
bible	presentation	title
collection, collection	printing	tome
of papers	proceeding	tool, training tool
compendium	reference, ready	treatise
compilation	reference	treatment
course, short course	resource	unique look at
directory	review	volume
edition, new edition	revision	work
exposition	standard	writing
guide, basic guide		

**13:15   Words and Expressions to Avoid
For More Effective Advertising Copy**

If you heed the sage advice of Caples and Ogilvy (cited in *Volume One*, 14:11), your advertising copy will be more effective if you use simple words and language used in everyday conversation.

In his classic best-selling handbook *How to Write and Publish a Scientific Paper* (ISI Press, 1979), Robert A. Day gives more than 100 examples of jargon frequently found in scientific writing, together with examples of preferred usage. We found the following sampling from Day's list to be particularly appropriate for professional and scholarly book copy. We repeat it here with his kind permission.

Avoid	Use Instead
a majority of	most
a number of	many
as a consequence of	because
despite the fact that	although
during the course of	during, while
end result	result
fewer in number	fewer
for the purpose of	for
from the point of view of	for
for the reason that	since, because
in a number of cases	some
in connection with	about, concerning
in order to	to

Avoid	Use Instead
in relation to	toward, to
in respect to	about
in some cases	sometimes
in terms of	about
in view of	because, since
inasmuch as	for, as
initiate	begin, start
is defined as	is
on the basis of	by
perform	do
prior to	before
subsequent to	after
sufficient	enough
take into consideration	consider
the great majority of	most
through the use of	by, with
utilize	use
with the possible exception of	except
with the result that	so that

13:16 More Jargon to Be Avoided in Copywriting

To Bob Day's 100 examples of jargon that are frequently found in scientific writing and are to be avoided, we would like to add two more that are commonly associated with newspaper, radio, and TV advertising: "act now!" and "simply."

Professional and scholarly book advertising copy should not, in our view, attempt to stampede a reader into a hurried buying decision with the instruction "act now."

The word "simply" is usually used incorrectly. A case in point is a recent letter mailed to medical school faculty that stated "To be considered for a complimentary copy, simply write on your school letterhead, listing the course title, enrollment, and the present text used."

Any action that requires writing a letter on letterhead to include specific information does not merit the word "simply." Perhaps the instruction "Attach your signed business card to this flier and return in enclosed postpaid reply envelope" might have merited the word "simply." However, a request for a letter on letterhead to meet specific requirements simply is not suited for the word "simply."

13:17 Alternatives for Sexist Expressions in Copy

Tradition dies hard, even in the writing of promotion copy. You can avoid sexist language in your copy by observing a few simple guidelines. If you are tempted to write "This handbook is for the chemist who wishes to upgrade his professional skills," remember that there are also female chemists.* Instead of "his," why not say "his or her"?

*According to the American Chemical Society, 88% of its members are male, 11% female, and 1% unknown.

Better still, change the copy to read "This handbook is for chemists who wish to upgrade their professional skills."

NONSEXIST ALTERNATIVES

Instead of	Consider Using
he	he or she (or she), he/she, one, you
his	his or her (or hers)
man	humankind, people
chairman	chairperson†
layman	layperson
manhood	adulthood
workmanlike	businesslike
businessman	business executive, manager
housewife	homemaker
salesman	salesperson, sales representative
workman	worker
foreman	supervisor
manpower	work force, personnel, workers
coed	female student
stewardess	flight attendant
mailman	postal worker
policeman	police officer

BIBLIOGRAPHY

APA Task Force on Issues of Sexual Bias in Graduate Education. "Guidelines for Nonsexist Use of Language." *American Psychologist*, 30 (1975) 682–684.

Burr, E., S. Dunn and N. Farquhar. *Guidelines for Equal Treatment of the Sexes in Social Studies Textbooks.* Los Angeles: Westside Women's Committee, 1973. (Available from Westside Women's Committee, Box 24D20, Los Angeles, CA 90024.)

DeBoard, D., A. M. Fisher, M. C. Moran, and L. Zawodny. *Guidelines to Promote the Awareness of Human Potential.* Philadelphia: Lippincott, n.d.

Guidelines for Equal Treatment of the Sexes in McGraw-Hill Book Company Publications. New York: McGraw-Hill, n.d.

Guidelines for Improving the Image of Women in Textbooks. Glenview, Ill.: Scott, Foresman, 1974.

Guidelines for Multiethnic/Nonsexist Survey. New York: Random House, 1975.

*The National Association of Parliamentarians (NAP) frowns on the use of "chairperson." It passed a resolution "to encourage the continued use of the word 'Chairman,'" resolving "That all NAP members should stress the principle that the word 'Chairman' belongs to the title of the office, and not the person, the same as the title of president or secretary." However, when we called this NAP resolution to the attention of a number of book marketers, they were unanimous in their feeling, NAP resolution not withstanding, that "chairperson" will continue to remain the accepted form for their catalogs and printed promotions.

Harper & Row Guidelines on Equal Treatment of the Sexes in Textbooks. New York: Harper & Row, 1976.

Henley, N., and B. Thorne. *She Said/He Said: An Annotated Bibliography of Sex Differences in Language, Speech, and Nonverbal Communication.* Pittsburg: Know, 1975. (Available from Know, Inc., Box 86031, Pittsburg, PA 15221.)

Lakoff, R. *Language and Woman's Place.* New York: Harper & Row, 1975.

Lerner, H. E. "Girls, Ladies, or Women? The Unconscious Dynamics of Language Choice." *Comprehensive Psychiatry* 17 (1976): 295–299.

Miller, C., & K. Swift. *Words and Women.* Garden City, N.Y.: Anchor Press/Doubleday, 1976.

Prentice-Hall Author's Guide. 5th ed. Englewood Cliffs, N.J.: Prentice-Hall, 1975.

The Treatment of Sex Roles and Minorities. New York: Holt, Rinehart & Winston, 1976.

Wiley Guidelines on Sexism in Language. New York: John Wiley & Sons, 1977.

13:18   An Indispensable Tool for Every Copywriter

Rodale's *The Synonym Finder* has been a constant desktop companion and aid to this writer in scores of writing assignments for more than 20 years. Given a random thought, idea, or weak word, *The Synonym Finder* has never failed to yield a better, more appropriate, or stronger word for the task at hand. The current edition is a revised and expanded version of this favored writing tool, which was originally issued in 1961. The 1979 edition contains more than one million synonyms.

Editor in Chief Laurence Urdang, the internationally esteemed lexicographer, has done a monumental job in the revised edition. You should not be without a personal copy, and it is advisable to opt for the slightly higher priced thumb-indexed version. For your copy of the *The Synonym Finder* by J. I. Rodale (completely revised by Laurence Urdang, 1979; hardcover $19.95, thumb-indexed $21.95) write to Rodale Press, Inc., 33 East Minor Street, Emmaus, PA 18049.

14

Headline Writing: Guidelines and Ideas for Sci-Tech, Professional, and Business Books

---

The headline is the telegram which decides the reader whether to read the copy.

David Ogilvy, *Confessions of Advertising Man,*
Atheneum, 1963.

14:01 Success Formula for Writing Potent Headlines

The effective headline is a vital ingredient of an offering for professional and reference books. It does for the scientist, engineer, or scholar what the newspaper headline does for a news story. It acts as a magnet to draw the reader's eye to the (often, very limited) block of copy immediately following it. At the same time, the headline focuses on a prime feature, offers a key benefit, or gives a compelling reason why the book offering merits the reader's attention. It often can provide sufficient incentive to order immediately.

The lively, appealing headline should provide a benefit, promise fulfillment of an existing information need, offer to give professionals an edge in their current work or research, supply up-to-date information in a rapidly changing area of science or scholarship, or provide new insights in an area closely related to the readers' profession. Headlines for books on business and investment should stress ways to increase profits or income and decrease risk, or they should furnish insights into the thinking of experts in a given area.

The following entries offer a compendium of action-packed headlines that are designed to give your book advertising copy an identity or personality, and to trigger response from the reader who might otherwise skim over an apparently innocuous title with little or no appeal.

176

These headlines will also equip you with a firm foundation for developing an expertise in creating headlines for your own specialized books.

14:02   **How to Trim Verbiage Out of Headlines:**
         Step-by-Step Examples

It is not wise to make a headline any lengthier than its primary function actually requires.

Victor O. Schwab, *How to Write a Good Advertisement*, Harper, 1962.

Headlines that are long winded or too long tend to lose readers and be counterproductive. It is relatively easy to trim most long headlines into much shorter ones without diminishing either the message or the impact. Here are some examples of actual headlines that were used to promote scientific and business books and were considered overly long, along with the step-by-step procedures used to shorten them.

EXAMPLE 1

The original headline used (26 words long):
    (Publisher) offers you, the scientist involved in
    polymer chemistry, these reference books as working tools
    to keep you abreast of developments in your fast-moving
    discipline.

The same headline shortened to 11 words:
    Working tools to keep you abreast of
    developments in polymer chemistry

Shortened to 7 words:
    Keep abreast of developments in polymer chemistry

Shortened to 5 words:
    New developments in polymer chemistry

EXAMPLE 2

The original headline used (24 words long):
    From Harvard to Ohio State to Stanford . . .
    From Wall St. to LaSalle St. to Montgomery St. . . . .
    "Texts"
    That Get Down to
    Business
    from (Publisher)

The same headline shortened to 8 words:
    "Texts"
    That Get Down to
    Business
    from (Publisher)

Shortened to 4 words:
    Business "Texts" from (Publisher)

14:03   More Than 300 Ideas for
Professional Book Promotion Headlines

Advance your career with _____
Advice on every facet of _____
All the basic techniques you need
The all-new edition of the classic best-seller
A _____ approach and exceedingly clear explanation that _____
At last!—Practical Guidance on _____
At last, a _____-oriented view of the subject

A basic, down-to-earth guide to _____
A basic rundown on what you need to know about _____

This book makes it easier than ever to _____
Benefit from the experience of leading experts
Brings you up-to-date on methods to _____
Brings together data from _____ and _____
Brings you up-to-date on important developments
Brings you up-to-date on methods to _____
A basic down-to-earth guide to _____
A basic but thorough rundown on what you need to know
    about _____
A basic down-to-earth guide to _____ for _____
Brush up your technique with this new guide
The book that can help you become an expert in _____
Be a better _____ in _____

A comprehensive synthesis of the subject
A comprehensive overview of _____
A clear, concise and highly readable account
A clear explanation in nonmathematical terms
A concise yet thorough account
A clear, easy-to-follow introductory text
Complete, easy-to-read coverage of _____
A complete survey of the field
Concrete, sensible guidance on _____
Covers the complete range of _____ and _____
A clear, concise way to learn all you need to know about _____
Catch up on the latest _____ techniques and their applications
Complete coverage of _____—in one volume
A clear, nontechnical account for _____
Complete information on _____
A comprehensive overview of _____
A concise introduction to _____
A concise basic guide for _____
A concise, illustrated introduction to _____
A complete introduction to _____
The most comprehensive and up-to-date text of its kind
A clear, nonmathematical how-to-do-it guide
Let __ authorities reveal and integrate the latest thinking and
    research for you

A comprehensive and in-depth review
Consistent commonsense guidelines for any questions you may have
on _____
A current, comprehensive, and authoritative perspective
A complete single-source guide to all aspects of _____
Complete coverage of techniques, applications, methods, and
equipment
A clear nonmathematical guide to _____
A clear explanation in nonmathematical terms
A clear understandable presentation of _____
The current state-of-the-art in _____
A complete survey of the field
A concise state-of-the-art review
Catch up with the latest _____ techniques and their applications
Catch up with sweeping technological changes in the industry
Current, authoritative information you can use

The definitive handbook on _____ . . . compiled by __ top
professionals
Detailed help on _____ practices and procedures
Discover the latest advances in _____
Discover the latest concepts in _____
Detailed guidelines for _____
Detailed information for more effective _____
Discover new _____ techniques

An easy-to-follow approach to _____
Extensive data on the _____ aspects of _____
An essential guide for engineers who _____
An essential tool for _____
Essential reading for _____
Essential information for _____
Exhaustive guide to the practical applications of _____
Everything you need to know to understand the mysteries of _____
Everything you need to know about _____
An easy-to-understand book that shows you how to _____
An excellent source of information and ideas on _____
Let the experts show you new solutions to practical problems in your
work
The essential reference for _____ in _____
Essential guide to _____
Expanded . . . More useful than ever before!
Expert advice for anyone involved in _____
Expert new solutions to practical problems
Extensive data on the _____ aspects of _____

The first comprehensive guide for _____
The first complete guide to _____
Fast answers to _____ questions
The first self-contained guide to _____
A fundamental resource for _____
First book to treat all aspects of _____

The first in a new series
Fills the gaps in _____ literature with one self-contained
    comprehensive volume
First time in book form—Important new material for/on _____
First-of-its-kind guide
Field-tested techniques to solve your _____ problems
First complete guide to _____
The first full-scale study of _____
The first new edition in __ years
The first book to cover these new theories
The first in-depth book on this subject

Gain a better understanding of _____
Gain a deeper understanding of _____
Gain a working knowledge of _____
Gain an in-depth understanding of _____
Gain quick access to _____ expertise
Get instant answers to questions on _____
A guide to the principal methods of _____
Get the latest developments in _____
Gain a basic understanding of current concepts in _____
A guide to the principal methods of _____
Gain a comprehensive understanding of _____
Get a detailed overview of _____
Get the latest data on _____ research techniques
Gain a solid introductory understanding of _____
Gain a working knowledge of _____
Gain a fuller understanding of the principles and techniques
    needed for _____
Gain a better understanding of the theory, design, and application
    of _____
Gain a better understanding of all aspects of _____
The greatest collection of _____ ever assembled under one cover

Handy reference and self-study review of _____
Help for anyone involved in _____
Helps you to isolate, measure, and solve _____ problems
How to get maximum benefits from _____
How to get the most from _____
How to cope with problems of _____
How to keep up with _____
How to use _____
How to use _____ techniques in your work
How to effectively use _____
How to set up and use _____
How to apply _____ to _____
How to better understand the _____ of _____
How to choose and use _____

Indispensable for anyone involved in _____
An indispensable manual for everyone concerned with _____

An instant-answer reference guide to help you in _____
An important new sourcebook . . . with more information on the
   subject than any other available work
Improve your ability to apply _____ technology to your _____
Ideal for teaching and self-study
Information you can put to immediate use
Ideal reference tool for _____
The ideal ready reference for the nonspecialist
Ideal ready reference to the _____ of _____ and _____
An ideal reference and learning aid for researchers and students
An ideal handbook for _____
Ideas you can use immediately
Important, ready-to-use facts on _____
Improve your ability to apply _____ to _____
The indispensable guide for the entire field of _____
An indispensable reference for everyone involved in _____
The indispensable reference for the industry
Information for virtually all uses of _____
Let internationally known authorities bring you up-to-date on recent
   advances
Innovative ideas to eliminate or minimize _____ problems
Instant access to information on every aspect of _____
Instant answers to your _____ questions
Instant answers to questions on _____
Innovative ideas to correct, eliminate, and minimize _____
   problems

Keep up-to-date in this exploding field
Keep up-to-date with _____
Keep up-to-date with this latest edition
The key elements you need to know to _____

The latest developments in _____
Latest edition of an established classic
Learn about the latest techniques and equipment for _____
Learn the "Hows" and "Whys" of _____
A fully illustrated up-to-date guide
Let the experts show you new solutions to practical problems
   in _____
Leading experts share their experience on advanced techniques
A leading authority shows you better ways to _____
The latest technology to help you solve _____ problems
A leader in the field brings you up-to-date on _____
The latest ideas and research on _____
Learn practical uses of _____ in your work
A logical, multiapproach explanation of the theory of _____
A lucid nonmathematical explanation of _____
Learn how to get the most out of _____

Master essential skills for _____
Master the essential skills for coping with _____

The master problem solver for every phase of _____
A mine of information
More exhaustive, more useful than ever before (new edition)
The most complete guide to _____ available/ever published
Most extensive collection of _____ information available in a single
    volume
A much-needed reference (of) (on) (for) _____
The most comprehensive treatment of topics pertinent to _____

A new and refreshing guide devoted to _____
The new "bible" of _____
A new edition of this authoritative guide
New edition of a standard guide/of an industry classic
A new strategy for solving _____ problems
Two new guides in a series devoted to _____
New information on _____ research
A new approach to _____
New methods to _____
A new, informed approach to _____
A new, more realistic approach to _____
New ideas for _____
New revision/edition of a classic
New techniques to help you solve problems in _____
New techniques to help you improve your _____
Now in one convenient volume—Basic source material for _____
Now you can understand and use _____
A new way of tackling _____ problems

The only resource on _____ you need
Offers you all current knowledge—with special money-saving features
This one-volume reference covers the entire field
The only reference on the subject
The only resource on _____ you need
On-the-job instant-answer reference work for coping with everyday
    problems
A one-volume library on _____
The only comprehensive treatment of _____
Over __ pages packed with detailed techniques on every aspect
    of _____
A one-volume examination of the basic principles of _____

A pioneering analysis of current research in _____
Practical in-depth coverage of _____
Powerful new skills for increased job effectiveness
A practical introduction to the entire _____ industry
Profit from the experiences of _____ experts
Provides you with a thorough understanding of the _____ of _____
Practical ready-to-use help on all aspects of _____
A practical guide to a variety of _____ methods
Practical details on key elements of _____
Practical guidelines to help you _____

Practical, proven ways to _____
Practical help on _____
A practical guide to _____
Practical guidance you can use to _____
Practical ready-to-use help on all aspects of _____
A practical new approach to _____
A practical guide to every aspect of _____
Practical, in-depth coverage of _____
Practical help on how to _____
Practical "know-how" to help you _____
This practical manual helps you understand the basics of _____
Practical step-by-step advice
Profit from the experiences of (#) _____ experts
A problem-solving approach to _____
Powerful ways to solve tough _____ problems
Practical, tested ideas for every _____ need
Practical "know-how" to help you _____

Quick answers to your _____ questions
Quick, expert answers to your _____ questions

Refresh your knowledge of _____
A refresher on the principles of _____
Now revised and expanded
Revised and expanded to reflect new developments
Refresh your memory . . . sharpen your skills with this exhaustive
    review of _____
Ready reference or self-study course on _____
Recommended practices and data for _____
Revised and updated guide to _____
Revised version of a widely acclaimed professional reference
Now!—A refresher of the principles of _____

Save time looking up facts about _____ by using this single source
Save time with this major reference for _____
Sharpen your skills in _____ with this self-study guide
Shows you the skills you need for _____
A single source for everyone who wants to _____
A self-contained guide to _____
A simplified, illustration-packed reference covering the full spectrum
    of techniques
A single comprehensive source covering every facet of _____
Shows _____ how to use _____ to _____
The skills you need for _____
A solid introduction to _____
A sourcebook of useful data and techniques
A simple, direct, and practical book that shows step-by-step the
    "how-to" of _____
The state-of-the-art in _____
State-of-the-art techniques for _____
A state-of-the-art synthesis of current information

Step-by-step guidelines for _____
Step-by-step guidelines for using _____
Now!—Share the experience of __ of the nation's top authorities on _____
A simplified guide to _____
A simple, concise, complete guide to _____
Now!—Solve any _____ problem with these tested methods
A single comprehensive source covering every facet of _____
The single source for anyone who wants to _____
A sourcebook and manual of _____ for _____
A solid introduction to _____
A staff of experts brings you help on every important area of _____
The skills you need for _____
Stay on top with the latest developments in _____
Summarizes the existing knowledge of the subject
Successful, time-tested methods for _____

A time-saving reference on _____ for _____
Takes the mystery out of _____
Time and money-saving solutions to your _____ problems
A time-saver you'll use every day in _____
A time-saving source of current information
A time-saving way to catch up on current ideas
A time-saving one-volume reference that summarizes existing knowledge of _____
A timely and informative new look at _____
A total systematic approach to _____
Teach yourself to _____ with _____

A unified treatment of _____
A unique new approach to _____
A unique and practical approach to _____
A unified approach to _____
An unparalleled overview of _____
A useful text for working _____
Update your _____ "know-how"/knowledge of _____
Up-to-date, accurate information on _____
Up-to-the-minute "inside" information on _____
Update your _____ "know-how"
An updated and expanded edition of the "classic" in the field
Updated!—A classic work for _____

Valuable help for the _____
Valuable lessons on _____
Valuable information on _____

Ways to benefit from _____
What you need to know to _____
Want a better, more comprehensive background in _____ ?
A work-saving, problem-solving guide to _____
A working reference for _____

A working aid for _____ that stresses _____
A world authority explains _____ so you can understand it
A wealth of techniques for dealing with _____

Your desktop guide to the basics of _____
Your complete guide to _____

Zero in on time and money-saving techniques in every facet of _____
Zero in on over ___ tested techniques in _____
Zero in on your problems in _____ with these tested methods

14:04   **Good Ad Headlines for Business-Oriented Books: A Rarity**

The abundance of powerful benefit-oriented selling headlines in advertising and promotion for scientific, technical, and professional books (see 14:03) does not seem to extend to advertising for books catering to the world of business, investment, and finance.

Can it be that copywriters for so many of these books believe the titles have a built-in selling pitch that requires little or no reinforcement? Or do they believe that an illustration of the book jacket, supported by the prestige of the publisher's imprint, will suffice? Or could it be just lack of imagination? Whatever the reason, the majority of headlines observed in recent years for books dealing with business, investment, and finance have been average to mediocre.

Headlines that rise above the mediocre are read, and, when outstanding, they are remembered and provoke responses. A case in point is this headline written by Louis Engel of Merrill, Lynch, Pierce, Fenner & Beane in 1948 for a full-page ad in the *New York Times:*

What everybody ought to know . . .
About This Stock and Bond Business

Some plain talk about a simple business
that often sounds complicated

The ad, probably the longest ever written, was a solid page of straight text that offered a free booklet. It produced more than 5,000 inquiries and was noted by half the *New York Times* audience, of which 37% read enough of the text to remember it on the day following publication and 20% read more than half the full-page text. The ad was repeated hundreds of times in various media.

When we discussed the scarcity of good headlines for business-oriented books with a copy professional at a major house, she agreed there was a problem and expressed the view that, unlike scientific and technical book advertising, "You can't sell business-type books with benefits. Your audience is too sophisticated. You have to capture their attention and their imagination."

Another book marketing professional with strong credentials as both an author and reviewer of books on business and investment responded this way: "The reason there are so few good headlines for business books is that most of the promotion is written by people who don't have the least idea of who buys business books and why." He offered this advice to copywriters for business-oriented books: "Appeal to the needs of the buyer in representing how the book meets these needs."

The next entry provides strong evidence that good headlines for business, investment, and finance books are being written but it has taken a long time to accumulate them.

14:05   **Successful Headlines that Have Sold Books on Business, Investment, Taxation, and Finance**

> Options without Ulcers
>
> How you can beat the experts at picking stocks that win
>
> Everything the IRS doesn't want you to know about your taxes
>
> How to reduce the danger of a tax audit
>
> How to preserve your money—come hell or high water
>
> Stop getting burned on market fluctuations
>
> Catch gold fever before it hits $1,000
>
> Let 38 experts show you how to do it right!
>
> Successful strategies to help you in your business
>
> 12 principles for art investment
>
> How to increase sales without increasing expenses
>
> The job you want is out there. The way to get it is in *here* . . .
>
> 3,147 legitimate tax strategies that are better than cheating
>
> For managers on the rise who want to be executives at the top!

14:06   **Headlines in Textbook Advertising: Why Many Are Ineffective**

> *When bookmen extol the high values and noble uses of their product, no one listens. . . . Let us leave the praising of books to others.*
>
> Curtis G. Benjamin, in *Scholarly Publishing*,
> October 1971.

It is disquieting when reputable publishing houses, particularly in the area of textbook publishing, sometimes seem to be in a competition to extol their virtues as "the best." Such breast-beating, in our view, is unnecessary and ill-advised.

When you have an imprint that enjoys a good reputation in a particular area of publishing or in general, headlines proclaiming "we're the greatest" will do little more for your advertising than just using the publisher's imprint by itself. In fact, such proclamations are, if anything, counterproductive. Here are a few examples of such headlines by prominent publishing houses in reputable scientific journals spotted at the time of this writing:

> The best science texts come from (name)
> Don't Experiment. Use the Best!
> The Best . . . from the Best

Examine book announcement advertising in the scientific and scholarly journals. By comparison, you'll notice that many prestigious houses list only their name in *Choice*, because the imprint carries its own message. In the same journals that carried the above "we're the best" headlines, here are examples of more appropriate ones:

> New and Forthcoming (name) Titles
> (name)—Where Biology Comes Alive
> Just Published by (name)

This philosophy for textbook announcement headlines also holds true for direct-mail promotion. An announcement from a respected imprint will be looked at even with a weak or ineffective headline.

Abbot Friedland, a veteran book marketer based at Princeton University Press, summed it up at a Society for Scholarly Publishing seminar in New York in October 1981, when he told an audience, "Anytime we advertise in a scholarly journal, we emphasize the (Princeton) imprint. The book(s) in that ad become incidental."

14:07 Headline-Writing Tips from a Member of the Copywriters Hall of Fame*

David Ogilvy, member of the Copywriters Hall of Fame, offers these tips for headline writers in his *Confessions of an Advertising Man* (New York: Atheneum, 1963):

1. The wickedest of all sins is to run an advertisement without a headline.
2. A change of headline can make a difference of ten to one in sales.
3. Do not say anything in your headline that is likely to exclude any readers who might be prospects for your product.
4. Try to inject news into your headlines.
5. Tricky headlines—puns, literary allusions, and other obscurities—are a sin.
6. It is dangerous to use negatives in headlines.
7. Avoid blind headlines—the kind that mean nothing unless you read the body copy underneath; most people don't.

---

*Additional tips for copywriters by Ogilvy appear in 14:11 in *Volume One* of *Book Marketing Handbook*, 1st ed.

15

Copy Fitting: Guidelines and Tables

Copy fitting—*Determining what area typewritten copy or other text will occupy after being set in a specific size and face of type; also, conversely, how much text will be required to fit a given space in an advertising or editorial layout.*

Appendix A, "Book Marketing Glossary:
The Vocabulary of Publishing and Promotion,"
in *Book Marketing Handbook*, 1st ed.
(*Volume One*), p. 382.

15:01   Copy Fitting: Use and Value for Copywriters

If you are involved in the production of copy for multititle printed book advertising and promotion, and especially if you operate on a scant budget, one of the most useful skills you can acquire is an adeptness at copy fitting. Many copywriters are ignorant of copy-fitting practices, weak in copy-editing skills, or just unsure of their subject matter and so most write overly long copy. This results in excess, costly composition that must then be cut or reset to fit the space available.

Copy fitting is not difficult and is a skill that can be readily learned without prior knowledge or experience. Let's assume, for example, you have a planned partial-page advertisement. Based on other similar advertisements of the same size, you see that such an advertisement will take 80 lines of 9 pt copy at 50 typewritten characters per line, with enough space left over for your establishment's standard advertising signature. You can save many composition dollars if your copy is written precisely to cover 80 typewritten lines of 50 characters or less.

Failure to write and/or edit copy to fit the maximum space available can eat up extra dollars in your budget by oversetting, then resetting copy. You may find it advantageous to use one to three typefaces, type sizes, and line widths, and to write copy to fit one of these established standard formats. Give yourself a choice of two or more standard type sizes so that when your copy will not fit even after careful trimming, you can try the same copy in the next smaller typesize. Sometimes, when your copy is only six or so lines over the space allotted, a simpler solution is to leave the composition intact and gain the needed additional lines by resetting the book titles in a smaller type size. When copy is very tight and the advertisement had planned to include a coupon, omit the coupon and include an 800 telephone number for orders.

15:02   How to Fit Copy for Your Printed Promotions: Simple Guidelines

The term copy fitting is a secret to many who write promotional copy. There is really no mystery to copyfitting, however. By applying the simple instructions in the following entry, you should quickly be able to fit copy with reasonable exactness to any desired area. To begin with, you should be familiar with these few simple typographic rules regarding the measurement of type or copy area on a printed page. Measurements are expressed in depth and width. Measurements of depth may be expressed in inches or picas, while measurement of width are usually stated in picas.

MEASURING DEPTH

There are 72 points to the inch. Since the height of a character type is expressed in points, a line of 9 pt. type will occupy 1/8 inch. Eight lines of 9 pt. type will be 1 inch deep, or nine lines of 8 pt. type will occupy 1 inch.

MEASURING WIDTH

Measurement of the width of type is generally stated in picas. Given that there are 12 points to a pica, there are six picas to the inch. The width of an 18-pica line is exactly 3 inches. A line set 21 picas wide will be exactly 3.5 inches. For precision in setting type or fitting copy to a precise measure, you may express widths in fractional picas, for example, 25½ picas.

CHARACTER COUNT

This refers to the number of typewritten characters (letters, numbers, or punctuation marks) that, when set in a particular typeface and size, will measure exactly 1 pica (1/6 inch). Your typewriter usually has the same number of characters per inch. However, the number of characters per pica in typeset copy will vary from one typeface to another. The character count for a particular typeface and size, as the tables in 15:03 indicate, is expressed as a whole and fractional number, such as 2.1, meaning that 2.1 lowercase letters in that typeface and size will measure 1 pica. For uppercase letters, figure a character count less one-third. Users of photocomposition sometimes allow an extra 10% for variations in width between photocomposition and machine-set type in the same typeface and size.

LEADING AS TOOL OF COPY FITTING

Leading (pronounced led-ing) in typography refers to the spacing between lines of type. (The traditional means of spacing when all composition was done with metal, was to use thin strips of metal—usually lead—in varying thickness from 1 pt. or 1/72 of an inch, to perhaps 8, 10, or 12 pts. Bear in mind that leading does not change the number of lines that have to be set; it only changes the measurement of depth. One "leads out" lines in a block of copy when it falls short of the depth desired for that block.

ESTABLISHING CHARACTER COUNT FOR A TYPEFACE AND SIZE

If you're fitting copy to an area in a layout, you fit to typeface and point size. For example, to fit the typeface Bodoni Book, the starting point would be to look in a book of typefaces containing Bodoni Book. Usually, with each typesize of a face, the character count is given.

If you have no typeface book, you can determine the approximate character count by taking a paragraph in the face and type size and counting the average number of typewritten characters per line and dividing by the number of picas in a line. For example, a line has 64 characters average and is set in 20 picas. The character count would be 3.2.

If you were to look up 8 pt. Bodoni Book in your type book, it would be found that the character count is 3.2, or that 3.2 (small) letters or characters when set in that typeface and size will occupy a width of 1 pica (1/6 inch).

COPY FITTING: A WORKING EXAMPLE

You have a job that calls for 8 pt. Bodoni Book. The designer of the promotion piece has indicated the copy area to measure exactly 3 inches wide (18 picas) by 2 inches (12 picas) deep. Here's how you would proceed:

1. You check your type book or otherwise establish that 8 pt. Bodoni Book has 3.2 characters per pica.
2. You know that 2 inches equals two times 72, or 144 points. Since 8 pt. type is 8/72 inch high, it will take 18 lines to fill the 2-inch space.
3. Now that you know that 8 pt. Bodoni Book has 3.2 characters per pica and that the line width is 18 picas, you refer to the table for 8

pt. type, look under the 3.2 column, and see that an 18-pica line will accommodate 70 typewritten characters. Therefore, you set your typewriter line width for 70. Your typewritten copy will take 18 lines to fill the 2-inch space.

4. Suppose you have written only 16 lines of copy and you want your copy, when set in type, to fit the 2-inch space precisely. Having fallen short by two lines of 8 pt. type, or 16 points, you can make up the 16 points by requesting the 16 lines of 8 pt. Bodoni Book to be set with 1-point leading. This means that each 8-point line will actually fill 9 points. Consequently, when the copy is set, the 16 lines will fill the 18 lines of space precisely.

NOTE ON LEADING

You can stretch any block of copy that falls short of a desired depth by leading between lines by 1 or more points. Where necessary or desirable, you can add leading between paragraphs. You might, for instance, wish to add in a three-paragraph block of copy only 6 points. You can do this simply by adding 3 points of leading between paragraphs.

USING THE COPY-FITTING TABLES

The universal copy-fitting tables in 15:03 give character counts for 6 through 12 pt. type sizes. Once you have obtained the character count for any typeface or for the typeface specified for the job at hand, use the appropriate table to locate the correct typewriter margin settings and you're ready to start fitting copy to any desired area.

The character counts indicated in these tables cover most line lengths up to 30 picas. Should an instance occur where you have to deal with a longer line, just take the character count for a line in the table half its length and double it.

15:03   Universal Copy-fitting Tables for Most Typefaces

If you wish to fit copy to any desired area, the following will guide you to the correct typewriter margin setting for virtually any typeface set in type sizes from 6 pt. to 12 pt. If you know the type size and approximate number of characters per pica for the typeface in which the copy is to be set, refer directly to the table for that typesize. By glancing at the column at the extreme left (the desired copy width), you will find on the corresponding horizontal line the correct margin setting.

Conversely, if you do not know the typeface or size and have a finite amount of copy you wish to fit to a certain area, you can use the copy-fitting tables to establish what type size in any given face will be required for the job. For example, assuming you have a block of copy with 500 typewritten characters and a copy area of 20 picas by 5/8 inch deep, here is how you could determine the type size that would be appropriate. Assume the desired typeface is Helvetica. In 6 pt. Helvetica has 3.5 characters per pica. A 20-pica line would utilize 70 characters.

If 5/8 inch is approximately 45 points (5/8 inch times 72 points to the inch), you could get seven 6 pt. lines into the 5/8 inch area. Seven lines would utilize 490 characters, or just about the total 500 units in the copy. Specifying 6 pt. Helvetica for the job would give you a precise fit on the first setting.

Average Number of Characters per Pica for 6 Pt. Type

Pica Width	3.1	3.2	3.3	3.4	3.5	3.6	3.7	3.8	3.9	4.0	4.2	4.4	4.8
1	3.1	3.2	3.3	3.4	3.5	3.6	3.7	3.8	3.9	4.0	4.2	4.4	4.8
10	31	32	33	34	35	36	37	38	39	40	42	44	48
12	37	38	39	41	42	43	41	46	47	47	50	53	58
14	43	45	46	48	49	50	51	53	55	55	58	62	68
16	50	51	52	54	56	58	59	60	62	63	67	71	78
18	56	58	59	61	63	65	66	68	70	71	75	80	86
20	62	64	65	68	70	72	73	76	78	79	84	89	96
22	68	70	72	75	77	79	81	84	86	87	92	98	106
24	74	77	78	82	84	86	88	92	94	95	100	107	116
26	81	83	85	88	91	94	95	100	101	103	109	115	126
28	87	90	91	95	98	101	103	108	109	111	117	124	134
30	93	96	98	102	105	108	110	116	117	119	126	133	146

Average Number of Characters per Pica for 7 Pt. Type

Pica Width	2.6	2.8	3.0	3.1	3.2	3.3	3.4	3.5	3.6	3.7	3.9	4.0
1	2.6	2.8	3.0	3.1	3.2	3.3	3.4	3.5	3.6	3.7	3.9	4.0
10	26	28	30	31	32	33	34	35	36	37	39	40
12	31	33	36	37	39	40	41	42	43	44	47	48
14	36	39	42	43	45	47	48	49	50	51	55	56
16	42	44	48	50	52	54	54	56	57	59	63	64
18	47	50	54	56	58	60	61	62	64	66	71	72
20	52	55	60	62	65	66	68	71	72	73	79	80
22	57	61	66	68	71	73	75	78	79	81	87	88
24	63	66	72	74	78	80	82	85	86	88	95	96
26	68	72	78	81	84	87	88	92	93	96	102	104
28	73	77	84	87	91	94	95	99	100	103	110	112
30	78	83	90	93	97	101	102	107	107	110	118	120

Average Number of Characters per Pica for 8 Pt. Type

Pica Width	2.3	2.4	2.6	2.7	2.8	2.9	3.0	3.1	3.2	3.3	3.4	3.5	3.7	3.8
1	2.3	2.4	2.6	2.7	2.8	2.9	3.0	3.1	3.2	3.3	3.4	3.5	3.7	3.8
10	23	24	26	27	28	29	30	31	32	33	34	35	37	39
12	28	29	31	32	34	34	36	37	38	40	40	42	44	47
14	32	34	36	37	39	40	42	43	45	47	47	49	51	54
16	36	38	42	42	45	46	48	49	51	53	54	56	58	62
18	41	43	47	48	50	51	54	55	58	60	60	63	65	70
20	45	48	52	53	56	57	60	61	64	66	67	70	73	77
22	49	53	57	58	62	63	66	67	70	73	74	77	80	85
24	53	58	62	64	67	68	72	73	77	80	80	84	87	93
26	58	62	68	69	73	74	78	79	83	87	87	91	94	100
28	62	67	73	74	78	80	84	85	90	93	94	98	101	108
30	66	74	78	80	84	86	90	92	96	100	101	105	108	116

Average Number of Characters per Pica for 9 Pt. Type

Pica Width	2.1	2.4	2.5	2.6	2.7	2.8	2.9	3.0	3.2	3.3	3.4
1	2.1	2.4	2.5	2.6	2.7	2.8	2.9	3.0	3.2	3.3	3.4
10	21	24	25	26	27	28	29	30	32	33	34
12	25	28	30	31	32	34	35	35	38	40	41
14	29	32	35	37	37	39	41	41	45	46	48
16	33	37	40	42	42	45	46	47	51	53	55
18	36	41	45	47	48	50	52	53	58	59	62
20	40	46	50	52	53	56	58	59	64	66	69
22	44	51	55	57	58	62	64	65	70	73	76
24	48	55	60	62	64	67	70	71	77	79	83
26	53	60	65	68	69	73	75	77	83	86	90
28	57	64	70	74	74	78	81	83	90	92	97
30	61	69	75	79	80	84	87	89	96	99	104

Average Number of Characters per Pica for 10 Pt. Type

Pica Width	2.0	2.1	2.2	2.3	2.4	2.5	2.6	2.7	2.8	2.9	3.0	3.1	3.2
1	2.0	2.1	2.2	2.3	2.4	2.5	2.6	2.7	2.8	2.9	3.0	3.1	3.2
10	20	21	22	23	24	25	26	27	28	29	30	31	32
12	24	25	26	28	29	30	31	32	33	34	36	37	39
14	28	29	31	32	34	35	36	37	39	40	42	43	45
16	32	34	35	37	39	40	42	43	44	46	48	50	52
18	36	38	40	41	44	45	47	48	50	51	54	56	58
20	40	42	44	46	48	50	52	54	55	57	60	62	65
22	44	46	48	51	53	55	57	59	61	63	65	68	71
24	48	50	53	55	58	60	62	64	66	68	71	74	78
26	52	55	57	60	63	65	68	70	72	74	77	81	84
28	56	59	62	64	68	70	73	75	77	80	83	87	91
30	60	63	66	69	73	75	78	81	83	86	89	93	97

Average Number of Characters per Pica for 11 Pt. Type

Pica Width	2.1	2.2	2.3	2.4	2.5	2.6	2.7	2.8	2.9	3.0
1	2.1	2.2	2.3	2.4	2.5	2.6	2.7	2.8	2.9	3.0
10	21	22	23	24	25	26	27	28	30	30
12	26	27	28	28	29	31	32	34	36	36
14	30	32	32	33	34	36	37	40	42	43
16	35	36	37	38	39	42	43	45	48	49
18	39	41	41	42	46	47	48	51	54	55
20	44	46	46	47	49	52	54	57	60	61
22	48	50	51	52	54	57	59	62	65	67
24	53	55	55	56	59	62	64	68	71	74
26	57	59	60	61	64	68	70	74	77	80
28	61	64	64	66	69	73	76	79	83	86
30	66	69	69	71	74	78	81	85	89	92

Pica Width	Average Number of Characters per Pica for 12 Pt. Type											
	1.7	1.8	1.9	2.0	2.1	2.2	2.3	2.4	2.5	2.6	2.8	2.9
1	1.7	1.8	1.9	2.0	2.1	2.2	2.3	2.4	2.5	2.6	2.8	2.9
10	17	17	19	20	21	22	23	24	25	26	28	29
12	20	20	22	24	25	26	27	28	29	31	33	34
14	24	24	26	28	29	31	32	33	34	36	39	40
16	27	27	30	32	33	35	36	38	39	42	44	46
18	31	30	33	36	37	40	41	42	44	47	50	52
20	34	34	37	40	42	44	45	47	49	52	56	57
22	37	37	41	44	46	48	50	52	54	57	61	63
24	41	40	44	48	50	53	54	56	59	62	67	69
26	44	43	48	52	54	57	59	61	64	67	72	74
28	48	47	52	56	59	62	63	66	69	73	78	80
30	51	50	56	60	64	66	68	71	74	78	84	86

15:04   Variables to Consider in Copy Fitting with Photocomposition

No copy-fitting formula is 100% accurate. Vivian Sudhalter, creative head of the McGraw-Hill Professional and Reference Book Division, cautions that in photocomposition a new set of variables tends to make existing copy-fitting procedures less precise. When first queried, she suggested a 10% allowance as a rule of thumb for variables in copy fitting. However, she proposed one take these points into consideration in determining a fit:

- The conscientiousness of the type house
- The size of the face (the bigger the size, the more the runover)
- The character of the face (the more extended, or "blockish," the more the runover)
- The pica width of the line (the longer the line, the better the fit)
- Whether the copy is justified (it shouldn't happen, but machines seem to be lazy with hyphens and there's more runover with unjustified lines)

Part III

Marketing and Promoting Professional and Reference Books

16

Marketing Strategies

16:01   The Marketing Plan: Blueprint for
Important Publishing Projects

In most publishing establishments, the launching of an important professional or reference work is preceded by a marketing plan. This plan serves as a blueprint and timetable for the launch. Once drawn up by the marketing department, it may go through several drafts and may have input from various other sources, including the author (author's questionnaire), the sponsoring editor, the public relations department, the outlet managers and field representatives, and sometimes an outside consultant.

The marketing plan accounts for both timing and goals of a launch, but is more often than not considered tentative and therefore not necessarily followed to the letter. Many factors can radically alter a marketing plan so that, although closely followed in its early stages, it may differ greatly later on. Timing plays a major role. If, for example, the planned campaign is based on seasonal timing strategies, major alterations may be required if there are production delays that will postpone publication—a situation common in many large-scale publishing projects.

Another campaign-altering factor is response to early stages of the promotion. If the first of a number of mailings in the plan to a segment of the principal market fails to be responsive, subsequent plans to mail to that same market segment must be changed or new approaches devised and substituted. Conversely, any marketing plan must have built-in flexibility to be able to take advantage of any unforeseen

197

promotional opportunities that may occur after the plan has been initiated.

Another factor is the need to observe and react promptly to early results from tests to peripheral markets. When test mailings to border-line markets during the early campaign stages are unsatisfactory, moneys designated for further promotion in these areas should be reallocated quickly to similar tests in other areas or to expansion of promotion in areas known to be more responsive.

However tentative the marketing plan, it is an essential ingredient in the launching of important professional and reference books and serves a multitude of useful purposes. One of the most important is the justification of a special promotion budget allocation for its implementation. Often, a promotion budget is not approved until after the marketing plan has been presented and accepted. The marketing plan also signifies to management that a well-conceived program is being designed to recoup the publisher's investment in the project as quickly as possible.

The marketing plan attests for both the author and sponsoring editor to the importance the project is being given in the publishing establishment's overall plans. And, lastly, it is the marketer's notice to all concerned that all of the factors that can or may contribute to the success of the publishing project are being orchestrated in a thoughtful and systematic, efficient, and cost-effective manner designed to realize the true potential of the project.

16:02   Input of Sponsoring Editor to Marketing Plan

At some presses, a marketing plan for a forthcoming title may be a joint effort of both the sponsoring editor and the marketing department. The "Promotional Plan" form on the following page is used by one business publisher where both the sponsoring editor and the marketing department contribute to promotional plans for a forthcoming book.

16:03   Way to Saturate a Large Field with a
Small Catalog Budget: Program/Guidelines

Here is a problem that comes up fairly often. The marketer has a strong list in a particular technical field that embraces about 60,000 to 70,000 individuals. A subject catalog is being printed for all the firm's books in the field, but the budget only allows for the printing and mailing of around 3,000 to 5,000 catalogs. How can one best cope with this situation?

There is a good chance that a card deck covers the 60,000 to 70,000 prospects. Check the offerings in the "Direct Response Section" of each issue of *Business Publication Rates and Data*, published by Standard Rate & Data Service, Inc. Buy a one-card participation and offer

PROMOTIONAL PLAN

Date Contract Signed   7/1/83
Mss to production _____
Tentative Price $55

Date   7/1/83
Author   Smith et al.
Title   Financial Report Manual

SPACE ADVERTISING: Applicable Publications

Editor	Marketing
Journal of Accountancy	Same: Planning done jointly w/editor
CPA Journal	
Practical Accountant	
Management Accounting	
Accounting Review	
Wall Street Journal (Eastern Ed'n.)	

MAILING LIST SUGGESTIONS

Editor		Marketing
AICPA Partners in Public Practice	31,000	Same: Planning done jointly w/editor
CPA Firms w/3 or more partners		
ATT: Managing Partner	6,000	
Corp. Controllers, largest firms	3,000	
CMG Accounting	12,500	
CMG Auditing Bookbuyers	4,500	
WGL Financial Bookbuyers (test)	5,000	

CONVENTIONS

Editor	Marketing
AAA—National and Regional Meetings	Same: Planning done jointly w/editor

the catalog free by return mail. Be sure the return card is postpaid. You are likely to receive requests from not more than 2 to 3% of the recipients, which will utilize up to 2,000 copies of your limited catalog supply.

Save your remaining inventory for these purposes:

- A mailing to technical libraries in the same field.

- Catalog requests received in the mail.

- Handouts at conventions reaching similar or related audiences (subject catalogs are popular at conventions).

16:04   Using an In-House Contact Name in High-Ticket Promotions

If you plan to launch an expensive multivolume reference or encyclopedic work that has a protracted publication schedule or involves a subscription plan that could result in a high volume of inquiries, be sure that your promotion includes the name and telephone number of a responsible, well-informed contact within your publishing establishment who will competently handle all calls or personally follow up all inquiries to a satisfactory resolution.

This individual should have contact with the editors, shipping department, production department, credit department, and others, so that all inquiries are handled promptly, competently and with a minimum of fuss or red tape. If the work involves a publication schedule over a number of years, a certain degree of imagination should be exercised by the informed contact, especially in cases where a subscription or order was cancelled or discontinued due to budgetary constraints, service problems, or possibly earlier disagreements with the publisher. The contact person should be able to sense when it would be appropriate to offer to reinstate a lapsed subscription or order so that the customer will suffer no penalty or embarrassment, or to otherwise salvage orders or subscriptions previously discontinued for whatever reason.

The practice of supplying the name and telephone number of an in-house contact in every high-ticket promotion can not only save you many otherwise lost sales but also win friends for your imprint.

16:05   **Technique for Keeping OP Titles Available Permanently at a Profit**

When a professional or scholarly title has been placed out of print, many publishers use a technique to keep the book available indefinitely at a profit. They submit it to the "Books on Demand" program of University Microfilms (UMI), which will fill all orders and pay publishers for the privilege.

Here is what you have to do: Supply one copy of your OP title, and UMI does all the rest. When an order is received, it will supply the customer with either a microform or a bound xerographic copy of the book. UMI's charge to the customer is calculated on a page basis, plus a binding charge, and the cost bears no relationship to the book's original selling price. You receive 10% of annual net receipts from all "on demand" sales of the book.

For details, write to University Microfilms International, Xerox Publishing Group, 300 N. Zeeb Road, Ann Arbor, MI 48106; 313-761-4700.

16:06   **Research Biologists: How to Reach This Affluent Book-Buyer Market**

Research biologists are prime prospects for your high-priced research monographs in their own and related areas. In a September 1981 study* of a publication reaching research biologists, 97.3% of the

*The study, "Survey of Federation Proceedings Recipients," was conducted by Health Industries Research, Stamford, Conn.

respondents reported having an average annual budget for book purchases in their own and related areas of $1,228.

One reason for the book-buying habits of this group is that 45 percent of all research grants issued by the National Institutes of Health (NIH) are given to research biologists who are members of the Federation of American Societies for Experimental Biology (FASEB) whose interest areas include these subjects: physiology, biochemistry, pharmacology, pathology, experimental therapeutics, nutrition, immunology, biomedical engineering, experimental biology and medicine, genetics, and mathematical biology.

Following are ways you can reach this major audience for your high-priced books:

1. Exhibit at the annual FASEB meeting. Meetings are held annually in principal exhibit cities and draw substantial attendance over a four-day period, which includes 35 hours of exhibit time. Apply early, as booths go quickly. Ask for a space in "Publishers' Row," where most book exhibits are situated side by side and face to face. Be prepared for substantial order taking.†

2. Advertise in *Federation Proceedings*, the FASEB monthly publication. The 18,000 researchers who receive this publication are awarded $867 million annually in NIH research grants.* One possible pitfall of advertising in *Federation Proceedings* is that about half of its readers search out articles related to their own special field of interest and go directly to those articles, rather than reading the entire issue.

3. Mail directly to the FASEB membership. For that mailing list, contact the Business Manager, Federation of American Societies for Experimental Biology, 9650 Rockville Pike, Bethesda, MD 20014; 301-654-3080. (A list of biomedical researchers who have NIH grants or are doctoral-level employees of NIH is also available from Eaton Publishing Co., 12 Overhill Road, Natick, MA 01760.)

16:07   Marketing Strategy of a Leading Medical Book Publisher

A stamp program has been the mainstay of the W. B. Saunders's direct-marketing strategy since the early 1970s. It marks the longest use of stamps as a promotional tool among the various medical publishers that rely on this device regularly in their promotions.

The stamp strategy at Saunders differs from that of other medical publishers in a very important way. Most other medical publishers use two or four-color illustrations of actual book jackets or covers. Saunders, instead, uses the stamp as an information as well as an ordering device. Each stamp contains the title, author, price, and ISBN of a book, and only one ink color is used for the stamps.

†The American Society of Biological Chemists (ASBC) meets jointly with FASEB in April about every three or four years (1985 is the next joint meeting). In other years, the ASBC meets independently, usually in May or June. Many of its members are also members of other FASEB affiliates and attend the FASEB meeting anyway.

Stamps are part of a conventional direct-mail package. For each of the approximately 110 titles published each year, an announcement flier is prepared for mailing to its special audience. Along with the flier is sent a sheet of 16 stamps, each of which contains a backlist title in the same field. No book is newer than 6 to 8 months old.

As many different books are published within each medical specialty, Saunders produces the stamp sheets in large quantities, sufficient to last for four to six months of mailings. Saunders has different sheets for different specialties, with about 12 to 14 sheets in all. Depending on the level of activity within each specialty, mailings may be made as frequently as twice a month or as infrequently as twice a year.

In addition to the new book announcement and the sheet of stamps, there is also an order card on which the new book or any four of the books on stamps may be ordered.

16:08   Direct-Mail Strategy of One Large University Press

How does one market a wide-ranging publishing program, mainly in the social sciences and the humanities, to cover effectively both front- and backlist? Princeton University Press (PUP) places the main emphasis of its direct-marketing program on a catalog that embraces its entire list. Here is how it works:

In addition to its general catalog, PUP issues on a cyclical basis one subject catalog approximately every month of the calendar year. It issues about 12 in all on a rotating basis. In this way, the same subject catalog is mailed about the same month each year. Infrequently, when the publishing program emphasizes a particular subject, more than one subject catalog may be issued during the same year.

Each subject catalog mailing is sent to approximately 25,000 names from lists rented from outside sources. PUP maintained its own lists up until about 1972, but found that it was more cost-effective for each once-a-year subject catalog mailing to rent fresh lists as needed.

All catalog copy is taken from the books' jacket copy. New titles are given prominent space on the front of each subject catalog. Among the subjects covered by the catalogs are art and architecture, history, political science, philosophy and religion, languages and literature, Middle East studies, and economics.

16:09   Marketing Strategy Based on Research Fails
to Produce: Lesson Learned

When a leading professional and reference book publisher initiated plans for a scientific encyclopedia in the 1950s, it surveyed a wide audience of professionals in engineering and technology to ascertain the need for such a work. The survey produced a highly positive response. Yet, when the work was published, response from this market was weak. As it turned out, the key audience for the reference work was libraries, both school and public.

The lesson learned here is that, although preliminary research can be a helpful indicator, it does not necessarily ensure results. Also, an indication by respondents to a survey of a "need" for a reference work may not necessarily be synonymous with a desire to purchase.

16:10   **Sold! 25,000 Copies of a Book Nobody Wanted:
Case Study/Strategies Used**

The book nobody wanted, but which was finally published by Crane Russak and the Institute of Physics in London, is now in its fourth printing.... Author Robert L. Weber, a physics professor at Pennsylvania State University, had his A Random Walk in Science, *an anthology of humor in science, turned down by 30 American publishers before it was accepted by The Institute ... [it] was selected last year as one of the 76 best books of the year ... by the British National Book League, and in March of this year by* Library Journal *as one of the 100 best sci-tech books of 1974.*

Publishers Weekly, June 2, 1975.

Robert Weber collected as a hobby humorous anecdotes of oddities in science to freshen up his classroom physics lectures. Someday, he had promised himself, he would assemble them and have them published under a title such as "Humor and Humanity in Science."

He made the move in the early 1970s. He was already well known as the leading author of a widely adopted introductory college physics text published by a leading commercial house, had served on important committees of the American Institute of Physics, and was a reviewer for a science periodical that featured book reviews.

However, after 30 rejections from American publishing establishments, he submitted his manuscript to the British Institute of Physics (IP) for consideration. It arrived at precisely the right time: the IP was about to celebrate its one hundredth anniversary and would make this a special centenary volume, retitled *A Random Walk in Science.*

The IP printed 4,500 copies and sought out an American copublisher. It sent a copy to Crane Russak & Co. and solicited interest in North American rights.

The book, with a red cloth, gold-stamped cover, captured the fancy of the marketing manager, who saw in the scores of interesting oddities a book of high sales and great publicity potential.* Many of the entries were gems from the past, long since forgotten, with the possible exception of "Murphy's law."

Crane Russak took 1,000 copies of the IP edition and published it in the United States in April 1974. Publicity releases were issued and review copies dispatched. One copy was sent to the *Village Voice*, a New York City weekly tabloid then read by many members of the publishing community, and captured the attention of Brian Vanderhorst, a columnist and science buff, who devoted an entire column to *A*

*This author was responsible for the marketing launch, and was recently awarded recognition at a Professional Publishers Marketing Group seminar for the "Most Successful Campaign."

Random Walk in Science. Orders followed and, better still, three separate inquiries ensued about book club rights.

One such book club sale was made to the Macmillan Library of Science, which printed 3,500 copies immediately for a fall selection. Crane Russak had sold out its initial 1,000 copies from IP and then printed another 3,000 copies of its own.

By September, Book-of-the-Month Club (BOMC) sought the book as a June (1975) alternate. The marketing manager at Crane Rusak obtained a release from the exclusive book club deal with Macmillan and closed a second deal with BOMC. In January 1975, more printing took place—the second each for Macmillan and Crane Russak and the first, for 5,000 copies, by BOMC.

The book continued to sell over the years for Crane Russak. At the end of 1982, Ben Russak, president of Crane Russak, surrendered North American rights to the book to the Heyden Book Co. in Philadelphia, which was planning to launch in 1983 a sequel by Weber published by the IP, entitled *More Random Walks in Science.*

At the time of its surrender of rights to Heyden, Russak said the book had sold more than 25,000 copies in its various U.S. printings. Its wide publicity had led to a Japanese edition and, finally, the sequel planned for 1983. Its success has been short of miraculous for what *Publishers Weekly* had called "the book nobody wanted."

MARKETING STRATEGIES USED

Interestingly, very little money was spent in the promotion of *Random Walk.* The book had been plugged (along with other books) into several list-type space advertisements that ran in library and scientific journals. It was also included in a "Previews" mailing that the publisher issued periodically to college, special, and selected public libraries. Each "preview" was printed on one side of an 8½" × 11" sheet.

Most of the book's exposure came from specially prepared and slanted publicity releases sent to various newspapers and publications and from extensive review copy distribution that led to numerous very positive reviews. A number of review copies were individually targeted to influential science reviewers. In some instances the review copy was preceded by a telephone call or letter, and in others, copies were sent by special messenger or with a personal cover letter signed by the marketing manager.

One of the important reviewers, to whom a copy was sent with a personal message, was also by coincidence on the selection panel for best sci-tech books of the year. *Random Walk*, which was worthy of the honor without a doubt, had reached the right hands at the right time, and so won one of awards for Best Sci-Tech Books of 1974.

Book club inquiries were handled with great expediency and agreements were concluded quickly. The marketer for *Random Walk* realized that the full-page ads devoted to the book in both book club offerings would generate many publisher sales, and, in fact, they did.

Random Walk was also prominently displayed in the company's exhibits at scientific meetings, and ample stock was on hand in the booth for cash-and-carry sales. At the 1975 Physics Show sponsored by the American Physical Society, the 20 copies sent to the meeting were sold out in the early hours. What the publishers didn't want, the physicists loved!

Because of the author's prominence in the physics community and the original British publisher's close ties with its American physics society counterpart, arrangements were made between the marketer and the American society for the society to offer the book to its membership at a special member price. Members were required to prepay orders and mail them directly to the society, which, in turn, forwarded orders to the publisher for prompt fulfillment. The society handling the orders received nothing.

The unique combination of strategies of a small publisher entailed virtually no outright expenditure of special promotion moneys, but it worked and the book was a success. Here is proof that initiative, imagination, and good exposure can sell books of merit, even when promotion funds are virtually nil.

**16:11   Prospectus Has Six Lives through
Imaginative Design Strategy: Case Study**

How do you plan a prospectus for an expensive multivolume work that will retain its basic size and format over the six years that the work is being published and still reflect periodic changes in price, content, and publication schedules without becoming obsolete?

Here is an outstanding example. This is a case study of a prospectus done in 1977 for the third edition of a 25-volume technical encyclopedia, which was to begin publication early in 1978. One new volume would be published each quarter over $6\frac{1}{4}$ years, or until sometime in 1984. Because thousands of dollars would be involved in such a purchase, most orders or subscriptions were based on prior examination of the prospectus.

It was highly desirable that the initial prospectus for this encyclopedia have a long life, yet this was not possible. The offering price was subject to change (and did a number of times), and the initial prospectus could not go beyond the contents of the first four volumes. Beyond the first four volumes, the breaks for subsequent parts depended on the length of the 1,000 contributions, which ranged from 4,000 to 10,000 words each.

The original eight-page prospectus went through five revisions* without changing basic appearance, page size, type size, cover, or format. Yet each revised printing, made at approximately one-year intervals, managed to include at least one additional year's contents (as well as the contents of all previously published volumes), reflect price changes as they occurred, and provide up-to-date publication schedules for unpublished volumes.

How was this accomplished? The original eight-page saddle-wire

*All design revisions were done by the author of this handbook.

stitched booklet was issued several months prior to publication of the first volume in 1977. Its 7″ × 10″ cover was a replica of the three-color (black, gold, and PMS 354 green) book jacket that would cover all 25 volumes of the technical encyclopedia. Eight sample pages from the first volume were included, as well as the complete tables of contents of the first four volumes. The back cover had a printed corner card and postal indicia for mailing as a self-mailer.

The first printing of the original prospectus was sufficient for the initial announcement and for inquiries for one year. An intensive space advertising campaign invited requests for the prospectus. Emphasis in the original prospectus was placed on new features and on the scope of subject coverage in the 25-volume work.

THE FIVE REPRINTED VERSIONS

The prospectus was first reprinted at the start of 1979, just after the first four volumes had been published. The cover and first two pages after the cover were essentially unchanged. This reprint, however, had the tables of contents of the first nine volumes. The eight sample pages were reduced to four. Excerpts from some early reviews were added.

The second reprinting took place early in 1980, shortly after the ninth volume was published. The cover and first two pages again were essentially the same. However, new and better review excerpts were added. Sample-page illustrations were moved to the outside back cover. The listing of contents was expanded to show the first 12 volumes. This reprint also contained the first price increase since the original announcement was prepared.

The third revised prospectus appeared at the start of 1981, after 12 volumes were published. The cover and two pages following were still virtually unchanged from the first printing, but reflected price changes. However, because a competitive work had suspended publication at about that time, a listing was included to show firm publication dates for the remainder of the 25-volume set. Listings of contents were expanded in this reprint to show the first 15 volumes. As the contents now spilled over onto the back cover (page 8), the earlier sample pages were dropped. To minimize the drabness of an all-text prospectus, spine-out silhouette illustrations of the multivolume encyclopedia were bled off the page in several available blank spaces on the pages containing the contents.

The fourth reprinting occurred at the start of 1982. Sixteen volumes had been published, and a second price increase was about to take effect. This fifth version of the prospectus still had the same eight-page format, same size and same cover. However, it now contained a complete listing of contents for 19 volumes (there would be 24 in all plus an index volume). It also confirmed the publication schedule for the remaining six volumes. To make possible the addition of contents listings for volumes 16 to 19, the illustrations were eliminated. Furthermore, the contents of each volume, which were previously listed in separate columns, were run in from end to end. There was no reduction in the type size used for the contents.

The prospectus was reprinted a fifth time in March 1983, to coincide with an inflation-related (third) price increase. The original eight-page format and cover were again retained, and, with no reduction in type size, the contents for the entire 24 text volumes were listed.

How was the seemingly impossible made possible? It was done by eliminating all subentries that had been included in the contents in the earlier prospectus for the first 19 volumes. For example, in all five previous versions of the prospectus, a subject heading such as "acetylene" would have five subentries that listed five different articles on acetylene. In the fifth and sixth versions of the prospectus, only the primary heading, "acetylene," was included. The omission of virtually all subentries except those deemed absolutely essential, in addition to the omission of running heads over the contents pages, vacated exactly enough lines of type (216) to fit the contents of the last five volumes.

The eight-page prospectus thus had six lives over a seven-year period. Yet it never changed its original cover, page size or count, general appearance, or format, nor was the type size of the contents entries altered. As a happy footnote, it should be added that by the time the sixth revised prospectus had been issued, the first volume of the encyclopedia had already come close to its lifetime sales projection.

17

Promotion Approaches in Different Publishing Projects and Markets

17:01   Successful Launching of a New American
            Reference Encyclopedia: Case Study

The Worldmark Press is distinguished for its highly regarded *Worldmark Encyclopedia of the Nations*. Soon to be in its sixth edition, it is an established standard reference work in libraries throughout the world. The publisher, Moshe Sachs, produces the encyclopedia in New York and has been selling territorial rights to various publishers throughout the world.

In 1981, Worldmark Press created a companion work to its *Worldmark Encyclopedia of the Nations*. Entitled *Worldmark Encyclopedia of the States*, it is designed in the same style and format as the other encyclopedia, but covers only the United States, with a separate section for each of the 50 states. Each section is divided into 50 keyed, uniform subject areas and gives information on each subject pertinent to that particular state.

Harper & Row won the U.S. distribution rights and launched the *Worldmark Encyclopedia of the States* late in February 1981 with an announcement mailing to 60,000 names on ten different lists. The mailing was timed to coincide with full-page announcements in *Library Journal*, *School Library Journal*, and Baker & Taylor's *Forecast*.

Although Harper & Row knew that the *Encyclopedia of the States* would have ready acceptance in the library market, based on its experience as distributor of the first four editions of the *Encyclopedia of the Nations*, it chose to test a number of other markets with its announcement mailing. The superb information contained in the new *Encyclopedia of the States*, much of which was available for the first time, suggested that it would be readily snapped up by business, government, and industry as a reference source.

208

To make the offering of the all-new work appealing, a special prepublication price of $54.95 was offered for five months until July 31, 1981, when the full list price of $69.95 would take effect. In most mail offerings for books, response virtually ceases after a dozen weeks and permits a campaign wrap-up. However, in the case of the *Worldmark Encyclopedia of the States* mail offering, order forms provided with the mailing continued to be returned for nearly six months, or until mid-August.

Moshe Sachs attributed this remarkable response to the prepub offer, which produced responses until two weeks into August that bore postmarks indicating they had been mailed prior to the July 31 cutoff date for the prepub offer.

Total response from the 60,000 mailing was 2.63%, or 1,583 orders. It was estimated that at least twice that number of orders were generated through library wholesalers and other outlets.

THE PROSPECTUS

The Harper & Row announcement for the *Encyclopedia of the States* was a self-mailer, printed in two colors of ink (maroon and blue) and measuring 8½" × 11" after folding (Figure 18). It opened vertically to reveal a continuous fact-filled sheet measuring 11" × 37", including a 4-inch removable flap that served as an order card at the bottom. The Harper announcement capitalized on strong reviews for the companion work in its announcement with great success. Copy on one panel reads ". . . in the world-acclaimed format of the *Worldmark Encyclopedia of the Nations*—used for over 20 years by librarians, educators, students, and researchers." The inside panel restates a similar premise: "Based on the same time-tested principles and presented in the same easy-to-use format as the *Worldmark Encyclopedia of the Nations*—a reference recommended by *Booklist, Library Journal, Wilson Junior High, Senior High and Public Library Catalogs.*" Still later in the announcement, this copy appears: "AN ENTIRELY NEW YET INSTANTLY FAMILIAR VERSION OF A CLASSIC REFERENCE."

Key elements of the prospectus were:

- Emphasis on factual content and the large number of sources from which the contents were drawn.
- Use of format that found approval by major library media in response to companion encyclopedia.
- More than 20 individual features of the encyclopedia listed.
- Listings of types of answers the encyclopedia supplied, using 14 examples.
- Illustration of the volume was nearly 50% of actual size.
- Illustrations of sample pages and maps with text large enough to read.
- Listing of 50 subjects for which information was provided by state, territory, and dependency.

FIGURE 18 Announcement used by Harper & Row to launch new encyclopedic reference work that was a companion volume to a related, successful encyclopedic work distributed by another publisher.

CAMPAIGN RESULTS

Here is a summary analysis of the response from the mailing date to the close of the campaign (end of prepub offer):

Responses first three months to May 18	70.4%
Response from May 18 to July 31 expiration	29.6%
Overall response (percentage of total mailing) for campaign	2.63%*
Response by Market	
Public libraries	5.9%
Junior and senior high school libraries	2.7%
College and university libraries	1.9%
Special libraries	.8%
Reference book buyers	.7%
Government offices	.6%
Commercial companies (sales directors)	.2%
Management consultants	.1%
Advertising agencies	.1%
Business and trade associations	.0%†

17:02 **High-Ticket Promotion Lacks Important Ingredient: Case History**

The prospectus for a multivolume business reference source was a beautiful piece of work: a 16-page booklet on coated stock with color illustrations and that stated many important benefits in its well-written copy, as well as excellent detailed credentials for the author. Only one ingredient was lacking: There was no order form in the prospectus and no mention of price. This was all the more puzzling because of the usually high, professional quality of the publisher's direct-mail efforts.

A search was made of the 9″ × 12″ white envelope in which the 8½″ × 11″ piece was mailed. Sure enough, nestled in the bottom of the envelope was a 5″ × 7″ BRC with the bold headline, "Special Pre-Publication Offer." It also contained a special price for the initial four volumes (priced over $200) that offered a $50 saving.

This mailing offered these lessons:

1. Avoid putting prices on your reply vehicle only; be sure also to include them in your main offering.
2. If for some reason you plan to use the same prospectus before and after publication and wish to avoid putting the prepublication price on the prospectus, bind in your prepub offer as a tearout reply card or envelope and state the postpublication price only on the prospectus.

*It should be noted that the responses in test areas were all modest, but the marketers felt the test of these areas were extremely worthwhile despite the small response.
†One order.

3. If the response card or envelope is to be loose, have it inserted into the prospectus before enclosing it in the mailing envelope so that the response vehicle will not be left inside the mailing envelope and discarded with the envelope.

Postscript When the contents of this entry were sent to the marketing head of the firm issuing this case history promotion, he reacted with the following reply:

The "mistake" was quite deliberate. Here are my reasons: First, the only reason for the prepub offer was that through an error in timing, the book was scheduled to appear at the very busiest time of the tax season, so an early mailing was essential. Second, in order to get agreement on the prepub offer, I had to build into the program a device to reduce the number of times this special offer would turn up after April. A key reason for allowing the price break is that a major supplement was planned for October, priced at $60. Anyone who bought less than three months before the supplement got it free; hence, the importance of getting the orders in as early as possible. Additionally, a review of promotions we had sent out in 9″ × 12″ envelopes over the preceding four years indicated that more than 95% of all orders came in on the separate order card, although normally there was also an order card on the circular. Hence it seemed clear, in planning this particular promotion, that our prospects look for the card. Finally, there was the element you identified of printing the circular for pre- and postpublication use. By buying in quantity, we were able to reduce the cost of the circular from $148 per M to $89 per M.

17:03   Use of Incentive to Attract Standing Orders for New Editions of Reference Works

If you are selling an annual or a reference work that is periodically reissued in a new edition, consider offering a standing order discount to single-copy buyers who agree to take automatic shipment of future editions as they are issued. The discount need not be great.

17:04   Can TV Exposure Help the Sale of Expensive Reference Works? Case History

Because of the wide general interest in the subject matter (an atlas containing rare old maps of historic and religious value), a reference work priced at over $100 was given a lengthy pitch by a noted television personality on a morning television network show. Yet, in the month following the TV exposure, no change resulted in the sales pattern for the work. The reference, which was expensive and had a short discount, was not stocked in any bookstore and found its market mainly among libraries and institutions.

The lack of sales from this television exposure (to an estimated audience of 6.5 million viewers) was subsequently commented on by Lee

Simmons, president of Franklin Spiers, the book advertising agency, in the April 11, 1980, issue of *Publishers Weekly*: "Television is a mass medium. Don't use it unless you have mass distribution." It follows also that if your book or author will be getting television exposure, preliminary arrangements should be made with major booksellers in the area to have stock of the book on hand for possible impulse sales.

18

Telephone Marketing:
Practices and Techniques
for Book Promotion

18:01   Publisher Benefits from Use of 800 Number in Book Promotion

The toll-free 800 number has become a standard component in the advertising and direct-mail promotions of an ever-growing number of publishers of business, professional, and scientific books. Use of the 800 number speeds response, produces larger orders, does not diminish other types of response, and has a better collection record.

The chief benefit of the 800 number seems to be that it does not seem to compete with other forms of response; orders phoned in are viewed as orders that might not otherwise have materialized. They are, for the most part, impulse purchases that happen at the time a customer views the advertising or promotion.

For example, a listing-type advertisement was run with regularity in a scientific journal over a number of years without ever producing a directly traceable order. It bore no coupon, just stating the publisher's name and address at the bottom. When a toll-free 800 number (together with an "order code number") was added in 18 pt. type just above the publisher's name, the traceable responses to the advertisement were nearly equal to the space cost.

A publisher of management-oriented books reported that when the toll-free 800 number was added to space advertising in business publications, many multiple-copy orders were received by phone from various business establishments.

For other entries in this volume related to telephone marketing, see 3:14, 22:22, 25:16, and 30:06.

18:02 Additional Benefits from Using 800 Number in Book Promotion

In *Volume One* we described some of the benefits derived from adding a toll-free number to space advertising and printed promotions. Some of these are covered in 18:01. Other benefits include the enhancement of response when used in conjunction with an order form or coupon, the number as a reminder to order, and its low cost when an outside answering service is used that charges only for calls received.

Some additional benefits are:

- Faster response than mail reply.
- Usable in small-space advertising.
- Usable in larger-space advertising lacking an order coupon to produce a traceable response.
- Provides 24-hour service 7 days a week for order taking (which most telephone answering services offer).
- Reduces billing/collection costs when used in conjunction with credit-card option.
- Better reporting of collections when the order is given to a person than when it is mailed in.
- Can be incorporated into advertising, promotions, and other printed matter (even shipping labels) as an added sales tool without taking up valuable space. (See Figure 19 for an example of how a bookseller offers toll-free ordering service on books.)

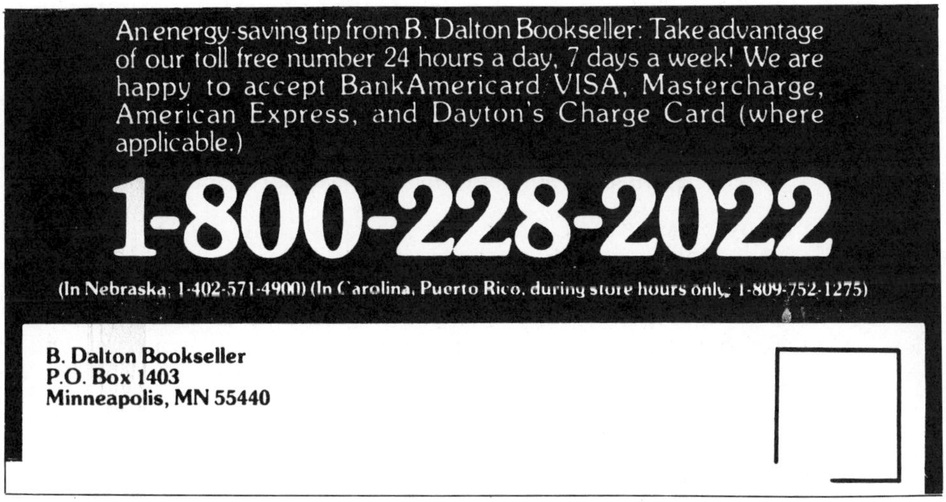

An energy-saving tip from B. Dalton Bookseller: Take advantage of our toll free number 24 hours a day, 7 days a week! We are happy to accept BankAmericard VISA, Mastercharge, American Express, and Dayton's Charge Card (where applicable.)

1-800-228-2022

(In Nebraska: 1-402-571-4900) (In Carolina, Puerto Rico, during store hours only: 1-809-752-1275)

B. Dalton Bookseller
P.O. Box 1403
Minneapolis, MN 55440

FIGURE 19 An example of bookseller use of telemarketing is this advertisement by the B. Dalton Bookseller chain that includes an 800 number. It invites readers to order any book by calling a toll-free number 24 hours a day, 7 days a week. Purchases may be charged to any of the popular credit cards. Dalton offers to ship directly to the customer or to someone else as a gift.

18:03   **Ways to Use Telephone as a Tool of Book and Journal Marketing**

- As a fast list-testing medium.
- As a great research tool that can be used to expedite direct-mail campaigns.
- For verification of orders before shipping when direct mail produces orders for high-ticket offerings. In addition to thanking the customer for the order, verify the purchase order number and the name of the individual (if unknown) placing the order.
- To make collection calls for unpaid shipments.
- To call buyers of a previous edition of a high-priced book to offer an examination copy of the new edition.
- As a variation of the "negative option" for periodical subscription sales; e.g., "I will send you a sample copy with memo invoice. You may mark 'cancel' on the invoice and return it, in which case the same copy is yours to keep without obligation."
- To research the market for high-ticket items prior to setting up the final marketing campaign.
- As a test of a list. A sample of 100 calls will generally give a response equivalent to a 1,000-name direct-mail test of the same list, according to one telemarketing expert.
- When you cannot afford to wait for response from a direct-mail test. A telephone test can do the same thing much faster.

18:04   **Advantages/Disadvantages of In-House Telemarketing System**

ADVANTAGES

- Total control of the operation
- Faster fulfillment and turnaround time
- Direct personal contact that can help your company image
- Use of in-house personnel that has better product knowledge

DISADVANTAGES

- Long-term funding
- Longer start-up time
- Personnel costs and considerations (recruiting, training, and the like)
- Space and equipment needs

18:05   **Advantages/Disadvantages of Outside Telephone Service**

ADVANTAGES

- You pay only a share of the telephone and personnel costs
- Fast start-up

- Professional dedication and experience of outside service
- Various levels of service obtainable, from simple order taking to complex selling situations
- No long-term commitment required
- Method for testing markets or lists

DISADVANTAGES

- Less control of the operation
- Slower turnaround time for orders
- May not be image building
- Outside service personnel will not have depth of product knowledge

18:06   Business and Professional Book Telemarketing Practices: The Salesperson and the Pitch

1. Your opening line should be: "I'm calling from (name of company; avoid using the word publisher in the company name) in (name of city in which publisher is located).

2. Your second line should be: "This is why I'm calling you." Then follow with a brief description of the product and make an offer. Try to close on the strength of the product's benefits. Don't try to close more than twice on a call.

3. Make the sales pitch very conversational. Speak at the speed you normally use. If the customer responds, you should endeavor to talk at about the same speed as the customer.

4. A sales call should not take more than one to two minutes.

5. Start each sales presentation with the same telephone sales pitch and try it for ten calls. If it is not working, modify the pitch and try it for another ten calls. If the pitch still does not work, modify it a second time and try this version for another 30 calls. If by the time you reach 50 calls you find it works, maintain the same pitch for the rest of the list. A telephone sales pitch that is working well after 50 calls will work well for 500.

6. Allow each telephone salesperson to work in his or her own modifications. Although a number of different salespeople will start with the same pitch, after completion of a telephone sales project each caller on that project will wind up with a pitch significantly different from that of other callers.

18:07   Tested Procedures for Selling Business and Professional Books by Telephone: The Book and the List

1. Be sure you have a product that is relevant to the person being called.

2. Try to tie in former purchases the buyer has made of similar titles (cross-selling). For example, "You bought John Smith's book on tax accounting. The author has now put together a new forms book on the subject."

3. The person making the call should quickly identify the reason for the call by introducing in the opening line both the caller and the company.

4. The caller must bear in mind that there is only one chance to call on a particular book (in contast with direct-mail efforts, which permit you to go back to the same prospect as many times as you like).

5. You can go back to a person on your list three, four, five, or even six times a year, providing you have a new book each time you call.

6. Rely on your own customer list. If you sell to individuals by phone, it is difficult to make outside lists cost-effective.

7. You have to start with the largest possible list for an ongoing operation.

8. By relying on your own lists, you are, to a large extent, relying on recognition for successful telephone selling.

9. For telemarketing, use much smaller lists. A list of 7,000 names is considered very large.

10. New York City is the toughest area for telephone sales. It is an area in which a telephone salesperson may have trouble getting past a secretary. Consider this in testing.

11. When you have a very diversified product, you would do much better to call 1,000 buyers of a similar product.

18:08   Personnel Selection Procedures for an In-House Telephone Selling Operation

Both men and women are equally effective in selling, although a telephone marketing pro says it helps if they sound mature. Above all, she advises, you should hire people who understand what they are saying and what they are hearing.

Salespeople work best when they have separate working stations, apart from other callers, but with ready access to floor supervisors who are on hand to answer questions. Here are some other tips on types of people to recruit:

- You need smart people. Look for schoolteachers, mothers, or people with some other interest in life who consider their telephone work a side activity.

- You need friendly people. Telephone callers help each other tremendously. In an effective telephone operation, everyone wants everyone else to do well.

- You need people who are willing to work only a few hours a day. This is not the type of work people can do full time and still be effective.

- You can expect telephone salespersons in an effective operation to last one or two years before they start to go stale.
- You get the best effort from a caller when you offer a modest salary plus commission.

18:09   Telemarketing: A Word of Caution

Telephone marketing campaigns have been used with great success in many areas of professional and reference book publishing. A key to this success has been that the calls were made to individuals to offer a product directly related to their interests, or to individuals with whom the publisher has had an ongoing or prior relationship, such as subscribers to loose-leaf publications, serials, or journals. With that key as an opener, the caller identifies him or herself and the organization that is currently offering or has previously supplied a product or service that will give or has given the recipient satisfaction.

A respected publishing authority has suggested that this chapter on telephone marketing also include mention of the fact that "an increasing number of people are irritated or incensed at telephone solicitation" and that its use "does incur a risk of generating bad feelings against the publisher who practices it."

Murray Roman, a telemarketing pioneer and widely known writer on the subject, counters with the statement that "generally customers don't object to calls." Writing in the "Telephone Marketing" chapter in Bob Stone's classic *Successful Direct Marketing Methods*, 2nd ed. (Chicago: Crain Books, 1979), Roman adds that a "carefully planned approach directed only to those prospects whose history, status, location, age, income, and related characteristics indicate their potential interest in the product or service is the key to successful cost-effective [telephone] promotion."

18:10   How to Improve Results and Reduce Costs of an
800 Number Answering Service

If you engage a telephone answering service, in conjunction with your toll-free promotion, you will have to pay for every call taken regardless of its value or nature. Here are some ways you can save time, money, and screening expense on such phone orders:

- Adding this line to your promotional copy, "For Book Orders Only," may help eliminate some nonrelated calls.
- Add an alternate number "for all other calls." This can help screen out nonordering calls.
- Do not rely on the answering service's standard form. Instead, design and supply one of your own, and provide appropriately identified blank spaces for all the information you desire for each order (including its source).

- If you supply your own form to the answering service, include on it for the operators' use separate direct-dial referral numbers for such things as rush orders, complimentary copy requests, complaints, foreign orders, and others.

18:11   Preliminary Steps to Ensure Reliability of 800 Number Answering Service

Not all 800 number telephone answering services are the same. The quality of service can vary widely. To save yourself future grief and a possible dilution of promotional efforts involving the use of a rented toll-free number, some preliminary investigation should be undertaken before you engage an answering service. If, as a starting point, you obtain positive answers to the following questions, you can be sure that you are dealing with a reliable service and thus reduce the possibility of future problems.

1. Is the service well established and financially stable?
2. Has it been serving other publishing accounts?
3. Have they (other publishing accounts) been contacted to verify that the service is/was satisfactory?
4. Will the service provide a statement prior to the start of your arrangement that the 800 number will not be changed without a minimum of, for example, 60 to 90 days' advance notice?
5. Will the service provide a statement prior to start of your arrangement that notices of price increase will be given at least 60 days in advance so that, if you do not agree to the increase, other arrangements can be made?
6. Is the per-call charge a flat fee for all calls, or will the service charge a somewhat lesser fee for a call that requires minimal effort, such as a referral to another number?
7. Is the service agreement with the telephone answering organization actually for handling calls, or is it being "brokered"?
8. How frequently are orders forwarded to you?
9. During what days and between what hours is the 800 number being answered?
10. Is the 800 number that you are utilizing a shared number for several accounts, or is it an exclusive line that may result in higher costs?

18:12   Source for Segmented Library Lists with Telephone Numbers

In 1982, several publishers that conducted telemarketing campaigns to libraries had to undertake the time and expense needed to compile telephone number lists. In 1983, this will no longer be necessary.

The R. R. Bowker Co. has long been publishing the *American*

Library Directory, which includes library telephone numbers. In 1983, the entries from this directory will become part of the data base of the Bowker Mailing List Department. This makes it possible for you to order any segmented list of libraries with telephone numbers for a small additional fee over the regular charge for the mailing list.

Numbers are included in the lower right-hand corner on regular (four-across, Cheshire) address labels. Because of the positioning of the telephone number, the address portion of the label cannot be used for mailing.

For prices and details on lists with telephone numbers, call Paulette Milata, Director, Mailing List Department, R. R. Bowker Co., 1180 Avenue of the Americas, New York, NY 10036.

18:13   Tracking Response from 800 Numbers in Book Promotions: Three Ways

If you plan to use an 800 number in your advertising through an outside telephone service, the calls are not difficult to track. To do so, here are three popular ways, in order of preference:

1. Add a line under the 800 number in each advertisement, for example, "Order Code #0000." Use the job number of the advertisement as the code. Have the answering service operators ask each caller, "What is the order code in the advertisement you are calling on?" Most callers will give the number if it is easy to spot and near the 800 number.
2. Include an extension number adjacent to the 800 number. When the operator answers, he or she will record the extension number given, which will change with each advertisement.
3. Include a department or operator number alongside the 800 number in each advertisement.

Answering services favor numbers rather than names for advertising tracking. Numbers are easier to spot in an advertisement, and names sometimes cause confusion.

18:14   Effect on Response When 800 Number Is Added to Book Promotions: Survey Results

What happens to ordering patterns when a toll-free number is added to promotions for business, scientific, and professional books? Marketers in two divisions of a New York publishing establishment found out in 1981, when they added an 800 telephone number to space and direct-mail advertising.

In the final quarter of the year, when promotions that included an 800 number averaged 500 calls per month, telephone ordering patterns were contrasted with simultaneous direct-mail offerings of essentially the same books, but without an 800 number. These were the results:

- In advertising and direct-mail offerings involving books in the natural sciences and engineering, a random selection of 100 telephone orders showed an average of 1.55 books per order.
- In advertising and direct-mail offerings of books in business, finance, and the social sciences, a random selection of 100 telephone orders showed an average of 1.78 books per order.
- In direct-mail promotions offering essentially the same titles as in the two categories above, but without an 800 number included, a random selection of 100 orders showed an average of 1.1 books per order.

SUMMARY

Orders placed through an 800 number for books in the sciences and engineering (1.55 books per order) were 40% higher than responses to offerings in which no 800 number was included. Orders placed through a toll-free number for books in business, finance, and the social sciences (1.78 books per order) were 60% higher than responses to offerings in which no 800 number was included.

CONCLUSIONS

It was the feeling of the marketers involved that most of the 800 number orders were incremental, i.e., orders from individuals who might not have ordered had it been necessary to complete and mail an order form or some other written communication. In the case of the business books, there was a strong indication that buyers in this area are more likely to order over the telephone than are buyers of books in the sciences and engineering. Other findings of this survey were that orders over the phone tend to be larger than written orders, and, last, that use and payment of an outside phone service on a per-call basis are cost-effective for advertising and direct-mail promotions, in terms of both the numbers of orders received and the size of individual orders.

18:15   **During What Hours Do Book Buyers Use 800 Number? Study Result/Indicators**

Buyers of professional and scholarly books who order through a telephone answering service most usually place such orders during normal (9 to 5) business hours. This was the result of a study of approximately 12,000 such calls during a seven-month period in 1982 by a service that operates 24-hours-a-day, seven-days-a-week, and has a number of book and journal publisher clients.

A study of 12,000 calls received on behalf of a book publishing client using the toll-free number was conducted by the National WATS Services of Fair Lawn, N.J. The study indicated that 82% of all calls were received during daytime business hours (9 A.M. to 5 P.M.), while the remaining 18% were received evenings and weekends (13.5% and 3.5%, respectively).

HOURS OF ORDERING FOR PROFESSIONAL AND SCHOLARLY BOOKS

Month (1982)	9 to 5 Orders	Evening Orders	Weekend Orders
January	79.4%	12.1%	8.4%
February	85.2%	10.9%	3.8%
March	79.7%	14.4%	5.9%
April	83.1%	13.1%	3.8%
May	85.2%	12.3%	2.5%
June	84.1%	12.8%	3%
July	83%	14.1%	2.9%
7-Month Average*	82.6%	13.5%	4.5%

*Based on approximately 12,000 calls.

Survey courtesy of National WATS Services, 39-40 Route 4, Fair Lawn, NJ 07410.

Although no differentiation was made between hours during the day, Charles R. Dall'Acqua, president of National WATS, said that a slightly higher percentage of the daytime calls was received in the afternoon.

The study suggests these useful indicators to book marketers:

1. If you are considering the installation of an in-house telephone answering service, you can assume that more than 80% of orders will come in during normal business hours.

2. The 18% of calls received during "off" hours confirms the claim by most telemarketing professionals that a large percentage of 800 number orders are made on impulse and might not have materialized had the caller had to complete and mail an order card or coupon with envelope.

18:16   **How Scientists and Engineers View 800 Number in Advertising: Two Surveys**

Science magazine asked readers of its October 9, 1981 issue how they would respond to an advertised product they might need in their laboratory in the next 30 days. 48% said they would dial an 800 number if one were available and 5% said they would dial the regular telephone number.

Plant engineering and purchasing executives who received the August 1981 issue of *U.S. Industrial Directory* were asked about 800 telephone numbers in another survey (Cahners Advertising Research Report No. 260.1). If two similar products were advertised in the same issue—one with a conventional phone number and one with an 800 number—which number would they call? 58% said they would call both, 41% said they would call only the 800 number, and 1% said they would call the conventional number.

Because many scientists and engineers buy or order books for their perceived immediate value to work or research, these survey results carry a message for book marketers, too.

18:17   **Library Reordering Process for New Edition of
Reference Work Can Be Speeded: Case Study**

In late 1981, the McGraw-Hill Book Co. inaugurated a telemarketing test to launch its monumental *Encyclopedia of Science and Technology*, 5th ed., due in spring 1982.

A telemarketing test campaign was launched to library buyers of the previous edition through an outside service. After a five-week test that drew $25 in firm orders for every dollar spent, a full-scale campaign was begun to reach other subscribers.

The telephone offer to libraries included savings of $90 off the publication price. Furthermore, the library could make payments over a two-year period while having full use of the new encyclopedia from 1982 onward.

No printed announcement preceded or accompanied the telemarketing campaign, so the results were not diluted or enhanced by any other effort. The beneficial results attained in this test were likely related to the fact that libraries, as a rule, will order the newest edition of any standard reference work in their collection if their budgets permit. However, the telemarketing campaign indicated that this reordering process can be considerably speeded.

Part **IV**

Book Publicity:
Ideas, Techniques,
and Guidelines

19

Book Review Practices, Procedures, and Insights

19:01   **Professional and Scholarly Book Reviews:**
Synopsis of Coverage

The first volume of *Book Marketing Handbook* made the point that because scientists and scholars are peer conscious, a review in a scientific or scholarly journal carries considerable weight in influencing the purchase of professional and scholarly books. *Volume One* described studies conducted by this author over a period of years that confirm this now widely recognized fact. It then provided detailed guidelines on the art of compiling, preparing, and processing review lists; discussed the reference tools needed for review list compilation; and gave advice on how to cope with review requests, maintain good relations with reviewers, and utilize excerpts from reviews to good advantage.

This new chapter on the book review as a marketing tool probes the subject in greater depth and answers questions regarding correct book review practices that trouble many a book marketer or publicist.

In addition to touching briefly on the mechanics of review list preparation, the following entries will probe the value of the review as a selling tool, describe how scientists rate book reviews in one leading scientific publication contrasted with the editorial matter, and suggest how you should deal with review copy requests after the initial mailing of review copies. This chapter also describes a system for checking for the appearance of reviews and suggests some ways to get extra mileage out of them once they have appeared.

The nagging question for many reviewers—whether to chase reviews after a review copy has been sent—is answered by an editor/book reviewer. Another such question frequently raised is also answered: Should you advertise in a periodical carrying a review of your book? Perhaps the most valuable entry in this chapter, and possibly in the entire book for some marketers, deals with the claim that a book listing that produces 10 orders by direct means can generate 60 more through the echo effect.

19:02   How to Compile a Master List of Book Review Policies for Media in Your Field

If you specialize in a particular field or in several areas in which there may be anywhere from a handful to several hundred assorted potential review media, it will be well worth your while to establish and maintain a file of review policies and practices of the publications to which you may be sending review copies.

Devise a form-letter questionnaire and send it to all potential review media for your books. Be sure to include a postpaid or stamped return envelope. A hand-signed letter is more appropriate, even if the letter is duplicated or printed.

As a rule, most editors will respond, and, for the relatively small cost of the mailing, you will have a file that is accurate and current and that reflects circulations, review policies, correct mailing addresses for the book reviewers, and as much additional helpful information as the periodical editor may wish to supply.

Such a list should be updated from time to time to clean the records and remove the deadwood. This is a relatively inexpensive way to keep your review list clean, although it may not be practical if you publish in a wide range of subjects and the review media possibilities are extensive.

The sample inquiry letter on the next page can be used on your own letterhead.

19:03   Touching All Bases in Review List Compilation: Major Sources of Information

Reviews are vital to the successful sale of most professional and scholarly books. Therefore, care should be taken that no periodical that reaches a potential audience for a particular new title is overlooked.

In the review list compilation process, check review suggestions made by the author in response to the author's questionnaire as well as any files you may have kept for prepublication requests received from journals and magazines. Also check your in-house master review list in the subject area and double-check *Ulrich's International Periodicals Directory* and possibly *Bacon's Publicity Checker.* You may want to avoid using your battered copy of *Advertiser's Guide to Scholarly Periodicals* (Ad Guide), as it has not been reissued in a new edition for many years and no plans were underway in early 1983 for an updated version.

SAMPLE LETTER

(date)

Dear Editor:

In order to ensure your prompt receipt of books for possible review, please provide us with the following information for our files:

Periodical _____   Circulation _____
Address   _____
           _____
           _____

Phone number _____
Frequency of book reviews _____
Book review editor _____
Book review editor's address (if different from periodical address)

           _____
           _____

If reviewer's term is for a stated period, indicate expiration date

           _____

Comments:

A postpaid return envelope is enclosed for your convenience. Thank you for your cooperation.

Cordially,

(name/signature)
Book Review Coordinator

You should also consult with the sponsoring editor, who may have a suggestion or two for an addition to the final list. If the book is important, you may want to heed the editor's suggestion to show the list to the author.

19:04   Review Copy Requests after the Initial Mailing: Guidelines for Handling

After the initial review copy mailing, requests that follow should be carefully screened. If a request is received from a publication on your original list, advise the inquirer that a copy has already been sent and specify to whom it was addressed. It may be that the original review copy was misdirected, or that the request was made as part of a routine when, in fact, the review copy already has been received.

When the request is made by a publication not on your original list, a review copy should be sent if the publication is deemed appropriate for the subject matter of the book. Some requests come from publications that previously did not review as a policy and now do; in such instances, it may be worthwhile to reconfirm the publication's review policy. Obviously, requests for review copies of books in areas totally unrelated to the subject matter of the periodical should be viewed with suspicion. Also, requests for an expensive book from international periodicals with a circulation of only a few hundred should be given thoughtful consideration, in view of the value of the copies.

Some publishers will not honor requests for review copies of books more than two years old, as such reviews are of little or no publicity value. Others may consider favorably a request for any book, no matter how old, in the hope that it might generate a favorable review that could boost sagging sales.

It has long been the author's feeling that any book listing in a periodical that has a valid circulation and that is related to the book in subject matter is worth at least the manufacturing cost of a book, and that all review copy requests deemed legitimate be honored at any time.

19:05   Review Copy Procedure at a University Press

The press maintains a comprehensive directory of all review media of primary importance for its publications. It is kept current and serves as a quick, uniform, and central source for all regularly used review information. Although the system lends itself to indexing on cards or computerization, this press prefers individual master sheets for each review medium, as follows:

1. Each review medium—journal, newspaper, radio station, and the like—is given a separate master sheet on which is listed the name and address of the book review editor or other person designated by the publication to receive review copies. The address often is different from that of the editorial office.

2. Each master sheet also lists subjects of interest to the reviewer or medium. It also provides such additional information as circulation, frequency of publication, and average number of books reviewed each year.

3. When a review copy is sent to the medium, the title of the book and the date mailed are recorded on the master sheet. When a review subsequently appears, the date of publication is noted alongside the date the review copy was sent.

4. Master review sheets are maintained in three categories: (1) Magazines and journals (filed alphabetically by name); (2) free-lance and other reviewers (filed alphabetically by name); and (3) newspapers and broadcast media (filed by state to facilitate regional distribution).

5. In conjunction with the review files in the three categories, a separate subject index is maintained for each of the subject areas in which the press publishes. The index has a separate entry for each subject that lists those media that review books in the subject area. (Unless it is obvious, a separate note may be added to distinguish special interests or focus.)

6. As not all reviews lend themselves to subject classification, there is also a separate file for "general interest" media, under which are listed major national magazines and journals, book review syndicates such as John Barkham Reviews, and newspapers.

19:06   Wording for Review Slip When Book Has Limited Territorial Rights

Reviews in international journals frequently generate both orders and inquiries from all parts of the world. When you are mailing review copies of a book for which you have only limited territorial sales rights, one way to prevent needless overseas correspondence is to add a note for the reviewer at the bottom of the review slip to this effect:

> Reviewer—Please note for your international circulation that outside the United States, this title is available from (name of originating publisher).

The line "outside the United States" can be altered to read "outside North America" or "outside the Western Hemisphere."

19:07   Should You "Chase" Reviews after Review Copy Has Been Sent? An Editor Replies

Some publishing establishments have a system for "chasing" reviews after a review copy has been sent to a periodical. This process, usually a form letter inquiring whether the book has been reviewed, takes place some six to twelve months after the review copy has been sent. University presses seem more inclined to follow this practice, whereas larger commercial houses are less inclined to do so for fear of antagonizing the review editor.

How do editors feel about receiving such follow-up letters? We asked one prominent journal editor in the social sciences. His view was that such letters tend to be counterproductive:

A book publisher sends out many review copies on an open solicitation basis. This means that the journal or magazine must make its own determination of the worthiness of the book, the availability of an appropriate reviewer (a problem equal to the value of the book), and above all, whether reviewing a particular title fits the theme(s) of any given issue. These decisions must remain unencumbered by pressure from [book] publishers.

A [book] publisher can exercise certain controls: above all, while heavy advertising may not (and should not) have a direct bearing on the book being reviewed, such a practice cannot help but influence a journal editor. Publishers can also begin to restrict or cut back drastically the sending of books to media that seem unresponsive over time.

Lastly, a publisher can exercise great control or leverage by the selective utilization of author(s). In professional publishing especially, authors and editors are close, or at least know each other personally as well as scholarly. Nicely crafted notes from authors to editors may serve as appropriate reinforcements.

But whatever mechanisms of persuasion exist, the publisher must always keep in mind the need to serve, and never coerce or unduly and unethically impinge upon the freedom of an editor to publish, no less than to publish.

ANOTHER EDITOR'S VIEW ON CHASING REVIEWS

When a publisher sends a copy of a book to either an individual or a periodical on an unsolicited basis, this becomes the property of the recipient. Such merchandise does not have to be returned. The sender is enjoined by legislation from in any way seeking recompense or harassing the recipient of the unordered merchandise. Thus, for a publisher to insist upon a review, a return of copy, or even an explanation for non-review might well be interpreted in legal terms as an infringement upon the rights of an unsuspecting recipient.

19:08   Ways to Obtain Copies of Reviews of Your Books

1. Request two copies of the review on an accompanying review slip.
2. Employ one or two press-clipping services.
3. Alert your editors and staff members to watch for reviews in their fields of interest.
4. Alert your order-processing department to forward copies of reviews that may be attached to orders.
5. When sending copies of reviews to authors, request that they send you copies of unduplicated reviews they receive from other sources. They usually have access to all the important journals in their own field as well as in many borderline areas.
6. Subscribe to one or more of the book review indexes. If you are affiliated with an institution, your institutional library may already be subscribing to such indexes.

19:09   System for Checking for Appearance of Reviews: University Press Approach

One university press maintains a record of all books sent for review, including the dates copies were sent to each review medium. When a review appears, the date of the review is recorded alongside the date the review copy was sent. This has the double advantage of indicating both approximately how long it takes for reviews to appear in each medium and which media do not review the press's books at all. After a period of time, if no reviews are shown to have been received, the press will contact reviewers to see if there is a problem. Often, such contacts disclose that review copies have been sent to an incorrect address, or that the medium no longer carries book reviews. Where other circumstances are involved, the inquiry may often clear up the problem and lead to future reviews.

19:10 Crucial Value of the Review as a Selling Tool for Small Publishers

As discussed earlier, a review in a respected scientific or scholarly journal, especially by an acknowledged authority or one with a prestigious affiliation, will carry a lot of weight in influencing professional and scholarly book purchases.

In *Volume One*, we posed the "rule" that the smaller the publishing establishment, the more dependent the publisher is on the book review, as the distribution mechanisms of larger houses are structured in ways that can overcome many shortcomings of an ineffective book review system. An important point worth adding with respect to the necessity for meticulous attention to book review practices by smaller publishers is that librarians and buyers of professional and scholarly works put more "trust" (see 38:13) in a work advertised by a prestigious publishing establishment with a reputation for quality publishing, or written by a reputable author in the field. Librarians may be less likely to order a book from a smaller or lesser known publisher, especially if the author is not well known (see 38:12), until after the appearance of favorable reviews.

19:11 How to Get Extra Mileage Out of Book Reviews

The fact that a review of your book has appeared and you have been sent a copy of it does not mean the process has ended. When a review is received, there are a number of ways you can get extra mileage out of it. For one thing, it makes good sense to send a copy to the author. Not only does it indicate that the book is being promoted but also that the author's review recommendations are being carried out. It may also trigger suggestions by the author for other review media in the same field that were not previously mentioned or considered. At the same time, you can acquaint the author with possible shortcomings of the book noted in the review, and these can be corrected in a subsequent edition.

In some publishing establishments, reviews are routinely filed for future reference and for possible excerpting in advertising or promotion copy. It is advantageous to copy and circulate these reviews (at least the good ones) to key people within your own publishing establishment—editors, trade reps, and others. Reviews or excerpts should also be circulated to your better library or bookstore accounts. The review is, after all, still the best selling vehicle for a professional or scholarly book, short of a personal recommendation.

If reviews are circulated periodically, design a cover sheet that is readily recognizable and establish a distribution list for all reviews. When circulating reviews in their original format, underline pertinent or quotable segments. Be sure each review carries the name and date of the periodical in which the review appeared.

19:12   Simple Way to Prevent a Negative Review

Occasionally a reviewer of a professional, scholarly, or reference book will inject a negative note into what might otherwise be an excellent review by noting that the most recent literature reference in the book is several or more years old. This can give the impression that the information in the book is based on outdated material. This type of negative review can be prevented in advance if the author is asked to provide one or more recent references to the manuscript before it is sent out for composition.

19:13   Should You Advertise in the Same Issue of a Periodical Containing a Review of Your Book?

This nagging question faces most book marketers at one time or another: Does a scheduled review of one's book warrant a supporting advertisement in the same issue? The question was posed to a number of experienced marketers of professional and scholarly books. Here's what they said:

- One favored the idea of an advertisement both before and after the review in the same issue (if budget and importance of the book warranted).
- Another marketer felt an advertisement was unnecessary in the same issue.
- Still another opined that it would be more advantageous to advertise in a later issue using a review excerpt from the previous issue. "Then you get exposure in two different issues," he said.
- One said she advertised a business book in the same issue with the review after obtaining prior agreement that the advertisement would face the review. (An 800 number in that advertisement produced more than 25 orders.)
- Another seasoned business book marketing pro indicated he would not advertise in the same issue "as the review is already giving me exposure where it really counts. If the publication is really targeted to the audience for my book and the review is very favorable, I would quote from it in a subsequent issue. The key to success is repetition."

The consensus of most book marketers, including this writer, seems to be that advertisement in an issue following the one carrying the review is more advantageous, especially if the ad carries a good quote from the review.

19:14   Value of "New Books" Listings In Periodicals

There is considerable value for publishers in the free book listings, usually found under "New Books" or a similarly worded heading, in many scientific, scholarly, or specialized periodicals.

Such nonreview listings may run in addition to the regular book review section, or in some instances, they serve as a substitute for reviews. Such listings provide basic information on books—title, author, page count, price, publication date, and name of publisher. They may also include several words or lines of nonevaluative descriptive matter under headings such as "Telegraphic Reviews," as used in the *American Mathematical Monthly*, or "New Scholarly Books," as used in *Chronicle of Higher Education.*

In some disciplines (mathematics is one), professionals rely heavily on this basic book information to keep abreast of the literature. The specialist within a narrow area of his or her discipline generally knows the leading authors in the specialty and, therefore, the information presented in such a listing is sufficient to induce the specialist to order the book, request an examination copy, or recommend for library purchase.

In the sciences and other rapidly changing fields where books date quickly, it is important for the review list coordinator to know which periodicals carry such new book listings and promptly supply a review copy—even if the periodical is known not to carry a full-scale book review section. This means that when you check *Ulrich's International Periodicals Directory* or *Bacon's Publicity Checker* and find that a specialized periodical that may be important to your book's market does not have a book review section, it is still worth your while to telephone the periodical and establish whether it carries informational listings of new books in its field.

In summary, new book listings are valuable and should be considered an integral part of the book review operation. A simple four-line listing in *Science*, for instance, reaches more than 150,000 scientists almost immediately after publication. Such a listing may precede a full-length review by 6 to 18 months, and may also be the only information to reach that audience if the book happens to be one of the 14 out of every 15 books received at *Science* that is not reviewed.

**19:15   Readership of Reviews Compared with Readership
of Editorial Content among Scientists: Study Results**

Subscribers to *Science* magazine read book reviews as much as they do the overall editorial content. These findings emerged from statistics obtained from readership studies of separate issues of *Science* in four different years. The studies were conducted by Ballot Research Co. of

SCIENCE READERSHIP STUDIES

Issue: Year and Date	Editorial Recognition Score	Book Review Recognition Score
1978 (June 23 issue)	67.9%	72.1%
1979 (Oct. 12 issue)	81%	70.8%
1980 (March 14 issue)	77.2%	81.1%
1981 (April 17 issue)	66%	67%
Average for all four studies:	73%	72.75%

Mamaroneck, N.Y. The score for recognition of overall editorial content in four issues was 73%. By contrast, the recognition score for book reviews only in the same four issues was 72.75%.*

19:16   Book Contents Listing Serving Scientific and Scholarly Audience Generates Many More Orders through Echo Effect

Current Contents (CC), a current-awareness publication of the Institute for Scientific Information (ISI) in Philadelphia, carries reproductions of the contents pages of scientific and scholarly journals in the natural sciences and engineering. Various editions of *CC* also include a section called "Current Book Contents," which lists the contents† of selected titles bearing a copyright from the current or preceding year. Selections are made from among publications in which articles, chapters, or sections have been written by different authors.‡ Books so listed are accompanied by a book order coupon returnable to ISI. In turn, ISI forwards such coupons to the publishers.

A communication from ISI to a book publisher stated, "Marketing surveys indicate that only about 14% of readers who order books after seeing a listing in *CC* use our order transmittal service. The rest order direct. . . . If we send you ten orders . . . you can be sure another sixty or so were generated by the listing."§

---

*The average advertising recognition score for the same four issues was 42.9%.

†Listings are selected from review copies sent to or requested by the Institute for Scientific Information. An exception is made for "Current Contents/Life Sciences," for which a placement fee ($150 minimum) is charged according to number of entries/chapters and other criteria. Complete details follow in Chapter 20.

‡The multiple-author rule applies to all editions of *Current Contents* except the *Life Sciences* and *Arts & Humanities* editions, which list books by only one author.

§For details of the echo effect of ISI "Current Book Contents" listings, see 12:18.

20

Book Review Policies of
Noteworthy Media

A favorable review of a demanding new science book in the Sunday Times Book Review *may not affect sales, but a rave review in* Science *can make a tremendous difference.*

Lewis Coser et al., *Books:*
The Culture and Commerce of
Publishing, Basic Books, 1982.

20:01 Science

Most authors of scientific books, irrespective of their specialty, include *Science*, a weekly publication of the American Association for the Advancement of Science, among the top two or three publications in which they would prefer to see a review of their books.

Your chances for getting a book reviewed in *Science* are generally much better if you limit your submissions to professional-level books in the basic sciences. This is not to say that *Science* reviews only such books. Actually, according to book review editor Katherine Livingston, professional-level books in the basic sciences constitute about two-thirds of the 250 to 275 books reviewed each year. The remaining third comprises mostly scholarly books in fields that are not technical in the usual sense, such as the history of science, public affairs, and the like. As a general rule *Science* will not review a textbook unless it is a first-of-its-kind work in an emerging branch of science. *Science* also will not review atlases, handbooks, or bibliographies.

Science receives about 4,000 books per year for review, so the 250 to

275 reviews represent about one published review for every 15 books received. Reviewers are carefully selected for the subject matter, and no reviewer is permitted to do more than one or two reviews a year.

Even if you think your book may not meet the criteria for a review in *Science*, it may be worthwhile to send a review copy anyway. If not reviewed, it will usually be listed under the "Books Received" column, which will bring your book to the attention of *Science*'s 150,000 or more readers. Such an announcement is invariably worth more than the cost of a single review copy.

When the *Science* book review department feels a review needs clarification before it can be published, the department occasionally will contact the publisher and request a second review copy. Don't delay when you receive such a request; it can hold up the review of your book!

20:02   Scientific American

Scientific American is one of the world's most prestigious publications for the well-informed and science-oriented lay reader. It reaches a monthly circulation of approximately 700,000, including more than 51,000 subscribers in libraries and education. Its full circulation page rate is approximately $16,000, so a feature length review can be of considerable value. Editor Dennis Flannagan says of the *Scientific American* book review policy: "Our review policy is to cover all of science. We have a book review columnist at MIT and he chooses about six books to review for each issue. In addition, once a year in December, we review leading children's books about science."

For a prompt response from *Scientific American*, send books for review directly to the reviewer, Philip Morrison, 11 Bowdoin St., Cambridge, MA 02138. Be prepared for a call from *Scientific American* if your book has been reviewed. Occasionally, you will be asked to send an extra review copy to *Scientific American* so the staff can check for additional bibliographic details. When such a call is received, respond promptly, or your review, worth many thousands of dollars, may be delayed.

20:03   American Scientist

A 12-person board of editors selects books it considers appropriate for review from among those received from publishers. Review copies are sent to expert reviewers. Except for lead reviews, most are 100 to 300 words in length. The six issues of *American Scientist* per year carry 500 to 600 reviews. Subjects reviewed include the physical sciences (physics, astronomy), earth sciences (geology, geophysical sciences, oceanography), life sciences (biology, biochemistry, medicine, ecology and environment), behavioral sciences (psychology, anthropology), mathematical and computer sciences, engineering and applied sciences (including some energy and environmental policy studies), and the history and philosophy of science. Subjects not covered in book reviews are other behavioral sciences, such as sociology and management. Reviews may appear from as soon as one month to more than six months after receipt of the review copy, six months being the average. Send review copies to Jane Hersey, Book Review Editor, American Scientist, 345 Whitney Avenue, New Haven, CT 06511; 203-624-2566.

20:04   American Reference Books Annual (ARBA)

American Reference Books Annual, a volume of close to 1,000 pages, is published each year in April and purchased mainly by libraries of all types. Approximately 2,000 book reviews are included and cover all new reference books and selected reference annuals published in the United States in the course of the calendar year. Annuals are reviewed every three to five years after their first issue. Foreign titles in English are included when there is an exclusive U.S. distributor. Selected reprints are also included.

Reviewers are mainly academic librarians (40%), library school faculty (20%), or special librarians (30%); about 10% are school and public librarians. Reviewers are given a December 15 deadline for each annual volume, so your review copies must be in by early November or else the review will be carried over to the following year. According to Bohdan Wynar, *ARBA*'s editor since its inception in 1970, many libraries view reference offerings for the year as a whole before making acquisitions decisions. Tearsheets of reviews are sent to the publisher upon publication of *ARBA* in April. Send review copies to Libraries Unlimited, Inc., P.O. Box 263, Littleton, CO 80160. For information, call 303-770-1220.

20:05   Current Book Contents

"Current Book Contents" is a section of the weekly current-awareness publication *Current Contents (CC)*, which is published in seven different sections by the Institute for Scientific Information (ISI) in Philadelphia. The readership of the various sections includes a dedicated book-buying audience comprising researchers, educators, librarians, and professionals in various fields.

The seven sections are: life sciences, social and behavioral sciences, engineering technology and applied sciences, arts and humanities, physical and chemical sciences, clinical practice, and agriculture, biology and environmental sciences. Each section carries reproductions of the contents pages of subject-related journals.

Book listings are free in six of the seven *CC* sections. The exception is "Current Contents/Life Sciences" (CC/LS). For this section, the fee is $85 for title and bibliographic entry plus $10 per chapter for multiple-author books of 39 chapters or less. Additional chapters are grouped and assigned a flat fee. The fee for single-author books in CC/LS is $85 for the title and bibliographic entry plus $5 per chapter. In both cases the minimum charge per book is $185.

An order coupon is included in each issue of *CC* and is returnable to ISI. Book orders thus received are transmitted to publishers without additional charge. Some listings can generate a considerable number of book orders. For information or to place a listing, contact Institute for Scientific Information, 3501 Market Street, University City Science Center, Philadelphia, PA 19104; 215-386-0100.

20:06   Datamation

Datamation is one of the leading periodicals in the electronic data processing industry. It reaches more than 130,000 information processing professionals monthly, and its international editions in even-numbered months swell this circulation by an additional 25,000. Of the total domestic readership (nearly 5,000 of the 130,000 are in Canada), approximately 25,000 are engaged in the design or manufacture of data processing equipment or components.

"We carry book reviews," says Debbie Sojka of *Datamation*, "[for] any kind of book relative to the computer industry. We run one review a month. Space permitting, we'll carry two. We'll look at anything that comes in and our editors on the staff will commission someone to review the book we want to carry. We don't want books with a lot of mathematics, or programming handbooks. But other than that, we're willing to take a look at anything."

In a publication such as *Datamation*, where a black-and-white page at this writing was $6,480, it will be worthwhile to invest a copy of your titles on information processing, considering the value of a page-long review.

20:07   Computer Decisions

Computer Decisions has a circulation of more than 117,000 individuals involved with management information systems (MIS), data processing management, and company management. It claims its circulation encompasses exclusively management-level personnel, and that this percentage is considerably higher than that of its three nearest competitors, *ComputerWorld*, *Datamation*, and *Infosystems*. A full-page, black-and-white advertisement in *Computer Decisions* as of late 1982 cost $5,445.

Mel Mandell, editor of *Computer Decisions*, says of his magazine's book review policy, "We review books if we think they are appropriate for our audience. We sometimes refer to books in our articles or list them as references. We like books that address themselves to management. We avoid technical books, how-to books on microcomputers. We average about two reviews a month."

20:08   Computer Design

Computer Design reaches 86,000 computer systems designers worldwide. Its readership is primarily concerned with the design and application of computer- and microprocessor-based systems. It did not have a book review section at the end of 1982, but was considering one for 1983. If you have books for this audience, *Computer Design* could be an important medium. To find out whether reviews are carried, call Peggy Killmon at 617-486-9501 or 800-225-0556, or write to Computer Design, 11 Goldsmith St., Littleton, MA 01460.

20:09   Engineering News Record

Engineering News Record reaches a weekly paid-circulation audience consisting of more than 100,000 engineers, architects, contractors, and other specialists in the construction industry in the United States and worldwide. Its readership is one that is ready to buy books of immediate benefit to them as guidance in their everyday work. *Engineering News Record*'s advertising rate had risen to $4,570 for a black-and-white page by January 6, 1983 (rate card 33). At that rate, book advertisements may not be feasible, but because the readership is so receptive to industry-related books, so is the editorial management. Editor Arthur Fox says, "We run a 'Just Published' listing of books received and from among these we run a book review section on a space-available basis, perhaps a dozen times a year. We're a weekly. We may run two or more reviews in a section, so the number of book reviews we will carry in a year may be two dozen or more. Address review copies to me. We're anxious to have a look at all books of interest."

Send books for review to Arthur Fox, Editor, Engineering News Record, 1221 Avenue of the Americas, New York, NY 10020.

20:10   Architectural Record

Architectural Record, with a circulation of more than 74,300 at this writing, is the largest of the three leading architectural periodicals. Its audience includes over 46,000 architects and engineers engaged in building design and product specification. It carries a book review department in every issue that leads off with a major review or feature article of approximately 1,500 words. In addition, it carries "telegraphic" reviews of about 10 to 15 lines each of books in the field. Per issue, there are five to ten short reviews, or 100 to 150 per year.

Associate Editor Charles Gandee, who is also book review editor, says he is interested in receiving review copies of books on any subject that will appeal to an architect—technical topics, building design, interior design, landscape architecture, engineering. "We try to get diversity into our review section," says Gandee, "and if we think a book is of major importance, we'll do a feature-length article including illustrations from the book itself. The lead time from when we receive a book until it appears in print is about three months. We like to see a finished book, although there have been some occasions when we have reviewed from galleys."

With the full-page, black-and-white advertising rate approaching $5,000, you should send review copies of pertinent books if you think you have potential feature material for this publication. Send books for review to Charles Gandee, Book Review Editor, Architectural Record, 1221 Avenue of the Americas, New York, NY 10020; 212-997-3450.

20:11   Heat Transfer Engineering

This relatively new journal reaches a select audience of more than 20,000 practicing engineers and industrial designers, researchers, and other personnel in companies using, designing, specifying, or manufacturing heat transfer equipment, components, or instruments. Published bimonthly by Hemisphere Publishing Corp., Washington, D.C., it lists all review copies of books in its "Books Received" section and carries numerous book reviews. If you publish books on thermal science, heat and mass transfer, radiation, fluid mechanics, numerical methods, energy conservation, alternate energy technologies, multiphase phenomena, and mechanical design, send review copies to Dr. R. L. Webb, Heat Transfer Engineering, Department of Mechanical Engineering, Pennsylvania State University, University Park, PA 16802; 202-783-3958.

21

Effective Book Publicity

It is true that the publisher must do both, but . . . inch for inch, column for column, publicity is far more cost-effective than space advertising.

Harlan Kessel, Marketing Manager,
University of California Press, at the
third Annual Meeting, Society for
Scholarly Publishing, San Francisco,
June 1981.

21:01 Special Approaches and Nature of Sci-Tech and Scholarly Book Publicity

In *Volume One* of *Book Marketing Handbook*, we outlined the basic precepts of publicity. We emphasized use of the word "news" rather than "publicity" in referring to news releases. The reason is that editors have no desire to print your publicity; their desire is, rather, to give their readers news. So you must supply the media with what they consider news—information that will appeal to them and that they think their readers will want to read. Do this and you will be successful; send them publicity and your efforts will fail.

In this chapter, you will find an explanation of how sci-tech and scholarly book publicity differs from trade book publicity. Most industry publicists are trade book-oriented, and many fail to comprehend the different approach required for sci-tech and scholarly book publicity to make it work effectively. The differences are explained.

Working tools for the professional and scholarly book publicist are listed (for detailed descriptions, see chapter 42 of *Volume One*). One of these, *Ulrich's International Periodicals Directory*, will be online in the Bowker data base as this book is published, and review lists to the most exacting specifications may now be obtained from more than 100,000 periodicals. Another of the six, *Ad Guide: An Advertiser's Guide to Scholarly Periodicals*, will not be reissued by AAUP in 1983 and, therefore, the old 1979–1980 edition is the final one, although still useful and a collector's item.

Another contribution of particular interest in this chapter deals with the special nature of the news release in professional and scholarly book promotion, and offers guidelines for its preparation.

21:02   Sci-Tech and Scholarly Book Publicity: How It Differs from Trade Book Publicity

Publicity for books in most scientific and technical fields, with notable exceptions in the social sciences, differs widely from that for trade books. The primary difference between the two categories of books lies in the nature of how each is marketed.

Trade books thrive on mass-media publicity, including radio and TV exposure, author appearances in the various media, lectures, and the like. They carry a large discount and are heavily advertised and publicized, and their authors are given repeated public exposures wherever possible. Such exploitation is an inducement for as many of the 19,000 U.S. bookstores as possible to order and stock the books on display racks and tables and to feature them in store windows.

Studies have proven that trade books are heavily bought by impulse shoppers, who, seeing the book on display in a bookstore, will buy it on impulse. The fact that a shopper in a bookstore saw an author on television, heard him or her on a radio interview, or read about the book in the *New York Times Book Review* is often enough to trigger an impulse purchase when that author's book is recognized in a bookstore.

Sci-tech and scholarly books, on the other hand, are likely to be found in stock in only a handful of the 19,000 U.S. bookstores at any given time. Unless a store specializes in the subject, or is known as a sci-tech bookstore, it is unlikely to carry such short-discount books in stock. Furthermore, even when a potential buyer specifically requests the short-discount title, the store may be reluctant to go through the bother and paperwork required to special-order it from the publisher.

Whereas the goal of the trade publicist is publicity for its own sake, the goal of the sci-tech and scholarly book publicist should be peer reviews in the specialized scientific, technical, and scholarly journals in the same field or in areas directly related to the book.

THE TRADE PUBLICIST

A trade publicist may try to establish a special relationship with editors and book reviewers, learn the editorial concerns of favored publications, and, from time to time, feed those concerns with their authors' views in these areas of concern. The trade publicist's hope is that the author can somehow be worked into editorial matter, even if it means only that the author's book is mentioned at the end of an article on the op-ed page. Such a result is enough to consider the placement a huge success.

For a book to benefit a publisher and generate sales in the sci-tech and scholarly world, a reviewer, who often has strong professional credentials in the same field as the author does, will write an in-depth chapter-by-chapter evaluation of the author's work, citing its contribution to the literature or its value as a text. In addition to a book's strengths as well as its weaknesses, the reviewer will often point out important omissions and thereby provide sound guidance for a succeeding edition. In other words, the sci-tech and scholarly book review is usually by a professional evaluating another professional's work for other professionals in the same field.

The trade book publicist will try to get to know the author of a trade book, find out what his speaking engagements are, and try to tie in local publicity. The publicist may also try to promote the book around the author's other activities.

THE SCI-TECH AND SCHOLARLY PUBLICIST

The sci-tech and scholarly publicist will rarely, if ever, try to get to know the author because most of the essential publicity material needed to promote the book will have been supplied by the author on the author/marketing questionnaire. In fact, many sci-tech and scholarly authors write for the prestige and recognition their books will give them in their own field and are often inclined to suggest more publicity efforts than the (often) short-run book will merit or than the publicist can afford to give it.

There is, as the preceding comparison indicates, a vast difference between publicity for the sci-tech and scholarly book and the trade book. The book publicist who serves both worlds, or who is making a career move from one to the other, must be aware of this difference and function accordingly if he or she is to succeed.

21:03   **Primary Information Source of the Book Publicist**

The average publicity person at a professional and scholarly book publisher is likely to have little or no familiarity with the wide range of subjects covered in a book publishing program. Most of the learning that is necessary to deal with the various subject areas is acquired by studying the author/marketing questionnaire for the book under consideration.

Obviously, the more information the questionnaire provides, the better the publicist is equipped to prepare an effective news release. Care must be taken to ensure that the author questionnaire asks the right questions to produce enough information to enable the publicist to be effective. If the right questions have been asked (and answered) on the questionnaire, it should not be necessary for the publicity person to contact an author. (For detailed information on the preparation of author questionnaires, see Chapter 37 of *Book Marketing Handbook, Volume One.*)

21:04   Working Tools of the Professional and Scholarly Book Publicist*

1. *Ulrich's International Periodicals Directory* (annual), R. R. Bowker.
2. *Ayer Directory of Publications* (annual), Ayer Press.
3. *Bacon's Publicity Checker* (annual), Bacon Publishing Co.
4. *Directory of Associations* (annual), Gale Research Co.
5. *SRDS Business Publication Rates and Data* (monthly), Standard Rate & Data Service, Inc.
6. *Ad Guide: An Advertiser's Guide to Scholarly Periodicals.* (1979–1980 edition was final issue), American University Press Services, Inc.

**21:05   The News Release in Professional and Scholarly
Book Promotion: Purposes and Guidelines for Preparation**

The professional and scholarly book news release should be designed for these purposes:

1. To generate requests for review copies from publications in fields related to the subject of the book that have a legitimate interest in examining books for possible review.
2. To provide busy book reviewers who already have the book with a brief synopsis of the book they can scan in advance of the actual review. This "preview" gives them a "handle" on the book's contents and its features. In many instances, busy reviewers will pick up factual matter from the news release verbatim and it becomes the review.†

Most news releases for professional and scholarly books should be directed to book reviewers or to editors responsible for assigning book reviews. Whereas the primary purpose of the standard news release is to obtain free space, generally, the primary goal of the professional or scholarly book news release is not to get published; rather, it is to arouse the interest of book reviewers or book editors enough to produce requests review copies of your book.

---

*For details on content, price, availability, and more, the reader is referred to Chapter 42 of *Book Marketing Handbook, Volume One.*

†The author recalls the practice of one publicist for a low-level technical book publisher in the electronics field who always included one or two "quoteworthy" phrases in the releases sent with review copies. When the releases were published virtually unchanged as "book reviews," the publicist would then excerpt from the "review" those same phrases and use them in the publisher's advertising, all the while attributing them to the technical periodical in which the release appeared as a review.

So, while the primary purpose of your news release is not to get editorial space, nevertheless its format should generally follow the rules for a standard news release. Bear in mind that the reviewer or book editor to whom you are sending your release is a professional and/or a specialist in the field. You must therefore keep your release factual and objective. Avoid hype—it is the fastest way to turn off a potential reviewer.

You can arouse the interest of the book reviewer or editor with the headline. Often, the headline can lead to a stronger, more intriguing, and more quotable release if you describe an aspect of the book's content rather than the book itself. For example, instead of "New Book on Medical Plants Published," why not use "Thousands of Plants Have Medical Potential Says New Book."

The release should describe the book, emphasizing its timeliness or primary contribution to the intended audience. Experienced publicists of professional and scholarly books usually place a "review copy request" coupon at the end of the release, which the reviewer or book editor (who receives the release without a book) can fill out to indicate a review copy is wanted.

Many publishers, especially those who put out high-priced or limited-edition books, automatically ship review copies to only the core or main journals in the field. All other review media will be sent a news release on the book, and will be required to request a review copy if they are interested in reviewing it.

21:06 **PR Aids Media System:**
How to Use It for News Release Dissemination

The PR Aids Media System for Effective Marketing of News Releases makes it easy—even if you are inexperienced—and inexpensive to order and use news releases effectively in conjunction with your book promotion efforts.

All ordering is done from a "Media System Order Book." PR Aids supplies you with a quantity of these order booklets, and you use one for each news release project and throw away the unused portions. The booklet system, introduced in mid-1981, replaced a system that began nearly a generation earlier and involved individual page selection from a large loose-leaf binder.

Each 32-page order booklet contains all the information you need to execute a complete order—order forms, count charts, instructions, tips, and prices—on perforated, removable pages. By placing your order with PR Aids, your news release can be produced and distributed to some 100,000 editors and writers at 26,000 media.

The PR Aids media system is kept current on a daily basis and provides a listing of more than 100,000 editors by name for trade and technical publications, professional and scholarly journals, consumer magazines, wire services, feature syndicates, Sunday supplements, syndicated columns, newsletters, the black press, foreign-language papers, local news bureaus, radio and TV networks and stations, and security analysts.

More than 3,000 interest categories, ranging from accounting, advertising, and architecture to vending, water, and wood, are grouped into sections and arranged alphabetically by title. Each category also refers you to related categories. The section on wood, for example, also refers you to construction, hobbies, and lumbering and forestry.

You also have many selection options within each category. For example, you can:

- Exclude daily, weekly, monthly, or less frequent media.
- Exclude media that charge for illustrations.
- Include only media published in selected languages.
- Restrict the distribution to media read, seen, or heard in specific state(s), province(s), metropolitan or trade areas, county, city, town, or ZIP code areas.
- Send photos to all, none, or only to those categories you have specified.
- Send photos to all media or omit media that do not use photos.

Once you have selected your media from the order book, PR Aids takes over the processing and distribution of your release—multilithing, photo prints, addressing, and mailing. PR Aids places no restrictions on the type of material you submit, and will handle anything from a one-paragraph release to a press kit.

The PR Aids order book includes a "release cost estimator" so you can estimate cost during planning stages. If you cannot figure out the cost because you have special requirements, PR Aids will give you an estimate over the phone.

Here are cities in which PR Aids has offices, together with phone numbers: New York (212-673-6363), Chicago (312-726-8693), Los Angeles (213-749-7383), Washington, D.C. (202-659-0627), Pittsburgh (412-471-9411), Southfield, Mich. (313-557-7474), and Atlanta (404-523-2515).

21:07   The PR Newswire

PR Newswire (PRN), a computerized news dissemination organization, can transmit your news releases to a wide range of media around the clock, seven days a week. The basic service, called "News-Line," reaches 150 key media in 50 cities in the East, Midwest, Southeast, and Southwest, at modest rates. Your press releases are transmitted into the NEXIS electronic news library for retrieval in full at any time by news editors and financial analysts.

This news dissemination service, in operation since 1954, provides a wide range of services. Among these are:

- "Feature News Wire," which guarantees overnight distribution of feature copy to some 400 media nationwide for less than the cost of postage.
- "Extended Coverage," which reaches media not in the PRN network or allows for saturation coverage in any of ten major U.S. cities via local PR wires.
- "Worldwide," which services media in Canada or any country, including translation when appropriate.

When your press release goes out over PR Newswire, it is stored in NEXIS, along with the full text of many of the world's leading newspapers, magazines, and wire services, including the Associated Press, United Press International, Reuters, the *Washington Post*, *Newsweek*, *U.S. News & World Report*, *The Economist*, and *Dun's Review*.

If you have a book with regional interest and wish selected regional coverage, these services are provided:

- "Metropolitan New York," which includes New York City (NYC) dailies, wire services, NYC bureaus of the *Los Angeles Times*, *Christian Science Monitor*, *Newsday*, and *London Observer*, in addition to suburban NYC dailies, radio and TV stations, and more than a score of special business and financial publications—about 60 in all.
- "Northeast Plus," which covers all of metropolitan New York (as above) and key cities in the Northeast Corridor from Washington to Boston.
- "Western," which is based in Los Angeles but is available from any PRN office, allows your release to reach some 80 leading media throughout the region, from the *Los Angeles Times* and the West Coast offices of all leading news media, including wire services, to the *Anchorage Times* in Alaska.
- "Investors Research Wire," which is available for the distribution of news releases to the investment community (banks, investment organizations, exchanges, and brokerage houses). Coverage is constantly expanding.

PR Newswire has offices in these cities: New York (150 East 58th Street, New York, NY 10155; 212-832-9400), Boston (State Street Bank Building, 225 Franklin Street, Boston, MA 02111; 617-482-5355), Los Angeles (Hilton Center Office Building, 900 Wilshire Boulevard, Los Angeles, CA 90017; 213-626-5501), and Miami (3892 Biscayne Boulevard, Miami, FL 33137; 305-576-5020).

21:08   Press Conference Planning Essentials: Checklist

- Is the book newsworthy?
- Is the author articulate?

- Have invitations been sent well in advance of the conference, giving the reasons for the conference and accompanied by a news release and copy of the book?

- Is the conference worth a phone call to all attendants the day before, both as a reminder and to ascertain whether they plan to be there or have representation?

- Will extra copies of the book and news release be freely available at the conference for those who have previously not seen them?

- Have plans been made to have half a dozen or more associates on hand as "audience-fillers" in the event that attendance is small?

- Has someone been designated to oversee the conference and keep the discussion moving and businesslike?

- Have plans been made for a news release to be prepared and issued promptly after the press conference? Will that release include newsworthy statements made by the author at the conference, and will it be distributed to those who did not attend?

21:09   Author Tours and the Scientific, Professional, or Scholarly Book

Author tours are a major marketing tool of many publishers of trade books.* However, there is virtually no potential benefit for publicity tours involving authors of scientific, professional, or scholarly works. There are rare exceptions where skillful planning and execution could make it work. For example, when your author is an authority in a particular field and has written about a major scientific breakthrough, or is a noted expert is in the field of business or investment, then a tour might succeed if your author is both articulate and personable and will agree to plug his or her book in scheduled appearances. If you are inclined to try a tour despite the high potential risk, plan well in advance of publication, and be absolutely certain that your title has a trade discount and the interest and support of larger general bookstores in the areas covered by the tour, which should agree to stock and display the book about the time your author's appearances are scheduled.

*"Organizing an Author Tour for Publicity and Perspective," The Huenefeld Report," December 22, 1980.

Part **V**

Outlets for Professional and Scholarly Books

22

Bookstores, Wholesalers, and Jobbers

22:01   **Facilitating Sales of Professional and Scholarly Books through Bookstores**

When stores encourage them, the percentage of special orders to total sales may run as high as 20%.

John P. Dessauer, in the
American Bookseller, January 1982.

Most publishers of professional and scholarly books do not consider the general trade bookstore as a source of sales. Most trade bookstores do not consider the usually short-discount professional and scholarly book as a source of profit. This seemingly hopeless situation can be remedied.

There are more than 19,000 retail book outlets in the United States. Only a minute fraction of them stock any professional and scholarly books, if at all. It is time that professional and scholarly publishers awake to the potential and opportunity that this vast network of outlets represents. Meet the bookseller halfway. Make a special effort to help make ordering hassle-free and profitable to the bookseller and then let him or her know that such orders are desired.

One means of encouraging such sales is to establish a bookseller discount policy on single-copy "special orders" that gives the bookseller a reasonable yield for a special order. A second is to establish a responsive order-fulfillment policy for bookstores, even for single-copy special orders. A third is to inform the bookseller that you welcome single-copy orders, will give them prompt attention, and provide a reasonable discount. It will also help if you indicate you provide a toll-free telephone number through which such orders can be placed.

To a bookseller, whose operating expenses may run from 25 to 35% of revenue, it is obvious that a 10% discount, coupled with a shipping charge, offers little incentive to special-order anything. However, with a toll-free telephone-ordering option and a 20 to 25% minimum discount on nontrade titles and at least 33⅓% on trade titles, many booksellers could be encouraged to become more involved with special ordering.

Your special order policy should be made known to the bookseller to indicate you want their special orders and have taken pains to encourage them. You should also supply the name of one individual or contact within your organization who is completely knowledgeable about your special order policies and to whom such orders or problems and questions can be directed for preferential handling. Such efforts can go a long way toward opening the door to special orders for your specialized professional and scholarly books from outlets that formerly refused to special-order and from which you would not normally expect to hear.

If credit is a problem, possibly booksellers could work out a bonding arrangement through the American Booksellers Association (ABA) whereby ABA would guarantee orders from a member store to a publisher up to a certain amount.

When it becomes easy for an individual to special-order any book on any subject in any area where there is a bookstore, the entire industry benefits. Booksellers can be greatly encouraged to handle and even welcome special orders—if you meet them halfway.

22:02   The Chains as Buyers of Short-Discount Professional/Reference Books

Don't overlook the large bookstore chains as potential outlets for your short-discount professional or reference books. It is a fallacy to presume that the chains will only consider books from publishers with trade discounts; in a great many instances they will carry nontrade titles. You may have to offer an agency plan that brings the base discount to a minimum of 30 to 33%, for starters. It may also be necessary to arrange your bookseller discount schedule so that several short-discount books can be purchased in groups of, say, 25 or more assorted titles at a time, at a somewhat more favorable discount than the 30 to 33% your agency plan offers.

However, chains such as Staceys on the West Coast and Kroch's and Brentano's in Chicago have a long history of success with professional and technical books and should not be overlooked. For some years now, one major chain has been offering professional and technical books at marked-up prices and encountered no serious problems with this practice. Another chain established professional/reference departments in selected stores in 1982 and has been expanding its activity in this area.

The two major chains, B. Dalton and Waldenbooks, both have specialist buyers with responsibility for buying scientific, technical, and other types of business and reference books. Dalton reorganized its buying staff in the late 1981, during which it designated one buyer for science and engineering, one buyer for electronics, computers, and medical subjects, and one buyer for books related to business/careers. Waldenbooks reorganized its book-buying staff early in 1983, so that all purchasing of books in science and technology, computers, reference, and study aids for its 770 stores now falls into a single buying category.

22:03 Incentives to Get Trade Bookstores to Stock Short-Discount Books

- Offer trade discounts on selected titles with wide appeal from your list.
- Offer paperbound editions at trade discount after the cloth edition has saturated its market.
- Offer an agency plan that provides 30% or more discount.
- Offer a discount of 30% or more on groups of assorted books.
- Run spring and fall stock promotions at a higher discount.
- If your program provides wide coverage of a particular field, offer to start the bookstore with an assortment of books in that field under an extended payment plan.
- Arrange with stores to run a "sale" on a wide assortment of your titles, say for one week, and offer cooperative advertising money in conjunction with any stock order for such an effort.

22:04 Trade Bookseller Benefits in Stocking and Selling Short-Discount Books

"I don't talk to anyone who offers books at less than 40% discount," the now retired buyer for a small trade bookstore chain once told me when I called for an appointment. I eventually got the appointment and was told I had three minutes to make my "pitch." After exactly three minutes, I was invited to leave. I couldn't think of too many good arguments for stocking short-discount books in so short a time, and I left with the feeling I had accomplished nothing (although the buyer did eventuallly stock a few of my books in one store).

It was a joy, therefore, many years later, to come across a sheet that Lyman Newlin, publishing consultant and longtime friend, had prepared for the American Booksellers Association. Entitled "On Selling Professional and Reference Books," the sheet listed benefits a trade bookstore would have by stocking short-discount books that any fast-talking marketer could easily fit into three minutes. Here they are:

1. Steady sales of comparatively high-priced books.

2. Stocking in quantity is not required. One copy of most titles will suffice in an average small store.

3. Profitability: With higher prices, a sale of one discounted (30 to 35% off) professional book at $50 gives a bookseller more dollars at less cost than would the sale of two or three trade discounted books.

4. The relatively small amount of space devoted to these books distinguishes a bookstore as one that deals in more than general trade books.

5. Once a bookseller is established as such a dealer, customers will usually special-order business and professional books not found in stock.

6. No special background is needed to handle such books—only source materials, such as *Books in Print* and *Subject Guide to Books in Print*, and a general knowledge of what publishers produce.

7. Special agency plans can provide better discounts. Most publishers of short-discount business and professional books offer a better discount to stocking booksellers through special agency plans.

22:05   ABA Handbook:
Vital Bookseller Reference Not to Be Overlooked

Ninety-seven percent of the respondents to an American Booksellers Association (ABA) member survey in March 1982 indicated they viewed the *ABA Book Buyer's Handbook* as the most valuable service of that organization. In a separate question, 98 percent said it was the ABA service they would be least willing to give up.

As a publisher, your entry in that annual publication obviously deserves prompt and serious attention. You should also not overlook the one advertising opportunity this handbook offers publishers—a listing of your ten best titles with trade appeal, whether new or backlist. Your paid entry in the *ABA Book Buyer's Handbook* gives you instant exposure to all booksellers that look at your listing.

22:06   National Association of College Stores:
Available Publisher Services

The National Association of College Stores (NACS) offers a number of publications and services of interest to publishers of professional and scholarly books. Some are available to publishers only with an associate membership. Publisher services include:

- Computer-generated labels of member stores
- A national trade fair with exhibits every April
- Eight to ten regional meetings in October and November with table-top exhibits

- Advertising space in *The College Store Journal*, published bimonthly
- *NACS NEWSCOPE*, a monthly newsletter on meetings and news from college stores
- Weekly *Confidential Bulletin* to college store managers lists changes in publisher policies, addresses, and the like
- *NACS Book Buyer's Manual*, updated and published annually as college store reference tool
- *List of School Opening and Other Dates* issued as an aid for publishers to determine deadlines for course adoptions

For details on associate membership and other NACS services, write to the National Association of College Stores, 528 East Lorain Street, P.O. Box 58, Oberlin, OH 44074; 216-776-7777.

22:07 AAP-NACS Fiche Service Now in Wide Use by College Stores

Providing details on approximately 40,000 titles, this monthly listing service is sponsored jointly by the Association of American Publishers (AAP) and the National Association of College Stores (NACS). The AAP-NACS Monthly Microfiche Service was in its start-up stage as *Volume One* of *Book Marketing Handbook* went to press (see *Volume One*, 21:20), but it is now an established and successful operation. It provides more than 500 college bookstores with updated monthly listings of in-print college textbooks of virtually all the textbook publishers.

Each listing includes title, publisher, author, edition number, ISBN, current price (list or net), anticipated new price (if any), stock status, original date of availability, out-of-print date (if applicable), binding (paper or cloth), and copyright date. The information is stored on 4″ × 6″ microfiche, readable by a 42X microfiche reader. The annual service fee to stores is economical to encourage the widest possible use. To inquire about participation in the program, contact Staff Director, Association of American Publishers, One Park Avenue, New York, NY 10016; 212-689-8920.

22:08 Functions of the Sales Rep

- Serves as an information specialist for the publisher's list.
- Builds a bridge between the publisher and the bookseller and explains house policies.
- Solves any problems existing between the bookseller and the publisher.
- Informs the bookseller of special deals or offers and promotional aids available from the publisher.
- Stimulates backlist sales by advising which titles are selling well in competitive outlets.

- Informs the bookseller of changing industry trends.
- Assists the bookseller in interpreting local market needs.

22:09   Essential Tool for Reps: The Basic Stock List

If you are using sales reps for the first time, be sure they are supplied with a seasonal basic stock list before they start making calls. Preferably your stock list or trade order form should be in two formats, first alphabetically by author and then by subject. Be sure you allow sufficient space on the form for your rep to not only write an order but also show the store's present inventory of your titles. If the stock list is compiled annually, rather than seasonally, allow extra lines under each subject category so the rep can add titles published since the list was last prepared. Some other entries your basic stock list or trade order form should include are:

1. Bill to
2. Ship to
3. Customer account number
4. Customer order number
5. Buyer's name
6. Salesperson's (rep's) name
7. Date of order
8. Blank space/lines for special information pertinent to proper fulfillment of the order.

22:10   Handles to Help Sales Rep Sell Professional and Scholarly Books

The sales rep can do most for your books when given a suitable "handle" on what to present to the bookstore. In the case of trade titles, the sales rep is likely to rely on such criteria as a book's prepublication selection by a major book club, sale of rights to a popular magazine, sale of movie or mass market paperback rights, or a large promotion budget.

But the sales rep selling professional and scholarly books looks for a different set of criteria. More often than not the salesperson is likely to use these standards for evaluating and communicating the potential of professional and scholarly books:

1. Sales record of the author's previous books or of the earlier edition of the same title
2. Availability of a successful hardcover title in paperback
3. Reputation of author as a leader or authority in the field
4. Author's professional or academic affiliation, especially if it is recognized for leadership in the field

5. Timeliness of the book's subject matter

5. Lack of new or updated material in competing works

7. Difference in approach (heavily illustrated or the like) compared to competitive works

8. Usefulness of format (for example, pocket-size handbook in flexible binding compared with larger competing work in hardcover)

9. Status of the publisher as a leader in the field of the book

22:11   Purposes of a Sales Conference

1. Present highlights of books to be published during the coming season.

2. Provide information on the list in general and on upcoming or needed changes in selling policies.

3. Indoctrinate new sales reps hired since the last sales conference.

4. Provide an environment in which there is dialogue and beneficial information exchange among reps.

5. Obtain feedback on trends and practices of the competition.

6. Obtain feedback on changing trends in the trade.

7. Allow for dialogue between the reps, editors, and sometimes management and staff.

8. Provide motivation for the reps.

9. Present selling techniques helpful to the reps in the field.

10. Permit reps to air grievances and resolve problems of mutual concern.

22:12   How to Make a Sales Presentation Go Over with the Reps

Commission reps may serve many different publishers and have looser ties with any one publisher's list than would a salaried rep, who is in frequent contact with the home office and under its supervision. However, both the commission sales representative and the full-time salaried salesperson share a common basic need: to have a "handle" on upcoming books with sales potential when selling to stores in their territory.

According to the classic *Klein's Comprehensive Etymological Dictionary of the English Language* (Elsevier, 1965), one of the derivations of the word "handle" is from the Swedish *höndla*, meaning "to seize, capture"; "to treat." This definition crystallizes the basic need of each sales rep: to have a few choice words that seize or capture the essence of each forthcoming title with bookstore potential.

The following comments stress the importance and value of the "handle" and reinforce the belief that long-winded, detailed descriptions at sales conferences may be counterproductive and turn the salespeople off.

What I look for at sales conferences . . . is the proper "handle" for each of the new books. We need a capsule description, the shorter the better, that puts the book in the most realistic light as far as potential bookstore sales are concerned.

> Commission rep George Scheer,
> *Book Traveler*, Dodd, Mead & Co., 1973.

When we make our calls, we have to find an expeditious, concise handle for a book that says a lot about it in as few words as possible.

> Sales rep Stanley Gould, San Francisco
> in *Publishers Weekly*, September, 3, 1982.

Find out . . . why this was a good book to publish and translate that to the sales reps so that [it] has a marketing and sales slant to it as opposed to a contents slant . . . our customers aren't looking for long scenarios for each book; they're looking for a handle on which to sell it.

> Al Reuben, Marketing Director, Simon &
> Schuster, in *Publishers Weekly*, September 3, 1982.

In summary, a sales presentation should tell the reps what a book is about, the audience for which it is intended, and what its bookstore potential may be—in words adequate to cover the subject and short enough to give the reps a "handle" on the book without having them mull over pages of notes.

22:13   **Bookseller Discount and Sales Rep Policy
of Handbook Publisher**

A short-discount publisher with a wide range of handbooks in the business and engineering disciplines successfully employed for many years a handbook discount schedule of 20% for orders of 1 to 2 copies, 33⅓% for 3 to 24 copies, and 40% for 25 or more copies of assorted titles.

For coverage by the publisher's salaried sales force of five, bookstore accounts were divided into three categories. Stores with greatest potential (category 1) were visited several times each year by the sales reps who also had responsibility for writing up orders, restocking, and returns. Category 2 stores, with less potential, were called upon about once a year, often when the salesperson was making a call on a category 1 store in the vicinity. Category 3 stores were not visited by the sales reps and were covered by mail and other means.

The 40% discount policy for 25 or more assorted titles proved very effective. The publisher reported that often, when a sales rep would write up an order that fell short of the 25, the bookseller would either increase the order to make the 40%, or else stall the order until an order of 25 or more copies could be placed. This kept the bookseller concentrating on a variety of the publisher's titles in order to maintain the maximum (40%) discount, and helped keep some of the publisher's older titles in stock in the stores.

22:14   **Solution to Sales Rep Calls during the Christmas Season**

A professional and reference book publisher with a salaried sales force
has found a useful way to keep the reps busy during the Christmas
season, when it is not possible for them to call on bookstores. The reps
volunteer to work a minimum of three days as nonsalaried salespersons
for several of their largest accounts. The rewards are considerable. The
reps are enthusiastic about the idea and gain new insights into both the
problems of the bookseller and customers' reactions to their own books
on display in the store. The bookseller develops a greater appreciation
for the publisher and a closer bond to the sales rep in future dealings,
and is grateful for help during the one time of the year when it is most
needed.

22:15   **Bookseller Follows Rep's Suggestion**
         and Has Windfall Profit on Handbook

A publisher was about to issue a new edition (the first in many years)
of a handbook that had been the bible of professionals and students in
the field for more than a generation. The publisher's rep was making a
periodic sales call on one of his accounts that regularly sold a substantial number of books in the subject area covered by the handbook.

"Why not," suggested the rep, "open the yellow pages of your phone
directory and call these people. Tell them the new edition is being
published shortly and ask how many copies they would like to
reserve." The bookseller followed the rep's advice, and found that it
worked. He subsequently placed a substantial prepublication order for
the new edition that netted him several thousand dollars in profit.

22:16   **Selling to the Bookstore by Mail When**
         You Have No Sales Reps: Guidelines

1. Compile a list of prospects from previous orders received and from
    such directory sources as the *American Book Trade Directory* and
    the *ABA Book Buyers Handbook*. If you have a common trade dis-
    count policy, a single list can include both retail booksellers and
    wholesalers.

2. As early as convenient, write to each outlet on your list to find out
    the name of the buyer for your type of books, and place that per-
    son's name on the list. Then monitor incoming orders to see that
    the name has not changed.

3. In an initial mailing or as new names are added, write to the
    bookseller to explain that although you employ no sales reps, you
    are interested in keeping the bookseller informed about your forth-
    coming publications, and that you will periodically issue bulletins,
    previews, announcements, and the like.

4. Include a list of pertinent backlist titles and/or titles in preparation. Also include a statement that clearly spells out your publishing direction, discounts, returns, and co-op policies (if applicable). Also supply detailed information on shipping—how you ship, origin of shipments, charges, and average turnaround time on orders received.

5. Include a catalog, if one is available, and one or two postpaid return envelopes.

6. In your initial mailing, offer an agency plan, if one is available. If not, offer incentives for stock orders, such as a larger discount for an initial order or any prepub order for forthcoming titles, free freight with or without special conditions, or a volume discount (for example, one book free with each order of ten).

7. Establish a standard, recognizable format for your announcements of forthcoming books that will readily identify each of your mailings.

8. Mail regularly, as well as in appropriate seasons or periods, so that your announcements are expected.

9. Monitor booksellers' ordering patterns. When any title on your list shows unusual activity, suggest compatible titles on your backlist. Also alert booksellers to forthcoming titles that are compatible with earlier titles that have sold well.

10. As finances permit, take a booth at the American Booksellers Association (ABA) annual meeting to display as much of your list as possible. Feature forthcoming titles with special incentives for placing orders at ABA. Then mail invitations to your accounts to visit your booth.

11. Be sure your sales policies and terms are listed in the *ABA Book Buyers Handbook*, and pay the small additional fee to include some of your better backlist titles in your listing. Also be sure you are listed in the *American Book Trade Directory* and in *Publisher's Trade List Annual*. All of these can generate mail orders from the book trade.

12. If appropriate, subscribe to ABA's STOP (Single Title Order Plan) and mention this in all of your mailings to booksellers.

22:17   **Building a Bookstore Mailing List for Professional and Scholarly Books**

At best, retail bookstore outlets in the United States that are consistently solid prospects for most professional and scholarly books number in the hundreds. If your publishing program is aimed at this selected group, your bookstore mailing list should include only those outlets whose wants are compatible with your publishing program. All wholesalers that handle books in your subject area should be included.

Initially, the names for your bookstore mailing list may be based on a list of bookstores that have previously ordered from you, augmented perhaps by entries selected from the most recent *American Book Trade Directory*. Avoid the "buckshot" approach by limiting your bookstore list to those that are active buyers. Be sure the address includes the name of the individual who signs the book orders.

Once your bookstore mailing list has been established, tailor an agency order plan that will provide a strong incentive for those on the list to place a standing order for all of your publications in their special-interest areas. Expand this list by adding names of booksellers who have contacted you by phone or mail for information on any of your books. Your agency accounts, as well as the nonagency accounts that order from you on an irregular basis, should ultimately comprise your basic bookstore mailing list. When you publish a book that has broader interest or trade potential, larger bookstore lists can be obtained from the R. R. Bowker Co. as needed for special mailings.

WHEN AND WHAT TO MAIL

For mailings to your bookstore list, develop an identifiable newsletter or "preview" format with matching envelope. Mailings of your newsletter, preview, special announcement, price list, or catalog—(if issued on a cyclical basis) will build recognition and identity for your company or list in the eyes of prospective bookseller accounts.

On a periodic enclosure, invite booksellers on your mailing list to indicate special interests or requests to be removed from your mailing list. The same enclosure should allow for address corrections or other notices of change (for example, the name of the new bookstore buyer).

When coding your bookseller list according to special interests, you should consult your records of past bookstore orders, particularly for nonagency accounts that have not specified areas of interest. A bookstore's failure to order directly from you may not necessarily mean it is not ordering your books and should therefore be removed from the list. The bookseller may be ordering your books from wholesalers, based on information it receives in your mailed announcements.

22:18   **Promoting Available Textbooks:**
Problem-Preventing Guidelines

If your list includes college textbooks, you can eliminate many service problems in advance by describing as explicitly as possible the availability of forthcoming titles in your promotional announcements to college stores. Following are problem-preventing guidelines:

1. When a forthcoming book has textbook application, promotion to college stores should clearly specify (by semester or season) whether the book can be delivered in time for the start of classes.

2. If you are promoting a new edition of a presently used text, specify in your promotional copy that orders for the coming semester will be filled with the new edition.

3. If delivery of the new edition cannot be guaranteed for the start of

classes, stores should be informed that the new edition is pending and the current edition will be supplied on all orders for the upcoming semester.

4. If both new and old editions will be available for the upcoming semester, specify that unless the old edition is specifically requested, the new edition will be shipped.

22:19   Should You Mail Those Semiannual Price Lists to Bookstores?

"No," says one trade sales manager. His trade reps report that, as a rule, the bookstores seldom refer to publisher price lists. If your price list is bound into *PTLA (Publishers Trade List Annual)*, additional mailings to bookstores are an unnecessary expense. You might make an exception for your agency bookstores or those stores that request such price lists. Stores favor price lists that contain a listing of out-of-print titles by product line or subject. A price list prevents occasional orders for a book already out of print.

22:20   Useful Tips for the Small Publisher

In his *Guide to Book Publishing* (Huenefeld, 1978), John Huenefeld advises:

Avoid creating specific promotions for single books—and concentrate instead on developing on-going contacts with audiences likely to buy more than one book, on more than one occasion.

If your list includes an expensive title with a number of pages in color that are important to the sales appeal of the book, overprint the color pages and include one or more sample pages with your bookstore promotion. If the book is already printed, utilize the pages from damaged books as mailing samples.

If your list includes a title with an extensive table of contents, such as a manual or handbook, have the contents set in such a way that they can be repositioned and used as copy for a promotional flier on the books.

Make the title of every book a selling tool, or mini-advertisement, for the book.

22:21   Small Mail-Order Publishers Favor USPS for Bookseller Contacts

Sixteen of 24 mail-order publishers of professional and scholarly books, responding to a survey (*The Huenefeld Report*, March, 31, 1980), reported they rely on the mail to announce new titles to major bookseller accounts. All of the publishers were in the $1 million annual sales range. Six in 24 reported using the telephone. Only 3 of the 24 had commissioned reps.

22:22   **Telemarketing System Boosts Sales to Small Trade Accounts:
Case Study**

This multiple-imprint publisher had thousands of bookseller accounts scattered throughout the country that were not visited by sales reps. Most accounts were too small, their activity too infrequent, or their locations so remote that sales calls would have been too expensive or impractical.

Could these small accounts be converted into greater revenue producers if a telephone channel were open to them? The idea was investigated and discussed with telephone company representatives by the publisher's director of distribution services, and in July 1981, a jointly designed telemarketing program was implemented.

The program was launched with the installation of a telemarketing department at the publisher's suburban distribution center. At the core of this telemarketing operation were seven special telephone lines. Three were used for incoming toll-free calls from booksellers and four were WATS lines, which permit large numbers of outgoing long-distance calls at low prices.

Simultaneously, a telephone sales department was started. Six telephone sales reps, after a brief training program, were engaged to operate the department. Three of these were individuals with customer-service backgrounds and the other three were hired specifically to sell over the telephone.

Here's how the telephone sales program was launched:

1. A letter was sent to all company accounts not called on by sales reps to announce the establishment of a telephone sales department. The letter stressed that calls or inquiries could be made to the telephone sales department via the toll-free number provided; that a telephone sales representative was available to handle bookseller calls or inquiries; and that the bookseller would shortly receive a phone call from the telephone sales representative handling his or her account.

2. Along with the letter, catalogs and descriptions of current publisher products were sent.

3. After the mailing, a telephone sales rep called the account. The purpose of the call was to qualify the account. Some of the accounts were so small or their activity so infrequent that company records did not even list a contact person for the account.

4. After the telephone sales rep's call, individual records were established for each bookseller to track orders and other activity.

How did this telemarketing program work? In comparison to sales for the first three months of telemarketing activity (July–September 1981), the publisher reported that sales activity during the July–September 1982 quarter in the same accounts increased by 62%. Even if your own publishing operation is modest, there are basic lessons to be learned here that can be applied by anyone.

22:23   **First Bookstore Sweepstakes Promotion for
Professional and Reference Books**

The first sweepstakes offering for professional and reference books
through bookstores was tried in late 1982 by John Stockwell of the
McGraw-Hill Professional and Reference Book Division. The promotion involved a mailing of sweepstakes kits to all of McGraw-Hill's
agency plan members who stock its professional and reference titles.

The kit consisted of a countertop poster offering prizes (the first
prize was a $6,000 Apple computer system), 500 sweepstakes entry
forms, and window banners inviting the public to enter the store and
enter the McGraw-Hill sweepstakes.

The entry form contained a listing of 30 best-selling professional and
reference titles that could be ordered, and asked the entrant whether
he or she had bought one of the books. Sweepstakes entrants were required to add their own postage and mail the entry form back to
McGraw-Hill.

Stores were invited to stock the books offered on the entry form and
could order by calling their McGraw-Hill rep or John Stockwell.
Reorders were rushed back to the stores by express mail.

22:24   **Assorted Bookseller Services Available from Trade Wholesalers**

- Across-the-board uniform discount on all trade titles
- Cash discount for prompt payment
- Free or reduced freight
- Toll-free or collect telephone orders
- Weekly microfiche service of available titles
- Books of small and hard-to-locate presses
- Catalogs and new-title lists
- Rapid order fulfillment
- Computer-assisted instant order verification
- Warehouse nearby
- Cooperative advertising policy
- Single invoice and payment for orders of assorted titles from various
  publishers
- Electronic hookup with stores for easier ordering
- Automatic new book order plans
- Programs for book advertising
- Open warehouse for bookseller shopping

22:25   **Library Wholesaling: Baker & Taylor Continues to Dominate**

The field of library wholesaling continues to be dominated by the Baker
& Taylor Companies, the nation's oldest and largest book wholesaler.

Baker & Taylor operated from a single location, in Hillside, N.J., until the early 1960s, when it decentralized. It presently serves libraries from regional centers in New Jersey, Illinois, Georgia, and Nevada, with executive offices in New York City. The four regional branches of this venerable supplier, founded in 1828,* carry in-depth stocks of important and reasonably active titles of virtually all publishers.

Much of Baker & Taylor's growth over the past quarter-century has been due to a combination of factors: extremely efficient service to libraries, decentralization, and the disappearance of many competing national and regional library jobbers. Among the largest were American News Co., A. C. McClurg, J. W. Stacey, Campbell & Hall, Inc., and Acme Code Co. Baker & Taylor's major New Jersey competitor had been A. H. Roemer & Co. of Summit.

Baker & Taylor's on-approval program for libraries was non-existent when this writer became sales and promotion manager of the company in 1959, and did not emerge for at least a decade thereafter. By mid-1982, the program was a more than $10 million operation and was still growing, aided largely by the demise of Richard Abel & Co., Inc.,† in 1974.

Baker & Taylor and Blackwell North America, Inc., both stepped in to fill the vacuum created by the loss of the "Abel approval plan," which was started in the 1960s by Richard Abel mainly for academic libraries. The plan provided the library with selected new books on approval in predetermined categories at the earliest possible date after publication.

Blackwell North America, as a second beneficiary of the Abel demise, continues to rank as the second largest library supplier for professional and scholarly books in the United States. Blackwell started its operation by acquiring the assets, premises, and records of the bankrupt Abel company.

22:26   **Competing against Medical Jobbers
Teaches Publisher a Lesson: Case Study**

The operations of a medical jobber are quite different from those of the typical trade or library jobber. First, the medical jobber is a trade wholesaler who serves booksellers in the area with the books of all medical publishers and who generally carries good inventories and gives fast, efficient service. Second, this jobber is a supplier for medical libraries and, third, functions as a direct seller, employing a sales force to call on accounts and serve the medical book needs of practitioners in the area.

---

*Originally a book publisher and then a combined publisher-wholesaler, Baker & Taylor ceased its book publishing operations in 1912 to devote its efforts exclusively to book distribution. For details, see Nat. G. Bodian, "More than a Century of Service," *The Book Buyer's Guide* Vol. 63, no. 784 (September 1960): 143.

†A detailed, authoritative account of this company's history may be found in "The Rise and Fall of Richard Abel and Co., Inc." by Lyman W. Newlin, veteran bookman and assistant to Richard Abel. The article appeared in *Scholarly Publishing* Vol. 7, no. 1 (October 1975): 55–61.

The college division of one large publisher learned the hard way in the mid-1970s that it is difficult to beat bookstore competition from medical jobbers. The company had a medical and nursing book line, and it was felt that sales in universities with medical schools could be greatly increased if college reps would make sales calls and promote medical and nursing books, thereby, in effect, competing with the medical jobbers.

But sales did not increase. What happened was that the bookstores ordered from both the publisher and the medical jobber, and in some instances they overordered. When the needs were not as large as the orders, returns were sent directly to the publisher for credit. The publishers' direct sales were small to begin with, and returns were erasing up to half of its sales. The publisher ultimately got the message and discontinued its college reps' sales calls on medical and nursing faculty and other attempts to compete for the college store orders.

Medical jobbers are favored as a source of supply in the textbook adoption market because they give prompt attention to orders and exert special efforts in emergencies. Marketers in the know learn quickly to work through, and not compete against, them.

23

Libraries

23:01   **Differentiating the Various Facets of
the Complex Library Market**

We wish to restate the premise stated in *Volume One* of *Book Marketing Handbook* that the library market must be a primary concern for the marketer of scientific, technical, professional, scholarly, and reference books. No marketer can hope to succeed without some understanding of the various facets of the library world and the different buying practices and requirements of each.

In this chapter, we dissect this diverse market—public, college and university, special, and school libraries—and provide you with clear insights into each, based on interviews, survey and study results, and the author's own experiences of more than twenty years.

We start by indicating the major influences that dictate the book-purchasing practices of each type of library, list the major promotional vehicles suited to most libraries, suggest formats and approaches that work best in the different types of libraries, and describe how the libraries view and make use of the materials that publishers send to them.

Supplied with this knowledge, even the most inexperienced marketer will understand how, in a universe of some 104,000 U.S. libraries, each segment can be approached in the most practical and cost-effective way. Case studies both in this chapter and throughout the book reinforce this information and provide examples of tried and tested approaches.

It should be noted that more than two-thirds of U.S. libraries are af-

269

filiated with schools, whether elementary, junior high, or high. Because of the size of this library segment and its special nature, separate treatment of school libraries as a market for professional and scholarly books is given in Chapter 25.

For other entries in this volume pertaining to libraries, see 4:07, 6:07, 7:02, 7:05, 10:06, 10:07, 18:12, 18:17, 22:25, 25:01, 25:02, 25:03, 25:04, 25:12, 25:14, 28:20, 32:08, 34:14, 34:17, and 36:02.

23:02 **Major Influences on Book Selection in Libraries**

- In academic libraries: Faculty and students
- In special libraries: Clientele
- In public libraries: Library staff, based on needs of community served
- In secondary school libraries: Teachers and supervisors and, to a lesser extent, students

23:03 **Librarians' Attitudes toward Purchase of Reference Books: Survey Results**

Librarians do not necessarily wait for reviews to buy new editions of reference works. They like to receive notice of forthcoming new editions of reference works at least three to six months before publication. They are not deterred from buying hardcover editions by the much lower price of a paperback edition. And they recognize no particular buying season for reference books.

These were some of the findings that came out of a survey of library practices for buying reference works. The study, conducted by Worldmark Press in late 1981, tallied the first 200 replies (35%) from a survey group of 560 libraries.

About 80% of the respondents in this survey were from an approximately equal number of public and secondary school librarians; the remaining 20% were divided between elementary school and college libraries. The answers that follow should provide guidance for the promotion of many types of reference works aimed at the broad library market.

Key questions in the survey (with responses) were:

Q. Do you rely on reviews before purchasing a new edition of a reference book when you already own the previous edition?
A. Yes: 27%   No: 64%

Q. Do you buy reference materials only after seeing a favorable review?
A. Yes: 40%   No: 54%

Q. When you have the previous edition of a major reference work, when do you like to be informed about a new edition?

A. 6 months in advance: 42%
   3 months in advance: 35%
   1 year in advance: 14%
   On publication: .5%

Q. Do you buy paperback reference books?
A. Yes: 61%   No: 27.5%

Q. If the price of the paper edition of a reference work is half the price of the equivalent hardcover, would you buy two paperbacks instead to increase circulations?
A. Yes: 23%   No: 33%

Q. What time of year are you most likely to purchase reference books?
A. Spring: 25%
   Fall: 24%
   Winter: 13%
   Anytime: 36%

Q. Which reviewing sources do you rely on for guidance in purchasing reference books:
A. *Booklist*: 66.5%
   Library Journal: 63%
   Wilson's Library Bulletin: 34.5%

23:04   **How to Increase Share of Library Market:
        Friedland's Prescription**

There is no advantage to pricing a book lower in order to increase your share of the library market. So says Abbot Friedland, marketing director of Princeton University Press: "If a library has $100 to spend and is considering ten books, five priced at $50 and five priced at $10, and if the two best books are in the $50 category, the library will buy the two best."

Friedland, speaking before a group of book marketers at a Society for Scholarly Publishing marketing seminar held in New York on October 21, 1981, made his point on pricing scholarly monographs for the library market with this example: You publish a book priced at $50. You estimate that, on the basis of the price and subject, 90% will sell to libraries and 10% to individuals. Using list prices for this example, your income will be as follows:

900 copies @ $50 to libraries	$45,000
100 copies @ $50 to individuals	$ 5,000
Total Income:	$50,000

You estimate that if the book were priced at only $25, you would sell 10% more to libraries and four times as many to individuals. At half price, with the increased sales, your income would be:

1,000 copies @ $25 to libraries	$25,000
400 copies @ $25 to individuals	$10,000
Total Income:	$35,000

Friedland concludes, "If you want to sell more books to libraries, don't reduce the price—produce a better book."

23:05   Basics of Library Promotion: A Checklist

1. Space advertising in library/publishing media
2. Book reviews in library/publishing media
3. Seasonal announcements
4. Subject mailings
5. Catalogs
6. Solo announcements/special projects
7. Inventory-reduction sales
8. Newsletters
9. Standing/selective-order programs
10. Exhibits at library conventions/meetings
11. Cooperative book exhibits at library conventions/meetings
12. News releases

23:06   The Importance of Price in a Library Promotion

"Why are you bothering me before I can order it?" This was the reaction of a librarian who was asked how he felt about book advertising in which no prices were given.

"When you're advertising a book for sale and soliciting orders, you should have the book reasonably close to publication and priced," according to this librarian.

Price is critical in any decision to order for most libraries. It is an essential piece of information for this market, and no selling can be done from a promotion that lacks prices. The author and title are important, but the next question every librarian asks is "How much is it?" Other questions may follow, for example, regarding the author's reputation or credentials. But if you promote to the library market and your books lack prices, try to at least include a tentative price that will give the librarian some idea of how much of a bite the book will take out of the budget.

23:07   A Library Professional Offers Advice to Library Marketers*

- Don't address a mailing to me with my name misspelled.
- Don't send me literature on books outside my sphere of interest.

*At a seminar of the Publisher's Library Marketing Group on "Direct Marketing Techniques to Libraries," which was held in New York on October 12, 1982. Additional tips on copy that will help sales of professional and reference books to libraries may be found in 13:03.

- Don't use a copy approach that will insult my intelligence.
- Don't make me tie up library funds to reserve a book you have indicated as being "in press" unless you intend to publish it.
- Don't try to sell me an important or expensive work without including some credentials of the author, unless he or she is nationally known.
- Don't fail to be clear in your opening statement if you expect me to read the rest of your literature.

23:08 Why This Library Promotion Was Bound to Fail: Case Study

The mailing was an attractive package that was sent to the membership of the Art Libraries Society of North America, a group of more than 1,000 career professionals in art librarianship. The acronym for this professional library group is ARLIS.

The opening of the letter read, "Dear ARLIC member." One librarian who received the mailing reported, "It immediately turned me off; they couldn't even get the organization acronym straight." The promotion offered a newsletter to this professional group and promised to provide an exclusive and unique source for information about art. No mention was made of author credentials, according to the recipient, who discarded the promotion piece without reading it and doubted whether anyone else in the ARLIS group reacted differently.

The lessons to be learned here are:

(1) When you address a professional group, be sure you spell the group's name or acronym correctly.

(2) When you are writing copy addressed to professionals, remember that they dislike hyperbole and superlatives and won't respond to this approach.

(3) If you are selling information to professionals about their own field, the author must be someone known and respected—if not within the group, at least in the field—if your book is to have credibility.

23:09 Notes on Catalog Use by Public Libraries

Librarians find publisher catalogs most effective when arranged by subject and then alphabetically by author, and when all new titles are clearly marked and show month and year of publication.

Librarians often rely on *Publishers' Trade List Annual* (*PTLA*) to ascertain a correct title or spelling of an author's name and, in the acquisitions departments of large public libraries, to verify orders. *PTLA* compiles annually 1,500 publisher catalogs and price lists, arranged alphabetically and bound into six permanent clothbound volumes. For details on participation in *PTLA*, contact R. R. Bowker Co., 1180 Avenue of the Americas, New York, NY 10036.

23:10   **Formats that Work Best for Public Library Promotions**

Do public libraries favor any particular format for publishers' promotional materials? Apparently not, if you heed the word of librarian Betty Gay, assistant to the library director of the Los Angeles Public Library. In a talk at the 1981 Society for Scholarly Publishing annual meeting in San Francisco, Gay said all formats for publishers' advertising materials are considered.

However, for whatever format you choose, one essential ingredient should be included in any promotional announcement: complete bibliographic information. These were some of Gay's further comments:

- Publication date must be present.
- An ISBN is helpful.
- An annotation, abstract, or evaluation helps attract attention to a particular book.
- Catalogs should be arranged by subject, then alphabetically by author.
- New-title entries should be so identified in the catalog and should show both month and year of publication.
- Expensive publishing projects should be announced as far in advance as possible to allow for proper budgeting.

Whatever the format, don't devote too much attention or effort in your public library promotion to the response vehicle. Your order will most likely come to you through a library jobber.

23:11   **Ways in Which Academic Libraries Use
Publishers' Seasonal Catalogs**

1. To prepare orders and/or for future reference
2. To note new volumes in series that are on standing order
3. To consult with faculty on certain titles
4. To circulate to selected faculty members
5. To place on faculty shelf in library
6. To send to college bookstore

23:12   **Formats and Approaches that Work Best for
Promotions to College Libraries**

1. Seasonal catalogs or consolidated announcements are favored over single-title announcements sent separately.
2. Other formats include consolidated announcements grouped by subject (subject catalogs), timely announcements in individual subject areas, and announcements sent in newsletter format at cyclical intervals.

3. A uniform format aids recognition of your imprint.

4. Include ISBN, LC number, and level of book.

5. Listing of related backlist titles with new-title announcements is considered helpful by librarians and may help your backlist sales.

6. Mail reasonably close to availability dates (for new titles).

7. Where special offers with expiration dates are involved, allow sufficient time for processing before the offer expires.

8. If "library recommendation" cards are sent simultaneously to faculty, librarians indicate a preference for $3'' \times 5''$ cards.

23:13   The Special Libraries Environment

"There are almost as many types of special libraries," says William A. Katz in *Special Collections: The Selection of Materials for Libraries* (New York: Holt, 1980) "as [there are] definitions of the term." "The special library," says Katz, "is usually part of a much larger unit, often another library, [such as] special collections within academic libraries . . . rare book rooms, map collections."

Staffed by information professionals, the special library may often specialize in a single subject, such as map collections, and must meet the particular information needs of its clientele. The acquisitions policy may be informal rather than explicit and is generally tied to the special library's aim of providing useful and important service to its clientele.

However, at another end of the special library spectrum is the corporate library, serving the diversified needs of the corporation and its various departments. The corporate library, even in a number of "Fortune 100" companies, is staffed by two professionals, one of whom would be the "manager" of the corporate library or information center. The other would have a title such as "information specialist."

Special librarians are resource specialists. They know how to search for and locate information quickly. Being information-service oriented, the special librarian does not necessarily view the special library as a depository for books; the physical objects that contain a library's information holdings are of secondary importance.* The special library's great dependency on current materials is reflected in the high rate of turnover of acquired materials. Most materials, says Katz in *Special Collections*, are retained for two to five years at best.

In any small special library, whether in a corporate or other environment, collection development is either handled by a single individual or is a shared responsibility. Therefore, your library promotion mailing is best addressed to either the library manager or librarian. So advises Debra Kaufman, former information specialist at the American Can Co. corporate library.

---

*According to Edythe Moore, manager of library services at the Aerospace Corp., in a statement she made at the Third Annual Society for Scholarly Publishing Meeting in San Francisco, June 1981.

For large libraries, or for a library where a single individual may be responsible for the development of a special collection within a larger environment, your promotional mailings should be addressed to the head of collection development if it is to reach the appropriate individual (titles for this position may vary from one library to another). Such individuals, while making the acquisitions, do discuss purchases with other staff members who are sensitive to the special information needs of the library's users.

23:14   **Formats and Approaches that Work Best for Special Library Promotions**

Special libraries collect, organize, and disseminate information on a special subject (or subjects) to a specialized clientele. The special library provides information to meet the immediate needs of members of its parent company or sponsor.

The special librarian is an information specialist or professional. Any time you as a marketer spend discussing your work with a special librarian will prove richly rewarding, for the special librarian, as a rule, has a tremendous grasp of all the literature and publishing output in his or her special field. On more than one occasion, this writer has learned new information about his own publications from talks with special librarians. Some special librarians have professional experience in their own special subject area in addition to an advanced degree in library science.

Your direct-mail promotion to special libraries, especially if you announce books and publications related to their special interests, is welcomed and usually fully utilized. Some of your efforts to promote to the special library will translate into immediate orders. Other promotional mailings or announcements, if not needed immediately, may be routed to other concerned individuals within the sponsoring organization or may be filed for future reference in the library.

What types of promotion do special librarians want from you? Here are a few:

- General announcements of forthcoming books
- Catalogs (both general and subject)
- Advance announcements of major reference works
- Special prepublication offers
- Information on subscription plans and offers
- Information on standing order plans

Unlike the public librarian who looks for complete bibliographic information (see 23:10), the special librarian is more concerned about having a detailed description of the information package being offered and an indication that the offering is up-to-date and reliable. Special librarians may assume that offers from some of the larger publishing houses are current and reliable, but smaller houses may have to offer more proof. This can easily be done by including on all offers the publication year (and month, if fairly recent) along with the author's business or professional affiliation and other credentials that imply authority or reliability.

Special libraries also buy paperback editions of peripheral reference materials, so if you have these available, include them in your promotions. Try to be as accurate as possible on availability dates for major forthcoming works. If the work is to be a serial, indicate the time span over which the serial will be published, the number of volumes planned (if known), and the number of volumes to be published each year. Also indicate whether the serial is sold by subscription, whether the subscription price is guaranteed for the entire work, and whether you offer a subscription discount that gives the librarian an incentive to order the entire work at once.

Another question you should answer in subscription offerings is whether payment must be made up front for the special subscription price, or whether individual volumes will be billed at the special subscription rate as each volume is published.

Lists of special librarians compiled by name should be avoided if you want to reach the special library with your announcement only once. Some companies and institutions encourage staff professionals to hold membership in the Special Libraries Association (SLA), whose membership directory may be a source for such lists. The pitfall of mailing to librarians by name is that companies such as DuPont, which has many libraries and perhaps 20 or more professionals, could receive multiple copies of mailings to individuals employed in the same library. The 11,500 SLA membership work at 6,800 different business addresses. To prevent duplications, mail to a list of libraries. If you want to reach a specific individual within that library, direct the mailing to the attention of the librarian you wish to reach by job function.

A final tip for special library promotions is this: Always include the name (and direct-dial number, if possible) of a responsible individual in your firm whom a librarian can call when there is a question about one of your mail or advertising offers. Special librarians make good use of the telephone and frequently order by phone, following up with a confirming order.

Inclusion of the name of a contact person in your space ad and mail promotions can provide the added benefit of cross-selling. Special librarians who telephone are open to suggestions about related pertinent publications on your list and frequently will order them on the strength of a recommendation made by the individual in your firm who takes the phone call. That individual should make it clear that such orders will be sent "on approval" and may be returned without obligation if unsatisfactory. Few are ever returned.

23:15   Guide to Special Libraries in International Markets with List Selection Options

If you wish to reach special libraries in international markets, a major source for such lists is the R. R. Bowker Co., in either New York or

London. Bowker's special libraries lists offer the greatest number of selectivity options, including type of library, geographic location, subject specialization, nonbook materials held, size (based on number of volumes), and multimedia facilities available. Additional features of the Bowker lists are:

- When different types of libraries are specified in a single order, duplicates are automatically omitted. Thus, if one order includes special libraries for both medicine and science and technology, you receive only one label if the library specializes in both subjects.
- You can screen out certain categories of libraries. For example, you can specify all art and architecture libraries in Italy, except university libraries.
- If you do not specify a position or title, your label will automatically be addressed to "Librarian." However, you may specify and receive as a substitute any of these 12 titles: Serials Librarian, Acquisitions Librarian, City Librarian, Divisional Librarian, Reference Librarian, Area Librarian, Regional Librarian, the Librarian, the Chief Librarian, County Librarian, Director of Libraries, and the Archivist.
- You may also specify a particular subject by Dewey decimal classification, using the numbers 0 through 999.

The accompanying tables indicate by country and subject the number of special libraries you can reach using Bowker's mailing lists.

23:16   Blanket-Order Plans for Libraries

The blanket-order plan, referred to by many as the "Greenaway plan,"* is an agreement between the publisher and the library whereby the publisher sends the library one copy of each title published prior to publication date and often at a higher library discount with no return privilege. Most such arrangements allow for limitations as agreed to by both parties. Such limitations may restrict plan shipments to trade titles only, to a particular type of trade title, to books on certain subjects only, to books up to a certain price ceiling, and other such variations as the participating library may request. Most plans involve trade titles only and are designed to aid larger public libraries and library systems in making a speedier decision on their multiple-copy orders.

23:17   Why Publishers' Continuation-Order Plans Fail to Thrive

Most libraries prefer to receive their books through their jobber or wholesaler and do so except when the works of a particular publisher offer a special incentive for direct ordering or when there are problems

*Named after Emerson Greenaway, former director of the Free Library of Philadelphia, who originated the concept of a blanket-order plan in 1958.

GUIDE TO SPECIAL LIBRARY LISTS EXCLUSIVE OF THE UNITED KINGDOM AND WESTERN EUROPE

By Subject, Count,* and Country or Area Specified

Country	Medicine	Law	Social Sciences	Religion & Philosophy	Business & Economics	Science & Technology	Music	Art & Architecture	Agriculture, Fisheries, Forestry	Literature & Languages	History	Geography & Environment	Politics & International Affairs
Middle East/North Africa	130	89	215	135	308	736	27	260	150	310	280	75	78
West, East, and Central Africa	65	55	90	45	140	160	19	120	118	175	125	55	29
Southern Africa	115	89	190	100	236	250	37	170	200	180	215	50	52
Hong Kong	28	15	60	35	45	42	7	27	9	145	35	30	10
Japan	153	110	200	100	476	500	18	135	130	165	155	33	77
India	99	65	125	70	175	245	34	170	160	165	165	55	40
Pakistan	20	18	35	100	50	35	1	23	15	35	49	9	26
Other Asia/Indian Ocean/Southeast Asia	200	140	300	20	340	550	45	290	300	325	320	140	100
Australasia	378	149	442	95	849	1,135	89	641	390	365	286	113	135
Total	1,188	730	1,757	700	2,719	3,653	277	1,836	1,472	1,860	1,630	560	547

*Counts shown are approximate; verify at time of use.

GUIDE TO SPECIAL LIBRARY LISTS IN THE UNITED KINGDOM AND WESTERN EUROPE

By Subject, Count,* and Country

Country	Medicine	Law	Social Sciences	Religion & Philosophy	Business & Economics	Science & Technology	Music	Art & Architecture	Agriculture, Fisheries, Forestry	Literature & Languages	History	Geography & Environment	Politics & International Affairs
United Kingdom	749	431	1,213	565	1,447	3,823	558	960	271	1,258	837	453	197
Austria	61	84	104	253	186	388	31	127	44	257	227	244	32
Belgium	168	81	250	94	390	1,141	16	162	75	169	104	62	66
Cyprus	—	—	10	2	9	—	—	2	—	20	19	14	—
Denmark	42	20	38	16	35	135	12	43	10	44	86	15	8
Finland	108	24	110	57	113	475	12	82	49	125	102	52	30
France	194	196	492	345	367	1,316	42	373	96	857	1,572	243	153
West Germany	305	320	702	462	584	1,556	80	421	108	632	468	195	119
Gibraltar	—	—	1	—	—	2	—	2	—	2	5	3	—
Greece	7	6	22	19	34	53	5	21	6	54	50	30	3
Iceland	3	2	6	2	9	16	2	4	6	15	15	5	2
Italy	239	92	266	311	346	773	49	235	113	431	383	152	70
Lichtenstein	—	—	—	—	—	—	—	1	—	1	1	—	—
Luxembourg	2	13	11	12	13	24	1	4	4	27	6	5	3
Malta	1	1	2	3	2	5	—	4	—	7	7	2	1
Netherlands	62	81	349	169	188	608	60	134	48	177	233	82	48
Norway	16	26	52	22	42	117	8	46	11	42	75	16	11
Portugal	35	14	57	12	60	137	5	52	28	73	66	20	12
Spain	59	46	100	75	103	217	12	88	27	136	173	59	17
Sweden	49	38	77	20	90	371	10	58	29	40	113	10	21
Switzerland	59	78	100	112	180	355	13	97	34	104	183	94	24
Total	2,159	1,551	3,962	2,551	4,198	11,512	916	2,916	959	4,471	4,725	1,756	817

*Counts shown are approximate; verify at time of use.

between the publisher and its supplier. For this reason, publisher-sponsored continuation- or selective-order plans are generally modest in number.

Here are some reasons why the library prefers to deal with a library supplier for continuation orders:

- Shipment is almost automatic and in larger quantities.
- Better discounts.
- Better selection. Jobber plans may include books from publishers that do not have such plans.
- Less paperwork and order processing. A single payment can cover the entire shipment, less rejects.

23:18   **Converting an Order for an Annual or Serial into a Standing Order**

For its annuals and serials, Gale Research sends a computer-generated renewal notice approximately 30 to 60 days prior to the availability of the new edition. It includes a printed notice (addressed to the librarian) advising that the renewal order form is for books purchased previously for which no renewal order has been placed. At the same time, the notice invites a standing order for the title, noting as an incentive that "All Standing Orders for Gale books are billed at a 5% discount." Gale offers another strong incentive for prepayment by picking up postage costs. The renewal notice used by Gale looks like the sample shown.

---

*Please route to Librarian: ORDER FORMS attached—not an invoice

---

Dear Librarian:

The attached renewal order forms are for books you purchased in the past. According to our records, you have not ordered the latest editions or volumes of these books.

By placing Standing Orders for these titles, you would save the time and expense of future renewal processing. All Standing Orders for Gale books are billed at a 5% discount.

To order, or place a Standing Order, just fill in the forms and return a copy to us. All books are sent on a 30-day approval.

GALE RESEARCH COMPANY # BOOK TOWER # DETROIT, MICHIGAN 48226

24

Colleges and Universities

24:01 **Textbook Adoption and Evaluation Practices: Study Result**

For marketers who seek an understanding of the college market of the 1980s, there are valuable lessons to be learned from "A Study for the Market for College Textbooks," prepared by Crossley Surveys, Inc., for the Book Industry Study Group, the Association of American Publishers, and the National Association of College Stores in March 1980. Here are a few highlights from this study:

• The single most important factor in textbook selection is the perceived quality of the book.
• In the largest courses, faculty requires a hardcover textbook.
• Faculty members select a textbook when they are ready, regardless of deadlines. (They recognize that being late in submitting adoptions creates a problem, but do not plan to change.)

FINDINGS ON TEXTBOOK EVALUATION AND ADOPTION PRACTICES (WITH CONCLUSIONS)

1. Most professors first learn about a new textbook through the publisher's own promotional efforts.
   Conclusion: Targeted mailings on pertinent titles to course instructors should not be overlooked.
2. Professional reviews and the recommendations of college travelers were less important in 1980 than in 1974.

282

3. A book becomes a candidate for adoption as soon as a professor seeks more information about it.
   Conclusion: Inquiries from college faculty merit priority handling. Failure to respond promptly can cost you an adoption.

4. Solicited and unsolicited copies are the most important source of this sort of information.

5. Circulars and brochures have become more effective and college travelers less effective, in recent years.
   Conclusion: At best, travelers can cover only a small percentage of faculty. Direct mail can make up for this shortcoming, but only by arousing interest in a book, not by leading to its active consideration.

6. A book receives active consideration due to word-of-mouth from colleagues; the impact of the author's reputation; and the professor's own impression based on a review of a copy.

7. The final adoption decision is based on the book's breadth and comprehensiveness; its suitability for the professor's teaching style; and the currency of information or approach.

8. Factors of only minor importance in adoptive decisions are student feedback; graphic layout or appearance; price; author's reputation; and reputation of publisher.

Copies of the 116-page study may be purchased from the Association of American Publishers, One Park Avenue, New York, NY 10016.

24:02 On Whom Does College Faculty Rely in Making Textbook Adoption Decisions?

Unlike librarians, who rely heavily on reviews in pertinent scientific and scholarly journals, college faculty place considerably more emphasis on the publishers' advertising and promotion.

If your publications are for the textbook market, the findings of a survey of 1970s college faculty should be of interest. The survey indicated that nearly three-fourths of the respondents reported receiving information on new textbooks first from publishers' advertising and promotion.

Some reported initial awareness of a textbook from more than one source. For example, one-third of the respondents indicated they were alerted initially through reviews in journals, whereas one-third cited contacts with college travelers as their information source. Only 4% learned of new textbooks first from libraries and only 3% from bookstores.

Faculty members making adoption decisions also showed they relied on multiple information sources to reach their decisions. Fifty-seven percent said they made adoption decisions after having reviewed requested examination copies; 48% adopted books for which they received unrequested examination copies, and 30% adopted on the basis of publisher-supplied information in circulars and brochures.

24:03   **Primary Market for Scholarly Books:**
         How Best to Reach It

Publishers of scholarly books have long recognized that the faculty members and affiliated libraries represent the primary market for their publications. Whether your establishment has a large staff of college reps or none at all, if you publish scholarly works, a major part of your marketing effort must be directed to this audience by mail.

The two largest and most reliable services offering mailing lists of college faculty are CMG (College Marketing Group, Inc.) and ED (The Educational Directory).

COLLEGE MARKETING GROUP

The College Marketing Group college faculty operation is described fully in 23:02 of *Book Marketing Handbook, Volume One.* The data base at CMG is updated weekly and many new list selectivity options have been added, including book-buyer names for the various college subjects listed. Additional details on CMG offerings are included throughout this volume and can be located in the index. Three separate faculty catalogs are available free from CMG.

THE EDUCATIONAL DIRECTORY

The Educational Directory college faculty operation is described fully in 23:03 of *Book Marketing Handbook, Volume One.* The data base at ED is updated constantly and many new list-selectivity options have been added in 1983. For a listing of new options, see 2:26 in this volume. The faculty catalog is available free from The Educational Directory, One Park Avenue, New York, NY 10016.

For additional details about the list services offered by College Marketing Group and by The Educational Directory, refer to the indexes at the back of this book.

24:04   **List Segmentation: The Vehicle that Changed**
         the Face of College Marketing

The precisely segmented mailing lists that marketers of college textbooks now take for granted did not exist a decade ago. Before that time, if you wanted to reach ornithologists, you had to mail to all biologists, or, to the only other type of college list segment available, heads of department. Thus, the only alternative to mailing to all biologists if you wanted to reach ornithologists would have been to direct your mailing to the chairs of all biology departments, in the hope that somehow your piece would ultimately find the instructor in ornithology.

College Marketing Group (CMG) solved this problem for the book marketer by introducing the segmented college faculty list in 1973, and this changed the way college texts were marketed through the mails. Marketers utilizing the segmented lists learned quickly that an inexpensive offset sales letter that contained simple descriptive copy and the full table of contents of a book pulled as well as an elaborate brochure—if the letter were directed to the right person.

Book marketers learned, too, that a brochure or catalog covering a broad range of specific subjects could be mailed with virtually no waste. This could be done by selecting from the CMG data base only those faculty teaching in the subject areas covered by the brochure or catalog and merging the names into a single composite mailing list. So grew the concept of targeted mailings to college and university faculty.

Today, the CMG data base for college faculty consists of more than half a million names segmented into the 3,500 college courses they teach, as well as thousands of librarians grouped according to the subject areas for which they are responsible for acquisitions. The data base also includes names of departmental library representatives in colleges and universities responsible for making recommendations for acquisitions within their subject area and names of continuing education coordinators by discipline.

24:05 Educational Software Use in Colleges: Study Result List Availability

Microcomputers are now widely used to aid classroom instruction, and the publishing community is moving rapidly to meet the growing need for educational software. Among college publishers already active in this area are McGraw-Hill, Addison Wesley, Harper & Row, Wiley, Wadsworth, Science Research Associates, and Southwestern. "There's no doubt," says one college marketer already involved in educational software, "that by the mid-1980s, nearly all publishers in the college area will be publishing microcomputer software."

How big is the educational software market already? A study by College Marketing Group, Winchester, Mass., in mid-1982 proved this market is very substantial. Of the 2,000 college department chairpersons CMG sampled from the U.S. college universe, nearly 1,000 responded. The size of the response is by itself indicative of the high interest.

Thirty-four percent of those who responded already were using microcomputers to assist them in instruction. Another 31% said they were planning to buy one or more microcomputers within a year. This would indicate that by mid-1983, 65% or more of the college departments that responded will have been using microcomputers.

As a result of this study, CMG has developed a computer-user list that is available to college marketers by discipline and by type of microcomputer used for instruction. For details on CMG's microcomputer lists, call Linnea Willman at 617-729-7865, or write CMG.

24:06   **Promoting a Textbook to the College Market:**
         Simplified Procedure

Because the college market is so segmented and the number of prospects often very small, most college promotions involving a single
book are generally very simple. Many consist of little more than an offset letter printed on letterhead in one color of ink, and a return order
card or envelope for examination requests.

Competition among major textbook publishers for a share of the
lucrative market for introductory textbooks continues to be waged
with increasingly expensive, full-color, and attractive brochures. However, this does not apply to upper-level textbooks.

Textbook promotion letters usually stress benefits to the student.
They emphasize content, features, and supplements for the instructor
and the student. They also cite advantages over competing works.
Such letters usually occupy a single sheet, on the reverse side of which
more copy and a coupon to request examination copies may be found.

The primary intent of such letters is to get the professor to request
an examination copy. The final goal, of course, is to have the book
adopted for the professor's course.

THE ADOPTION DECISION

The adoption decision is usually made by the professor. In some instances, such as for larger introductory or basic courses, a committee
or group of professors may be involved in an adoption decision. Irrespective of how the adoption decision is made, almost invariably the
purchase order to the publisher will originate from the college bookstore or another bookstore near the campus.

Orders for the fall term are usually placed in June, July, or August.
The adoption decision, however, is usually made by the professor in
the spring—March, April, or May. If your promotions reach the professor in January or February, this will allow ample time for that instructor to request, receive, and examine a copy of the book before it is
time to make a decision.

A second buying season precedes the winter and spring term. The
order will usually reach the publisher in December after adoption decisions have been made by professors in October and November. Your
mailings to professors for this term should be timed for September.

Although adoption orders come in on a (college) store purchase
order, it is relatively simple to relate such orders to schools where complimentary copies were sent. Many publishers of upper-level college
texts send copies for examination only and require either adoption or
return of book for cancellation of the invoice. If the book is retained,
payment is required. Invoice cancellation requests in these instances
indicate that adoptions have been made.

COLLEGE STORES DO NOT INFLUENCE

College stores, as a rule, do not influence textbook selection; they
function as a service. Titles stocked in quantity are those that have

been adopted. Some stores/schools adopt books for a minimum of two years, and some community colleges for three years. Many college stores carry a selection of professional and reference books and, occasionally, a copy or two of a potential textbook. This is particularly true for professional or reference books that are also appropriate as graduate-level texts.

Not all college textbooks merit a full-scale promotion effort. If you publish only an occasional college-level text, or if you publish no textbooks and wish to reach only a part of the college market with a particular book, this can easily be done. Instructor lists are available for any segment of the college market at any level, for specific courses, for schools by size of enrollment or geographic location, or any combination of these. For more details, see 24:03.

24:07   Uses of Personalized Letters in Textbook Promotion

Mail to professors in the following cases:

- At schools your reps do not call on
- On whom your reps plan to call later
- Whom your reps have called on but didn't see
- In advance of a planned telemarketing campaign
- Who have already adopted one of your books, in order to call attention to a related title

24:08   How Academics Regard Publishers' Mail Promotions in the United States and the United Kingdom

College faculty members rely heavily on publishers' direct-mail promotions in both the United States and the United Kingdom to keep informed of new books. This was proven conclusively in two college faculty surveys conducted during the 1970s—one by The Educational Directory (ED) in the United States and the other by Social Surveys (Gallup Poll), Ltd., on behalf of IBIS in Great Britain and Ireland.

In the early 1970s, ED asked college faculty members to indicate subject areas in which they would like to receive direct-mail advertisements from book publishers. Writing in the July 1973 issue of *Scholarly Publishing*, Curtis Dewees of ED reported that of the more than 100,000 American faculty contacted, "not more than ten individuals [requested] their names be removed from all ED lists"—less than 1/10,000 of 1 percent!

A different study was conducted among academics in Great Britain and Ireland in 1976 to evaluate their attitudes toward receiving advertising information sent by mail. In this study, Gallup Poll selected 1,000 academics from a systematic sampling of more than 90,000 names on the IBIS list. The survey found 72% viewed publishers' direct-mail promotions as a valid source of information, and 62% regarded the information as useful in book-buying decisions.

24:09   **Winning Letter Technique for Textbook Promotion
with Complimentary Copy**

Academic educators are extremely peer conscious. Therefore, a statement by a fellow educator about a potential textbook will carry
more weight than an advertising blurb, signed or unsigned, by the
publisher.

On page 289 is an example of a promotion letter for an introductory
chemistry text that demonstrates how this technique can be used in
practice. Written by the author on the author's institutional letterhead, it was addressed to "Dear Fellow Chemist and Educator."

There is a ring of sincerity and credibility to the author's words "I
have attempted to write an easily understandable text" that is rein-
forced by his invitation to send comments and specific suggestions
"regardless of your plans for adoption."

24:10   **Test Mailings to College Faculty
with and without Routing Slips**

When Allen & Unwin began its U.S. operations, seven mailings were
made to college faculty during its first season. The first three were
sent without library routing slips and the last four with routing slips.
The first three mailings produced a single direct response pattern.
However, the mailings with library routing slips showed three distinct
response waves in different periods: first from the addressees, then
from college libraries, and finally from jobbers and wholesalers. The
addition of library routing slips obviously produced additional sales
for Allen & Unwin.

24:11   **Unique Marketing Mix: New Dimension in Textbook Publishing**

What happens when a series of textbooks is developed in which all the
authors are based on a single university campus, and the editorial and
production work is done on campus by the university's press while the
marketing to colleges is undertaken by a major commercial publisher?
The partners in this arrangement are MIT Press and McGraw-Hill.
The ultimate success of this experiment may well alter the future textbook publishing programs of both organizations.

Under a co-publishing arrangement between McGraw-Hill and MIT
Press in 1982, eight college- and graduate-level textbooks in computer
science and electrical engineering will be published. Authors of all
eight books are MIT faculty members, and all editorial and production
functions are being carried out locally by MIT Press. The marketing of
these texts to the college market will be done exclusively by McGraw-
Hill through its College Division sales reps. Concurrently, the MIT
Press will market the same books through its regular direct-mail
promotions.

SAMPLE PROMOTION LETTER

Dear Fellow Chemist and Educator:

By this time you should have received from McGraw-Hill a complimentary copy of my new text, *Introduction to Chemical Analysis.* I am writing to thank you for considering the text for your course in chemical analysis.

I have spent a great deal of time preparing a text which I believe is the best available teaching tool for analytical chemistry. I would like to point out a few of the features of the text.

Chapter 6, entitled "Error in the Chemical Analysis and Sampling," is a discussion of several topics that are generally applicable to all methods of analysis. The text has been written so that Chapter 6 can be taught prior to Chapters 2 through 5 if desired. Nothing in Chapter 6 requires knowledge of the material covered in an earlier chapter. I think you will find the chapters on molecular spectroscopy, atomic spectroscopy, potentiometry, nonpotentiometric electroanalysis and chromatography (Chapters 8 through 13) to be particularly thorough and current. The separate chapter on curve fitting, the working curve method, and the standard addition technique (Chapter 7) is designed to demonstrate the general utility of those techniques.

Chapters 2 through 5, on chemical equilibrium, gravimetry, acid-base reactions and volumetric analyses, contain a balanced treatment of the important classical methods of analysis. The chapter on analytical automation and process-control analyzers (Chapter 14) is a brief introduction to the design and use of analytical equipment that is commonly used in hospitals, governmental laboratories, and industrial laboratories.

I have attempted to write an easily understandable text that covers the major areas of analytical chemistry. After you have had an opportunity to review the text (regardless of your plans for adoption), I would like to hear your comments. Specific suggestions are especially appreciated.

If you have not received a copy of the text, please write or phone (318-231-6737) me and I will see to it that you get one. For faster service, contact your local McGraw-Hill representative or Mr. James A. Dodd, Marketing Manager, Science and Mathematics, College Division, McGraw-Hill Book Company, 1221 Avenue of the Americas, New York, NY 10020. Thank you for considering the text and for your assistance.

The co-publishing arrangement between a commercial publisher and a university press gives both publishers the best of both possible worlds—editorial and production work takes place on campus and allows for convenient access to authors, and the large marketing staff of a major college publisher will enhance the sales effort. This idea, if properly applied, can expand the programs and add a new dimension to the marketing program of every university press.

24:12   Information Source for Continuing Education Programs

If you market or promote textbooks or reference materials appropriate for any noncollege, postsecondary occupational program, complete data on the more than 10,000 schools offering these programs is available in the *NCES Directory*, published biennially in even-numbered years by the National Center for Educational Statistics, 400 Maryland Avenue SW, Washington, DC 20202.

The directory lists all public and private schools by category in these classifications: public schools approved by a state department of education; public and private schools approved by a regional accrediting association recognized by the U.S. Office of Education (OE); private schools offering programs approved by an accrediting association or agency recognized by OE; public and private schools meeting the Veterans Administration requirements or the eligibility requirements of OE's Federal Insured Student Loan or Basic Educational Opportunity Grant programs.

Indexes in the directory list schools both alphabetically and by program offerings. Among the program offerings listed are business, associate degree in nursing, anesthesiology, cosmetology, animal technician, certified laboratory assistant, dental assistant, dental hygienist, dental technician, engineering technology, histologic technician, interior design aide, medical assistant, medical laboratory technician, and practical nurse.

The *NCES Directory* is available from Superintendent of Documents, U.S. Government Printing Office, Washington, DC 20402.

24:13   Continuing Education Market: Copy Approach and Timing of Promotions

If you plan to promote to the continuing education (CE) market, your copy should be oriented to the segment of the CE market being solicited and the aims of the CE program. Essentially, CE courses are targeted to these four groups:

1. Professionals (doctors, teachers, engineers, businesspeople, nurses) taking vocational or professional retraining courses
2. Persons attending school nights or weekends to obtain a college degree
3. Day students taking some courses at night to avoid conflicts in schedule or to get their degree more quickly.
4. People taking recreational courses

TIMING AND TARGETING OF PROMOTIONS

Over half the courses taught in college and university continuing education programs are taught by daytime faculty members who may already be receiving your mailed promotions for courses they teach. Rather than risk duplication of effort by mailing to complete lists of CE instructors just in order to reach part-time faculty, consider instead mailing to the CE area coordinator for the subject or discipline, and group all your titles within that subject area in a single promotional mailing. (A list of CE coordinators by subject area is available from College Marketing Group.)

CE coordinators assemble the fall program during the summer months. Often they may decide on textbooks to be used in the school's CE programs. However, your promotion piece should ask them to route your mailing to the appropriate part-time or full-time instructor if they do not control adoptions.

24:14 Ways to Track and Evaluate Promotions to College Faculty

1. Direct orders.
2. Note number of requests for examination copies received.
3. Note number of classroom adoptions resulting from examination copies sent.
4. Watch for inclusion of promoted titles in college bookstore orders.
5. Faculty recipients of your promotion pieces often order for departmental libraries through the institutional library. Such departmental library orders may be reflected in orders from library jobbers.
6. Watch for increase in orders from government or industry sources. More than 50% of college faculty do research for industry or government* and can influence purchases by these sources.

24:15 First All-Book Card Deck to Offer Everything Gratis: Case History

In December 1980, a New York publisher of technical and occupational textbooks issued a card deck in which every book was offered gratis. The card-deck mailing, offering 34 texts in electronics and electronic technology, was mailed to 4,039 instructors of related courses in high schools and colleges.

A white kraft mailing envelope was used that bore printed postal indicia for third-class bulk mail. On the outside of the mailing envelope, copy imprinted in the corner was "Top-Quality Texts in Electronic Technology."

More than 4,000 deck mailings produced 3,473 requests for complimentary copies. Respondents had to supply course title, title of current textbook used, name of instructor, school, and department, as well as address.

Result   Responses on the 33 "shop" books varied from .2% to 3.3%. The thirty-fourth title was not a "shop" text, but rather a technical mathematics book on calculus. This card drew a 15.15% response.

Return   On the basis of a total of 137,326 cards mailed in the 4,039 decks, the 3,473 requests for complimentary copies represented a 2.5% return. A good number of the requests resulted in adoptions during the fall 1981 semester. Many of these adoptions were for secondary schools, institutions not visited by the publisher's college sales representatives.

*According to studies by Robert Linnell of the University of Southern California, reported in the *New York Times*, November 16, 1981.

24:16   **Special Discount Offer Stimulates
Summer Orders from College Stores**

An academic publisher of study guides, solution manuals, and student workbooks endeavors to stimulate summer sales to college stores by mailing to the stores at the outset of summer an order form with the heading "Special Summer and Fall Discount Offer." The student guides and manuals are offered with full returns privilege at a discount that betters the normal college bookstore discount by 7%. The mailing is sent to all NACS member stores, and forms are also carried by the publisher's sales reps.

24:17   **College Traveler Bookmobile Program Terminated**

The College Traveler Bookmobile Program ceased operation on October 26, 1981. Its final owner, Drake Bush of Knoxville, Tenn., said he suspended operations "due to increased operating costs, insufficient participation by publishers, and lack of interest by colleges." The program, which had served publishers in the college marketplace for more than a decade and through three changes of ownership, consisted of three bookmobiles that were operated by experienced college travelers and that visited college campuses, displaying books of interest to faculty members on behalf of participating publishers. Each campus visit was sponsored by the college bookstore, which notified faculty in advance of the visit. The bookmobile concept was originated by Glenn Matthews of College Marketing Group, Winchester, Mass.

25

The School Market

25:01 The Secondary School Library as a Market for Professional and Scholarly Books

Many involved in professional and scholarly book marketing underestimate the potential market for their books among secondary or senior high schools in general and high school libraries in particular. This is a sizable market that is easily reached by mail through a vast selection of lists, many of which have selection criteria that enable you to focus on narrow segments of the market with pinpoint accuracy. Following are some factors that make the high school library an attractive market for many types of professional, reference, and scholarly books:

- The high school library is essentially a reference collection.
- Librarians are constantly on the search for supplementary titles that support studies in the major disciplines.
- Serious consideration is often given to low-level college texts that will appeal to students in honors programs.
- Book buying is especially heavy in science, mathematics, engineering, literature, history, economics, and practical how-to books in mechanics.

25:02   School and Public Library Buying Patterns: Sales Study

If you plan to promote a high-priced reference work to school and public libraries, you have the best chance for success if you reach them before their peak buying periods. These periods seem to fall in the second quarter of the calendar year. This conclusion is based on a study of the long-term sales results of a classic multivolume encyclopedic reference work that was sold almost exclusively to the school and public library markets.

The study of sales to these two markets indicated the heaviest buying periods for the reference work were in the second quarter in each of the five years projected as the life cycle of the work.

April was the best month in three of the five years and the second heaviest buying month in a fourth year. May was the second best month for two years and third best month for two years. June ranked as the best month for sales in the second and fifth years. The high sales figures for June are due, we think, to the fact that some librarians delay purchase of relatively high-priced reference works until the final month of their fiscal year and then buy if the remaining funds in the budget permit such purchases.

Sales results for second-quarter months (April through June) are shown for the five-year period in the accompanying table.

LIBRARY BUYING ACTIVITY: PEAK MONTHS
OVER FIVE-YEAR LIFE CYCLE OF REFERENCE WORK

1st Year	2nd Year	3rd Year	4th Year	5th Year
April	June	April	April	June
January	April	May	May	March
May	May	February	July	February
February	September	March	January	April

25:03   The Confusing Terminology of the School Library Market

The school library is a major buyer of many types of reference books and materials. But many marketers are confused by the complexity of terms used to describe what was formerly called the school library.* If you are among the confused, you should remember that even terms that include the word "media" or "resources," still denote a library. The most popular term for the traditional school library seems to be school library media center. The key word is media, for it signals the expanded role of the school library as a learning center that is concerned not only with books and periodicals but also a widening range of other learning tools such as films, recordings, videotapes, and other nonprint materials.

When promoting to the school library or school library media center, you should consider not only the library that serves one school but also

*William A. Katz, *Collection Development: The Selection of Materials for Libraries* (New York: Holt, Rinehart and Winston, 1980).

the growing number of school district media centers, which may feed materials to all of the schools within an entire school district. Some other terms replacing the traditional designation for school library include school media center, media center, media resource center, multimedia library, library media center, school learning resource center, instructional materials center, and audiovisual center.

25:04 Promotions to the High School Library: Useful Ingredients

- Keep promotional copy simple and understandable.
- Keep book description short and, if possible, include table of contents.
- Biographical information on the author should be included, where pertinent.
- Include Library of Congress (LC) catalog card number.
- Supply Dewey decimal number, if possible.
- Show publication date, price, ISBN, and page count.
- Indicate whether the book is available in both paper and cloth.
- If your promotional offering includes many books, group them by subject.
- Include positive reviews; they will help the selection process.
- Include a simple checklist order form.
- Be sure to mention whether a title is an annual, serial, new edition, or part of a series; for series, give the name of the series.

25:05 How to Reach the Cream of the High School Market: Guidelines for Test Mailing

If you publish for the college market and wonder whether one of your promotions might be appropriate for the high school market, here's a way you can run a test at relatively low cost. On your next planned promotion for what you consider an appropriate title or titles, overrun the printing by a little more than 2,000 copies.

College Marketing Group can supply you with a list of approximately 2,200 high schools that will enable you to reach the cream of the high school market—schools with enrollments over 500 that spend more than $60 per pupil for instructional materials.

Mail your promotional piece together with a cover letter that stresses the value of your book(s) for the more motivated, college-bound, upper-level students. Restate the educational benefits and features that will help the teacher prepare for or instruct the course.

Address your letters and promotion pieces to department chairpersons by title. Ask them to route the mailing to instructors of courses in their department for which the book(s) may be appropriate. The most common departments in high schools are art, business education, English, languages, industrial arts, music, social studies, and science.

For more information, write to College Marketing Group, 50 Cross Street, Winchester, MA 01890.

25:06   Co-op Postcard Mailings to the High School Market

If you want to reach selected segments of the high school market at relatively low cost, be sure to look into the semiannual direct-response postcard mailings sponsored by Co-op Mailings, Inc., of Hillside, N.J. These mailings, made in September and January, include:

- High school science teachers: 60,000 (by name).
- Industrial arts/vocational ed teachers: 52,000 (by name), of whom 39,000 teach in high schools, 12,000 in junior and community colleges, and 1,900 in vocational and trade schools.
- Career Guidance Counseling: 37,000 (by title), of whom 34,000 work in secondary schools and 3,000 on the district level.
- Home Economics Teachers: 58,000 (by name), of whom 47,000 teach in high schools and 6,000 in colleges, and 5,000 are county and extension agents.

Suppliers of educational materials participate in Co-op Mailings' postcard mailings year after year. Rates are reasonable. With your participation you receive samples and proof of the mailing. If you have any questions, call Irv Berkowitz at 201-666-3111, or write to him at Co-op Mailings, Inc., Box 248, Hillsdale, NJ 07642.

25:07   Best (and Worst) Months for School Mailings

The two major mailing seasons for school-funded purchases are spring and fall. Those who aim for spring season buying begin mailing in January and continue through June.

For supplementary classroom materials requiring no preview, the best months to mail are February and March for spring buying and August and September for fall buying.

The two worst months for school mailings are October and May. By October, most of school budget is committed. By May most schools are preparing to close and are preoccupied with that activity.

Seasonal buying patterns for schools and related valuable information are reported regularly in *Direct Response to Schools Marketing Newsletter*, from which information in this entry was derived. The address for this newsletter is School Market Research Institute, Box 160, Chester, CT 06412.

25:08   Experiment with Off-Season Mailings to School Market

When a newly established California company began promoting to the elhi school market by mail, it was at a loss as to when to time its offerings of special education materials. After a year of experimentation, the firm decided to restrict its mailings to two cycles—one at the beginning of the school year and again in March.

The results of the two-cycle approach seemed satisfactory, but the company was troubled by the large time gaps in between mailings. By its third year in business, the firm dropped the two-cycle approach and began mailing to schools year-round. To the delight of all, it found that the continuous promotions brought in orders throughout the year.

The valuable lesson learned here is that, even when you believe the buying practice of a market to be seasonal, you should experiment with mailings during off-seasons. Sometimes, if you use the right approach, the possibility of year-round sales does exist.

25:09   Mailing to Educators at School vs. Mailing to the Home

Generally, professional offerings to teachers fare better when they are addressed to teachers at their school addresses. Mailings received at school usually reach a wider audience because of the pass-along effect. However, some marketers favor the idea of reaching the teacher at home where the competition from other mail is not as great. For this reason, some school list specialists such as Market Data Retrieval offer lists with both school and home addresses. In the school environment, a mailing piece will command more attention if you address it to a person, rather than a job title.

If you are new to mailings at the secondary school level, a valuable free tool to help you off to a good start is "Market Finder," available from Market Data Retrieval, which is perhaps the largest compiler of lists for the school market. (See 25:06, 25:11, 25:12, and 25:13 for additional information and addresses.)

25:10   Which Works Better in School Mailings—Names or Titles?

In mailings to schools, names work better than titles, says Terry Coen of Market Data Retrieval. He gives these reasons: First, names make mail sorting and delivery easier, and, second, names give the recipients the feeling that the message is meant specifically for them. This can affect the way the recipient will receive and act on the mailing.

Coen's reasoning is supported by a three-way controlled test mailing that was sent to schools by a publisher of supplementary materials. One segment was addressed to "School Secretary" with routing instructions. A second list was addressed to teachers by title and grade level. The third segment was addressed to teachers by name.

Result   The list segment that addressed teachers by name outpulled the segment addressed to teachers by grade and title by 50%. It outpulled the mailing addressed to the school secretary by 100%. The second segment (teachers by title/grade level) outpulled the third by 42%.

25:11   **List Selection Options for Promotions to the Secondary School Market**

1. Public senior high schools (grades 7–12)
2. Public senior high schools (grades 9–12)
3. Public senior high schools (grades 10–12)
4. Public senior high schools by expenditures per student for instructional materials
5. Public senior high schools by enrollment sizes: 1–100, 100–199, 200–299, 300–499, 500–999, 1,000–2,499, 2,500 and over
6. Public and/or nonpublic high schools offering special programs for academically talented pupils
7. Public high schools with special programs for the handicapped
8. Public high schools with vocational education
9. Catholic high schools by enrollment size
10. Private high schools by enrollment size
11. Canadian high schools
12. Public high school libraries/media centers
13. Regional media centers
14. Public high schools with courses in special subjects (by subject)
15. Secondary school teachers in science, mathematics, social science, by subject taught
16. Secondary education book buyers
17. Libraries at senior high schools with 250–499 and 500 or more enrollment
18. Senior high school teachers by name and subject taught
19. Senior high school teachers (by name and subject taught) who are mail-order buyers of books and supplementary teaching materials
20. Selected public high school libraries with full-time librarians

Note: For complete details on all high school lists, refer to *Direct Mail Rates and Data*, Standard Rate & Data Service, Inc., 5201 Old Orchard Road, Skokie, IL 60077.

25:12   **Major List Sources for the High School Library Market**

A pioneer in the development of lists for the school library market is the R. R. Bowker Co., which, through its publications *School Library Journal* and *American Library Directory*, maintains the most accurate data base possible in this area. Among the school library lists available from Bowker are:

- Public high school libraries (approximately 16,500)
- Selected public high school libraries with full-time librarians (approximately 10,300)
- Junior high school libraries (approximately 13,500)
- Selected junior high school libraries with full-time librarians (approximately 8,300)
- Catholic high school libraries (approximately 1,500)
- Private high school libraries (approximately 1,800)

For information, contact Paulette Milata, Director, Bowker Mailing List Department, 1180 Avenue of Americas, New York, NY 10036; 212-764-5223.

Market Data Retrieval offers the following lists of the public school library market (see 23:13 for detailed description of list services for the elhi market):

- School district personnel (by name) involved in the purchase of library materials (approximately 2,500). Selection options available by enrollment sizes (under 3,000; 3,000–9,999; over 10,000)
- Junior high and senior high school library personnel. Selection options available by name, job title, size of school enrollment
- Junior high school libraries/media centers (approximately 10,000)
- Senior high school libraries/media centers (approximately 14,000)
- High-expenditure public high school libraries (over $60 spent per pupil)

For information, contact Market Data Retrieval, Ketchum Place, Westport, CT 06880.

25:13   **Market Data Retrieval:**
Primary List Source for the School Market

If your plans include the elhi school market, one of the largest and most reliable sources of lists is Market Data Retrieval (MDR), which has offices in Westport, Conn., Chicago, and Denver and direct-dial numbers in San Francisco and Los Angeles. MDR maintains an up-to-the-minute data bank of more than two and one-half million names of teachers and administrators, with addresses both at home and at school, as well as more than 250 educators who are known mail-order buyers.

MDR lists are updated by telephone and maintained by job title or function. The lists offer a wide selection of options, including enrollments, budgets, and personnel assignments. Account executives at MDR are assigned to specific accounts and will provide personalized attention. Orders are shipped and guaranteed completely, usually within ten days. The MDR catalog with its bound-in "Market Finder" is a must if you plan to mail to the school market.

MDR has offices in Westport, CT (Ketchum Place, ZIP 06880, 203-226-8941) (headquarters); Chicago, IL (59 East Van Buren Street, Suite 2506, ZIP 60605, 312-461-9580); Denver, CO (1615 California Street, Suite 623, ZIP 80202, 303-573-7617); and numbers in Los Angeles, CA (213-625-7750, connected to Denver office), and San Francisco, CA (415-956-2067, also connected to Denver office).

Market Data Retrieval elhi lists are also available from College Marketing Group, 6 Winchester Terrace, Winchester, MA 01890.

25:14   Tracking Response to High School Library Promotion: Guidelines

You've unleashed your major school promotions in the fall or winter, given it your best effort, followed up with a catalog, and the library response is weak at best or even poor. Take heart! Your promotion was not a flop. In fact, it may have been a huge success, but you may have to wait until late spring or even midsummer before you will know about it. Even then, you cannot be sure because even though sales of the promoted books suddenly took off, they were from jobbers—not from the schools. The following timetable provides a picture of how many school librarians function and also a clue as to why your "successful" promotions have had a delayed reaction:

HIGH SCHOOL LIBRARY MARKET: PROMOTION AND ORDERING CYCLE

- Time your major promotions for delivery in January, February, and March.
- In many schools, librarians commit a major portion of their budgets on orders prepared and submitted during May and June, based on promotional materials received from publishers during the school year.
- Orders are submitted to jobbers or processed through boards of education to reach jobbers in May, June, or even July. In turn, jobbers will order for delivery in July or August.

25:15   Response Rate on Promotions to School Faculty

In the school establishment, often several individuals are involved in most buying decisions. Consequently, response may be slow or difficult to trace to the specific individual to whom the mailing was made.

25:16   Telephone Technique for Marketing Texts to Business and Vocational Schools

A successful telephone marketing approach was used by a publisher to sell books to business and vocational schools. Utilizing an independent telemarketing service, it consists of a series of three calls: (1) a qualifying call to establish the name of the instructor and relevance of a book for a specific course, including an offer to supply a free examination copy; (2) the follow-up call giving highlights of the book; and (3) follow-up/reminder.

Here is a brief outline of the program:

- First Call (to department chairperson or curriculum coordinator)

  "We are publishing (name of book). What is the name of the person who is giving this course, or who decides on the textbook for this course? We'd like to send that person a copy of the book."

  (Upon receipt of instructors' names, send complimentary copies.)

- Second Call (to recipients of books four or five weeks after book was sent)

  "Recently we sent you a copy of our new book (give book title). Did you by any chance have an opportunity to look at the new chapter on (one of the featured chapters mentioned). We'd like your opinion on it."

  (Teacher will usually admit he or she read book and give an opinion, or say he or she has not had a chance to look at it yet.) Caller: "Well, then, I wonder if I could call you back in a week or two." (Usually teacher will make an appointment for the return call.)

- Third Call

  (Caller telephones teacher about the date mentioned in the second call, or on the specific date suggested by teacher. The salesperson will repeat the name of the book and remind the teacher that he or she recommended a return call to solicit an opinion of the book. By that time, usually, the teacher will also advise whether he or she is considering use of the book or not.)

25:17   Premium Offerings to Schoolteachers

Premiums, special discounts, and other incentives are often important considerations in direct-response offerings to teachers. However, if the premium offering is to have credibility, it must be one related to the offer so as not to appear to be a thinly disguised bribe.

25:18   Publicity and Product Advertising Medium for Reaching the School Market

An effective and penetrating medium for reaching the K–12 market if you have reference or learning materials is *Curriculum Product Review*. This product-information–oriented tabloid, published monthly from August through April, reaches more than 50,000 curriculum coordinators and specialists, media centers, and selected principals. Its coverage includes more than 98% of all school districts. More than 350 products are publicized in each issue. If you send publicity, include a photo. For advertising, contact Bobit Publishing, 2500 Artesia Boulevard, Redondo Beach, CA 90278; 213-376-8788.

26

Cooperative and Special Sales

_____

26:01   **Present and Future Prospects for**
         Special Sales as Publisher Market

Cooperative and special sales agreements in areas outside the traditional book outlets—bookstores, wholesalers, and libraries—have existed in various forms for many years. However, in the years between
this volume and *Volume One* of *Book Marketing Handbook*, publishers' activity in special sales has greatly accelerated. Presently,
many publishers are seeing special sales for the first time as a major
source of new income.

No longer the orphan or stepchild of the marketing department,
separate departments have been created in many publishing establishments to penetrate and tap the full potential of this largely unex-
ploited market. One important factor in the great appeal of this
market is that it relies heavily on backlist titles, many of which have
already exhausted the largest part of their library and bookstore sales
potential.

In the recent past, nontraditional sales in some publishing establishments were considered "over-the-transom," miscellaneous transactions and were often relegated to clerical staff for handling. In some of
these same houses, as we approach the mid-1980s, specially designated
managers are plotting strategies and implementing full-scale programs for a larger share of this market.

At a 1982 seminar on special sales, a book marketer on the speaker's
panel told the assembled audience he envisioned that by 1990 some 10
to 15% of publisher sales would occur through this medium.

In 1982, the American University Press Services polled its membership in an endeavor to compile a list of nontraditional outlets, and the 30 different presses that responded (see 26:13) provided the names of 600 such outlets. The Association of American University Presses (AAUP) now has a program to expand this list in an effort to aid all its members in embarking on a campaign to expand sales of its scholarly publications through nontraditional outlets.

The era of special (nontraditional) sales is at hand. Its potential is unlimited to those who exploit it properly.

26:02   **Areas that Offer Good Potential for Special Sales**

1. Professional associations and societies
2. Business publications, special-interest publications, and journals
3. Catalog houses
4. Other book publishers with limited lists
5. Manufacturing companies that issue catalogs
6. Mail-order booksellers
7. Specialist booksellers serving a particular industry
8. Seminar sponsors
9. Specialist book clubs
10. Museums
11. Nonbook wholesalers and retailers
12. Premium users

26:03   **Problems in Professional and Reference Book Cooperative Sales: Checklist of Ways to Cope**

Most publishers of professional and reference books have a uniform discount schedule they offer on cooperative sales agreements with catalog houses, periodicals, mail-order sellers, and the like. These discounts are likely to range from 30 to 40%. Sometimes there will be a slightly larger discount for quantities or, possibly, a two-tiered discount—higher if shipped directly to the co-op account, somewhat lower if shipped to the co-op account's customer and billed to the co-op account. Some houses will offer a better discount if the buyer agrees to give up the return option.

One recurring problem with publishers that have a co-op sales program is that, inevitably, a prime prospect will come along who will insist on a discount larger than the prevailing one, and who will not deal on any other basis. Such prime prospects often make all sorts of alluring sales claims. They may cite sales of other publishers' books in the hundreds or thousands. Or they may say they can offer access to a specialized market that would be difficult for you to reach, but where your books would get repeated exposure.

Both legally and ethically, a publisher cannot offer different discounts to different co-op accounts. Sections 2(d) and 2(e) of the Robinson-Patman Act prohibit a seller from granting advertising and promotional allowances to customers unless they are available to all competing customers on proportionally equal terms.

However, there are ways to sign up a choice prospective co-op account on terms that ultimately will be found acceptable and that will not violate any laws. These ways involve building into your existing discount structure a group of discount incentives that will be available to all co-op accounts on an equal basis.

Let's say you have a prospective co-op account who demands 40% or else "no deal," when your best discount on professional and reference books is 33%. How do you cope with this situation? Here are some suggested solutions to such problems. The actual possibilities are limited only by your imagination, but remember—the discount variations must be equally applicable to all co-op accounts.

- Specify a larger discount on orders for certain quantities if placed prior to publication.
- Specify a larger discount when a title is reordered in certain quantities (for example, in even 100s).
- Specify a larger discount when a certain number of assorted titles are ordered at one time.
- One copy free with every (specify quantity) of books ordered at one time.
- Specify a larger discount when orders are prepaid.
- Specify a larger discount when books are purchased on a no-returns basis.
- Year-end rebate when annual purchases reach a certain (specified) level.
- Advertising allowance—specify a rate or volume of annual purchases.
- P.I. (per inquiry) arrangement—a commission paid on every order received.

With all of these arrangements, some co-op accounts will attempt to take advantage of the publisher or will misinterpret the terms offered. For this reason, whatever your co-op discount policy, the terms should be spelled out carefully and precisely, and penalties for returns clearly cited. Any extra effort given this activity in advance will pay handsome dividends later on.

26:04 Publisher and Co-op Account Share Special Market under Unique Arrangement

A unique cooperative sales arrangement has worked successfully for many years. The partners in this arrangement are a publisher of business books aimed at a specialized segment of the investment market and a monthly periodical that covered the specialized market and was the publisher's co-op account.

The arrangement was as follows: The book publisher inserted paid space advertisements in the investment periodical of his co-op account in alternate months. Each one-page advertisement carried five or six current best-sellers or forthcoming books, and the periodical billed the book publisher for each ad. In the alternate-month issues in which the book publisher did not advertise, the periodical publisher repeated the advertisement, changing only the headline and inserting his own name and address as the source for the books. Orders received by the periodical were then drop-shipped by the book publisher, and the business periodical earned the co-op discount on each sale.

The arrangement worked equally well for both, inasmuch as it gave double exposure to each of the advertisements while at the same time ensuring the periodical publisher a virtually ready-to-use advertisement on which it could earn in excess of 30% on all orders received.

26:05 Drop-Ship Order Fulfillment under Cooperative Sales Agreements

When a cooperative sales agreement has been established with a periodical or catalog house, the ideal arrangement is for the co-op account to stock a minimal quantity of each title so that orders can be filled promptly. However, more often than not, most co-op arrangements require that the publisher drop-ship to the co-op account's customer from a mailing label supplied by the co-op account. When such a co-op drop-ship arrangement exists, it is advantageous to instruct the co-op account to submit mail orders immediately as received and not to accumulate them. It is also desirable for the publisher to establish a prompt order-fulfillment arrangement for this type of order.

One reason drop-ship co-op orders should receive speedy fulfillment is that any unusually lengthy time lag in the delivery of the book to the customer could lead to complaints from the postal service, as most of these orders are prepaid, and regulations require refund if prepaid orders cannot be filled within a specified period of time.

26:06 Guidelines for Approaching and Dealing with Mail-Order Catalog Accounts

In *Volume One* of *Book Marketing Handbook*, we discussed in detail the practical approaches for pursuing cooperative sales arrangements with professional associations and societies and with business publications and journals. In this volume, we offer a set of practical approaches and guidelines for dealing with a different class of cooperative sales account, the mail-order catalog account.

Before going into the details, two important factors should be remembered:

1. Credibility is very important in all your dealings with a catalog account.
2. Catalog accounts will invariably want to see your book before they commit themselves to it.

When approaching a prospective catalog account, you must bear in mind that the arrangement you are proposing may be new to the other party. The prospective account may never have handled professional or reference books before, and therefore has no idea of what to expect from such an arrangement. In other cases where the catalog account has had such experience, books may be a very low priority item.

A new or inexperienced catalog account will order very conservatively. The older, more experienced catalog houses may order more liberally, but they have a lot of experience in estimating how much return they can expect per page and what your books can contribute to that return.

When you approach a potential catalog account, especially one that has had no prior experience with professional and reference books, make it as easy as possible for it to enter a cooperative agreement.

One way is to guarantee prices for a stated period or for the life of the catalog. Another is to offer a very liberal returns policy so the other party feels it has a way out, even if it has no intention of using the option. Offer free artwork or offer to subsidize some of the artwork up to a percentage of the initial order so the catalog can become involved with your books with a minimum of expense.

Once established, keep the catalog account constantly informed of new books of possible interest to its clientele. Give plenty of advance notice about impending price increases. Sometimes a catalog house will want to stock up on a title that has sold well and either continue selling it at the lower price or else sell at a higher new price and pocket the extra profit.

Contact your catalog accounts by telephone as frequently as you can. Be friendly in approach, and soft-sell. Many such accounts operate in rural areas where the tempo is very slow. Be accessible when they have questions or concerns. Try to make each contact a pleasant and enjoyable conversation.

Make an effort to maintain contacts with catalog houses even when there is no interest initially. Get them to think of you and your product line. Sometimes just keeping the contact alive can lead to a future relationship as your list keeps changing and as the catalog houses seek new products related to their clientele's interests.

**26:07   Catalog Account Problems:
Dealing with Competitors/Price Protection**

Most scientific and technical publishers rely heavily on direct-mail promotion to reach their specialized audiences. Mail-order catalog houses have also discovered the financial advantages of offering books to these same audiences. Bridging these two is a certain category of book publisher that, itself limited in output in certain subject areas, will enhance a mail promotion by including selected, better titles of other publishers on a dealer arrangement. These inclusions may or may not identify the imprint of other publishers.

Should a fellow publisher establish a dealer arrangement for your better selling titles, it is recommended that the publisher be required to identify each of your titles so promoted in order not to imply that these are publications of the mailer. A one-word identification in parentheses after the copy should suffice.

PRICE PROTECTION TO CATALOGERS

Some catalog houses will ask for price protection on offerings of your books. With ever-increasing reprint costs, it is difficult to guarantee price for an unlimited time. The suggested procedure, since most mail-order catalogs are issued quarterly, is to give price protection for a maximum of 90 days from the catalog issuance date. One major publisher has been doing this and has found this period to be generally acceptable to the catalog houses.

26:08   **Pricing Policies for Industrial Bulk Sales**

The industrial bulk sale falls into two basic categories: (1) a quantity of a title taken from stock or a reprint of an upcoming title; and (2) a customized special edition in which changes may be made in the cover and/or text. On sales of a title taken from your stock, your standard quantity discount should be applied. In the case of a special or customized edition, a special price will have to be negotiated based on the size of the edition, necessary changes, and amount of royalty involved. Because many special or customized editions are the result of an author's efforts and come up at the time the contract is signed, or at least prior to the first printing, it is usually possible to arrange with the author for a reduced royalty on this edition, which will allow you to set a more attractive price. It may be worthwhile to have a reduced-royalty clause in your standard contract to account for special editions.

26:09   **Bulk Sales to Industry for Premium Use**

Many companies have bought and used books as premiums in quantities ranging from dozens or hundreds to the tens of thousands. Most buyers of books as premiums had not previously considering using a book as a premium until they were presented with the idea. The likeliest prospect for the book premium is the employer of an author of a specialized book, which may wish to use the book because it identifies the employer's product. However, other prospects may have to be solicited. If your list contains specialized books that lend themselves to premium use in a particular company or industry, a small letter mailing can test this potential market for you.

The letter may be as simple as the accompanying example, or it may

SAMPLE LETTER

Dear Premium Buyer:

If you are looking for an effective marketing tool that can identify and promote your products and that will have lasting value to your customers, why not consider using a book as a premium?

Many companies already use books as premiums with their products. Others have their representatives leave behind a book bearing their company name after a sales visit. You are invited to make use of this effective marketing method by selecting a book from our list that identifies your products and also appeals to your customers' interests or information needs. You may choose books from stock, or order a special premium edition that will bear your company name and logo.

Contact us today. We'll be pleased to provide you with a complete list of books available as premiums, as well as quantity discounts.

Sincerely,

---

be a personalized letter to a specific individual within a specific company about a specific book. The letter may be sent by itself or with a more elaborate brochure or catalog. If your books are right and your solicitation is correctly targeted, the channel of premium sales may be opened to you.

A Word of Caution   Don't try to offer as a premium a book of poor sales potential. Your best-selling book is your best prospect for a premium sale.

26:10   Book Used as Premium to Enhance Company Image

An encyclopedic reference work devoted to the accomplishments of a minority group was used by a company in a highly competitive industry as an image-building public relations device. In 1976, when a new edition of the reference work was issued, the company purchased a large quantity from the publisher at a substantial discount and made the books available at close to cost to schools sponsored by that minority. The publicity generated by the premium enhanced the image of the company as one that was sympathetic to the aspirations of the minority. The premiums also substantially increased the distribution of the reference work in an area where purchases at full price might otherwise have been very limited.

26:11   Publishing a Sponsored Book: What You Should Know

The sponsored book has long been a way of life for some university presses. Without such outside help, many meritorious works of scholarship would never have been published. However, in some commercial houses, especially those with independent special sales departments, the sponsored book is a sought-after source of income. Such projects occasionally fall in unexpectedly. However, to achieve any volume, publishers have to solicit actively these projects as a source of risk-free, immediate income.

What types of books are most frequently sponsored? Often they represent an authorized history of a company or organization, a biography of the sponsor's founder or an individual closely identified with the sponsor, or a treatment of a product or process in which the sponsor has a major interest. Professional research organizations have an interest in having their research published, both to please existing clients and to attract new ones.

How does the publisher benefit from a sponsored book?

1. There is no risk. The sponsor usually agrees in advance to buy an agreed-upon quantity (sometimes the entire edition), or may provide a specific sum of money toward the publication cost. Where there is a purchase agreement, a price is usually agreed upon in advance of publication and may be about 50 to 65% off the established list price.
2. The sponsored book is usually profitable immediately upon publication.
3. No advances are required prior to publication.
4. No royalties are paid after publication.
5. The sponsored book is usually written by an accomplished writer and based on sound research. Usually all writing and manuscript preparation costs have been covered by the sponsor.
6. The sponsor, especially if a commercial organization, often will spend its own money to help advertise and promote the book, or will mention it in its regular advertising.

What are some disadvantages of the sponsored book?

1. Unless they tell the story of a major scientific contribution, such books usually have little or no review potential.
2. Library sales potential is modest or virtually nonexistent, except possibly in special collections within the same business or industry or in businesses that have a relationship with the sponsor.
3. There is no trade sales potential, except in rare cases.
4. If the sponsored book is a blatant commercial push for the sponsor, it could harm the publisher's image.

What advantages can the publisher offer to the potential sponsor of a subsidized book?

1. The book may be used by the sponsor as a marketing tool. (For example, one manufacturer offered a book describing practical applications of its electronic product as a premium with each unit sold; an instrument manufacturer offered for sales leads a book of instrumentation technique in which most of the illustrations utilized instruments of its manufacture; another manufacturer

distributed a book on the history of a manufacturing process that was in wide use and that had been developed by that manufacturer; and a professional research organization distributed published works based on its research to potential clients.

2. The book may enhance the company's image among potential clients, customers, investors, or its own employees.

3. The book presents the sponsor's story in a favorable manner.

4. The book may promote a cause or concept in which the sponsor has an ongoing interest.

5. The book may project a favorable image of the sponsor among specialized audiences it wishes to influence.

6. The book carries the prestige of a recognized publisher's imprint.

26:12   Major Sales Outlet for Computer Books: The Computer Store

The computer store is a major sales outlet for computer books. Many computer stores offer a wide array of computer-related books and magazines and, hence, will be receptive to your offerings in this area.

According to George Stanley, manager of new market development at Prentice-Hall, computer books represent only 1 to 3% of computer stores' sales, yet these stores like to carry and feature computer books because:

1. They reinforce the store's image as a complete computer center.

2. They help increase store traffic.

3. They help develop an educated consumer.

4. Books are hassle-free, as most suppliers have liberal return privileges.

Stanley described the Prentice-Hall sales operation in computer stores at a special sales panel discussion sponsored by the New York chapter of the Women's National Book Association. Speaking at the Women's City Club of New York, on February 16, 1982, he said his company uses its own salaried reps rather than commission reps to sell to computer stores. The reason for this is that commission reps have too many high-ticket items to sell and would therefore not get the attention they require.

According to Stanley, his company offers liberal trade discounts and cooperative advertising, as well as support advertising in consumer computer publications—all demonstrating the publisher's commitment to the retailer.

26:13   Nontraditional Sales Outlets for University Press Books: AAUP Program

An important development in university press publishing in 1983 is the ongoing program of American University Press Services to cultivate an awareness among its member presses of the potential of non-traditional or special sales. Members are being encouraged to tap fully this market for the sale of university press publications.

In a first step in 1982, the Association of American University Presses (AAUP) assembled from 30 member presses a list of 560 non-traditional outlets through which university press books were being sold. Additionally, when these 560 outlets were contacted, they suggested (at AAUP's request) additional outlets that further expanded the list to 665 verified outlets.

These names were published in "Directory of Nontraditional Outlets for University Press Publications" and distributed to the AAUP membership in the latter part of 1982. (For a detailed description of the directory, see 42:05.)

Patricia McHugh, publications coordinator at AAUP, says: "We have received enthusiastic support for this project. We believe it is a unique and exciting aid to marketing university press books and will consider continuous expansion of the directory and computerization as mailing lists within The Educational Directory."

Book marketers interested in details on the availability of this list of nontraditional outlets for university press books, including selectivity options, should contact The Educational Directory at One Park Avenue, New York, NY 10016; 212-889-3510.

26:14   Society Membership Incentive Offers Publisher Sales Opportunities

If you publish books of interest to organic chemists, you may want to consider participation in the special membership incentive plan of the Division of Organic Chemistry of the American Chemical Society. Under the plan, the division gives each of its members a number of order coupons for books with membership renewal. The member signs the coupon and sends the order with prepayment to a participating publisher to receive a discount, usually about 25%.

For details of publisher participation in the Discount for Members plan, write to Walter S. Trahanovsky, Secretary-Treasurer, American Chemical Society, Division of Organic Chemistry, c/o Department of Chemistry, Iowa State University, Ames, IA 50011.

26:15   Cooperative Advertising Opportunity for Science Publishers

A little known or understood cooperative advertising program at *Science News* can produce substantial revenue if you have a list of scientific books that will appeal to a lay or professional scientific audience.

Under its cooperative advertising program, *Science News* will accept your one- or two-page camera-ready mechanical and run it with a bind-in removable post-paid order card, which is returnable to *Science News*. Orders will be forwarded to you in exchange for payment of your standard bookseller discount to *Science News*.

Your advertising can state your usual terms of payment (prepayment, charge cards, or purchase orders) from companies, libraries, or schools. All advertising is subject to approval by *Science News* for suitability. Do not include anything dealing with mysticism, sex, the occult, or other nonscientific topics.

Among past participants in the program are McGraw-Hill, Van Nostrand Reinhold, TAB Books, Inc., and W. H. Freeman. The bind-in order cards were added in 1976, although this cooperative advertising program had been in effect since early 1972 under the direction of Fred Dieffenbacher. A two-page spread advertising appropriate titles will reach the *Science News* circulation of 172,000 and can generate upwards of $10,000 in orders.

For details, contact Fred Dieffenbacher, P.O. Box F, Dorset, VT 05251; 802-867-5581.

**26:16   Society Apprehensive of Publisher's List Rental
Learns Lesson: Case History**

A professional society received a mailing list rental request from a publisher whose books it offered for sale to its membership. The society turned down the rental request on the premise that the publisher's promotion would be competing with the society for the same customers.

Then the publisher explained to the society's list manager that the anticipated return from such mailings was only approximately 1 percent, and that approximately 99 out of every 100 members would still be left as prospective customers of the society. Furthermore, under the society's cooperative program, only current titles of the publisher were offered, whereas the publisher's promotions were to include a substantial portion of its backlist titles.

The society list was finally released to the publisher with the understanding that, in lieu of list rental, the society would receive from the publisher a credit equal to the profit earned by the society had it made the sale on all duplicated titles. It was further agreed the publisher would make up the difference if the credit did not equal the list rental.

After the mailing was made and returns were evaluated, the society found that the actual "commission" generated by the duplicated titles was approximately one-third less than the amount the society would have received under a conventional list rental. The society then agreed that such rentals were not detrimental to its own co-op sales efforts and that future list rental requests would be honored.

27

Book Clubs

27:01   How Soon after Publication Should You Sell Book Club Rights? Guidelines

If you have a title with broad general appeal, an early book club sale may be desirable. Some book marketers do not agree: They say an early book club offer might cannibalize sales from their own direct-mail efforts or from bookstores. However, others say it is desirable for a book to receive the maximum promotion possible during the book's introductory period, and that book club offers, through their initial and residual mailings, actually help direct-mail and bookstore sales.

As a rule, early book club offers aid the sale of professional business books. The exception is a book that appeals to a specific group or to members of a specific profession modest in number who represent virtually the entire market for the book. When such is the case, it is prudent to withhold the book from any book club offer for at least a year, or until the book has achieved a high degree of saturation among its primary audience.

Illustrating the principle of broad general appeal are three successful books on mail order by three different publishers: *How to Start and Operate a Mail Order Business* (McGraw-Hill), *Successful Direct Marketing Methods* (Crain), and *How I Made One Million Dollars in Mail Order* (Prentice-Hall). All three were offered by book clubs within the first six months after publication and all three are reported to have sold well over 100,000 copies.

In timing the release of book club rights, consider this rule of thumb:

The broader the appeal of the book, the sooner you can release it to a book club. The more specialized the book and its audience, the longer the book club rights should be withheld.

27:02   Timing for Release of Books in Fast-Changing Fields to Book Clubs

How soon is it "safe" to release to a book club a book that has broad appeal and deals with a subject in an area that changes quickly, such as engineering or technology? This is a much-debated question in many publishing establishments and is answered in many different ways.

As a rule, fast-changing fields have a proliferation of new titles that often deal with the same narrow subject area, and their book clubs have a capacity for many new titles. Such books' sales soar during the first year and then fade abruptly, and the titles virtually cease to be active by the end of the third year (see 39:03 and 39:04).

Authors in these fields love early release to the book clubs because it gives their books sudden wide distribution. Some publishers fear book club distribution because they believe the early competition from the club will depress sales of their own edition. One marketer, who is a staunch advocate of early release of such books, gives these reasons:

1. You cannot afford to wait a year. Usually the material is outdated by then and the club won't touch the book.
2. You may lose some sales by early release to the clubs, but you gain them back in other ways. One important factor in book club distribution is that the clubs get the books into the hands of members, for example engineers, very quickly. These engineers work with other engineers, and exposure of one copy of a book to colleagues is likely to generate orders directly from the publisher.
3. The clubs reach engineers where they work or live, which may often be hundreds of miles away from the nearest technical bookstore where the book may be stocked or ordered.

The advocate of early club release advises, "If you're determined to hold a 'hot' book off the club market for a while, release it in six months instead. This gives you time to sell off the largest share of the potential market and still have it in the hands of the club while it is still 'hot.'"

Here, then, are the benefits to the publisher, aside from royalties, of sharing a book with a book club in a fast-changing area of engineering and/or technology:

- It enables the publisher to increase the pressrun on an initial or subsequent printing and reduce unit cost.
- By joining the initial pressrun, the book club copies can help keep book prices down.
- It pleases the author by giving his or her book wider distribution.

- It helps the publisher's sales through the echo effect, because colleagues will order their own copies from the publisher after seeing the book in the hands of a coworker.

27:03   What Happens When Book Club Withdraws Your Title from Sale?

When interest in a book club offering wanes, the club will obtain a bid from a remainder dealer for its remaining stock of the title. As the publisher of the title, you will be given an opportunity to buy the club's stock at the remainder dealer's bid price. If you elect not to buy, the book will then be sold at the price bid by the remainder dealer. If the title in question is still active on your list, it may be worth the small amount of money involved to keep the book out of the remainder market, or to expand your existing stock at a small fraction of manufacturing cost.

27:04   Club Seeking Higher-Priced Books Aimed at Home Handyman

The home handyman is paying more for tips on how to make better use of tools or make repairs around the house. This is evidenced by the changing pricing criteria of the Popular Science Book Club (PSBC), the largest specialized book club in the United States. PSBC is now seeking books priced over $20 for main selections, in contrast to its pricing of main selections at $12 in 1979. PSBC buys 15* main selections a year. It seeks books priced over $15 as alternate selections (up from $10 in 1979) and buys 120 alternates a year.

Keep PSBC in mind if you think you have a winning book on woodworking, furniture making, wiring, plumbing, house building, and related subjects. Contact Leonard Malleck, Director of Book Clubs, 380 Madison Avenue, New York, NY 10017; 212-687-3000. Malleck says a successful main selection has a long life with sales potential approaching 100,000.

27:05   Criteria for Starting a Professional Book Club

1. Is the field constantly developing and expanding?
2. Has the field been researched to ascertain whether it is receptive to a book club? Has a test offering been made?
3. Is the field of a type in which the individuals would respond to offers of books for refresher courses or career advancement?
4. Are there enough books being published in the field to sustain such a club?
5. Will other publishers agree to sell book club rights to you for your offerings?

*The club works on a cycle shorter than a full calendar month, giving members 15 rather than 12 selection periods a year.

6. Are the professionals in the field of a type to maintain their membership in such a book club once they have joined?

7. Does any other book club currently serve this field?

8. Do you have access to experts in the field who will identify topics of maximum interest to prospective club members and recognize classics in the field that should be considered?

9. Do you have assurances that you can obtain enough new and recent titles and current editions of established classics in the field to make offerings that will attract club members?

10. Can you come up with enough of a selection to make offerings on a cyclical basis (monthly, bimonthly, quarterly) for a sustained period while the club is getting underway?

27:06   Simplified Operational Guidelines for Positive-Option Club: The AMACOM Story

Launching a book club need not be expensive or complicated. The positive-option book club operation of AMACOM, the publishing division of the American Management Associations (AMA), parallels similar efforts that were tried with success over the years with minimum effort, investment, or commitment.

The AMACOM Book Club is aimed mainly at the more than 80,000 members of the AMA, to whom it sends mailings offering its own publications. AMA members receive approximately 10% discount off the list prices. Non-AMA members pay list price. AMACOM pays shipping and handling for prepaid orders.

Each book purchase earns the buyer a dividend voucher, based on the price paid, not the list price. Dividend vouchers are issued with a face value of from "one" for books priced up to $16.66, to "ten" for books priced from $64.70 to $70.50. Buyers of books through the club may then use the dividends in lieu of cash for further book purchases according to an established scale of dividend values stated in each announcement. Ten dividend credits will be accepted as payment for a book priced from $15 to $17.49, on up to 44 dividend credits, which will pay for a book priced from $55 to $59.99. The club permits book returns, but not for AMA books purchased with dividends.

Psychologically, the dividend credit idea is a valuable incentive because it places in the hands of the book buyer an uncashed check that can only be applied to a future purchase. If you plan to follow the idea, an expiration date on dividend credits would be advisable.

27:07   University Press Succeeds with Book Club Exclusively for Alumni: Case Study

One of the more innovative book clubs in recent memory is the one started by the University of Notre Dame Press in 1980, under press director Jim Langford. The club is directed solely toward the nearly

75,000 members of the Notre Dame Alumni Association and has, in less than two years of operation, attracted 3,000 members.

The club offers a range of books, mainly in history, literature, business, economics, law, and contemporary issues. It will consider books in philosophy, but rarely poetry, and little or nothing in sociology or the physical sciences. To retain membership in the Notre Dame Alumni Book Club, a member need only place a minimum order of $10 a year.

Langford sees an eventual growth to 5,000 members and is convinced that, although the program will never be a big money-maker, it will keep Notre Dame alumni informed about and reading university press books.*

Book club offerings are drawn from the University of Note Dame Press and about 15 other university presses as well. Offers are usually made at 10 to 15% off list price. A good offering will sell about 400 to 500 copies. Other publishers with suitable works in the areas covered by this book club will have their works considered.

Mailings are made in October and May to the entire University of Notre Dame alumni body and in January and July to book club members only. For information on book participation, contact James R. Langford, University of Notre Dame Press, Notre Dame, IN 46556; 219-239-6346.

27:08 Professional Book Club with Imprecise Approach Discontinued

Membership in the eight specialist book clubs sponsored by McGraw-Hill Book Clubs continue to grow. Each is targeted to a specialized audience within an engineering discipline or business profession, for example, the Mechanical Engineer's Book Club, Civil Engineer's Book Club, and the like.

However, the McGraw-Hill Management Book Guild, which aimed at a general management audience and offered books on topics ranging from accounting, marketing, and career advancement to money management, mergers, and estate planning, has been discontinued.

27:09 The Book Club of 1874: Composition and Operations

Although the book club as presently known in the United States first appeared on the scene in 1926, the idea of a book club was suggested over a century earlier, as the following excerpt from the January 1874 issue of *Scribner's Monthly* indicates:

No investment with which we are acquainted pays so large an intellectual dividend as a Book Club. Three dollars a year is very little to pay for one's intellectual nourishment; by itself it will not secure even a good magazine; but if forty

*Another university press offering books under a special program is Harvard University Press. The Harvard Alumni Library, started in 1981, mails to the alumni body twice a year offering 20 to 25 of its own titles at an average discount of 20%. There are no membership requirements.

persons will give as much for their united pleasure, it will be enough to furnish as much reading for the same number of persons as is easily digested in a season.

A Book Club is the simplest of societies to manage; it will, in fact, almost manage itself. When the Club is formed, a president, vice president, secretary, and treasurer,—generally united in one,—and a committee of buyers are chosen. The secretary really does the business, the other officers being mainly nominal; he receives the books, has them neatly covered with paper, marks the length of time each person may keep the volumes, delivers them to a member entitled to the earliest perusal, and takes charge of them when the round of the Club has been made. . . . the books ought to be started on the circuit by different persons, that all may have equal chances for some first perusal. At the end of the year, when all the volumes have been read, a capital custom is to hold a private auction, and sell them at low rates to the members.

Part VI

Medical Book Marketing and Promotion

28

Medical Book Promotion
Tips and Techniques

28:01   Medical Book Defined

In different publishing establishments, many different types of books are classified under the broad heading of "medical books." We asked a veteran medical marketing professional for her definition of a medical book. This was her response:

A medical book is designed for someone in medical practice or research. It must have clinical application, i.e., apply to the care of people who are sick, and be of interest to practitioners, nurses, or students.

28:02   Uniqueness of Medical Book Market and Best Way to Reach It

The single unique feature of medical book marketing is that the marketplace is so well defined that you don't have to locate the market. The entire field of interest for a particular book may be confined to 6,000 people in the United States. This means that your medical promotions must be fine-tuned to its highly specialized and easily reachable audience.

You need a high degree of saturation of your market so you can mail to it repeatedly, without becoming boring. You may have to go after the same audience many, many times before you can achieve a book's potential share of that market.

Medical publishers reach the medical marketplace in a variety of ways. Some of these include:

1. Direct-mail promotion
2. Space advertising
3. Medical book distributors
4. Sales representatives
5. Exhibits at conventions and medical meetings and in hospitals
6. Cooperative book exhibits

The best and least expensive way to reach a high percentage of the potential medical audience is through direct mail. For the small publisher or the larger publisher with only an occasional title in a particular medical specialty, direct mail is the way to go. Space advertising can inform a potential audience, but it will not produce book sales the way direct mail does. Direct mail provides all the essential data needed for a buying decision, asks for the order, and provides a convenient response vehicle—order card, envelope, or toll-free number.

If you do promote your medical books by direct mail, bear in mind that your mailings will not work if you rely on backlist promotions. For a mailing to be successful, it must lead off with an appealing new title (see 2:17 in this volume).

For other entries in this volume relating to medical book promotion, see 3:11, 3:13, and 5:03.

28:03   Book-Buying Practices of Doctors: Survey Finding

How desirable are medical book-buyer lists? Doctors who have bought one or more books in the previous year are prime prospects for additional purchases of books in the same field. This was the outcome of a survey of medical doctors in both private practice and academic settings who had purchased a high-priced medical reference work. Ninety-eight percent of the survey's respondents indicated they had purchased at least one other professional reference book during the preceding year.

SURVEY FINDINGS

- Doctors in a university setting, using organizational funds, buy more professional books than doctors in private practice.
- Doctors who purchase with research grant funds are likely to buy more professional books than doctors in either university settings or private practice who do not have grant funding.

ENVIRONMENTS OF MEDICAL BOOK BUYERS

- Among private-practice respondents, 69% purchased 1 to 10 books in the previous year; 29% purchased 11 or more books in the previous year.
- Among respondents affiliated with a university, 75% purchased 1 to 10 books in the previous year; 24% purchased 11 or more books in the previous year.

FUNDS USED FOR BOOK PURCHASES

- Of the book buyers using personal funds, 71% purchased 1 to 10 books in the previous year; 26% purchased 11 or more books in the previous year.
- Among book buyers using organizational funds, 76% purchased 1 to 10 books in the previous year; 22% purchased 11 or more books in the previous year.
- Of the book buyers using grant funding, 65% purchased 1 to 10 books in the previous year; 33% purchased 11 or more books in the previous year.

CONCLUSIONS

- If you promote professional books to doctors, book-buyer lists in any medical specialty will provide a better mix than just lists of doctors in that specialty.
- If you are aiming for multiple-book purchases, lists of buyers with grant funds available will produce more of these purchases than will other types of buyer lists.

28:04   Book-Buying Practices of the Nursing Market: Survey Findings

The nursing market represents one of the largest professional book-buying audiences in the United States. Collectively this professional group buys substantial quantities of nursing and other benefit-oriented materials, particularly those related to psychology (both personal and group) and management techniques.

A study of the universe of over two and a quarter million nurses, of whom more than 60% work full time, was made in the fall of 1980.* Here are some of the findings of that survey:

- 64.8% of those surveyed purchased an average of 3.7 books related to their work during the previous 12-month period.
- 49.9% of book-buying nurses purchased an average of 1.8 hardcover books over a 12-month period.
- 36.4% of these book buyers purchased an average of 2.1 paperback books.

Among the hardcover book buyers, nurses averaged one-third fewer book purchases when the price was over $20 than when the price was under $10.† As to paperback books, the average number of book purchases in the $20 or higher price range was less than 14% smaller than the price range under $10.

*The 1981 Survey of the Universe of Nurses was conducted by Audience Analysts, Inc., Bala-Cynwyd, PA 19004, in fall 1980.

†Taking into account both the date of the study and inflation, a present-day comparison should allow for price increases of about 50%.

28:05   Novel Scheme for Identification/Marketing of Medical Books

At the 1982 meeting of the (British) Publishers Association (PA) Medical Group in Normandy, France, a proposal was circulated for an international code for medical books.* The proposed code would be in two parts: a group of letters defining the subject and a number (or group of numbers) defining the level. Thus, by the code a bookseller could identity both its audience and its level. An example was given of a book on diagnosis and treatment of immunodeficiency diseases with the code LTM4.

The "L" would indicate the book should be classified under laboratory medicine; the "T" that the book would also interest pediatricians; the "M" that the book would also interest general physicians; and the "4" that it was a reference book. (A basic undergraduate text would have been coded with a "1".)

A strong argument in support of the novel proposal was that it might convince nonspecialist medical booksellers to display and distribute such books if they were already selling trade books to doctors. The proposal is being further researched by the PA Medical Group. In the summer of 1982, the board of the American Medical Publishers Association was queried about its interest in the proposal, and overwhelmingly turned it down.

28:06   Another Unique Promotion Technique Popular with Medical Marketers

Among the medical book marketing and promotion tips in *Volume One* of *Book Marketing Handbook*, we described the practice of publishers who exhibit at medical meetings and display their books on a high table in the aisle with all books lying flat, readily exposed to passersby. Their reasoning for doing so was that doctors, who are always rushed, must be caught on the run if any of their precious time is to be seized for examining displayed books.

Now we would like to share with you a direct-response technique that is used by many medical marketers and was designed with the same purpose in mind—and it works! We refer to the widespread practice among a number of medical publishers to mail book promotions to doctors in the form of a sheet of colorfully printed stamps. Each stamp illustrates a medical book jacket or cover, an order number is identified at base of stamp, and an order card is included in the mailing. All the busy doctor has to do is lick the stamp representing the book of his or her choice, paste it on the reply card, and drop the card in the mail.

Among the medical publishers who have been using this device are W. B. Saunders, F. A. Davis, Little, Brown, and C. V. Mosby. At the time of this writing, stamp mailings were also under consideration by Medical Economics Books.

*Such a medical subject classification system would be applied as rigidly as the ISBN system. The proposal, by Andrew Bax of Blackwell Scientific, was reported in *The Bookseller*, May 15, 1982.

For complete details on how stamps can be used in medical promotions, see 5:03 and 16:07.

Most medical marketers use two-color stamps. However, one of the medical houses that started modestly in 1980 with a test mailing of 8,000, using two-color stamps, was mailing in quantities of up to 140,000 three years later, using four-color stamps.

28:07 How Frequently Can You Mail to Same List in Medical Book Promotion?

There is no rule on how often you can mail to the same medical list. One medical marketer says, "I continue mailing to the same list until the response ceases to be cost-effective."

Obviously, a first announcement of an important new medical title will outpull a follow-up mailing made several months later for the same book. One medical publisher estimates her follow-up mailings produce about half the response of her initial mailing. To avoid this large falloff in response to follow-up mailings, mix a follow-up mailing with new lists not previously tried. The fresher list will increase the overall response of the total mailing and permit you to make repeated mailings to previously used lists without loss.

28:08 Sources of Medical Book-Buyer Lists

A list of known buyers of sci-tech and professional books will outpull an association or society list.

"Laws" for Successful Direct Marketing (1:07),
Book Marketing Handbook, 1st Ed. *(Volume One)*

A by-product of the multimillion-name data base available from CMG, the Data Base Division of College Marketing Group, is a list of 60,000 medical book buyers, segmented by medical specialty. There are individuals who have purchased professional-level titles at prices exceeding $30 each from the various medical book publishers, nearly all of whom are commercial and participate in the CMG data base. Most of the names are of recent (within the last two years) book buyers and are guaranteed 100% deliverability.

Another prime source for names of buyers of books on general medicine is The Educational Directory (ED), owned and operated by the Association of American University Presses. It offers the names of more than 3,000 buyers, which are supplied by some 35 member university presses. These medical book-buyer names can be merged with any other list in the ED data base.

28:09 Source of Nursing and Allied Health Book-Buyer Lists

College Marketing Group (CMG) now offers list segments from its enlarged data base for 23,000 buyers of nursing books and 6,000 buyers of allied health books. These buyers have purchased professional and reference books priced at more than $25 within the two most recent years.

The 23,000 buyer universe for nursing books is augmented by separate list selections for nursing professors in medical surgical nursing, obstetric and newborn nursing, pediatric nursing, psychiatric nursing (coordinators), community nursing, nursing leadership/administration, and nursing education.

The book-buyer segments for allied health include groupings in physical therapy, biomedical technology, and medical photography and illustration.

28:10   Understanding the Medical School Curriculum: What Books Fit What Levels

When you promote your medical books to the school environment, bear in mind that the program of medical studies is regimented. The first year entails mainly lectures, labs and basic science courses emphasizing the normal human anatomy. By contrast, the second year is partly clinical in nature, and emphasizes the pathology of the body. The third year is devoted mostly to required clerkships. The fourth year offers electives in the subspecialties of medicine and surgery, which include such subjects as radiology, pediatric subspecialties, child psychiatry, obstetric and gynecologic subspecialties.

Medical schools vary in their organization of the various medical and surgical specialties, which may exist either as autonomous departments or as sections within the department of medicine or surgery. The major subspecialties of medicine are allergy-immunology, cardiology, dermatology, endocrinology, gastroenterology, hematology-oncology, infectious disease, neurology, pulmonary disease, renal medicine (nephrology), and rheumatology. The major subspecialties of surgery are anesthesiology, cardiovascular-thoracic surgery, gastrointestinal surgery, neurosurgery, ophthalmology, orthopedics, otorinolaryngology, plastic surgery, and urology.

28:11   A Department Store of List Options for Medical Marketers: The CMG Medical Data Base

The CMG medical mailing list data base, now fully described in a separate catalog, provides the marketer of medical texts and reference works with a "department store" of lists available in all aspects of medical, nursing, and allied health education and research.

The various components of the CMG data base are listed individually. However, any of the components can be mixed, matched, integrated, or broken out by the medical marketer according to any promotional aims or budgetary limitations.

The medical school faculty lists, for example, cover courses offered in the basic sciences in medical schools. However, selection options within each course include total faculty, chairpersons or medical school section heads, course coordinators, nonmedical school faculty, book buyers, or Canadian faculty.

The clinical sciences list segments provide even more selections for the marketer: total faculty, chairpersons or section heads, course coordinators, clerkships or subinternships (clinical courses held at inpatient hospitals and various outpatient settings where students become actively involved in patient care), clerkship directors, residency coordinators (those responsible for direction of post medical school programs), nonmedical school faculty, book buyers, and Canadian faculty.

Faculty list segments and book buyer lists are also available for courses in humanities in medicine, health care management, health science and education, and pharmacy. In nursing, course lists are available for associate and baccalaureate degrees and graduate-level programs, as well as for registered nurse and licensed practical nurse diplomas and book buyers. Allied health course lists can be broken down to proprietary and vocational-technical hospital schools; two-year, four-year and graduate programs; and book buyers. Canadian nursing faculty names are also available.

For the CMG Medical List Catalog, write to CMG, Data Base Division of College Marketing Group, Attention: Glenn Matthews, 50 Cross Street, Winchester, MA 01890; or call Linnea Willman at 617-729-7865.

28:12 Alternate Approach to Targeted Mailings for Medical Texts

Although precise lists of medical school teaching faculty can be obtained for mailing, at least one medical publisher prefers a different route for launching a new medical text.

Prior to publication of a new text, a letter is sent to the appropriate department chairperson with complete details of the forthcoming title. The letter says a complimentary copy will be sent to the department head when the book is published. It also asks for the names of instructors in the department who might use the book in a specific course, and the name of the course, so that complimentary copies can be sent to other faculty as well.

When the names are received (and most usually supply an average of one to four names), the book is subsequently sent. Along with each copy goes a letter indicating the book has been sent at the suggestion of the department chairperson (name used), who thought it might be useful in the course (name of course as supplied by department chair is used).

Although this personalized approach takes a certain amount of individualized effort, its advantage is that it does tend to carry the authority of the department chair, on whose suggestion the book was sent. It works.

28:13   List Selection Options for Medical Laboratories

The expanded College Marketing Group (CMG) medical data base includes the names of more than 30,000 laboratory personnel. They are subdivided into 23 different selection categories. It should be noted that, as part of the overall medical data base, book-buyer names from the CMG Lablist can be added to any other mailing list segment in the CMG data base you request for a mailing. For example, if you mail to CMG lists of hematology faculty or hematology clerkships, you may also add on the 2,300 hematology book buyers from the CMG Lablist.

The Lablist provides the names of the director, chief technologist, and main buyer or supervisor for 12 different medical test categories. Eight other selection options are available, ranging from hospital or nonhospital setting to number of employees in the lab (from under 5 to over 50).

28:14   Source of Medical Lists for Overseas Markets

If you wish to target promotions for medical books or journals to overseas markets, a reliable, long-established medical list source is IBIS Information Services in New York. IBIS offers a list of names for more than 80,000 physicians, both general practitioners and medical specialists, who are either in practice or in teaching or research. Medical lists are also available for various other countries worldwide, and include doctors, medical school faculty, and medical libraries. Contact IBIS Information Services, Inc., 51 East 42nd Street, New York, NY 10017; 212-687-9150. For additional details on IBIS list, see 2:01.

28:15   Lists Available for Other Segments of the Health Care Market

In addition to medical practitioners, there are a number of other health-care audiences that are prime prospects for many different types of books. Accurate, reliable lists are available for all of these audiences, and a wide range of selection options makes it possible to reach select groups within the various audiences with extreme accuracy. Here are some of these audiences* and selection options:

PHYSICIAN ASSISTANTS (AMERICAN ACADEMY OF PHYSICIAN ASSISTANTS)

Physician assistants work closely with physicians, and in some states they prescribe drugs, administer treatment, and perform diagnostic tests. They are interested in medical books, journals, and other

*Most lists are available from the Direct Marketing Handbook of Healthcare Audiences, Fisher-Stevens, Inc., Totowa, N.J. Other list sources include the College Marketing Group (see Nurses) and Mailing List Marketing (see Laboratory Operations Management).

materials that will help them meet their certification requirements. List selection options: members of AAPA, nonmembers; also by state.

DENTISTS

Selection options: by city, state, county, and ZIP Code; geographic region, size of city; general practice plus nine dental specialties; year of graduation, name of school; or any combination of these.

PHARMACIES

- Selection options: by state, county, city, or ZIP code; by type of store: independent retailers, chain stores, chain headquarters, and wholesalers.

- American Pharmaceutical Association (APhA) list. Available by home address. Selections can also be based on the membership of two academies: the Academy of Pharmaceutical Sciences, which includes six sections (basic pharmaceutics; economic, social and administrative sciences; industrial pharmaceutical technology; medicinal chemistry and pharmacognosy; pharmaceutical analysis and control; and pharmacology and toxicology), and the Academy of Pharmacy Practice, which includes five sections (clinical practice, federal pharmacy, long-term care, nuclear pharmacy, and practice management).

- American Society of Hospital Pharmacists (ASHP) list. Available for selection by special-interest group and type of membership. Be sure to specify U.S. only or total list, as about 40% of membership is outside the United States. Membership is divided into these groups: pharmacists currently practicing in a hospital or related institution, associate membership for graduate students, and allied health practitioners contributing to hospital pharmacy. Special interests or subcategories of pharmacy include administrative, adult clinical, ambulatory care, clinical pharmacokinetic, drug and poison information, geriatric, psychopharmacy, oncology, pediatric, radiopharmacy, and intravenous therapy.

HOSPITALS

Selection options: by number of beds, type of service management, ownership and population, ZIP Code, city, state, county.

- *Health Care Product News* circulation list offers names of general administration, professional, and service personnel for hospitals by number of beds; also general administration at nursing homes by number of beds. List selection options available for 24 professional functions/titles, including hospital administrator; nursing home administrator; chief pharmacist (hospital); director of nursing services (hospital); director of nursing services (nursing home); director of in-service education; chief engineer/maintenance chief; food service manager/chief dietitian; local, state, regional, and federal health officials; architects and consultants.

NURSES

- *Medical Economics* list of registered nurses. Selections available by state and sectional center facilities.
- *RN Magazine* circulation list. Selections available by name, state, ZIP Code, type of nursing practice, and position/responsibility.
- *Nurse Educator* circulation list. Selections available: nursing educators who are faculty members of state-approved schools and department heads of in-service education in hospitals of 75 beds or more.
- *Nursing Dimension* circulation lists. Selections available: nurses practicing in health-care and educational facilities. Selections for these specialties: directors of nursing, assistant directors, administrators, supervisors, head nurse and assistants; by practice setting (hospitals, nursing homes, extended care facilities, schools of nursing, public health nursing, occupational health nursing, school nursing, nursing school libraries).

College Marketing Group also offers a full range of nursing educator lists with many course and selection options. Nursing educators' lists may be obtained by course name, as well as by program (associate degree, baccalaureate, graduate, RN diploma, LPN, allied health, or for all categories). Nursing education course lists are grouped under seven headings: basic sciences, fundamentals of nursing, medical surgical nursing, maternal/child nursing, psychiatric nursing, community health nursing, advanced and clinical nursing, and allied health. Canadian lists also available. For course names and current counts, refer to CMG's current catalog or call CMG at 617-729-7865.

LABORATORY OPERATIONS MANAGEMENT

More than 58,000 names are available in this major segment of the health-care field, yet each segment of this widely dispersed group can be reached with pinpoint accuracy, from the 6,253 pathologists in hospitals to the single nuclear medicine supervisor in a blood bank. List segments available from Mailing List Marketing, Oradell, N.J., cover 18 different occupational categories of specialists in laboratory operations management and are available on a selective basis in seven different work settings, including hospitals (by total or bed count), private (independent) labs, government labs, group practice, blood banks, biomedical industrial labs, and university and college labs. For details, contact Janet Doka, Manager, List Marketing, Mailing List Marketing, Medical Economics Co., Inc., Oradell, NJ 07649; 212-262-3030.

28:16   **Available List Options for Promotion
to Medical Professionals**

If you publish books for the medical market and you cannot afford large mailings, medical mailing list houses, through a combination of computer and ZIP codes, have available a wide variety of list options that enable you to target even your smallest mailings with maximum effectiveness.

Whether you are new to or experienced in medical promotion, you should always remember that the list is the single most important element in any medical direct-mail promotion. Try to be fully aware of all the list segmentation options available to you through the various brokers who specialize in medical and allied health lists.

28:17 **New Direct-Mail Program at Saunders**
Shares Spotlight with Active Backlist: Case Study

The direct-mail program at W. B. Saunders Co. in Philadelphia must be highly effective. It has been in use since 1974 and uses a combination of fliers, stamps, and postcards in a most interesting and unusual way.

When a mailing is done on a new book, the envelope package includes a two-page flier/brochure about the title and something extra. That something extra is a sheet of stamps, 20 in all,* and a postpaid order card on which four stamps can be pasted.

The sheet of stamps contains related backlist titles in the medical specialty treated by the new book on the flier. The sheet folds into thirds to fit neatly into the envelope. The stamp portion of the sheet occupies only two-thirds, the remaining third is a free bookplate or, occasionally, an illustration possibly of historical interest and related to the topic of the mailing. The 20 stamps do not always promote books. Sometimes several of the spaces are occupied by Saunders's medical journals.

Stamp sheets are printed in two colors of ink, and each stamp contains an outline of a book 1 inch high (see Figure 20). Inside the book outline a second color of ink, usually light blue or yellow, or a screened picture related to the subject matter of the mailing (a child for pediatrics, or a pregnant woman for obstetrics) may be used.

COPY ON STAMPS

Because medical book jackets do not reduce to a 1-inch height and remain legible, the Saunders practice of using a black-bordered book outline works exceptionally well. Inside the book outline are printed the title of the book and name of author. Directly under the book outline on each stamp the page count, price, and order number are given. Directly above each book outline on the stamp the year of publication or the word "NEW" appears in boldface.

Susan Hunter, Saunders marketing director, says "The key to successful use of the stamps is selecting titles that are recognizable either by the author's name or by the number of previous promotions on the title. In other words, I don't think the [stamp] technique is a good one

---

*Saunders had been using sheets of 16 stamps for years, but switched to the 20-stamp sheet in late 1982.

FIGURE 20 A sheet of stamps accompanies each new book flier mailing at W. B. Saunders. Each sheet contains approximately 20 books in the same medical specialty as the new book offered. The illustrated sheets also contain a free bookplate.

for a publisher trying to establish a new list. It is really a backlist promotion vehicle."

Saunders, which according to *Literary Market Place* published 110 titles in 1981 and has a substantial backlist, uses a dozen or more stamp sheets in various medical specialties. It mails as frequently as twice a month and prints sufficient quantities of each sheet at a time to last four to six months. Usually, a title is not added to a specialty stamp sheet until after the title has been available for at least four to six months.

28:18   Medical Book Marketers' Comments on Use of Stamps in Promotion

"The key to successful use of stamps in medical book promotion is selecting titles that are recognizable, either by the author's name, or by the number of previous promotions on the title."

"Stamps encourage people to buy more books. While they are searching the cover illustrations on the stamps for the book of their choice, they see other titles and order them as well."

"I don't think the [stamp] technique is a good one for a publisher trying to establish a new list. It is really a backlist promotion vehicle."

28:19   Medical and Health-Care Cooperative Book Exhibits

The cooperative book exhibit is one of the most cost-effective ways of reaching specialized audiences in the medical and health-care fields, especially when you have only one or more books in a particular medical specialty. Conference Book Service (CBS) is a specialist in co-op book exhibits.

Following is a list of cooperative book exhibits CBS traditionally holds at annual medical and health-care meetings. You can participate for approximately $20 per book, and features of the service include face-out display of each book, coverage by a booth attendant and feedback on your book(s), and distribution of a printed catalog and any literature/catalogs you may wish to disseminate in conjunction with your books. These conferences are covered by CBS:

- American Association of Medical Microbiology chairpersons
- Annual Brain Research Conference
- Hospital Purchasing Exposition and Nursing Congress
- International Academy of Pathology
- American Society of Neurochemistry
- Medical Library Association
- Society on Nuclear Medicine
- Society of General Physiologists
- American Psychoanalytic Association

Various other medical or related meetings are added to the CBS schedule each year as publisher interest warrants. If you have a medical conference you would like to suggest for inclusion, or for a schedule of medical exhibits, contact Conference Book Service, Inc., 80 South Early Street, Alexandria, VA 22304; 703-823-6966.

28:20   Timing of Mailing to Medical Librarians

If you plan to exhibit at the Medical Library Association convention, usually held in early June, a mailing timed for about one month prior to the convention will enable those librarians planning to attend to preselect those books they want to look at more closely.

28:21   Advertising Sources in Medical and Allied Health Fields

If you advertise in the medical and allied health fields, you'll find *The Media Guide*, issued annually by Steven K. Herlitz, Inc., a convenient, information-packed reference source. *The Media Guide* provides a wealth of information in convenient tabular form on more than 300 publications in the medical and allied health fields that accept advertising.

Periodicals are grouped under such subject headings as clinical journals, limited mass journals, mass medical journals, surgical journals, medical newspapers, hospital journals, nursing journals, biomedical journals, regional journals, osteopathic journals, laboratory journals, and pharmacy journals. Each journal entry includes advertising page rate, additional cost for color ads, circulation, cost-per-1,000 circulation, and frequency of publication. Entries also indicate whether a journal is an official publication.

The Herlitz organization has been publishing *The Media Guide* for more than 25 years. It is free for the asking. Write to Steven K. Herlitz, Inc., 404 Park Avenue South, New York, NY 10016 (212-532-9400); or to 731 Market Street, San Francisco, CA 94103 (415-777-2050).

28:22   Medical Wholesaler, Jobber, or What? The Preferred Term

Many librarians indicate they prefer to order through a jobber, and categorize all library suppliers that are not publishers as jobbers. However, in the medical book supply field, the specialist book supplier is not categorized as a jobber but rather as a book distributor.

The term "distributor" is perhaps most appropriate because the medical specialist is at once many things, as we discussed in *Volume One* of *Book Marketing Handbook*: a trade wholesaler that supplies bookstores, a library jobber that serves libraries, a direct seller that sells by mail and engages a sales force, and a book supplier that serves the medical book needs of nearby medical practitioners.

Says one medical book distributor about the three choices, "I prefer 'distributor' over jobber, but 'jobber' over 'wholesaler,' in that order."

28:23   The Medical Book Distributor: How Best to Reach

If you publish an occasional medically oriented book, you don't have to search out a medical distributor. If a demand develops for your book, the distributor will come to you. However, if you want to reach the medical distributor, here are the key contacts, with telephone numbers for the leading medical distributors:

- Massachusetts: Bill Brown, President/Owner, Brown and Connolly, Inc., 2 Keith Way, Hingham, MA 02043; 617-749-8570.
- Illinois: Stan Weiss, Owner/President; Barry Shreibstein, Vice President, Logan Brothers Book Co., 1450 West Randolph Street, Chicago, IL 60607; 312-733-6424.
- New Jersey: Ed Rodham, General Manager, Logan Brothers Book Co.,* 135 New Dutch Lane, Fairfield, NJ 07006; 800-526-3025.
- Ohio: Bob O'Connell, General Manager, Logan Brothers East, 7230 Northfield Road, Walton Hills, OH 44146; 216-439-7500.
- Missouri: John Marcus, Owner/President, Matthews Book Co., 11559 Rock Island Court, Maryland Heights, MO 63043; 314-432-1400.
- Texas: John and Bill Majors, Owners; Albert Majors McClendon, General Manager, J. A. Majors Co., 221 Walnut Hill Lane, Irving, TX 75061; 214-659-0666. Also Anne Ellison, J. A. Majors Co. (Houston Branch), 1806 Southgate, Houston, TX 77030; 713-526-5757.
- Georgia: Gary Brooks, J. A. Majors Co. (Atlanta Branch), 3770 Zip Industrial Boulevard, P.O. Box 82685, Atlanta, GA 30354; 404-768-4956.
- Louisiana: Warner Pope, J. A. Majors Co. (New Orleans Branch), 3903 Bienville Street, New Orleans, LA 70119; 504-486-5956.
- California: Bob Ruby, Owner/President, Medical & Technical Books, Inc., 11511 Tennessee Avenue, Los Angeles, CA 90064; 213-879-1607.
- Pennsylvania: Tim Foster, Owner/President, Rittenhouse Book Distributors, 511 Feheley Drive, King of Prussia, PA 19406; 215-277-1414.

*Successor to Eliot Books, Inc.

Part **VII**

Book Promotion
in the
Social Sciences

29

The Social Sciences

29:01 The Future of Social Science Publishing

It is the failure of many publishers to spot ... shifting trends that have led them to surrender their social science lists.

Irving Louis Horowitz, Hannah Arendt Distinguished
Professor of Sociology and Political Science,
Rutgers University.

In *Volume One* of *Book Marketing Handbook*, Dr. Irving Louis Horowitz, authority on the social sciences and social science publishing, provided a detailed definition of the boundaries of social science publishing, which he summarized as "the study of the human condition in the process of interaction."

For this chapter, we again sought the advice of Dr. Horowitz, who is editor in chief of *Society*, president of Transaction Books, publishing consultant, and author or contributor to scores of books in the social sciences. To the question "What is the future of social science publishing?" Horowitz replied:

Contrary to the common wisdom—social science is not collapsing or dissolving, but it is becoming more specialized. The key to marketing books in this area is to follow the bouncing professional ball; i.e., the "action" is no longer in the large, omnibus organizations like the American Political Science Association or the American Sociological Association; but rather such newer social science outfits like the Society for Scientific Religion, Association for Public Policy Analysis and Management, Institute of Information Scientists, etc. ad infinitum. It is the failure of many publishers to spot such shifting trends that have led them to surrender their social science lists.

29:02   Current Trends in the Social Sciences

Valuable insights on present and future trends in social science publishing may be gained by reading the October/November 1981, issue of *Public Opinion*, bimonthly publication of the American Enterprise Institute for Public Policy Research. A panel of distinguished social scientists was asked this question by the editors of *Public Opinion*: Is social science a god that failed? Brief, selected excerpts from their answers follow:

- Walter Berns, American Enterprise Institute: "To the extent that the social sciences set themselves up as hard sciences, they have failed. . . . They cannot provide the kind of hard information about human behavior that physics provides about the behavior of atoms. But social science with more modest goals can be useful."

- Irving Louis Horowitz, Rutgers University: "Today you have to look at social science innovation where the action is taking place. . . . If anything, social science is undergoing a renaissance. People have not been able to see it because they have locked into old professions, old organizations, and old ways of thinking. Meanwhile there has been a pluralization and a multiplication of the organizational forums to which social scientists now belong."

- Alice Rossi, Professor of Sociology, University of Massachusetts, and President-Elect, American Sociological Association: "The social sciences overreached their potentialities when they looked for universal laws of social behavior that would hold at all times and in all places like the laws of physics. One of the important things that has developed in the last ten or fifteen years within the social sciences is the realization that we're really historical sciences."

- Irving Kristol, Editor, *The Public Interest*: "Behind much of social science in the last 150 years is the belief that its practitioners can create a more rational, orderly world. It has turned out, however, that social science simply does not have such a capability . . . as far as sociology and political science are concerned, they should . . . really try to understand society, rather than to take it upon themselves to become masters of social change."

- David Reisman, Henry Ford II Professor of Social Science, Emeritus, Harvard University: "[The social sciences] include many different fields, some of which are thriving . . . the social sciences have been politicized and . . . except for economics, the direction has been leftward. . . . To refurbish their image, social scientists should . . . get out of the hothouse of academia and have some contact with the people social science tends to ignore."

- Kenneth Prewitt, President, the Social Science Research Council: "I don't think the social sciences failed . . . ; indeed I would argue that social science is in a very healthy state. . . . If we really look at what we've accomplished over the last fifty to seventy years, it's a much stronger record than social scientists have proclaimed."

- Robert Nisbet, American Enterprise Institute (and author, *The History of the Idea of Progress*): "The social sciences were absolutely saturated with liberalism from about the middle 1930s into the middle 1970s. . . . It was the liberal core that did more lasting harm to social science than anything from the outside. . . . But there have been some very real and salutary changes during the last few years. . . . A conservative, or nonliberal, nonradical, perspective in the social sciences is not only possible these days but formidable."

29:03   Book Pricing in the Social Sciences

To achieve any measure of success, a book must be priced within its market. That is, it must be offered at a price that seems reasonable to potential buyers within its market, that is competitive with like books, and within its readers' ability to pay. All of these criteria are particularly true of books in the social sciences.

A social science book intended as an undergraduate text, where most books might fall into the $7 to $15 range, will have virtually no acceptance if priced at $25 to $30. This writer recalls two instances in the 1970s involving social science book pricing. In one instance a book in sociology, intended mainly as a textbook, was produced in a dual edition, with one publisher offering an inexpensive paperbound textbook edition and the other offering a considerably higher priced cloth edition intended mainly for the library market. When both editions were advertised jointly, virtually all of the response was for the paper edition.

In the other instance, a textbook on international relations was imported from the original British publisher in a cloth edition priced approximately 60% higher than competing works in the same area. Although the book attracted a considerable amount of favorable attention when displayed at a political science meeting and advertised, sales were virtually dormant. When, following the meeting, a mailing to political scientists offered the same book at a special (competitive) textbook price on adoption orders only, the book readily found its way into the classroom.

29:04   Promotion Approaches for the Social Science Research Monograph

The social science research monograph represents a theoretical, speculative, or substantive contribution to social science knowledge and generally can be promoted to a widely varied audience that includes policymakers, researchers, practitioners, and intelligent, well-informed laypersons. Your promotion should aim to convince the potential reader that the book makes a significant contribution to social science, explain the implications of the research presented, and stress the permanent value of the book for archives. If the book offers numerous citations to other relevant research, the number of literature references should be mentioned, as should the number of tables or appendixes if either is an important or sizable part of the book's content.

**29:05   Major Source for College Faculty and Book-Buyer Lists
in the Social Sciences**

Among the services that offer lists in the social sciences for both college faculty and book buyers, a major supplier is the Data Base Division of College Marketing Group (CMG). Based on contracts with 16
mainly commercial book publishers who have supplied customer data,
CMG now offers from a single source consolidated book-buyer lists of
more than 100,000 names in the social sciences, along with its traditional lists of instructors.

The faculty lists are compiled from class schedules or other lists of
teaching assignments, from colleges and universities, and from sales
reps working for four major textbook publishers. The lists are augmented by mail and phone inquiries to department chairpersons.

Social science faculty lists are available by course(s) taught at two-
year, four-year, and graduate schools. Names of bookbuyers in the
same subject areas are also available. Groups may be mixed to include
or exclude any category. One may, for example, buy a list of names of
sociology instructors at two-year colleges, adding to it a selection of
names from the list of 10,000 buyers of sociology books. Additional
list selection options are offered by size of school enrollment.

A feature of the CMG social sciences lists is that they also include
departmental library representatives, library book selection personnel,
library periodicals selection personnel, and library nonprint selection
personnel. As many libraries buy on recommendations from departmental library representatives, these segmented lists provide a degree
of coverage almost unimaginable a decade ago.

For targeted book marketing, the CMG catalog presents a working
tool of immense value to the marketer of texts and reference works in
the social sciences as well as in the arts, humanities, and education.
For a copy of the CMG Social Science Mailing List Catalog, write to
Data Base Division, College Marketing Group, 50 Cross Street, Winchester, MA 01890; 617-729-7865.

30

Business, Law, Economics

**30:01 Business and Management-Oriented Books:
How to Integrate in Sci-Tech Mailings**

Don't hesitate to include books on business and management in your
sci-tech mailings, especially if those books are directed to scientists,
engineers, and researchers in such rapidly changing fields as computer
science and electronics. Workers in high-technology areas, advises one
specialist, "are hungry for information and they are anxious to keep up
with every type of management technique they can get their hands on
so they can keep things from flying apart."

They are also interested in self-help books and books that offer
career guidance or tips on improvement of personal skills. The author's
experience with mailings to this group has proven this time and again.
Books on business and self-improvement, when included in mailings to
sci-tech audiences, have not only held their own with the sci-tech titles
in the mailings but, in some instances, have outsold featured sci-tech
titles.

Where you do include business or self-improvement books in a
nonrelated mailing, avoid integrating them by theme with other titles
in the mailing if they will look out of place. Instead, group them under
a common heading such as "Reference Sources for Your Professional
Library," or "Useful Professional Reference Works" or "Professional
Reference Works, Handbooks."

30:02   A Marketing Plan for a High-Ticket Book
Aimed at Auditors and Accountants

You are asked to come up with a marketing plan for a reference work priced at $85 and aimed at auditors and accountants, and your budget is not to exceed $35,000. Here is a plan that would give you fairly good coverage of the market and, at the same time, allow you to test the much larger buyer lists of two other publishers in the field for a follow-up mailing.

BUDGET ALLOCATIONS

Direct mail (initial announcement, see breakdown below)	
60,000 pieces mailed at $300/1,000	$18,000
Space advertising (see breakdown below)	$ 7,500
Telephone follow-up on 200 to 300 names	$ 3,000
Direct mail (follow-up)	
22,000 pieces mailed at $300/1,000	$ 6,500
Total cost (budget)	$35,000

Direct-mail campaign (initial announcement)	
AICPA partners in public practice	30,000
CPA firms with three or more partners:	
Att: Managing Partner	5,000
Corporate controllers, largest firms	3,000
Buyers of accounting books (house list)	9,000
Buyers of books in financial management (house list)	3,000
Financial book buyers: test of larger list from	
Publisher A	5,000
Financial book buyers: test of larger list from	
Publisher B	5,000
Total for mailing per budget	60,000

Space advertising (within $7,500 budget)
Journal of Accountancy
CPA Journal
Practical Accountant
Management Accounting
Wall Street Journal (Eastern edition)
Accounting Review

30:03   Books for the Corporate Middle Manager:
Suggested Copy Approach

Promotion copy for books aimed at a corporate audience, mainly staff and middle-management personnel should be conservative, says one marketer of such books. "It should have an air of stability and practicality. Both the book and the advertising for it," he adds, "should include information a subordinate can comfortably present to a boss for consideration or approval. Copy emphasis for books directed to the corporate middle manager should be [applications-] and problem-oriented. In such business areas as business data processing and accounting, copy should be more conservative than for books on such subjects as management, marketing, and investment."

30:04   **Best Advertising Medium for Books on Business, Investment, Finance**

If you publish in the areas of business, investment, or finance, the *Wall Street Journal*, with a circulation of more than two million, ranks first as a space advertising medium. The newspaper has long been acknowledged as the primary publication in the United States for mail-order advertising. One expert* has claimed that a quarter-page ad in *WSJ* will produce as many orders as would a full-page advertisement in any other publication. At *WSJ*'s high rates, however, if a quarter-page seems a luxury, go for a smaller space as your budget permits. Even small ads can pull extremely well.

If you can't afford the *WSJ* national edition and want to test the circulation for a particular book, try one of the regional editions printed in 17 printing plants across the country. By testing one regional edition at a time, it may be possible to ascertain if your book has regional appeal and to repeat in that region only. Place your insertion order extra early. Advertising space in some issues is sometimes sold out, and you may not get the first insertion date you ask for.

For additional information on advertising for business or related books, see 14:04 and 14:05.

30:05   **Why a Good Review in a Mass-Circulation Periodical Sometimes Fails to Help Sales**

From time to time, professional book publishers come up with a title that has strong trade potential, and so they aim for reviews in mass-circulation business periodicals as a sales booster. Then, when the review does appear, it does not seem to have any influence on the book's sales. Why?

The answer lies in the way mass-appeal books sell in bookstores. Quite often, such reviews, although quite favorable, appear long after bookstore sales have peaked and stores have already made their returns to the publisher. Once returned, bookstores are reluctant to restock or reorder a previously held book that was considered overstock.

One possible solution would be to supply the periodical with galleys before publication. But most mass-circulation periodicals want to see a finished book, so instead, copy what trade houses do quite successfully.

*Joseph Sugarman, *DM News*, September 15, 1980.

Set a publication date for about six weeks after the review copies have been sent. Most trade houses set pubdates for a substantial time after bound-book date in order to be sure that the books are in stock in the stores before the promotions break. This practice also gives the important periodicals a chance to review the book as close as possible to the official publication date.

30:06   Tandem Mail and Phone Strategy Solves Problems in Portfolio Promotion: Case Study

A marketer of business publications had a 20-portfolio series in real estate that he planned to sell by direct mail. He launched his campaign with a major mailing to supposedly good lists and offered the 20 portfolios on a no-risk 30-day examination basis. Mail response was high. But the offer was deemed a flop and further promotion postponed until a better marketing approach was prepared. Despite the high response, about 30% of the portfolios sent on examination were returned, and another 20% proved to be uncollectible.

Ultimately, a new twofold strategy was devised that, if successful, would radically cut down on the high percentage of examination-copy returns and, at the same time, reduce the bad debt ratio to almost zero. This was the plan: Instead of offering the entire 20-portfolio series, a 20-card deck was sent out, with each card offering only one portfolio, at $28, for a 30-day free examination. The response for the 20 individual cards/portfolios was considerably greater than the response to the earlier 20-portfolio offer, and the bad-debt ratio was also considerably reduced. But the marketer's promotion did not end there!

In a second step to the promotion, each paid buyer of a portfolio from the card-deck offer was then contacted by phone, using an in-house telephone sales force. The telephone salesperson thanked the caller for the purchase and then offered the entire 20-portfolio package at a 50% saving off the established list price. Furthermore, the buyer was told that the $28 already paid would be credited against the purchase. The unique sales approach worked surprisingly well, and sales of the 20-portfolio series were resumed with great success.

30:07   Single Line on Order Form Sparks Growth for Business Book Publisher

A major publisher of business books and loose-leaf services sold primarily by mail attributes a large measure of the company's growth to the use of this single line on the order form of promotional literature:

"I understand that subsequent volumes in the series will be sent on approval."

As virtually all of the publications of this publisher are followed by supplements, each sale is magnified many times by the subsequent addition of supplements.

The company's marketing head cautions that the inclusion of this line tends to diminish to some extent the response one might receive from a one-time purchase. On the other hand, the credit risk on sending subsequent volumes or supplements is small, as the recipient has established a credit record by receiving and paying for the initial shipment.

If you publish supplements or serials and are concerned that the line as worded above may tend to diminish response substantially, or that the procedure will create problems in your credit department, you might alter the line to make subsequent shipments optional:

( ) Please see that I receive subsequent volumes in this series on an approval basis.

30:08 Unique Arrangement Sells More than 1,000 Copies of Business Book: Case Study

An airline in-flight publication* contacted a business publisher and asked for permission to serialize portions of a book oriented toward business managers over several issues of the magazine.

The request was referred to the marketing manager for recommendation of a rights fee. He suggested that no fee be charged, but instead, that the in-flight publication add a paragraph after each excerpt giving the publisher's name and address, book price, and ordering information. In addition, the reader would be given the option of ordering by circling a designated number on the magazine's reader's service card.

This was found acceptable. The result was a flow of orders through the reader's service card that went well beyond 1,000 copies. Orders that came through bookstores or directly to the publisher by mail were impossible to trace. However, the book sold well beyond its sales estimates during the months it was excerpted and for a number of months thereafter.

30:09 Prescription for Recycling Business Textbooks into Trade Books

A prominent publisher of business books has developed an interesting procedure for recycling textbooks into successful trade books. The routine more or less follows this pattern: A reasonably successful textbook on a business subject is the first prerequisite. The first and last chapters are removed and rewritten with a "trade" slant. At the same time, all questions, problems, and other textbook aspects of the book are removed. If deemed necessary, illustrations are added and certain portions of the book are rewritten for a nonstudent audience. The

*Airline in-flight publications reach an educated, affluent, and captive audience that offers substantial sales potential for publishers of many types of self-help, self-improvement, and business-oriented books. Circulations for the more than a dozen monthly airline publications range from as few as 40,000 to 50,000 ($4,000 to $5,000 per-page advertising rate) to those with circulations approaching 300,000 (per-page advertising rate of $11,000 to $12,000).

retitled book, to which an attractive jacket is added, is then reissued as a new trade title with all the attendant advertising and publicity. Such recycled textbooks are reported to enjoy sales of 8,000 to 14,000 copies, mainly through bookstores.

30:10   Technique that Prevents Misshipments of Annuals to Business Professionals

One publisher of annual volumes for professionals in various areas of business, accounting, and taxation has developed a highly effective technique for reducing risk in the shipment of upcoming volumes. When an initial sale is made, the order form states that new annual editions will be sent automatically unless the customer specifically requests on the order form that new annual editions not be sent. Then, two to three months before each annual is published, an address correction mailing is made to customers. No mention is made in that mailing of the new edition. If the returned form indicates the customer is still at the same address, the new edition is sent.

30:11   Origin of Loose-Leaf Publishing

In 1913, a young law student, Richard Prentice Ettinger, and his professor at New York University, Dr. Charles W. Gerstenberg, collaborated on a book on business law. They decided to publish it themselves after having engaged a friendly printer who would extend to them $10,000 in credit. As a name for their new publishing venture, they used the combined maiden names of their mothers, Prentice-Hall.

With the publication of their third book, disaster struck. As the 4,000-copy edition was published, they learned that the law on tax regulations in one of the chapters had just been changed. Ettinger, thinking of ways to solve the problem, came up with a solution. The binding was removed, the obsolete chapter replaced, and the corrected book issued in a loose-leaf binder.*

At the same time, the decision was made to offer a loose-leaf subscription service so that the book would never be out of date. The publisher would simply send a new chapter whenever changes in the law were made. Thus, the loose-leaf publishing concept was born.†

We are indebted to Kenneth T. Hurst, president of Prentice-Hall International since 1974, who supplied background data for this entry, and especially for this noteworthy comment: "Gutenberg claimed to have invented . . . movable type; Ettinger claimed to have invented the movable page."

*The loose-leaf binder was an invention of Charles E. Sheppard. He founded the C. E. Sheppard Co. in New York City in 1900 to manufacture these binders. He actively headed the company until 1958, when he sold it to Yawman & Erbe Manufacturing Co., and retired at the age of 85.

†In recognition of "the unique nature of publishing loose-leaf services" and its growth as an important segment of book publishing, the AAP's Professional and Scholarly Publishing Division established the PSP Looseleaf Committee in October 1981. Ted Caris of Aspen Systems Corp. was its first chairman.

30:12   Advertising Tips from a Loose-Leaf Legal Publisher

- All-type ads sell better than ads containing graphics.
- Book illustrations produce better results than illustrations of people.
- Local and regional law journals are more effective than national journals for law book advertising.
- Special issues of law journals offer no advantage over regular issues.
- Advertising in directories is not as effective as advertising in regular periodicals.

30:13   Loose-Leaf Legal Publishing:
How Space Advertising Can Support Program

1. For outright orders (not very effective)
2. To introduce a new product
3. To give exposure to a product already well known and selling well
4. For image building/public relations purposes
5. For speed—space advertising is fastest if you can reach your market through newspapers
6. To support direct-mail promotion, which has been found to be more effective when supported by space advertising
7. To generate leads—advertisement should offer "more information," and a salesperson following up, either in person or by phone, to close a sale

30:14   Effective Media for Generating Leads
for Legal Publication Sales

In loose-leaf legal publishing, where a sale is often a subscription rather than an outright purchase of a single book, and may involve an annual payment of hundreds of dollars, a certain amount of selling must be done before a sale can be consummated. Telephone selling has been found adequate by some publishers. Others employ salespeople to follow up leads generated by advertising and to call on the prospects at their business premises. A list of media found effective by one loose-leaf publisher for generating leads follows:

1. *Lawyers Marketplace* (bound book postcards)
2. *National Law Journal*
3. *Legal Times of Washington*
4. *American Bar Association Journal*
5. *American Lawyer*

For other entries in this volume relating to sales of law books, see 6:05 and 6:10.

30:15   **Reply Format Change in Law Book Promotions**
         Causes Prepaid Orders to Soar

A California law book publisher had been issuing self-mailers on coated cover stock with postpaid business reply cards. In 1977, a typical mail offering was produced in two formats for test purposes.

Half the mailing utilized an 8½″ × 14″ promotion piece on 8 pt. coated cover stock that folded down to a 5½″ × 8½″ self-mailer. The perforated postpaid business reply card was attached. The other half of the mailing utilized an 11″ × 17″ piece, using the same copy and offer, but included a perforated order coupon, printed on 70 lb. uncoated stock, that required customer-supplied envelope and postage.

Both portions of the mailing were mailed on the same day.

RESULT

The mailing with postpaid BRC generated 828 orders. 362, or 44% of the total orders received, were accompanied by payment. 466, or 57% of the total orders received, were without payment.

The mailing that was printed on lighter stock and had a coupon requiring the customer to provide envelope and postage produced 880 orders. 585, or 66% of the total orders received, were accompanied by payment. 295, or 34% of the total orders received, were without payment.

CONCLUSION

When lighter-weight paper was used by the law book publisher and a coupon was used that required the customer to supply envelope and postage, the number of prepaid orders increased 50%. As a result of this test, the publisher changed its long-standing business reply card mailing format to one requiring the customers to provide their own envelope and postage. When the test was repeated two years later, the test results were about the same. The publisher now retains this format as standard policy.

SIMILAR CHANGE PRODUCES SAME RESULT FOR
NEW YORK LEGAL JOURNAL PUBLISHER

A New York City publisher of legal journals made the same change in reply format and discovered that requiring customers (attorneys) to supply envelopes and postage increased prepaid orders by an average of 30%. In this test, the paper stock used was changed from 7 pt. bulk stock to 60 lb. white offset paper. A key-coded label was affixed to the order form. Aside from the 30% increase in prepaid orders, the change also produced these benefits:

• Reduced billing expense
• Lower rate of returns/cancellations
• Lower collection and bad debt expense

Postscript Since the changes were made by the aforementioned legal publishers, several other law book and periodical publishers have also found that prepaid orders were up when customers were asked to supply envelope and postage. It should be noted that all of the tests and changes involved attorneys or law firms.

Part VIII

Exhibits and Conventions

31

Booth Exhibits

31:01 **Tips for Profitable Book Exhibits:**
Findings of Survey on Impulse Book Buying

Can you profit from the sale of books at an exhibit or convention? The
answer is yes, even if you don't have a wealth of new titles to exhibit.
A survey* entitled "The Impulse Buying of Books" suggests you
stand a chance of doing pretty well on sales if certain criteria are met.

The study on impulse book buying found that more than half of the
purchases in 60 bookstores surveyed were made by individuals who
had not previously planned on buying. The findings can easily be
related to the sale of professional and scholarly books at exhibits and
conventions, as the circumstances and motivation for most of these
purchases generally prevail at exhibits. Here are some of the survey
findings and parallels relating to convention exhibits:

- Finding 1: Ten in 25 browsers surveyed purchased a book.
  Parallel: Convention exhibits lend themselves to browsing, hence
  book buying.
- Finding 2: The longer a browser spends in a bookstore, the greater
  the likelihood there is for a book purchase.
  Parallel: Open and inviting book exhibits facing wide aisles and
  with good selections of pertinent titles encourage pro-
  longed browsing, which can result in book purchases.
- Finding 3: Impulse purchases result when there is a "visible presentation of a range of books understandable to the
  customers."

*The study was conducted by the Book Marketing Council and the Booksellers
Association in March 1982, and reported in *The Bookseller*, July 24, 1982.

Parallel: A book exhibit at an association or society meeting affords an excellent opportunity to display a range of books
compatible with the professional interests of the attendees in a relaxed environment that is highly conducive
to impulse buying. Furthermore, the usual convention discount provides a strong buying incentive.

31:02   How to Select a Good Booth Location from a Floor Plan: Criteria

- Near elevators
- Adjacent to registration area
- Aisles to the right of the exhibit entrance
- Ends of aisles
- In "publisher's row," or adjacent to booths of other major pub-
lishers
- In the room most accessible to the building entrance (if exhibit is in
more than one room)
- In the larger of the two exhibit rooms (if exhibit is in two equally ac-
cessible rooms of different size)
- In the room with a higher ceiling or that is better lit (if exhibit is in
two rooms of same size and accessibility)
- In the room on the ground-floor level (if exhibits are on both lower
and upper levels)

31:03   How to Reduce Risk at Industrial Exhibits

In large industrial shows, where book publishers' exhibits are few
and scattered, participation may be risky and likely not to be cost-
effective. With rare exceptions, the few publishers of scientific or
technical books who take a chance on such meetings are often sandwiched in between large industrial exhibitors with spacious, elaborate
displays that sometimes feature visual and sound effects. In these conditions, the publisher's exhibit tends to be easily overlooked.

If you do plan to exhibit at a large industrial show that has no special arrangements for book publishers, you should contact a book exhibitor listed at the previous year's show and ask how it fared (there
are exceptions, such as the annual Pittsburgh Conference for analytical chemistry in Atlantic City). With no prior information, you should
request a location opposite or adjacent to the booth of another exhibiting publisher, preferably one with an imprint well known in the field.

For more information on booth exhibits at trade or professional
meetings, see 42:09.

31:04   More Nonbook Materials to Include When You Pack for an Exhibit

Volume One of *Book Marketing Handbook* provided a checklist of ten
nonbook materials to be included with your book shipment when you

pack for an exhibit. It included such essentials as a list of books on display, catalogs and special fliers, posters, ad reprints pertinent to the display, page proofs of important forthcoming books, and mailing list and examination-copy request forms.

These additional materials, experienced exhibitors have advised, are also frequently omitted from the exhibit materials:

1. An up-to-date printout or list giving current prices and inventory.
2. Preaddressed return shipping labels, preferably pressure-sensitive. If the labels are adhesive-backed, arrange in advance to have a moistener available for packing.
3. Pressure-sensitive filament or other strong sealing tape to reseal book cartons for return shipment. Avoid using gummed paper tape. It often adheres poorly to dust-coated book cartons.

31:05   Reminder for Advertising in Convention Program

If you are of the school that favors advertising in the convention/ meeting program, plan early for your advertisement. Most programs have closing deadlines as far as six months in advance of the meeting. Insertion should be made early and orders placed well in advance of deadline. Most exhibit advertisers learn this only by planning, producing, and placing an advertisement for a program only to find that it was submitted two months after the deadline.

31:06   More for Your Exhibit Dollar: Display Technique

When you exhibit at an interdisciplinary meeting, it is a good policy to ship considerably more titles than you can normally display at one time. Your initial setup should, of course, feature your new and best-selling titles deemed most appropriate for the meeting; the surplus titles should be stored out of sight. Then, as the show progresses, shuffle the books on display, removing those of little or no interest and replacing them with others previously not displayed that you believe might be of interest.

Also bring to your exhibit and store a few titles of general interest. After a couple of days into a lengthy meeting, some booth visitors may suffer from information "overload" and respond favorably to books of general interest.

Be sure to include the extra (stored) titles on your preprinted order form with prices so that the form can accommodate any sale, regardless of which titles are on display at any one time. Also, many meeting attendees take home exhibit order forms and place orders after the meeting, so a full listing of all titles ensures maximum coverage and consideration.

An additional benefit of the surplus-stock technique is that it often enables you to please an author of one of the "extra" books who shows up at the booth unexpectedly.

31:07   **Ways of Grouping Books in Convention Display**

Display practices for scientific, technical, professional, and scholarly books vary from publisher to publisher and sometimes from show to show. Here are some of the more popular book-display methods:

1. Feature the newest title or titles, either face-out or as a special display. Secondary treatment should be given to books by more important authors or those who are prominent but sensitive and might be at the meeting. Spine-out display for the older but steadily selling backlist titles.

2. All titles arranged alphabetically by author, with newest and best-selling books displayed face-out. This works particularly well at a single-discipline meeting.

3. Books grouped by subject, but arranged alphabetically by author within the subject grouping. This type of display works well at a multidisciplinary meeting such as FASEB (Federation of American Societies for Experimental Biology), where a number of different research societies meet jointly.

4. If only a segment of the booth display is devoted to undergraduate textbooks, these can often be displayed as a single group so that attendees with specific textbook interests can locate books of interest in a single, convenient booth location. Face-out display of the newest and most important texts is the general practice, with little attention to subject grouping. Occasionally a special floor display (pyramid stacking) is used for a new or forthcoming text, when extensive sampling is planned.

31:08   **Selling the Display Books after the Exhibit: Guidelines**

If you choose to sell off your display stock at the end of a meeting, establish a time after which the sale will begin, preferably the last hour or two before closing, and stick to your schedule. If you start your sale too soon, it will conflict with normal booth traffic and hamper the main purpose of the exhibit, which is to exhibit (and establish editorial contacts). Furthermore, it should be made clear that the sale will continue until a fixed hour, say, 30 minutes after closing or precisely at the closing hour. This will save you the trouble of reopening a packed carton to locate a book that may have been promised during the course of the meeting.

On occasion, you may be approached by a local librarian or bookseller who is seeking to buy your entire exhibit at a bargain price. Such sales to libraries are both useful and convenient, since often the displayed books may not be in resalable condition. Furthermore it is likely the library would not have purchased many of the titles. As for sales to booksellers, on the other hand, if your publishing establishment has a policy of accepting returns from booksellers for full credit, it makes little sense to sell off exhibit stock at a substantial discount when, conceivably, some of it could be returned at a future date for full credit.

31:09   Exhibit Report Form: Sample Format

To: Exhibit Coordinator

From: Booth Manager _____

Re: Name of Meeting _____

      Location   _____

      ʹ Dates _____

REGISTRATION:

Estimated Attendance: _____
Est. % Academic _____ Est. % Professional _____

BOOKS:

Best-selling titles and/or titles that generated most interest:

1.
2.
3.
4.
5.
6.

Suggested titles to be added (or deleted) for next year

1.
2.
3.
4.
5.
6.

EXHIBIT MATERIALS:

Indicate below if supplies were adequate/inadequate/too much

1. List of books on display
2. Catalogs
3. Mailing list request forms
4. Catalog request forms
5. Comp copy/exam copy forms
6. Other (specify)

SALES:

Est. net sales at this meeting: $_____

GENERAL COMMENT, CRITICISM ON BOOTH SETUP, FURNISHINGS:

Meeting location next year: _____

Should we exhibit at this meeting against next year?   ___Yes   ___No
Why_____

If "yes," what suggestions to improve next year's exhibit?

31:10   **Characteristics of Booth Visitors at
Professional and Scholarly Meetings**

When you display professional and scholarly books at meetings and
conventions, you learn eventually that most booth visitors fall into
a number of definable categories. Here are some of the more
recognizable stereotypes:

- *The Keeping-Up Crowd:* They come into the booth only when it is
  crowded and they can rub elbows with others.
- *The Me-Myself-Aloners:* They come into the booth only when it is
  empty. They browse quietly until someone else enters the booth and
  then move on quietly.
- *The "I'm Invisible" Browsers:* They don't want to be noticed or
  even, heaven forbid, approached. At the slightest chance they will
  receive attention or recognition by the publisher's representative,
  they make a hasty retreat out of the booth. (If left alone long enough,
  they'll get more bold and may get up enough courage to ask a question.)
- *The "Don't Fence Me In" Bunch:* Usually visible when you have a
  corner booth. They stand outside, or alongside, the booth and reach
  in to get a book and examine it. Rarely can they be coaxed into the
  booth.
- *The Too-Busy-to-Stop Bunch:* They only stop when the book is on a
  table at the aisle, and then only when they can examine it "on-the-
  fly," so to speak. This type is prevalent at medical meetings.
  Publishers who exhibit are aware of this type and often have books
  on tables 36 inches high or higher, where they can be reached by the
  hurried doctors/attendees as they pass by the booth.
- *The "Collector":* Often a graduate student, he invades your booth
  weighed down with a foot-high stack of books, catalogs, and literature in hand. He lays his stack on a table, often on top of an important or expensive display title, while he browses leisurely. Occasionally, when a Collector has left with his pile, it is discovered that
  the display title is nowhere to be found, and one may presume that
  Collector's pile is now about 1½ inches higher.
- *The Literature Accumulator:* He strides down the aisle, shopping
  bag in hand, too busy to stop, pausing at your booth just long
  enough to collect samples of every piece of literature and order form.
  You wonder if he's visiting the show to study book literature in his
  hotel room.
- *The "I'm a Very Important Person" Type:* He strides into your
  booth, confirms that you're in charge, and proceeds to drop the name
  of your company president, board chairman, or publisher and lets
  you know he is well connected with important people in your company. He wants you to show a certain amount of awe and respect for
  his importance. Rarely will he look at the books on display or ask
  questions about your publishing program.

- *The "Can I Take This with Me" Type:* They're too busy to look at your book, but convincingly assure you that if they can take it with them, it will be given serious consideration as a textbook for their class, which is given at least twice a year and has a student enrollment of at least 50 each time.

- *The "Move In and Take Over" Browser:* He literally invades your booth by placing his literature, coat, and other miscellaneous possessions on one of the two strategically placed chairs in the booth. Then he selects a key title in your display—usually an only copy—and proceeds to read it for the next hour or so. He rarely orders the book.

- *The "Oh, I Didn't Know You Were Closing" Crowd:* They usually show up at the booth at closing time, often as the lights are flickering to indicate exhibit hours are over. Following a quickly muttered apology, "Oh, I didn't know you were closing," they keep you hanging around for an extra 15 or 20 minutes while they look at one or more books, often in near darkness. They rarely order.

- *The Hawk-Eye Competitor:* He works for another publisher exhibiting at the same show. He slips into your booth when it is busy, often with badge off or concealed behind a jacket lapel, and carefully sizes up your titles that compete with his. He also collects samples of all your literature and a copy of your catalog before leaving.

- *The Last-Minute Shopper:* He must have the book for a class starting the day after show closing and "reserves" your display copy for a purchase/pickup at noon on closing day. He arrives at your booth, breathless, after the show has closed and after you've just packed your last carton. His empassioned pleadings compel you to unpack two cartons until you locate the badly wanted book for him. Then he has the nerve to offer you a $50 traveler's check for the $9.50 book, and when he's cleaned out all your traveling cash to make the change, he asks for a bag!

- *The Bargain Hunter:* He enters the booth and confronts the representative with a loud, "Are these books 50% off at the end of the show?" Told "no," he will often counter with "But XYZ (another publisher/exhibitor) is giving 50% off on their books." When convinced that your policy won't change to match the "competition," he may either walk out or return later holding one of your books. His second approach, usually, is to point out a purported flaw in the book, either from handling, packing, or manufacture, and then ask for a special reduced price.

31:11 Converting a Modest Offering into an Exhibit Attraction: Small Publisher Makes Big Showing

How do you fill a convention booth when you're a new publisher with only three titles to show? When Don Dellen planned his first exhibit at the American Mathematical Society Meeting in Atlanta in 1978 for the newly started Dellen Publishing Co., he came up with this unique solution: Authentic, giant-sized replicas of his first 3 titles were made large enough to fill the entire booth. His leadoff title (Raymond A. Barnett, *Calculus for Management, Life and Social Sciences*) was duplicated in a four-color, 6-foot high model, 4 feet wide and 1 foot thick. A second title, converted into a replica 5 feet high and three feet wide, faithfully duplicated the cover design of the book. The third title was a replica 3 feet high, 2 feet wide, and in one color. The total cost to Dellen of the three exhibit attention-getters was $3,500, and the giant books were used for a number of years.

31:12 Catalog Handout at Consumer-Oriented Computer Show Produces Echo Response

In late 1981, the Combined Book Exhibit, Inc. (CBE), set up a complete, well-stocked "mobile" computer bookstore at a large consumer-oriented computer show in Boston. The bookstore display represented the books of many publishers. Visitors to the "store" were given a catalog of all books in the store. More than 25,000 of the catalogs were handed out in all. Order forms were given only to potential buyers.

CBE accepted payment for the books and then passed the orders on to the publishers for fulfillment after deducting their agreed-upon discount (30%). Aside from the sales made by CBE (both cash and credit card), "we saw something else happen," says Ed Malinowski, president of CBE. "We saw how a new market is created. We started to get orders from schools, from institutions, from companies, and from all of the segmented markets across the boards."

There are some lessons here for the convention book exhibitor: Catalogs, exhibit lists, and other book literature handed out at a convention or exhibit ultimately will generate orders through the echo effect. Consequently, the dollar value of orders should never be taken as a sole criterion of a show's effectiveness; a large measure of the benefits from convention book exhibits may never be traceable to the exhibit that generated the ordering.

32

Cooperative Book Exhibits

32:01 Cooperative Book Exhibits:
Important Part of the U.S. Publishing Scene

As discussed in *Book Marketing Handbook, Volume One*, the cooperative book exhibit is an important part of the U.S. publishing scene because it frequently affords the only opportunity for many professionals, educators, and librarians to see, examine, and make buying decisions about a wide array of new and important books in their fields.

The two major cooperative book exhibit sponsors who continue to dominate the American scene for scientific, technical, professional, and scholarly publishers of books and journals are Conference Book Service (see 32:04), an Alexandria, Va., based exhibit service founded in 1952 by Jack Cameron, a retired U.S. Army officer who still directs the service; and the Combined Book Exhibit, Inc. (see 32:05), the Hawthorne, N.Y., based exhibit service that originated the concept of the cooperative book exhibit in 1933.

A newcomer to the U.S. cooperative exhibit scene at the end of 1982 was the program launched by the Association of American Publishers (AAP), which was designed not to compete with the established giants in the co-op exhibit field, but rather to augment the coverage available to book publishers, especially in fields not touched by the larger services that have tended to specialize in selected areas.

The AAP Book Stop program (see 32:06) will, for example, go to meetings dealing with the humanities and will also be covering most of the regional bookseller meetings.

As the cooperative book exhibit continues to evolve to meet the changing needs of the publishing industry, so, too, are the cooperative exhibit service programs evolving to meet these needs. The following entries provide a state-of-the-art look at cooperative book exhibits as practiced by the major service organizations.

It should be kept in mind that in addition to the major exhibit organizations and the emergence of the AAP Book Stop program, Academia Book Exhibits of Fairfax, Va., continues to excel under the direction of Emmy Jacobious at a limited number of international scientific and scholarly meetings, and that many professional societies sponsor their own cooperative book exhibits. A listing of many of these may be found in *Volume One* of *Book Marketing Handbook* (see 31:03).

32:02   How to Use and Get the Most out of a Cooperative Book Exhibit: Guidelines

1. Be sure all correspondence and packages intended for a specific exhibit are clearly labeled with the exhibit code words or name of meeting for which they are intended. Many meetings are closely related and have similar-sounding names.

2. Send the cooperative book exhibitor a list of the books you are exhibiting, indicating exactly how you wish them to appear in the exhibit catalog. Be sure to include the ISBN and the price for each title.

3. Exhibit attendees like and expect discounts. A discount offer on your exhibited books at a meeting encourages orders and can enable you to track the exhibit's effectiveness through orders received.

4. Along with your exhibited books send catalogs, promotional literature, and, if you have sufficient books, separate order forms. The separate order form is particularly appropriate if you are offering a convention discount.

5. The cooperative book exhibitor is prepared to give personalized service. If you have a particular title you want to receive individualized attention, call and tell the cooperative book exhibitor. Conference Book Service says it invites calls from exhibitors with suggestions that will help make the exhibit more effective.

6. It is possible through most cooperative book exhibitors to have a separate tabletop display just for your own books. Conference Book Service will mount a separate table display, if requested to do so, for any exhibitor displaying 25 or more books at a meeting.

7. You can participate in a cooperative exhibit with a large number of books at a meeting you do not plan to attend, even when no cooperative book exhibit has been announced. Conference Book Service will, on request from any publisher with a sufficient start-up quantity, schedule a cooperative book exhibit for any scientific, technical, or medical titles you have in large quantity. A minimum of 20 different titles is sufficient.

8. When you participate in a cooperative book exhibit, alert your editors who will attend the conference or meeting. If your press has

no other exhibit there, the cooperative book exhibit booth can provide the editor with a home base and message center for contacts with authors and prospective authors.

32:03 How Booth Attendants at Cooperative Book Exhibit Serve Publisher

Conference Book Service instructs and provides clear guidelines for its representatives on how to act on behalf of publishers participating in a cooperative book exhibit. Some of these guidelines are presented here to give those unfamiliar with the cooperative book exhibit concept an indication of what they can expect from such participation.

The booth attendant, after introducing him- or herself to visitors, will invite them to browse and say, "If you find any titles you like, note them in the catalog and order them directly from the publishers. If you'd like to place the order here, simply fill in the requested information on the back page of the order form and we'll be glad to forward it to the publisher or a qualified bookseller at the end of the show."

Attendants are instructed to arrange for booth coverage by a neighboring exhibitor if they leave the booth unattended and to accommodate the special requests of an author or publisher's representative who may show up at the booth. If the latter brings additional promotional literature, catalogs, or order forms, the attendants will incorporate these into the display. They are instructed to work in the best interests of the participating publishers and are told that while no selling can take place at the booth, the end goal of their efforts must be to achieve sales for the publishers they represent.

32:04 Conference Book Service: Its Changing Role as Publishers' Aid Over 30 Years

Conference Book Service (CBS), organized in 1952, continues to grow and evolve in its proclaimed role as "an educational arm of the publishing community." In 1982, after 30 years at one location, CBS moved to a new larger location at 80 South Early Street in Alexandria, Va. 22304; 703-823-6968.

In its new, expanded quarters, CBS continues to grow and change with the evolving needs of the publishing industry. Although it continues to mount 100 to 120 cooperative book exhibits each year, roughly 25% of each year's schedule is changed from the preceding year.

One major change in the way that Conference Book Service now functions is that, while the price per book for exhibiting is still close to $20, more than 50 percent of the total number of CBS book exhibits are presently offered to publishers at a flat fee of usually $150, for which a publisher can exhibit as many titles as wanted. Thus, for as little as $150, a fraction of the cost of a booth, a publisher could conceivably have its entire list on display at a meeting where the exhibit cost may otherwise be prohibitive.

PRESENT CHARGE SYSTEM

According to Mark Trocchi, CBS schedule manager, the price to exhibit in 1983 was $20 per book, with a minimum fee of $35 for the first book. For two books, the fee is $40. Says Trocchi, "for the cost of the smallest classified ad in a small daily newspaper, a publisher can have his book or journal in front of a specialized audience . . . , often displayed face-out, and [have] an attendant present with a broad knowledge of books to discuss it with attendees and provide orders or feedback to the publisher."

How are scientific, technical, medical, and scholarly publishers using cooperative book exhibits these days? According to Trocchi, exhibitor patterns have changed radically in recent years. Whereas in previous years a typical exhibit had 100 books from 20 different publishers, presently an exhibit is likely to display 50 books from 20 publishers. There is more participation by smaller presses that don't have a large promotion budget or large personnel staff. Houses that used to exhibit both current and backlist titles are concentrating on books published during the current year. At medical meetings, which Conference Book Service covers well, the average exhibit has about 75 titles from 15 to 20 medical publishers.

ADVANTAGE OF COOPERATIVE EXHIBITS

A big advantage of the cooperative exhibit, says Trocchi, is the following:

We represent ourselves as an educational, noncommercial exhibit—an educational arm of the publishing community. Consequently, we get a better reception from scholarly exhibitors who frown on commercial activities and may not normally permit book exhibits. We've opened up many areas for the publishing industry that were against commercial exhibitors but were receptive to us.

We have made a great effort to improve the quality of the booth personnel we use. Most have some background in books. We try to get retired librarians or schoolteachers, or people with an academic background . . . people with a knowledge of books in the broadest sense of the term.

It is impossible to get a person [who is an] expert in plasma physics, but not difficult to get a person with a knowledge of books from a scholarly angle. By definition that person can present a publisher's books or journals just as effectively as a person from the publisher's own promotion department. Many times a retired librarian has a better background than someone with a liberal arts degree, two years out of college, working in a publisher's promotion department.

HOW EXHIBITS ARE MOUNTED

Trocchi continues:

The decline in the number of books being shown at a meeting is, in a sense, better for the publisher-exhibitor. When you have a tabletop booth display with 40 books on it, every book stands out.

On smaller displays, we face-out a number of titles. We can't face-out every title, so we have a revolving display. About twice a day, the booth attendant rotates the face-out titles, so that by the end of the day's exhibit hours, most of the books in the exhibit will have been face-out for part of the time.

One message I'd like to get across to the publishing community, is that we're [a] small business dedicated to giving personal service. We like to keep the channels of communication open to all publishers. Don't be afraid to get on the phone and tell us you have a meeting and that your author is a featured speaker and you have 20 books in the area you'd like to exhibit. If there's a chance for heavier participation by other publishers, we'll follow up, make contacts, and try to arrange a special book exhibit.

32:05 Combined Book Exhibit Launches Different Showcase —and Finds It Sells Books

After more than 50 years of experience exhibiting books at conventions and exhibits, the Combined Book Exhibit, Inc. (CBE), has learned something its publisher-clients have known all along: It's easy and profitable to sell books when you match the right product with the right audience. And CBE is doing something about it.

CBE learned the lesson in a very practical way in late 1981, when it set up a mobile bookstore at a consumer-oriented computer show in Boston. Catalogs were handed out (more than 25,000 of them) and orders with payment were taken and transmitted to publishers for fulfillment.

However, by 1982, at a second consumer-oriented computer show, CBE took a different approach. This time there were books for sale on the spot, ample reserve stocks, two cash registers to ring up sales, two people to restock empty shelves, and two more for crowd control (only a limited number were allowed to enter the store at one time). At the end of the show, total sales, in both cash and credit-card charges, came to $35,000. "We could have done $50,000" said Ed Malinowski, president of CBE, "with more cash registers."

The Combined Book Exhibit, according to Malinowski, will continue to set up its mobile bookstore at the heavily attended computer shows. He also anticipates this showcase for publishers will be expanded into other "hot" subject areas. Under consideration at the time of this writing was the annual meeting of the American Society of Interior Designers (ASID). The regular CBE exhibit schedule will not be affected.

32:06 The AAP Book Stop Program: New Co-op Exhibit Opportunity for Publishers

The Association of American Publishers (AAP) has become a new and growing force on the cooperative book exhibit scene with its AAP Book Stop program, launched in late 1982. Its schedule includes meetings of the National Council for Social Studies, National Science Teachers Association, American Psychological Association, American Educational Research Association, Eastern Sociological Association, and Organization of American Historians.

The AAP Book Stop exhibit list, which included 13 meetings in its first year, will be revised annually and expanded to include such special markets as international and special sales, as well as most of the regional booksellers meetings.

Each exhibit accommodates a minimum of 150 to a maximum of 200 titles, is professionally staffed, and provides an exhibit checklist. In addition, an exhibit report and all sales leads and inquiries are promptly forwarded to each participating publisher after the show. The cost per title is $25* for each show. Major titles in each exhibit are featured in photo blow-ups, which cost $35* each.

The program was organized for AAP by Marilyn Abel. For additional details, contact Marilyn Abel or Ray George at AAP, One Park Avenue, New York, NY 10016; 212-689-8920.

32:07   Checklist for AAP Book Stop Participations

If you wish to participate in any of the meetings scheduled as part of the AAP Book Stop exhibit program, following is a checklist of the information AAP requires. Each book must be submitted on a separate sheet giving the name of the meeting, and all participations must be prepaid ($25/book for AAP members, $35 for nonmembers in 1983).

( ) Author's name
( ) Coauthor's name
( ) Book title and subtitle (if applicable)
( ) Publication date
( ) New or revised edition
( ) Number of pages and trim size
( ) Binding
( ) ISBN
( ) Brief description
( ) Market for book
( ) Promotion materials available
( ) Subject classification(s)
( ) Special reason to feature
( ) Name of contact person

32:08   Three Exhibit Options for Publishers at
ALA Combined Book Exhibit

The Combined Book Exhibit, Inc., long a mainstay at annual conferences of the American Library Association (ALA), now offers publishers cooperative exhibits in three separate sections at this an-

*Prices shown are for AAP members. Nonmembers are charged $35 per book for participation and $50 per book for featured treatment, payable in advance.

nual meeting: the Combined Book Exhibit (also for catalogs) for adult and juvenile books; the Periodical Display Services (also for catalogs) for journals, magazines, business publications, newsletters, and newspapers; and the Computer Information Exhibit (again, also for catalogs), covering books and periodicals about computers for users. For details, call Ed Malinowski at CBE, 212-733-4888. The Computer Information Exhibit was introduced at the 1982 ALA meeting in Philadelphia and repeated at the 1983 meeting in Los Angeles; it will be continued indefinitely while the publishing boom in computer technology continues. More than 175 publishers now offer books in computer science.

32:09   When No Cooperative Book Exhibits Are Scheduled: Alternatives

Your list does not warrant your own exhibit at a scientific or scholarly meeting. Your author is attending, possibly to present an important paper and insists the book be on display. You check and find there is no cooperative book exhibit. What are the alternatives?

1. Offer your author promotional leaflets and a copy of the book and suggest that the author make his or her own display arrangements.
2. Check if the sponsoring organization has a free literature table and supply fliers about the book for that table.
3. If your author is well connected with the sponsoring organization, arrangements may be possible for the leaflet to be an enclosure in the kit given to each registrant.
4. Arrange with another publisher to include the book in that publisher's exhibit, and promise to reciprocate.
5. If your author is affiliated with an exhibiting industrial firm, arrange for it to include the book and leaflets in its display.
6. As a last resort, offer one of the professional cooperative exhibit services a guaranteed minimum number of titles* to set up a cooperative exhibit at the meeting.

---

*Conference Book Service will consider launching an exhibit for 20 or more titles. Contact Mark Trocchi for details.

Part IX

Scientific and
Scholarly Journals

33

Origin and Definitions

The scientist ... must always be up to date. Thus, the book cannot be his ever alert, knowing-what-goes-on companion: it serves as a cluster of information. To know the latest moves in the laboratory, he needs separate bits of information. This function is met in the main by the scientific journal.

Maurice Goldsmith, Editor of
Science and Public Policy,
at STM meeting in Frankfurt/Main,
October 11, 1977.

33:01 Origin of Journal and Journals

The word "journal" comes from the French cognate derived from the Latin *diurnal*, meaning "daily," wrote Eli Chernin in *Scholarly Publishing* (7, no. 1, October 1975). He went on to explain, "A journal is a daily record of events, and by extension a newspaper or periodical." "Journals as we know them," Chernin added, "were spawned by savants in the mid-seventeenth century and arose from desperation these men felt in attending meetings of their 'invisible colleagues' and in keeping up with their personal correspondence about new discoveries."

What prompted the beginning of scientific journals? Chernin, then vice chairman of the Council of Biology Editors, cites the explanation provided by D. A. Kronick in *A History of Scientific and Technical Periodicals* (Scarecrow Press, 1962): "the books and pamphlets of that era were inadequate because in its search for truth, science had evolved a new formula: 'one experiment or observation equals one ... publication.' "

33:02   The Evolution of Scientific and Medical Journals*

"In the beginning was the General Scientific Journal. And the General Scientific Journal begat the Specialty Journal, and the Specialty Journal begat the Subspecialty Journal. And the Subspecialty Journal begat the Single-Subject Journal, whether according to class of compound, specific disease, or methodology. And the Single-Subject Journal begat the Interdisciplinary Journal to link up the specialties separated at an earlier evolutionary date. And the scientific community saw that the journals were good, and they were fruitful and multiplied. So the National Journals (e.g., British, American, and Canadian) begat the Supranational Journals (e.g., European and Scandinavian). And the Supranational Journals begat the International Journals of many of the subjects catalogued thus far. And the whole scientific literature became overweight, unreadable, and impossible to collate, and therefore the scientists looked at the situation and saw that it was bad. And so they created other journals to help them, and they called these journals Progress, Review, Advances, and Abstracts Journals. And the General Abstract Journal begat the Specialist Abstract Journal. . . ."

33:03   Magazine or Journal: How to Distinguish between the Two

When is a periodical a magazine and when is it a journal? Ask and you will get a variety of answers. We like the clarification offered by a representative of the American Chemical Society (ACS), an organization that publishes both magazines and journals.

ACS bases the distinction between a magazine and a journal on editorial content. ACS journals publish research papers and other high-level research material that has not appeared previously. Magazines published by the ACS have broader editorial scope than journals and rarely include research papers, with the exceptions noted below. ACS magazines (*Chemtech*, *SciQuest*, and *Chemical and Engineering News*) include material that may or may not be research-oriented and that may have been published elsewhere.

Two ACS periodicals (*Analytical Chemistry* and *Environmental Science and Technology*) are hybrids. Each functions as a journal in its respective field, but also has a magazine section up front.

It should be noted, however, that the ACS designation of research as the basis or criterion of a journal may not hold true for journals in the social sciences, whose entries tend to be scholarly rather than research-oriented.

Maive O'Connor, in *The Scientist as Editor: Guidelines for Editors of Books and Journals* (New York: Wiley, and Kent, England: Pitman Medical, 1979), defines a journal as "a third kind of multi-author book . . . that appears weekly, monthly, quarterly, or perhaps ir-

*Reprinted by permission of *The New England Journal of Medicine* 305 (1981): 400–401.

regularly, with most of its contents submitted by authors for their own reasons rather than solicited by editors for theirs."

William Begell, journal publisher and author of numerous articles on journal publishing, says that a journal is neither a book nor a magazine. "The best test of whether a publication is a journal or magazine is to ask the publishers," says Begell. "If they refer to their periodical as a 'book,' then you know they publish a magazine."

33:04 In Business, Journal May Mean Magazine, and Vice Versa

In many business disciplines, journals are not always research-oriented and magazines are often referred to as journals. In accounting, for example, two periodicals, both of which have the word "journal" as part of their title, pretty well cover the field.

One is *Journal of Accountancy*, whose primary audience is practitioners. Despite its designation as a journal, it contains little pure theory. The other, *The Accounting Review: Quarterly Journal of the American Accounting Association*, has as its stated purpose "the wide dissemination of the results of research and other scholarly inquiries." It closely adheres to the journal precept.

A third national periodical in the field, the *Practical Accountant*, has 40,000 subscribers and makes no claim at being a journal; rather, it is essentially a professional newsmagazine. Yet, most of its accountant/ subscribers, if asked which journals they read, will invariably include *Practical Accountant*.

33:05 Difference between a Book and a Journal: A Definition

William Begell, president of Hemisphere Publishing Co., and at this writing chairman of the AAP Professional and Scholarly Publishing Division, draws on both his experience as longtime publisher of scientific and scholarly books and journals and his engineering background to provide this unique explanation of the difference between a book and a journal for readers of this handbook:

The basic difference between a book and a journal is that the former is produced by the "batch" and the latter by the "continuous" process. Batch process is usually an industrial operation in which a batch of starting material is mixed, processed, and packaged. Baking a cake is a good example. Each time a new batch of flour is needed. Books are produced by the batch process. Each book is a separate entity; different author, different editor, different size, different print run, different jacket, and different design. It is "mixed" and created within the publishing house as a separate item, with its own ISBN, and sold primarily on its own merits.

Journals, on the other hand, are produced by the continuous process. A continuous process, industrially speaking, is one where a steady stream of starting material is fed into the initial stage and the final product emerges continuously from the last stage of the production line. Fluidity is generally a good description of a continuous process and journals are essentially "fluid." The fluid or continuous aspects of journal publishing can be simplistically represented by the "steady" flow of manuscripts from the journal's editor, through the internal "workings" of a production/manufacturing team, and emerging through the fulfillment operation to reach the same subscriber at a predetermined periodicity. Unlike books, and in most cases, each journal issue looks like its predecessors and has the same editor, same print run, same ISSN, same design, and is not sold on its own merits but on the merits of the journal as a whole.

33:06   Criteria for Starting a New Primary Scientific Journal*

1. Is there a need for this new journal?
2. Does it fit into an existing program, or will it be isolated so that promotion will be excessively expensive?
3. Is it for an emerging new field?
4. Are there existing journals that cover the same field?
5. Are the institutes' or research centers' interest in this subject identifiable?
6. Is there a body of active researchers working in the field?
7. Is there some assurance of a sufficient flow of material to keep such a journal viable?
8. Can you obtain the right editor in chief, who will be supported by a committed editorial board?
9. Does the editor in chief have a sense of the need for quick publication, with good reviewers available to him or her?

33:07   Way to Reduce Risk of Starting New Journal

One way to reduce the risk of starting a new journal is to take over an existing society journal. Dan Fischel raised this prospect at the AAP Midwinter Meeting, February 1982, in Washington, D.C. He pointed out that when you take over an existing society journal you are likely to have a profit from the start because you have a circulation base from which to achieve profitability. Furthermore, he said, there is less risk of failure. With the start-up risk of a new venture reduced, you may achieve profitability from the very beginning.

Many society journals that operate either on a marginal basis or at a loss may not be thinking about making a change. However, if properly approached, they may be open to a takeover bid by a commercial publisher—especially one with an ongoing journals program.

Another approach is that taken by the periodicals consortia of Johns Hopkins University Press and of the Transaction Periodicals Consortium at Rutgers, which provide services for small scholarly journals that must rely on others to assume the publishing role.

*From a talk given by Ben Russak entitled "The Economics of Journal Publishing," at the Third Annual Society for Scholarly Publishing Meeting, San Francisco, June 1981.

34

Journal Marketing and Promotion Strategies

34:01 Differences in Direct-Mail Promotion of Scholarly Books vs. Journals: One Manager's Point of View

"The single most valuable lesson I've learned," says the journals promotion manager at a major university press, "is the value and importance of using direct-mail promotion to its utmost the way people in the commercial world do."

In a prior promotion job she held at a large, well-known book publishing establishment, direct mail was a relatively unknown quantity. This professional and reference book publisher utilized five different styles for mailing pieces, one standard-format catalog, and several small flier formats. All mail promotion utilized one of these standard formats.

"This rigid form of promotion does not work for journals," she adds. "Journals need flexible promotion formats, and in houses where books and journals are in the same subject areas, they should also be promoted together as part of an integrated program.

"In journals promotion we are very conscious of direct-mail techniques. Many book promotion people are distracted by the large volume of trade sales their books enjoy and they never think seriously about direct mail. And when they do think of journal promotion, they think it is just like promoting books, only you ask for a subscription.

"We in journals promotion have to think of ourselves more as selling magazine subscriptions than as being scholarly publishers. It's a straight selling job. Some book promotion people get confused at the different approaches we must take to do our kind of selling."

**34:02   When Journal Has Undefinable Audience:
How to Develop Lists of Prospects**

How does one create a continuous source of names of prospects for a journal that has an undefinable audience? This question was posed by Norman Cohen of Baywood Publishing Co., publisher of a quarterly journal appealing to those interested in the topic of death and dying.

Cohen was put in contact with Willis Walker at Van Nostrand Reinhold, who had faced the same problem—and solved it—for the *International Journal of Eating Disorders.* The solution in this case was a subscription to Automatic Subject Citation Alert (ASCA), a monthly service of the Institute for Scientific Information (ISI), in Philadelphia. This service screens the contents of some 9,000 scientific and scholarly publications that are fed into the ISI data base from the Current Contents service of ISI, which lists the full table of contents of these publications in its current awareness publications.

The information is furnished on a printout based on a profile supplied by the inquirer. In the case of *International Journal of Eating Disorders*, the profile called for printouts of any published articles containing such words as weight, obesity, starvation, vomit, anorexia nervosa, hunger, bulimia, and appetite (see Figure 21). Printouts were supplied in duplicate with a carbon interleaf.

From this monthly printout, the journal's marketer has thousands of prospects to contact each year to solicit subscriptions. In addition, the printout also shows a substantial part of the back section of each journal issue, which includes much material under the heading "Recent Research Bibliography."

34:03   The Seven Deadly Sins of Promoting a Journal*

1. Rely on libraries as primary markets.
2. Design for content, not an identifiable market.
3. Depend on the editor for pricing and marketing.
4. Publish early issues on time, no matter what.
6. Believe librarians and scholars are turned off by Madison Avenue techniques.
5. Keep marketing budget below 20% of total.
7. Depend on submitted papers.

34:04   Targeting Your New Journal Promotion: Guidelines

When you are preparing a mailing on a new scientific journal in a specialized field, how do you address your mailing labels so that they reach the appropriate individuals? Here are some suggestions:

*Presented by Edward Langer of the American Society for Metals on June 3, 1980, as part of the Second Annual Society for Scholarly Publishing Meeting in Minneapolis. Langer spoke on journal marketing strategies as seen through the eyes of a professional society publisher.

FIGURE 21 Sample printout page from Automatic Subject Citation Alert (ASCA) supplied to a journal dealing with eating disorders. The marketer has marked with a pen those names on the printout that seem likely prospects to be solicited with a subscription offer. Sample profile words supplied by the journal marketer appear on the printout sheet: overweight, weight, and obesity. Each listing gives the name of the article, number of literature references, and name, professional affiliation, and address of the author.

- For academic libraries, address your new journal announcement to the serials librarians, although the final subscription decision is likely to be made by the library director.
- For academic fields where there is likely to be a departmental library, also mail to the serials librarian, (department name) library.
- For academic fields where your new journal may have appeal across various branches of a single discipline, mail also to the department chairperson.
- If your new journal deals with a narrow area within a specific discipline in which perhaps a single course may be given, or if the subject of the journal is included as part of a larger course, address your journal promotion to Instructor (subject covered).

34:05   **Package or Self-Mailer:**
        Which Is the Better Promotion Format for Journals?

You are launching a new journal that has a subscription price of $50 and a prepublication subscription offer of $40. Which format would be better for your announcement mailing—self-mailer or package? When this question was posed at a symposium for journal marketers, the consultant-speaker proceeded to present his views.

The proposed new journal was described as having an audience of approximately 50,000 professionals to whom the launch mailing would be made. An argument was presented to explain why the standard package (defined as #10 envelope, letter, two-color flier, order card) is better, even though it will cost approximately $100 more per 1,000 than a self-mailer (defined as four 8½" × 11" pages in that size or folded down to 5½" × 8½"). The speaker's contention was that the standard package would outpull the self-mailer sufficiently to overcome the $5,000 cost differential. But will it?

The speaker's reasoning was that, in a mailing to 50,000 prospects, where you offer a $50 subscription with a $10 prepublication saving, one can expect "that if the self-mailer pulled 2,000 subscribers, the standard package will pull 2,200." Having presented this hypothesis, he continued with the question, "What makes the standard package so powerful?" He then detailed the special benefits of each component in a package mailing.

But the presentation has a fallacy! When and where did any announcement of a new professional or scholarly journal with a $50 subscription price mailed to 50,000 prospects within any given field ever produce a response of 2,000 subscriptions, let alone 2,200?

Experienced journal promotion pros will tell you they would be happy with a 1% direct response on a 50,000 launch promotion, and some would be satisfied with much less. There are others among seasoned marketers who would advise that response should not be evaluated on the basis of just one year, and that you should use at least a five-year revenue estimate, coupled with conversion and renewal rates. For instance, the proposed new journal at $50, with an 80% subscription renewal rate, would bring in $159 (after deducting the $10 prepublication discount) over five years with no additional promotion cost.

Consequently, if one follows the speaker's hypothesis that a package will outpull a self-mailer by 10% and produce a 1.1% response, the first-year yield would be $22,000 (instead of $20,000), while the extra cost of the package over the self-mailer, using the speaker's cost figures, would be $5,000.

Conclusion For professional and scholarly journal promotions, the lower cost self-mailer format will suffice for most efforts, unless you have one so unusual that you feel it must have a special letter. In all other instances, however, opt for a self-mailer.

If you are keen on the idea of a letter with the presentation, work the letter into one of the panels of the self-mailer at little or no additional cost. If the logic here is not convincing and you can afford it, test both self-mailer and package and run with whichever you find to be most cost-effective.

34:06   Format Preference for Journal Promotions at University Press

"We've tried various formats for journals promotion," says Julie Zuckman, MIT Press journals promotion manager, "and we've found the Reply-o-Letter format the most innovative. What we like about the Reply-o-Letter format is its very businesslike format; it doesn't resemble most other book promotion formats. We've used it for some time and it's been very effective. It always does well for us."

34:07   How to Get Extra Mileage from the Journal Promotion Flier

When your flier or promotion piece is for a journal that is two or three years old, include on the order form subscription options for all preceding volumes from the first to the current volume. Where funds are available, a library will want to have all issues of a journal for the archives, even if it is starting its subscription in the second or third year of the journal's publication.

If you are promoting a journal with limited subscription potential and would like the flier to serve for two or three years without becoming obsolete, allow for ordering of current and future volumes into the next couple of years. For example, if your current volume is volume 5 (1985), show on the order form

( ) Vol. 5, 1985 $00.00
( ) Vol. 6, 1986 $00.00
( ) Vol. 7, 1987 $00.00

If prices are known for the next three years, the flier you prepared to announce volume 5 will still be useful during the life of volumes 6 and 7.

34:08   Dealing with Postage Charges in Journal Promotion

Some U.S. journal publishers include delivery charges in the subscription price for subscriptions originating in the United States (or North America), but add a postage-and-handling charge for journal subscriptions originating elsewhere. Others add a postage charge in addition to the subscription price, regardless of the country of the subscription's origin. These discrepancies tend to be confusing and can lead to unnecessary correspondence and possible collection problems. Thus, you should clearly spell out your postage charges in all promotional literature.

34:09   Why It Pays to Show Postage Cost as an Additional Charge

When U.S. and foreign subscription prices for a journal are the same and the postage cost is included in the U.S. subscription price for a journal, it may appear that you are charging foreign subscribers a higher price (because foreign postage costs more). On the other hand, when postage is an additional charge for both foreign and domestic subscriptions, prices can be shown to be the same, with the difference indicated only in the postage charges.

34:10   Journal Promotion as Adjunct to Book Promotion

Journal promotion is often more feasible (and profitable) when done in conjunction with a book promotion in the same discipline or subject area.

Example   A publisher of books with a strong position in psychology and psychiatry markets did a major combined mailing in these subject areas and included an announcement of a related journal. The journal portion of the mailing, which was incidental to the mailing, produced 200 new $25 subscriptions, or $5,000 in income. Had the journal been promoted by itself, the return would probably have been only a small fraction of 1 percent and therefore considered unsuccessful. However, at virtually no cost and in tandem with the larger book promotion, the mailing was an unqualified success.

**34:11   Journal Promotion Echo Effect Boosts
Society Membership: Case Study**

A new journal was started by a commercial publisher on behalf of a professional society in the social sciences. Society members were to receive the new journal as part of their membership. However, the publisher launched a concentrated direct-mail and space advertising campaign just prior to the start of publication to generate paid circulation among nonmembers and institutions.

During the period before and just after publication of the first issue, the publisher's 80,000 mailed promotion pieces produced a traceable response of one-half of 1 percent. During this same period, untraceable subscription orders amounted to another half of 1 percent.

The publisher was interested to know how the promotion had affected the sponsoring society's membership during the launch period, as the membership fee was only $8 more than just the subscription alone, and it seemed logical that many recipients of the promotion would opt for membership.

The publisher learned that a membership-renewal mailing sent two weeks prior to the journal promotion had resulted in less than 100 responses. In the six months subsequent to the journal launch promotion, during which only one additional renewal mailing was made, the society's membership, including renewals and new members, rose to nearly 500.

The society was convinced that the new journal, as an incentive to join, was the primary force behind the sharp increase in membership. However, the journal publisher was equally convinced that a good portion of that membership increase was the result of echo effects from the simultaneous advertising and direct-mail campaigns.

34:12   Combining Related Journals in Single Prospectus: Case Study

If you publish a number of journals in a single discipline or subject area, you can trim printing and mailing costs by producing a single mailing piece incorporating all of them. This procedure not only has the advantage of cost-savings but it also gives the recipient several options instead of a straightforward "yes" or "no" in the case of a single-journal offering.

One journal publisher has had success with a combined journals flier produced in a self-mailer format. One such offering was printed in two colors on 90-lb. white offset stock. Measuring 8" × 22" when flat, it folded down to 5½" × 8" to provide eight panels of printing area.

One face-out panel was the mailing cover with a printed corner card, space for the mailing address, and printed postal indicia. An inside panel had a perforated business reply card on the lower two-thirds of the panel. Above the BRC, on one side a symposium proceeding was offered, and a line of copy read "Please . . . Pass this brochure along to your colleague or library." On the other side above the card, ordering information appeared that listed the publisher's name and address and a toll-free number.

Each of the remaining four panels was devoted to a single journal. Each panel gave the name of the journal, editorial board members, and complete data on the journal (including ISSN) and cited places where the journal is abstracted and/or indexed. Most of the journal descriptions also carried a listing of recent and forthcoming articles.

34:13   Circulation Promotion Issued in Publisher's Name Only: Case Study

When the U.S. publisher of *Nature* (until early 1983) tried a circulation promotion in 1981, his #10 envelope bore only his name, Robert Ubell, on the envelope corner card. The mailing, sent to lists of U.S scientists, offered a subscription for one year at half the usual price.

The response, according to Publisher Ubell, was a little over 1%, which he said was no better or worse than circulation promotions conducted by U.S. consumer periodicals. Our feeling was that the response was significant in view of the price, which, even at 50% discount, was still $86.50.

The package's enclosure consisted of an insert, printed in script on white coated card stock measuring 8½" wide and 7½" long, folded in half to 8½" × 3¾". The cover copy, printed in black ink, read:

An Invitation

from

the American Publisher of

Nature

The inside copy, a four-paragraph message, was set ragged left and right and centered, and included at the bottom an invitation to respond using an enclosed reply envelope. The black-ink-on-white wallet-flap reply envelope had these ordering options printed on the back: (1) one year of *Nature* at half price ($86.50); (2) six months for $50; or (3) three months for $30.

A toll-free number was also printed in boldface on the BRE for credit-card orders only.

34:14   Uses of Library Routing Slip in Journal Promotions

A package promotion for a scientific journal subscription was mailed to a list of psychologists. The package included letter, flier, reply card, and a library routing slip on a separate piece of paper (50 lb. stock). Although the intent of the routing slip was to have the mailing's recipients complete and forward the package to their institutional librarian, a few completed and mailed the routing slips back with personal subscriptions.

Another journal publisher who promotes to this same audience places the subscription order form (BRC) and the library routing/recommendation slip side-by-side as segments on a single foldout flap that is part of the journal prospectus. With this procedure, none of the routing slips has been mailed back to the publisher.

34:15   How Stamp Sheet Was Used for Premium Offer
on Journal Subscription Renewal Campaign

In conjunction with a subscription renewal promotion campaign for the medical journal *The Lancet*, the publisher of the North American edition included a stamp sheet containing four-color illustrations of the covers of the Little, Brown Spiral Manual series, a group of books on various topics of interest to the medical generalist (i.e., doctors who do not specialize but see a variety of patients).

At the head of the stamp sheet was this copy: "Choose any one of these manuals (valued from $12.95 to $15.95) as your free bonus for resubscribing to *THE LANCET*. Just affix the appropriate stamp to your subscription form."

A subscription card was included along with a letter. The mailing with stamps was done in October 1982, by the Medical Division of Little, Brown, publisher of the North American edition of *Lancet*, the prestigious British medical journal.

34:16   Can a Scientific Journal Be Sold by Sales Representatives?
Survey Findings

A prestigious scientific journal conducted a field survey to determine the potential for subscription sales to libraries and institutions through field representatives. The survey found that calls by field representatives can have a public relations value, but are not cost-effective. Such calls also run contrary to established library ordering patterns for periodicals.

Other findings of the survey were as follows:

- Libraries traditionally order periodicals by mail, either directly or through a subscription agent.
- Libraries rarely enter a periodical subscription through a salesperson.
- Libraries order periodicals at individually regulated times of the year. These times will not be altered by the visit of a salesperson.
- Periodicals with high subscription prices (usually more than $100) are rarely ordered without discussions with staff or administration.
- Entry of a subscription frequently follows some form of promotion received from the publisher.
- Libraries have to cope with inflation and tight budgets and are likely to weed out one or more existing subscriptions in order to add a new one.
- Journals eliminated are those for which there is little demand, and that may be expensive or take up space on shelves, and that are available from other institutions with which the library has cooperative arrangements.
- Entry of a subscription is likely to be preceded by some kind of demand or request.
- Periodicals most likely to be considered are those readily accessible through indexes, abstracting resources, and the like.

34:17   Unique Low-Budget Library Contact
Program for Scientific Journals

A publisher of hundreds of scientific research journals maintains contact with the library market in a unique manner and on a relatively modest budget.

The publisher is Pergamon Press. In 1980, we heard about its program of hiring retired librarians to call on libraries as its "goodwill ambassadors." For ten calls a month within a radius of 50 miles of their home, the librarians were given a monthly "salary" of $250.

These "good-will ambassadors" do no selling, but they do present themselves on behalf of Pergamon Press in the library and invite customers to air any Pergamon-related problems. These are referred back to the publisher for handling and resolution by a qualified member of the sales or marketing staff.

One can be sure these representatives—mature, seasoned librarians—are effective in calling on libraries, and that they project an image for the publisher no other type of representation could buy at any price. And the total cost of the program for 30 library representatives was $100,000 per year!

34:18 Budgeting the Cost of a Book Used as a Premium: Guideline

If you should offer a book from your own press as a premium in a journal subscription campaign, how do you budget the cost?

In one prestigious house, where the press's books are used as premiums in subscription campaigns, the cost to the journals department for the books is the manufacturing cost plus full royalty to the author.

"The book is going to someone in [a] field . . . where we would normally sell the book," says the journals marketer, "so the book's author gets the same royalty he would get if we sold the book to the same individual."

34:19 Preliminary Bid to Agencies Prevents
Complaints on Special Offer

A publisher of scholarly and professional journals decided to offer its overstock of back issues of one of its journals at a 30% discount. Before making the offer, it contacted the subscription agencies, told them of the planned offer, and advised them they would be given the first option to purchase outright any of the back issues at 50% discount. The agencies could then make the same 30% discount offer to their customers and still retain their usual 20% discount. Response from the agencies was negligible, so the publisher subsequently made the 30% discount offer to the entire subscription list, including agency customers, and no complaints were heard from the subscription agencies.

34:20 Does It Pay to Woo Individual Subscription
Cancellations for a Specialized Journal?

Individuals usually subscribe to a scientific or scholarly journal because it is pertinent to their professional areas of interest. New subscribers are most easily obtained from among professionals just entering the field. Conversely, subscribers are extremely difficult to retain when they have left the area of specialization covered by the journal.

Newcomers to the field are the best prospects in subscription promotions. Efforts to reach those who have left the field will produce minimal results. When individuals cancel personal subscriptions to a professional or scholarly journal, they rarely continue to read it through other sources. One study found that less than one in twelve former subscribers still read with any regularity a journal they had previously subscribed to.

34:21   Journal Discount/Price Protection on Extended Subscription

One major publisher of international scholarly research and review journals (Pergamon Press) offers libraries a price reduction of 5 percent when subscriptions are placed for two years. Publisher Robert Maxwell said of this policy in a letter, "this two-year rate also protects the libraries against any increase in price resulting from inflation or increases in number of pages, or from any charges for the supply of additional volumes not previously announced."

34:22   Promise of Listing by Name Entices New Subscribers: Journal Subscription Idea

The old adage "names make news" also applies to journal subscriptions. A new scholarly journal in the social sciences, seeking to establish a strong subscriber base early on, included with its announcement mailings a discount of 25% off the first-year subscription price for prepaid three-year subscriptions.

Then it went a step farther. In some promotions, it also promised that "charter subscribers" would be listed in one issue yearly in the first three years. The promotions promising "charter subscriber" listing by name drew greater responses than those that did not offer listing.

34:23   Idea for Upgrading Journal Subscription

When the first payment is received from a new individual or institutional subscriber, acknowledge promptly with a "thank you" letter. As a postscript, offer to upgrade the subscription, for example, by offering to extend the subscription for any number of years at a discount. Mention that the extension offers an immediate saving and also gives protection against possible future price increases.

34:24   Photocopy Permission Fees: Additional Income Requiring No Effort

Journal publishers have access to an additional source of income involving no cost and requiring virtually no effort. That income can be realized by registering with the Copyright Clearance Center (CCC). The CCC logs and credits to participating publishers photocopying transactions reported by more than 1,000 registered user organizations that voluntarily report and pay fees to CCC for photocopies.

After deduction of its modest service charge, CCC issues payments to publishers quarterly. Nearly 3,000 scientific, technical, and scholarly journals are registered to receive these photocopying permission fees.

To have your journals participate in the CCC system, you submit, without charge, a registration form (which CCC provides) for each serial or separate publication title. You must then include on the masthead of each journal a statement indicating your prior registration with the CCC, and also print an article fee code at the bottom of page one of each article. The fees can vary from article to article.

Your registration with the CCC need not interfere with arrangements you now have to supply reprints, or with other ongoing photocopying licensing arrangements you may have with other organizations.

For complete details on how you can register your journals with CCC, write to Copyright Clearance Center, Inc., 21 Congress Street, Salem, MA 01970; 617-744-3350.

34:25   Gimmicky Presentation of Readership Study has Negative Effect

The thin-walled carton was placed on the book marketer's desk with the incoming mail. The top flap had no seal and opened easily to reveal a pile of tiny glass fragments in the interior. The carton had come from the advertising management of a group of scientific research journals. The promotion carton was to contain the results of a college market readership study that had been wrapped around a glass laboratory beaker. Ultimately, the delivery of a box of broken glass destroyed whatever value the study may have had, for the recipient's only concern was to get the small fragments of broken glass off the desk. The attempt here to deliver a readership survey in a cute and gimmicky way to potential buyers of advertising had backfired and, if anything, been counterproductive. The same information would have fit as easily on two sides of an 8½″ × 11″ sheet of paper mailed in a #10 envelope.

The lesson to be learned here is: Communicate information in a simple, straightforward manner. The chances of it being read may be far greater than when you present the same data in a much more expensive, gimmicky way that could offend recipients or otherwise backfire on you. This lesson is particularly valuable for promotions to the library, academic, or bookstore markets. Factual, straightforward information of potential usefulness will receive attention even when it is presented in an unpretentious and unglamorous manner.

34:26   Microform: Unacceptable Alternative
Format for Printed Journals

Many publishers of scientific and scholarly journals have long viewed microform as a desirable and considerably less expensive format for journals printed in paper editions. However, users of journals are not that anxious to share the same view. Speaking on alternative journal formats at the annual meeting of the Society for Scholarly Publishing in Minneapolis in June 1980, Judy C. Holoviak, journals manager of the American Geophysical Union, cited the experience of the *Journal of Geophysical Research*. After that journal was available in microform for seven years, only between 1 and 2% of the subscribers to the paper edition had entered subscriptions for the microform edition.

35

Journal Advertising and Publicity

35:01 Value of Exchange Advertising for Scholarly Journals

1. It fills up unsightly blank pages at the end of a signature.
2. It gets exposure for your journal in related journals in the same or closely related fields.
3. If you have a journal of international scope, it provides a cost-free means of advertising in European journals.
4. It can get your journal advertised in other journals that do not sell or accept advertising but will place an exchange advertisement.
5. It will please journal editors. Most editors in the same or complementary fields know each other and often will feel you have an effective marketing program for their journal if they see exchange advertising in other journals.
6. When you have a special issue, you can do spot exchange-ad placements with journals related to the subject of the special issue for extra publicity on that issue.

35:02 Journal Advertising Exchange: Techniques and Procedures

Most knowledgeable journal marketers carry on an active advertising exchange program with other journals in the same or related fields. Because journal promotion budgets are tiny and produce small results over long periods of time, the advertising exchange program is the only vehicle for stretching the small budget to fit the demanding job journal promotions require.

At one university press, a full-time assistant is assigned to journal exchanges—and justifiably so. The exchange program is very time-consuming and requires a lot of record keeping and clerical maintenance.

Very often handling a journal advertising exchange program is a matter of having the right person for the job. The reason, quite simply, is that there are no rules or guidelines for such exchanges. Much depends on just having a friendly telephone voice and a winning personality, which will often get the party at the other end to agree to the exchange on mutually acceptable terms. Other than personality, the prestige of the journal and/or publisher may help you in soliciting advertising exchanges.

What constitutes a good exchange? Most often advertising exchanges are made on a per-page basis, i.e., one page of advertising space for another. However, a few journals like to exchange on a dollar-for-dollar space basis. If your journal charges $200 a page for advertising and the other party charges $500 a page, it may ask for two and one-half pages in your journal for one in its journal.

On rare occasions, journal advertising exchanges may be made on the basis of circulation. If one journal has twice the circulation of another, it may demand twice the space or even more. Large circulation periodicals in some fields will ask for two pages of advertising or more in exchange for the single, partial-page ad insert it gives to a prestigious but very small circulation journal in the same field.

One journal trades advertising space in its journal in exchange for space in other journals that it uses to advertise the book publications of its sister division in the same professional society.

As there are few rules for exchanges, you are limited only by what you can arrange, how well you can wheel and deal, and what you are prepared to give in the way of advertising space in order to get what you want from the other journal. On occasion, negotiating exchanges can be fulfilling, as this writer once learned when he arranged an ad exchange on a three-to-one basis (in favor of the writer) with a periodical that had a dozen times the circulation of his own.

35:03   Journal Advertising Exchange Program at a University Press

"The hardest part of . . . running a journal exchange advertising program," says the journal promotion manager, "is to initiate brand new exchanges. You have to find the right person, explain the exchange program (some never heard of it), and then get them to agree to the exchange.

"You've got to hit it off with the person you're calling, get them to like you and to give you the space you are asking for.

"I generally exchange with journals with about the same circulations as the journals that I handle. I try to avoid the ones with larger circulations. They don't want to exchange; they want to sell advertising space. So I try to stay in my own ballpark.

"Once you've set up an exchange and you've worked out an agreeable exchange that works well, it can go on for years and years.

"I like the challenge of going into a market with a one-shot exchange that I normally wouldn't bother with. It's those special ones where you make the money, especially if you can hit it off with one phone call."

35:04   Journal Advertising Exchange Program at Large Commercial Publisher

"We have a very active journal exchange program. I generally base exchanges with other journals on circulation. It is my feeling that the number of people I reach in an exchange should be approximately equal to the number of people that the exchange ad in my journal will reach.

"I go by numbers. A lot of journal exchange people go by [advertising] page rates. What's important to me is how many people I'm reaching, and how new is the journal.

"If it's a new journal, for example, and it's the first issue and somebody has 300 and I have 5,000, I'd probably say 'no.' But if those same numbers prevailed and the journal had been around a long time and it was a really hot journal, I'd consider it, even if the circulation was much lower. Sometimes good will will be a factor in an exchange. If it's a publisher that is doing great things and I feel I may need them in the future, then I will exchange, even when the numbers aren't right.

"I'd be more inclined to say 'yes' to a request from a prestigious house where the same request from a house with a bad reputation would get a quick 'no.'

"My feeling is I'm not going through the production and detail unless I'm going to get something out of it. My time is very important and I have to be very discriminating."

35:05   Problems and Pitfalls of Exchange Advertising: Advice from a Professional

This entry was specially written for this volume by Julie Zuckman, Journal Promotion and Advertising Manager at MIT Press.

1. Don't make too many commitments: Do not promise to run ads in any particular issue. Make commitments by the year or volume. You should never promise to run more ads than you will have blanks, and since you can't know in advance how many blanks you will have, you should not overextend yourself.

2. To avoid problems, make sure your exchange proposal and/or rate card spells out your production needs very carefully. Failure to observe this fundamental requirement can result in receipt of unacceptable camera copy, including:

- Photocopies, material to be pubset, materials of the wrong size or shape
- Items that are expensive to produce: halftones, dropouts, stripping, not camera ready, bleeds
- Stale ads that are two or more years old
- Incompetent ads with misspellings, blotches, stray marks, objectionable copy

Bear in mind that things you would not tolerate from a paid advertiser should not be acceptable from an exchange advertiser. These problems crop up frequently if you do exchanges with small, fly-by-night journals, especially in the arts and other underfunded disciplines, that cannot afford professional services such as typesetting.

3. Control your own production costs:
    - If possible, standardize your entire exchange-ad format so that ads can be easily updated from one volume to the next with just a few copy changes.
    - Design a flexible format that can be easily adapted to fit a variety of shapes and sizes by adding or taking away rules, decorative devices, and various sizes of headlines. Most journals are 6″ × 9″, but there is a lot of variety in trim size for journals in the sciences and arts. A 6″ × 9″ ad can, with some imagination, be made to fit an 8½″ × 11″ page, without the expense of setting a new ad.
    - When there is a wide range of choice in possible exchanges, consider selecting journals that are all the same size so that you can use one ad format for all of them. Don't sacrifice quality for convenience, though.

4. How to deal with book ads when you thought you were exchanging journal for journal: This is liable to happen when dealing with a promotion department that handles both book and journal advertising. I do not allow this because it is not fair to my paying book advertisers, because it reduces my ad sales income, and because once you let publishers get away with it, you will never see a paid ad from them. To avoid this, state your terms of exchange clearly in your proposal—journal for journal. Exceptions to this rule may be made if you are desperate to get your advertisement into a journal and it won't exchange on any other basis. But this is a bad precedent.

5. Controlling the paperwork monster: Exchange programs generate mountains of time-consuming paperwork. To handle this load:
    - Establish orderly files for each journal, with neat records so you can find out at a glance who owes what to whom and what the deadlines and ad specs are. Note and file names, addresses, phone numbers, and exchange information carefully and promptly.
    - Adhere to the convention of sending tearsheets and confirmation that you are running the ad. You should expect the same; otherwise, you have no record.

6. Preventing an old ad with incorrect prices from running: Be sure to send out new camera copy at least three months before the date your new volume price or price changes become effective. Tell the other journal to destroy your old camera copy. Establish yearly updating and renewal schedules for exchange agreements with all journals and try to stagger these throughout the year so you will not have to make up ten new ads in one month.

7. Questioning the utility of exchange advertising: Code your ads and track the response, but accept the fact that you still need exchanges to fill up the blanks. If you do not want to spend the time and money, create a series of in-house ads for your own books and journals and run them over and over again; you'll soon discover that exchange ads look better.

35:06   Journal Advertising Exchanges: Alternatives to Space

Another journal contacts you for an exchange of ad space in one of your journals, but you see no value in taking space in theirs. Perhaps the circulation of the journal is too small, or you have no advertisement available, or don't want to take the time and expense to bother. What alternative forms of "payment" are available to you that will enable an "exchange" to take place on mutually beneficial terms?

Here are some alternatives to exchanging advertising space:

1. Space in exchange for so many thousand names of their book buyers.
2. Space in exchange for circulation lists of one or more of their journals.
3. Space in exchange for a list of names of buyers of a particular book on their list who may be prospective subscribers to your journal.
4. Space in exchange for free participation in one of their sponsored card decks.
5. Space in exchange for book advertising for another division of your company.
6. Space in exchange for their agreement to show your journals, offer literature, and accept orders at a show that they will be attending but you will not.
7. Space in exchange for a per-inquiry arrangement in which you will be paid for each subscription resulting from the advertisement.

35:07   More Ways to Advertise Your Journals at No or Low Cost*

- Arrange subscription list exchanges or one-time use of your list for advertising space.

*In addition to journal advertising exchanges (for information on ad exchanges, refer to 35:02 through 35:06 in this chapter).

- Have a recent or impressive issue of your journal reprinted in miniature, perhaps on a scale of one-fourth, and use it as a souvenir handout at conventions or as an enclosure with a mail promotion. Be sure to indicate that it is a scaled-down version and give the true size.
- Include bind-in or freestanding subscription order cards in your journals.

35:08 Do Free Subscriptions to Abstracting and Indexing Services Pay Off?

Does it pay to give free subscriptions to abstracting and indexing services? The question has come up time and again without a satisfactory answer. More often than not, the more affluent journals do continue such complimentary subscriptions; some of the less affluent may elect not to. A possible clue to the answer may lie in "Standards for College Libraries," which appeared in *College Research Libraries News* (October 1975, p. 290), and said in part about periodicals, "It is good practice for a library to own any title . . . needed more than six times per year."

It follows that if citations in abstracting and indexing services turn scholars and researchers to library periodicals in search of information, then such services certainly help increase the number of "uses" journals have in the library and, therefore, make a contribution to the value of continuing the subscription for the library. Conversely, some librarians are swayed in subscription decisions by such considerations as when and where a journal is indexed, as they believe indexing helps research needs.

Likewise, in starting a new journal, it makes good sense to obtain recommendations from the editors and editorial board for important abstracting and indexing services in the field(s) covered by the new journal and to make advance arrangements for such services so that a listing of publications in which the new journal will be abstracted and/or indexed can be made part of the journal's prospectus. It is this writer's feeling that free subscriptions are warranted for any abstracting and indexing service in the same or related field of the journal.

35:09 Publicity Sources for New Science Journals

BIOSCIENCE

If your new scientific journal is of interest to *BioScience*'s multidisciplinary readership in biology, send your announcement to Features and News Editor, BioScience, 1401 Wilson Boulevard, Arlington, VA 22209. Your new journal will be listed in the People and Places section, which follows the Book Review section. The listing will include title, name of publisher, description of general content, format, and subscription information.

NATURE

This prestigious scientific weekly originates in the United Kingdom, but has a U.S. edition and a large and growing North American circulation. An annual review supplement, which appears in the first weekly issue in October, is devoted to new science journals. New journals for any annual supplement should have begun publication between January of the preceding year and May of the year of the issue. In order to qualify for consideration, a journal must be of professional interest to scientists (but not an abstracts journal), must be in the English language, and must be published at least three times a year. If your new journal meets these criteria, send before the end of June four sample issues, including the first and most recent issues, to Review Editor, *Nature*, 4 Little Essex Street, London WC2R 3LF, England. If you have a question, call *Nature* in London at 836 6633, ext 2570.

THE CHRONICLE OF HIGHER EDUCATION

This weekly newspaper on news and trends in higher education has nearly 70,000 loyal subscribers in colleges and universities. Each issue contains a section on publishing with extensive new book listings. In addition, the highly popular "Footnotes" column on the first page of the publishing section in each issue includes announcements of new journals under that heading. Inasmuch as more than 50% of U.S. college faculty were found in a study to do outside consulting, you should consider this publication for announcements of your new journal, whether academically oriented or not. Write to The Chronicle of Higher Education, 1333 New Hampshire Avenue NW, Washington, DC 20036.

35:10   Periodicals of the Larger Periodical Subscription Agencies

- Ebsco Subscription Services, P.O. Box 2543, Birmingham, AL 35202
  Publication: *Ebsco Bulletin of Serials Changes* (monthly)
- McGregor Magazine Agency, Mount Morris, IL 61054
  Publications: *McGregor Periodicals Bulletin* (three or four times per year)
  Librarians' Reference Catalog (annual)
- Moore-Cottrell Subscription Agencies, Inc., North Cohocton, NY 14868
  Publication: *Periodicals Update* (monthly)
- Swets North America, Inc., P.O. Box 417, Berwyn, PA 19312
  Publication: *Swets Info* (monthly)
- Turner Subscription Agency, Inc., 234 Park Avenue South, New York, NY 10003
  Publications: *Turner Periodical Catalog* (annual)
  Turner School Periodical Guide (annual)

- F. W. Faxon Co., Inc., 15 SW Park, Westwood, MA 02090
  Publication: *Serials Updating Service* (quarterly)
- Read-More Publications, 140 Cedar Street, New York, NY 10006
  Publication: *Read-More Newsletter* (bimonthly)

35:11   Is a Separate Journal Catalog Necessary?

The question of a separate catalog for journals is one that some journals promotion managers often ask. Should we have one or shouldn't we? If we do, will it pay off for all the effort and expense?

One journal marketer, whose list consists of 16 journals, says a full catalog is not necessary. She says a descriptive folder will serve just as well, and for periodical subscription agents, a detailed sheet giving essential basic subscription data, prices, and discounts will suffice.

Another journal marketer, who has responsibility for promoting more than 75 journals of an international publishing organization, sees a journal catalog as a necessity and revises and reissues one annually. It contains 16 pages stitched in a hard cover and fits into a #10 envelope and is useful as a handout at exhibits and conventions.

A serials librarian said she wouldn't think of looking into a catalog when she was interested in a journal in a single subject area. However, she felt it was useful to have a publisher's book catalog containing a separate listing for journals in the same subject area, and a listing of all the publisher's journals in the general book catalog.

Our opinion is that if you have a small journal list, a folder or informational sheet is usually adequate. For a larger list, a sheet or folder may be unwieldy and a catalog format becomes essential.

36

Subscription Studies

36:01 More on Why Journal Subscriptions Are Dropped by Institutions

In *Volume One*, we reported on the principal reasons why institutions
drop subscriptions, based on a telephone survey of subscriptions by a
journal publisher. The reasons, in order of importance, were budget
cuts, reduced demand, price, the ability to share a subscription with
another institution, and the closing of some institutions.

Additional reasons for journal subscription cancellations included
the following:

- The journal does not support the collection.
- The subject matter covered by a particular journal has diminished in
  importance or timeliness, leading to subscription to a more appropriate journal.
- Certain subscriptions are cancelled to make funds available for new
  subscriptions.
- A journal has a poor showing in citation studies.

For additional information on reasons for journal cancellations by
institutions, see the results of a National Science Foundation study in
36:02.

**36:02 Why Libraries Enter and Cancel Subscriptions
to Scholarly and Research Journals**

These findings on the subscription practices of libraries emerged from
a study funded by the National Science Foundation (NSF) and conducted by the Indiana Research Center for Library Information
Science. Published in 1980 in *Library Quarterly**** (vol. 50, no. 3), the
study found these to be the principal reasons why libraries enter new
subscriptions (in descending order):

1. Evaluation by a user group, or departmental recommendation
2. Recommendation based on library staff evaluation
3. Specific recommendation of a continuing user
4. Appropriateness of journals for new areas of specialized collection
   development
5. Specific request of a new user

These were found to be the principal reasons why libraries cancel an
existing subscription (in descending order):

1. Budget cuts
2. Recommendation based on staff evaluation
3. Shifting priorities
4. User recommendations
5. High price

**36:03 Why Individuals Enter and Cancel Subscriptions
to Scholarly and Research Journals**

These findings on the subscription practices of individuals also
emerged from the Indiana Research Center Study published in *Library
Quarterly* (vol. 50, no. 3) in 1980.

The principal reasons why individuals subscribe (in descending
order) are:

1. They are relatively new to a profession and want to keep up with activities or developments.
2. They now feel able to afford a subscription.
3. They previously used a library copy, but now find it impractical.
4. They recently changed to an area of specialization covered by the
   journal.
5. They received the subscription as part of a society membership.

**Marketers of scholarly and research journals are well advised to obtain this issue of
Library Quarterly and enjoy the complete results of that study, reported on pages
287–309.

The principal reasons why individuals cancel subscriptions (in descending order) are:

1. The individuals' interest changed.
2. Content of the journal failed to meet expectations.
3. Individuals switched to a more appropriate journal.
4. Individuals were no longer members of the society through which the journal was received.
5. Lessened finances caused individuals to cut back on expenditures.

36:04   Geographic Trends in Subscriptions: Implications for Journal Promotion

When a study was conducted by STM* in 1978 of geographic trends in subscriptions to international scientific journals, the results bore an important message for U.S. publishers. The study covered 403 journals from 30 publishers. Of these, 87 were published in the United States and 85 in the United Kingdom. The study examined foreign journal subscriptions to U.S. journals in 1971, 1974, and 1977.

There was an upward trend in subscriptions during the 1970s. Foreign subscriptions to U.S. journals examined in the study were 17.9% of total circulation in 1971, 19.2% in 1974, and 19.9% in 1977. These three figures, if plotted on a chart, would indicate a foreign subscription base for the U.S. journals of 23.5% by 1982.

In late 1982, we queried a publisher with more than a score of international scientific journals in its foreign subscription base. Instead of the projected 23.5%, it was actually 33⅓%. In high-technology areas, the ratio of foreign to domestic subscriptions was 60–40 in favor of foreign subscriptions. The indication is clear: Foreign subscriptions to international scientific journals are growing at a much more rapid rate than are domestic subscriptions.

Marketers of such international scientific journals must bear in mind that most of these subscriptions come through subscription agencies. When a foreign subscription is received from any agency, care must be taken to ensure that that agency is on the publisher's mailing list to receive all journal announcements.

Each subscription agency has its own subscriber group and, for the most part, can be relied upon to reach its customers with information on journals pertinent to its clients' special interests.

However, in the scientific specialties, journal promotions should also strive to reach the memberships of foreign professional groups and societies. Often the members of these societies decide for the institutions with which they are affiliated which journals will be subscribed to. Promotion budgets must take into account the relationship of

---

*STM is the International Group of Scientific, Technical, and Medical Publishers. Its secretariat is located at Keizergracht 462, Amsterdam 1016 GE, The Netherlands. STM's membership is drawn from more than 20 countries.

foreign subscriptions to the overall circulation, and promotional efforts must be directed accordingly.

What holds for the sciences does not hold for other areas. As journals move into such areas as investment and finance, foreign circulation tends to be smaller, perhaps 25% or less. One exception would be a journal with a good international economics outlook. Where such journals present a balanced international overview, foreign and domestic circulations may be relatively equal.

36:05   How to Deal with Subscription Agencies on Special Offers

Most special journal subscription offers are planned with the idea that orders will come directly back to the publisher. However, many libraries rely exclusively on a subscription agency for their journal subscriptions.

To maximize the return from a special subscription offer, plan to include as part of the special-offer package an order form or coupon with a fixed expiration date. Have the copy on the form state that it can be sent either to the publisher or to the library's subscription agency. Prior to the promotion, you should inform the subscription agencies about the special offer and advise that you will honor orders from them for the special offer at their usual discount, provided they are accompanied by the coupon or order form that is part of the special offer.

36:06   Agency Discount Used as Subscription-Building Device: Case Study

Can a publisher of scientific and business journals use discounts to enlist the aid of subscription agents in increasing subscriptions? One publisher tried it and reported it was working satisfactorily and would be continued indefinitely. Here's what was done:

Five months before the start of the new subscription year, subscription agents were informed that a new discount policy was being instituted, and that under the new policy the older journals with well-established subscription bases would have a reduced discount for new and renewal subscriptions. On newer journals, i.e., those three years old or less, the discount for new subscriptions would be doubled for the first year only.

The change, the agents were told, was "an incentive to help build subscriptions" and "encourage widest possible publicity."

36:07   How to Cut Postage Cost of Renewal Campaigns

As growing postage costs become an increasing problem for journal publishers, one move to diminish postage costs took place quietly on December 6, 1981. On that date, the requirement that first-class mail not be attached to or enclosed in other than first-class mailings ended.

Thus, since December 6, 1981, it has been possible (and many publishers have taken advantage of this) to enclose with the mailing of a journal a subscription renewal notice, which postal regulations previously required to be sent with first-class postage. Under the changed regulation, first-class mail that is incidental but related to the matter mailed via another class requires no additional postage.

One fulfillment professional says there is a decided benefit to sending the renewal notice with the journal, because seeing the notice with the journal gives it a sense of immediacy it would not have had it been delivered separately.

It is a relatively simple matter to separate labels due for renewal notices and to mail them in a separate batch with the renewal invoice. You can avoid having the postpaid renewal notice get lost or overlooked by putting it in an envelope, as you would any first-class mailing, and setting the postage meter at $.00. This will give the notice the look and feel of a first-class letter.

36:08   Low-Cost Subscription-Building Device
Frequently Overlooked by Journal Marketers

One low-cost subscription-building device that is largely overlooked by most journal marketers is the inclusion of a removable subscription order form in the journal itself.

Bearing in mind that many journals have their widest readership through library subscriptions, the removable subscription card makes it easy for the reader of the library copy to have in his or her hands a convenient vehicle for placing a personal subscription, or for recommending a subscription to a friend, colleague, or departmental library or to a company or institutional media or resource center.

Consumer periodicals already make heavy use of removable subscription order cards, and for good reason. In a *New York Times* report of December 31, 1981, by Philip H. Dougherty, a monthly consumer magazine stated its primary circulation tool was a removable subscription card in each issue. The second and third best circulation builders were direct mail and television, in that order—despite the fact that the latter occupied most of the annual circulation-promotion budget of almost $6 million! (The publication was *Money* magazine, which has a circulation of close to one million, about 13% of which is sold on newsstands.)

Part X

Marketer-Author Relations

37

Working with Your Author

Authors in specialized markets are at the same time readers of other books and know the readership for these particular markets. They can be actively "employed" for the marketing of their books and they usually appreciate it. Some of them even turn out to be their own best salesmen on the occasion of conferences and other meetings with colleagues.

Albrecht von Hagen, McGraw-Hill
International Book Co., Hamburg,
at STM Conference,
Basel, Switzerland, November 1979.

37:01 Author Questionnaire Procedures: When Author Fails to Respond

The author (or marketing) questionnaire is vital to planning promotion for any professional or scholarly book. Consequently, one individual within your publishing establishment should have total responsibility for ensuring completion and internal distribution of completed questionnaires to concerned individuals within the organization. Logically, the sponsoring editor should issue the questionnaire at the time of contract signing. If not, the one to issue it should be someone in the marketing department (often, a person with a secretarial or assistant job function). As many authors are slow in returning such questionnaires, requests for completion and all follow-ups should bear the signature of someone of authority, logically the sponsoring editor or marketing manager.

When a request is sent to an author, a follow-up copy should be

405

scheduled for mailing in, say, four or five weeks. If no reply has been received, the second request for the completed questionnaire should be sent. By the end of eight weeks or so, if the questionnaire has not been returned, an urgent request should be made to the sponsoring editor for his or her personal attention and follow-up in the matter. (The sample form demonstrates how such a request might be worded.) This practice will ensure that questionnaire data will be in the hands of the marketing department for planning purposes well in advance of publication.

37:02   Keeping Your Author Questionnaire Current

Some houses use an author questionnaire that has been carried over for countless years without charge. Others may use a format that was picked up from another house and adapted because of its thoroughness of coverage. Many such author questionnaires carry questions that call for responses of little or no value from the author. For example, one house requests a glossy photograph, although it stopped using illustrations of authors on its jackets years ago. Another asks for mailing lists that might be used to promote the author's book. When such lists are received, they are rarely ever used and more often than not have to be returned to the author. If you do request lists, ask for recent lists, i.e., ones no older than two or three years. Better still, ask about list availability; then, when you know what is available, ask only for what you intend to use.

Check your present author questionnaire periodically. Are there questions that should be modified or dropped entirely? Have you modified your publishing program so that new information should be requested? A few minutes spent updating or reviewing your questionnaire can save time, effort, and money.

37:03   Author Requests Large Quantities of Literature: What Action to Take?

Occasionally, an author of a professional or reference work will ask the publisher to provide a large quantity of promotional literature that the author says she or he will distribute personally, through business affiliation or through friends or professional connections. Often, fulfilling such requests can be productive. However, the marketer should be aware that such a request can also be an ego trip for the author and have little basis in fact.

In one instance, the author of a professional book issued an "order" to his publisher that 20,000 fliers on his book be sent to a specific publication headed by a friend, who would distribute them to the circulation of that publication. A note at the bottom of the letter indicated a copy had also been sent to the intended recipient of the fliers. Because shipping instructions were not included, a call was made to the intended recipient for clear instructions. The call revealed that, although the author was known to the publication, no commitment

---

MEMORANDUM

Date:

To: Sponsoring Editor

From: Marketing Department

Subject: Failure of Your Author to Return Marketing Questionnaire
after Two Requests

Author:

Title:

After two requests over an approximate ___ week period, your author has failed to complete and return the Marketing Questionnaire.

It is absolutely essential that we have this questionnaire if any planning is to be done for the marketing and promotion of the above-mentioned book. This information is also essential for the design of the jacket.

You are urgently requested to initiate whatever action you deem necessary to obtain the Marketing Questionnaire for our use at the earliest possible date.

It would also be appreciated if you would inform me of whatever action is being taken so that we can make our plans accordingly.

(Signature)

Reply:

---

had been made for a mass mailing, but that "a couple of hundred" fliers, if sent, might be used.

In another instance, one author requested huge quantities of a promotional insert about his book for inclusion in his company's regular mailings to its lists of prospects. As it turned out, the inserts tended more to reinforce the firm's expertise for its consulting service, the primary subject of the mailing, than to act as a selling vehicle for the book.

Most experienced book marketers can recall at least one instance in which fulfilling an author's request for a large quantity of literature proved unproductive. The lesson here is that major book promotion is best kept in the hands of the publisher's marketing and promotion staff, and that authors' requests for large quantities of literature should be handled cautiously.

37:04 **Quick, Simple, Inexpensive Way to
Generate Extra Sales through Author**

Many authors of scientific, professional, and scholarly books are also prolific writers of articles and lecturers. Consequently, they have numerous opportunities to promote their books to individuals who write to request reprints of their published articles or who attend seminars at which the authors are speakers.

Where it may be the publisher's policy to promote books in groups or by subject, it is not always feasible to have a flier made up on a specific title available on short notice to fulfill an author's request.

A simple, inexpensive way to deal with such requests is to type up such a flier on the publisher's letterhead, showing the title, author and affiliation, publication date, price, short synopsis, and table of contents. If the book has a jacket, most likely the information for the flier can be lifted from it word-for-word or in abbreviated form. The contents can be adapted or abbreviated from the contents page.

The lower 20% or 25% of the letterhead can contain a coupon-type order form addressed to the publisher. If an attractive multicolor letterhead is available, the flier might be run off on preprinted letterhead to give it a more professional appearance.

As most requested involve no more than perhaps 200 to 500 such fliers, these can be run off on in-house copying facilities, or by inexpensive neighborhood printing services, many of which provide same-day or overnight service.

As orders generated by these fliers are at list price, in some instances the first order can offset the small cost of the flier. And, having such a flier in hand, many authors become conscientious promoters of their own work.

37:05   Persuading the Reluctant Author: How the Marketer Can Help

Sooner or later, you may, in your capacity as a book marketer, be summoned to an author-recruitment session. Generally, such sessions are convened when your acquisitions editor has a potential author in the office whose manuscript has been favorably evaluated, but the author is reluctant to sign. He or she either already has offers from two competing publishers, or else plans to call on one or more others before selecting a publisher. Your acquisitions editor's anxious face appears in your doorway. The editor wants that contract, and asks if you can spare a minute or two with the prospective author to help convince him or her that your publishing establishment is best for the book.

We like to call this an "arm-twisting" session, although in reality, its purpose is more to instill confidence in your operation and persuade the prospective author you can do the best job for his or her book.

How do you handle an "arm-twisting" session? First, you convey the impression that you see a substantial potential market for the author's work and will make a conscientious effort to promote it to its intended audiences, should he or she select your company to be the publisher. You then make the strongest possible case for what your publishing establishment can actually do—by enumerating the proven strengths that it has to offer any author. Never exaggerate or overstate! The prospective author will take your statements as gospel* and expect everything you promise. So present only your establishment's true strengths, and don't try to stretch them.

No two publishers have the same strengths. Some establishments may have a strong publishing program in a particular field in which the prospective author's book may fall. In this instance, the following statements might be apt to persuade an author:

"We are the world's leading publisher in the field of interferon research, and your book will become part of that distinguished list," or "Because we have a large number of titles in the area of your book, we can reach its markets in the following ways: (give examples)."

The prestige of your imprint, rather than your marketing approach, may be a principal strength, so you drop a few names: "We've been publishing more than 100 years. Our authors have included many Nobel Prize winners, and such other distinguished names as _____ , _____ , and _____ ."

For university presses in particular, the prestige of the press's imprint may be the strongest selling point. Academic authors in particular like the idea of being published by such imprints as Harvard, Chicago, or Princeton, and others that are particularly prestigious in specialized areas.

Your special position in a potential author's field may be tied to your position as publisher of specialized journals in that or other closely related fields. In that case you may wish to capitalize on the fact that the author's book will receive considerable exposure in its field through advertising in these journals.

Be alert to things that can turn a prospective author off as well. Consider the prospect of an author who is opposed to ownership of publishers by conglomerates. If it is possible to ascertain what the author expects of a publisher, it is best to gear your approach to these issues, if you can do so in a truthful manner.

Most authors have two common interests: (1) whether your promotion will reach everyone who could be interested in their book, and (2) whether those who want to buy it will be able to do so without difficulty. Can you meet these interests? Does your shipping center have fast turnaround on orders received? Will the book be kept in print for a reasonable time? The right answers to these questions will convince authors of your abilities as a publisher.

Many authors and potential authors are anxious for bookstore exposure. (How many times has an author complained, "None of my friends have been able to find my book in any bookstore"?) If you have sales reps and good bookstore distribution, this can provide motivation for a prospective author. A large number of "agency" accounts that will automatically stock a book upon publication is also helpful.

---

*An acquisitions editor reviewing this entry recalled that, in more than 18 years with four large publishing houses, nine out of ten problems with authors were related to marketing functions, i.e., promises the authors felt were not kept.

Be aware of the author of a social science book who thinks his or her book has the makings of a best-seller. It may be necessary to explain that the potential audience for the book is segmented, so your job as a marketer will be to bring the author's expectations for the book's sales into true perspective. Sell the author on the real market for the book, for example, with the following: "Perhaps there are hundreds of thousands of people who will be interested in your book, *The Decline of the Family*, but only a small fraction of that number will be sufficiently interested to actually buy the book."

A note of caution: Many authors of professional books write to enhance their standing within their profession or to establish themselves as authorities on the subject of their book. However, be wary of the prospective author who sees or intends the book as an ongoing vehicle to advertise his or her services. Authors with such expectations occasionally become troublesome with their constant suggestions for exploiting the book, their expectations of rapid high-volume sales, their requests for special attention, advertisements, literature, exposure of their books at numerous exhibits and conventions, and the like.

Such authors create more trouble for the publisher than their books are worth, and perhaps should be avoided altogether. Invariably this type of author, when you first fail to meet his or her expectations, will fire off a letter of protest—not to you or to the editor but usually to the company president or board chairman (if you're owned by a conglomerate, it might even be the board chairman of the conglomerate)—citing the promises you may have actually made or others the author perceived you made during the "arm-twisting" session and your failure to live up to those promises. In such cases, even your slightest exaggerations are cited as legally binding commitments that you have failed to honor.

So the marketer should approach author-recruitment sessions with care and caution and state actual strengths firmly and forthrightly. Never go one iota beyond what you are actually prepared to do. Failing that, be prepared to eat your words!

37:06   When an Author Seeks Name/Address of Local Bookseller for Referrals: How to Cope

Of the more than 19,000 bookstore outlets in the United States, only a handful stock professional and scholarly books to any degree. This poses a problem time and again for book marketers when the author of a limited potential scholarly reference work is about to give a talk at a symposium or university on a topic closely related to the book's subject, and asks for the name and address of a nearby bookseller to which potential buyers can be referred.

Here are some ways to handle such a situation that have worked for others:

1. Ask the university bookstore or bookstore in the area if it will stock a quantity of the book for 30 days from the date of the talk. Offer to

pay return freight on unsold copies or, if you consider it worthwhile, offer to pay the freight both ways.

2. Prepare a flier on your standard letterhead with an order coupon on the bottom returnable to you. An alternative is to issue a news release describing the book that has a returnable order form at the bottom. In either case, give the author a quantity for distribution or pickup in the area.

3. Print descriptive information about the book on a postpaid reply card (returnable to you) for distribution by the author.

4. Give the author a name and phone number to announce that will accept collect or toll-free telephone orders.

5. If the author is agreeable (some may even suggest it), send books directly to the author (at author's discount), and allow the author to make his or her own selling arrangements. Offer returns protection.

37:07   How and When to Approach an Author When the Book's Title Is Unsuitable

In the film industry, a movie that fails to attract an audience when released is sometimes withdrawn and later reissued under a different (better) title. In professional and reference book publishing, you have only one chance to make your author's book successful. A good book with a weak or belabored title, or one that does not deliver the book's intent or major benefit, can suffer seriously, especially if its content is targeted to a specialized audience.

Once a manuscript has been approved for publication, the marketer should ask: Is this the most appropriate title for this book? The choice, in the long run, will be up to the author. However, although most authors give care and painstaking attention to every detail in a manuscript, such is not always the case for the book's title. Often an author will consult about the title with family members, office staff, or other associates, whose aim is to choose something "cute" or "catchy."

Where circumstances permit, the marketer should be involved in the selection of a title, even though an author's contacts, at least in the early stages, are almost entirely with the sponsoring editor. There are times when a proposed alternate title will be appropriate. At other times, it may be more appropriate to prepare a variety of title suggestions (see 38:15). The variety makes it possible for an author to respond with his or her own new title, which, more often than not, is a composite of two or more of the suggestions prepared by the marketer.

Rarely will an author reject a proposal for a more desirable title. A title proposed by the marketer in concert with the sponsoring editor may not be the one finally selected by the author, but usually the title agreed upon reflects the marketer's and editor's line of thinking. Either way, a professional or reference book with a good, meaningful title, i.e., one that speaks directly to the book's audience, will attract more attention and achieve a better share of its market potential much more quickly. Because of this, your author will usually welcome your title-change proposal and accept it as a vehicle for faster or greater sales.

37:08 Marketing Information Requirements for a Revised Edition

When submitting a questionnaire to the author of a revised edition for completion, make it clear that the information supplied for the earlier edition will not suffice for the revision and that a new questionnaire is required. Here is how one publisher words such requests:

As the author of a revision, you may have supplied some of this information before. However, we will be using THIS questionnaire to build a NEW MARKETING FILE as a source for all advertising, sales, and promotion activity for your text. It is essential that throughout this questionnaire you give us COMPLETE AND UP-TO-DATE INFORMATION regarding yourself, your book, its market, etc.—if necessary, duplicating information you may have provided several years ago."

Some specific questions to ask the author of a revised edition are:

- What specific changes in structure and content does the revised book have?
- What are some of the key new features in this edition?
- What distinguishing features of the earlier edition have been retained?
- If the book is intended as a textbook, indicate pertinent department(s), course title(s), level, and semester(s) usually offered.
- If the book is intended as a textbook, indicate its appropriateness for nonacademic use such as secondary schools, technical institutes, government, industrial, and union training programs.
- Can the author supply names of contacts in societies or associations who might be contacted regarding use of the book as a textbook?

Part **XI**

Book Marketing
and Promotion Cogitation

38

More Shoptalk: A Potpourri

There is no known system of training in methods that can assure a neophyte of becoming certified as a skilled practitioner of the art of publishing.... We become experienced not through training in an accredited institution of learning but through the process of apprenticeship. We learn by doing, by imitating, by intuition: by trial and error.

Morris Philipson, Director,
University of Chicago Press
(adapted from a paper presented to the
Chicago Book Clinic, February 6, 1979;
reported in *Scholarly Publishing*, July 1979).

Too many publishers ... function with the peculiar notion that publishing isn't marketing—it's printing books.... And so eager but untrained young kids are grossly underpaid to do a professional marketing job, and books don't sell anywhere near their potential.

Bruce W. Markus, in "Letters,"
Publishers Weekly, February 5, 1982.

38:01   Publishing Directions for Professional and Scholarly Books

The major consumers of business and professional books in the mid- and late 1980s will be the college graduates of the early 1980s. Their career choices as college seniors, therefore, offer useful guidelines for what might be the growing (and declining) areas of professional and scholarly publishing during the years ahead.

415

A study,* conducted by the National Center for Education Statistics, U.S. Department of Education in 1982, examined the career choices of U.S. college seniors in the year 1979–1980 in various subject areas and compared these with the choices of college graduates of a decade earlier. Here is what the survey disclosed:

- One professional career that students increasingly are choosing and that was chosen by 1.2% of 1979–1980 college seniors is computer and information sciences. Of the nation's 929,400 seniors, 1.2%, or six times the number of students from a decade earlier (.2%), chose this major.
- Another major growth area is engineering, up 33.9% as a college major from what seniors were choosing in 1969–1970.

Publishing in these areas should hold great promise through the end of the decade and beyond (see 39:03 and 39:04).

Traditionally strong areas in which publishers have had a substantial interest—i.e., the physical sciences and fine and applied arts, including architecture—maintained their position over the decade with only a small downward trend.

- Fine and applied arts majors were 4.4% of the total 1979–1980 college senior population, down only 2.2% from 4.5% a decade before.
- Physical sciences majors were 2.5% of the total student population, down 7.4% from 2.7% in 1969–1970.

The most severe falloff in career choices occurred in foreign languages, the social sciences (including economics), and education. All of these were down by substantial amounts.

- As English increasingly becomes the acknowledged international language of science and scholarship (see the second chapter-opening quote in Chapter 43), there seems to be diminishing interest in foreign languages as a major. This subject had a 55.6% decline in the ten-year period studied, from 2.7% of total college senior majors in the earlier period to 1.2% in 1980. Still, the 1.2% figure matches the number choosing computer and information sciences as areas of concentration.
- The social sciences were chosen by 19.4% of college seniors in 1969–1970, but only accounted for 11.2% of the 1979–1980 college majors. The number of majors dropped 42.3% over the decade, but still constituted a substantial segment of the total student population.
- Education, shaken by diminishing student populations and school closings at the rate of 5% a year or more (see 4:15), was down to

*The study, "Earned Degrees Conferred, 1979–1980," is available from U.S. Department of Commerce, National Technical Information Service, 5285 Port Royal, Springfield, VA 22161; order accession no. 82165044. Price: $7.50 postpaid.

12.8% from the 20.9% of a decade earlier. The ten-year decline was 37.8%.

The table below summarizes the information contained in the U.S. Department of Education study.

Subject or Discipline	1979–1980* % of Total College Seniors	1969–1970† % of Total College Seniors	Change over 10-Year Period	
			Increase (%)	Decrease (%)
Computer & information sciences	1.2	.2	600. +	—
Social sciences (including economics)	11.2	19.4	—	42.3
Education	12.8	20.9	—	37.8
Engineering	7.5	5.6	33.9	—
Physical sciences	2.5	2.7	—	7.4
Foreign languages	1.2	2.7	—	55.6
Fine & applied arts (including architecture)	4.4	4.5	—	2.2

*1980 universe: 924,000 seniors.

†1970 universe: 792,300 seniors.

Source: National Center for Education Statistics, U.S. Department of Education, "Earned Degrees Conferred 1979–1980," February 4, 1982.

38:02 Murphy's Law, Pareto's Law, and Book Marketing Professionalism

There's an old story about the schoolteacher who, after one of her pupils had given an oral report, admonished, "Johnnie, there are two words I wish you wouldn't use: One is 'swell' and the other is 'lousy.' "

"Okay teacher," Johnnie replied, "What are they?"

Analogously, there are two "laws" that have become part of the vocabulary of book marketing professionals: One is Murphy's law and the other is Pareto's law. Murphy's law—"If anything can go wrong it will"*—is used frequently by book marketers to excuse a promotion that went bad. Pareto's Law—the 80-20 principle—is being beaten to death in various other ways—not so much by name, but by connotation. Vilfredo Pareto (1848–1923) was an Italian economist who observed that in any given situation involving people, things, or circumstances, 20% of the known variables will produce 80% of the results.†

Book marketers have now adopted Pareto and toss about such phrases as "20% of the books are bringing in 80% of the money," or "20% of the sales reps are doing 80% of the business," or "20% of the names in any given mailing list will bring in 80% of the responses," ad infinitum. We have learned to live with Murphy, who has become part

*"The Contribution of Edsel Murphy to the Understanding of Behavior in Inanimate Objects," *EEE: The Magazine of Circuit Design*, August 1967.

†P. Mali, *Management Handbook: Operating Guidelines, Techniques and Practices* (New York: Wiley, 1981).

of the established vocabulary. But we should bury Pareto, once and for all. There are no sure rules about which percentage of books, salespeople, or names on a mailing list will bring about a fixed percentage of the anticipated total.

Let's abandon platitudes and get back to using numbers that reflect research, intelligence, and serious thought based on experience and known factors. We are, after all, marketing professionals.

38:03   More "Laws" for When Things Go Wrong*

1. *Glyme's formula for success:* The secret of success is sincerity. Once you can fake that, you've got it made.
2. *Finster's law:* A closed mouth gathers no foot.
3. *Lynch's law:* When the going gets tough, everybody leaves.
4. *First rule of history:* History doesn't repeat itself—historians merely repeat each other.
5. *Stewart's law of retroaction:* It is easier to get forgiveness than permission.
6. *Green's law of debate:* Anything is possible if you don't know what you're talking about.
7. *Conway's law:* In any organization there will always be one person who knows what is going on. This person must be fired.
8. *Denniston's law:* Virtue is its own punishment.
9. *Lieberman's law:* Everybody lies; but it doesn't matter since nobody listens.
10. *Oliver's law of location:* No matter where you go, there you are.

38:04   Survival Factor in Sci-tech and Medical Publishing

"Book publishing," says Dan Fischel, "is one of only a few industries that depends for its survival on an extremely high volume of new products. That makes it impossible to predict sales with any degree of dependability. Nor can the publisher afford to conduct market research studies for each book."

In a "Point of View" article in the August 1, 1980, issue of *Publishers Weekly*, Fischel opined, "What has kept technical, scientific and medical publishers from foundering altogether is the fact that although books of this kind may often sell slowly, they do at least continue to sell, year after year. That slow trickle builds what is known as backlist strength and yields small but necessary profits.

"The continuing sale of these books, although disappointing in itself, helps the publisher bring out new titles that are otherwise doubtful. The extra sale not only helps improve the publisher's finan-

*From Arthur Bloch, *Murphy's Law Book Two/More Reasons Why Things Go Wrong!* (Los Angeles: Price/Stern/Sloan Publishers, 1980), one of a three-book series.

cial strength, but also permits joint advertising and promotion of the old and new titles together. When the campaign for a new book also sells a number of old titles in the same field, it helps to defray costs and often to extend the campaign into additional media or mailing lists."

38:05 Advantages of Marketing Scholarly Books over Trade Books

1. Primary markets are usually well defined.
2. There are usually periodicals closely related in subject to the book in which it can be advertised and reviewed.
3. Most fill an information need and encounter little sales resistance.
4. Most have a longer life than trade books. This is especially true of university press books, where often two-thirds or more of annual sales are for backlist titles.
5. The scholarly publisher enjoys strong imprint loyalty. If known for high quality and standards, or if strong in the subject area, the publisher's books encounter little sales resistance.
6. Scholarly books within the same subject area are not competitive. There is room for different books on the same subject.
7. Usually, manuscript review by specialists in the field is sufficient justification for publication. Market research is not necessary.

38:06 Innovation in Book Marketing: Experts' Tips for Preventing Failure

Because professional and scholarly book marketing has traditionally been learned on the job, mainly by following established patterns or through trial and error, book marketing practices have tended pretty much to follow similar paths. Yet, those who have dared to innovate often have come up with startling results.

Card decks, originally used exclusively to generate requests for literature and sales leads, in the past decade have evolved into one of the most cost-effective means of selling certain types of professional and reference books. Yet, many publishers have still to try this means of promotion.

Innovators in selling professional and reference books to individuals by telephone have been meeting increasing success. Telemarketing has evolved from a hit-or-miss effort to an almost precise science (see Chapter 18) that, when certain procedures are followed, produces a highly cost-effective means of selling books. In some instances, telephone selling has proven superior to direct-mail marketing.

Offbeat promotional efforts, such as simulated stamps and sweepstakes, have, when properly tried, been found to work with great success on professional, reference, and business books.

The answer to innovation in professional and scholarly book marketing lies in buying "failure insurance" by engaging outside experienced professional help for your innovative effort. Such help may be brought in-house as a consultant who has had prior experience with the activity under consideration, and who will provide guidance in launching the operation. Or the professional help may be an outside service that is able and willing to handle the entire effort.

McGraw-Hill, when it launched a new edition of a science encyclopedia, was prepared to promote by direct mail using a colorful prospectus. It first tried a telephone marketing effort to a major segment of its market and found it worked so well that the prospectus was never mailed to that group—telemarketing did it all! Likewise, the Boston-based publishing firm of Warren, Gorham & Lamont, Inc. (WGL), credits innovative marketing and success in telephone selling in particular as major factors in its meteoric rise to its current status as a successful publisher of books and periodicals in banking, taxation, investment, and real estate.

Says Arthur Rosenfeld, WGL president,* "When you consider marketing in a new area, there is usually someone who is meeting your problem or something quite like it. It is helpful to start with an outside service and watch from a vantage point how they do it." Speaking before the AAP Midwinter Meeting in Washington, D.C., in February 1982, Rosenfeld recalled how "When [WGL] wandered into telephone marketing, we made a deal with a phone service, and we have continued to use them over time."†

John Stockwell, a seasoned book marketing pro in the McGraw-Hill Professional and Reference Books Division, affirms Rosenfeld's advice: "If you're doing something different, get expert professional help. They have gone through this before and know the pitfalls." Stockwell's comment was made while he described his success with a sweepstakes conducted earlier in 1982. Addressing a marketing seminar of the Professional Publishers Marketing Group in May 1982, Stockwell outlined details of the sweepstakes effort, adding this note of caution: "When you try something different, be sure to check with your attorney or legal department."

Stockwell has this advice for book marketers on innovation in book marketing: "Regardless of how hokey it is, an idea in some other field can be made to work for you."

38:07   Growth of Book and Journal Marketing Seminars and Workshops

In our preface to *Volume One*, we lamented the lack of a medium in which the skills of book marketing professionals could be presented and shared by other practitioners and by those seeking education in

---

*To November 1, 1982, then president and editorial director of International Thompson Professional Publishing.

†Detailed guidelines for operating an in-house telephone room, based on the Warren, Gorham & Lamont telephone selling operation, may be found in 18:07.

book and journal marketing. We cited the scarcity of seminars designed specifically for the specialized needs and tastes of scientific, technical, professional, and scholarly books and defined the purpose of this handbook as a move toward meeting that need.

Since 1982, perhaps inspired, or at least encouraged, by the appearance of *Volume One* of *Book Marketing Handbook*, a growing number of excellent topical seminars and workshops have been conducted within and for the publishing community. They have been tailored to the most specialized needs of book (and journal) marketers, and have presented expert counsel on such wide-ranging topics as journal promotion, electronic marketing, loose-leaf publications, special sales, telephone marketing, special and premium sales, direct-mail technique, and more. In the area of direct-mail technique, there have been numerous panel discussions and all-day seminars, some finely tuned to such narrow topics as "The Offer."

Much credit for the increasing attention to education in marketing for publishers is due the various divisions of the Association of American Publishers (AAP), which have been conducting luncheon workshops and/or day-long meetings on topics geared to divisional interests. Each has brought together a panel of experts on the topics covered.

Additionally, the Society for Scholarly Publishing has introduced speakers at its annual meetings and at all-day marketing seminars. The Professional Publishers Marketing Group, with some 60 publishing company members, has focused its interest mainly on direct-mail techniques at luncheon meetings and all-day seminars featuring various panels and guest speakers who address themselves to specialized narrow areas of direct marketing.

For the marketing of scholarly books and journals, seminars and workshops for staff members of university presses have been conducted by the Association of American University Presses (AAUP). In addition to sponsoring one-, two- or three-day seminars held in several cities, it has also included how-to-do-it workshops in the annual regional meetings of AAUP members, and sometimes in connection with AAUP national annual meetings.

For additional information, or to be placed on the mailing lists of any of these groups, direct your inquiries to the groups at the following addresses:

- AAP: Staff Director, AAP, Professional and Scholarly Division, One Park Avenue, New York, NY 10016.
- AAUP: American Association of University Presses, One Park Avenue, New York, NY 10016.
- Society for Scholarly Publishing: Executive Director, 2000 Florida Avenue N.W., Washington, DC 20009.
- Professional Publishers Marketing Group (PPMG), P.O. Box 511, Essex Station, Boston, MA 02112.

38:08 **University Press and Learned Society Publishing: How They Differ from Commercial Publishing**

THE UNIVERSITY PRESS PUBLISHER

The university press publisher is a not-for-profit operation with the primary mandate of making widely available the best of scholarly knowledge and the most important results of scholarly research.* Major publishing fields emphasized by university presses† (in descending order) are literature, philosophy and religion, political science, economics, history and archaeology, art and art history, anthropology, sociology and urban studies, and music.

 The clientele of the university press is chiefly academic. Because much of the university press output does not sell in the commercial marketplace, university presses rely on subsidies from the institutions they serve as well as from private foundations and government agencies.‡ University press print runs are much smaller than those of commercial publishers—about 1,500 to 2,500 clothbound and 2,500 to 3,500 paperbound. If supplied camera-ready copy, a university press can afford to publish 1,000 clothbound copies and often, with subsidies, as few as 750 copies.§

THE LEARNED SOCIETY PUBLISHER

For the learned society's publishing program, the primary market is its membership. The publishing mandate of the learned society is the dissemination of scientific knowledge without regard to marketability or profitability. This is the interpretation of one learned society publisher, Tom Houston of the New York Academy of Sciences, who commented at the third annual meeting of the Society for Scholarly Publishing, held in June 1981 in San Francisco. Said Houston: "Book publishing programs in learned societies may be in effect to keep alive the membership program."

 Reinforcing Houston's statement is the program of the 190,000-member Institute for Electrical and Electronic Engineers (IEEE) which publishes more than 400 nonperiodical titles annually in addition to the 45 IEEE periodicals. Its book publishing program adds up to more than 60,000 pages each year and covers core developments in the fields of its membership.

*According to the *Association of American University Presses Directory* (New York: AAUP, 1979).

†Fritz Machlup, *Information through the Printed Word*, Vol. 1, *Book Publishing* (New York: Praeger, 1978).

‡*The Humanities in American Life* (Report of the Commission on the Humanities) (Berkeley and Los Angeles: University of California Press, 1980).

§Richard P. Barden, Assistant Director, University of Washington Press, in a talk at the third annual meeting of the Society for Scholarly Publishing in San Francisco, June 1–3, 1981.

38:09   A Word of Caution for Marketers: Antitrust Guidelines

While the Association of American Publishers (AAP) makes it possible for members of the publishing industry to share useful information and to act in a unified manner on issues of common concern, there are many problems that cannot be solved by joint action or discussed and resolved by agreement among competitors.

Marketers should be aware of the severe penalties to which they and their companies could be subject if certain business practices are deemed not to be in compliance with federal and state statutes. The following AAP antitrust policy guidelines provide useful information on topics to avoid in discussions with other publishing establishments.

- Do not discuss or disclose information about competitive policies or practices such as: prices, pricing formulas, bids, markups; discounts or discount schedules; credit or freight terms; returns policies; profit or other margins, royalty rates, fees and other individual costs; and advertising or promotional assistance policies.

- Do not discuss specific customers, suppliers or competitors, their terms of sale or purchase, or whether you will or will not do business with them.

- Do not engage in informal or social conversation about antitrust-sensitive issues. Discourage those who do from continuing, or leave the discussion and state your reason for doing so.

38:10   Is Net Pricing Right for Sci-Tech, Professional, and Scholarly Books?

Is net pricing an answer for more effective marketing of scientific, technical, and scholarly books through booksellers and jobbers? We think not. In fact, it could slow the flow of such books through this outlet. Here's why.

With net pricing, the bookseller or wholesaler's markup can vary greatly. Librarians, already troubled by shrinking book budgets and rising book prices, as well as cost-conscious individual buyers, will be quick to realize that substantial savings may be attained by shopping around for the best price before buying.

Because such price comparisons take time, this could slow the ordering process from booksellers considerably.* Also, because getting price quotations is both costly and time-consuming, it can add to library overhead and eat into funds designated for book purchases. For the bookseller, the quotation process diminishes the profit margin and could even threaten business prospects.

Publishers who promote books without prices will be considerably

---

*College stores—a primary market for scientific, technical, and scholarly books—indicated in a survey by Knowledge Industry Publications, Inc., in August 1980, they were opposed to net pricing.

less effective, and, when they do suggest prices, risk antagonizing the bookseller by becoming a face-to-face competitor. Also, consider the diminished effectiveness of a book review without a price in it!

In the end, no one benefits. In our belief net pricing is a vehicle that poses too many dangers for all concerned to merit serious attention by any intelligent marketer of sci-tech, professional, or scholarly books.

38:11 Pricing of Technical Books in the Natural Sciences: Study Result

In the course of a calendar year, *Science* magazine receives review copies of virtually all technical books published in the natural sciences. From among these, the best are selected for the publication's book review section. Pricing studies have been conducted by *Science* for all books priced in U.S. currency that have been reviewed in *Science* over the four-year period from 1977 through 1981.

The prices per page of these technical books in the natural sciences were 6.8¢ (1977); 7.8¢ (1978); 8.6¢ (1979); 9.0¢ (1980); and 11.3¢ (1981). Annual percentage increases were 14.7% (1978); 10.3% (1979), 4.7% (1980), and 25.6% (1981). Average book price increases from 1977 through 1981 were 10.2% for 1978, 8.7% for 1979, 8.8% for 1980, and 24.7% for 1981.

Results of the pricing studies conducted by *Science* are summarized in the accompanying table.

SCIENCE MAGAZINE STUDY OF ALL TECHNICAL BOOKS REVIEWED OVER FIVE YEARS

	1977	1978	1979	1980	1981
Average price per book	32.70	36.04	39.18	42.61	52.76
Percent increase over prior year		10.2%	8.7%	8.8%	24.7%
Average price per page	6.8¢	7.8¢	8.6¢	9.0¢	11.3¢
Percent increase over prior year		14.7%	10.3%	4.7%	25.6%

38:12 The Value of a Publisher's Imprint Defined in Three Words

A publishing house's reputation is important . . . libraries will rely on publishers with a reputation for, and a tradition of, publishing good scholarship.

Lewis Coser et al., in *Books: The Culture and Commerce of Publishing* (New York: Basic Books, 1982).

Professional and scholarly publishers are in the business of communicating information and serving the need for knowledge. People throughout the world make use of their publications. Over a period of time, by offering completely reliable information services, publishers establish a position of trust with their readers. This is clearly shown by the example in 1:21, in which part of a promotional mailing used the letterhead of an established, highly regarded publisher, and the balance was reproduced on the letterhead of a new imprint owned by the same publisher. The first portion of the mailing, which used the known publisher's imprint, outpulled the other by a rate of 2–1.

That is why publications from prestigious university presses, noted for their high degree of scholarship, will outsell similar works from lesser known or less prestigious presses, even though the works may be of equal quality.

Harold W. McGraw, Jr., chairman of McGraw-Hill, expressed the value of a publisher's imprint in a message to McGraw-Hill employees in September 1982, in these three simple words: "We are trusted."

38:13   Value and Importance of Authors' Names in Book Promotion

There are at least two major areas of publishing in which a book's title may be of secondary importance. They are educational publishing, especially at the undergraduate level, and advanced reference materials. In both of these areas of publishing, book buyers and users generally refer to a particular book by the author's name, rather than by the book's title.

The explanation for textbooks is simple. In any given field, there may be dozens or even hundreds of books with virtually the same title. In a field like organic chemistry, virtually every textbook is titled *Organic Chemistry* or something very close to it. In the social sciences, one publishing establishment determined that there were more than 150 introductory psychology texts and more than 220 in sociology.

This sameness of title may be found in any of the basic college courses in the physical or social sciences, hence the preference by instructor and student alike to refer to the book by the author's name. The author's name as a means of identification is considered so important in some textbook houses that its appearance on a book jacket, particularly on the spine, may be as prominent and set in as large a type size as the book title. A title stands as a descriptive device for catalog listings and advertising, but not as the identifying device for many users. To them, the author's name identifies the book.

Use of an author's name as a book title also applies to advanced reference books, at the other end of the publishing spectrum. This is especially true when the author's name may be associated with codification of the discipline, or when the author is identified with the whole discipline. In such cases, professionals in the field almost always refer to work by the author's name, rather than by the book's title, at least through the first or early editions.

Ultimately, as the author's name becomes increasingly identified with the book as a short description, the name is incorporated into the title. By making the author's name an official part of a classic reference work or textbook, the work is ensured perpetuity even after an original author has retired or died and succeeding editions of the work have been carried on by others.

Here are a few examples of books known better by the author's name than by title:

- *Architectural Graphic Standards*, the standard work in the field of architecture for two generations, is referred to by virtually everyone as "Ramsey/Sleeper."
- *Reagents for Organic Synthesis*, the classic reference work by Fieser and Fieser, has been published in a series since 1967 and became *Fieser and Fieser's Reagents for Organic Synthesis* in 1981 with publication of the ninth volume.
- *Encyclopedia of Chemical Technology* by Kirk and Othmer was universally referred to as "Kirk-Othmer" by users of two editions over 30 years. With the third edition, published from 1978 to 1984, the work was retitled *Kirk-Othmer Encyclopedia of Chemical Technology*.

38:14   The Publication Date as a Sales and Promotion Tool

Many professional and scholarly publishers set as the publication date the date the book is received from the bindery and, theoretically, enters into stock at their warehouse or shipping center. For general professional and reference titles, where the date is not critical, it is more beneficial to set a formal publication date that is about two months after the date the book is available for actual shipment. This practice should not apply, of course, to any book with textbook potential and for which an early availability date may be a critical factor in its adoption.

A publication date at least two months beyond the availability date gives reviewers an opportunity to receive and prepare reviews on books not yet published. And the stocking bookseller will be able to have the book in stock, ready for sale on or before the announced publication date. The prepublication status gives the book special importance and encourages the bookseller to promote the already available book as a forthcoming event.

Certain review media will not consider for review a book received after publication, and the advance setting of publication dates in some instances may enhance the possibility of reviews.

38:15   The Book Title: Checklist of Ideas
to Help Make It Meaningful

You have been asked to suggest a title change or to come up with one more meaningful than the working title the author has submitted with the manuscript (see also related entry, 37:07). The following checklist offers guidance for suggesting a title that can help make your book come alive to the professional, scholarly, or business audience for which it is intended:

- Describe content. Example: *Handbook of Engineering Fundamentals*

- Promise a benefit. Example: *How to Find the Job You Always Wanted*
- Identify the book's audience. Example: *Clear Technical Writing for Engineers and Scientists*
- Establish credibility. Example: *Official National Atlas of Israel*
- Question and involve. Example: *Do You Make These Common Writing Mistakes?*
- Show level of content. Example: *Introduction to Algebra*
- Demonstrate Continuity. Example: *American Library Directory 1984, 37th Edition*
- Stress its completeness. Example: *Encyclopedia of Composite Materials*
- Stress location. Example: *Geology of California*
- Focus on time. Example: *Yearbook of the United Nations, 1984*
- Focus on a narrow topic. Example: *Hypoid Gear Tooth Design*
- Focus on a broad field. Example: *Encyclopedia of Chemical Technology*
- Present research findings. Example: *Interferon Research, 1983*
- Update obsolete information. Example: *Your Income Tax, 1984 Edition*
- Provide an industry or discipline standard. Example: *Architectural Graphic Standards*

38:16 Use of Colons in Titles and the Length of Book Titles

Increasingly, scholarly books bear titles with a lengthy statement. Many often have two related statements separated by a colon. A study of such compound titles, reported in the August 1981, issue of *American Psychologist*,* found that fully two-thirds of all book titles reviewed in *Contemporary Psychology* (*CP*), a journal of book reviews in psychology, contained a colon. The two-thirds of the book titles with "titular colonicity," i.e., having a colon, did not take into account any compound titles in the remaining one-third of the reviewed titles that were separated by commas, semicolons, and periods, which were not considered "colonic" for the study.

In science and technology, published reports in narrow areas often defy description in a short, easy title. As the *American Psychologist* study on book titles indicates, publishers are accepting longer titles without apparent damage to the publishing process.

A title, regardless of length, is critical to the salability of professional and scholarly books because many professionals often order or recommend a book on the strength of its listing in the "books received" section of a professional journal or periodical. If such titles

*J. T. Dillon, "The Emergence of the Colon: An Empirical Correlate of Scholarship," *American Psychologist*, August 1981.

fail to portray the book accurately, they will often be returned as unacceptable. The effective book title should not imply content it does not contain, nor should it imply more than its true coverage. It should be clear enough to interest a potential buyer, and as long as it needs to be to be understood.

38:17   How to Clarify Book Titles Containing Acronyms: Examples

If one accepts the premise that the title of a professional or scholarly book should serve as mini-advertisement for the book, it follows that a book title containing an acronym could be counterproductive in markets where the acronym is not known. Within a relatively short span of time, this writer encountered four scientific book titles that used an acronym as part of the title and that most likely would not have been understandable to a bookseller, acquisitions librarian, or purchasing agent.

There are many ways of getting around a confusing acronym in a book title. Usually in consultation with the sponsoring editor and/or author, such problems can be resolved, as the following examples show:

Book as Titled	Suggested Alternate
Analog MOS Integrated Circuits	Analog Metal-Oxide Semiconductor (MOS) Integrated Circuits
VHSIC Technology and Approaches	VHSIC (Very High Speed Integrated Circuits) Technology and Approaches
Maintenance and Troubleshooting HPLC Systems: A User's Guide	Maintenance and Troubleshooting HPLC Systems: A User's Guide to High Pressure Liquid Chromatography Apparatus
EMP: Radiation and Protective Techniques	Electromagnetic Pulse (EMP): Radiation and Protective Techniques

When it is not possible to change a title in order to clarify a not widely understood acronym that is an integral component of the title, the solution can be found in advertising and promotion copy, where the acronym should be followed by a spelling out of the term, either immediately adjacent to the title or early on in the copy.

38:18   Binding Color Favored over Book Title to
Identify Series Volumes: Case Study

In some fields, color rather than the name of an author or editor is used to identify a book or series. Perhaps the most notable example is the series of books on industrial electric power published by the Standards

Department of the Institute of Electrical and Electronic Engineers (IEEE), the world's largest professional society.

When publication of the various IEEE standards was begun in 1959, the first "standards" reference volume was issued in a red cover. It was followed shortly thereafter by another volume in a green cover. As these reference volumes were advertised, both mail and phone orders identified the books as the "red book" and the "green book."

As a consequence of such identification, by 1973–1974, the names of the colors were added to the book spines of the various standards volumes as they were published. Today, the IEEE standards volumes available include the *Gold Book*, the *Gray Book*, the *Green Book*, the *Brown Book*, and the *Buff Book*. By the end of 1984, additional volumes to be published will include the *Blue Book*, the *Black Book*, the *White Book*, and the *Lavender Book*.*

Each published volume is identified according to its binding and has its own permanently assigned identifying color, representing the ten different IEEE industry-standards volumes to be available by the end of 1984.

38:19 First Book on Subject or Improved Competitive Book: Which Does Better?

Does the fact that a book is the first on the subject assure success? Most authors of such books are firmly convinced that, because their book is a "first," everyone will want it. But if you ask the same question of John Stockwell, a veteran marketer of professional and reference books at McGraw-Hill, you'll get an entirely different point of view.

When you publish the first book on a subject, Stockwell says, you will be a missionary in this field, and missionaries as a rule do poorly. He prefers competition. His view, expressed at a seminar of the Professional Publishers' Marketing Group in New York in 1982, is: "When you have a competitor with a similar product, bear in mind there is always room for a competitor who can do it better." His advice to would-be publishers of missionary-type products is: "Go out and find a product that is doing well and do it better."

38:20 How One University Press Makes Scholarly Books Affordable: Case Study

It is a fact of life that many books written by scholars for other interested scholars reach only a minute segment of their intended audience because of their high prices and wind up mainly on library shelves.

One university press has been solving this problem for many years

*Lavender is tentatively the designated color. Other names being considered include violet and purple, with the final choice to be made by the Industrial Power Systems Department of the Industrial Applications Society.

through a program in which selected scholarly monographs are published simultaneously in cloth and paper. The press has been able to do this because it found that libraries, given a choice between cloth and paper editions, almost invariably buy the cloth. The income from library sales of the cloth edition makes it possible to offer a much lower priced softcover edition for purchase by individuals.

The publisher is Princeton University Press and the program is called the Limited Paperback Editions program. Abbot Friedland, marketing director of Princeton University Press (PUP), cites these two examples that illustrate how the program works. He takes the case of a hypothetical monograph that is 400 pages in length and has a print run of 1,500 and a price of $32. Based on the press's experience with this type of monograph, 1,200 will be purchased by libraries and 300 by individuals. This will produce the following sales:

Libraries:	1,200 copies × $32	$38,400
Individuals:	300 copies × $32	$ 9,600
		$48,000

Then he shows how this title would be produced and sold under the PUP Limited Paperback Editions program. The same 400-page monograph would be printed with the 1,200-copy library edition bound in cloth and priced at $35 (instead of $32), and an additional 1,000 paperbacks would be produced and priced at $14.50. The sales picture would then look like this:

Cloth (libraries):	1,200 copies × $35	$42,000
Paper (individuals):	1,000 copies × $14.50	$14,500
		$56,500

The difference in the net dollar sales between publishing simultaneous editions (cloth at $35 and paper at $14.50) and publishing a cloth edition only at $32 is as follows:

Simultaneous cloth @ $35 and paper @ $14.50	$56,500
Cloth edition Only @ $32	$48,000
	$ 8,500

Even with the additional manufacturing costs, order-fulfillment charges, and higher royalties, the net income from simultaneous cloth/paper editions is slightly more favorable than revenues for publishing in cloth only. "More importantly," Friedland points out, "it widens the distribution of the scholarly book to the scholar for whom the work is primarily intended." Friedland adds, "The Limited Paperback Edition is not the answer for every book, but a widening number of Princeton University Press titles [is] being produced in simultaneous cloth and paperback [editions] because it makes them available to a wider range of scholars at affordable prices."

38:21 Alternative Solution to Dual Editions: One Publisher's Approach

The practice of producing a hardcover institutional edition and a lower priced (usually paperbound) edition for individuals was solved by ISI

(Institute for Scientific Information) Press in an interesting, simple way. It offers the same hardcover volume at a dual price.

When ISI Press issued its *Atlas of Science* in a hardcover, 542-page volume in 1982, it offered the work at $90 to institutions and at $45 to individuals. Institutional orders required a purchase order number for billing. Individual orders required prepayment by check or payment by VISA or MasterCard. This dual pricing system has been used in the past for scholarly journals and by associations and societies for member and nonmember orders, but this was the first application we had seen for offers of a hardcover book to all buyers.

38:22 A Lucrative Yet Frequently Overlooked Market for Your Books

Authors of professional and scholarly books are usually also substantial buyers of books within their field or discipline. Yet many publishers, having signed a contract to publish, often overlook the author as a major prospect for the purchase of other related books in the list. Publishers invariably have an author's discount that enables an author to buy, at a discount of from 25 to 33⅓% additional copies of his or her own book beyond the usual allocation of free copies. Yet this same discount offered to the author on any book in the entire list can result in considerable repeat sales of current and forthcoming titles. Follow these three rules to convert your author universe into a separate, profitable market:

1. Establish a favorable discount for authors that applies to the entire list.
2. Establish eligibility for the discount as soon as the author signs a contract, and make the author aware of it.
3. Add the author to your mailing list to receive announcements of all forthcoming publications in or related to the author's special field of interest.

38:23 Book Made Obsolete by Change in Law: How Two Publishers Coped

How do you cope when your recent book is made obsolete by a change in the law? Here are two case histories, one of which made publishing history. In the 1970s a reference work on real estate was made obsolete by a newly enacted law, and the publisher learned that the law would be treated in depth in a competing work that was about to be issued. He solved the problem with this simple solution: All of the changes in the law were incorporated into a single chapter, and the revised chapter was incorporated into a scheduled reprint. He also corrected the preface to call attention to the book's coverage of new law. And, to ensure that the reprint would not be confused with earlier printings, he covered the book with a redesigned jacket that identified it as revised edition.

Over half a century earlier, in 1913, a book issued on taxation was made obsolete by a change in the law the year following publication. To save the edition, the covers were stripped, the binding removed, and corrected pages were inserted in the proper sequence. The corrected work was then resold in a loose-leaf binder. This act gave birth to the concept of loose-leaf publishing, which has since then expanded to such a degree that the Association of American Publishers established a Loose-Leaf Publishing Committee in October 1981.

38:24   Copyright Date Procedure for Books Produced Late in Year

In its first five editions, *Worldmark Encyclopedia of the Nations* was published at five-year intervals. It was sold mainly to libraries. When the fifth edition was published, it carried a 1976 copyright date, although distribution, in fact, did not begin until early 1977. In 1981, a number of librarians, using the 1976 date as a criterion, reordered the *Worldmark Encyclopedia of the Nations* and were greatly dismayed when they received the still-current fifth edition.

Difficulties resulting from an improper copyright date can be avoided if publishers establish a cutoff date near the end of the year, say October 1 or November 1, after which the following year's copyright date will be used in all publications.

Because of the importance of having books reach reviewers or potential adopters well in advance of publication date, some marketers use a copyright date of the following year for books available at varying times during the second half of the calendar year, but set official publication dates for the same year. Clarification of the use of copyright dates may be found in Section 406 of the Copyright Act of 1976.

38:25   The Book Industry SAN Program: Purpose and Origin

The book industry Standard Account Number (SAN) program is now an established fixture among U.S. book-buying and selling establishments and institutions. A brief account of its purpose and origin follows:

A SAN is a unique seven-digit numeric identifier preceded by the letters SAN and used by book-buying and selling organizations to permit easier and more accurate communications. Its use has been found especially effective in communications involving computer and telecommunications where the SAN format (SAN XXX-XXXX) serves as complete identification for a single street or mailing address involved in book buying or selling. Organizations with multiple locations have a separate SAN for each address. The SAN program is applicable only to those engaged in repeated book-buying and selling transactions; it does not apply to one-time buyers or consumers.

The SAN program was initiated in 1980 by the R. R. Bowker Co. following approval in December 1979 by the American National Standards

Institute (ANSI). The ANSI standard was developed by the ANSI Z39 subcommittee made up of representatives of publishers, distributors, wholesalers, bookstores, libraries, and schools and school systems.

You can get details about the SAN program and SAN number assignments from R. R. Bowker Co., 1180 Avenue of the Americas, New York, NY 10036.

39

How to Estimate a Book's Lifetime Sales Potential

39:01 How to Project Yearly Sales for Technical, Professional, and Reference Books

If your marketing duties call for you to make sales estimates for professional and reference books and to produce annual sales projections, the accompanying table may save you untold hours and much effort. The sales projections have been tabulated based on an estimating formula successfully used for a wide range of technical, professional, and reference books from elementary to advanced levels.

You can quickly verify the relevance of these figures for your own books by matching the sales histories of several of your backlist titles with similar first-year and lifetime sales in the table. Bear in mind that the annual sales patterns for your book can be drastically different from those indicated in the table if it is a yearbook, a book of current or popular interest, or one involving special circumstances.

Entry 39:03 demonstrates clearly how a rapidly growing field requires special estimating guidelines, and suggests ways in which to think about such sales when estimating.

39:02 How to Estimate a Book's Sales Potential: Guidelines

1. Avoid pulling a number out of the air that seems right.
2. Search out another, preferably recent, book on your backlist that is comparable, or at least within the same subject area, and that has a proven sales history.

SALES PROJECTIONS FOR TECHNICAL, PROFESSIONAL, AND REFERENCE BOOKS: INSTANT CALCULATOR

If 1st Year Sales Est. Is:	and Lifetime (5 yr.) Est. Is:	2nd Year Est. Sales Should Be:	3rd Year Est. Sales Should Be:	4th Year Est. Sales Should Be:	5th Year Est. Sales Should Be:
500	1,000	260	135	70	35
500	1,200	319	191	118	72
700	1,800	466	310	197	127
750	1,500	390	203	105	55
800	1,600	415	215	112	58
800	2,000	515	332	214	139
900	1,500	366	149	61	24
1,000	1,500	337	114	38	11
1,000	1,800	462	213	89	36
1,000	2,000	519	269	140	72
1,000	2,500	644	415	267	174
1,200	2,400	623	323	168	86
1,200	2,500	652	354	192	102
1,200	3,000	773	498	321	208
1,500	2,500	611	248	101	40
1,500	3,000	779	404	210	107
1,500	3,500	918	549	332	201
1,500	4,000	1,043	683	461	313
2,000	3,000	674	227	77	24
2,000	3,500	878	385	169	68
2,000	4,000	1,038	539	280	143
2,000	4,500	1,184	701	415	200
2,000	5,000	1,238	829	534	349
2,500	3,500	718	206	59	17
2,500	4,000	950	361	137	52
2,500	5,000	1,298	673	349	180
3,000	4,500	1,011	341	115	33
3,000	6,000	1,558	808	420	214
3,500	5,000	1,050	325	100	25
3,500	7,000	1,817	943	489	251
4,000	8,000	2,076	1,077	559	288

3. Tie your sales estimate to the sales record of the comparable book.

4. If the book under consideration has textbook adoption potential, whereas the compared book did not, allow a little extra for adoptions.

5. If the book under consideration is priced considerably higher than the earlier book, allow for sales shrinkage due to price resistance.

6. If other books on your backlist that cover the same subject area as the book under consideration have not sold well in general, keep your sales estimate compatible with the general sales histories of that type of book. Estimate sales for the new book based on the average of the sales of all (or many) of the other books in its category.

7. If the book is a new edition, be guided by the sales history of the previous edition. If the book is oriented to professionals working in a fast-changing field, allow for an increase in sales over the previous edition to account for heightened information needs of profes-

sionals who wish to update their knowledge of developments in that field. If the field or subject covered by the book experiences little change, allow for fewer sales because satisfaction with information provided in the previous edition may diminish desire for the newer one.

8. Consider the competition. Have other books on the same subject been published recently that will reduce the sales potential for your book? If your book is primarily a library item, will libraries be satisfied with another recent title on the same subject and shun your forthcoming title?

39:03   How to Estimate Sales of Books in the Computer Sciences: Different Formula

The sales projection chart for technical, professional, and reference books in 39:01 is not applicable to books in the computer sciences. This is a fast-changing field. Books in computer science that provide a practical, state-of-the-art approach may sell in surprisingly large numbers for a relatively short span of time and then come to a virtual halt.

In terms of numbers, such books may take off in this booming field and surpass all expectations the first year. By the second year, sales will drop off by as much as 50% and drop to practically nil by the third year.

If you're looking for a sales pattern, think in terms of three-year sales: 60% the first year, 30% the second year, 10% the third year. In many instances, rapidly changing technologies will have made the book obsolete by the end of the third year.

If you have an effective marketing/distribution system for this type of book, you should think in terms of a minimum of 3,000 units for first-year sales. At one publishing establishment, where the marketing head made a "liberal" first-year sales projection of 7,000, the book actually sold 32,000 copies. Rules do not apply to a book in the computer sciences when it takes off.

This estimating procedure is meant for the most current computer science books, not the theoretical books that tend to follow more traditional sales patterns.

39:04   Books on Electronics: Comparison with Sales Patterns of Computer Sciences Titles

As in the computer science field, there are a number of "hot" or rapidly developing areas of electronics for which sales patterns for related books differ widely from the estimates charted in 39:01.

There are a number of reasons why sales patterns for books in these areas, like the computer science titles discussed in 39:03, take off rapidly, enjoy the bulk of their sales in the first year, drop rapidly in the second year, and virtually cease selling by the end of the third year. One, of course, is that they are heavily promoted. Another is that they go out of date very rapidly. Still another is that, even in some houses, several books on the same topic may be published within a very short time. Simultaneously, in other houses the same thing may be happening. As a consequence, for some of the so-called "hot" topics in electronics, there may be as many as 10 to 20 new titles issued within a short span of years.

Most such titles are a year out of date when published, and with new material reaching the market at a frantic pace, at the end of the third year after publication, they are largely obsolete. A possible sales pattern for books in the most popular areas of electronics, suggested one marketer at an establishment where multiple publications on the same subject are a common occurrence, is to use a three-year sales life of 70–30–10, i.e., 70% the first year, 20% the second year, and 10% the third year.

39:05   How to Cope with High Inventories of Slow-Moving Backlist Titles

A problem for many marketers of professional and scholarly books is what to do with the high-inventory, slow-moving professional or scholarly titles whose sales have come to a near standstill or that contain outdated material and have dim future sales prospects.

One useful practice for reducing such surplus inventory is the three-for-one formula, i.e., retain three times the number of copies sold in the preceding 12-month period, theoretically a three-year supply, and eliminate the balance. If the book has had diminishing sales over the preceding year or two, the retained inventory may actually cover considerably more than three years. In such cases where warehousing and handling costs to keep the title on the active list exceed yearly income, it may be advantageous to place the title out of print.

On the other hand, even with the best of formulas, your once best-selling professional or scholarly title with sales of 60 or 70 copies a year may go on selling that number for many, many years. In such cases, and especially where the book carries a high list price, it may be profitable after several years when inventory is reduced and the stock on hand is sold out to reprint in small quantities, perhaps 150 or 250 copies, to fill the continuing small but steady demand. A prudent practice on such reprints that will prevent unnecessary expense is to wait until sufficient back orders have accumulated to cover most if not all of the cost of the reprint.

Part **XII**

Job Talk: Book Marketing and Promotion

40

Ideas and Concepts about Jobs
in Publishing

There is something special about publishing people. For these people, working together with books compensates for wages and hours customarily not governed by union contracts. Publishing is the lowest paid segment of the communications world, and although there is some evidence of change, people who could make more money elsewhere stay in it because of its special nature made so notably by their fellow workers.

John Tebbel, at the second annual meeting of the
Society for Scholarly Publishing in
Minneapolis, June 1980.

40:01 Publishers: Why Blame the Conglomerates? It May Be You!

At a time when managerial jobs in promotion in the New York area were being advertised in the $25,000 to $40,000 range, one reputable publisher advertised a job in the Sunday *New York Times* for $11,500, less than the salary paid a good secretary in the same area!

Such job advertisements for book promotion personnel at substandard salaries inevitably attract a good number of applicants. And someone, usually with a reasonably good academic background, is employed and given a budget to administer while he or she is learning the basics of the job.

The salary saving gained from hiring at substandard salaries will be offset many times over by badly timed mailings to the wrong lists in badly prepared formats for overpriced promotions. How much more sensible it would be for the management to have spent a fraction of this wasted money on an adequate salary that would have bought a qualified practitioner of book promotion, one who has a proven track record and experience in book marketing practices and techniques.

Marketing veteran Bruce Marcus summed it up in the "Letters" column of *Publishers Weekly* (February 5, 1982). He alluded to hiring practices in which publishers seemed to be saying:

Books don't have to be marketed by professionals, they merely have to be signed . . . And so eager but untrained young kids are grossly underpaid to do a professional marketing job, and books don't sell anywhere near their potential, and profits drop, and everybody yells that the conglomerates are ruining the business.

To Marcus's remarks, we add a hearty "amen," and this note: Publishers, why blame the conglomerates? It may be you!

40:02   Job-Hopping: Fast Route to Advancement in Publishing

Comparisons of company affiliations for publishing professionals listed in *Literary Market Place* show an annual job-change rate of about 25%. There's no question that job-hopping is an established way of life for the upwardly mobile publishing professional, and this is particularly true for those involved in various aspects of marketing and promotion.

Frequently, each job change represents a new level of experience, new challenges, and a higher salary than the professional would have achieved through normal merit increases in the previously held position.

In a mail survey sent to 400 job appointees whose positions had been announced in *Publishers Weekly, PW* reported in its December 19, 1980, issue that the one-fourth who responded provided the following details:

- More than half were in marketing and promotion.
- Those with six to ten years in publishing spent 2.6 years with each employer.
- Those reporting salaries over $35,000 all had less than 15 years publishing experience.
- The word "marketing" as part of a job title was no indication of salary level. "Marketing" respondents reported salaries as low as $11,700 and as high as $57,000.

Respondents reported these earning levels for years of experience indicated:

2 years experience or less	$10,000–$15,000
2–5 years experience	$15,000–$20,000
6–10 years experience	$20,000–$25,000
11–15 years experience	$30,000–$35,000

40:03   **Career Patterns of University Press Directors:**
        Could You Qualify?

Would your marketing background qualify you for that job of university press director that shows up in *PW* or the Sunday *New York Times* display ads from time to time? A 1981 study of university press directors, conducted by David Gilbert of the University of Nebraska Press and reported in the April 1982, issue of *Scholarly Publishing*, disclosed this profile:

- Age at time of appointment: 45
- Sex: male: (over 90%)
- Sixteen years' publishing experience, 11 years at a university press
- Bachelor's degree
- Immediately previous job at a university press
- Prior experience in both editorial and marketing with two other houses
- Some experience in commercial publishing (over 63% of those appointed during 1976–1981, compared with only 25% for those appointed before 1970)

Relatively few in the study came directly to a directorship from a previously held marketing position. Only 2 of 45 who rose to the directorship of a university press advanced directly from a marketing position. Only one of ten directors advanced directly from a previously held marketing position at commercial houses.

40:04   **The Job of College Traveler:**
        One Path to a Marketing Career in Publishing

Book marketing is not part of the traditional college curriculum. It is more likely to be learned on the job by someone who has held one or more prior publishing positions.

In publishing, one primary channel to a position in marketing is the job of college traveler or college sales representative.* This background is almost a prerequisite for a marketing manager's job in college textbook publishing. Many of those in publishing who hold key marketing positions, and numerous others in high positions in the world of professional and educational publishing, started their publishing careers as college travelers.

This could be your entry to a career in marketing if your other efforts to break into book marketing fail. What do you need to become a college traveler? You'll need a college education, intelligence, imagination, a tolerance for a high volume of paperwork, and a lot of self

---

*The term "college traveler" is still most commonly used in the industry, although many publishers have opted for "college sales representative" and refer in conversation to their travelers as college reps.

motivation. Most of the time your work as a college traveler will be done without close supervision.

What will your job be as a college traveler? What are the demands and benefits of such a job? You can learn much from a letter written many years ago by a college sales manager to a job applicant who answered an advertisement in the *Philadelphia Inquirer* for a college representative. Excerpts from that letter follow:

[As scientific and technical publishers,] we issue between 100 and 150 new books and revisions each year, both textbooks and professional, at the college level and above. A vital part of our work is concerned with the discovery, development, and acquisition of suitable manuscripts, and the sale of books to colleges and universities. . . .

Our college representatives are responsible for an assigned territory which could range from an area around a large city to five or six states, for calling on instructors and promoting the use of [our] new and current textbooks. We are interested in quantity sales to students rather than single copies. Our men do not take orders or carry samples, but are recognized as associates in the academic world, visiting and talking with teachers of science and engineering. By this and through providing copies of appropriate books, we attempt to convince them to adopt a textbook, discuss forthcoming titles, and see to it that their teaching needs are attended to insofar as possible. Much of this, of course, is pure public relations and may not result in an immediate sale. Equally important is the discussion of instructional problems, trends in education, needed books, and suggested authors. The [college] representative is responsible for constantly reporting this information and for finding and helping to develop manuscripts for publication in conjunction with the editorial department.

This man, therefore, must have a special combination of talents. He must be able to work and live in an academic atmosphere with all of its restraints and yet be an aggressive sales-minded person. He must have an interest in teachers as individuals—their concern with educational standards, enrollment problems, teaching needs, and so on. He must also be able to deal with ideas—the basis of our thinking and our future publishing plans. He is a reporter, salesman, and field editor.

This is a job with a future for the right man.† . . . Most promotions within the company are made from the college staff, since only with this experience can a man acquire the specialized background and training needed in other phases of educational publishing. This includes advancement to editorial, production, sales, and management positions.

[The] prerequisites then, are maturity, an ability to work hard under sometimes difficult conditions and often long hours, an aptitude for educa-

---

†The letter describing the job of college traveler is dated October 27, 1955, and was prophetic in more ways than one. As this entry was written, the author of the letter, Andrew H. Neilly, Jr., was president and chief executive officer of John Wiley & Sons, Inc. After graduating from the University of Rochester, he took his first job at Wiley as college traveler. The recipient of the letter, George Thomsen, was only a short time out of Valparaiso University and was subsequently employed as a college traveler at Wiley. At this writing, Thomsen had held a number of managerial positions, including that of college marketing manager. He was currently marketing systems manager in the College Division of Wiley.

tional work, and willingness to travel. [This is a position] for a man‡ who wants a career rewarding in its daily associations with persons of the highest professional caliber, with the promise of adequate financial return.

The college traveler of yesteryear called on schools spread over a sizable segment of the country. He left home in September and, except for a brief vacation during the Christmas season, was on the road until June. If he were married, he would be accompanied by his wife, who shared the driving during the long-distance traveling and provided companionship.

Today's college representative has a much smaller geographic area and spends a considerably larger percentage of time on actual campus visits. At Wiley, for example, the traveler's territory consists of about 45 schools with a total enrollment of 150,000 students and several thousand professors. All of his or her contacts must be efficiently accommodated in 145 available working days.

40:05   **Why Applicants Failed in Bid for
High-Salaried Marketing Spot: Case History**

A West Coast publisher of professional and educational books and related materials, seeking to fill its top marketing position, sought applicants through a display advertisement in the *New York Times*. The salary offered was well above East Coast salary levels for an equivalent position. Less than a dozen applications were received, apparently reflecting the preference of many marketing executives for a base closer to the heavier concentration of publishing firms in the East. All applicants considered were given a hypothetical set of conditions relating to one of the publisher's products and were asked to draw up a marketing plan as part of the interview. None of the candidates produced anything that, in the publisher's view, reflected an ability to develop an effective marketing program, and so none was hired.

---

‡The rigorous life of a traveler in the 1950s favored the employment of men. However, with the changing social and economic climate and the emergence of women into the labor force, a considerable number of women entered the ranks of publishing as college travelers. Presently a number of publishing houses have sales staffs that are equally divided, and a few have more women than men.

41

More Tips on Job Hunting

41:01   How Long Should a Job Search Take? An Authority's Formula

The brutal and fundamental truth about job hunting is that "the most qualified person" is not necessarily the person who gets the job. It's the person best able to convince the people doing the hiring that he or she is the right person for the job.

Robert Half, *The Robert Half
Way to Get Hired in Today's Job Market*
(Rawson, Wade Publishers, 1981).

Robert Half, noted authority on employment, poses an interesting formula for estimating the length of time your job search should take. He suggests you take your present or last salary, including bonus and fringes, drop the last three digits and divide by two. The resulting net figure is the approximate number of weeks for your search. But he makes provisions for certain other factors that can affect the net figure, for example:

- If your competitive qualifications are high, deduct 20% from the net. If they are low, add 50%.
- If you're looking for an increase of 20% or more over your previous salary, add 50% to the net figure; if you're willing to take a 10% decrease in salary, deduct 20% from the net.
- If your appearance, personality, and communications skills are excellent, deduct 20% from the net figure.

**41:02   The Head Hunter: What Happens and What to Expect
if You Are Called**

Even if happily employed, you may, in the course of your career, receive a *sotto voce* call from an executive search organization or agency "head hunter" asking whether you would be interested in an attractive job opportunity at more money. Flattering as it may seem to you, chances are you have not been singled out for your special talents or reputation. Most likely, the caller from the executive search organization has your name from *Literary Market Place* or some other directory, or from someone who has mentioned your name in a conversation. The head hunter will be calling because your employment experience and record are compatible with the types of positions the agent is trying to fill for a client.

WHAT HAPPENS AFTER THE CALL

1. If, as a result of the call, you agree to an interview with the prospective employer, bear in mind you are perhaps one of four or five candidates who have also been called and who have agreed to the same routine. This interview is likely to be with the potential employer's screener, perhaps someone in the personnel department. Your comments should be strictly limited to facts regarding your background, experience, and possibly education.

2. If, after the initial interview, you are called back for a second interview, it is likely that you are still under consideration and that the field has now been narrowed down to perhaps two or three candidates. The second interview gives you your first exposure to the person to whom you may be reporting if you are hired. This interviewer has your resume and perhaps comments from both the screener and the executive search organization. Of primary importance here is not only whether you indicate you can handle the job but also whether you will fit in, and whether you show the kind of interest or enthusiasm that indicate you will fit in.

3. If, after the interviews, there are indications that you are being favorably considered, your contact from the executive search organization may take up the matter of your salary expectations. You can feel reasonably confident that the head hunter will try to arrive at an offer that will meet or come close to your expectations. The agent will do this not only because he or she is anxious to complete the placement but also because the executive search organization will probably be paid a percentage of your first year's salary as a commission if you are hired.

4. If, on the other hand, you have gone through the preliminary screening and perhaps one or two interviews with the individual who makes the hiring decision, there is no assurance that your chances for getting the job are good. Not infrequently, none of the candidates is found acceptable, and the position may be filled from other sources.

41:03   Best Type of Resume for Your Job Application

Whatever the ultimate format of the resume you prepare, it must follow certain basic prerequisites to succeed. It should:

- Be concise, interesting, relevant
- Be neatly produced and arranged
- Avoid misspellings or grammatical errors

Management consultant Burdette Bostwick, in his *How to Find the Job You've Always Wanted*, 2nd ed. (New York: John Wiley & Sons, 1982) describes ten basic resume styles. Here, we discuss four that lend themselves to adaptation for the wide range of marketing jobs in publishing.

1. *The Basic Resume:* This one is best for you if you are seeking to enter publishing, or if you have had very limited work experience. It should contain your name, address, personal data, job objectives, education, and such things as summer jobs, hobbies (if you think them appropriate), and the like. Limit to one page.

2. *The Chronological Resume:* If you have job experience, this may be best for you. Your work experience is listed in reverse chronological order, followed by education and personal data. Bostwick recommends the resume be preceded by a summary that briefly states the material to follow.

3. *The Functional Resume:* In this one, you organize your work experience by function, such as promotion management, copywriting, book review coordination. In this type of resume, you stress work experience, and it is useful to have had different types of experience within the same company. It is more beneficial when you have had this experience in a reputable establishment. If you have had varied experience in different companies, you may want to consider a functional resume that lists job functions according to the company for which they were performed.

4. *The Professional Resume:* In some publishing establishments, great emphasis is given to academic qualifications (this is perhaps more true of editorial than marketing positions). If your qualifications are considerable, the professional resume may be best for you. In it you place emphasis on your academic qualifications and the background that such training has given you for the job you seek.

For detailed descriptions of all ten types of resumes and samples of each with suggestions and criticisms, refer to Bostwick's book.

41:04   Can You Get Away with Misstatements on Your Resume?

In a March 30, 1982, *Wall Street Journal* report, a midwestern search firm reported only one in three companies attempts to verify facts presented in a resume. However, eight out of ten said they would fire anyone found to have made a false claim. In book publishing, your chances for getting away with a false statement are practically nonexistent. Ours is a relatively small community, and the mobility rate of personnel between companies is high, so that misstatements are likely to be discovered quickly.

41:05 Preparing for an Interview: How to Gain a Competitive Edge

If you're preparing for an interview for any book marketing position, it will pay you to spend some time and effort researching the company you will be visiting and its publishing program. Your answers during the interview will be weighed against how closely they match the needs of the publisher's ongoing program or future publishing aims. If you can answer interview questions with a mixture of poise and enthusiasm that reflects an awareness of the publisher's program and ongoing needs, you will have a decided advantage over other applicants who are not similarly prepared.

On the lighter side of preparing for a job interview, the figure speaks for itself.

Job interview, huh?

FIGURE 22   Reprinted by permission from *Optical Spectra*, February 1979.

41:06 If You're Asked about Yourself at a Job Interview

Your job interview may well open with the question, "Tell me about yourself." How you answer will be crucial in that it will set the tone for the entire interview. Answer forthrightly and with self-confidence. It may be wise to write out your answer ahead of time, so that, while seemingly spontaneous, your reply will be organized to highlight your strengths and accomplishments that are pertinent to the job at hand. Caution! This question is meant as an interview opener. Don't string out your answer. Give it a few minutes at most.

41:07   Should You Register with an Employment Agency?

It may help, but your chances of finding a job in publishing through employment agencies are remote at best. In large publishing centers such as New York City, competition is very keen and marketing-related jobs that might be listed with employment agencies are relatively scarce. For such jobs, employers usually pay the agency fees (in New York, usually one percentage point for each $1,000 of salary, or 20% for a job paying $20,000).

In recent years some larger New York publishers, reluctant to pay the large agency fees, have instead begun to rely more on unsolicited resumes and employee referrals. Many companies in publishing offer a cash reward to an employee who makes a referral leading to employment. For this reason, if you are presently in publishing, maintain contacts with former colleagues and others you know in publishing. When you are job hunting, be sure to let these contacts know; it could be mutually beneficial.

An employment counselor at a New York agency told a newspaper interviewer, "We're a sales agency. We rent and sell people." This view suggests some employment counselors may be more interested in completing a "sale," or filling an existing order, than in helping to put you in touch with a job that is compatible with your experience, aspirations, and/or salary level.

41:08   If You're Fired without Prior Warning

Take it gracefully. Remember, your record and references are at stake and these will be important to your next employer, advises the head of an executive recruiting firm.* Furthermore, he says, by remaining calm and composed, you may be able to stay on the payroll a little longer, or use the office during your job search. And associates in the company may be helpful.

*Frank Beaudine, president of Eastman & Beaudine, in the May 19, 1980, *Wall Street Journal.*

Part **XIII**

More Tools of the Trade for Professional and Scholarly Book Marketers

42

Reference Tools and Periodicals

42:01   Basic Reference Tools of the Trade: Time and Work Savers

Whether new to the field or experienced, many book marketers, because of specialization, are often unaware of key basic reference tools that can make their work much easier. These reference sources frequently provide information that will enable marketers to achieve their desired goals with less effort and in much less time. This chapter lists and describes some of the basic working tools.

Volume One listed and provided detailed information on such basic tools of the trade as *The American Book Trade Directory, The American Library Directory, Literary Market Place, Magazine Industry Market Place*, and *Ulrich's International Periodicals Directory* (all from R. R. Bowker Co.); *Directory of Special Libraries and Information Centers, Encyclopedia of Associations* (both from Gale Research); the *Ayer Directory of Publications* (from Ayer Press); *Bacon's Publicity Checker* (from Bacon Publishing Co.); the *National Trade and Professional Associations of the United States & Canada & Labor Unions* (from Columbia Books); and the SRDS publications: *Business Publication Rates & Data*, and *Direct Mail Lists and Data* (from Standard Rate & Data Service). All are published annually or more frequently.

The earlier volume also listed *Ad Guide: An Advertiser's Guide to Scholarly Periodicals* (1979–1980 edition), published by American University Press Services. Unfortunately, the scheduled 1981–1982 edition of this invaluable working tool for book marketers did not appear, and AAUP reported that the publication was being discontinued for financial reasons.

The Education Directory (*ED*) catalog, offered free in loose-leaf form, has been expanded considerably since 1979, and many categories of university press book buyers have been added along with lists of new course offerings. The catalog also offers subscription lists for more than 200 scientific and scholarly periodicals, which ED "brokers" for the various publications listed.

42:02   The Bowker Mailing Lists Catalog

Bowker Mailing Lists, a comprehensive catalog covering libraries, schools, and booksellers both in the United States and abroad, includes selections from U.S., Canadian, and foreign publishers; U.S. book reviewers; and subscribers to *Publishers Weekly*, *Library Journal*, and *School Library Journal*. Lists of U.S. libraries are available by book budget, branch, level, and specialty. Library selection options include these categories: main public; government, federal, and armed forces; municipal, county, and regional; branch public; college and university; junior college; religious (by religion); law; medical; and U.S. school (by grade level or with full-time librarian). Lists of Canadian libraries are available by book budget, branch, level, and specialty; foreign library lists are grouped by type of library, subject, and country.

U.S. bookstore lists are available by types of books carried and by types of bookstores. Canadian bookstores are included in lists, along with foreign booksellers by country.

For a copy of the Bowker Mailing List catalog, write to Paulette Milata, Director, Bowker Mailing List Department, 1180 Avenue of the Americas, New York, NY 10036.

42:03   The CMG Mailing List Catalog

The CMG Mailing List catalog, a 60-page work in 1979, has now been greatly expanded into three separate subject catalogs. Through contractual agreements with more than 30 publishers, the CMG data base has been expanded by several million names and now offers not only college faculty, medical, and educational lists but also mail-order book-buyer lists in virtually all of the categories in which it previously had offerings. College Marketing Group (CMG) now offers these three catalogs, free upon request: CMG Science, Engineering, Vo-Tech & Business Mailing Lists; CMG Medical Mailing Lists; and CMG Mailing List Catalog for Arts, Humanities, Education, and Social Science.

For catalogs write to CMG at its new location, 50 Cross Street, Winchester, MA 01890; 617-729-7865.

42:04   Subject Directory of Special Libraries and Information Centers,
7th ed. Edited by Lois Lenroot-Ernt. Gale, 1982. Five volumes (by subject). 1,738 pp. $95 per volume; set: $460.

An invaluable reference work for marketers that provides convenient access to more than two dozen useful facts about 16,000 special libraries. Each volume covers a broad group of libraries at an economical price. Volume 1 covers business and law; Volume 2, education and information science; Volume 3, health sciences; Vol. 4, social sciences; and Vol. 5, science and technology.

Volume 4, in 528 pages, includes the subject headings area/ethnic, art, geography/map, history, music, religion/theology, theatre, and urban/regional planning. Volume 5, in 426 pages, includes agriculture, energy, environment/conservation, and food sciences. In addition to the subject index, each volume contains an alternate name index for cross-references to variant names for libraries. These volumes provide an indispensable reference tool for marketers, whether it is used for inquiries, order verification, list compilation, or telephone marketing (telephone numbers are included).

Order from Gale Research Co., Book Tower, Detroit, MI 48226.

42:05 **Directory of Nontraditional Outlets for University Press Publications.** American University Press Services, Inc., 1982. $10.

This directory was assembled in June 1982 and contains detailed information on 665 nontraditional outlets for university press publications. The entries are presented in eight general subject categories: humanities; social sciences; natural sciences; applied sciences; arts; regional/ethnic; other; and nonbook publications. Outlets of equal interest in multiple categories are listed under "other," which is subdivided into general interest, reference/text, and sports/hobbies/outdoors.

Each entry provides such details as account name, address, phone number, and name and title of contact person; subjects of interest; type of outlet; how frequently books are reviewed; submission requirements; methods of promotion used by outlet; size and frequency of catalogs issued (if a mail-order outlet); number of titles handled; and more.

Send orders to American University Press Services, Inc., One Park Avenue, New York, NY 10016, att: Patricia McHugh, Publications Coordinator; or to Larry M. Fees, Director, The Education Directory, at the same address.

42:06 **Directory of Directories, 2nd ed. 1983: An Annotated Guide to Business and Industrial Directories, Professional and Scientific Rosters, and Other Lists and Guides of All Kinds.** Edited by James M. Theridge. Gale, 1982. 1,017 pp. $90.

Encompassing more than 7,000 directories arranged in 16 separate sections, this reference tool provides complete data in virtually every area in which a directory is published, including business, science and engineering, and education. Each listing includes title, subtitle, full publisher address (for both editorial and order-fulfillment personnel), telephone number, description of contents, entry arrangement, usual season or month of publication, pages, indexes, price, editor's name, ISSN or other identification, and more. The detailed subject index contains 2,600 headings with numerous cross-references. A valuable tool for direct-mail efforts, this directory covers many different areas of industry, banking, finance, education, the sciences, engineering, medicine, the arts, and more.

42:07   DMMA Fact Book on Direct Response Marketing. 1983 ed. Direct Mail/Marketing Association, Inc. Annual statistical update. Approx. 250 pages. $39.95 ($29.95 to DMMA members).

This annual statistical update is a handy reference tool for various aspects of the direct marketing industry. The 15 sections and numerous appendixes present a broad overview of the field, from its history, definition, and state of the art to various useful media for direct marketing, mailing lists, promotion, delivery systems, emerging technology, government regulations, education, ethics, and a direct marketing glossary. For the first time since the *Fact Book* was published in 1978, the 1983 edition will contain an index. The international sections in 1983 have been greatly expanded and will be available separately, probably at $13 to nonmembers, $10 to DMMA members. In 1984, for the first time, the DMMA will publish the first *International Fact Book* as a companion volume to the totally revised 1984 edition of *Fact Book*.

   Available from the Publications Department, Direct Mail/Marketing Association, Inc., 6 East 43rd Street, New York, NY 10017.

42:08   International Literary Market Place (ILMP).
R. R. Bowker Co., 1982. Annual. 531 pp. Paper, $52.50.

A practical guide to the book world outside the United States and Canada, this comprehensive volume surveys 159 countries and provides detailed information on key people in 9,000 international publishing establishments and 3,500 book-related organizations. Under each country's heading, you will find general information on the book trade and customs, as well as specialized information on book trade organizations, book trade reference books and journals, publishers, literary agents, book clubs, major booksellers, major libraries, library associations, library reference books and journals, literary associations and societies, literary periodicals, literary prizes, and translation agencies and associations. If you intend to do any business overseas or to have any working relationship with any international publishing operation, this is a basic, essential reference.

   Order from R. R. Bowker Co., Box 1807, Ann Arbor, MI 48106.

42:09 **Trade and Professional Exhibits Directory**, 1st ed.
Gale, 1983. 412 pp. in three parts. Paper, $75.

The 3,500 listings provide an invaluable reference source for the exhibits manager and others who seek detailed information on participation in exhibits and conventions. The 8½" × 11" paperbound directory includes a wealth of information on each show, including name of convention or show, and sponsor; names of exhibits manager or managing agent; type of audience (professions or groups attending); principal categories of exhibitors; dates and locations of exhibits for next five years; and special features of exhibit.

Much of the material in this new directory is not available from other sources, such as five-year coverage of exhibit dates and locations, notes on cost of exhibit space, and details on audiences attending. The directory is arranged according to business classifications of the sponsoring groups. Four separate indexes are provided, keyed to entry numbers: (1) geographic, by convention location for the current year, with the name and date of the show; (2) chronological index for five years by date and name of show; (3) business activities index by products or services offered by the exhibitors; and (4) index of show sponsors by name. This is truly a needed and useful tool for all exhibit planners.

42:10 **The Canadian Report: The International Newsletter of the Publishing Industry in Canada.** Biweekly.

Providing an up-to-the-minute overview of all aspects of business and subsidiary rights activities of publishers in Canada, these reports feature writing that is low key and extremely readable. Publisher Glenn Edward Wirmer gives more emphasis to bookselling activity than to publishing management and often provides highlights of U.S. bookseller activities. Activities described often include contact names and phone numbers. Issued on the first and fifteenth of each month, except in January, July, August, and September, when it is issued only on the first.

To order, write to The Canadian Report, 17 Queen Street East, Suite 439, Toronto M5C 1P9, Canada.

Part XIV

International Book Marketing and Promotion

43

Guidelines for Reaching International Markets

Science books travel easily across frontiers. . . . There are well over a hundred different countries in which regular readers of academic books in the English language are to be found; the publisher of science books needs to have access to machinery for reaching all of these.

Anthony Parker, Science Editor, Cambridge University
Press, in *Scholarly Publishing*, April 1972.

English has established itself as [the] "lingua franca" of science, engineering, medicine, and business, which in turn allows for growing international sales potential. . . . For this reason . . . co-publishing has become a way of life in specialized STM publishing.

Albrecht von Hagen, McGraw-Hill
International Book Co., Hamburg,
at STM Conference, Basel, Switzerland, November 1979.

A comprehensive study by the English department at Jyväskylä U., Central Finland . . . based on responses from 539 college students in three Finnish towns . . . shows that the overwhelming majority—91%—would like to command English as well as they do Finnish.

Times Higher Education Supplement
(London), September 18, 1981, p. 7.

43:01   Guidelines for Marketing Books Overseas

1. High-level texts in science, technology, and medicine always do best in overseas markets. Always stress those titles on your list that fit these categories.

2. Textbooks and professional and reference titles in business and economics also have strong appeal when the approach is general. Avoid including books that deal with U.S. federal taxation, U.S. statutes, or strictly domestic issues.

3. Books on ecology in all subject areas travel well to overseas markets.

4. High price tags do not diminish the sales appeal of professional and reference books in overseas markets. In some instances, they even enhance the sales appeal.

5. Encyclopedias, dictionaries, and handbooks of good quality in virtually all subject areas and academic disciplines have strong overseas potential.

6. Nursing texts in the English language have little appeal overseas (except in U.S. territories and possessions).

For other entries in this volume relating to reaching international markets, see 2:05, 7:03, 23:15, and 28:14.

43:02   **The Overseas Market for Scientific, Technical, and Medical Books**

There are two paths that the U.S. publisher of scientific, technical, and medical books can take to penetrate overseas markets. One approach involves a marketing mechanism for the entire list; the other involves the overseas marketing of individual titles. This chapter will attempt to describe and define both approaches and some of the advantages and disadvantages of each.

• Overseas Marketing Approaches Involving Entire List

1. A subsidiary company
2. A local agent (also called a sales representative)
3. A local distributor
4. An export sales agent

• Overseas Marketing Approaches Involving Individual Titles

1. A co-edition
2. Sale of rights or translation rights
3. Direct-selling/mail order
4. International journals/periodicals

43:03   **Overseas Marketing of List through a Subsidiary Company**

ADVANTAGES

1. A subsidiary company can fill orders immediately from stock on hand. One international marketer says, "There is no substitute for immediacy, which I estimate adds 10% to sales."

2. A subsidiary company may often have close connections with review media, and the review slips that accompany the book give local prices.

3. A subsidiary company can publish its own books for the home market and, therefore, provide a better environment for the sale of your books.

4. A subsidiary company may employ a local sales force that can service bookseller outlets on the spot.

5. A subsidiary company can sell in local currency.

6. A subsidiary company can expedite collection.

7. A subsidiary company can attend special conferences and other types of book exhibits in its home territory.

8. A subsidiary company can give you early warning of market changes.

9. A subsidiary company may also serve as an outlet for publications of other U.S. publishers and enjoy a strong position in a field in which your own position is weak, or in which you publish very few titles that do not merit individualized promotions.

DISADVANTAGES

1. The subsidiary company may not give your publications the same effort as it gives its own publications.

2. If on consignment, the subsidiary company may be inclined to overstock your publications, leaving you in short supply of salable books that may date rapidly.

3. The subsidiary company may have to mark up price to cover overhead, thereby making the book less attractive due to the higher price.

4. The subsidiary company may sell to markets to which you prefer to sell directly.

5. The subsidiary company may harm your image by taking on too many outside agencies.

43:04 Overseas Marketing of List through a Local Agent

ADVANTAGES

1. Arrangements with a local agent offer a broad range of possibilities and can be tailored to what you consider your best advantage. For example, your arrangement with a local agent might include these variations:
   - Stocking, order fulfillment, billing, and marketing
   - Stocking, order fulfillment, and billing, but not marketing
   - Stocking, order fulfillment, and billing, with nonexclusive marketing rights
   - Stocking, order fulfillment, and billing with marketing rights, exclusive of certain segments of the market (for example, libraries)

2. Discounts can be established based on the amount and type of services the local agent renders for your list.

3. As with subsidiaries, a local agent carries stock and can fill orders for your titles immediately.

DISADVANTAGES

1. Agents cost money. You may be able to do a better job yourself for less.

2. Any difficulties or problems, however temporary, in your relations with an exclusive agent can lead to your being cut off from the market(s) the agent is serving.

3. The agent may be handling too many companies and may not be able to do the job you expect or require.

4. The agent may not be reaching certain segments of the market in its territory that you consider important for your books.

5. The agent may not be doing a satisfactory job in some respects for its present clients. Any alleged shortcomings in service should be investigated before you set up any agency arrangement for your list.

6. Many of the disadvantages listed in 43:03 for subsidiary companies are applicable to local agents as well.

43:05   Overseas Marketing of List through a Local Distributor

ADVANTAGES

1. A local distributor, unlike some local agents, can exist solely as a warehousing service that handles only order fulfillment and billing.

2. Because its services are limited, you retain the right to promote to the local distributor's area from the United States and can still be sure of prompt local fulfillment.

3. In responding to overseas inquiries, you gain considerable credibility when you are able to assure potential buyers that the book is available from a local source and can quote prices payable in local currency.

43:06   Overseas Marketing of List through an Export Sales Agent

A number of export sales agents operate out of the United States and have offices worldwide. The New York firm of Feffer & Simons, Inc., for example, has branch offices in England, Australia, India, Japan, Mexico, the Netherlands, the Philippines, and Switzerland. For a complete listing of export sales agents, refer to "Export Representatives" (section 66) in *Literary Market Place*, or study how other publishers with lists similar to yours distribute their books overseas by reference to *Who Distributes What and Where* (R. R. Bowker, annual).

ADVANTAGES

1. The export sales agent takes the credit risk on overseas accounts.
2. Overseas buyers can send orders to the export sales agent's local office, as a general rule.
3. The publisher is responsible for its own order fulfillment.
4. The export sales agent does all the billing and collection (for a discount).
5. The publisher can promote by direct mail to areas covered by the export sales agent, either to complement the sales agent's efforts or to replace them.

43:07   Overseas Marketing through a Co-Publication

ADVANTAGES

1. The co-publisher will consider the book its own and make the same marketing and promotion effort it would for its other titles.
2. The co-publisher is likely to join your print run and increase it, thus reducing unit cost considerably.
3. Promotion efforts by the co-publisher may have a spillover effect that will enhance sales of your own edition of the book in markets not covered by the co-publisher.
4. The success of the co-publisher in selling your book to its market may prompt reverse co-publishing agreements for its books in your market.
5. Co-published works, particularly in the scientific, technical, and scholarly areas, please authors, who like to see the widest possible dissemination of their research through published works.

DISADVANTAGES

If world markets are divided between co-publishers, and your publishing partner does not have effective coverage of what you consider to be an important segment of its market, it may be necessary to declare such (geographic) segments "open markets" in which both co-publishers may offer the book for sale.

43:08   Overseas Marketing through Sale of Reprint or Translation Rights

ADVANTAGES

1. You receive cash up front for rights sales.
2. Even if you have sold translation rights in a country, territory, or for a particular language, you still can sell the English-language edition in the same area(s).

3. Promotion of the translated edition may generate additional sales · for the English-language edition.

DISADVANTAGES

1. Your per-unit profit is less for the sale of a translated or a reprinted copy.
2. Unless you select and deal with reliable publishers, you cannot effectively control the print runs.
3. With a reprint sale, the possibility always exists that reprints will extend beyond the authorized markets.

43:09   Overseas Marketing through Direct Selling or Mail Order

ADVANTAGES

1. English-language books can be sold in overseas markets. English is the international language of science, technology, and higher education.
2. Good overseas markets exist in the United Kingdom, the European continent, Scandinavia, Australia, South Africa, and Japan, and can be reached by mail.
3. Smaller markets do exist for English-language scientific, technical, and medical books in Scandinavia, Germany, Holland, Latin America, the Far and Near East, and Africa. These markets can be reached by mail.
4. There are established, reliable sources (for example, R. R. Bowker and IBIS) for lists of many book-buying groups in foreign markets.
5. Low-cost, air mailings can be made to overseas markets through ISAL (International Surface Air Lift).
6. Surface-mail postage costs to some European countries from the United States is less expensive than identical mailings made locally.
7. Cooperative mailings can be made to overseas libraries and other groups (through IBIS) at very low cost.
8. You are in total control and are the direct beneficiary of all direct-response marketing to overseas markets.

DISADVANTAGES

1. Payment problems can arise with various foreign currencies. It is best to insist on payment in U.S. dollars.
2. Direct response is often difficult to trace since book-buying in the United Kingdom and Europe is usually done through booksellers.

43:10 Overseas Marketing through Advertising in International Journals or Periodicals

ADVANTAGES

1. A single advertising insertion can provide broad exposure to specialists in a number of countries.
2. The cost per contact is considerably less than costs for mailings.
3. The response is measureable. With pro-forma invoicing you receive payment and postage charges before shipping.
4. Ordering patterns can provide clues to potential new overseas markets.
5. Prices can be marked up to cover overhead.

DISADVANTAGES

1. Lost shipments or slow overseas delivery may result in extra correspondence and expense.
2. Shipments to some countries may result in undue paperwork for filing forms and claims.
3. Overseas shipments could be unprofitable unless prices have been marked up to cover the extra costs resulting from additional paperwork, handling, and lost or stolen books.

43:11 Prime Source of International Mailing Lists

A prime source in the United States for international mailing lists is IBIS Information Services, Inc., the New York City–based subsidiary of IBIS Information Services Limited, established in April 1980. Staffed by international list experts, the New York office of IBIS supplies a wide range of mailing lists and mailing services to U.S. publishers. The parent company in England was formed in 1968 by a group of prestigious British publishing houses for use by the worldwide publishing community. Current sponsors of IBIS include Cambridge and Oxford University Press, Pitman Publishing, Blackwell Scientific Publications, and Associated Book Publishers. The New York office is located at 215 Park Ave. S., New York, NY 10003. For a portfolio of IBIS lists and mailing services, call 212-505-7620.

43:12 How to Send International Mailings Inexpensively: Guidelines/Details

"Whether you supply the international market through agents, distributors, or ship directly from the U.S.A.," says Steven Lustig of IBIS Information Services, "direct mail is the single most important advertising medium."

The IBIS list organization, with quarters at 51 East 42nd Street in New York City, has in its data base of a million addresses lists of overseas college faculty members, scientists/engineers, schools, bookstores, libraries, association members, conference delegates, professionals, companies, and more.

For about 12¢, you can send a half-ounce flier anywhere in Europe, and it will be delivered almost as quickly as by airmail. For a mailing to Australia, the cost is about 15¢. These rates are offered by a New York City mailing service that consolidates mail for the U.S. Postal Service's International Surface Air Lift (ISAL). The mailing organization is Expediters of the Printed Word, Inc., located at 527 Madison Avenue, New York, NY 10022; 212-838-1364. The contact person is Andy Curshen. The ISAL service is also available at the airports in Chicago, Houston, and Dallas. USPS is considering other major cities for inclusion in ISAL service. To find out if your city has been or will be added, call USPS at 202-245-5757.

The inexpensive rates offered by Expediters of the Printed Word include filling in forms, bag-tagging, permit applications, airfreight reservations, delivery of mail to JFK Airport in New York, and postage. All this comes to you at less than the cost of surface mail. All you do is send your stuffed envelopes, sorted by country, to Expediters and it does the rest. It bills you later.

43:13   **Order Form Copy that Prevents Problems
on International Orders**

If your printed promotion offers free shipping with prepaid orders and you mail internationally, be alert for potential problems arising from foreign orders. Since surface mail is slow, many foreign buyers who remit payment with their orders specify airmail or other means of shipment. You can avoid delays in order fulfillment by stating in your promotion copy that you pay "normal book rate" on prepaid orders, and that any other means of shipment requires an additional charge. Showing a fixed charge for overseas airmail shipment can often save unnecessary correspondence.

43:14   **Lists with Addresses in Canada or Mexico:
USPS Special Mailing Requirements**

Any lists that include addresses in Canada or Mexico will require treatment different from that which applies to the balance of the mailing. For example, self-mailers are not permitted for Canada and Mexico, and each piece must be sealed in an envelope. Mail these pieces by first-class mail. Letter rates for first-class mail to either Canada or Mexico are the same as those for the United States.

If you mail first class to Canada or Mexico (or any international destination) and you request that postage stamps be used for the mailing, the stamps must, under the guidelines of the Universal Postal

Union, bear postage that denotes the amount paid by the mailer.* This was cited by the U.S. Postal Service because it occasionally issues first-class stamps (such as Christmas stamps or stamps bearing a letter of the alphabet when increases are anticipated) that bear no notation of value.

43:15   The Market for English-Language Books in Japan

There is substantial library funding in Japan for journal acquisitions that, in some instances, amounts to as much as 70% of the budget; the balance is used for books. The rising costs of journal subscriptions have diminished moneys available for books, and purchasing is becoming very selective. Book purchasing is channeled through four or five major library suppliers (refer to listings in *International Literary Marketplace*). For good scientific and technical books in the English language that sell in Japan, there are about 20 good booksellers, many of which serve a specific territory and all of which use travelers. These booksellers' sales of English-language reference works are made primarily to libraries in these categories: university (departmental and research), government research institutes and other government institutions, and industry. The types of reference books that sell are encyclopedias, handbooks, and titles on a very advanced level that are not available in the Japanese language. There is virtually no market for textbooks, and the markets that do exist are restricted mainly to professional, reference, and medical books.

Libraries purchase on recommendation from departmental researchers or, in the case of educational institutions, from the departmental or specialized book-selection committee. In college faculty recommendations, quality, and seldom price, is a major factor in the recommendation process. The Japanese market seeks books that have no counterpart in the Japanese language and important titles in all areas of research.

43:16   Rule of Thumb for Estimating Canadian Market

Some U.S. book marketers who include Canada in market planning are prone to use as a rule of thumb 10% of U.S. market, based on a comparison of the populations of the two countries. However, one should bear in mind that half of the Canadian market may be French-speaking. Better use 5% and be more realistic.

43:17   How to Reach Overseas Markets for
Business and Professional Books: One Approach

Publishers of business books have been reluctant to explore overseas markets, fearing language barriers would diminish the potential of

*USPS *Memo to Mailers*, December 1981.

their professional book offerings. One publisher overcame this fear and has achieved a degree of success. Here's how he did it.

He initiated mailings to the names of foreign subscribers to U.S. publications in the same fields as those covered by his own books and also mailed to the foreign membership of U.S. professional associations and societies in related fields. The response to such mail offerings proved to be on a par with the responses to his domestic direct-mail offerings.

Have no fear that foreign lists are too small to bother with. Substantial lists are available. Several prestigious U.S. periodicals offer substantial foreign coverage, as these examples indicate:

- *Harvard Business Review* has more than 30,000 foreign subscribers, in addition to some 18,000 in Canada.
- *The New England Journal of Medicine* has 30,000 foreign subscribers.
- *Spectrum*, a publication of the Institute of Electrical and Electronics Engineers, has more than 20,000 foreign subscribers, in addition to more than 10,000 in Canada.

43:18   Canadian College Faculty Lists

An updating program for lists of Canadian college faculty will be completed by mid-1983 by the Education Directory (ED). Because of the considerable revisions, ED Director Larry Fees says the list of more than 25,000 faculty names is "in effect a new list and will include the full Canadian postal code for speedy and accurate delivery."

Appendix A
Book Marketing Glossary:
An Enlarged Vocabulary of
Publishing and Promotion

The special language of book marketers, especially those dealing with scholarly, sci-tech, and professional books, comes from many trades and professions.

- Book marketers deal with editors, and must know the terms related to manuscripts, editing procedures, and editorial planning.
- They deal with authors and therefore must have some familiarity with the language of the scholar, researcher scientist, engineer.
- They deal with various levels of graphic arts and therefore must be acquainted with the vocabulary of art, typography, printing, paper, and related terms of the printer and lettershop.
- They are involved in or responsible for advertising, selling, and publicity and must be familiar with specialized terminology peculiar to these professions.
- They must be familiar with mailing procedures and the various facets of direct marketing and with the work of the retail bookseller, the campus bookseller, and the various types of wholesalers who serve as vital links to many of the publisher's outlets.
- They must be familiar with the language of the social scientist or researcher in understanding and dealing with the psychological motivations inherent in good advertising copy and headlines.

In other words, they should know or have ready access to practical explanations of many of the terms they are likely to encounter. This enlarged glossary takes into account *all* of the areas in which marketers may have to deal. In providing definitions, it aims not so much at the dictionary meaning as it does at the meaning the term will have for the marketer in his or her everyday activities.

Using the Glossary: Aims and Intent   This enlarged glossary is both a reference and teaching tool. Many glossaries share a common fault—that of providing explanations of trade, professional, or technical terms in specialized language and without providing interpretations of the specialized language, so that the explanations are less meaningful to the reader. This glossary provides explanations or cross-references to the linking terms, and describes practices associated with the terms. In this way, the reader at any level of experience can readily comprehend each term presented.

See also, for some 1,800 terms related to book publishing, production, bookselling, collecting, library work, and other book-related activities, *The Bookman's Glossary*, edited by Jean Peters, 6th ed., 224 pp., Bowker, 1983, $21.95.

AAIP   American Association of Independent Publishers.

AAP   Association of American Publishers.

aa's   Author's alterations to text material already typeset.

AAUP   Association of American University Presses.

ABA   See **American Booksellers Association.**

ABC   Audit Bureau of Circulation.

ABPA   See **American Book Producers Association.**

acetate overlay   A sheet of clear plastic superimposed in register on an art mechanical for a color separation, or other modification, of the base mechanical.

acquisitions librarian   Usually a technical services professional on a library staff who handles the paperwork for book orders after a decision to buy has been made.

ACRL   Association of College and Research Libraries.

active list, active titles   Books on a publisher's list both old and new, that are stocked, sell, and are deemed profitable to keep in print.

add-on sales   Sales of related titles recommended at the time a telephone order is received for a particular book or publication.

Address Correction Requested   A line added to a mailing piece requesting the Postal Service, for a fee, to supply correct address where addressee is no longer at address on the mailing piece. See also **Return Postage Guaranteed.**

Ad Guide   Short title for *An Advertiser's Guide to Scholarly Periodicals*, published irregularly. First edition 1960–61, discontinued with 1979–80 edition. "... had a very loyal vocal audience," says AAUP, "but too few sold to make economic sense."

adopt   To choose as a basic or required textbook in a college or university course.

Advertiser's Guide to Scholarly Periodicals, An   See **Ad Guide.**

affiliated relationship   A contractual arrangement between a small publisher (affiliate) and a (usually) larger publisher who agrees to handle all details of warehousing, shipping, and billing for an agreed-upon percentage of the net billing. See also **distribution deal.**

AFIPS   American Federation of Information Processing Societies.

agate line   Unit of advertising measurement equal to $1/14''$ by usual column width of the publication. Used by some magazines and most newspapers as standard unit of advertising measurement.

ALA   American Library Association.

American Book Producers Association (ABPA)   An association of individuals who "package" or create ready-to-publish books for publishers. Organized in New York City in 1980. See also **book packager.**

American Booksellers Association   A national organization of firms and persons engaged in the retail sale of books.

AMPA   American Medical Publishers Association.

approval copy   A book accompanied by an invoice seeking payment or return of the book within a specified period, for consideration for purchase by or recommendation to students. See also **complimentary copy, desk copy.**

approval plan   See **on-approval plan.**

ARL Association of Research Libraries; a division of American Library Association (ALA).

ASIS American Society for Information Science.

attention line Job title or function, usually printed on an envelope when a mailing label has only the name of a company or institution.

Audit Bureau of Circulation (ABC) An organization of publishers, advertisers, and agencies to standardize and check the correctness of the circulation of publisher-members.

author-prepared copy; author-supplied composition (reproducible camera-ready copy) See **camera-ready copy (author-prepared)**.

author questionnaire, marketing questionnaire A multipage form that an author is asked to complete and return to publisher after the manuscript has been put into production. The answers provide guidance on where to market and promote the book and are also used in the preparation of the jacket copy.

automatic shipment A procedure in book clubs whereby, as part of the original order, the club ships each new selection automatically until requested to stop (in contrast to negative or positive option book club shipments whereby the customer is informed of each shipment). Also known as "till-forbid" offer.

BABT Brotherhood of Associated Book Travelers.

backlist Older titles kept in print by the publisher. Books not of the current season. Some publishers consider a book a backlist title after six months or a year.

back order An order for a book not yet published or out of stock, to be shipped when the book becomes available.

basic rate See **one-time rate**.

basis weight The traditional pound designation for a ream of paper in a standard size (basis size). The term "60 pound paper" usually means that 500 sheets of the traditional 25″ × 30″ basis size weigh 60 pounds.

Benday (or Ben Day) A "screen" or pattern of lines or dots, applied to an area of reproduced art by the printing-platemaker, to fill in areas that would normally reproduce in a solid color or as pure white.

best-seller Applicable to a sci-tech, professional, or scholarly book, the term refers to a title that has gone through several printings and/or editions and retains a steady sales pattern over a protracted period.

b.f. Boldface type.

big ticket A term borrowed from the merchandising field and used in publishing to indicate a book or series being offered at a high price, or at a higher price than the usual price for a comparable item. Term interchangeable with *high ticket*.

bind-in card A detachable reply card bound into a particular issue of a periodical. If sold to an advertiser, it usually supports an accompanying advertisement. Some periodical publishers restrict bind-in cards to "in-house" promotions only. See also **blow-in cards**.

bingo card A term commonly used among advertisers for a reader's service card (qv).

blanket order An order from a library authorizing a publisher or jobber to send one or more copies of every title published according to certain agreed-upon criteria—for example, in a specific subject area. See also **on-approval plan**.

bleed Any printed matter (most often an illustration) that extends to the full limit of the trimmed size in any print job. It "bleeds off" the edge of the paper.

blow-in cards Single, loose cards inserted in periodicals to solicit subscriptions. The term comes from the fact that the cards are often "blown in" by machine between the periodical pages by air pressure. See also **bind-in card**.

blow-up A photographic enlargement of any copy.

blueprint See **blues**.

blues (blueprint) A same-size contact print made from a film negative or positive for final check and proofreading purposes before platemaking. Also called a *silver print* or *vandyke*.

blurb A short sales pitch or review of a book usually printed on its jacket flaps, or in an advertisement of it.

body type Type used in text matter, as opposed to display type.

book insert See **insert, book.**

book jacket See **jacket.**

book packager An independent individual or organization that produces books off the premises for distribution by a book publisher. The "package" may be a finished manuscript, camera-ready copy, or a complete book. Also called *book producer*. See also **American Book Producers Association.**

book producer See **book packager.**

bookstore chains A group of bookstores owned and operated by the same company. "The chains" generally refer to the two largest, B. Dalton Bookseller and Waldenbooks, although for professional and scholarly books other important chains include Kroch's and Brentano's, and Staceys.

book that travels well A book whose sales will hold up in overseas markets.

bottom line An accounting term that in publishers' marketing refers to the net result of an activity or promotion.

BPA See **Business Publications Audit of Circulation, Inc.**

BRC Business reply card. See also **business reply envelope.**

BRE See **business reply envelope.**

broadside A single sheet of advertising, usually large in size and printed on one side. A useful device when a publishing project has a large story to tell, as with an encyclopedia. Often folded down several times and used as a self-mailer.

bulk mailing The mailing of third-class matter in quantities or weights exceeding minimums established by the Postal Service, at a special bulk rate lower than the established rate for regular third-class mail.

Business Publications Audit of Circulation, Inc. (BPA) A not-for-profit, independent organization that provides independent verification of all paid and controlled circulations for nearly 800 business publications and professional journals.

business reply card mailing See **card deck.**

business reply envelope A return envelope used as a mailing enclosure, and bearing a printed insignia, special vertical-bar insignia, and permit number obliging the mailer to pay the letter rate of postage (20¢ for the first ounce as of early 1983) for its return. New Postal Service regulations, effective July 15, 1979, require a standardized design, the addition of a bar-code pattern, a Facing Identification Mark (qv), and a size no smaller than $3\frac{1}{2}'' \times 5''$ and no larger than $6\frac{1}{2}'' \times 11\frac{1}{2}''$. See also **return envelope.**

buy campaign "A buy campaign exists when a movie company (there are other culprits also) arranges for its employees or employees of distributors in key market cities to actually buy a large number of copies of a given title from a reporting bookstore during a brief period, so that its sales will seem to zoom to the (sometimes) innocent bookseller, who then reports it to a bestseller list" (according to Sol Stein, ("How to Make Trade Book Publishing Profitable," *Publishers Weekly*, May 23, 1980, p. 37).

buying around The (legal) bypassing of an exclusive distributorship arrangement: the buying of books published abroad from a distributor in the country of origin to avoid an importer's price markup.

calendar-year basis (journals) The subscription basis for most scientific and other scholarly journals is on a calendar-year basis. Therefore, subscriptions placed between January and December will bring all back issues.

camera-ready copy A piece of copy ready to be photographed for reproduction without further alteration.

camera-ready copy (author-prepared) Authors' typed manuscripts, used by some book and journal publishers. Copy is photographed for offset printing, after being supplied by the author according to publisher's specifications, and assumed to be error-free.

campaign A promotion effort aimed at a specific objective, over a given period of time, such as launching a new edition of a best-selling reference, handbook, etc.

campaign, direct-mail A series of mailings designed to achieve an express objective for a specific book or group of books over a stated period of time. See also **campaign evaluation, period of.**

campaign evaluation, period of For professional-book direct-mail promotion, various publishers use different periods. Most responses come in within 12 weeks of the date on which the mailing was completed. Allow one week less for a first-class mailing.

c & lc Capitals and lowercase letters. (Also u & lc, for upper- and lowercase).

c & sc Capitals and small capitals.

caps Capital letters of a typeface. Indicated in proofreaders' marks by three lines under all letters to be capitalized.

card deck Also expressed as direct-response advertising, business reply card mailings, co-op mailings, loose-deck packets, action postcards, postcard mailings, product information cards, product inquiry service, etc. The card deck is a collection of business reply cards usually in loose-deck or booklet format, each containing an advertisement that recipient can complete and mail back (usually postage-free) to an advertiser to receive a product, service, or additional information. A useful medium for selling many types of appropriate professional books.

Carrier Presort A subclass within bulk third-class mail that offers mailers a minimum per-piece charge of 6.9¢ for advertising mail prepared by Postal Service carrier routes in contrast to the minimum per-piece charge of 8.4¢.

casting off Estimating the number of pages or amount of space that typewritten copy will occupy when it is set in a specific size and measure of a given typeface; or how much copy must be written to fill a specific area. See also **copy fitting.**

catalog List of all of a publisher's books currently in print. Usually organized by subject area, and within subject area by author. Usually contains book description or table of contents. See also **short-title catalog.**

Cataloging-in-Publication (CIP) Program A program initiated by the Library of Congress in 1971 that allows books to be cataloged while they are in publisher's proof forms. A similar program exists in the United Kingdom through the British Library. See also **Library of Congress Proof Slips.**

cathode ray tube (CRT) A high-resolution TV screen used in high-speed electronic type composition. See also **CRT composition.**

C.C.C. See **Copyright Clearance Center.**

center spread An advertisement on facing center pages in a publication.

certified mail First-class mail of no intrinsic value sent with a receipt, which recipient must sign.

chain See **bookstore chains.**

character count A count of all letters and spaces (using line averages), to be used in determining the area that text copy will occupy when set in type.

checking copy A copy of a specific issue of a publication in which an advertisement has been inserted. See also **tear sheet.**

Cheshire A labeling machine. Also refers to type of label used.

cheshiring Term used by lettershops and others involved in machine-addressed mailings to indicate label addressing done with a Cheshire machine.

CIP See **Cataloging-in-Publication Program; Library of Congress Proof Slips.**

CLA Canadian Library Association.

closed-end series A series of books with a finite number of volumes. See also **open-end series.**

closing date Last date on which a publication will accept an advertisement for a specific issue.

co-edition See **co-publishing**.

cold-type composition Composition in which no molten metal is involved. Usually created by either "strike-on" or photographic methods. See also **hot type**.

college library collection A book collection designed to support, primarily, the curriculum needs of the college. See also **university library collection**.

college representative See **college traveler**.

college store A book-stocking facility on or near a college campus, whose primary activity is to supply the book needs of students and faculty. The store may be affiliated with the school or privately owned.

college traveler A textbook publisher's representative who calls on college instructors in an assigned territory to promote the use of the company's new and current textbooks.

colophon Trademark or device used in some books or on promotional matter to identify a particular publishing house or imprint. Also, a description of how the book was designed or manufactured. (Originally, printer's statement at the end of a book.)

column inch Advertising space equal to publication's usual column width by 1″ of depth. Often the smallest unit of advertising space sold by some magazines and newspapers.

combination plate A photoengraving or offset plate made from copy combining both line and halftone.

combination rate Special advertising rate offered by a publisher of two or more periodicals to advertisers as an incentive to contract for space in more than one publication.

commissioned rep A book salesperson covering an agreed-upon territory for one or more publishers, receiving a commission from each publisher he or she represents, based on either all sales or sales from specific accounts assigned to him or her within a designated geographic territory. A commissioned rep is considered to be self-employed, or a member of a sales group, rather than an employee of the publisher(s) he or she represents. See also **house rep**.

comp Term used as a verb to indicate a free copy will be given: "comp" it. Also, a comprehensive sketch of art or design. Also, a compositor (person).

comp copy See **complimentary copy**.

compiler (mailing list) Owns and maintains one or more lists of names and addresses, extracted and compiled usually from printed sources to reach a given market or audience; does not, as a rule, work with original data or do original research.

complimentary copy A book sent free to a faculty member for evaluation as a required or supplemental text in a course. See also **approval copy, desk copy**.

composition The setting and arrangement of original manuscript text into type in a form suitable for platemaking and printing.

compositor One who sets type or a company performing composition services.

comprehensive layout See **layout**.

computer-printed letter A letter printed by any high-speed computer printout machine. The entire letter is produced in seconds, in upper- and lowercase, including inserted salutation and PS, if desired. Very similar in appearance to a typed letter. See also **word-processed letter**.

computer terminal See **terminal**.

Conference Papers Index A monthly index of published papers from conferences in the life sciences, chemistry, engineering, and related fields, indexed by subject, author, title, format, availability, and source.

conference proceedings A book consisting of papers presented, usually with related statements made, at a scientific or scholarly meeting or conference.

consignment See **on consignment**.

consolidated shipment The practice by publishers of combining back orders with new releases in a single shipment to reduce freight and postage cost to booksellers.

continuation order An order to supply, automatically on publication, each succeeding volume of a series, or each new volume of an annual. See also **on-approval plan.**

continuous tone A photograph or illustration with continuously differing black-and-white (or color) tone values. See also **screen.**

contract rate A special discounted rate given a periodical advertiser for advertising placed within a specified period, usually a year. See also **contract year; frequency discount; short rate.**

contract year A twelve-month period, effective with insertion of the first advertisement, that a space advertising contract will run. See also **frequency discount.**

controlled circulation A business publication containing at least 25% editorial matter, issued on a regular basis, and circulated free or mainly free to individuals within a particular profession, business, or industry.

cooperative advertisement Advertisement placed by bookseller over his or her own name, advertising a publisher's book or books. The publisher and bookseller share the costs of the advertisement, frequently on a 75-25 basis, the publisher paying the 75%, the dollar amount usually limited to a percentage (5%, 10%, etc.) of the bookseller's purchases from the publisher or of the publisher's books and other conditions. See also **Robinson-Patman Act.**

cooperative mailing A mailing to a specialized market containing advertising from more than one advertiser.

cooperative sales agreement Sales agreement between publisher and a society, association, periodical, or other nontrade bookselling medium that agrees to advertise and/or promote and sell, at its own expense, a publisher's books. The discount may be the same as that given the publisher's bookstore accounts.

co-publishing The sharing of an edition of a book between an originating publisher and one or more other publishers, each having exclusive marketing and distribution rights within a territory. The book may carry the title-page imprint of the originating publisher only, the joint imprint of the co-publishers, or the imprint only of the publisher taking the book for a specific territory. The originating publisher may arrange for the simultaneous (initial) printing of the co-edition. Subsequent printings may be done jointly or independently.

copy The "manuscript" text (usually typewritten) to be converted into printed matter. Illustrations are also referred to as camera copy. See also **composition.**

copy fitting Estimating the type size and line width necessary to fit a piece of typed copy into a prescribed space on a printed promotion; also the space a piece of copy will occupy when set in a prescribed type size and line width. See also **casting off.**

copyright Protection of an "intellectual work" reserving to the author or other owner the right of publication. A copyright protects the work as a whole, but not the concept, idea, or theme if expressed another way. Definitions and information about fees and other services are available from: Copyright Office, Library of Congress, Washington, DC 20559. Ask for Circular R4, *Copyright Fees Effective January 1, 1979.*

Copyright Clearance Center (C.C.C.) A payment center created in 1978 to collect and make payments to a publisher for the right of photocopying. Over 800 photocopy users are registered. Address: 21 Congress St., Salem, MA 01970.

core journal A journal in a discipline or research area in which the most significant work is published.

core market The primary market for a book or journal.

cost-to-net-sales ratio The relation between the cost of a promotion and the net sales realized from it, usually expressed as a percentage. Used by many as a yardstick to measure results of mail-order campaigns, book sales, etc.

cover Any of the outer four pages of a paperbound periodical, book, booklet, or catalog. The outside front cover is called the first cover (or cover 1); the inside front cover is called the second cover (cover 2); the inside back cover is called the third cover (cover 3); the outside back cover is called the fourth cover (cover 4). Advertising rates on periodical covers are usually higher than regular page rates because readership is believed to be higher. Not to be confused with jacket (qv).

cover rate (advertising)   Advertising rates for covers in periodicals are generally billed at a premium over the advertising rate for inside pages.

credit hold   Withholding of credit to an account pending receipt of payment for previous shipments. Book trade credit holds are usually not threatened or applied until after 45 to 90 days.

crop marks   Guidelines on a piece of artwork or printed area indicating the precise area to be reproduced (placed outside the area to be reproduced).

cross-marketing   Selling a book in various markets other than its primary market.

CRT   See **cathode ray tube; CRT composition.**

CRT composition   Computer-controlled type composition, produced by photographically exposing letter forms slashed on a cathode ray tube.

ctr   Designer instruction to compositor or platemaker to center type or illustration copy between understood limits.

cut   A printing plate, usually metal and usually for an illustration, used in letterpress printing. Sometimes loosely used to signify any illustration, copy, or reproduction.

data base (publishing applications)   Digitally stored and indexed information about one subject accessed by computer programs.

decoy   A name, usually fictitious, inserted in a mailing list to monitor list usage.

dedicated system   A subscription-fulfillment system totally independent of any other system in the publishing organization.

delete   To remove.

delivery guarantee   See **mailing-list guarantee.**

demographic edition   Circulation of a publication reaching a segment of the field served by the publication. It may be a geographic segment, or that portion of the circulation working in certain occupations or professions or using specific equipment.

demographics, demographic characteristics   The social, economic, and geographic characteristics of a group. See also **psychographics.**

departmental library representative   A professor in a college department responsible for liaison with the library staff, recommending acquisitions, channeling acquisition requests from others in the department, and administering the departmental library budget.

desk copy   A book furnished free to serve as the instructor's copy when copies have been ordered for students' use in a specific course. A complimentary copy may be considered a desk copy upon the instructor's decision to use it as a required/supplemental text. See also **approval copy, complimentary copy.**

deterioration index   A term and concept for the annual rate at which a mailing list deteriorates or becomes ineffective, expressed as a percentage.

direct advertising   Advertising in any printed form, reproduced in quantity and distributed to prospects, usually by mail.

direct-impression composition   See **cold-type composition; strike-on composition.**

direct-mail advertising   Advertising sent through the mails or other direct delivery service.

Direct Marketing Association (DMA)   Oldest and largest international trade association representing users, creators, and suppliers of direct-mail advertising and other direct-marketing techniques. Headquarters: 6 E. 43 St., New York, NY 10017; Washington, DC, office: 1730 K St. NW 20006.

direct-mail testing   Testing a segment of a market with different variables—format (package vs. self-mailer), copy, price offers, single-book offering vs. list offering, reply devices, ink color, paper, postage, etc. See also **mailing-list testing; market testing.**

direct marketing   The selling of books, goods, or services directly to the consumer.

direct-response advertising   Advertising through any medium designed to generate a measurable response.

direct-response mailing   See **card deck.**

direct subscriber   A journal subscriber who enters a subscription directly with the publisher (as opposed to subscription through an agency).

discount from list price   The traditional billing formula of most publishers used to determine the selling price to booksellers or, in some instances, to libraries and nonprofit institutions. See also **list price, net price.**

display type   Usually type 14 points or larger, or not available on a text-setting machine. Used for headlines, as distinguished from body type. See also **body type.**

distribution deal   An arrangement between two publishers under which one, usually the larger, agrees to warehouse, distribute, and handle billing for the books published by the other. Sales may be generated by the larger publisher's sales force. See also **affiliated relationship.**

DMA   Direct Marketing Association.

documentation   A branch of librarianship dealing with the materials and needs of researchers and scholars, and the improvement of graphic communication; also, citation of sources in a book or journal.

dropout halftone   Halftone with no dots in the highlight areas.

drop ship   To ship an order to one address (e.g., a customer) while billing it to another (e.g., a retailer).

drop-shipment   Order placed by bookseller with publisher whereby book is sent directly to the customer, but billed to the bookseller.

dual imprint   See **joint imprint.**

dummy name   See **decoy.**

duotone   A two-color reproduction printed from two halftone plates made from one original.

dupe-elimination   See **merge, purge.**

dust jacket   See **jacket.**

dust wrapper   See **jacket.**

earned rate   An advertising rate "earned" in a publication by the use of a number of insertions within a period of one year. An advertiser billed at the one-time rate would receive a rebate to the earned three-time rate by placing three insertions within a year.

echo effect (of direct-mail promotion)   The "spillover" or indirect sales effect from a publisher's direct-mail (or space) advertising campaign. Various studies have shown that in addition to the keyed or directly traceable returns, publisher's direct-mail promotions produce indirect and untraceable sales, called echo.

edition   One of the different forms in which a book is published (as applied to original, revised, reprint, textbook, etc., or paperbound, deluxe, library, large-print, illustrated, etc.).

800 number   See **Inward-WATS.**

electronic publishing   A process involving computer composition, digital transmission of the published information to a customer, and screen display or printout capability at customer's location. Also the dissemination of the works in whole or in part from a data base that can be manipulated by computer. Such works are distributed by electronic means to a distant receiving unit.

em   The square of any type size. A 10-point em measures 10 points by 10 points.

endpapers   Four pages, two at the beginning and two at the end, of a casebound book. One at each end is pasted to the inside of the cover board.

envelope stuffer   Advertising enclosed with statements, bills, or correspondence.

examination copy, exam copy   Book sent to an educator for examination and consideration as a possible classroom text. Examination periods of many publishers are 30 to 60 days. Exam copy invoices for professional and graduate-level books should state terms, period of examination, and that invoice will be canceled on adoption or return of book. See also **desk copy.**

exchange ads   Advertising exchanged between periodicals in the same or related subject areas without payment. Such ads are generally aimed at attracting subscribers from the circulation of the periodical in which the advertisement appears.

Exclusive to   A heading used on a news release written exclusively for one publication. The sender is obliged to issue no other publicity on the subject until the "Exclusive" release has appeared, or he or she has definite word that it will not be used. See also **Special to.**

expires   Former subscribers to a publication.

Express Mail   A class of mail in which next-day delivery is guaranteed.

face   In letterpress printing, the raised portion of type that receives the ink and produces printing. See also **typeface.**

Facing Identification Mark (FIM)   A series of vertical lines or bars required on all business reply mail (cards and envelopes) since July 15, 1979, under revised postal regulations.

faculty committee   (In the context of library acquisitions) individuals within a college or university who assist in or make recommendations for the development of the library collection.

faculty editorial committee   University faculty members designated to advise on the publishing program of a university press.

f and g's   See **folded and gathered sheets.**

festschrift   The practice of paying homage to a scholar with a volume of essays by former students, friends, and colleagues, upon the scholar's retirement or on special occasions (e.g., his or her 70th birthday).

floppy disc (or mini-floppy)   A flexible disc, resembling a 45 RPM phonograph record, used for magnetic storage of computer data. A single disc of the usual size (5¼″ diameter) can store up to 60 pages of text. Its entire contents may often be effectively accessible without the need for sequential search to reach a particular location, as is required with computer tape.

folded and gathered sheets   All the signatures (folded printed sheets forming the various sections of a book) assembled in the sequence in which they are to be bound into a book. Also called *f and g's*, folded and gathered sheets are often sent to reviewers, book clubs, and exhibits to meet deadlines when bound books are not yet available.

folio publishing   Print on paper. See also **tele publishing.**

font   The complete assortment of type characters for one design or style of type, usually roman and italic caps and lowercase, small caps, figures, points, and a few common fractions. See also **wrong font.**

footnote reference system   A system for citing references in a scholarly book where the references, in numerical sequence, appear at the bottom of the page where cited. This system is not favored by publishers because it is more expensive to set than other systems. See also **Harvard system; name-and-date system; sequential numbering system**

foreign publication rights   See **translation rights.** Also, rights granted to a publisher in another country to publish a book in the language of original publication (including, for example, rights granted to a publishing house in Great Britain to be the British publisher of an American book).

FPT   See **freight pass through.** See also **FPT price.**

FPT price   A price carried on the jacket or cover of a book (sometimes accompanied by the letters "FPT") that reflects the publisher's retail or catalog price plus an additional charge to help the bookseller recoup freight costs from the consumer. (Publishers' discount is based on catalog retail price, not FPT price.)

freight pass through   A pricing system used by some publishers whereby the price shown on the book is higher than its catalog retail price. The amount added on enables the bookseller to recoup freight costs from consumers. See also **FPT price**.

frequency discount   A discounted advertising rate in a publication for a given number of insertions stipulated by the publisher within a contract year. See also **contract year**.

fully protected (list)   See **protected**.

galley proof (galley)   (In traditional letterpress context) a proof taken from type standing in a metal tray (galley) used to hold and store type. The term is still frequently used to refer to the first set of type proofs irrespective of the method of composition used.

gang run   Two or more jobs "ganged up" or printed simultaneously on the same press for reasons of economy.

geographic and/or demographic edition   An edition of a publication in which the advertiser may advertise to a specific geographic area or segment of the total circulation, or to a demographic segment of the total circulation that will reach individual subscribers by job title or function, type of industry, instrumentation used, etc. Approximately 250 business publications offer geographic/demographic editions. Some card-deck sponsors also offer demographic options.

going online   Electronic delivery of information normally offered as a printed product.

grain   The direction in which fibers run in paper. When heavier weight papers are folded against the grain, the fold is sometimes uneven. See also **score**.

gripper edge   The leading edge of a sheet of paper going through the printing press, which the grippers take hold of to carry it through. See also **grippers**.

gripper margin   See **gripper edge**.

grippers   A printing term for the mechanical fingers that grip the leading edge of a sheet of paper as it passes through the press. See also **gripper edge**.

gutter   The inside margin of a bound page from the printed area to the binding edge.

gutter bleed   Printed or illustrative matter that extends to the center or binding edge of a publication, book, or booklet. See also **bleed; gutter**.

halftone   A reproduction of a continuous tone image in which the image is formed by very small dots of various sizes. See also **continuous tone; line copy**.

halftone screen   See **screen**.

handbook   A comprehensive compilation of practical information and data, organized for quick and efficient use and designed to provide ready solutions to problems, e.g., for engineers, students, mechanics, editors.

handle   A strong, concise summary of selling features of a book used by a rep in sales calls on booksellers and subsequently by the bookseller to describe the book to a potential buyer. A handle, says one rep, "says a lot about a book in as few words as possible."

hard copy   Copy printed on paper, as opposed to electronically stored or displayed copy. See also **soft copy**.

Harvard system   Method of citing papers in scientific books and periodicals. In lieu of footnotes, citations given at end of article or chapter, arranged alphabetically by author, include author(s), year, title, name of periodical or book publisher, volume number, and page number. References in the text consist only of author's name and date of publication in parentheses. See also **footnote reference system; name-and-date system; sequential numbering system**.

heads (headlines)   Secondary headlines are referred to as "subheads."

highlight halftone   See **dropout halftone**.

high opacity paper   Paper with little show-through of printing from the opposite side of the sheet.

high-ticket item   See **big ticket**.

hot type   Type cast from molten metal. Some forms of hot metal composition are Monotype, Linotype, Ludlow, foundry. Today almost no composition uses hot type. See also **cold-type composition**.

house list   A company-owned mailing list.

house rep   A book salesperson who is an employee of the publisher, and who is usually on salary and bonus. He or she represents only one publisher. See also **commissioned rep.**

IIA   See **Information Industry Association.**

imposition   The prefolding press-page arrangement of a multipage printing job to be printed on a single sheet. The arrangement is such that the printed sheet can be folded and bound with maximum efficiency, and with pages appearing in correct numerical sequence. For types of imposition, see **sheetwise imposition; work-and-tumble; work-and-turn.**

impression   All copies of a book printed at one time. See also **edition.**

imprint   The name of the publisher on the title page of a book. Also the name and address of an advertiser on its advertising material. Many publishers offer advertising material to booksellers with *imprint omitted.* The bookstore may then add its own imprint and use the material for promotion to its own customers and prospects.

income-to-cost ratio   A method of evaluating a mail-order promotion, especially in a multibook mailing. Some professional-book publishers consider a mailing effective if the cost does not exceed 33–40¢ of each sales dollar. See also **echo effect (of direct-mail promotion).**

information center   See **special library.**

Information Industry Association   Association of commercial producers of timely information or products designed to fill information needs.

ink jet printing   A computer-controlled direct printing method; first developed mainly to address envelopes. The impression is put directly on the envelope (rather than on a label) with a spray of ink.

inquiry-response mailing   A mailing aimed at eliciting inquiries rather than direct orders.

insert, book   An advertising piece that accompanies an outgoing book shipment. Some publishers use insert advertisements of related books or journals in all copies of a book printing, or as a stuffer in outgoing shipments or invoices. Also a separately printed section of a book, usually illustrations, inserted in the book at binding stage.

insertion order   A set of instructions to a publication by an advertiser or its agency requesting insertion of an advertisement of a stated size and on a particular date or in a specific issue, and frequently indicating position desired (right-hand page, book review section, page facing editorial matter, as far forward as possible, etc.).

insert, package   An advertising piece that accompanies any outgoing shipment of product.

instant publishing   See **on-demand publishing.**

interlibrary loan   A transaction in which library material is made available by one institution to another.

international co-edition   A book, usually heavily illustrated, issued in various countries and languages by publishers cooperating to spread the costs. See also **co-publishing.**

International Standard Book Number   An established international system of book numbering, providing a ten-digit identifier unique to each book title published. The ISBN system is administered in the United States by R. R. Bowker Co. See also **International Standard Serial Number.**

International Standard Serial Number   A unique number assigned to a serial publication that remains unchanged as long as the title of the serial remains unchanged. Administered by the Library of Congress, which assigns numbers. Under U.S. Postal regulations, the ISSN must appear on the outer wrapper of all periodicals.

International System of Units (SI)   Derived from Système International d'Unités, the SI metric system is the generally preferred system of weights and measures.

Inward-WATS The 800 number telephone system that permits reception of telephone calls from anyone in the service area selected. See also **Outward-WATS; Wide Area Telecommunications Service.**

IN-WATS See **Inward-WATS.**

ISBN See **International Standard Book Number.**

ISSN See **International Standard Serial Number.**

IST Division of Information Science and Technology. National Science Foundation.

ital Italics.

jacket Paper cover around a bound book originally used to protect a book prior to sale. The jacket now serves primarily as an advertisement, giving information about the book and its author. Text, professional, and reference books are often published without jackets.

jobber; book jobber; library jobber See **wholesaler.**

joint imprint The imprint of two publishers on the title page of an edition of a book being marketed and distributed by each in a different country. See also **co-publishing.**

justify Instruction to indicate that type composition is to be set flush left and right (justified on both sides).

key An identifying device in an advertisement to indicate the source of the response. See also **keyed advertisement.**

keyed advertisement A letter, number, code, or mark used in print or mail advertising to identify the source of the response. If different mailing lists have been used, a different *key* may be used for each list. The best location for a key is on the back of a business reply card, or in the upper left-hand corner on a business reply envelope.

laid paper Paper marked with a pattern of close parallel lines or watermarked as if ribbed.

language rights The granting of a license to a foreign publisher to translate and publish a book in a foreign language. The licensee usually has world rights on the edition in the specific language of the translation (Spanish is an exception: The Spanish American rights and rights for Spain may be sold separately).

layout A type specification diagram showing arrangements of elements of printed matter—page, piece—for a printer to follow. A preliminary quick pencil sketch is called a *rough* layout. A more precise drawing, closely approximating a final advertisement, for example, is called a *comprehensive.*

LC Library of Congress. See also **Library of Congress Proof Slips.**

lc Lowercase; small letters.

leaders Dots (. . .) or short strokes (- -) used in copy to direct the reader from one part of the copy to another. Usually specified in linear measurement, such as 2, 4, or 6 units per em.

leading The extra white space between printed lines, usually expressed in points, to permit easier reading, achieve an aesthetic effect, or pad out copy space (e.g., "10-on-12" or "10/12" signifies 10-point type on a 12-point body). See also **set solid.**

lead time The time needed from implementation of a promotion job to deadline.

letterpress Printing process in which ink is transferred from metal type or plates directly onto the paper.

lettershop A business equipped to handle the mechanical details of mailings, such as printing, collating, folding, inserting, addressing, imprinting, sorting, mailing, list maintenance, etc.

Library of Congress Proof Slips Descriptive book cataloging copy sold by the Library of Congress to public and academic libraries for their use in cataloging and book selection. The CIP Program enters information into the proof slip system in advance of publication.

line art See **line copy.**

line copy Any copy suitable for reproduction without using a halftone screen: solid blacks or whites. Also referred to as *line art.*

list   See **mailing list.**

list ad   An advertisement containing a number or list of books as opposed to an ad featuring a single book.

list broker   Represents all list owners; rents lists to advertisers.

list cleaning   See **mailing-list cleaning.**

list compiler   See **compiler (mailing list).**

list exchange   A list that is available, not for payment but usually in exchange for other names or advertising space.

list maintenance   See **mailing-list maintenance.**

list price   Suggested resale price. See also **discount from list price; net price; net pricing.**

list rental   See **mailing-list rental.**

list salting   See **salting.**

list segmentation   A means of targeting a mailing to a selected segment of a larger mailing list, from which one or more common characteristics can be isolated, such as buyers of books in a certain subject area or above a certain price, buyers from a given geographic region or from a certain year, and the like.

list selection   A selected part of a mailing list that may be rented separately from the entire list. See also **list segmentation.**

list sequence   The sequence or order in which names appear on a mailing list.

list testing   A sample mailing to a portion of a mailing list to determine its responsiveness. Many list owners set minimums on orders for test mailings, which may be in names, such as a 3,000 or 5,000 minimum, or in dollar amount, such as $100 or $150. Minimums vary with each list.

lithography   Abbreviation: litho. See **offset printing.**

logotype   Identifying device or trademark. Abbreviation: logo. See also **colophon; signature (in advertisement).**

long discount   See **trade discount.**

loose-leaf publishing   Publication of information of a current nature useful to business and professional people in their everyday activities. Because it is an ongoing publication service with updates issued at stated intervals or as required, it is usually stored in a loose-leaf binder.

loose-leaf reference   One or more volumes on a specific topic published in a loose-leaf binder, updated by supplements and revisions, either on a regular basis or as required.

machine readable   Information encoded in any form readable by a machine (usually digital computers), e.g., as holes punched on cards (punch cards) or as electronic signals on magnetic tape or disc. See also **photocomposer.**

McNaughton Plan   A rental plan through which public libraries rent high-demand books fully cataloged and processed for immediate circulation.

magazine subscription agency   See **subscription agency.**

magnetic tape   A plastic tape, with a surface capable of storing magnetic patterns, on which data may be stored via electrical impulses.

mailing list   A collection of names derived from a common source.

mailing-list broker   An independent agent who represents either buyer or seller in the supplying of mailing lists to direct-mail advertisers.

mailing-list cleaning   Removing from a mailing list those names and addresses that have ceased to be of value. See also **Address Correction Requested; Return Postage Guaranteed.**

mailing-list guarantee   A guarantee from a list owner to refund within a given period of time (usually 30 days) a given amount of money per piece for each name on the rented list that was undeliverable over a certain percentage (93%, 95%, etc.) of the total list. Envelopes bearing undeliverable names (nixies) must be returned to list owner to collect on guarantee.

mailing list maintenance   An ongoing program for making changes in existing names and addresses on a list as they occur, converting information from typed or written sources into additions to the mailing list, correcting ZIP Codes, deleting names that have ceased to be useful, etc. See also **merge, purge; purge.**

mailing-list profile Common characteristics of a list.

mailing-list rental The rental of a mailing list from its owner or compiler, for one-time use only, for a specified fee.

mailing-list sequence The order in which names and addresses are arranged in a list. The most frequently used sequence is by ZIP Code.

mailing-list testing A sample mailing to a portion of a list to test the responsiveness of the total list. See also **direct-mail testing; market testing.**

mailing package See **package.**

mail-order A book order received by mail, phone, or other medium and shipped to the customer through the mail or another carrier such as United Parcel Service (UPS).

mail-order advertising A method of sales promotion in which the entire sales transaction is done through the mail.

mail-order publication A book, series, or set with broad appeal to consumers that is designed and produced primarily for sale by mail.

Mail Preference Service (MPS) A centralized delisting program operated by the Direct Marketing Association for individuals who do not want to receive unsolicited mail. The information is circulated to 1,200 DMA members.

mail-responsive list A list of people who have previously responded to a mailing offer.

MARC MAchine Readable Cataloging.

market clustering Publishing in closely related areas or disciplines. This enables a number of different titles to share promotional costs, making for greater marketing strength and editorial visibility.

marketing (in publishing) All activities related to directing the sale and movement of books and publications from publisher to user, either directly (as in mail order) or through others, such as booksellers, jobbers, professors, etc. See also **direct marketing; mail order.**

marketing questionnaire See **author questionnaire.**

market segmentation See **list segmentation.**

market testing Direct-mail tests to small segments of new, different, or untried markets in fields related to a book to ascertain whether the tested market has potential for the book(s) in the mailing offer. See also **direct-mail testing; mailing-list testing.**

mass market paperback Paperbound books, usually of standard rack size (4¼" × 7"), relatively low priced, and distributed to newsstands and various mass-market outlets by local wholesale distributors.

matchcode A coded distillation of the elements of a name and address, which enables a computer to match identical addresses on different lists and cast out duplicates in a merge, purge operation. See **merge, purge.**

mechanical; mechanical paste-up The elements of an advertisement or other printed piece pasted into position to conform to layout or dummy, and ready to be photographed for platemaking. The finished mechanical is said to be camera ready. See also **camera-ready copy.**

medical book distributors Suppliers of medical and allied health books to retailers, students, and professionals in the health services fields.

medical jobbers See **medical book distributors.**

merge, purge To combine two or more mailing lists into a single list with duplicate names eliminated.

microcomputer A small computer, usually a portable or desk-top unit with a keyboard and a CRT display. It may also be connected for a television display.

microfiche A plastic sheet of photographic negative film, usually 4" × 6" in size, on which up to 98 pages are stored, greatly reduced in size. They can be seen enlarged on a projection machine or reader. See also **microform.**

microfilm A type of microform on which images are stored on a film roll, greatly reduced in size. See also **microform.**

microform General term embracing both microfilm and micro-opaque processes; graphic materials photographically reduced to extremely small size.

micropublishing The publishing of information in microform.

monograph A treatment, usually short, of a single subject by an author or a group of authors. See also **treatise**.

Murphy's Law "If anything can go wrong, it will."

NACS National Association of College Stores.

name-and-date system A system for citing references in books and journals in which the surname of the first author, followed by year of publication, is placed in parentheses within the text. Complete citation is provided in a bibliography. Comparable to Harvard system (qv). See also **footnote reference system; sequential numbering system**.

National Periodicals Center See **National Periodicals System**.

National Periodicals System A concept calling for a program or center, funded by the federal government, that would maintain a comprehensive collection of periodical titles and provide on-demand document delivery service by loan, photocopy, or microform to participating libraries.

negative check-off option An option given to customers or periodical subscribers by list renters to check off on their order or subscription renewal form if they object to having their names rented out.

negative option The successful mail-order technique used by most book clubs whereby a book is shipped and billed to a member automatically unless the member writes in advance and asks that it not be sent.

negative-option publishing Sometimes used as another name for book clubs. See also **no-commitment book club**.

nesting An enclosure, placed within another (nested), before being inserted into a mailing envelope.

net Price to be paid; no further discount. See also **net price**.

net price The bookseller's cost for a book, usually the list or suggested resale price less discount. Shipping or transportation charges, when levied, are usually added onto the net price. See also **list price; net; net pricing**.

net pricing Publishers' billing for a book at an established net price, with no suggested retail price. Booksellers then set retail selling prices on an individual basis. See also **list price**.

net profit The "paper" profit a publisher makes when the sale of a book is made, regardless of whether payment is ultimately collected.

new edition An edition containing substantial changes from the previous edition and printed from new, revised plates.

newsletter A concise periodical, often using typewriter type and mailed in a #10 envelope to simulate a letter. Provides late-breaking information in a particular area of interest. Most newsletters are sold by subscription, and generally do not contain advertising.

nixie A piece of mail returned by the post office because it is undeliverable.

NMA National Micrographic Association.

no-commitment book club A book club that requires no commitment of a minimum purchase of books as a condition of membership. See also **negative-option publishing**.

NOP Publisher's abbreviation for "not our publication."

nth name A method of selecting a portion of a mailing list (every sixth name, every eighth name, etc.)

NYP Abbreviation for "not yet published."

OCR See **optical character recognition**.

offprint Copies of a journal article made available in quantity, apart from the original journal issue. Offprints are made from sheets run simultaneously with and in addition to journal printing. They may start with the last page of the previous article, and may also contain the first page of the article following. See also **reprint (journal)**.

offset printing Offset lithography; a process in which a plate, wrapped around a cylinder (plate cylinder), transfers an inked image onto a sheet or rubber blanket wrapped around another cylinder (blanket cylinder), from which it is then transferred (offset) to the paper. See also **web offset**.

on-approval plan Books sent with the understanding that any not wanted may be returned. A number of jobbers ship new books on requested subjects automatically as received, "on approval." See also **continuation order**.

on consignment Books supplied with the understanding that they be paid for when sold. Supplier retains title until sold and can recall books not paid for.

on-demand publishing Reprinting of a book, document, or partial document to order, from a microform reproduction or magnetic storage.

one-time rate Basic advertising rate in a publication. Rate applied to advertising in a publication when the number of insertions is insufficient to earn a contract or frequency discount. See also **earned rate**.

one-time use An understanding that a rented mailing list will not be used more than once without the consent of the list owner.

online access Information retrieval from a data base through a computer terminal.

on-request publishing See **on-demand publishing**.

OP Abbreviation for "out-of-print"; publisher has no more copies for sale, no intention to reprint. See also **OS**.

opacity The property of paper that prevents the printing on one side of the sheet from showing through to the other. See also **show-through**.

open-end series A series with an indeterminate length. Volumes may be published irregularly or annually. See also **closed-end series**.

optical character recognition (1) Copy prepared using OCR-readable typefaces can be "read" by electronic scanning machines (optical readers). This information can then be used to produce photocomposition. (2) Optical character readers are used by the U.S. Postal Service to read ZIP numbers for mail-sorting . (3) Some scholarly journals ask authors to prepare submissions in an optical character recognition (OCR) typeface, which can be machine read by scanning. See also **camera-ready copy (author-prepared)**.

optical reader See **optical character recognition**.

OS Abbreviation for "out-of-stock"; new shipment or new printing awaited. See also **OP**.

outlet manager The coordinator for all sales and promotion activities related to a specific book sales outlet, such as trade sales manager, library sales manager, college marketing manager, etc.

out of print See **OP**.

out of stock See **OS**.

Outward-WATS A telephone company service that enables the customer to place calls to any telephone number in the service area selected on a fixed monthly charge. See also **Inward-WATS; Wide Area Telecommunications Service**.

overlay A protective covering for artwork or photographs. Also, a transparent covering, usually of tracing paper or plastic. It is sometimes used to show corrections, placement of colors, and other instructions to the platemaker. Also, a sheet carrying a copy for a separate color, in register.

overrun The practice of printing a larger quantity than ordered to compensate for spoilage during the press run and binding operations.

over the transom A book proposal or manuscript received unexpectedly or without prior solicitation or invitation.

package (direct mail) The most popular mailing format used in publishing promotions. Consists of envelope, letter, folder, and reply device. See also **self-mailer**.

packager See **book packager**.

page charges   A fee paid by the author of an article to have the article printed and published in certain society-sponsored journals.

Pareto's Law   A general law stating that 80% of the total results in a given situation are produced by 20% of the participants. For example, 80% of sales come from 20% of the titles, or 80% of the orders are brought in by 20% of the sales reps. Also referred to as the "80–20 principle."

pass-along reader   Reader of a publication who has not purchased or received the publication from the publisher by request.

pass-along readership   Total number of readers beyond the paid circulation of a business or professional publication.

peel-off label   A self-adhesive label that can be removed from a backing sheet, usually affixed to a mailing piece.

per inquiry   See **P.I. deal.**

permission   The granting of permission by a copyright owner to quote from a book or article, usually for a fee.

personalized letter   A letter used in mailing in which the name of the recipient has been included in both the salutation and the body of the letter. See also **personal letter.**

personal letter   Letter in which recipient's name is given in the heading and salutation but not mentioned elsewhere in the letter. See also **personalized letter.**

photocomposer   A photo-mechanical machine used to set type, in position, on photo-sensitive paper plates. See also **machine readable.**

photocomposition   Text set by photographic means.

photocopy   A photographic copy of an existing photograph. Such a print may be enlarged, reduced, or screened.

photo offset lithography   See **offset printing.**

photostat   Abbreviation: stat. A fast method of making photocopies of black-and-white original copy. Photostats may be direct positive (DP) or negative-to-positive (negative made first). A photostat may be made larger, smaller, or the same size. A requested change in size is usually expressed as percent of original copy (e.g., photostat to 85% size). If used for reproduction, a glossy stat is to be specified.

pica   A standard unit for measuring type matter, either line width or copy depth. A pica measures 12 points or about $\frac{1}{6}$". See also **point.**

P.I. deal   Payment for advertising based on the number of orders or inquiries received. Payment is a fixed amount per inquiry.

pilot club   A book club with the minimum number of members necessary to reveal predictable behavior characteristics in such things as sales, returns, payments, resignations, etc.

piracy   The act of reprinting and issuing a copyrighted book without permission or payment to the copyright owner.

point   A unit of type measurement equal to $\frac{1}{72}$" (.0138"). See also **pica.**

positive option   Technique of certain book clubs that send announcements of new selections, rather than books. The member must send back an order before the club will ship. See also **negative option.**

postcard mailing   See **card deck.**

PPMG   See **Professional Publishers' Marketing Group.**

PR Aids   A computerized system of PR Aids, Inc., for distributing news releases and announcements, as well as review copies, to critics and editors in all media.

preferred position   A desired position for which an advertiser must pay a premium over the basic rate. For magazine covers a premium over the earned rate is almost always charged. See also **earned rate; run-of-paper position.**

prelims   The preliminary pages or front matter of a book, usually identified by roman lowercase page numbers.

prepub   Prior to publication. A prepub order is one received prior to publication; a prepub price is a price in effect before the designated date of publication.

prepublication price   A special price usually at a discount off the publisher's list price, to encourage buyers to place orders prior to publication.

press kit   An information package, usually a folder with flaps or pockets, containing (for book-promotion applications) a news release, a glossy photo of author, information from the book, an author biography, and quotes or reviews about the book.

primary journal   A journal meant primarily for archival use and purchased mainly by libraries.

printing (2nd, 3rd, etc.)   Reprinting of a book after the initial printing, using the same type, print negatives, or plates. Also called second impression, third impression, etc.

proceedings   See **conference proceedings**.

product manager   Marketing coordinator for a specific product line within a publishing house. The product manager may also be involved in many nonmarketing activities such as planning, contract approval, inventory control, etc.

professional books   Books directed to a professional audience and specifically related to its work.

Professional Publishers' Marketing Group (PPMG)   An organization of marketing executives concerned with improving technique for the marketing of professional books and journals. Organized Jan. 16, 1981, in New York City, its originator was Peter Hodges of Warren, Gorham & Lamont, Boston. For membership information, write PPMG, Box 511, Essex Sta., Boston, MA 02112.

professional trade title   Book that is intended for use by professionals but that has sufficient appeal to be stocked in stores that normally do not carry professional and scholarly books. Such titles carry a trade discount.

pro forma invoice   A vehicle for informing a prospective book buyer of the total cost, including any applicable charges. Shipment is not usually made until payment is received. Pro forma invoicing is used when a publisher will not ship on an open credit basis.

program (computer)   A collection of instructions designed to make a computer perform a specific task.

protected   A book trade term meaning a book that may be returned to the publisher for credit if unsold. The term "fully protected," when applied to a publisher's list, means all unsold books are returnable.

PSP   Professional and Scholarly Publishing Division of the Association of American Publishers.

psychographics   Study of differences in personality and life-style (psychographic characteristics) within a demographic group. Provides insights into individual psychological characteristics and their possible influence on buying patterns and preferences. See also **demographics**.

PTLA   See **Publishers Trade List Annual**.

pub date (publication date)   The publisher's official or record date a book becomes available for sale. A publisher often ships a book to the trade in advance of this date with instructions not to release until publication date.

Publisher's Alliance   Formerly Small Publisher's Association. A group of small publishers, organized for the purpose of pooling resources and manpower.

Publishers' Trade List Annual   A compilation of catalogs and publication lists from some 1,500 publishers, arranged alphabetically and bound into six permanent clothbound volumes. A basic reference tool for many libraries and booksellers, published annually in September by R. R. Bowker Co.

publishing-on-demand   See **on-demand publishing**.

Pubmart   An annual three-day program in New York City consisting of approximately 100 concurrent half-day sessions covering various aspects of book publishing. Started in 1977, it is jointly sponsored by R. R. Bowker Co. and Knowledge Industry Publications.

pubset type (publication-set type)   Type matter set by a periodical or newspaper from copy supplied by the advertiser, for an advertisement to be published at a future date. Most newspapers and larger periodicals will charge only for the space purchased, the composition being supplied free when requested by the advertiser. Most smaller-circulation and scholarly periodicals charge for composition at their cost, or at a nominal fee.

purge Eliminating duplicate or undesirable items from a file (e.g., unwanted names from a mailing list). See also **merge, purge.**

pyramiding Testing a mailing list by mailing to increasingly larger quantities of the same list, based on success of the smaller samples.

questionnaire, author See **author questionnaire, marketing questionnaire.**

rag rt Instruction used by artists and type specifiers to indicate composition is to be set flush left and ragged (unjustified) right.

ragged right, rag right Copy with unjustified right-hand margin.

rate See **contract rate; short rate.**

rate card A card issued by a publication giving advertising rates and related pertinent information—mechanical requirements, closing dates, etc.

reader's service card A business reply card on which many numbers are printed in grid formation; the card is bound into a publication, and enables the reader to request literature, information, or other services by circling a key number on the card corresponding to a number identifying a product mentioned in an advertisement or in the editorial matter. Some periodicals also use the key numbers as a means of ordering an advertised book. Also called bingo card (qv).

reduction Photographically decreasing an image to a desired size. An 8″ × 10″ photo or block of copy reduced to 4″ × 5″ would be "scaled 50%." See also **scale.**

referee An expert on a subject to whom an editor sends the manuscript of a journal article or book for evaluation.

regional book A book designed to appeal to readers within a specific area of the country. Usually offered at a trade discount, such books are sold through book outlets and by direct mail to individuals within that region.

register Exact alignment of two or more printing images on one surface.

remainder house A specialist dealer who buys publishers' overstock and sells to bookstores (and sometimes also to individuals by mail).

remaindering The practice of selling, at greatly reduced prices, all or part of a publisher's overstock of a slow-moving book, or of one being dropped from the list.

Reply-O-Letter A patented mailing format with a die-cut opening on the face of the letter and a pocket on the reverse side. An addressed reply card or envelope inserted into the pocket shows through the die-cut opening, providing an address for both the letter and the window mailing envelope.

reprint book A book consisting of a collection of journal articles in which the original articles were used as camera-ready copy.

reprint (journal) Pages of an article removed from a journal and reimposed in such a way that only the text of the article is supplied. See also **offprint.**

reprint publisher A publisher that specializes in reprinting, usually in small editions, older titles of value that have gone out of print. See also **on-demand publishing.**

repro, repro proof See **reproduction proof.**

reproduction proof Clean and sharp typeset copy suitable for photographic reproduction and platemaking.

response device The BRC (business reply card) or BRE (business reply envelope) within a package-format mailing.

response rate Percentage of return from a mailing, in direct-response marketing.

return envelope A self-addressed envelope used as a mail enclosure, to facilitate a reply, order, or payment from the addressee.

Return Postage Guaranteed A line added to pieces in a third-class bulk mailing that instructs the Postal Service to return any undeliverable mailing piece. The straight third-class postage rate is charged for the return. See also **Address Correction Requested.**

reverse, reverse plate   Negative-image copy, or printing plate, in which whites come out black and vice versa.

review slip   An enclosure in a book sent by a publisher for review. Usually includes such information as title, author, pub date, and price; also a request that the publication send copy(ies) of published review.

Robinson-Patman Act   A law passed in 1936 calling for a seller to treat all competitive customers of a product on proportionally equal terms with regard to discounts and cooperative advertising allowances, and other terms, for the purpose of prohibiting discrimination or favoritism "in restraint of trade."

roman   An upright type style, as opposed to a slanting or italic style. Normal text style.

ROP   See **run-of-paper position.**

rough layout   See **layout.**

rule of nine   Publisher's discount policy that assumes that an order for more than nine copies of a title suited for use as a textbook is considered an adoption and invoiced at textbook discount.

run-around   Usually, an illustration set into the type area. Lines of type in a column are shortened at either left or right to allow space for the illustration or other featured material. The type runs around the illustration. Sometimes called *set-around.*

run-of-book   See **run-of-paper position.**

run-of-paper position   Placement of an advertisement in a publication anywhere in the edition, at the publisher's discretion. *Run-of-book* has the same meaning, but usually applies to magazine advertising only.

saddle wiring   Binding method for a booklet by which wire staples are driven through the back fold of the booklet. (This enables booklet to lie flat when open.) If booklet is too thick for saddle wiring, it may be *side wired.* For this, heavier staples are used. See also **side wiring or side stitching.**

sales conference   A forum used by most publishers for presenting forthcoming books to the sales force.

salting   Decoy or dummy names inserted in a mailing list to test for delivery of mailings, or unauthorized use of list. Also called *seeding.*

sample   A representative portion of a total group involved in a survey.

SAN   See **Standard Address Number.**

sans serif   A typeface without serifs. See also **serif.**

SBN   See **International Standard Book Number.**

sc   Proofreader's mark for small caps (small capital letters). These are capital letters approximately the height of lowercase (small letters). See also **x height.**

scale   Term used in preparation of printing or advertising to denote size of reduction or enlargement. When expressed as a percentage, "scale 50%" would be used for a reduction to 50% of size before reduction. See also **reduction.**

SCF (Sectional Center Facility)   A centralized mail-processing hub in the U.S. Postal Service. The first three digits of the Zip Code identify the sectional center area; the last two identify the associate offices, and also stations and branches of the sectional center. There are 313 SCFs in the Postal Service.

Scholar's Bookshelf   Princeton, NJ–based mail-order operation originated by Abbot M. Friedland that offers sharply discounted publishers' overstock titles in the humanities and fine arts, science, and technology. Catalog mailings are made to scholars and institutions throughout the world.

score   To emboss or impress a rule on a thick sheet of paper, or several thicknesses, so that it will fold evenly without cracking or distorting the paper.

screen   A term used when a continuous tone photograph is converted or broken into dots. Screen-line number signifies number of dots per inch. Most frequently used screens are 120-line and 133-line screens, for magazines and direct mail. Screens in newspaper advertising are coarser—65-line or 85-line. See also **Benday; halftone.**

screen print   See **Velox.**

seeding   See **salting.**

segmentation See **list segmentation.**

selectivity Selection options of certain mailing lists that enable the list user to focus on a desired segment of a market.

self-cover A printed piece with a cover of the same paper as the inside text pages.

self-mailer Any direct-mail piece without an envelope or special wrapping.

sequential numbering system A system for citing references in numerical sequence in the text. See also **footnote reference system; Harvard system; name-and-date system.**

serial A publication issued in successive parts or issues, usually at regular intervals and meant to be continued indefinitely. Serials include periodicals, annuals, and proceedings and transactions of societies.

series A collection of books or monographs within a defined discipline or subdiscipline.

serif A bracketed cross stroke or projection at the extremities of type of letter forms. There are many varieties: square serif, old-style serif, modern, etc. See also **sans serif.**

set-around See **run-around.**

set solid To set type without any leading, or spacing between lines. See also **leading.**

sheetwise imposition Printing one side of the sheet from one plate or set of plates, and then the other side from another plate or set of plates. See also **work-and-tumble; work-and-turn.**

short discount A discount at a relatively low scale given to booksellers and wholesalers for handling textbooks and those professional books, reference books, and other specialized works that are primarily sold directly to users. See also **trade discount.**

short rate An advertising rate billed to an advertiser that is higher than a lower rate previously billed because the advertiser has not purchased the amount of space or met the minimum insertion requirement on which the lower rate was based. See also **contract rate; contract year; frequency discount.**

short run publishing The practice of publishing a book economically in a reasonably short time for a small market, often from unedited typewritten sheets supplied by the author. See also **camera-ready copy (author-prepared).**

short-title catalog A list of all of a publisher's titles, giving author, title, price, publication date, and order numbers or reference codes.

show-through The degree to which printing on one side of a sheet can be seen from the other side. See also **opacity.**

SI See **International System of Units (SI).**

SIC See **Standard Industrial Classification.**

side wiring or side stitching Method of binding thick booklets or periodicals with wire or thread going from one side of booklet or periodical to the other. See also **saddle wiring.**

signature (in advertisement) Name and address at the end of an advertisement usually accompanied by the publisher's colophon or device. The signature is sometimes called a logotype or logo.

signature (in bound publication) Section of a book or catalog, obtained by folding a single sheet of paper into 8, 12, 16, or more pages.

silver print See **blues.**

simultaneous publication Publication of a book in cloth and paper editions at the same time.

Single Title Order Plan (STOP) A special order form used by booksellers to facilitate delivery of special book orders from publishers at lowest cost to both bookseller and publisher, and to speed delivery of books to the customer. Forms are available from the American Booksellers Association.

sinkage, sink The amount of space left blank at top of page before the first line of type, properly measured from the top of the normal text page (not the top of the paper).

sizing of paper Treatment of the surface of a paper to prevent penetration of water. Offset papers are rather heavily sized.

SLA Special Libraries Association.

slippage (of titles) Delay of books in production beyond the originally scheduled publication dates.

slug A whole line of traditional line-cast composition. Also, a temporary line inserted as an identifying reminder of a line or lines to be supplied later.

small caps Small capital letters; shaped like capital letters but about the size of the lowercase (small) x. Indicated in copy by two lines drawn underneath. See also **sc**.

Society for Scholarly Publishing (SSP) An international interdisciplinary organization for those involved in the production and use of scholarly works in commercial, academic, society, or governmental settings.

soft copy Information displayed visually on video terminal, from digital storage, or in microform; also unedited manuscript copy. See also **hard copy**.

software Computer programs.

solo mailing A mailing in which only one book is offered.

special library A library or information center maintained by an individual, corporation, association, government agency, or any group, or a specialized departmental collection within a library responsible for the organization and dissemination of information on a specific subject, primarily offering service to a specialized clientele through the use of varied media and methods. See also **SLA**.

special sales Publishers' sales made to or through a nontraditional outlet, i.e., any outlet other than a bookstore or library.

Special to A heading used on a news release written in a nonexclusive but special way for the publication to which it is being sent. Releases to other publications can be sent simultaneously, if written in a different format. See also **Exclusive to**.

specs Type specifications.

spinoff A book excerpted or resulting from a previously published larger or encyclopedic work; also a periodical article expanded to book length.

split-run test An option offered by some magazines permitting two different advertisements, copy approaches, or coupon offers to run in alternate copies of the same issue for testing purposes. Split-run can also be used in direct mail with alternate mailing list names, or to reach two distinct groups both included in the same circulation of a particular promotion.

sponsored book A book sometimes issued by an established publishing house in behalf of a company or organization with a special interest in having it published. Sometimes a payment is made to insure the publisher against loss from a small sale through normal channels; or the sponsor may agree to buy a sufficient number of copies at an agreed-upon price to insure profitable publication. Not to be confused with vanity publisher (qv).

spread An advertisement on two facing pages. See also **center spread**.

SSP See **Society for Scholarly Publishing**.

Standard Address Number (SAN) A unique seven-digit number assigned to organizations regularly involved in buying or selling books, to assist in computer-to-computer ordering, invoicing, and information-updating formats. SANs are issued by the Standard Address Numbering Agency, which operates within the ISBN Agency at R. R. Bowker Co.

Standard Industrial Classification A government-assigned code number by function and product for every U.S. business. Many compilers rent mailing lists by SIC classification.

standing order See **continuation order**.

stat See **photostat**. Term sometimes used as a verb (e.g., stat to 85% of copy size).

stet Proofreading term for "let it stand as it is."

STM International Group of Scientific, Technical, and Medical Publishers. Based in Amsterdam, the group was established in 1969 in Frankfurt and now has nearly 150 member companies. Paul Nijhoff Asser is its executive secretary.

STM publisher/company   One engaged in the publication of scientific, technical, and/ or medical books.

stock-holding bookshop   British term for a full-line bookstore that carries a good back-list stock or titles.

STOP   See **Single Title Order Plan.**

strike-on composition (direct-impression composition)   Copy prepared for platemaking and printing using a typewriter or other keyboard device that makes a physical impression on the paper. See also **cold-type composition.**

strip-in   See **stripping.**

stripping   The assembling, usually in negative form, of the elements that are to appear on the printing plate.

stuffer   See **insert, book.**

sub rights   Commonly used term in publishing for subsidiary rights.

subscription agency   The principal medium through which libraries place periodical subscriptions. Agencies receive orders for periodicals from libraries, and group them by publisher before forwarding them. Most publishers allow a small discount for this service, as it saves them the time and expense of billing subscriptions individually. The library benefits by having a single periodical source and a monthly billing for all its periodical requirements.

subscription (book)   Order for a defined series of titles published at variable intervals but with a predefined life span. Payment may be in advance, or as each book is invoiced. Price is often fixed throughout the subscription period. See also **continuation order.**

subsidiary rights   For scholarly, sci-tech, and professional-book publishers, this is usually limited to book club, translation, reprint, or paperback rights. Were it not for book club participation in the press run, many small publishers could not afford the high unit cost of publishing. Trade houses also sell TV, movie, and serialization rights.

subsidy publisher   See **vanity publisher.**

substance   Abbreviation: Sub. See **basis weight.**

supplements (book)   Published products related to a previously published work. Supplements, when free, are sent automatically. If charged, they may be requested at the time of original purchase, or by notification from the publisher when issued.

surprints   Combining of two negatives on the same printing plate. See also **dropout halftone; reverse plate.**

synoptic format   A synopsis of a larger work; a brief summary of the most important features of the full text.

synoptic journal   A publishing format used in some scientific or scholarly journals in which only summaries of the authors' full papers are presented. Full copies of any paper are supplied on demand from a data bank.

synoptic/microform journal   A journal that prints only synopses or summaries of scientific papers. It simultaneously publishes the full papers in a microfiche edition of the journal.

tagline   A line added to a mailing piece to help direct it to a specific job title or function (marketing director, publicist, vice-president, etc.).

tear sheet   A page torn from a specific issue of a publication containing an advertisement and sent to an advertiser or agency as proof of insertion.

teaser   An advertisement or promotion to generate curiosity for an advertisement or promotion to follow.

teaser copy   Copy on an envelope that attempts to capture the attention of the recipient and to stimulate interest in the envelope's contents.

telemarketing   Use of the telephone as a sales vehicle. Most often associated with the use of toll-free telephone numbers. See also **Inward-WATS.**

teleordering   An ordering system linking bookseller to wholesaler by a computer terminal in the bookstore that is connected to the wholesaler's main data-processing installation.

tele publishing   Electronic means of disseminating information, in contrast with print on paper. See also **folio publishing.**

terminal   A device by which information can be sent to or received from a computer. Operation is governed by a typewriter-like keyboard. Information received can be automatically typed on paper, or displayed on a video screen.

test mailing   See **list testing.**

theoretical text   Usually an advanced-level text by an authority on the subject, useful for graduate study and professional reference.

third-class bulk rate   Special postage rate for mailings of 200 or more identical pieces and/or weighing 50 pounds or more, and meeting other special postal requirements.

till-forbid offer   See **automatic shipment.**

tint   A pattern of dots that reproduces as a tone.

tip-in   A page pasted or glued into a bound or stapled book.

trade discount   A discount given by publishers to booksellers and wholesalers on general trade fiction and nonfiction of the kind ordinarily sold in bookstores. Trade discounts differ according to publisher; they are variously scaled, according to quantity, over a range of about 33⅓ to 45%, or more.

trade title   Popular fiction or nonfiction book sold in the average bookstore or carried in a well-stocked public library. Trade titles carry a trade discount. See also **trade discount, professional trade title.**

translation rights   The licensing of a publisher to publish a translation of a book. See also **foreign publication rights.**

treatise   An edited volume in which each chapter is identified with its author. See also **monograph.**

trim   To reduce overlong copy. Also, abbreviation for "trimmed size" of a printed piece.

trimmed size   Page size, or final size of any printed job. See also **type area.**

TSM   Former name of the Technical, Scientific, and Medical Division of the Association of American Publishers. Division was renamed Professional and Scholarly Publishing Division in November 1979.

tsm publishing   Generally used as a reference to technical, scientific, and medical publishing.

twig books   Advanced treatises and monographs with limited markets, deriving from increasingly specialized subbranches, or "twigs," of broader disciplines. From twigging (qv).

twigging   The proliferation of publications in progressively narrow, specialized areas of a scientific or scholarly discipline. A term coined by Curtis Benjamin.

type area   The type page size or other area (within the trimmed size) that the composition and illustrative matter will occupy. See also **trimmed size.**

typeface   A style or design of type, sometimes named after its designer.

type page   Area of the page that type will normally occupy, margins not included.

typescript   See **copy.**

typewriter composition   Composition prepared for reproduction with a typewriter or similar strike-on device. See also **camera-ready copy (author-prepared); strike-on composition.**

typo   Typographical error.

typography   The selection and arrangement of type for use in printed matter. Less frequently, the business of typesetting.

underrun   Shortage from the number of printed copies requested, usually caused by spoilage in printing and binding.

unduping   See **merge, purge.**

university library collection   A book collection designed to serve the needs of the university, especially in research. See also **college library collection.**

university press   A not-for-profit publisher of scholarly books and journals, which is owned by or related to a university or group of institutions of higher learning.

USPS   U.S. Postal Service.

value pricing   The price of a book based on what the publisher considers the value of its use. "You charge what you think the traffic will bear," according to Frank L. Greenagel, former president of Arete Publishing Co.

vandyke   See **blues.**

vanity publisher   A firm that exists to produce books, whatever their subject matter or literary value, at the *author's* risk and expense. Sometimes referred to as a subsidy publisher, but not to be confused with a publisher funded in part by institutional grants or subsidies for scholarly purposes. See also **sponsored book.**

VDT   See **Video Display Terminal.**

vellum overlay   A sheet of semitransparent paper, used mainly for protection or for color separations. See also **overlay.**

Velox   A screened black-and-white photoprint that can be pasted on a mechanical and used as line copy. (Screens usually have less than 100 lines per inch.) See also **Benday; screen.**

videodisc   A picture playback system that can be used to present a standard color picture on a conventional television set or display monitor. Some publishers view the videodisc as an educational and instructional tool utilizing original material or material transferred from existing texts.

Video Display Terminal   A CRT (cathode ray tube) used to view and edit material existing in computer-controlled magnetic storage.

wafers, dots, seals   The pressure-sensitive "circles" or adhesive labels used to seal envelopes and self-mailers.

WATS   See **Wide Area Telecommunications Service.**

web offset   A high-speed form of offset printing, utilizing paper fed from rolls rather than single sheets. See also **offset printing.**

web press   A printing press fed from large, continuous rolls (webs) of paper.

weight   The basis on which paper is sold; 60-lb. (or 60 substance) means a ream of paper in a certain size (usually 25″ × 38″) that weighs 60 pounds. See also **basis weight.**

wf   Proofreader's mark for wrong font (qv).

white mail   Orders not traceable to any promotional effort or source. The term is derived from the fact that such orders are frequently received on plain white sheets of paper. However, they may also include untraceable purchase orders or orders by telephone.

wholesaler; wholesale bookseller (jobber)   A supplier of the books of many different publishers to libraries and bookstores. Provides the convenience of a single invoice for shipments of different titles from different publishers, and often toll-free ordering service. The preferred means of book buying for most libraries.

Wide Area Telecommunications Service (WATS)   A direct-dial service which permits telephone customers to place or receive long-distance calls at established monthly hourly rates. There are two types of WATS—interstate and intrastate. See also **Inward-WATS; Outward-WATS.**

widow   A nondialog short line of type, usually less than ¾ of a line, starting a page or or column.

WISP   Women in Scholarly Publishing, an organization formed in Spring Lake, NJ, on June 21, 1980.

word-processed letter   A letter prepared through a word-processing machine. Process uses two discs—one containing the addresses to be used for mailing, and the other containing the letter. Letter is produced automatically by combining text with address information. See also **computer-printed letter.**

word-processing machine   A machine that prepares text by manipulating it in magnetic storage. See also **word-processed letter.**

work-and-tumble   The same as work-and-turn, except that after one side of the sheet is printed, it is tumbled side to side instead of end for end. See also **sheet-wise imposition; work-and-turn.**

work-and-turn   A sheet printed from a press form so arranged that the one form can be printed on one side of the sheet. The sheet is then turned end for end and printed on the other side. This gives two copies of the pages when the sheet is cut in half. See also **sheetwise imposition; work-and-tumble.**

wrong font (wf)   Letter from one type size or style of type mixed with those of another. See also **font** and **wf.**

x height   May refer to capital or lowercase x: the height of a small (or lowercase) letter typically the letter x in a type font; also for the capital X. See also **sc.**

ZIP   See **Zoning Improvement Plan.**

ZIP Code   A five-digit numerical code that identifies a specific geographic area. The first ZIP digit divides the country into ten major areas, of which zero is New England; nine is the West Coast. The first three ZIP digits identify a smaller area within a single state. The last two digits stand for either (1) a postal zone within the limits of a major city; or (2) a small city or town in which all addresses have the same ZIP Code.

ZIP Code analysis   Evaluation of a mail campaign return by ZIP Code to ascertain the most responsive areas.

ZIP + 4   A bulk subclass of first-class mail under which a rate reduction is allowed for 500 or more first-class letters mailed at one time bearing the nine-digit ZIP + 4 code that can be read by optical character-reader equipment. The code utilizes the standard five-digit ZIP Code followed by a hyphen and an additional four digits.

Zoning Improvement Plan   A five-digit system introduced by the U.S. Postal Service July 1, 1963, to improve mail sorting and distribution. See also **ZIP Code.**

Appendix B
Index to Book Marketing Handbook, Volume One

Note: References are to numbered entries within chapters. Each entry number consists of a chapter number followed by the number of the entry within the chapter. Page numbers are given for entries appearing in the Glossary.

Formats (cont.)
  for journal promotion flier, 33:04
  for library sales, 22:06
  magazine format for prospectus to promote
    Atlas of Israel, 16:01
  newsletter favored in mailings to physi-
    cians, 27:01
  for presentation to potential industrial ac-
    count, 22:08
  for regular mailings to bookstores, 21:04
  standard news release, 20:10
Forward and Return Postage Guaranteed, use
    of line in third-class mail, 6:06
Frankfurt Book Fair, 31:02, 43:06
Free delivery, as wholesaler incentive, 21:13
Free 800 telephone number. *See* 800 tele-
    phone number
Free examination copy. *See* Examination copy
Free examination period, as mail-order op-
    tion, 1:16
Free freight. *See* Free delivery, as wholesaler
    incentive
Free postage, offer with library sales, 22:06
Free publicity. *See* Publicity
Free shipping
  as incentive for prepayment in direct-mail
    promotion, 1:16
  with prepaid orders, 1:15
Free trial examination, offers in direct-mail
    promotion, 1:15
Freemont, Robert, 1:35
Frequency discount, glossary (p. 385)
Freiberger, Walter F., 19:10
Friedland, Abbott, 11:02
French, fading as language of science in
    Middle East, 43:05
Fry, Bernard M., 36:06
Fry Report, The, 32:01
Full-service subscription agency. *See* Sub-
    scription agency, full-service
Fulfillment cycle, in journals subscription
    processing, 35:07
The Futurist, 20:16

Gale Research Company, 5:03, 26:06
Galley proof (galley), glossary (p. 385)
Gang printing. *See* Printing, gang
Gang run, glossary (p. 385)
General Agreement on Tariffs and Trade, Ca-
    nadian, 43:12
General-interest books
  at convention exhibits, 30:13
  promotion of in single-subject mailings,
    1:21
General Medical Book Co. (NY), 28:08
General Science Index, 19:18
Geographic advertising editions, 12:10

Geographic edition and/or demographic edi-
    tion, glossary (p. 385)
Geographic mailing-list test, 1:09
Geographic option, in card-deck mailing, 8:11
George Madden and Associates, 23:07
  as college faculty mailing-list source, 2:03
  specialized list source, 11:05
Geotimes, 4:12
  foreign circulation, 43:01
German, replaced by English as international
    language of science, 43:02
Gordon Publications, Inc., as mailing-list
    source for chemical process industries,
    2:03
Government agencies, quantity purchases
    from, 24:06
Government contracts, and red tape in book-
    selling, 21:14
Graduate students, book buying practice at
    conventions, 30:15
Grain
  glossary (p. 385)
  paper, 7:10
Graphic material, for sales presentations,
    21:22
Gratis copy requests, 23:05
  See also Complimentary copies; Desk copy
    requests; Examination copy; Review
    copies
Great Britain. *See* England; United Kingdom
Green borders, use on third-class mail, 7:07
Greenwood Press, Inc., 26:06
Gripper edge, glossary (p. 385)
Gripper margin. *See* Gripper edge
Grippers, glossary (p. 385)
Guide to American Directories, 5:03, 42:20
Guide to Scientific Instruments, 12:10
"Guide to World's Abstracting and Indexing
    Services in Science and Technology,"
    19:16
Gutter, glossary (p. 385)
Gutter bleed, glossary (p. 385)

Halftone, glossary (p. 385)
Halftone screen. *See* Screen, glossary
Handbook, glossary (p. 385)
Hand-inserting. *See* Envelopes, hand-
    inserting
Handout for press conference, 20:13
Hard copy, glossary (p. 385)
Hard sell copy, avoidance of in sci-tech ad
    copy, 14:08
Hard-to-locate books, bookseller purchases of,
    21:13
Harper & Row, 16:02
Hart, Beverly, 8:09
Harvard Cooperative Society, Cambridge
    (MA), 28:08

Industrial mailing lists, international, 43:08
Industrial Marketing, 42:12
Industrial publications
  advertising response from, 13:09
  See also Business publications
Industrial quantity discounts, schedule of,
  24:09
Industrial Research/Development, foreign subscription list, 43:09
Industrial Research Magazine, 12:10
  chromatography demographic advertising
    edition, 12:10
  as mailing list source, 2:03
Industrial sales
  by booksellers, 21:09
  copy for back of sales letter, 24:09
  letterwriting approach, 24:08
  presentation format, 24:08
  quantity sale, reasons for, 24:06
  See also Industrial accounts
Industrial training programs, book sales for,
  24:06
Ineffective promotion, discontinuance of,
  16:02
Influence
  of book reviews, 18:01
  of opinion leaders in books field, 20:15
Information, newsworthy, 20:01
Information center. *See* Special libraries
Information Reports and Bibliographies, 36:06
Ingram Book Company, as major growing
  power in trade wholesaling, 21:13
Initial stock orders
  placed by retail booksellers, 21:13
  with agency plan, 21:02
Ink
  color preferred by doctors, 27:01
  two-color effect with one color, 7:11
Ink jet printing, glossary (p. 386)
Inorganic Chemistry, ACS combination adver-
  tising rate applicable to, 12:09
Inquiry followup procedure, from encyclopedia
  advertising, 16:04
Inquiry-response mailings, 1:03
Insert, book, glossary (p. 386)
Insertion order, glossary (p. 386)
Institute for Scientific Information, 19:06,
  19:09
Institute of Electrical and Electronic Engi-
  neers, 4:21, 12:12
  as mailing-list source, 2:03
Instrument and Apparatus News, 4:10
Instruments & Control Systems, 4:10
Insufficient promotion, 38:07
Interlibrary loan, glossary (p. 386)
Internal mobility, of bankers within own or-
  ganization, 29:03
International Aerospace Abstracts, 19:16

International Book Information Service
  (IBIS), 43:08
  list-ordering information, 43:08
International book marketing
  lists available for, 43:08, 43:09
  See also Book marketing;
    Names of countries or regions
International Book Trade Directory, 44:06
International co-edition, glossary (p. 386)
*International Directory of Acronyms in Li-
  brary, Information and Computer Sci-
  ences,* 42:21
International Directory of Booksellers, 44:07
International division, to handle overseas
  sales, 43:03
*International Guide to the Academic Market-
  place. See* International Book Informa-
  tion Service
International Literary Market Place, 44:07
International marketing. *See* Markets, over-
  seas
International operations, of U.S. publishers,
  43:03
International orders. *See* Foreign orders, convention
International sales, overseas market potential
  for U.S. produced books, 28:03
International scientific communications, 8:12
International Standard Book Number, glos-
  sary (p. 386)
International Standard Serial Number, glos-
  sary (p. 386)
*International Subscription Agents and Anno-
  tated Directory,* 34:02
International System of Units (SI), glossary
  (p. 386)
Inventory requirements, for professional and
  scholarly books with trade appeal,
  21:05
Invitation-type format, in direct-mail format
  test, 1:10
Invoice clarity, in college examination-copy
  offer, 23:06
Inward-WATS, glossary (p. 386)
In-WATS. *See* Inward-WATS, glossary
Iowa Book and Supply Co., Iowa City (IA),
  21:08
Ireland, annual mobility rate of, 4:25
Iron Age, 4:10
Israel
  defense forces, effect on *Atlas of Israel,*
    16:01
  as market for U.S. produced books, 43:06
Ital, glossary (p. 387)

Jacket, glossary (p. 387)
Jacobius, Emmy, 31:02

text potential for, 21:19
treated as trade books, 21:05
which should be withheld from book clubs,
25:03
Professional associations and societies
American Anthropological Association,
4:08, 28:10
American Association for the Advancement
of Science, 19:13
American Association of Cost Engineers,
19:04
American Association of Law Libraries,
10:04
American Booksellers Association, 10:04,
12:16, 21:09, 38:08
American Chemical Society, 4:05, 12:09,
12:17
American Dental Association, 27:05
American Economic Association, 28:10
American Geological Institute, 4:12
American Historical Association, 28:10
American Industrial Hygiene Association,
16:03
American Institute of Aeronautics and As-
tronautics, 19:16
American Institute of Architects, 2:03, 4:09
American Institute of Biological Sciences,
4:14
American Institute of Chemical Engineers,
19:04
American Institute of Industrial Engineers,
19:04
American Institute of Mining, Metallurgi-
cal, and Petroleum Engineers, 19:04
American Institute of Physics, 4:22, 32:02
American Library Association, 10:04, 19:08,
22:08
American Mathematical Society, 4:20, 19:10
American Medical Association, 27:03, 27:05
American Meteorological Society, 19:16
American Osteopathic Association, 27:05,
27:06
American Political Science Association,
4:23, 28:10
American Psychological Association, 4:15,
28:04, 28:05, 28:06, 28:10
American Society for Engineering Educa-
tion, 19:12
American Society of Civil Engineers, 4:13,
13:13, 19:04
American Society of Heating, Refrigerating
and Air-Conditioning Engineers, 19:04
American Sociological Association 4:07, 28:10
American Statistical Association, 4:16
American Vacuum Society, 19:16
annual rate of change in membership, 2:02
approaches for establishing cooperative
sales arrangement, 24:02

Association for Computing Machinery,
19:16
Association of American Publishers, 1:01,
3:02, 14:00, 21:19, 21:20, 22:08
Association of American University
Presses, 38:08
Association of College and Research Librar-
ies, 18:04, 19:02
Association of Energy Engineers, 19:04
Association of the Learned and Professional
Society Publishers, 18:01
Direct Mail Marketing Association, 2:02,
4:02
Electrochemical Society, 4:17, 19:04
Illuminating Engineering Society, 19:04
Institute of Electrical and Electronic Engi-
neers, 2:03, 4:21, 12:12, 19:04
international mailing lists, 43:08
mailing list comparison with lists of known
book buyers, 1:07
Medical Library Association, 10:04
members from foreign countries, 43:01
National Association of College Stores,
21:20
publications of, mailing lists of, 2:02
as original mailing list sources, 2:05
as prospects for cooperative sales arrangement, 24:01
Society for Scholarly Publishing, 32:02
Society of Automotive Engineers, 19:04
Special Libraries Association, 10:04, 12:17,
19:07, 22:03
World Future Society, 20:16
Professional journals, advertising readership
in, 39:02
Professional Mailing Lists, Inc., 22:03
Professional monitoring service, use for direct
mail, 1:23
Professional societies. See Professional asso-
ciations and societies
Professionals, book marketing, criteria for,
38:10
*Professional's Guide to Public Relations Ser-
vices*, 20:06
Professionals, without university affiliation,
28:04
Professors. See College faculty
Profit, bookseller, 21:09
Profitability of journals, 32:01
Profitable mailing, as guide to percentage of
return, 1:07
Progressives, requirement for four-color advertising, 12:11
Promotion
author recommendations for, 37:02
in ineffective markets, 16:02
to library and school media, 16:02
of new journal, 32:01

as communications medium for scholarship, 32:02

defined by H. William Koch, 32:02

destined to remain in present printed form, 32:02

fact of life for scholarly societies, 32:01

survival vehicle for, 28:11

See also Scientific and technical journals

Scholarly Publishing: A Journal for Authors and Publishers, 42:33

Scholarly Reprints, Inc., 26:06

Scholar's Bookshelf, book-buyer mailing list, 11:02

School Library Journal, 22:02

Schwab, Victor O., 12:01

Harry Schwartz Bookstore, Milwaukee (WI), 21:08

Sci-tech and professional books

advertising, things to avoid in, 12:02

book marketing strategy, importance of reaching opinion leaders, 20:15

buyers, results of study on, 12:04

list brokers for, 2:04

mailing lists, quality variation among different groups and disciplines, 2:02

selling by mail successfully, 1:05

stocks carried by library jobbers, 1:02

value of book reviews in, 18:01

See also Professional and scholarly books; Scientific books

Science, 12:10

foreign circulation, 43:01

interdisciplinary appeal of, 12:03

as leading science book reviewing medium, 18:05

Science Books and Films, book review policy, 19:13

Science editors, news releases to, 20:01

Science News, 19:09

as leading science book reviewing medium, 18:05

Science periodicals, leading for book reviews, 18:05

Scientific American, 20:16

illustration of pubset advertisement in, 12:18

as leading science book reviewing medium, 18:05

in noncoupon advertising test, 39:02

Scientific and technical bookstores, 61 leading, 21:08

Scientific and technical journals, 32:01

See also Scholarly journals

Scientific and technical societies, that sponsor cooperative book exhibits, 31:03

Scientific book publisher, awareness of increased interest by libraries in journals, 32:01

Scientific books

movement in and out of U.S., 43:02

overseas sales, 43:02

that should be withheld from book clubs, 25:03

See also Professional and scholarly books

Scientific disciplines, promotion timing for, 10:03

Scientific-Technical Books, Irvine (CA), 21:08

Scientists

availability of mailing lists by profession, 2:03

mailing-list selection options for, 2:15

peer conscious, 18:01

Sci Quest, ACS combination advertising rate applicable to, 12:09

Score, glossary (p. 393)

Score, paper, 7:10

Scotchprints, as format for submitting space advertising, 12:07

Screen, glossary (p. 393)

Screen print. *See* Velox

Scripts

model, for selling diretory by telephone, 17:09

prepared, in telephone selling, 17:05

Season or time-of-year test in direct-mail promotion, 1:09

Seasonal catalogs, for bookstores, 21:04

Secondary effect. *See* Echo effect

Security-outlook envelopes. *See* Envelopes, security-outlook

Seeding. *See* Salting

Selective-order plans, library, 22:05

See also Standing-order plans, library

Selectivity

in college-faculty lists, 22:02

glossary (p. 393)

See also List selection factors

Self-cover, glossary (p. 394)

Self-improvement books, best seasons for direct mail (table), 10:06

Self-mailers

components, 1:32

glossary (p. 394)

use of, for economy, 1:21

Selfridge, John L., 19:10

Seminars, publishing, for promoters of sci-tech and professional books, 38:08

Sentence structure, in direct-mail letter copy, 14:04

Sequence option, in card-deck mailing, 8:11

Sequential numbering system, glossary (p. 394)

Serials

continuation orders for, 22:05

glossary (p. 394)

U.S. Bureau of the Census 4:02, 4:24, 4:25,
4:26
figures on population mobility, 2:02
U.S. Department of Commerce, 38:09, 43:02
U.S. Department of Labor, study of how jobs
are obtained, 41:10
U.S. Government Printing Office, 5:04
U.S. Monitoring Service, 1:23
U.S. Postal Service, 5:04, 30:09
See also *Memo to Mailers*
U.S. Publications Catalog for China, 43:07
University Book Center, Boulder (CO), 21:08
University Bookstore, Madison (WI), 21:08
University Bookstore, OHS, Columbus, 28:08
University Bookstore, Seattle (WA), 21:08
University library collection, glossary (p. 397)
University Microfilms International, 26:07
University of Alabama Bookstore, Birming-
ham, 28:08
University of Alberta Bookstore, 43:10
University of British Columbia Bookstore,
43:10
University of Chicago Bookstore, Chicago
(IL), 21:08
University of Chicago Press, 22:03
foreign circulation of journals, 43:01
journals subscriber mailing lists, 28:09
University of Hawaii Bookstore, Honolulu,
28:08
University of Manitoba Bookstore, 43:10
University of Pennsylvania Bookstore, Phila-
delphia (PA), 21:08
University of Southern California Bookstore,
Los Angeles, 28:08
University of Toronto Bookstore, 43:10
University of Toronto Medical Bookshop,
43:10
University press
glossary (p. 397)
marketing seminars and workshops, 38:08
University Press of America, 26:06
University Store, Amherst (MA), 21:08
Unrealized markets, identifying and reaching,
40:01
Unwin, Sir Stanley, 12:01
dealings with author, 37:06
on length of book titles, 38:02
The Urban Edge, 28:11
Urban Innovation Abroad, 28:11
The Urban League Review, 28:11
Used books, sales in U.S. bookstores, 21:19
Used texts, in college stores, 21:19

VDT. *See* Video Display Terminal, glossary
Vaillancourt, Pauline M., 42:21
Vandyke. *See* Blues, glossary
Vanity publisher, glossary (p. 397)

Vellum overlay, glossary (p. 397)
Velox
as format for submitting space advertising,
12:07
glossary (p. 397)
Venezian, Angelo R., Inc., 2:04
Verbs, action, in promotion copy, 14:06
Verification of mailing size, date, delivery,
1:23
Video Display Terminal, glossary (p. 397)
Visa credit-card option, in test against on-
approval offer, 1:30
Vocational and technical schools, best and
worst months for mail promotion to,
10:04

WATS. *See* Wide Area Telecommunications
Service, glossary
wf, glossary (p. 397)
Wall Street Journal, 14:11
McGraw-Hill study of echo in, 12:15
Warehousing and shipping, foreign, 43:03
Warren, Gorham, and Lamont, Inc., 14:09
business list source, 29:02
as mailing list source for names in real es-
tate, finance, banking, 2:03
*The Washington Quarterly: A Review of Stra-
tegic and International Studies,* 28:11
Web offset, glossary (p. 397)
Web press, glossary (p. 397)
Weekly Exchange, section in *Publishers
Weekly,* 18:04
Richard Weiner, Inc., 20:06
Sam Weller's Zion Bookstore, Salt Lake City
(UT), 21:08, 28:08
Wells, Robert, 19:14
Weight (paper), glossary (p. 397)
West Coast trade wholesaling, 21:13
Western Union, 6:09
Westvaco, USEnvelope Division, 7:08
Westview Press, 1:01
Wharmby, E., 36:06
White, Herbert S., 36:06
White mail, as vehicle for discovering unreal-
ized markets, 40:01
Wholesale booksellers. *See* Wholesalers
Wholesalers
American, directory of, 42:06
in book trade, 21:11
comparison with jobber, 21:10
discount advantage over publisher, 21:13
discounts to retail booksellers, 21:13
glossary (p. 397)
incentives to retail booksellers, 21:13
single monthly payment as trade incentive,
21:13
Wholesalers, academic library, 21:15

Index

Microfiche, glossary (p. 485)
Microfilm, glossary (p. 485)
Microform
    copy of out-of-print book, 16:05
    glossary (p. 486)
Micropublishing, glossary (p. 486)
Milata, Paulette, 18:12, 25:12, 42:02
Military career personnel, good prospects for
    telephone marketing, 4:11
Mini-floppy. *See* Floppy disc, glossary
Mobility, among scientists in leadership
    roles, 4:04
Money magazine, 36:08
Monitoring of list rentals, 2:07
Monograph, glossary (p. 486)
Moore, Edythe, 23:13
Moore-Cottrell Subscription Agencies, Inc.,
    35:10
More Random Walks in Science, 16:10
Morrison, Philip, 20:02
Morton, Joseph, 7:02
Mosby, C. V., 28:06
Movable page, invention of, 30:11
Mover rate for U.S. households, 4:22
Multibook buyers
    in medical market, lists for, 28:03
    in nursing market, 28:04
Multimedia library. *See* School libraries
Multiple-book buyers, added value over
    names of one-time book buyers, 2:12
Multiple-copy book buyers, 1:05
Multiple-copy orders, discount or special
    price as order inducement for, 12:12
Murphy's Law, 38:02
    glossary (p. 486)
Murphy's Law Book Two, 38:03

NAC NEWSCOPE, 22:06
NACS
    glossary (p. 486)
    See also National Association of College
        Stores
NBL. *See* National Business Lists
NBL Marketing Guide, 4:21
NCES Directory, 24:12
NEXIS electronic news library, 21:07
NMA, glossary (p. 486)
NOP, glossary (p. 486)
*NPTA Directory. See The National Profes-
    sional and Trade Association (NPTA)
    Directory*
Nth name, glossary (p. 486)
NYP, glossary (p. 486)
Name-and-date system, glossary (p. 486)
Name, personal
    commands more attention than job title,
        25:09
    use of in school mailings, 25:10
Name, use of as a key in advertising, 12:03

Nash, Ed, 1:29, 13:06
National Association of College Stores, 10:02,
    10:05, 22:07, 24:01, 24:16
    publisher services, 22:06
National Association of Parliamentarians,
    13:17
National Business Lists, 4:21
National Center for Educational Statistics,
    24:12, 38:01
National Council for Social Studies, 32:06
National Institutes of Health (NIH), 16:06
National Law Journal, 30:14
National Periodicals System, glossary
    (p. 486)
*The National Professional and Trade Associa-
    tion (NPTA) Directory*, annual rate of
    changes in, 4:16
National Science Foundation, 36:02, 36:03
National Science Teachers Association, 32:06
National Society of Professional Engineers,
    12:19
*National Trade and Professional Associations
    of the United States and Canada &
    Labor Unions*, 42:01
National WATS Services, 18:15
Nature
    case study of circulation promotion, 34:13
    new journal publicity source, 35:09
Negative check-off option, glossary (p. 486)
Negative option, glossary (p. 486)
Negative-option publishing, glossary (p. 486)
Neilly, Andrew H., Jr., 40:04
Nesting, glossary (p. 486)
Net, glossary (p. 486)
Net price, glossary (p. 486)
Net pricing
    attitude of college stores toward, 38:10
    dangers posed by for professional and
        scholarly books, 38:10
    effect on library buying, 38:10
    glossary (p. 486)
    for professional and scholarly books, 38:10
Net profit, glossary (p. 486)
Neu, D. Morgan, 12:11
"New Books," listings in periodicals, 19:14
New edition
    glossary (p. 486)
    of library reference work, sold through
        telemarketing campaign, 18:17
New England Journal of Medicine, 33:02
    foreign subscribers, 43:17
New title, essential ingredient in medical
    book promotion, 28:02
New York Academy of Sciences, 38:08
New York Law Journal Seminars-Press,
    mailing format test, 3:09
The New York Review of Books, 6:09
The *New York Times*, 6:09, 12:24, 14:04,
    24:14, 36:08
    Book Review, 20:01, 21:02